International Conference on Information Science and Technology (IST 2017)

ITM Web of Conferences Volume 11 (2017)

Wuhan, China
24 - 26 March 2017

Editors:

Hui Yang

ISBN: 978-1-5108-4117-8

Printed from e-media with permission by:

Curran Associates, Inc.
57 Morehouse Lane
Red Hook, NY 12571

Some format issues inherent in the e-media version may also appear in this print version.

Printed by Curran Associates, Inc. (2017)

For additional information, please contact EDP Sciences – Web of Conferences at the address below.

EDP Sciences – Web of Conferences
17, Avenue du Hoggar
Parc d'Activité de Courtabœuf
BP 112
F-91944 Les Ulis Cedex A
France

Phone: +33 (0) 1 69 18 75 75
Fax: +33 (0) 1 69 28 84 91

contact-edps@webofconferences.org

Additional copies of this publication are available from:

Curran Associates, Inc.
57 Morehouse Lane
Red Hook, NY 12571 USA
Phone: 845-758-0400
Fax: 845-758-2633
Email: curran@proceedings.com
Web: www.proceedings.com

TABLE OF CONTENTS

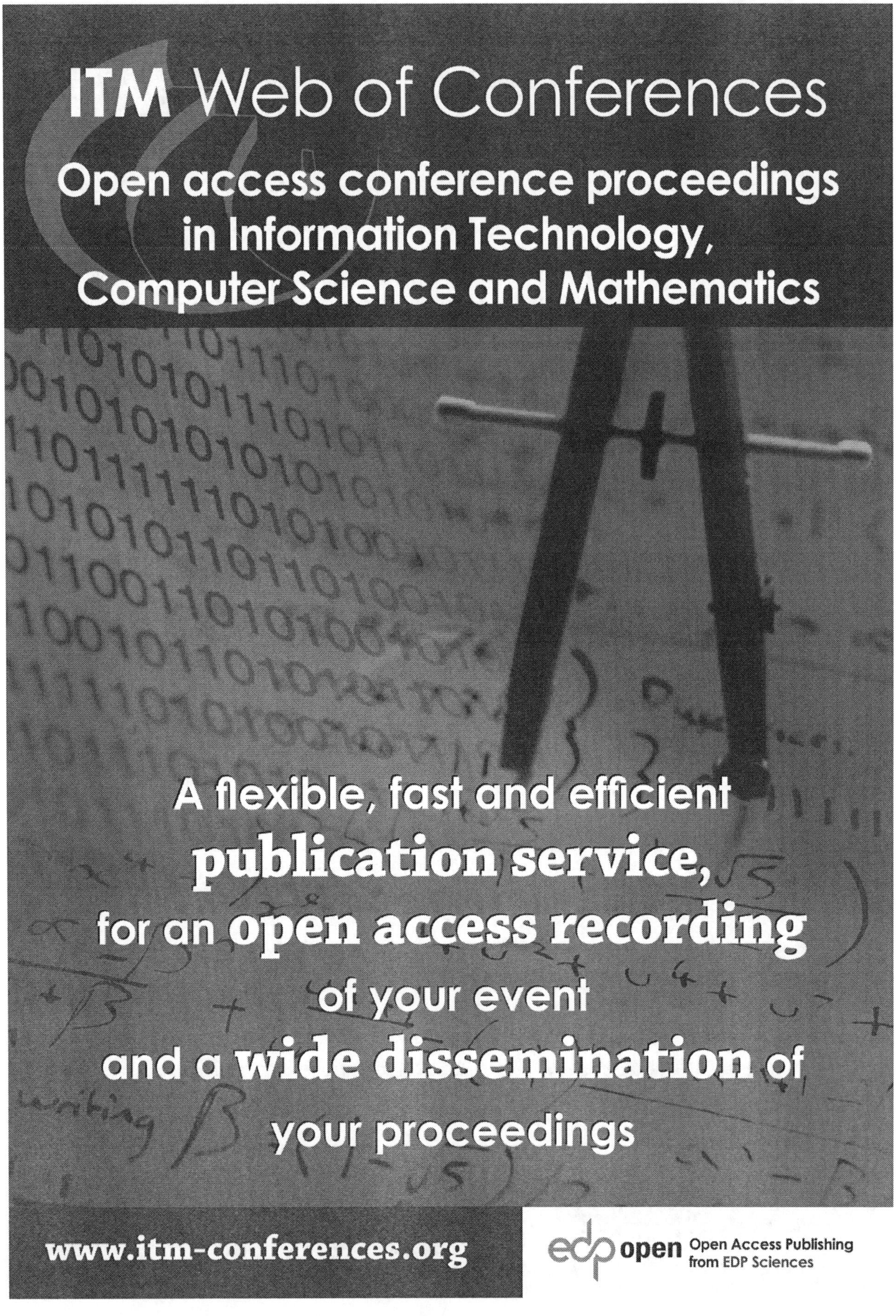
ITM Web of Conferences
Open access conference proceedings in Information Technology, Computer Science and Mathematics
A flexible, fast and efficient publication service, for an open access recording of your event and a wide dissemination of your proceedings
www.itm-conferences.org
edp open Open Access Publishing from EDP Sciences

Preface

The 2017 International Conference on Information Science and Technology [IST2017] was held in Wuhan, China, from March 24th to March 26th, 2017. IST2017 aims to bring researchers, engineers, and students to the areas of Information Science and Technology. IST2017 features unique mixed topics of Information Theory and Application, Intelligent Sensing Technology, Computational Intelligence, Computer Vision and Image Processing, Network and Communication, Speech and Natural Language Processing, High Performance Computation, Bioinformatics and Biomedical Engineering, Theoretical Computer Science, Control and Automation, Signal Processing, Automotive Electronics and Electric Vehicles, Robotics, Big Data Processing and Management. We received a total of 100 submissions from various parts of the world. The Technical Program Committee worked very hard to have all papers reviewed before the review deadline. The final technical program consists of 66 papers. There are five keynote speeches and oral sessions. All the keynote speakers are internationally recognized leading experts in their research fields, who have demonstrated outstanding proficiency and have achieved distinction in their profession. The proceedings were published as a volume in EDP Sciences on ITM Web of Conferences Publishing Company series. Some excellent papers were selected and recommended to the Engineering Index and Science Citation Index Expanded Journal. We would like to mention that, due to the limitation of the conference venue capacity, we are not able to include many fine papers in the technical program. Our apology goes to those authors.

We would like to express our sincere gratitude to all the members of Technical Program Committee and organizers for their enthusiasm, time, and expertise. Our deep thanks also go to many volunteers and staffs for the long hours and hard work they have generously given to IST2017. We are very grateful to EDP Sciences on ITM Web of Conferences Publishing Company for their support in making IST2017 possible. Finally, we would like to thank all the authors, speakers, and participants of this conference for their contributions to IST2017.

IST2017 Organizing Committee

Committees

General Chair

Prof. Jietai Jing, East China Normal University, China

Co-Chair

Prof. Hui Yang, Beijing University of Posts and Telecommunications, China

Prof. Jinglei Tang, Northwest A&F University, China

Prof. S. Ganesh Kumar, Anna University, India

Editor

Prof. Jietai Jing, East China Normal University, China

Prof. Hui Yang, Beijing University of Posts and Telecommunications, China

Technical Program Committee

Prof. Hui Yang, Beijing University of Posts and Telecommunications, China

Prof. Dongming Chen, Northeastern University, China

Dr. Yanyan Han, Beijing Electronics Science & technology Institute, China

Prof. Jinglei Tang, Northwest A&F University, China

Prof. Wei Wang, Chongqing University of Posts and Telecommunications, China

Prof. Yinghua Zhou, Chongqing University of Posts and Telecommunications, China

Prof. Yongming Han, Beijing University of Chemical Technology, China

Prof. Chaoyang Chen, Wayne State University, USA

Prof. Jingsha, Beijing University of Technology, USA

Prof. Jiadi Yu, Shanghai Jiaotong University, China

Prof. S. Ganesh Kumar, Anna University, India

Prof. Jietai Jing, East China Normal University, China

Prof. Ke Wang, Huaqiao University, China

Prof. Zheng Guo, Fujian Medical University, China

Prof. Jianwei Liu, China University of Petroleum, China

Prof. Zhonghua Li, Sun Yat-sen University, China

Prof. Xiaoying Wang, Qinghai University, China

Dr. Jin Hu, Chongqing Jiaotong University, China

Prof. Bingwei He, Fuzhou University, China

Prof. Yu-En Wu, National Kaohsiung First University of Science and Technology, Taiwan

Prof. Tahir Yavuz, Başkent University, Turkey

Prof. Wanbo Yu, Dalian University, China

Prof. Turgay IBRIKCI, Cukurova University, Turkey

Prof. Humar Kahramanli, Selcuk University, Turkey

Prof. Huey-Ming Lee, Chinese Culture University, Taiwan

Prof. Lily Lin, China University of Technology, Taiwan

Dr. Low Loi Ming, The National Energy University (Universiti Tenaga Nasional), Malaysia

Prof. Quanyi LIU, Civil Aviation Flight University of China, China

Prof. Cheng-Yuan Tang, Huafan University, Taiwan

Prof. Carlos Eduardo Cadenas Román, Universidad de Carabobo, Venezuela

Dr. Imran Memon, Zhejiang University, Pakistan

Chair I

Jie-Tai JING

Professor, East China Normal University, China

Academic Appointments and Employment

1999/9-2004/7 State Key Laboratory of Quantum Optics and Quantum Optics Devices, Institute of Opto-Electronics, Shanxi University, Taiyuan, China

2004/7- Ph.D. in Optics

1995/9-1999/7 National Training Base for Physics Researchers and Teachers, Department of Physics, Shanxi University, Taiyuan, China

1999/7-B.S. in Physics

Professional Experience

2008/4- Present Department of Physics, State Key Laboratory of Precision Spectroscopy, East China Normal University, Shanghai, P. R. China

2006/9-2008/4 University of Maryland, College Park, MD 20740, USA.

Postdoctoral Research Associate

2004/8-2006/9 Lab of Quantum Optics and Quantum Information, Department of Physics, University of Virginia, Charlottesville, VA 22903, USA.

Selected Recent Publications

Zhongzhong Qin, Leiming Cao, Hailong Wang, A. M. Marino, Weiping Zhang and Jietai Jing*, "Experimental generation of multiple quantum correlated beams from hot rubidium vapor", Physical Review Letters 113, 023602 (2014)

F. Hudelist, J. Kong, C. Liu, Jietai Jing, Z. Y. Ou and W. Zhang, "Quantum metrology with parametric amplifier based photon correlation interferometers", Nature Communications. 5, 3049 (2014)

Jietai Jing, Zhifan Zhou, Cunjin Liu, Zhongzhong Qin, Yami Fang, Jun Zhou and Weiping Zhang, "Ultralow-light-level all-optical transistor in rubidium vapor", Appl. Phys. Lett. , 104, 151103 (2014)

Jietai Jing, Cunjin Liu, Zhifan Zhou, Z.Y.Ou, and Weiping Zhang, "Realization of nonlinear interferometer with parametric amplifiers", Appl. Phys. Lett. , 99, 011110 (2011)

Jia Kong, Jietai Jing*, Hailong Wang, F. Hudelist, Cunjin Liu, and Weiping Zhang, Experimental investigation of the visibility dependence in a nonlinear interferometer using parametric amplifiers, Appl. Phys. Lett. ,102, 011130(2013)

Zhifan Zhou, Cunjin Liu, Yami Fang, Jun Zhou, Ryan T. Glasser, Liqing Chen, Jietai Jing*, and Weiping Zhang, "Optical logic gates using coherent feedback", Appl. Phys. Lett., 101, 191113(2012)

Zhongzhong Qin, Jietai Jing*, Jun Zhou, Cunjin Liu, Raphael Pooser, Zhifan Zhou, and Weiping Zhang, "A compact diode-laser-pumped quantum light source based on four wave mixing in hot rubidium vapor", Optics Letters, 37, 3141(2012)

Cunjin Liu, Jietai Jing*, Zhifan Zhou, R. C. Pooser, F. Hudelist, Lu Zhou and Weiping Zhang, "Realization of low frequency and controllable squeezing based on a four-wave-mixing amplifier in rubidium vapor", Optics Letters, 36, 2979(2011)

Co- Chair I / Editor I

Hui YANG

Assistant Professor, Beijing University of Posts and Telecommunications, China

Biography

Hui YANG received B.E and Ph. D degree incommunication and information systems from Beijing University of Posts and Telecommunications (BUPT), Beijing, China, in 2009 and 2014. He is currently an assistant professor of Institute of Information Photonics and Optical Communications at BUPT, working on many China national (including NSFC, 973, 863, etc.) and international projects regarding optical networking and communication technologies. His main research interests include network architecture, software defined optical network (SDON), dynamic optical network, flexibleb and width optical network, cross-stratum optimization (CSO) and network protocols and algorithms. He has authored or coauthored more than 60 peer-reviewed papers related to the previously mentioned research topics in prestigious international journals and conferences, and he is the first author of more than30 of them. He presented several invited papers in international journals and conferences, including many prestigious ones such as Scientific Reports, IEEE Communications Magazine, Optics Express, IEEE JOCN, Optical Switching and Networking, INFOCOM, OFC, ECOC and GLOBECOM etc. He got the Best Paper Award in NCCA 2015. Also, he is an active reviewer for several international journals, and I have previously reviewed more than 30 manuscripts in the following journals.

Co- Chair II

Jing-lei TANG

Associate Professor, Northwest A&F University, China

Dr. Jinglei Tang received her PhD from Northwest A&F University (NWSUAF), Shaanxi,China, in 2010. She is currently associate professor at College of Information Engineering (CIE), Northwest A&F University (NWSUAF). Her research interests include decision support, information management, computer vision, pattern recognition, machine learning, image analysis, etc. She is reviewer for Natural Science Foundation of China (NSFC) proposals, and reviewer for a lot of journals such as Computers and Electronics in Agriculture, etc. She also is TPC member for a lot of International conferences. Dr. Tang have published more than 40 papers in recently five years, including 16 papers in the international journal of Science Citation Index(SCI).

Education

2006.03–2010.12: PhD in Electronic Engineering, National Key Lab on ISN, College of Mechanical and Electronic Engineering, Northwest A&F University, Yangling, China.

2003.09–2006.06: MEng in Computer technology application. School of Computer Science and Technology, Southwest University of Science and Technology, Mianyang, China.

1993.09–1997.06: BEng in agricultural mechanization, College of Mechanical Electronical and Engineering,Hebei Normal University of Science & Technology, Qinhuangdao, China.

Professional Experiences

2012.01–now: Asso professor and MEng tutor (since Oct, 2010)), College of Information Engineering (CIE), Northwest A&F University (NWAFU).

2009.04–2010-04: Visiting Scholar, School of Information,University of Sydney, sponsored by the China Scholarship Council (CSC).

2006.06–2009.02: Lecturer, College of Information Engineering (CIE), Northwest A&F University (NWAFU).

1997.07–2003.09: Technician, Shijiazhuang Aircraft Industry Co., Ltd. Shijiazhuang, China.

Co- Chair III

S.GANESH KUMAR

Assistant Professor, DEEE, College of Engineering Guindy, Anna University, Sardar Patel Road, Chennai. India

Biography

S. Ganesh Kumar was born on May 25, 1977 in India. He completed his B.E., M.E. and Ph.D. degrees from Madras University and Anna University in 1998, 2005 and 2014 respectively. He has seventeen years of teaching and research experience. He has delivered lecture through satellite on the subject Electrical Machines I. He has published many number of papers in referred journals and prestigious conferences (IEEE PEDS, IECON, APEC etc..). He has delivered many number of lectures in various engineering colleges in Tamilnadu, India. He has chaired the two national and one international conferences.

He is an Editorial Board member in The Journal of Engineering and Fundamentals, International Journal of Electrical Machines & Drives, International Journal of Analysis of Electrical Machines, International Journals Power Electronics Controllers and Converters, International Institute of Engineers ,VSRD international journal of Electrical, Electronics & Communication Engineering, Journal of Electrical and Power System Engineering, Journal of Digital Integrated Circuits in Electrical Devices, Journal of Advances in Electrical Devices, International Journal of Electrical Components an Energy Conversion, International Journal of Research Studies in Electrical and Electronics Engineering, International Journal of Electronic Design and Test (JEDT),

He has reviewed papers in IEEE transactions on Industrial Electronics, IET power Electronics, ISA transactions, Electric Power Components and Systems, Journal of Circuits Systems and Computers, Journal of Electrical Engineering & Technology, Universal Journal of Mechanical Engineering. Universal Journal of Electrical & Electronic Engg, WSEAS, Maejo International Journal of Science and Technology, Advances in Electrical and Electronic Engineering, British Journal of Applied Science & Technology, International Journal of Measurement Technologies and Instrumentation Engineering (IJMTIE), IECON,APEC, PEDSTC, EESED, ICCA and EDEP.

He has organized three Faculty Development Training Programmes (Solid State Drives, Design of Electrical Machines and Power Electronics. He was served as a member of conferences held in DEEE, Anna University (ICPCES-2010, ICPCES-2014, NCEEE'08, NCSGRES-2015)

He is presently working at Anna University, Chennai as Assistant Professor in Department of Electrical and Electronics Engineering. His areas of interest are Electrical Machines and Drives. He is a member of ISTE, IE and IAENG.

Keynote Speaker I

Prof. Wen-Tsai Sung

The Department of Electrical Engineering, National Chin-Yi University of Technology, Taiwan

Wen-Tsai Sung is working with the Department of Electrical Engineering, National Chin-Yi University of Technology as a professor and Vice-Dean of Academic Affairs. He received a PhD and MS degree from the Department of Electrical Engineering, National Central University, Taiwan in 2007 and 2000. He has won the 2009 JMBE Best Annual Excellent Paper Award and the dragon thesis award that sponsor is Acer Foundation. His research interests include Wireless Sensors Network, Data Fusion, System Biology, System on Chip, Computer-Aided Design for Learning, Bioinformatics, and Biomedical Engineering. He has published a number of international journal and conferences article related to these areas. Currently, he is the chief of Wireless Sensors Networks Laboratory. At present, he serves as the Editor-in-Chief in three international journals: International Journal of Communications (IJC), Communications in Information Science and Management Engineering (CISME) and Journal of Vibration Analysis, Measurement, and Control (JVAMC), he also serves as the other international journals in Associate-Editor and Guest Editor (IET Systems Biology).

Keynote Speaker II

Dr. Amol R. Madane

Tata Consultancy Services Ltd., India

Dr. Amol R. Madane has completed Doctorate of Philosophy (PhD) under the guidance of Dr. Uttam D. Kolekar in Image/ Video Security area in Jan 2015. He holds Masters of Engineering degree in Electronics Engineering from Mumbai University, India. He is an associate of Tata Consultancy Services Ltd. from last 9+ years. His main area of research is Image Watermarking, Object Detection and Tracking, Body Segmentation and Pose Estimation, Activity Recognition, Semantic Interpretation, Advanced Driver Assistance System (ADAS). He has published research papers in international journals, conference. He has published technical book on "Design and Performance Evaluation of Image Encoders in View of 4G Applications" by Lulu book publishers, Raleigh, NC 27607, United States. He is working as Editorial Board Member, Reviewer of various international and national journals, conferences etc. He is member of professional institutes such as IEEE, IETE, ISTE, IEI, ISTD, CSI, ACM etc.

The 2017 International Conference on Information Science and Technology

Wuhan, China. March 24th-26th, 2017

IST
Conference on Information Science and Technology

The Statement of Peer Review for IST2017

The 2017 International Conference on Information Science and Technology [IST2017] was held in Wuhan, China, from March 24th to March 26th, 2017, which aims to bring researchers, engineers, and students to the areas of Information Science and Technology.

IST2017 proceeding tends to collect the most up-to-date, comprehensive, and worldwide state-of-art knowledge on Information Science and Technology. All the accepted papers have been submitted to strict peer-review by 2-4 expert referees, and selected based on originality, significance and clarity for the purpose of the conference. Each accepted paper at least has two review reports, and the authors modified according to the review reports, and submitted a modify report.

The Technical Program Committee members have been working very hard to meet the deadline of review. We sincerely hope that the conference would not only show the participants a broad overview of the latest research results on related fields, but also provide them with a significant platform for academic connection and exchange.

Editor's signature:

Date: April 28, 2017

Security Isolation Strategy Mechanism for Lightweight Virtualization Environment

Qian LIU[1], Xiao-Yong LI[1,a], Jian DU[2] and Gang LIU[3]

[1]*Beijing Jiaotong University, School of Computer and Information Technology, 100044, Beijing*
[2]*China Transport Telecommunications & Information Center, 100011, Beijing*
[3]*China Railway Corporation Transport Bureau Information Sector, 100844, Beijing*

Abstract. For cloud service providers, lightweight virtualization is a more economical way of virtualization. While the user is worried about the safety of applications and data of the container, due to the container sharing the underlying interface and the kernel, therefore the security and trusted degree of lightweight virtualization container isolation mechanism is critical for the promotion of lightweight virtualization service. Because the user cannot directly participate in the process of the construction and management of container isolation mechanism, it is difficult for them to establish confidence in the security and trusted degree of container isolation mechanism. Based on the research and analysis of system credible and virtualization isolation mechanism, this paper puts forward a set of lightweight virtualization security isolation strategy mechanism, divides lightweight virtualization container storage address space into several parts, puts forward the definition of lightweight virtualization security isolation, gives the formal description and proof of container security isolation strategy, and combines with related technology to verify the feasibility of lightweight virtualization security isolation strategy mechanism. The mechanism has important guiding significance for cloud services providers to deploy container security isolation.

1 Introduction

These Cloud computing generally adopt virtualization technology to support themselves, the traditional virtualization technologies include Xen hypervisor, VMWare, and Linux kernel Virtual Machine (KVM) and so on, these virtualization technology can achieve extension, control computing resources, and can securely isolate Virtual Machine (VM), while the resources they consume is large, and the performance and economic benefits they bring are relatively low. With the increased number of cloud users, the demand for physical resources is growing at an order of magnitude, so from the perspective of reducing the hardware cost, people hope for the appearance of a more economical virtualization solutions.

In recent years, operating system-level virtualization which based on the Linux Containers (LXC) technology is becoming more and more popular, such lightweight virtualization has many advantages compared to the traditional way of virtualization. First of all, container can start in the second level, it is much faster compared to the traditional way of virtualization. Second, container run on a shared operating system kernel, this allows multiple virtual environment to share the underlying operating

[a] Corresponding author: 14120354@bjtu.edu.cn

system interface and a public host kernel, therefore the system resource utilization is very high, and virtual machine density that single server can support is big, so as cloud service providers can have better profit space.

The problem lightweight virtualization bringing is users worrying about whether the strength of container isolation mechanism is safe enough, and whether or not they can ensure the security of user's application and data. So the method of lightweight virtualization technology attracting more users is to prove the effectiveness of their isolation, enabling users to establish enough confidence level for the services it provides.

At present domestic research, the lightweight virtualization field focus on implementation method, lacking of basic research such as container isolation mechanism security policies. This paper proposes a safety isolation strategy mechanism under lightweight virtualization environment with the help of lightweight virtualization containers technology and virtualization isolation mechanism, aims to solve the problem of container security isolation.

Innovation point of this article is: 1) based on the characteristics of lightweight virtualization, putting forward the address space division of lightweight virtualization storage resources and the definition of isolation; 2) adopting the trusted computing technology, turning it into the formal security isolation strategy, providing guidelines for developing container, and improving the user's confidence in lightweight virtualization technology.

In this paper, the first chapter introduces the research status of the related technology, including the current research status of the system trust and virtualization isolation mechanism; The second chapter embarks from dividing the address space of lightweight virtualization storage resources, researches lightweight virtualization security isolation strategy mechanism, proposes lightweight virtualization security isolation definition, formally describe container security isolation strategy; The third chapter certificates the strength of these container security isolation strategy; The forth chapter analyzes in detail the technical feasibility of above-mentioned lightweight virtualization security isolation strategy mechanism. the publisher.

2 Correlation Study

2.1 Trusted System

Trusted computing group described credible as "an entity' behavior is always carried out in accordance with the expected targets and the way", whether the system is trusted or not, it can guaranteed from two aspects: one is the system to act in accordance with the code of conduct, only within the scope of the code of conduct, the behavior of the system is considered credible. Second, conduct itself needs to meet the requirements of people's confidence level.

For the first assurance requirements, through the trust root and trust chain mentioned in the basic consider of the trusted compute to ensure that the system runs in accordance with the code of conduct, Trusted Computing Group (TCG)put forward the Trusted Computing platform [1-3][technical specification.

Technology needed by second assurance requirements is relatively a bit more complicated, such as through the precise formal verification [4]to describe behavior standards, such as ensure that the source (developed in-house or a third party)of the specification is transparent controllable[5-7]: if from developed in-house , the user can through process management, code size control methods to minimize or eliminate potential errors or bugs in code of conduct; if from a third party, the user can through other ways to evaluate the credibility of the code of conduct [8-10], such as the evaluation of others, such as solve the operation control issues of the user program with reference monitor [11,12]. System credible guarantee are shown in Figure 1 below:

DOI: 10.1051/itmconf/20171101001

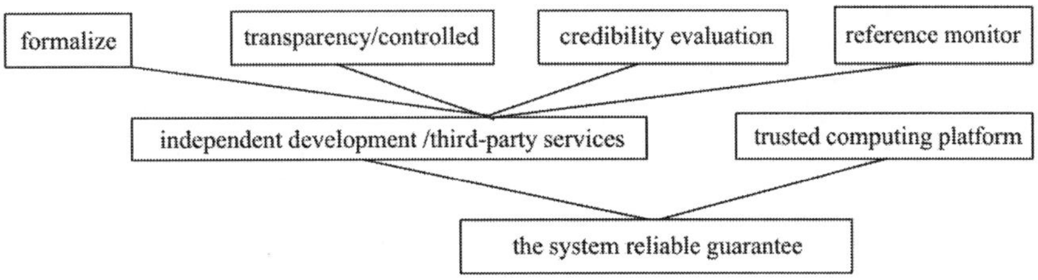

Figure 1. The system reliable guarantee.

2.2 Virtualization Isolation

Traditional virtualization is also called heavyweight virtualization, typical heavyweight virtualization methods includes KVM, Xen, VMWare, VirtualBox and other virtualization, etc. The machine which traditional virtual machines (VMs) running on is usually referred to as the host machine, the virtual machine is often referred to as the client. VMs are created and ran by the Virtual Machine Monitor (VMM) .The VMM has three basic characteristics: 1) the equivalence, the VMM provides an environment almost equaled with the host machine;2) the effectiveness, the program running in the virtual machine environment shows the performance of the minimum punishment;3) safety, VMM can completely control system resources.

In the early study of isolation, Rushby proposed "separation kernel" [13] on a single machine hosting multiple isolation environment to protect context. In 2008, on the basis of prior work experience, Rushby [14]summed up three kinds of the isolation technique: spatial separation, this kind of isolation is a direct implementation for resources which without sharing policy framework, each component of resource in physics are independent; Temporal isolation makes resources in a certain period of time only used by a component, wipes clean after using it, and then assigns them to another component, so always; Encryption isolation uses encryption signatures or calibration approach to strengthen the protection of reading and writing.

In the study of spatial segregation, Chen haibo et al. [15]of Fudan University used the nested virtualization technology to solve virtual security problem under the mega tenancy environment of cloud computing, putted forward the overall solution Cloudvisor, the main method of this mechanism was using the security protection of virtualization layer to achieve the isolation of resource management. In the study of temporal isolation, David Lie et al. [16] of Stanford university designed a kind of CPU architecture based on "the Execute - only the Memory" (XOM).In this kind of CPU architecture, data in cache and memory include tags used to bind data to a specific XOM isolated partition and MAC value for integrity protection .In the study of encryption isolation, Sahai et al.[17] proposed a called Attribute-based Encryption (ABE) Encryption access control method, which can provide fine-grained control for sharing data, but can only support threshold access control policy. To show more flexible access control policy, Bethencourt et al.[18]further putted forward the key-policy ABE (KP - ABE) and ciphertext-poicy ABE (CP - ABE) two types of ABE mechanism.

Lightweight virtualization is also called operating system-level virtualization, based on Linux Containers (LXC) technology. The earliest container technology can be traced back to the chroot tool series of Unix operating system. UNIX seventh edition in 1979 introduced the chroot (Change Root) mechanism. Chroot is a process making the specified directory as the root directory, all of its file system operation can only in the specified directory, so as not to harm the host system. Chroot existed the flaw like classic jump out of the holes, and it provided no segregation for any resources such as process and network .Early container implementation technologies also include the FreeBSD jail on FreeBSD operating system and Linux - VServer on GNU/Linux, and Sun Solaris Containers on the Solaris operating system. These techniques have been developed very mature, but do not have any of their containers integrated into the mainstream Linux kernel, therefore the LXC is currently the only operating-system virtualization technology for the Linux.

LXC was incorporated into the kernel thread from the beginning of Linux version 3.8, it packages what needed by the operation of the application into a container, such as the external environment, internal code, components and package dependency, allocates available hardware resources for different container through the common Application Programming Interface(API) and other tools, creates independent sandbox environment for running application, makes Linux users easily create and manage system or application container. By using Namespace and control group (Cgroups) function, LXC provides applications with an independent operating system environment.

In 1992, aiming to solve the problem of resource isolation based on the process, Namespace [19] have been proposed for the first time, it is an operating system level environment isolation method for Linux to achieve the lightweight virtualization (containers) service. Process under the same Namespace can sense the change of each other, and ignore the process's change from the external, so that the container in the process feels as if itself in an independent system environment, so as to achieve the goal of independence and isolation. Namespace like PID, NET, IPC, MNT, UTS and USER, segregate the process, the network, the message, the file systems, the UTS (" UNIX Time - sharing System ") and the USER space of the container.

3 Lightweight virtualization security isolation strategy mechanism

To simplify the problem, this paper hasn't take the above time isolation, encryption isolation into consideration, only focus on the study of lightweight virtualization storage resource address space isolation in the study of the lightweight virtualization space isolation .The host creates a new container meaning to assign it an independent storage resource address space.

3.1 Lightweight virtualization security isolation definition

Lightweight virtualization system includes two kinds of subject, respectively is: 1) the Host, the Host machine provides system services for containers, such as container disk read and write, network transmission, etc.;2) Containers, information cannot read and write between different containers.
Based on the structure of lightweight virtualization system, system storage address space can be divided into: 1) the host storage address space, which all belonged to the host machine.2) the container storage address space, each container has their own separate storage address space. Among them, based on access permission, the host storage address space can further be divided into three categories: the first kind of address space is closely related to all containers privacy protection, any container cannot read and write the content of this address space portion; The second type of address space has nothing to do with privacy of specific container, all containers can read the content of this portion, but can't write, such as public image resource information, etc.; The third type of address space is closely related to the privacy protection of particular container, in addition to the host machine and the container, other containers can't read and write, such as the container configuration information.

The letter S represents subject of the system, $S=\{Ho、Co_1、Co_2、...、Co_n\}$, of which: Ho represents the host machine, $Co_i\,(1\le i\le n)$ represents container i. The letter L represents system storage address space, $L=\{H、C_1、C_2、...、C_n\}$ denotes a division, of which: H denotes the storage address space corresponding to the host machine, $C_i\,(1\le i\le n)$ denotes the storage address space corresponding to the container i.

$H=\{H_x、H_{ro}、H_{1c}、H_{2c}、...、H_{nc}\}$ represents a division of H, of which: H_x denotes the first kind of address space of H, any containers can not read or write on this part of the address space; H_{ro} denotes the second category of address space in H, the content of the address space for this part can be read by all containers, but no container can conduct write operation; $H_{ic}\,(1\le i\le n)$ denotes the third type of address space, only the container i can read and write the contents of this part of the address space.

The above discussion towards the relation of system storage address space partitioning is shown in Figure 2.

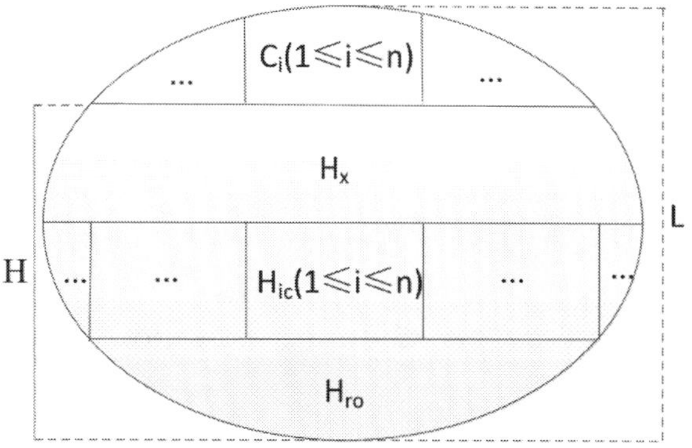

Figure 2. Lightweight virtualization storage address space division relations.

$R: S \rightarrow 2^L$ denotes the storage address space which the subject can read, $W: S \rightarrow 2^L$ denotes the storage address space which the subject can write.

In system, the direct information exchange between the two subject show up as a subject write information to the storage address space where another subject can read, for any two different subject s and t, if $R(s) \cap W(t) \neq \varnothing$, then t can pass information to s. Such as a container in the system through the system call request the host machine services, is through writing system call parameters, then these parameters are read by the host kernel so as to complete the service request.

Isolation between the two subject means there is no direct or indirect information exchange between them, but in this article, the container isolation we discussed is relatively weak on demand, because all containers need to exchange information with the host machine, to apply for the system service. Given this, lightweight virtualization system isolation requirements between the container is limited to no direct exchange of information between any two containers, for this reason, this paper gives a container isolation definition as follows:

Definition 1. In lightweight virtualization structure, security isolation between containers refers to: For $\forall i, j, 1 \leq i \leq n, 1 \leq j \leq n, i \neq j$, have: $R(Co_i) \cap W(Co_j) = \varnothing$

Definition 1 refers to the meaning of no one container can directly read other containers address space, or they can be used to realize information exchange for both reading and writing.

3.2 Lightweight virtualization security isolation policy

Based on Figure 2 about lightweight virtualization storage address space partition method, this paper puts forward a set of security isolation rules, in order to realize the security isolation between different containers.

Rule 1: $\forall Co_i (1 \leq i \leq n) \in S \Rightarrow R(Co_i) \in C_i \cup H_{ro} \cup H_{ic}$

Rule 2: $\forall Co_i (1 \leq i \leq n) \in S \Rightarrow W(Co_i) \in C_i \cup H_{ic}$

Rule 1shows the address space that any containers $i(1 \leq i \leq n)$ can read include the container storage address space corresponding to the container i itself $C_i(1 \leq i \leq n)$,the address space H_{ro} in H which can be read but can't be write by all containers, and the address space $H_{ic}(1 \le i \le n)$ in H which can only be read or write by the corresponding container.

Rule 2 shows the address space that any containers $i(1 \le i \le n)$ can write include the container storage address space corresponding to the container i itself $C_i(1 \le i \le n)$, and the address space $H_{ic}(1 \le i \le n)$ in H which can only be read or write by the corresponding container.

If a lightweight virtualization system adopt as shown in figure 2 storage address space partition method, and satisfy the rules 1 and 2, then the system's isolation between all the containers is security, namely for $\forall i, j, 1 \le i \le n, 1 \le j \le n, i \ne j$, $R(Co_i) \cap W(Co_j) = (C_i \cup H_{ro} \cup H_{ic}) \cap (C_j \cup H_{jc}) = \varnothing$.

4 Lightweight virtualization security isolation strategy mechanism security

As mentioned above, isolation strategy mechanism is guaranteeing different containers isolated in the host machine level, but the host machine will inevitably consciously or unconsciously run some unsafe applications, including the program code which containing trojans, worms and other malicious code, the vulnerability of the these unsafe applications may tamper with mechanism, and result a certain destruction to the effectiveness of the mechanism.

Basing on the analysis of the system safety mentioned above, this chapter will ensure the safety of isolation strategy mechanism from two aspects, on the one hand is the safety of isolation strategy mechanism itself, by using formal formula to prove that isolation strategy set is meeting the requirement of container security isolation definition; On the other hand is the security isolation strategy mechanism at run time, with the help of white list of trusted computing platform technology. The guarantee of mechanism safety is shown in Figure 3:

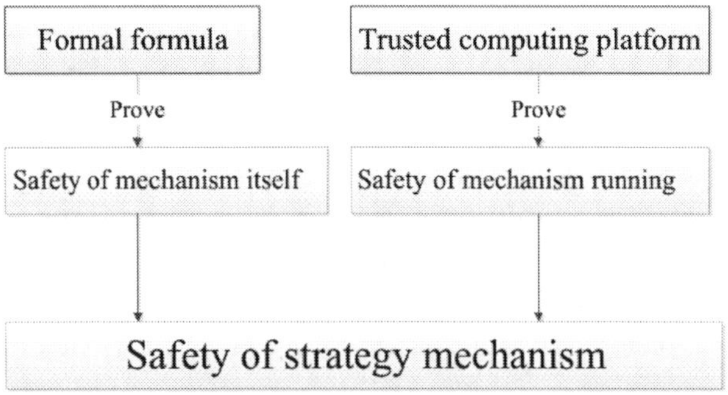

Figure 3. The guarantee of mechanism safety.

4.1 Safety of isolation strategy mechanism itself

As mentioned above, isolation strategy mechanism is guaranteeing different containers isolated in the host machine level, but the host machine will inevitably consciously or unconsciously run some unsafe applications, including the program code which containing trojans, worms and other malicious code, the vulnerability of the these unsafe applications may tamper with mechanism, and result a certain destruction to the effectiveness of the mechanism.

According to lightweight virtualization security policy, the readable storage address space of the container i is $R(Co_i)=\{C_i、H_{ro}、H_{ic}\}$, the writable storage address space of the container j is $W(Co_j)=\{C_j、H_{jc}\}$.

And by the system storage address space partition, we know $H.C_1.C_2.....C_n$ is a partition of the lightweight virtualization storage resource address space L, that is to say $L=H\cup C_1\cup...\cup C_n$.We know $H_x.H_{ro}.H_{1c}.H_{2c}.....H_{nc}$ is a partition of the host storage address space H, that is $H=H_x\cup H_{ro}\cup H_{1c}\cup H_{2c}\cup...\cup H_{nc}$.

According to the definition of division, there is no overlap between these address space to each other, there is no public read/write address space, so the intersection between any two address space among all the address space is an empty set.

That is $\forall l_1,l_2\in L, l_1\neq l_2\Rightarrow l_1\cap l_2=\varnothing$.

$$R(Co_i)\cap W(Co_j)$$
$$=(C_i\cup H_{ro}\cup H_{ic})\cap(C_j\cup H_{jc})$$
$$=(C_i\cap C_j)\cup(C_i\cap H_{jc})\cup(H_{ro}\cap C_j)$$
$$\cup(H_{ro}\cap H_{jc})\cup(H_{ic}\cap C_j)\cup(H_{ic}\cap H_{jc})$$
$$=\varnothing\cup\varnothing\cup\varnothing\cup\varnothing\cup\varnothing\cup\varnothing$$
$$=\varnothing$$

To sum up, for $\forall i,j,1\leq i\leq n,1\leq j\leq n,i\neq j,\forall s\in S$, we have: $R(Co_i)\cap W(Co_j)=\varnothing$.

The above formally proofs lightweight security isolation strategy is credible. At the same time, the Trusted Platform technologies such as the Core Root of Trust for Measurement (CRTM) and Trusted Platform Module (TPM), etc., can guarantee the host machine itself runtime to be trusted.

4.2 Safety of isolation strategy mechanism at run time

In order to implement the isolation strategy mechanism, and guarantee mechanism not been tampered, which means the container subject can only access the address space in permissions. In this paper, the idea of the trusted application white List technology (Trusted Software List, TSL) in trusted computing platform is used to deal with the problem, the TSL in this paper including: all safe executable files in system and its integrity check values (hash value).

Once a subject launch the system call, according the system call information, the first step is to determine whether this executable file in TSL: if in, then go to the next step; Otherwise, return to ban. Second step is to compute the hash value of the executable file, and comparing with the credible hash value in the TSL: if same, return to allow, continue system call to normal execution; Otherwise, return to ban, system call failed.

TSL = {E, H}denotes a credible white list in the host machine system, of which E = {e_1, e_2,..., e_n} said executable file collection in TSL, H = {h_1, h_2,..., h_n} said the integrity of the calibration value of collection corresponding to TSL executable file. With function In (E) = {1, 0} said whether an executable file in TSL: if in, then return to 1 on the result, can go to the next phase of judgment; If not, then the result return 0, calls are forbidden to perform. Function (E, H) = {1, 0} said whether an executable file hash value is consistently with the hash values corresponding to TSL, if can the result return 1, the system calls continue normal execution; if can't the result return zero, the system call failed.

The process discussed above is shown as follows:

if:

$$\forall e_1 \in E, \; In(e_1) = 0 \Rightarrow return \;\; 0;$$

else if:

$$\forall e_1 \in E, \; \forall h_1 \in H, \; Equal(e_1, h_1) = 0 \Rightarrow return \;\; 0;$$

else:

return 1.

This method can realize the effective operation of isolation strategy mechanism, on the premise of security, and ensure the isolation strategy mechanism of unity between safety and efficacy, to enhance the user's confidence in lightweight virtualization technology.

5 Lightweight Virtualization Security Isolation Strategy Mechanism Feasibility

According to the characteristics of the lightweight virtualization, security isolation strategy mechanism proposed in this paper can be realized by Namespace and Copy-On-Wirte(COW) technology. Namespace is an operating system level environmental isolation method provided by Linux, in order to realize the lightweight virtualization services. COW is only in the process of paragraphs in the space content will change, will be a copy of the contents of the parent for the child process technology.

Of which PID is used to isolate the process of different containers; NET makes the container has an independent Network Devices, IP Addresses, IP Routing Tables, /proc/net directory, that each container network can be isolated; MNT makes the process of different Namespace see file system is different, so that the file system saw by process in different Namespace is isolated from each other.

The biggest difference between COW file system and other systems is that: COW never overwrite the existing content of the file system. COW makes container to read or write its own address space rather than to read-only storage address space of a host computer, can be used to separate the container storage address space and the hosting read-only storage address space. COW will merge two address space (the hosting read-only storage address space and the container storage address space) into one, therefore the angle of view on the container is all content of combined address space. If the container needs to update its perspective /etc/hosts file, the file happens to be contents of the hosting read-only storage address space, COW will firstly not overwrite /etc/hosts file on the read-only storage address space in the host machine, secondly it will copy the file to the container storage address space, namely copy to/etc/hosts file on the container storage address space , and then conduct update operation on the latter .In this way, even if the host machine read-only storage address space and the container storage address space both have /etc/hosts file ,and COW can ensure that container only read or write contents of /etc/hosts file on the container storage address space , namely the updated content.

Acknowledgement

In this paper, the research on security isolation under lightweight virtualization environment involves multiple levels, on the basis of the lightweight virtualization environment storage address space division, proposed lightweight virtualization security isolation definition, formally described security isolation strategy, proved that lightweight virtualization security isolation strategy for security isolation between the container is credible, and combined with related technical to verify lightweight virtualization security isolation strategy mechanism this paper proposed is feasible. The significance of this paper is to provide system with an isolation strategy mechanism, deploy a system without this isolation strategy mechanism may exist a potential safety hazard like covert channel. And the method of translating the abstract container isolation credible and feasible requirements into specific formal rules is a kind of innovation, provides a reference for future similar research.

References

1. Perez R, Sailer R, van Doorn L. vTPM: virtualizing the trusted platform module[C]. Proc 15th Conf on USENIX Security Symposium; 2006; 2006. p. 305-20.
2. England P, Loeser J. Para-virtualized TPM sharing[C]. Trusted Computing-Challenges and Applications: Springer; 2008: 119-32.
3. Stumpf F, Eckert C. Enhancing trusted platform modules with hardware-based virtualization techniques[C]. Emerging Security Information, Systems and Technologies, 2008 SECURWARE'08 Second International Conference on; 2008: IEEE; 2008. p. 1-9.
4. Greve D, Wilding M, Vanfleet WM. A separation kernel formal security policy[C]. Proc Fourth International Workshop on the ACL2 Theorem Prover and Its Applications; 2003: Citeseer; 2003.
5. Pauley WA. Cloud provider transparency: an empirical evaluation [J]. Security & Privacy, IEEE 2010; 8(6): 32-9.
6. Whaiduzzaman M, Gani A. Measuring security for cloud service provider: A Third Party approach[C]. Electrical Information and Communication Technology (EICT), 2013 International Conference on; 2014: IEEE; 2014. p. 1-6.
7. Wüllenweber K, Weitzel T. An empirical exploration of how process standardization reduces outsourcing risks[C]. System Sciences, 2007 HICSS 2007 40th Annual Hawaii International Conference on; 2007: IEEE; 2007. p. 240c-c.
8. Chakraborty S, Roy K. An SLA-based framework for estimating trustworthiness of a cloud[C]. Trust, Security and Privacy in Computing and Communications (TrustCom), 2012 IEEE 11th International Conference on; 2012: IEEE; 2012. p. 937-42.
9. Zadeh LA. Probability measures of fuzzy events [J]. Journal of mathematical analysis and applications 1968; 23(2): 421-7.
10. Shapley LS. A value for n-person games[R]: DTIC Document, 1952.
11. Anderson JP. Computer Security Technology Planning Study. Volume 2[R]: DTIC Document, 1972.
12. Peter Loscocco N. Integrating flexible support for security policies into the Linux operating system[C]. Proceedings of the FREENIX track: USENIX Annual Technical Conference; 2001; 2001.
13. Rushby JM. Design and verification of secure systems [M]: ACM; 1981.
14. Rushby J. Separation and integration in mils (the mils constitution)[J]. Computer Science Laboratory SRI International, Technical Report 2008.
15. Zhang F, Chen J, Chen H, Zang B. CloudVisor: retrofitting protection of virtual machines in multi-tenant cloud with nested virtualization[C]. Proceedings of the Twenty-Third ACM Symposium on Operating Systems Principles; 2011: ACM; 2011. p. 203-16.
16. Lie D, Thekkath C, Mitchell M, et al. Architectural support for copy and tamper resistant software [J]. ACM SIGPLAN Notices 2000; 35(11): 168-77.
17. Sahai A, Waters B. Fuzzy identity-based encryption[C]. Advances in Cryptology–EUROCRYPT 2005: Springer; 2005: 457-73.
18. Bethencourt J, Sahai A, Waters B. Ciphertext-policy attribute-based encryption[C]. Security and Privacy, 2007 SP'07 IEEE Symposium on; 2007: IEEE; 2007. p. 321-34.
19. Pike R, Presotto D, Thompson K, Trickey H, Winterbottom P. The use of name spaces in Plan 9[C]. Proceedings of the 5th workshop on ACM SIGOPS European workshop: Models and paradigms for distributed systems structuring; 1992: ACM; 1992. p. 1-5.

A Container-based Trusted Multi-level Security Mechanism

Xiao-Yong LI[1], Chen JI[1,a] and Gang LIU[2]

[1]*School of Computer and Information Technology, Beijing Jiaotong University, Beijing, China*
[2]*Information Technology Center, China Railway Corporation, Beijing, China*

Abstract. Multi-level security mechanism has been widely applied in the military, government, defense and other domains in which information is required to be divided by security-level. Through this type of security mechanism, users at different security levels are provided with information at corresponding security levels. Traditional multi-level security mechanism which depends on the safety of operating system finally proved to be not practical. We propose a container-based trusted multi-level security mechanism in this paper to improve the applicability of the multi-level mechanism. It guarantees multi-level security of the system through a set of multi-level security policy rules and trusted techniques. The technical feasibility and application scenarios are also discussed. The ease of realization, strong practical significance and low cost of our method will largely expand the application of multi-level security mechanism in real life.

1 Introduction

Multi-level security (MLS) refers to the ability to process information with different security levels in a computer system. It was originally used to support the security and confidentiality of military systems and databases. In a multi-level security system, the subject can't read the object of security level is higher than it and can't write the object of security level is lower than it. The implementation of multi-level security system can effectively guarantee the confidentiality of the application software and data, restrict illegal attacker, and prevent attackers from arbitrarily destructing system information. Moreover, it can also be easy to configure and manage the system policy.

In the past research, there are a lot of achievements about MLS have been made. Many research institutions and scholars try to support multiple security through a platform based on secure operating system, such as Adept-50, safety Xenix, SE-Linux, etc. However, the current development statuses of these systems prove that it was not successful in practical application. In order to resolve these problems, this paper proposes a trusted multi-level security container mechanism. This mechanism is based on lightweight virtualization technology and reference the idea of multiple independent levels of security and safety (MILS)[1, 2]. In section 3, we also prove the safety of it.

The innovations of this paper are: 1) This mechanism can be used directly in most commercial systems, and improve the problem of poor usability of traditional MLS mechanism; 2) the implementation of this method is not only simple but also diverse. It can meet different MLS requirements, and has a strong practical significance; 3) the safety of the trusted multi-level security container mechanism is proved in this paper, and the credibility of this method is improved.

[a] Corresponding author: 14120352@bjtu.edu.cn

In Section 2 we introduce the related research, including the latest research of MLS, lightweight virtualization technology and trusted system. According to the actual requirements of security applications, we propose the definition of multi-level security based on the lightweight virtualized environment in Section 3, and then propose a set of multi-level security policy rules. We also prove that these rules meet the definition of multi-level security, and analyses technical feasibility of the mechanism. We present several application scenarios of this mechanism in Section 4, and conclude this paper in Section 5.

2 Related works

2.1 Container and lightweight virtualization technology

Lightweight virtualization is relative to the heavyweight virtualization terms. Heavyweight virtualization usually refers to the KVM, VMware, etc. which based on the virtualization of hardware. Lightweight virtualization based on container technology refers to the operating system-level virtualization technology, such as Docker [3], Linux Containers (LXC) and so on.

Recently, most of cloud service providers provide a complete operating environment serves to running applications by using traditional virtualization technology, and the entire operating system running on a virtual hardware platform. But this approach greatly consumes and wastes systems resources, brings greater cost, and has higher demands on the server, so more and more enterprises are choosing to use lightweight virtualization technology. Lightweight virtual machines (called "container") can load applications directly on the host platform, use the same kernel with the host, and lead to a small performance loss. Lightweight virtualization technology uses lightweight isolation. In order to share resources between the host and containers, it also provides a shared mechanism.

In summary, for one host, using lightweight virtualization will virtualize more virtual machines than using traditional virtualization. It greatly improve the resource utilization and system overhead, and is a more economical way for enterprise and cloud providers.

2.2 Multi-level security

According to the importance and sensitivity of the information, the information will be divided into different security level. By dividing security level, multi-level security policies can ensure that the information can only be used by the people whose security level is higher than or equal to it. There are a lot of well-known multi-level security models have been proposed, such as BLP [4], Biba [5], clark-Wilson [6] and so on. In 2005, Jim Alves-Foss et al. propose the concept of multiple independent levels of security and safety (MILS). MILS is originally based on the Rushby's idea of isolation [7, 8], and is a high-security system. It can build a set of credible security solution by using several management units which can be independent analysis.

In addition to these classic multi-level security model, the development of cloud computing and virtualization technology provide more favorable conditions for a multiple single-level (MSL) system's implementation. MSL [9] use isolated computing or virtual machine for different security level data to separate these data. The purpose is to implement the multi-level security mechanism without special modification of operating systems or applications. References [10] propose an action-based multi-level access control (AMAC) model and gives the formal description of the policy. This model considers many information such as characteristics of structured document, changes of document's security level, changes of the user's security level, system status information and so on. It implement multi-level security access to structured documents in a cloud computing environment, and prove the security of multi-level access control policies of AMAC model. References [11] proposed a multi-level security mechanism based on virtualization technology. It avoids cross-contamination issues and hidden channels of different security levels through strong security isolation mechanism, and reduce difficulty and costs of multi-level security's implementation by its seamless support for existing commercial operating systems and applications.

2.3 Trusted system

Trusted system can guarantee credibility from two parts: trusted source and trusted running. First, the source of the system determines the requirements and methods to ensure credibility of the system. For a third-party system, the credibility of the system can be achieved through process transparency [12] of system behavior specification's production and management, and the user can also refer to other users' reviews to evaluate the credibility of the system [13]; for the system developed by users themselves, possible errors and vulnerabilities in the system design process should be reduced or eliminated as much as possible. For example, formal description [14] can be used to regulate the production process and code size control [15] can be used to reduce the possible risks.

In addition to the problem of trusted sources, the trusted running is also important. We can use trusted computing platform (TCP) technology to ensure the trusted running [16], and ensure the system running as expected by a trusted root and trusted delivery mechanisms.

3 Container-based trusted multi-level security mechanism

3.1 Confidentiality Requirements of multi-level security

Multi-level security confidentiality policies divided the information into different security levels based on the importance and sensitivity of the information. The information can only flow from low security-level to high security-level. That is, a subject with high security level can read an object with low security level, a low security level subject can write a high security level object, and a subject can read or write an object if there security levels is equal. By this way, it can ensures that the information can only be one-way flow from low to high, and avoids the disclosure of information from high to low.

Depending on the above, we propose formal definition of the Multi-level security confidentiality requirements. This paper use S denotes the set of all domains of the safety system, use A denotes the set of entire address space of the security system, and use L denotes a set of security tags which have a partial order relation$\preccurlyeq$. $l_1 \preccurlyeq l_2$represents $l_2$has a higher security level than l_1. Function level: $S \rightarrow L$denotes the security level of domain S. Function alter: $S \rightarrow A$ denotes the address space which is writable by domain S. Function observe: $S \rightarrow A$ denotes the address space which is readable by domain S.

Definition 1 For $\forall u,v \in S$ and $level(u) \preccurlyeq level(v)$, we say that the security policy meets the multi-level security confidentiality requirements if

$$alter(u) \cap observe(v) \neq \emptyset \tag{1}$$

$$observe(u) \cap alter(v) = \emptyset \tag{2}$$

For two domains with different security levels, if the intersection of the writable address space of the low security-level domain and the readable address space of high security-level domain is not empty, the information of the low security-level domain can flow to the high security-level domain. If the intersection of the readable address space of the low security-level domain and the writable address space of high security-level domain is empty, the low security-level domain can't read the information which is written by a high security-level domain. All above meet the basic idea of multi-level security confidentiality requirements.

There are differences between definition 1 and traditional models of multi-level security. Definition 1 supports the idea that low security-level can preserve their privacy. As shown in Figure 1, M and N are two arbitrary domain and N has higher security-level than M. $M = \{M_c, M_p\}$ is a division, in which N can read area M_c and can't read M_p. It means that M_p is M's private area. In this case, M can not only report information to N through M_c, but also protect its privacy by M_p, which meets the practical safety requirements of many systems. If $M_c = M$, N can read all the information in M.

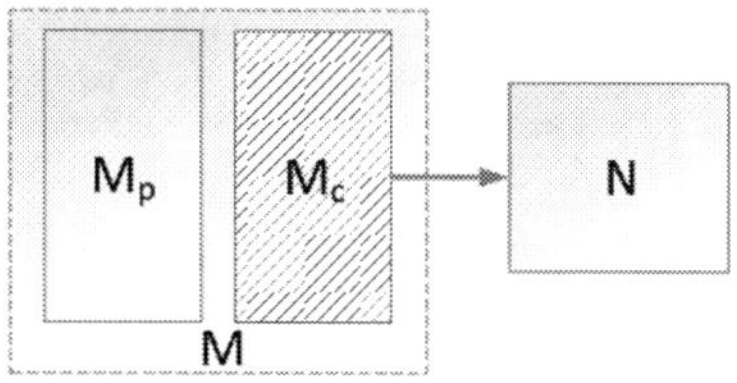

Figure 1. Schematic diagram of multilevel security policy.

3.2 Container-based trusted multi-level security mechanism

This section proposes a trusted multi-level security container mechanism. The purpose of the mechanism is to support that information flow between different security level containers meets the confidentiality requirements of definition 1.

1) Division of address space

In the lightweight virtualization environment, the system is divided into two domains: a) container domain: It is the private portion of each container, and a container domain usually corresponds to a container; b) host machine domain: The other parts of the system except for container domains. In this paper, different domains can access different address spaces according to their permissions.

According to the division of the domain, The system address space is divided into two categories: a) container domain address space (C_i): It is assigned to different container domains; b) host domain address space: including all address space of the system except for container domain address space, which is assigned to host domain. Because of different container domains has different permissions for the part of host domain address space, the host domain address space are further divided: a) host-sharing area (SA), each container can read the contents of this area, such as images, related information of basic software and so on; b) host-container area (CA_i): The content of this area is only related to the specific container, only corresponding container domain can read or write the corresponding host-container area, each container corresponds to a host container domain; c) host-private area (PA): No containers can read or write this area. It can only be accessed by the host. The four parts is a division of the system address space, the address space in each part is not overlapping, as shown in Figure 2.

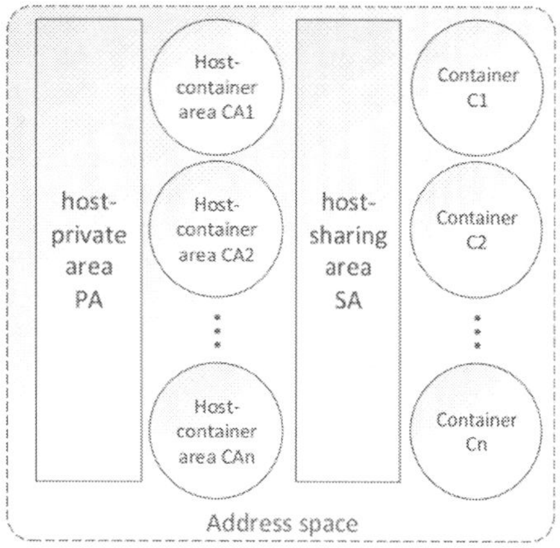

Figure 2. Address space partition in lightweight virtual environment

2) Security policy and proof

Based on the division of the address space in Figure 2, the container environment is defined as follows:

In this paper, we use $\text{Container}(S, A)$ denotes the container environment $\text{S} = \{HD, CD_1, CD_2, \ldots, CD_n\}$. Among them, HD denotes the host machine domain, $CD_i(1 \leq i \leq n)$ denotes the container domain i and CD represents the set of all container domains. $\text{A} = \{SA, \text{PA}, CA_1, CA_2, \ldots, CA_n, C_1, C_2, \ldots, C_n\}$, where SA denotes the set of address space of host-sharing area, PA denotes the set of address space of the host-private area, $CA_i(1 \leq i \leq n)$ denoted the address space of host-container area which can be accessed by the corresponding container domain i, and $C_i(1 \leq i \leq n)$ denotes the set of container domain address space which is corresponding to container domain i.

According to definition and, the following rules about trusted multi-level security policy are proposed:

Rule 1:

$$\forall i,, 1 \leq i \leq n, C_i \cup CA_i \cup SA \subset observe(CD_i) \tag{3}$$

Rule 2:

$$\forall i,, 1 \leq i \leq n, alter(CD_i) = C_i \cup CA_i \tag{4}$$

Rule 3:

$$\forall i,j, 1 \leq i \leq n, 1 \leq j \leq n, i \neq j,\ level(CD_i) \preccurlyeq level(CD_j)$$
$$\Rightarrow C_i \subset observe(CD_j) \wedge C_i \not\subset alter(CD_j) \tag{5}$$

Rule 4:

$$\forall i,j, 1 \leq i \leq n, 1 \leq j \leq n, i \neq j,\ level(CD_i) \preccurlyeq level(CD_j)$$
$$\Rightarrow C_j \not\subset observe(CD_i) \wedge C_j \not\subset alter(CD_i) \tag{6}$$

Rule 5:

$$\forall i,j, 1 \leq i \leq n, 1 \leq j \leq n, i \neq j,\ CA_i \not\subset observe(CD_j) \wedge CA_i \not\subset alter(CD_j) \tag{7}$$

Rule 1 means that the readable address spaces of a container domain include the host-container area, host-sharing area, and the container domain address space which is corresponding with it. Rule 2 means that the writable address spaces of a container domain include corresponding container domain address space and corresponding host-container area. Here container domain CD_i can be understood as the domain M in Figure 1, and C_i, CA_i can be understood as M_c, M_p. Rule 3 means that if the security level of two container domains is different, the container domain with high security level can only read the container domain address space of the container domain with low security level, and can't write it. Rule 4 means that if the security level of two container domains is different, the container domain with low security level can neither read nor write the container domain address space of the container domain with high security level. Rule 5 means that for an arbitrary host container area, in addition to corresponding container domains, the other container domains cannot read and write the address spaces of these areas. The following is a proof of the security.

Proof:

According to the definition 1, for $\forall u, v \in S$ and $level(u) \preccurlyeq level(v)$, we say that the security policy meets the multi-level security confidentiality requirements if

$$alter(u) \cap observe(v) \neq \emptyset \tag{8}$$

$$observe(u) \cap alter(v) = \emptyset \tag{9}$$

So, for the trusted multi-level secure container policy, it is needed to prove that:

For $\forall i,j, 1 \leq i \leq n, 1 \leq j \leq n, i \neq j$ when $level(CD_i) \preccurlyeq level(CD_j)$

$$alter(CD_i) \cap observe(CD_j) \neq \emptyset \tag{10}$$

$$observe(CD_i) \cap alter(CD_j) = \emptyset \tag{11}$$

1). According to the rule 2,

$$alter(CD_i) = C_i \cup CA_i \tag{12}$$

$$\because \forall i,j, 1 \leq i \leq n, 1 \leq j \leq n, i \neq j,$$

$$level(CD_i) \preccurlyeq level(CD_j) \tag{13}$$

According to the rule 3,

$$C_i \subset observe(CD_j) \tag{14}$$

$$\therefore C_i \subset alter(CD_i) \wedge C_i \subset observe(CD_j) \tag{15}$$

$$\therefore alter(CD_i) \cap observe(CD_j) \neq \emptyset \tag{16}$$

$\therefore$ (10) is proved

2). According to the rule 2,

$$alter(CD_j) = C_j \cup CA_j \tag{17}$$

$$\because \forall i,j, 1 \leq i \leq n, 1 \leq j \leq n, i \neq j,$$

$$level(CD_i) \preccurlyeq level(CD_j) \tag{18}$$

According to the rule 4,

$$C_j \not\subset observe(CD_i) \tag{19}$$

According to the rule 5,

$$CA_j \not\subset observe(CD_i) \tag{20}$$

$$\therefore observe(CD_i) \cap alter(CD_j) = \emptyset \tag{21}$$

$\therefore$ (11) is proved

In conclusion, the trusted multi-level security container policy proposed meets the multi-level security requirements.

In addition, we can also ensure the credibility of the method from two aspects: trusted source and trusted running. On the one hand, we can ensure the credibility by using trusted computing platform technology when the system is running. Trusted computing platform technology use trusted platform module (TPM) as the core, and ensure the trusted running through the trust transfer mechanism, identity authentication, safe storage mechanism and so on. On the other hand, because this method is developed and designed independently, we can use the idea of reference monitor to complete the design and development, and as far as possible to reduce the size of key code in the process of implementation.

3.3 Feasibility analysis

According to the discussion in the section 3 and the structural characteristics of this method, we can use the union file system[17] (UnionFS) technology to implement the mechanism. UnionFS is a layered, lightweight and high performance file system, which can merge multiple file systems together and allowing the coexistence of read-only and read-write directories. By using the copy-on-write function, it allows virtual modification of the read-only file system, and the real modification will be saved to the read-write file system. The principle is shown in Figure 3.

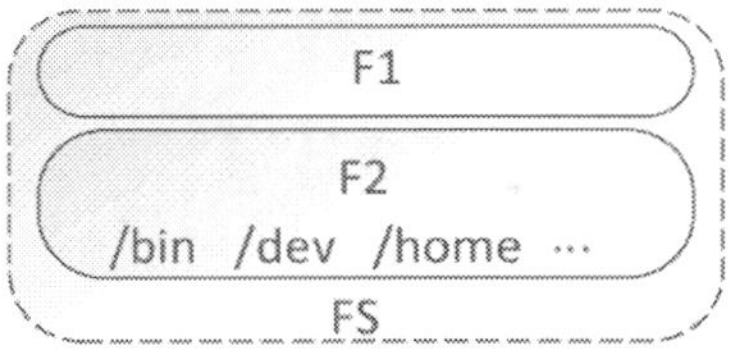

Figure 3. Schematic diagram of UnionFS

F1 and F2 formed a union file system FS through the method 'mount', where F1 is considered as a read-write layer and F2 is considered as a read-only layer. FS can only read the contents of F2. When FS wants to modify the file in F2, F1 will creates a file corresponding to the file in F2 and FS is actually modify the F1.

The trusted multi-level secure container mechanism proposed in section 3 can be implemented by using UnionFS technology. As shown in Figure 1, we can considered the file system Mc as the read-only layer of the UnionFS, and file system N itself as the read-write layer of the UnionFS. In this way, all changes of Mc can reflected in the file system N, and M can't know any changes in N. All above meet the requirements of the multilevel security model.

For example, Docker is a typical container-based lightweight virtualization system, the AUFS (Another UnionFS) it uses is a union file system. In addition to AUFS, the union file system types that Docker supports also include btrfs, vfs and DeviceMapper. Therefore, in most of the lightweight virtualization systems, such as docker, we can use the characteristics of the union file system to implement the trusted multi-level security container mechanism directly.

4 Scenarios

Trusted multi-level security container mechanism combines the traditional multi-level security policy and lightweight virtualization environment, and using the formal method proves its security, which has a strong application significance. In the reference[18], Rushby is divided multi-level security policy into two types: transitive model and intransitive model. The two kinds of models can be implemented by this mechanism. The following are explanation of implementation of these two models.

1) Transitive model

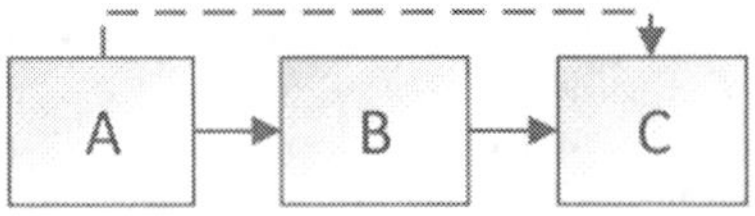

Figure 4. Transitive model

As shown in Figure 4, for three different domains A, B and C, the security level relationship of A, B, C is $A<B<C$. $A \rightsquigarrow B$ denotes the information can flow from domain B to domain A. Then, the model can be referred to as $A \rightsquigarrow B, B \rightsquigarrow C, A \rightsquigarrow C$. The file A can be considered as the read-only layer of domain B, and the file system is considered as the read-only layer of domain C. According to the characteristics of the union file system, domain B can know the changes in domain A, domain C can know the changes in domain A and domain B. Conversely, the lower level domain will not aware of the changes in high level domain.

This implementation way has more practical significance than the traditional BLP model. In practical application, the lower security level user can report information to the higher security level user, but it doesn't mean that he can write something on the contents of the higher security level user. For the organization with security requirements, the high security level user can know the low security-level user's modify of files, and low security level user can not know the high security level user's file system. In addition, high security level user can modify files of low security level user, and this modification will not affect the original file system of low security level user.

2) Intransitive model

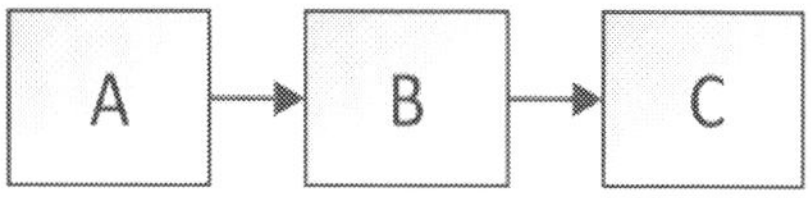

Figure 5. Intransitive model (1)

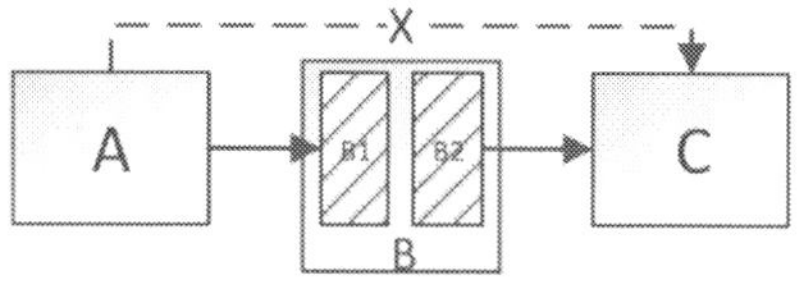

Figure 6. Intransitive model (2)

As shown in Figure 5, for three different domains A, B and C, the non-transitive model can be referred to as $A \rightsquigarrow B, B \rightsquigarrow C, A \not\rightsquigarrow C$. According to characteristics of non-transitive model, B divided into two disjoint domains: B1 and B2. A is considered as the read-only layer of B1, and B2 is considered as the read-only layer of C, as shown in Figure 6. B acts as a middleman or arbiter to judge the information in B1. If the information meet the requirements of C to read, B will copy the information of B1 to B2, then C can read these information. If not, nothing to do. In this way, the information can flow from A to B, from B to C, but can't directly flow from C to A. This model is widely used in practical applications. B can be considered as a confidential department of a unit or organization. It can examine and verify the information of user A, and judge whether user C can read the information. If the requirement is met, the information from A will be written in the area which is readable for user C. This method can avoid the information leakage caused by the direct communication between user A and C.

Conclusion

Trusted multi-level security container mechanism is aimed at the problem of data protection in container-based lightweight virtualization environment, overcome the limitations of the current mainstream MLS in application. At the same time, the trusted multi-level security container mechanism adopt formal description and other trusted computing technologies to ensure the credibility of this method. In addition, the trusted multi-level security container mechanism fully take into account the implementability and flexibility in the practical application, and has a strong guiding significance in design and implementation of the relevant multi-level security container system.

References

1. Alves-Foss J, Oman P W, Taylor C, et al. The MILS architecture for high-assurance embedded systems.[J]. International Journal of Embedded Systems, 2006, 2(3/4):239-247.
2. W. Scott Harrison, Nadine Hanebutte, Paul W. Oman, Jim Alves-Foss. The MILS Architecture for a Secure Global information Grid [J].The Journal of Defense Software Engineering, 2005(10):20-24.
3. Anderson C. Docker[J]. IEEE Software, 2015, 32(3).
4. Bell D E, Padula L J L. Secure Computer System: Unified Exposition and Multics Interpretation[J]. Secure Computer System Unified Exposition & Multics Interpretation, 1976:161-161.
5. Biba K J. Integrity Considerations for Secure Computer Systems[J]. Electronic Systems Div Air Force Hanscom Afb, 1977.
6. Clark D D, Wilson D R. A Comparison of Commercial and Military Computer Security Policies[C]// IEEE Symposium on Security & Privacy. IEEE, 1987:184-184.
7. Rushby J M. Design and verification of secure systems[M]// ACM SIGOPS Operating Systems Review. 2010:12-21.
8. Rushby J M. Proof of separability A verification technique for a class of security kernels[M]// International Symposium on Programming. 1970:352-367.
9. Wikipedia editor. MSL. Available from: https://en.wikipedia.org/wiki/Multiple_single-level.
10. Xiong Jinbo, et al. Action-Based Multilevel Access Control for Structured Document [J]. Journal of Computer Research and Development, 2013, 50(7):1399-1408.
11. Cheng Jing, Shi Yong. Study on Multilevel Security Mechanism based on Virtualization[J]. Communications Technology, 2013(1):35-39.
12. Chen Qingzhang. Characteristics of transparent environment[J]. Application Research of Computers, 1990(5):18-19.
13. Jurca R, Faltings B. Eliciting Truthful Feedback for Binary Reputation Mechanisms[C]// Ieee/wic/acm International Conference on Web Intelligence. IEEE Computer Society, 2004:214-220.
14. Kelly J C, Lead T, Kemp K, et al. formal methods specification and verification guidebook for software and computer systems volume i: planning and technology insertion[J]. 1998.
15. Anderson J P, Anderson J P. Computer Security Technology Planning Study. Volume 2[J]. Computer Security Technology Planning Study, 1972.
16. Group T. TCG specification architecture overview. TCG Specification Revision. 2007;1:1-24.
17. Quigley D, Sipek J, Wright C P, et al. Unionfs: User and Community-Oriented Development of a Unification File System[J]. Proceedings of the Linux Symposium, 2006:349--362.
18. Rushby J. Noninterference, Transitivity, and Channel-Control Security Policies[J]. 1992.

User-Authentication on Wearable Devices Based on Punch Gesture Biometrics

Guan-Cheng LIANG[a], Xiang-Yu XU and Jia-Di YU

Department of Computer Science and Engineering, Shanghai Jiao Tong University, Shanghai, China.

Abstract. Due to commoditization and convenience, wearable technology are interwoven with our daily life. However, privacy sensitive data stored on those devices such as personal email, message can be easily stolen. Most devices require a PIN input to unlock. However, this mechanism is vulnerable to shoulder surfing attack. Thus many novel authentication approaches have been proposed to solve this problem. And biometric-based methods have been adopted by many researchers because of the efficiency and excellent performance. In this paper, we propose a new biometric-based authentication system. We focus on how the user performs a straight punch gesture subconsciously. By analysis the acceleration data from the smartwatch when user performing the gesture, we are able to profile the user. And we authenticate the user according to the biometrics of this action. This mechanism is light-weighted and do not require user to remember any secret code. We develop an authentication system on Samsung Gear Fit 2 and conducted a real-world experiment on 20 volunteers. And we collected 13000 gesture samples to evaluate our system. Results show that our system can achieve a classification accuracy of at least 95.45%. In attacking scenario, our system can achieve an equal error rate lower than 4%. The maximum number of samples required by a well-trained classifier is 25.

1 Introduction

Wearable devices have growing popularity in recent days. Products such as smartwatch and smartband are inexpensive and provide good usability. People are allowed to access social media, e-pay apps through these equipment. However the personal information within brings us the security concern. Attackers may steal the device to snoop sensitive information which results in fatal aftermath. Hence recognizing the identity of the user has great significance.

Unlike smartphone or tablets, wearable devices are usually equipped with small touchscreen, which is only sufficient to perform PIN input. This scheme is defenseless against shoulder surfing attack. Recently, Huawei or Apple enable smartwatch and smartphone to unlock each other after they are paired [1, 2]. This approach leads to more severe consequences for both devices once either the smartphone or wearable device is stolen. Due to resource constraints for wearable devices, researchers turned their focus to biometric-based authentication. For example, resonant properties of human hand are used to establish a secure channel between two devices [4]. However this method is sensitive to the location of the hardware on human hand. Meanwhile Gait based recognition suffers from long training process[5–7].

[a] Corresponding author: liangguancheng@sjtu.edu.cn

For practical use, the authentication system should be light-weighted, e.g. no extra hardware involved and easy to use. Therefore we focus on using hand gesture as a unique behavior of user for authentication. However previous gesture based system requires user to perform very complicated gestures which can be quite cumbersome[3].

In this work we identify the user based on the biometrics generated by punch gesture. Since each person has a unique way of doing a punch gesture which reveals the information of one's identity. And this gesture depends on wingspan, strength, and personal habit et.al. Moreover, the punch gesture is a subliminal action that doesn't need to remember.

There exist several challenges of realizing this system. First, the accelerometer data contains some noise that may cause uncertainty in our system. Thus we apply a low pass filter to remove high frequency noise. Second, we need to identify the features within the recorded data we should use to distinguish different users. To this end, we conduct a close analysis on the collected data to extract useful features for authentication. Third, the attacker may imitate the gesture performed by the legitimate owner to get access to the device. Thus we evaluate the effectiveness of our system in such scenario. The results show that our system can effectually defeat against the imitation of the attackers.

In particular, the legitimate owner wearing a device performs a punch gesture while we collect the readings from accelerometer. Then we use the collected data to extract training dataset and train an effective classifier offline. Later the data is collected from the unidentified user who wears the device, if it matches the pattern of the legitimate user, the user is authorized. In real world the user can perform a punch gesture at any place any time.

We summarize our contribution in this work as follows:

- We conduct a close analysis on the accelerometer data generated by punch gesture to demonstrate biological diversity among different users.
- We propose and implemented a novel authentication system based on biometric of punch gesture.
- We evaluate our system on collected traces of 20 volunteers during 20 days.

The rest of the paper is organized as follows: Section II reviewed the related work on wearable authentication. Section III conducted a close analysis on biometric of punch gesture. In Section IV we present the implementation of our system. Then we perform evaluation for authentication and display the result in Section V. Finally, we draw a conclusion in Section VI.

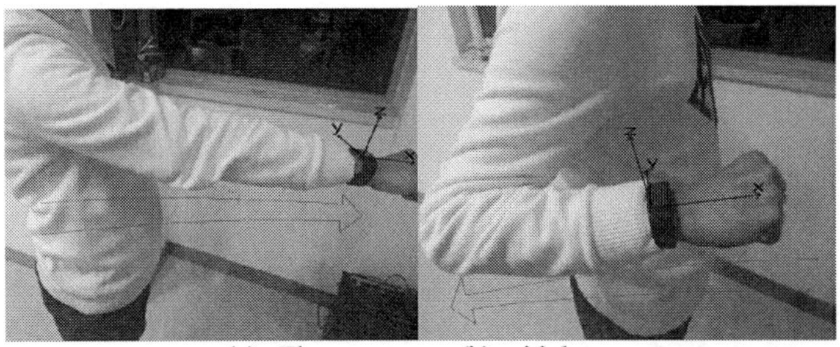

(a) Throw (b) withdraw

Figure 1. Punch gesture.

2 Related work

In this section we review previous works on biometric-based authentication system for wearable devices.

Since wearables are always attached to user's body, gait data can be extracted to identify user. Before smartwatch and other wearables are available, researchers have been studying gait based authentication using wearable motion sensors such as accelerometer or gyroscope[5, 7]. In those works, a wearable sensor is located on a specific area on human body to collect motion data[8–10]. Most recently, a gait based authentication system on smartwatch has been proposed [6]. However gait is

 DOI: 10.1051/itmconf/20171101003

inconsistent when user walks on different kind of surfaces, resulting in low true positive rate. And time consuming training and recognition process are needed for these methods, which is not user-friendly.

Meanwhile, using hand gesture as a biometric for authentication is a promising solution. The sweep or swing of action user while holding the mobile device can be used as biometric for authentication [12, 14]. Yet it's not suitable for wearables since the device is not fixed on the wrist. Continuous gestures of the user, as an out-of-band communication channel, are used to pair wearables and other devices [3]. However those gestures are too complex to perform. For simplicity and usability, we use simple punch gesture as biometric to authenticate the user in this paper.

3 Data collection and analysis

In this section, we give a definition of the punch gesture first. Then we describe the data collection procedure with a set of volunteers. And we conduct a close analysis on the collected accelerometer data.

3.1 Defining punch gesture

The punch gesture is a simple 3D space gesture. We notice that there exist different types of punch gesture in martial arts and combat sports. However, we only adopt the straight punch gesture in this paper. And we assume everyone perform this gesture with the right hand. A person can perform a straight punch gesture as follows: First stand straight and hold the fist within the right chest area. Then throw and withdraw the fist with the way he or she feels comfortable. We present the punch gesture in Fig. 1. The trajectory of throwing and withdrawing almost follows a straight line. This gesture possesses many advantages. First, everyone can perform this gesture in a subconscious way without any specific instruction. Second, it isn't limited to any specific scenario to perform this gesture.

3.2 Collecting data

We developed an application on the Samsung Gear Fit 2 for accelerometer data acquisition. The data are stored locally on the smartwatch. We set the sample rate of the accelerometer to 100 Hz. This

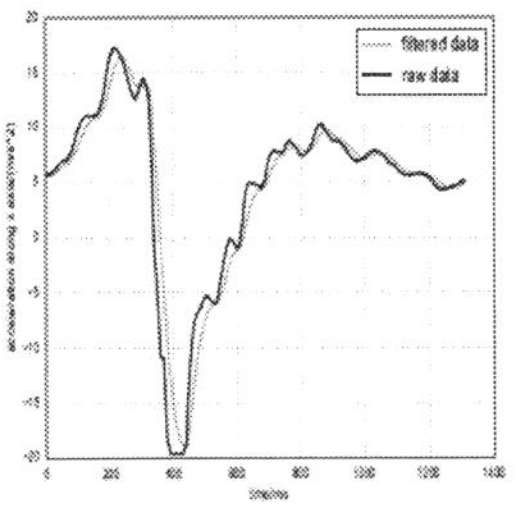

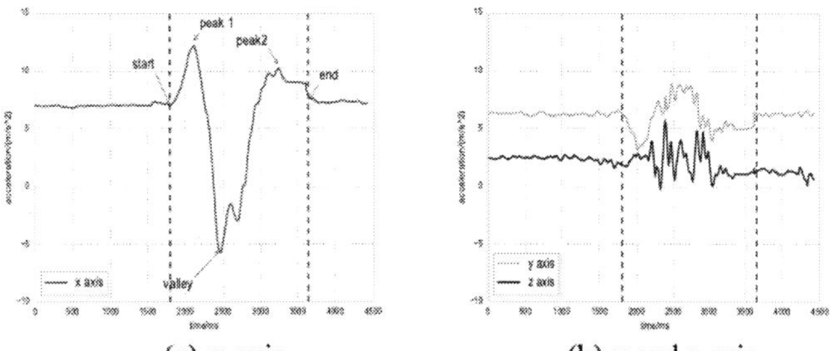

(a) x axis

(b) y and z axis

Figure 2. Low pass filter.

Figure 3. Acceleration data of volunteer 5 performing punch gesture

application will record the accelerometer data when the volunteer performs the gesture. After one gesture is finished, an assistant will press a button on the smartwatch's touchscreen to save the data while the volunteer holds the hand still. The recorded data file is defined as one observation. After 10 observations are complete, the assistant will press a button on the touchscreen to exit the application. The collected data will be transferred to the laptop for further analysis. We recruit 20 graduate students (8 female, 12 male) in the CSE department for our experiment. We label each of them with a unique number. Every day each of them were asked to perform the punch gesture for 10 times, and all observations are labelled with their number. We execute this experiment for 10 days. Together we collected 2000 observations for analysis.

3.2 Analysing data

Accelerometer readings are always containing noise, since the wearable device can sometimes be slippery on the wrist. Thus we need to eliminate noise to obtain more accurate data. We apply a low pass filter on the readings since human action always produce low frequency noise. As we depicted in Fig. 2, the filtered data are smoother than the original data.

We randomly choose 5 out of 20 volunteers, denoted as {V1, V2, V3, V4, V5}, to demonstrate our observation. In our settings, the moving direction of the fist keeps consistent with the x-axis of the accelerometer. Since the moving direction of the fist is almost a straight line, the acceleration produces the most significant change on the axis parallel to this direction. As we depicted in Fig. 3, when V5 perform the punch gesture, we observe a remarkable shift along x-axis while the readings from y and z axis presents inconsistency. This originates from the fact that the acceleration change on y and z axis comes from the slipping on the direction perpendicular to the punch direction. Thus the readings from x-axis retain clearness while the readings from y and z axis suffer from randomness. Therefore we choose the readings along x-axis to detect the beginning and finish time of the gesture by calculating the energy levels[11]. We denote the beginning and the finish time as T0 and TN. We plot 10 segmented observations of V3 in Fig. 4. And one observation for each volunteer is depicted in Fig. 5. We observe that all volunteers share some similar features while at the same time can be distinguished from each other.

First, there exist two peaks and a valley on the segmented data. We label them as ρ_1, ρ_2 and υ. As we can see in Fig. 4, the punch gesture can be divided into two phases, throwing and withdrawing. The volunteer first accelerates to push the fist, and then decelerates in order to change the moving direction at the end of the former phase. Thus we observe an increase follow by a reduction between T_0 and T_{υ}. Similarly, the second phase of withdrawing the fist experiences an almost symmetrical process. This compliance with our intuition since withdrawing a fist is symmetric with throwing. However, we make some observations on Fig. 4 and Fig. 5. First, we notice that the value of ρ_1, ρ_2 and υ is different among all volunteers. Second, the speed of and decreasing the acceleration shows diversity for different volunteers but maintains consistency for the same volunteer. Third, the duration of the gesture of the same volunteer may varies between gestures, yet is still a good indicator of different volunteers. Finally, when a volunteer starts the gesture, the initial acceleration along 3 axes indicates how the volunteer

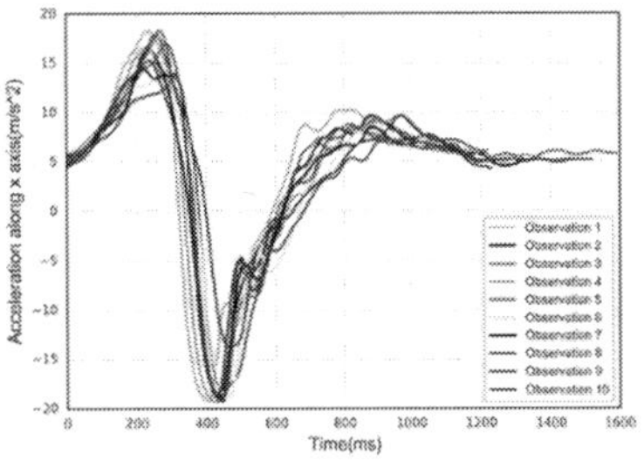

Figure 4. Ten observations of Volunteer 3

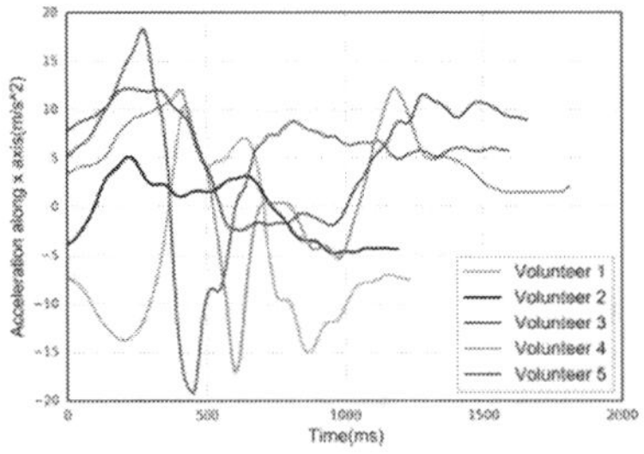

Figure 5. Observation of 5 Volunteers

prefers to hold the fist on still. We define this initial position of the fist as a triple <acc^I_x, acc^I_y , acc^I_z >. Therefore, we can leverage the biometrics to recognize the legitimate user and attackers.

4 System design

In this section, we design an authentication system for wearable devices to identify the legitimate user who owns the device and prevent attackers from accessing the device. We only use the acceleration data from accelerometer that is available on all wearable devices.

4.1 System overview

The system architecture consists of two parts. We first collect observations from the legitimate owner

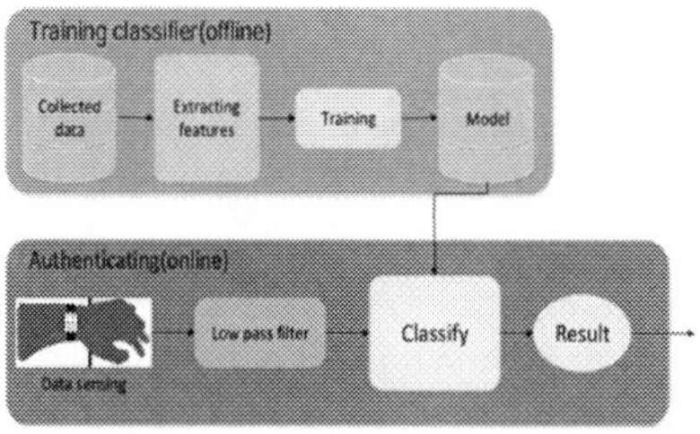

Figure 6. System architecture

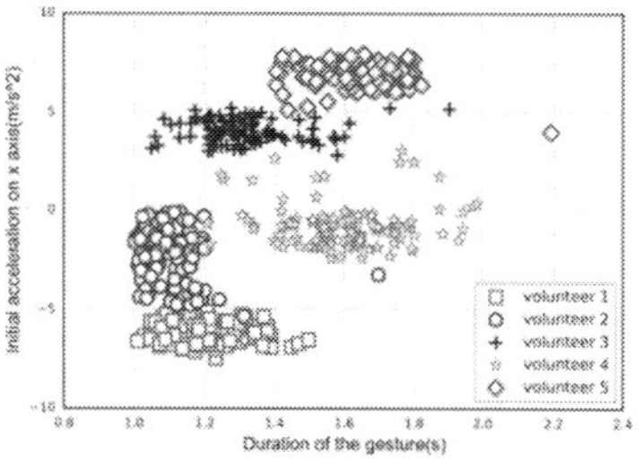

Figure 7. Distribution of feature tuple <T,acc^{I}_{x}> for 5 volunteers

and extract training dataset to learn a classifier in the offline part. Then we utilize the classifier to recognize the identity of the user in online part. We depict the work flow of our system in Fig. 6.

In the offline part, we train an efficient classifier for the legitimate owner. First we collect sufficient observations. For this purpose the legitimate owner is asked to wear the device and perform the gesture for several times. Then we extract effective features from each observation to form a feature vector. Afterwards, the dataset is fed to a machine learning framework thus a classifier for the legitimate owner is obtained.

In the online part, a well-trained classifier is stored on the device ready for authentication. The user is asked to perform the punch gesture to unlock the device. The authentication system first collects the readings of accelerometer and applies a low pass filter to remove noise. Then the feature vector is extracted from the readings. Finally we authenticate the user by feeding the feature vector to the classifier of the legitimate owner. If the result is positive, then the user is authorized to access the device. Otherwise it stays locked for security. As more observations are collected in authenticating process, we add these data to the training dataset to improve the performance of the classifier. However we will show that a small amount of observation is enough for training a useful classifier.

4.2 Feature extraction

Table I. Feature list

Feature	Description	Feature	Description
$acc^{\rho}_{x,1}$	Value of peak 1	T	Duration of punch gesture
$acc^{\rho}_{x,2}$	Value of peak 2	acc^{I}_{x}	Initial acceleration on x axis
b_1	Bandwidth of peak 1	acc^{I}_{y}	Initial acceleration on y axis
b_2	Bandwidth of peak 2	acc^{I}_{z}	Initial acceleration on z axis
μ_1	Mean of peak 1	acc^{υ}_{x}	Value of valley
μ_2	Mean of peak 2	b_{υ}	Bandwidth of valley
σ_1	Standard deviation of peak 1	μ_{υ}	Mean of valley
σ_2	Standard deviation of peak 2	σ_{υ}	Standard deviation of valley

To train an efficient classifier, we need to extract useful feature. By analysing the collected data in Section III, we choose to use statistical features relevant to ρ_1, ρ_2 and υ, 3 features relevant to the initial position, and the duration of the gesture. We list 16 features we find useful to classify different volunteers. In particular, we provide a description of the features. (1)Acceleration Value: We extract the acceleration of ρ_1, ρ_2 and υ which we denote as $acc^{\rho}_{x,1}$, $acc^{\rho}_{x,2}$ and acc^{υ}_{x}. (2)Bandwidth: For ρ_1 and ρ_2, we define the Bandwidth as:

$$\min_{0\leq t\leq T_\upsilon} acc_x^t < acc_x^\rho \cdot \alpha - \max_{T_\upsilon\leq t\leq T_N} acc_x^t < acc_x^\rho \cdot \alpha \quad (1)$$

Intuitively, we search from the peak to both sides until the value drops below a threshold. It reveals how fast a user performs the gesture. This threshold is relevant to the value of the peak. And we empirically select $\alpha = 0.5$ in our work. Moreover, the valuence of acc^{υ}_x varies from volunteer to volunteer. Thus we define the left side of the Band of υ as:

$$\min_{T_\upsilon\leq t\leq T_{\rho_2}} acc_x^t < acc_x^\upsilon + \beta - \max_{T_{\rho_1}\leq t\leq T_\upsilon} acc_x^t < acc_x^\upsilon + \beta \quad (2)$$

It's similar to Bandwidth of a peak, but both positive and negative value of acc^{υ}_x can be dealt with. Here we choose $\beta = 2$ empirically. (3)Mean, Standard deviation: We calculate the mean value and standard deviation within the bandwidth of ρ_1, ρ_2 and υ, which we use as statistical features. (4)Duration: The duration of the gesture is extracted using the segmentation method we describe at Section III. (5)Initial acceleration: We define the acceleration value along 3 axes before the user performs the gesture as the initial acceleration, e.g. the readings when user's hand holds still. The time user starts the gesture is T_0, thus we calculate the initial acceleration by average:

$$acc_x^I = \sum_{t=0}^{T_0} acc_x^t / T_0 \quad (3)$$

And acc^I_y , acc^I_z are obtained using the same method. We plot the distribution of all volunteers in 2-dimensional feature space in Fig. 7. It can be seen that we can possibly separate each volunteer from others efficiently utilizing a simple feature tuple.

4.3 Classifier training

In practical scenario, we will only obtain the training data from the legitimate user. Therefore we utilize one-class SVM to train the model. One-class SVM learns a decision function for novelty detection. First we feed the extracted training dataset from the legitimate owner to the algorithm. Here the samples of this dataset are considered as normal observations. The SVM learns a decision boundary that enclose as much as normal observations while excludes outliers. After training process, we can use this model to classify a new data. If a new data is identified as a similar one to the training set, e.g. lies within the closure we learned, we recognize the user as the authorized user. Otherwise we recognize the data as an illegal user's, and reject the user from accessing the device.

We choose the one-class SVM with the Radial Basis Function (RBF) kernel implemented in scikit-learn python package to train the model. In order to find the optimal parameter ν and γ for the model, we perform a grid search on the ranges $2\text{-}18 \leqslant \nu \leqslant 20$, $2\text{-}18 \leqslant \gamma \leqslant 20$. And we do a 10-cross validation on the training dataset. Since the training dataset are all from the legitimate user, we can select the parameters which provide the highest true positive rate (TPR). Even through high TPR is usually accompanied by high false positive rate (FPR). We show in the evaluation section that FPR is totally acceptable in our system.

5 Evaluation

In this section, we evaluate the performance of our system. We ask 20 volunteers to wear a smartwatch on the right hand, and the experiment is conducted for 20 days. The experiment is divided into two sessions. In the first session during the first 10 days, each volunteer is asked to perform 10 gestures for each day. And we train a particular classifier for each volunteer V_i using the data from V_i. Then we test the classifier on the data that are not used in training process. For example, after the classifier for V_i is obtained, we test it on the data of$\{ V_j \mid 1 \leqslant j \leqslant 20 \text{ and } j \neq i\}$. In the second session during the last 10 days, first we ask one volunteer to perform the gesture for 5 times and we record the volunteer's action. Afterwards, we show the video to 5 of other volunteers and ask them to imitate the gesture of the volunteer in the video for 10 times. In this scenario other volunteers are attackers. We repeat this process for each volunteer at each day. Together we obtain 13000 observations.

Table II. Total accuracy

Volunteer	**1**	**2**	**3**	**4**	**5**	**6**	**7**	**8**	**9**	**10**
Accuracy(%)	99.43	99.13	95.45	97.72	98.24	98.77	96.52	98.35	99.11	99.17
Volunteer	**11**	**12**	**13**	**14**	**15**	**16**	**17**	**18**	**19**	**20**
Accuracy(%)	99.32	95.83	97.65	98.73	97.18	98.53	99.62	97.22	97.19	98.04

5.1 Metrics

We define the metrics as follows to evaluate the performance of our system:

- *Accuracy*: The probability that the classification of an observation A is actually the label of A.
- *Precision*: The probability that an observation A accepted by the classifier is actually an observation of the legitimate owner.
- *Recall*: The probability that an observation A of the legitimate owner is accepted by the classifier.
- *False positive rate(FPR)*: The probability that an observation A of the illegal owner being accepted by the classifier.
- *Equal error rate(EER)*:The value of FPR such that 1-TPR equals FPR.

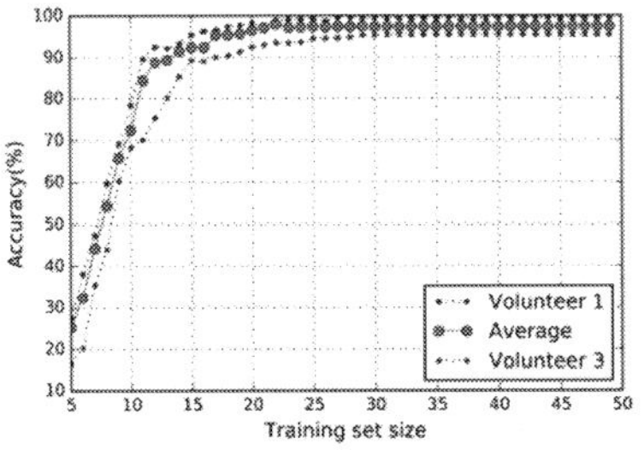

Figure 8. Accuracy under different size of training set.

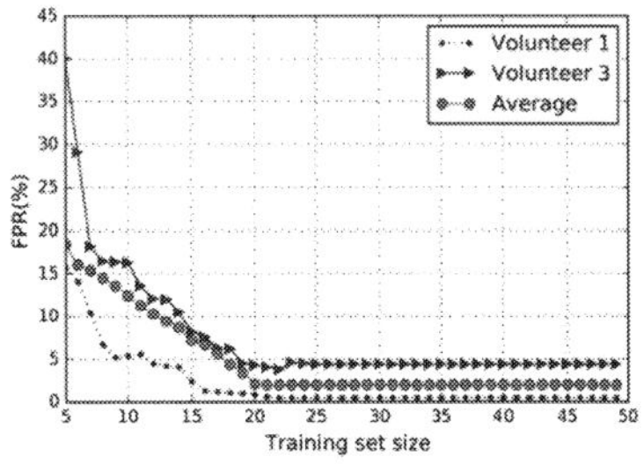

Figure 9. FPR under different size of training set.

5.2 Attacking without imitation

First we evaluate our system on the dataset collected from the first session. We report the result in TABLE II. It can be seen that the lowest accuracy is 95.45% for volunteer 3. The total accuracy for all volunteer is above 95%. Despite that we only use the observations from the legitimate owner in training phase, the one-class SVM can guarantee the exactness of the system. Although more observations from the legitimate owner gives better result in our system, it's practical to use as less as observation to achieve the appropriate accuracy. In this way, the training process can finish quickly and the legitimate owner can use our system in real world. We can feed more observations from the legitimate owner to the SVM for better performance later. Therefore, we show the performance of our system when using different size of training set in training process in Fig. 8. We notice that the classifier of Volunteer 1 can achieve 99% accuracy using only 25 observations. Moreover, Volunteer 3 can achieve 94% accuracy using at most 30 observations. On average, each volunteer can obtain the highest accuracy using at most 25 observations.

However, since we choose the parameters to obtain highest TPR in training phase, more observations is needed to decrease the FPR of the system. Fig. 9 shows that although the FPR can be beyond acceptable when we own few observations from the legitimate owner, it will drop to the lowest value using a small number of observations. In worst case scenario, i.e. for Volunteer 3, FPR drop below 5% using at most 25 observations. This indicates that even we miss the negative observations from the illegal owners, a well-trained classifier for the legitimate owner can separate illegal owners from the authorized one effectively.

5.3 Attacking with imitation

In this scenario, we have 20 group of 6 volunteers. Within each group there are one legitimate owner and 5 attackers. We exploit the well trained classifier for each legitimate owner from the first session and test it on the data collected from the second session. We present the results for each group in Fig. 10. We observe that the recall is above 95% for each group, indicating that the identity of the legitimate owner

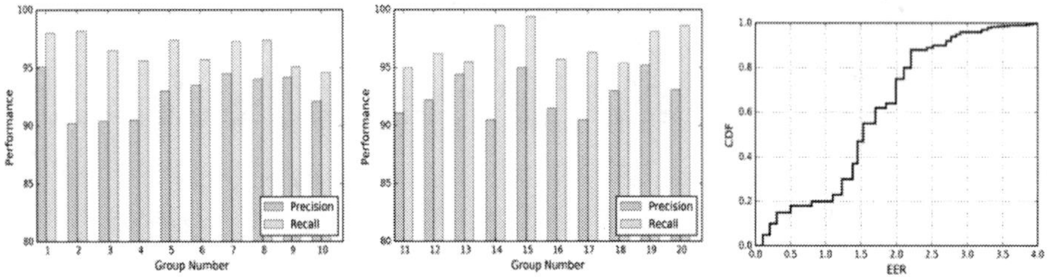

(a) Group 1 to 10. **(b)** Group 11 to 20. **(c)** CDF of EER.

Figure 10. Performance

can be effectively recognized. And the precision is slightly lower since the attackers are now able to observe the legitimate owner closely for imitation. However the attackers can rarely hack into the device by imitation since the precision is above 90%. Therefore the device is safeguarded.

To better demonstrate the usability as well as security of our system, we calculate the EER for each group. Since lower TPR results in lower FPR, we preserve some classifiers with lower TPR during grid search. We test those classifiers on the collected data to calculate FPR. Afterwards we have several TPR-FPR tuples. Using ROC curve we can calculate the EER [13]. We plot the cumulative distribution function(CDF) of the EER in Fig. 10(c). It shows that our system can achieve an EER lower than 4% which is good enough for practical use.

Conclusion

This paper presents a novel authentication system using single punch gesture. The intuition that each person performs this gesture in a unique way leads to this work. We first collect observations of volunteer performing this gesture and recognize the characteristic. Then we build a classifier for each volunteer based on one-class SVM to recognize the legitimate owner. We evaluate the performance of our system on 20 volunteers in two sessions. We collect 13000 observations in total and the results show that our system can achieve an accuracy of at least 95% using at most 25 observations from the legitimate owner. When the attacker access the system by imitation, our system can achieve an EER lower than 4%.

References

1. Apple watch. http://www.apple.com/watch/
2. Huawei watch. http://consumer.huawei.com/en/wearables/ huaweiwatch/index.htm
3. I. Ahmed, Y. Y, S. Bhattacharya, N. Asokan, G. Jacucci, P. Nurmi, and S. Tarkoma, Proc. UbiComp 15, 391-401(2015)
4. W. Wang, L. Yang, Q. Zhang, Proc. UbiComp 16, 670-681(2016)
5. J. Mantyjarvi, M. Lindholm, E. Vildjiounaite, S. M. Makela, and H. J. Ailisto, Proc. ICASSP 05, 973-976(2005)
6. A. H. Johnston, G. M. Weiss, Proc. BTAS 15, 1-6(2015)

7. D. Gafurov, K. Helkala, T. Sondrol, J. Computers **1**, 51-59(2006)
8. M. Derawi, P. Bours, K. Holien, Proc. IIHMSP 10, 312-317(2010)
9. R. Liu, J. Zhou, M. Liu, X. Hou, Proc. ICIEA 07, 2654-2659(2007)
10. T. liu, Y. Inoue, K. Shibata, Measurement **42**, 978-988(2009)
11. J. Liu, Y. Wang, G. Kar, Y. Chen, J. Yang, M. Gruteser, Proc. MobiCom 15, 142-154(2015)
12. F. Okumura, A. Kubota, Y. Hatori, K. Matsuo, M. Hashimoto, A. Koike, Proc. ISPACS 06, 45-50(2006)
13. K. Murphy, Machine Learning: A Probabilistic Perspective. MIT(2012)
14. K. Matsuo, F. Okumura, M. Hashimoto, S. Sakazawa, Y. Hatori, ICB 07, 211-221(2007)

iPark: Parking Management System Based on Arduino and Cloud Platform

Lin-Xian WEI, Yan-Li YANG, Ling-Jun DENG[a], Liang-Hai YANG, Yi-Xuan CHEN and Ao LI
ShenZhen University, ShenZhen, GuangDong, China

Abstract. In order to have a better use of cross-platforms. We adopt the B/S architecture design and implement a parking management system. This system can not only view parking spaces, but also meet other needs, such as parking reservation and position recording. The node-based development can realize a flexible changing function that adds or removes nodes at any time. Based on cloud platforms, sever is built by PHP, MySQL database and other technologies and tools. Sensor networks are established relied on Arduino and nRF24L01 model.

1 Introduction

With the development of the Internet technology and embedded technology, as well as the increasing demand of intelligence and facilitation from society, the convenience of online management system becomes evident. The high development of the Internet is bound to make type and quantity of its terminals grow faster and faster. The internet changes from previous PC as a main networking tool to the mobile phone terminal, even up to now, "everything is connected." The parking management system can achieve the purpose of information collection, data processing and data real-time transmission via sensor, micro controller and communication module. Finally, dealing by a control center, information feedbacks to users then interacts with users, too.

Because the traditional parking management fails to connect to the Internet, it cannot interact with owners. That failure brings difficult for owners to find parking spaces. As the internet of things technology continues to mature, it gets rid of complex and inconvenient of the traditional parking management. This paper, based on wireless communication, combines the Internet with the embedded technology, and then designs a parking management system. The cloud platform completes parking information visualization, parking occupancy information and parking lot reservation and other functions.

2 System architecture design

According to data transmission, processing and feedback process, the system is divided into three parts: car park internal network, cloud platform and mobile terminal.

[a] Corresponding author: deng497@outlook.com

Those three parts are developed individually, and do not affect each other. They all use open and call interface to interact with information, which can increase system stability. The system structure diagram is shown in Figure 1.

The terminal is controlled by users. First, it transmits data to cloud platform, and data processed by the cloud platform will go through a router in the parking place. Second, gateway nodes obtain data and instructions which will be sent to every perceptual control node in the parking lot through a wireless module. Ultimately, we achieve the purpose of sensing surveillance and controlling equipment. The level of hardware system structure is shown in Figure 2.

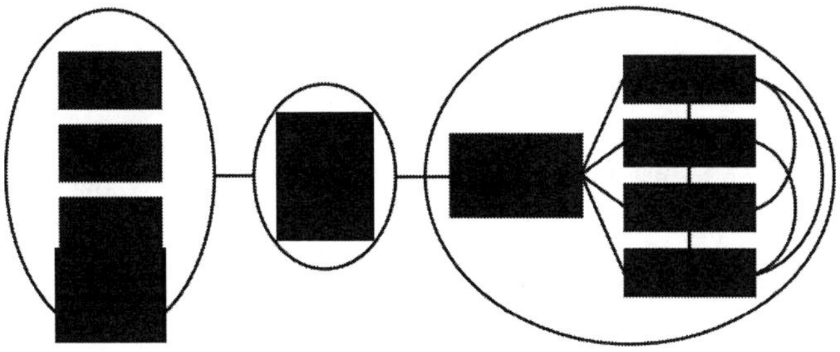

Figure 1. The system structure diagram.

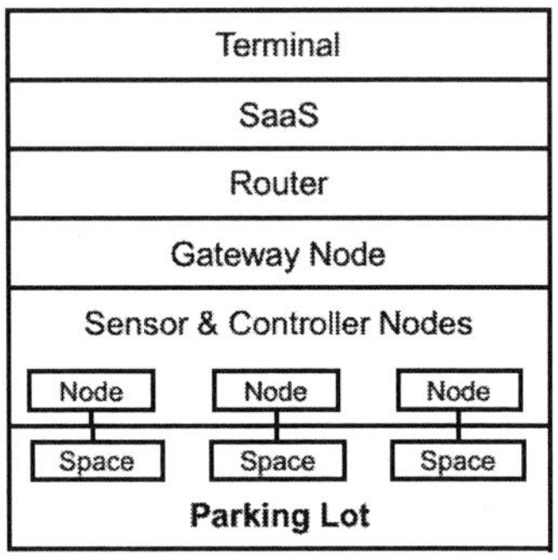

Figure 2. The hardware system structure diagram.

2.1 Parking lot sensor node network

Setting the micro controller with the nRF24L01 module as basic configuration, defining a node according to different sensors and modules by functionality, an internal distributed network is built in the park. Data processing is independent of each other, and they have a direct communication through the 2.4G band or have an indirect communication through the parking gateway. If a single node is destroyed, it is not going to affect the whole network.

Every network node has a unique identification number that can collect and process related data independently. For instance, parking lot nodes collect and process occupancy data and that information are sent to cloud server through parking gateway.

The distributed network is an important basis for incremental development of intelligent parking field, which can dynamically add or delete nodes without affecting original functions. A new node accesses the network gateway without confirmation, which can communicate with servers by gateway identification and password.

The gateway node is a bridge between the internal distributed network and Internet communication. In addition to the nRF24L01 module, the gateway node also has a W5100 Ethernet module for connecting Internet.

2.2 Cloud server

The robust stability of cloud server also provides protection for high concurrency, which has become the first choice for control center.

Cloud server uses PHP, MySQL database to build a control center. It is used to manage users' account information, integrate and process datum from network nodes, and provide a remote management system.

The Cloud server stores a unique ID number of all nodes in database, and it establishes a table to associate users' account with related nodes. That method brings convenience to manage, and users can flexibly increase or delete nodes.

2.3 Mobile terminal

Through browser on the mobile terminal accessing to cloud serve, we can obtain real time data and realize remote real-time monitoring by running JavaScript code, and using ajax technology. The user interface applies the JQuery Mobile, which imitates the style of mobile terminal APP, to improve user's experience. Through the ajax technology to achieve a seamlessly transfer page without refreshing [2].

Benefitting from B/S architecture, the mobile terminal platform has no restriction. Whether PC or intelligent mobile phone, or any kind of operating system, the browser is just supported by JavaScript can manage and use the intelligent parking lot system, and also meets the demand of users on each platform.

3 The realization of sensor node network in parking lot

3.1 Node of platform

Nodes use Arduino as a development platform. The Arduino includes software and hardware which are Arduino IDE and a variety of Arduino boards (using AVR chips). The flexibility and convenience of platform for post-packaging of the AVRGCC library allows developers to pay more attention on creativity and implementation. Thus the Arduino IDE cross-platform can run on following three systems: Mac OS, Windows and Linux [1].

Selection of Arduino boards depends on the function of nodes. Gateway nodes use the Arduino UNO board equipped with Ethernet Shield and nRF24L01 wireless module in some of the more stringent requirements on the size of environment. For example, the smart node switch adopts the smaller volume of Arduino Pro Mini, so it can be easily embedded into various products.

The high flexibility of node development is usually to develop nodes quickly with specific function under specific demands. At the same time, nodes also comply with the independence of platform. If they obey the system construct, nodes can also be exploited by other platforms. Nodes among different platforms communicate with each other, which can also be composed of the distributed network. The deployment of experiment is shown as Figure 3.

Figure 3. The Parking space node deployment.

3.2 Headings Nodes based on Arduino platform realization

All nodes have at least a microcontroller and an nRF24L01 module to achieve the network, and each node has a unique identifier. Nodes are equipped with a variety of function and different sensors and modules. All notes constitute a parking lot internal network, which sets node as a unit for development to ensure the stability of system and the diversity of function. The new developed nodes can also be seamlessly added into the existing nodes' network that is flexible and convenient. Nodes' development should focus on specialized functions. Amounts of function of one node are available but might destroy the stability, so we promote to use specialized function of node. Nodes can be divided into two categories: the gateway node and the sensor control node. Those two types of nodes form a star network, and the structure of P2P is used between sensor control nodes.

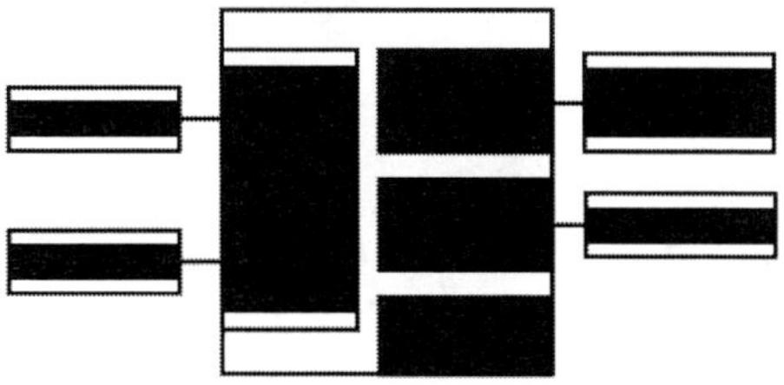

Figure 4. The hardware architecture of node

3.3 Hardware architecture of node

A node is consisted of Arduino board and nRF24L01 module. According to special need, it adds different devices, such as W5100 Ethernet Shield, ultrasonic distance measurement and other sensors. Among them, the nRF24L01 module and W5100 are essential modules of network management class nodes. It is a bridge connecting the Internet and the node network. Arduino connects the Internet through W5100, and nRF24L01 is responsible for communicating with other nodes. The hardware architecture of the node is shown in Figure 4.

In the node development, you should pay more attention to select multiple subordinate devices, so that you can avoid conflicts. For example, when you use nRF24L01, SS stitches of SD and W5100 linking Ethernet Shield should be set as a high level output, and the CS stitches of nRF24L01 should be set as a low level of output. On the contrary, the Ethernet Shield will be used in the same way.

3.4 Software architecture of the node

Each node on devices, have written a corresponding driver, and export interface for system calls. According to the function of node, when the system is written, the required interface is selected to call. nRF24L01 commonly used third party libraries have Mirf and RF24, etc.; While W5100 uses the official library Ethernet, on the basis of the preparation of the project dedicated HTTP_Client for access to the cloud platform. The software architecture of the node is shown in Figure 5.

The gateway node is the most important kind of node, which is responsible for connecting internal network with the internet. It adopts Arduino UNO board [3], Ethernet Shield and nRF24L01 as the basic configuration, and uses the official Ethernet Shield library files, and even connects to the Internet to create a Socket completing TCP connection with servers. Based on that, iPark project specially prepared a HTTP protocol database for data interaction with the server. After completing this server response, connections are broke down to save server resources, and the next connection request is initiated by a node again. Using the POST method in HTTP, the unique identifier of gateway node and data transmitted by other nodes are submitted to a server. The server judges and verifies the node identifier and returns to instruction. After a gateway node receives returned instructions, node identifiers and instructions are parsed, and instructions are sent to relate node identifiers to complete a communication between internal network and cloud server. A real project will package the HTTP protocol into a new library and apply that into gateway nodes considering Ethernet library. And then error handling mechanism and reconnection mechanism are written.

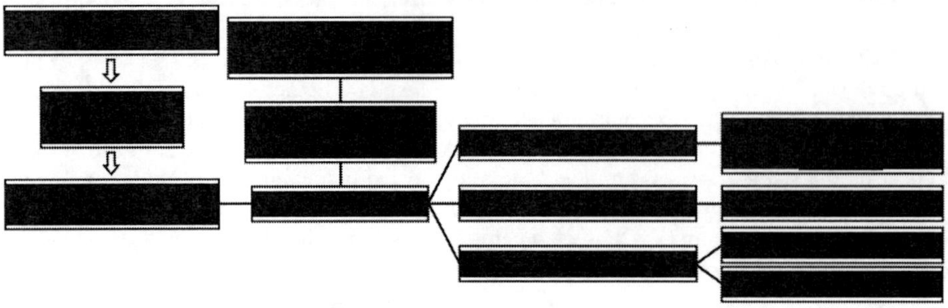

Figure 5. The software architecture of node

3.5 Wireless network based on nRF24L01 module

In the application scenario of intelligent parking, the distance between two nodes in general is from ten meters to 100 meters. So considering cost conditions, the use of nRF24L01 module can meet a variety of demands. The distance between two nodes is short, and nodes can communicate directly with each other wirelessly.

nRF24L01 works between 2.4GHZ to 2.5GHz with low current consumption and small size. The operating frequency, protocol address, transmission rate and data packet length all can be set by software, and the nRF24L01 supports automatic response. As the application applied for the parking lot with advantages of short-distance transmission, wireless network can be regarded as a fully connected network where each node communicates directly. The gateway node plays an important role in wireless network when communication among remote control nodes is required. After getting remote instruction and node address, those gateway notes send instruction to the assigned node. Nodes analyze the address of the other nodes in the instruction, and start to communicate with it according to the instruction. Nodes can also send broadcasts to each other to identify "neighbor" nodes.

4 Cloud platform control center implementation

By Adopting MySQL database and PHP to build the cloud control center, we use the form, which makes the car park node network to call control center API, to achieve monitoring and management of network nodes in parking lot.

MySQL is one of the most popular relational database management systems. It has the characteristics of small size and fast speed, so that it attracts many developers. Compared with CGI or Perl, PHP can implement dynamic web pages rapidly. Matching MySQL and PHP together is a mainstream.

The control center stores parking information of users in a database. Users can book a parking space in user interface. When the user operates and manages parking space remotely in control center, the server will find gateway node which is bound with the user's parking place in MySQL database. And then operation instructions and identifiers of gateway nodes are written in an instruction table in the database. Through constant polling server, gateway nodes query instructions issued by the bound account, after being acquired, and they are forwarded to a wireless network inside the parking lot to complete user's remote management. When the internal network node of the parking lot uploads data, data will be sent into servers by POST in HTTP through gateway notes. Eventually, the server responses the treated content to gateway nodes. All of those complete a data collection of control center.

The control center connects the user's mobile terminal and internal network nodes in the user's parking lot. Therefore, there are two kinds of API for external calls. One is the interface for the mobile terminal calls, and the other is for internal network of the parking lot. After opening the API in control center, you can allow more developers to develop third party nodes to rich application.

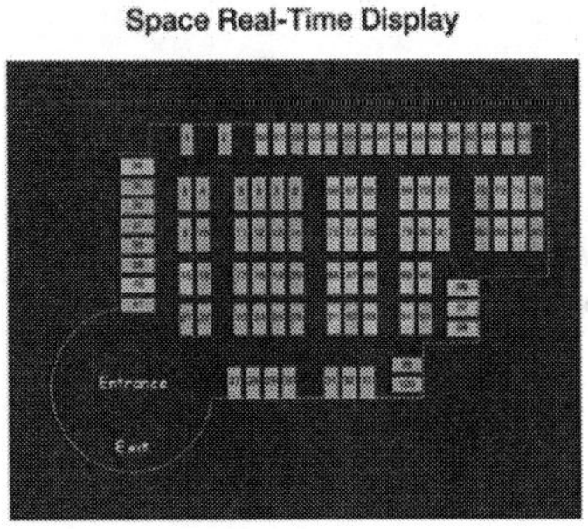

Figure 6. Parking space information interface

5 Mobile terminal implementation

User interaction in iPark system is based on B/S architecture that is Browser/Server architecture with good cross platform. A browser which only supports JavaScript can complete node management on the network. Currently, on the market, most of the browsers support it.

In data interaction, data can be accessed and submitted by AJAX technology in real-time. In pages switch, the experience of native App switches without refreshing can be achieved by JQuery animation effect. AJAX allows asynchronously transmit data between browser and server without reloading the entire page and without blocking users, and it receives data returned by the server and then processes and displays them on the page, as shown in figure 6.

When users log in to the iPark, the browser will encrypt users' information and store them in local cookies. It is easy to automatically login in the next time and reduce the cumbersome procedures. Cookies is a kind of data, which a website uses to identify the user's identity and stores in the user's local terminal. Sites cannot extract Cookies information from other sites other than they place.

In security, because of the AJAX technology, every time the user account and encrypted password are summited to verify that each operation is carried out by the user himself. That approach can prevent hackers from intercepting packets to steal passwords and prevent unnecessary security holes due to stateless HTTP protocols.

Conclusion

Nowadays, sensor technology and wireless network technology are becoming more and more mature in the age of information, so Internet of Things is bound to become a hot spot to meet the people's pursuit of quality of life, intelligent life, and the demand for convenience. Thus, the Internet of Things market owns characters of vast, potentially and huge application value that arouse the concern of much more manufacturers. The emergence of Arduino, with its good support for each sensor, has become the first choice for the rapid development of prototypes related Internet of Things. In this paper, a kind of intelligent parking management system based on nodes is designed, and a feasible, fast and effective scheme is proposed based on Arduino implementation.

References

1. Dale Wheat, Arduino internals. Apress: 20-180 (2011)

2. Xiaojuan.Luo. & Li.Xu, Real-time Supervisory Based on AJAX and B/S Architecture: 64-65 (2013)
3. Ruiyan.Cai, Principle and application of Arduino: 155-157 (2012)
4. Zhiyun.Shi, Jianping.Gai, Daihua.Wang, Zhjie.Zhang, A new kind of high speed wireless RF transceiver--nRF24L01 and its application: 42 – 44
5. John W. Satzinger, Systems Analysis and Design in a Changing World [M]. Cengage Learning EMEA: 22-190 (2008)
6. Thomas M. Connolly, Carolyn E. Begg, Database systems: a practical approach to design, implementation, and management [M]. Addison-Wesley: 97-142 (2009)
7. Matthew MacDonald, Beginning ASP.NET 4.0 in Java: 96-102 (2010)
8. Andy Oppel & Robert Sheldon, SQL: a beginner's guide BEGINNER'S GUIDE [M]. McGraw-Hill Professional: 50-180 (2008)
9. J.F.Di Marzio, Android: A Progammer's Guide. New York Mc-Graw-Hill: 869-876 (2008)
10. J. D. Owens, D. Luebke, N. Govindaraju, M. Harris, J. Krger, A. E. Lefohn, and T. J. Purcell, A survey of general-purpose computation on graphics hardware (2005)
11. W. Mark, R. Glanville, K. Akeley, and M. Kilgard, Cg: A system for programming graphics hardware (2003)
12. Rick Rogers, Jhon Lombardo, Zigurd Mednieks, Blake Meike, Android Application Development.Sebastopol (2009)
13. Thompson T, The Android Mobile Phone Platform. The World of Software Development (2008)
14. GEO matching regions: multiple regions of interests using content based image retrieval based on relative locations. Multimedia Tools and Applications, 1-35
15. Contemporary integration of content based image retrieval. Wavelet Active Media Technology and Information Processing (ICCWAMTIP, 2014)
16. Content based image retrieval based on geo-location driven image tagging on the social web. Wavelet Active Media Technology and Information Processing (ICCWAMTIP, 2014)
17. Travel recommendation using geo-tagged photos in social media for tourist. Wireless Personal Communications 80 (4), 1347-1362
18. Dynamic path privacy protection framework for continuous query service over road networks. World Wide Web, 1-34
19. Efficient object identification and multiple regions of interest using CBIR based on relative locations and matching region. Wavelet Active Media Technology and Information Processing (ICCWAMTIP, 2015)
20. Unsupervised feature approach for content based image retrieval using principal component analysis. Wavelet Active Media Technology and Information Processing (ICCWAMTIP, 2014)
21. Database Technology on the Web: Query Interface Determining Algorithm for Deep Web Based on HTML Features and Hierarchical Clustering. Sindh University Research Journal-SURJ (Science Series) 48 (1)
22. Enhanced privacy and authentication: An efficient and secure anonymous communication for location based service using asymmetric cryptography scheme. Wireless Personal Communications 84 (2), 1487-1508
23. Authentication User's Privacy: An Integrating Location Privacy Protection Algorithm for Secure Moving Objects in Location Based Services. Wireless Personal Communications 82 (3), 1585-1600
24. A secure and efficient communication scheme with authenticated key establishment protocol for road networks. Wireless Personal Communications 85 (3), 1167-1191

Prediction of Postpartum Hemorrhage Volume of Pregnant Women Based on GA-SVM Algorithm

Ren-Jun SHUAI[1], Yang HE[1] and Ping CHEN[2]

[1]*Nanjing Tech University, University, 211816, China*
[2]*Nanjing Health Information Center, 210003 China*

Abstract: To take most advantage of the medical data resources from maternal and child health information platform and to improve the medical level, the team bring up a method based on support vector machine (SVM) algorithm which is aimed at predicting blood flow and blood pressure within 2-24 hours after parturition. We cleaned up the extracted data, determine the linear correlation via Pearson correlation coefficient, and utilize the significance to test and justify the relevance of data. Also, genetic algorithm is used to optimize the parameters. Then, we filter out the data with strong correlation coefficient and make predictions through the SVM algorithm. Finally, we determine the effectiveness of the prediction by doing the comparison between predicted results and the real data. The experiments show that, SVM is valid and feasible for the prediction of postpartum hemorrhage and the blood pressure.

1. Introduction

Postpartum hemorrhage (PPH) refers to a serious childbirth complication where the amount of bleed flow of pregnant women within 24 hours after delivery is more than 500ml. Postpartum hemorrhage often happens suddenly and may lead to death if pregnant women cannot be treated on time. Postpartum hypertension is also a serious complication of maternal mortality. So, if blood pressure and the amount of blood flow can be predicted, proper measures can be taken to avoid death of pregnant women.

As early as 20 years ago, our country has developed a 'Postpartum hemorrhage prediction score table', which has played an important role in prediction of postpartum hemorrhage. Yan Jianying and Huang Kehua screened out high risk factors by analyzing 212 cases of postpartum hemorrhage and 424 healthy cases from Provincial Maternity and Child Care Center of Fujian province. They establish the high risk scoring system for postpartum hemorrhage based on 'Postpartum hemorrhage prediction score table'. By comparison, they found that scoring system provides more accurate prediction than scoring table[1]. However, because of development and changes of people's lifestyles, factors of postpartum hemorrhage increased as well as maternal complications. With enhancement of medical level and improvement of data analysis skills, all stages of maternal data can be used, through algorithm, to predict the amount of maternal postpartum hemorrhage, doctors can be able to take appropriate emergent measures to reduce the possibilities of maternal mortality. The study of postpartum blood pressure are mostly based on the productive process of blood pressure changes.

2. Algorithm Background

2.1 Pearson Correlation Coefficient

There exists certain connections among things and Pearson correlation coefficient is used to describe them through quantitative indicators.

When analyzing, we should pay attention to an important basic principle: correlation is not equal to cause and effect. Correlation analysis in part shows correlation between the two variables, but not a certain type of this correlation. In other words, correlation analysis doesn't reveal which is cause and which is result[2].

As to two variables x and y, after several groups of tests for multiple sets of data, we mark them as(x_i , y_i)(i =1,2,3⋯ n),then the expression of correlation coefficient is as follows:

$$r = \frac{\sum_{i=1}^{n}(x_i - \bar{x})(y_i - \bar{y})}{\sqrt{\sum_{i=1}^{n}(x_i - \bar{x})^2 \sum_{i=1}^{n}(y_i - \bar{y})^2}} \quad (1)$$

In the formula, $\bar{x}$, $\bar{y}$ respectively represents average value of x , y .The value range of r is(-1,1),and the positive and negative signs in front of r represent the directions of the association, the absolute value indicates the intensity of the association. The closer to 1, the higher the degree of linear correlation is. If $r = 1$ or -1 , then there is a perfect linear correlation between x and y [3].

2.2 Significance test of r

The correlation coefficient r is calculated by the data, so it will be affected by the randomness and the number of samples. So, we need to examine the reliability of the sample which justifies the significance of the experiment.

First, the null hypothesis for the sample is H_O.Second, we calculate the statistics for the test. Usually we describe the test by using t-distribution, and the formula is:

$$t = |r|\sqrt{\frac{n-2}{1-r^2}} \sim t(n-2) \quad (2)$$

Finally, with T-distribution table, we determine the linear relationship and find the critical value between variables according to the pre-determined significance level α and degrees of freedom $d_i = n-2$ [4,5].

2.3 Support Vector Machine

SVM (Support Vector Machine) is a neural network model of small probability events proposed by Vapnik

The core idea of SVM is to maximize the classification interval. Taking the two classification problem as an example, we hope to find a super plane, which can successfully separate the sample points of the two categories, and ensures that the point-to-hyperplane spacing is maximized. Compared to other similar machine learning algorithms (eg, Perceptron, Logistic Regression), SVM has more generalization ability[6].

2.3.1 Basic Theory of SVM

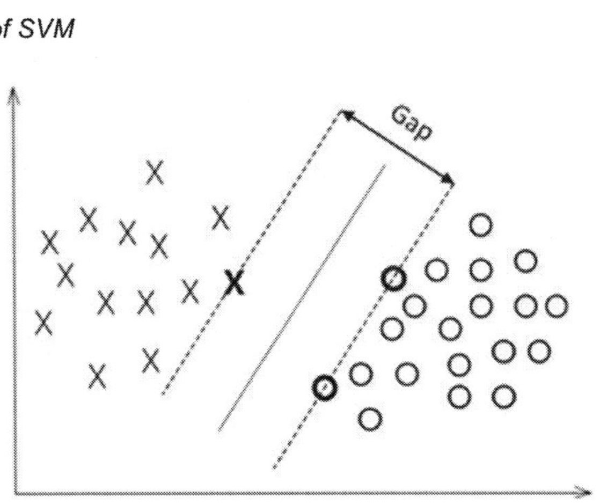

Figure 1. SVM algorithm idea

As shown in Figure 1, in the two-dimensional space, SVM algorithm is committed to find such a line, which can classify the data points and require data points to the distance of the straight line. The greater the distance is, the more improved accuracy will be. Therefore, we need to find such a plane that making this accuracy as high as possible. That is, we want to solve the optimization problem: $\max \gamma$.

In addition, some conditions need to be met:

$$y_i(w^T x_i + b) = \gamma_i \geq \gamma, i = 1,2......n \tag{3}$$

Let $r = 1$, then this hyper plane can be expressed as:

$$\max \frac{1}{\|w\|} \tag{4}$$

$$s.t, y_i(w^T x_i + b) \geq 1, i = 1,2......n \tag{5}$$

equivalent to:

$$\min \frac{1}{2}\|w\|^2, s.t, y_i(w^T x_i + b) \geq 1, i = 1,2......n \tag{6}$$

According to the solving method of convex quadratic programming in optimization theory, we define the Lagrangian function:

$$L(w,b,\alpha) = \frac{1}{2}\|w\|^2 - \sum_{i=1}^{n} \alpha_i (y_i(w^T x_i + b) - 1) \tag{7}$$

we also defined:

$$\theta(w) = \max_{\alpha_i \geq 0} L(w,b,\alpha) \tag{8}$$

When the above constraints are met, $\theta(w)$ is the same as $\frac{1}{2}\|w\|^2$, so the original problem is equivalent to:

$$\min_{w,b}\theta(w)=\min_{w,b}\max_{\alpha_i\geq 0}L(w,b,\alpha)=p^* \quad (9)$$

In order to facilitate the solution, the problem is transformed into a dual problem:

$$\max_{\alpha_i\geq 0}\min_{w,b}L(w,b,\alpha)=d^* \quad (10)$$

This optimization needs to satisfy the KKT condition:

$$1.\ h_j(x_*)=0, j=1,2......p, g_k(x_*)\leq 0, k=1,2......q \quad (11)$$

$$2.\ \nabla f(x_*)+\sum_{j=1}^{p}\lambda_j\nabla h_j(x_*)+\sum_{k=1}^{q}u_k\nabla g_k(x_*)=0,\ \lambda_j\neq o, u_k\geq 0, u_k g_k(x_*)=0 \quad (12)$$

To solve this equation, we need to seek the minimum of w and b .That is $\nabla_w L(w,b,\alpha),\nabla_b L(w,b,\alpha)=0$, then we get the results: $w=\sum_{i=1}^{n}\alpha_i x_i y_i$, $\sum_{i=1}^{n}\alpha_i y_i=0$.Into the formula,we get:

$$\max_{\alpha}\sum_{i=1}^{n}\alpha_i-\frac{1}{2}\sum_{i,j=1}^{n}\alpha_i\alpha_j y_i y_j x_i^T x_j, s.t, \alpha_i\geq o, i=1,2......n, \sum_{i=1}^{n}\alpha_i y_i=0 \quad (13)$$

For nonlinear functions, the SVM algorithm approach is to choose a kernel function K, which projecting data into higher dimensional space. In order to achieve this transformation which from high to low dimensional space conversion, we need to use kernel function $k(x,x_i)=\phi(x)\phi(x_i)$.The common kernel functions are shown in Table 2, Corresponding linear separable equation (13) we will eventually become non-linear problems:

$$\max_{\alpha}\sum_{i=1}^{n}\alpha_i-\frac{1}{2}\sum_{i,j=1}^{n}\alpha_i\alpha_j y_i y_j K(x,y), s.t., \alpha_i\geq 0, \sum_{i=1}^{n}\alpha_i y_i=0 j=1,2......n \quad (14)$$ [7,8].

Table 2. Common kernel functions

Name	Expression
Linear kernel function	$K(x,y)=x^T y+c$
Polynomial kernel function	$K(x,y)=(rx^T y+c)^d$
Radial basis function (RBF) kernel function	$K(x,y)=\exp(-r\lVert x-y\rVert^2)$
Sigmoid kernel function	$K(x,y)=\tan r(a(x,y)+c)$

2.3.2 Regression prediction of SVM

In order to use the support vector machine for regression analysis, Cortes and others add the penalty term C to the objective function, and set the threshold to control the proportion of the error and convert the above equation into:

$$\max_{\alpha}\sum_{i=1}^{n}\alpha_i-\frac{1}{2}\sum_{i,j=1}^{n}\alpha_i\alpha_j y_i y_j K(x,y),\ s.t., 0\leq\alpha\leq C, \sum_{i=1}^{n}\alpha_i y_i=0, i=1,2......n \quad (15)$$

$K(x, y)$ represents the kernel function type of the support vector machine from the low-dimensional to the high-dimensional space conversion, which describes prediction expression of SVM.

2.3.3 Realization of SVM Prediction Based on Genetic Algorithm Optimization

Genetic algorithm is an adaptive searching technique based on a selection and reproduction mechanism found in the natural evolution process, and it was pioneered by Holland in the 1970s.It has become very famous with its global searching, parallel computing, better robustness, and not needing differential information during evolution.

SVM algorithm needs to determine the three factors in dealing with the prediction of nonlinear function:1.Selection of kernel function;2.Parameters of the kernel function r;3.Penalties C. If the results are predicted without these factors, results will be ultimately affected. Genetic Algorithm is a method by using the evolution in biology sphere, that is, the natural selection of the biological world and the natural genetic mechanism of the randomized search method. The algorithm was proposed by Professor J. Holland of the United States in 1975. Its superiority lies in the use of probabilistic optimization method where it doesn't need to determine the rules, instead you can automatically get and guide the search space optimization. So, it is very suitable for large-scale parallel computing. It has the inherent heuristic stochastic search characteristic and is not easy to fall into the local optimum. The kernel function parameters and the penalty term are determined as follows:

Step 1: Coding, the kernel function type, the kernel function parameter and the penalty item in the SVM prediction algorithm are encoded by binary coding;

Step 2: Initialization, we need to select a group and extract a certain amount of individuals, then forms a population. The choice of individuals is to take a uniform distribution of methods rather than random methods, which ensures that the selected kernel function parameters and penalty terms are distributed evenly in the parameter space;

Step 3: Selection, crossover and mutation. Individual selection is based on the individual fitness of the population. The standard of individual fitness is the standard deviation of the prediction model. Crossover and mutation are used to process the population of the current generation, resulting in a new generation of population;

Step 4: Determine the best global convergence. If the selected individuals reach the expected threshold that the distance between the populations is less than the accepted value, the iteration process converges and the algorithm ends. Otherwise, it returns to step 3 and continues to cycle[9,10].

3.Data analysis

Data analysis is a process of gathering data, analyzing data, and making it become useful information. The main process of data analysis is:1.data collection;2.data storage;3.data extraction;4.data filtering;5.data analysis;6.data presentation;7.data applications.

The data of this experiment come from Nanjing Maternal and Child Health Care System. The subjects were collected from the Gulou Hospital from 2014 to 2015[11].

3.1 Data acquisition and storage

Data collection refers to the acquisition and collection of data. Doctors or pregnant women take the information of maternal and child into the system by using mobile Internet technology.

Data storage means that the data is stored in a certain format. Since Women and children's data are regarded as privacy, it must be stored on the database of personal sensitive privacy information (including patient privacy information related to the name, ID number, contact telephone, address, medical history and other data) for encryption. Nanjing Maternal and Child System uses M2-S5100 database security gateway to store and encrypt information of women and children.

3.2 Data extraction and data filtering

Data extraction traverses the entire database and extracts the relevant data from the cloud storage platform based on the data table name. Query the database, such as: AGE, PREGNANCIES (Pregnancy times), CGAGEW(Childbirth Week (Week)), CGAGED(Delivery Week (days)), MODELIVERY(Mode of delivery), THBPHIGH(2 hours postpartum blood pressure - high), THBPLOW(Two hours postpartum blood pressure - low), TWFBLEEDING(2-24 hours postpartum hemorrhage)...,a total of 8629 data is exported.

Data filtering is to delete, organize, and exclude useless data. Delete the entire data-free row, then we get the remaining 7833 data. We use K-means algorithm to select the most extreme clustering, and the data in the cluster is deleted by the whole row, remaining 5036 data. Finally, the CGAGEW, CGAGED integration components delivery days (DAY).

3.3 Experimental setup

We calculate the correlation coefficient and the significance level of TWFBLEEDING, THBPHIGH, THBPLOW,MODELIVERY,PREGNANCIES,DAY and two-tailed test was used for significance test.

We use SVM to predict the amount of blood loss and blood pressure. In the experiment, the original data were transformed into two sets of data samples with the class of subject. The first set of data is labeled the amount of bleeding, that is, each sample can be expressed as (xi, yi), xi is the input eigenvector, yi is bleeding. The second set of data is labeled with blood pressure, the same as the first set, xi is the input eigenvector, yi is the blood pressure value.

In addition, in order to test the prediction effect of the algorithm in this experiment, we use standard deviation to measure the performance of the forecast(the range of predicted average error).Otherwise,5- fold cross validation was used. The data was divided into 5 parts at random and the experiment was repeated 5 times. In each experiment, 4 training sets were selected and 1 were tested. The results are the average of the 5 experiments.

Genetic algorithm is used to optimize the experimental parameters to determine the kernel function, the kernel function parameters r and penalty items C .Repetitive use of SVM to predict maternal postpartum hemorrhage and blood pressure.

The experimental results were compared[12-16].

3.4 Data analysis

To determine the linear relationship between TWFBLEEDING and other data, the data were first analyzed for Pearson's coefficient and the significance test. The results in Table 3.

Table 3. Pearson correlation coefficient calculation results

		PREGNANCIES	MODELIVERY	DAY
TWFBLEEDING	Pearson	0.048**	0.131**	-0.048**
	Significance (two-tailed)	0.001	0.000	0.001
THBPHIGH	Pearson	0.001	0.027*	0.032*
	Significance (two-tailed)	0.923	0.045	0.023
THBPLOW	Pearson	-0.223	0.063**	0.029*
	Significance (two-tailed)	0.107	0.000	0.042

Notes:** Correlation is significant at 0.01 (double tail), * Correlation is significant at 0.05 (two tails).

Table 3 shows that TWFBLEEDING and PREGNANCIES, MODELIVERY is positively correlated and the DAY is a negative correlation, association is very significant, but very small. THBPHIGH and PREGNANCIES, MODELIVERY, DAY is positively correlated. THBPHIGH and PREGNANCIES is not significant. THBPHIGH and MODELIVERY, DAY association is significant, but very small. THBPLOW and PREGNANCIES is negative correlation, but MODELIVERY, DAY is positively correlated, THBPLOW and PREGNANCIES has no significant. The association of THBPLOW and MODELIVERY is very significant, but very small, THBPLOW and DAY association is significant, but very small.

Then, the postpartum hemorrhage and postpartum blood pressure were predicted by using the formula (14) and radial basis function (RBF) kernel function. TWFBLEEDING was predicted by PREGNANCIES, MODELIVERY, DAY according to the two-tailed significance test, THBPHIGH and THBPLOW were predicted by MODELIVERY and DAY. The prediction results are shown in Table 4.

Table 4. SVM algorithm prediction results (standard deviation)

	TWFBLEEDING	THBPHIGH	THBPLOW
SVM	49.2564	7.8239	7.2667
GA-SVM	30.1586	5.1257	5.3574

As can be seen from Table 4, the use of SVM and GA-SVM algorithm to predict TWFBLEEDING, THBPHIGH, THBPLOW is feasible, and the results are within the acceptable range. SVM prediction based on genetic algorithm has less error than traditional SVM prediction.

4 Concluding remarks

This study shows that the Pearson correlation coefficient and significance test were used to eliminate the factors which may influence the blood loss and blood pressure. Finally, the SVM prediction model based on the genetic algorithm was used to predict the hemorrhage and blood pressure. The results of this study show that SVM algorithm for maternal postpartum hemorrhage and blood pressure prediction is a viable method for improving the survival rate of pregnant women and it has a certain practical significance. In this paper, the data used in the prediction of the results is not a lot, and the object of predict is relatively simple, we remove some special circumstances, so the future can use more data, a better algorithm for postpartum hemorrhage and blood pressure prediction.

References

1. YAN Jian-ying, HUANG Ke-hua, LIU Qing-min, HUANG Xiao-yan, XU Rong-li. Study on risk factors of high risk postpartum hemorrhage and its clinical value [J].Chinese Journal of Practical Gynecology and Obstetrics, 2014,10: 791-797.
2. David de la Mata-Moya; María Pilar Jarabo-Amores; Jaime Martín de Nicolás; Manuel Rosa-Zurera. Approximating the Neyman–Pearson detector with 2C-SVMs. Application to radar detection[J].Signal Processing.2017:364-375.
3. Hogan, Anna1;Sellar, Sam2;Lingard, Bob2.Commercialising comparison: Pearson puts the TLC in soft capitalism[J].Journal of Education Policy.2016,Vol.31(No.3):243-258.
4. Zhao, Sen1;Shojaie, Ali1.A significance test for graph-constrained estimation[J]. Biometrics.2016,Vol.72(No.2):484-493.
5. Adam Claridge-Chang1, 2, 3,;Pryseley N Assam4, 5,.Estimation statistics should replace significance testing.[J].Nat Methods.2016,Vol.13(No.2):108-109.
6. Milad Jajarmizadeh, Elham Kakaei Lafdani, Sobri Harun,Azadeh Ahmadi. Application of SVM and SWAT models for monthly streamflow prediction, a case study in South of Iran[J]. KSCE Journal of Civil Engineering,2015,191:.

7. David de la Mata-Moya; María Pilar Jarabo-Amores; Jaime Martín de Nicolás; Manuel Rosa-Zurera.Approximating the Neyman–Pearson detector with 2C-SVMs. Application to radar detection[J].Signal Processing.2017:364-375.
8. Abbas M. Abd;Suhad M. Abd.Modelling the strength of lightweight foamed concrete using support vector machine (SVM)[J].Case Studies in Construction Materials.2017:8-15.
9. Aslahi-Shahri, B.1;Rahmani, R.2(r.r.rahmani@ieee.org); Chizari, M.3;Maralani, A.4;Eslami, M.5;Golkar, M.5;Ebrahimi, A.1.A hybrid method consisting of GA and SVM for intrusion detection system[J].Neural Computing and Applications.2016,Vol.27(No.6):1669-1676.
10. Nadeem,Mohammad1(mail.mdnadeem@gmail.com);Banka,Haider1;Venugopal,R.2.SVM-Based Predictive Modelling of Wet Pelletization Using Experimental and GA-Based Synthetic Data[J].Arabian Journal for Science and Engineering.2016,Vol.41(No.3): 1053-1065.
11. Francesco Di Tria;Ezio Lefons;Filippo Tangorra.Cost-benefit analysis of data warehouse design methodologies[J].Information Systems.2017: 47-62.
12. Yan-Qing Zhang;Nian-Sheng Tang.Bayesian local influence analysis of general estimating equations with nonignorable missing data[J].Computational Statistics and Data Analysis.2017: 184-200.
13. Shirong Denga;Kin-yat Liub;Xingqiu Zhaobc.Semiparametric regression analysis of multivariate longitudinal data with informative observation times[J].Computational Statistics and Data Analysis.2017: 120-130.
14. V. Bhanu Prasada; Supriya Mallicka; Ashish Dutt Upadhyayb; G.K. Ratha. Systematic review and individual patient data analysis of pediatric head and neck squamous cell carcinoma: An analysis of 217 cases[J].International Journal of Pediatric Otorhinolaryngology.2017: 75-81.
15. G.S. Vyasa(Assistant Professor);K.N. Jhab(Associate Professor).Benchmarking green building attributes to achieve cost effectiveness using a data envelopment analysis[J].Sustainable Cities and Society.2017: 127-134.
16. Shu-yi Guo;Qi Si.Mechanical hydraulic characteristic analysis scheme based on lightweight crowd data in mobile embedded devices[J].EURASIP Journal on Embedded Systems.2017,Vol.2017(No.1)

 DOI: 10.1051/itmconf/20171101006

Application of the Improved Differential Evolution Algorithm in Portfolio

Gui-Ying NING[1,a], Dun-Qian CAO[2], and Yong-Quan ZHOU[3]

[1]*Lushan College of Guangxi University Science and Technology, Liuzhou, Guangxi 545616, China;*
[2]*College of Mathematics and Computer Science, Guangxi University for Nationalities, Nanning 530006, China;*
[3]*College of Information Science and Engineering, Guangxi University for Nationalities, Nanning, Guangxi 530006, China*

Abstract. Aiming at the NP hard problem of portfolio optimization, an improved differential evolution algorithm is proposed. In this algorithm, the mutation operator and crossover operator are set up adaptively, and then according to the characteristics of the mutation itself, two kinds of mutation operators with global search ability and local search ability are improved .The improved algorithm can improve the convergence speed and ensure the precision of the algorithm. Through five stocks of the same type and 20 different types of stocks for empirical analysis, the results show that the proposed algorithm has a certain guiding role in solving the problem of portfolio optimization.

1 Introduction

With the rapid economic development, emerging assets constantly emerging financial markets, more and more families, companies keen on capital investment, the inherent risks of financial markets and the resulting revenue has always been one of the focuses of the investors. In the market operation, anyone with an investment in its earnings also associated with certain risks at the same time, different ways of investment profit is different also. In order to find the optimal investment scheme, we need to make a trade-off between costs and benefits. The theory of portfolio comes into being.

The earliest theory of portfolio theory was proposed by American economist Markowitz [1] in 1952, which proposed mean-variance (M-V) by using two concepts of expectation and variance in mathematical statistics. Once the model is put forward, which is widely applied to portfolio selection and asset allocation. The M-V model measures the overall level of the real rate of return with the expected rate of return (mean of return), and measures the uncertainty (risk) of the rate of return by the variance (or standard deviation) of the yield. The model is:

$$\min\sum_{i=1}^{N}\sum_{j=1}^{N}W_iW_jCov(x_i,x_j) \tag{1}$$

$$s.t\sum_{i=1}^{N}W_i\mu_i = R \tag{2}$$

[a] Corresponding author: guiyingning@126.com

$$\sum_{i=1}^{N} W_i = 1 \tag{3}$$

$$0 \le W_i \le 1, i = 1,2,\cdots,N. \tag{4}$$

In which: W_i denotes the proportion of the funds invested in the security of i in the total investment, u_i denotes the expected return rate of the securities of i , $Cov(x_i,x_j)$ denotes the covariance between the i and the j securities, N denotes the number of total investment securities, R is the expected rate of return target. (1) represents the minimum total risk required to invest, (2) shows the expected to achieve the total revenue, (3) is the ratio of all the securities investment and is 1, (4) shows that the investment ratio of each security is between 0 and 1. The model indicates that the total risk to the investor is minimized when a certain return is satisfied.

The M-V model is established with gains and risks predictable1.

However, in actual operation process, due to the uncertainty of market factors, the risk and return of investment are often difficult to predict. Therefore, many scholars have improved the model and put forward some new models, such as semi-variance model [2], the mean absolute deviation model, such as the literatures [3-7], these methods are for the actual transaction there are some restrictions on the problem raised by the problem, which is not starting from the problem of solving the difficulty. It is proved that no matter what kind of model of portfolio optimization problem is a NP hard problem, with the continuous expansion of market investment, the traditional method can not get satisfactory results. Finding an effective solution to this problem is also of great importance.

The group intelligent algorithm is a new kind of optimization algorithm, which has achieved a very good effect in the function optimization problem. At present, some scholars have applied the algorithm to portfolio optimization problems, such as the literatures [8-12]. These methods are based on actual situation to some improvement after solving the model. The practice shows that these methods also achieved good effect. In this paper, the modified MV model is reconstructed and the improved differential evolution algorithm is used to solve it. The empirical analyses show that the proposed algorithm is effective.

2 Basic differential evolution algorithm

Differential evolution algorithm (DE) [13] was proposed by Storn and Price in 1995, which uses real number coding. The algorithm is simple and easy to implement. It has significant advantages in solving some complicated optimization problems.

2.1 The basic specific operational process of differential evolution algorithm

2.1.1 Mutation operation:

The purpose of the mutation operation is to generate a mutation vector which can disturb the target vector. The specific process as follows:

$$v_{ij}(t+1) = x_{ij}(t) + F(x_{p1,j}(t) - x_{p2,j}(t)). \tag{5}$$

In which: x_{p1} and x_{p2} are any two selected difference vector in the generation t , p_1 and p_2 are an integer of $[1, M]$,which were randomly selected random integers that are not equal to each other, F is a factor of the variation, it is usually a real number of [0,2]. x_{ij} is the jth component of the ith individual. $i = 1,2,\cdots,M$, $j = 1,2,\cdots,n$.

 DOI: 10.1051/itmconf/20171101006

2.1.2 Crossover operation:

The purpose of crossover operation is to increase the diversity of the population. The specific operation is:

$$u_{ij}(t+1)=\begin{cases} v_{ij}(t+1) & randl_{ij} \le p_c \\ x_{ij}(t) & randl_{ij} > p_c \end{cases}. \tag{6}$$

Where p_c is the crossover probability factors, usually taking a real number of (0, 1], $randl_{ij}$ is a random number of [0, 1].

2.1.3 Selection Operation:

The selection operation is based on the evaluation of fitness; the purpose is to determine which individuals to enter the next generation. The specific operation is:

$$X_i(t+1)=\begin{cases} U_i(t+1) & if\ J(U_i(t+1)) < J(X_i(t)) \\ X_i(t) & otherwise \end{cases} \tag{7}$$

Like other evolutionary computation, the DE algorithm simulates the evolution of organisms, which makes the evolution of the population towards a better direction. The new population after mutation operation and crossover operation will choose excellent individuals into the next generation by greedy choice way .This method can guarantee the superiority of the group and accelerate the speed of searching, but also make the algorithm falls into local optimum easily. In addition, DE as a random search algorithm, the population diversity is good in the beginning, but with the increase of the number of iterations, the generation between the distributions of population density is high and the exchange of information is less and less. So as to make the global optimization ability gradually decline, despite the global optimal search can be realized, but also can appear the phenomenon of premature convergence.

3 Improvement of basic differential evolution algorithm

3.1 Parameter settings

The influence of parameter setting of differential evolution algorithm on its overall performance is very big. Variation factors F determine the deviation vector amplification ratio, the larger the F, the higher the mutation strength, the global search ability is stronger, but the slower the convergence speed. On the contrary, F is smaller, the lower the strength of individual variation, accelerate the search speed, but it may cause algorithm trapped in local optimal solution, the crossover factor CR controls whether the vector is derived from the individual or the parent of the individual variation, CR is larger, the smaller the degree of individual difference, the faster the convergence speed, but also easily caught in the local excellent. Research shows that so far $F \in [0.4,1]$ is effective, and $F = 0.5$ is usually a better choice. In order to keep the global searching ability and improve the convergence speed and precision of the algorithm, the mutation operator and the crossover operator are set as follows:

Mutation operator: $F = 1 - \dfrac{t}{t+T}$,

Crossover operator: $CR = e^{\frac{t-T}{T}}$

In which t is the current evolution generation, T is the maximum evolution generation, in this setting, mutation operator decreases in [0.5, 1] with the evolution generation increase, crossover operator exponential increases in (0, 1]. This setting can guarantee the individual diversity in the early stage of evolution and improve the global search ability. In the later stage, the degree of difference among individuals will be reduced to speed up the convergence speed.

3.2 Mutation operation settings

Differential evolution algorithm for each generation of individual x_i^t mutation to get a new individual v_i^{t+1}, commonly used mutation operations are:

1.DE/rand/1/bin, which is:

$$v_{ij}(t+1)=x_{ij}(t)+F(x_{p1,j}(t)-x_{p2,j}(t))$$

2.DE/best/2/bin, which is:

$$v_{ij}(t+1)=x_{best,j}(t)+F(x_{p1,j}(t)-x_{p2,j}(t)+x_{p3,j}(t)-x_{p4,j}(t))$$

3.DE/rand/1/bin, which is:

$$v_{ij}(t+1)=x_{i,j}(t)+F(x_{p1,j}(t)-x_{p2,j}(t)+x_{p3,j}(t)-x_{p4,j}(t))$$

The DE / rand / 1 / bin is helpful to keep the diversity of the population and improves the global searching ability, but reduces the convergence speed, the DE / best / 2 / bin reduces the differences between individuals, improves local searching ability and accelerates the convergence speed, but also accelerates the algorithm into the possibility of local optimum. Experiments show that 3.is better than 1.in enhancing the diversity of population. The 2.is very good results in improving the convergence speed and accuracy, according to the above analysis, in order to guarantee the diversity and improve the convergence speed of the algorithm, an improved mutation strategy was proposed .The new mutation operation is:

$$v_{ij}(t+1)=\lambda x_{ij}(t)+(1-\lambda)x_{best,j}(t)+F(x_{p1,j}(t)-x_{p2,j}(t)+x_{p3,j}(t)-x_{p4,j}(t)) \quad (8)$$

In which $\lambda\in[0,1]$ and $\lambda=\frac{T-t}{T}$, t is the current evolution generation, T is the maximum evolution generation.

In the above formula, with the increasing of evolutionary algebra t, the value of λ gradually changes from the maximum value 1 to 0 gradually. At the beginning of evolution, $\lambda=1$,the formula becomes 3, it can guarantee the algorithm in the evolutionary initial stage has stronger global searching ability, as much as you can find the global optimal point, to the late evolution of the maximum evolutionary algebra, $\lambda=0$,(8) becomes 2, it can guarantee the algorithm has stronger local search ability in the stage, improve the precision and convergence speed of the algorithm. The experiments results show that this setting can not only guarantee the algorithm has stronger global searching ability, and can guarantee the convergence speed and accuracy of the algorithm.

4 The application of improved differential evolution algorithm in portfolio optimization problem

In fact, the two objective functions of risks and benefits of the standard M-V model is a pair of opposite direction problem, it is not easy to solve in the process of actual operation. In order to better evaluate the contradiction between the risks and benefits. This paper considers the non-radix and the quota. A new risk weighting factor p $(0\le p\le 1)$ is introduced, the objective functions of the risk and the benefits were combined into a target function to discuss. The combined model is as follows:

 DOI: 10.1051/itmconf/20171101006

$$\min(p\sum_{i=1}^{N}\sum_{j=1}^{N}W_iW_jCov(x_i,x_j)-(1-p)\sum_{i=1}^{N}W_i\mu_i \tag{9}$$

$$\sum_{i=1}^{N}W_i=1 \qquad 0\le W_i\le 1, i=1,2,\cdots,N.$$

For a specific portfolio optimization problem, we define Eq. (9) as the objective function.

4.1 Algorithm specific process:

Step1: Initialize, randomly generates the initial population of size N , and determines the maximum evolutionary algebra T ;

Step2: Calculate the fitness value of individual species and select the best individual;

Step 3: The population is mutated according to (8);

Step 4: The crossover operation of the transformed individuals is performed according to the new crossover operator;

Step5: Calculates the fitness value of the new individual after crossing and does selection operation;

Step6: Determine whether the termination condition is reached, if so, evolution terminates, and the individual is output as the optimal solution. Otherwise, go to step7;

Step7: Sets the evolutionary algebra $t=t+1$, and into step2.

5 The empirical analysis

In order to test the effectiveness of the proposed algorithm in solving the portfolio optimization problem, we select the opening price of five Shanghai stocks, namely, Bank of China, Dongfeng Motor, China Unicom, Guodian Nanzi, Sichuan Changhong, form January to December in 2015 as the effective numerical of the test, the basic information in Table 1. In addition, select the opening price of the deep stock of four small plates, four motherboards, two gem and 10 stocks in Shanghai a total of 20 stocks from January 2015 to June 2016 in 12 months as a reference data, all the data from the Star of the Securities. In the test, we solve the optimal portfolio of each stock by calculating the monthly benefits of each stock and the covariance matrix between the two. In order to reduce the accident, each group of test data are running 10 times, the largest evolutionary algebra is 100, the population size is 10 times of the stock quantity, and take the optimal solution of 10 times as the solution result. Table 2 shows that when the risk weight factor takes different values, the fitness value and benefits / risk ratio after running 10 times, the benefits / risk ratio reflects the return on the unit risk.

Table 1. The basic information of 5 stocks

Serial number	Stock Name	Opening price (January to December)
1	China Bank(601989)	4.18; 4.24; 4.12; 4.38; 4.83; 4.34; 4.87; 4.42; 3.81; 3.79; 3.87; 4.11
2	Dongfeng Motor(600006)	5.96; 5.81; 6.21; 7.01; 8.58; 9.75; 12.48; 9.00; 13.19; 8.70; 9.52; 8.84
3	China Unicom(600050)	4.97; 4.45; 5.65; 5.46; 9.35; 8.45; 7.33; 6.12; 6.30; 6.17; 6.53; 6.23
4	Guodian Nanzi(600268)	7.35; 7.93; 8.30; 9.18; 12.12; 16.48; 14.68; 10.30; 8.55; 7.73; 9.55; 9.70
5	Sichuan Changhong(600839)	4.66; 5.69; 5.17; 5.99; 8.03; 8.52; 9.72; 7.29; 6.90; 6.10; 6.48; 6.04

Table 2. Portfolio results of five stocks

p	0	0.3	0.5	0.8	1
fitness value	-1.7897	-0.0136	-0.0050	9.1821e-005	5.7842e-004
risk	0.0204	0.0205	0.0210	0.0216	0.0268
benefits	0.0180	0.0219	0.0235	0.0246	0.0273
benefits / risk	0.8839	1.0665	1.1176	1.1401	1.0189
Optimal solution	0.2004 0.0936 0.5993 0.0817 0.0250	0.0901 0.0717 0.3008 0.3781 0.1593	0.0331 0.0994 0.3075 0.2763 0.2837	0.0365 0.1465 0.0974 0.2842 0.4354	0.1441 0.5970 0.0120 0.0546 0.1923

As we can see from the Table 2, when the risks are not taken into account, namely, $p=0$ the benefits are very little. With the increase of the risk, the benefits are also gradually increase, when only considering risk regardless of benefits, namely, $p=1$, although revenue, but earnings per unit risk declines. This shows that in the investment in stocks, income and risk is directly proportional to, so-called "high risk high reward" principle.

According to Table 2, Figure1 shows the effective frontier of the investment with different returns and corresponding minimum risk.

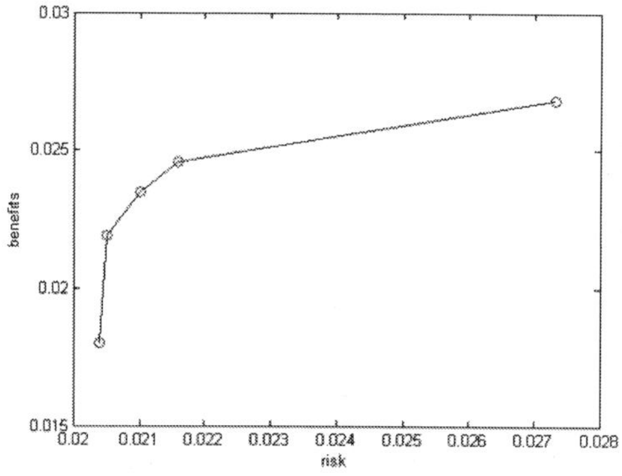

Figure 1. Effective frontier of portfolio

Table 3 presents the returns of the 20 stocks in the risk weighting factor $p=0, p=0.5, p=1$, which does not consider risk, risk and income are equally important and does not consider earnings yield per unit risk and the corresponding optimal portfolio solution.

Table 3. The results of different portfolios of 20 stocks

p	0	0.5	1
fitness value	-0.0848	-0.0369	6.9569e-004
risk	0.0108	0.0124	0.0187
benefits	0.0026	0.0094	0.0112
benefits /risk	0.2427	0.7566	0.6001
Optimal solution	0.0438 0.0270 0.0395 0.1801 0.2256 0.0001 0.0247 0.0555 0.1017 0.0031 0.0336 0.0825 0.0004 0.0062 0.0052 0.0674 0.0587 0.0361 0.0012 0.0076	0.0212 0.0001 0.0080 0.0363 0.0086 0.0491 0.0647 0.0022 0.0110 0.2137 0.0092 0.0095 0.0575 0.1795 0.0091 0.0012 0.0023 0.0125 0.0180 0.2863	0.0305 0.0197 0.1322 0.0329 0.0784 0.0834 0.0184 0.2190 0.0477 0.0879 0.0989 0.0571 0.0003 0.0501 0.0084 0.0044 0.0043 0.0210 0.0038 0.0016

 DOI: 10.1051/itmconf/20171101006

Looking at the optimization results in Table 2 and Table 3, we can see that in only five small portfolio, generally high yield per unit risk, at around 1, when stock quantity increases to 20, revenues per unit risk generally dropped, which shows that the stock investment profit is associated with the number of shares, the greater the number of reduced profits, which is consistent with existing research [14]. In addition, Table 2 shows the same type of five Shanghai stocks, while table 3 is from different types of stocks. When selecting any of the five stocks in Table 3 for a combined test, we found that the return on unit risk is higher than in table 2. This shows that under the same conditions, investment stock returns are also related to the type of stock, investment in different types of stocks, the risk is relatively reduced, that is, decentralized investment is less risky than the overall investment. Figure 2 to figure 5 shows the corresponding evolutionary curves under different weights in Table 3:

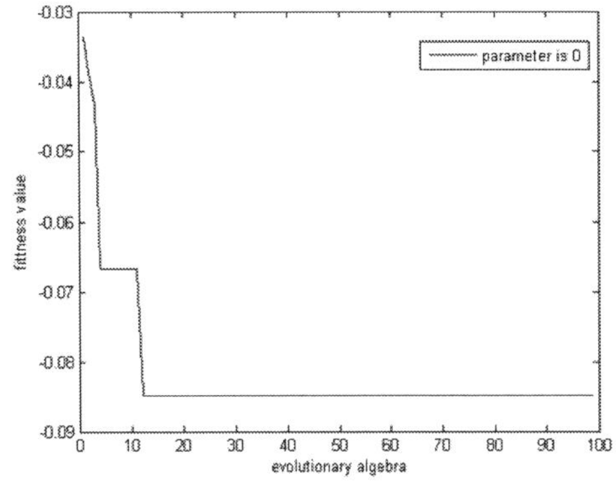

Figure 2. Evolution curve of the risk weight factor $p=0$

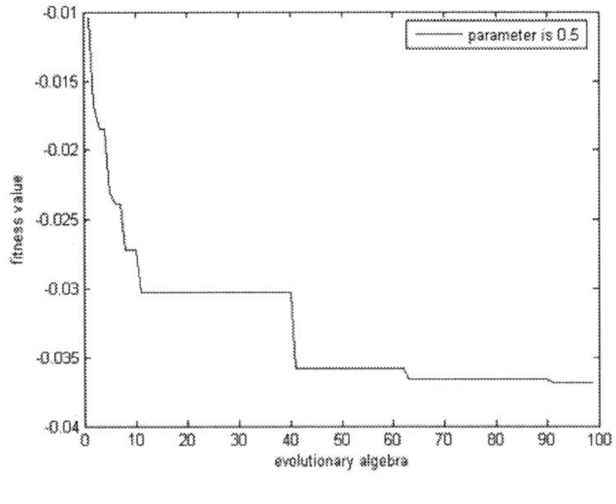

Figure 3. Evolution curve of the risk weight factor $p=0.5$

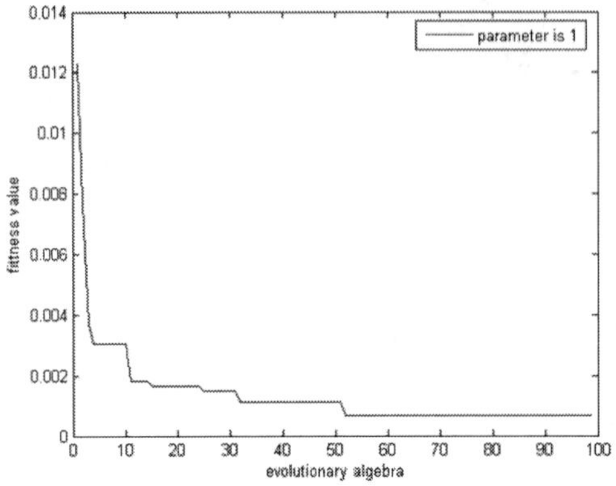

Figure 4. Evolution curve of the risk weight factor $p = 1$

Conclusions

Against the standard DE is slow convergence speed, easily into local optimum, this paper improves the mutation and crossover factors of standard DE, and improves the mutation operation formula. The improved DE is used to solve the NP hard problem of portfolio optimization. Through five stocks and 20 stocks for empirical testing, the test results show that the proposed algorithm can effectively guide the portfolio optimization problem.

In the actual investment portfolio, due to various factors, there will be a variety of constraints. The follow-up work of this paper is to study how to use this algorithm to solve the portfolio optimization problem under the real constraints.

Acknowledge

National Natural Science Foundation of China (61165015) ;Education Department of Guangxi Zhuang Autonomous Region universities scientific research items (KY2015YB521) ; Education Department of Guangxi Science Research Project (KY2015YB081).

References

1. Markowitz H.: Portfio selection.J.J.FIN.**7** (1), 77-91 (1952).
2. Peng, Z., Zhang, W.: The positivistic multi-period mean-semi variance portfolio selection.J. Nat.Sci. S.CHN.Univ. Techn.**16** (5), 21-27 (2014).
3. Qing, Z., Wang, Z.: Robust optimization strategy of mean-semi absolute deviation model under transaction costs.J. Nat.Sci.Ludong Univ. **31**(1), 27-31 (2015).
4. Peng, Z.: The optimization on the multiperiod mean semi-absolute deviation fuzzy portfolio selection.J. F.Syst.Math.**27** (1), 168-175 (2013).
5. Jing, Y.: Mean-Variance-Approximate skewness portfolio model and empirical analysis.J. OR TRANSACTIONS.**12** (1), 107-113 (2010).
6. Peng, Z., Shu, Y.: Optimization of mean-absolute deviation fuzzy portfolio selection with transaction cost .J. Wuhan Univ. Sci.Techn. **38**(3), 235-239 (2015).
7. Lian, R., Xu, R.:.A portfolio model based on transaction costs and absolute deviation.J. Nat.Sci. Shaoyang Univ.**7** (2), 18-21 (2010).
8. Li, M., Li, Y., Fan, S.: Application of the improved artificial fish swarm algorithm in foreign exchange forecast and portfolio.J. Syst.Eng.Th. &Pract., **35**(5), 1256-1265 (2015).

9. Ma, Y., Wang, Y.: Genetic algorithm of portfolio optimization with cardinality constraint and its empirical analysis.J. Nat.Sci. N.W. Norm. Univ. **47**(2), 26-30 (2011).
10. Jiang, J., Liao, W.: Portfolio optimization based on quadratic particle swarm optimization.J. Comput. Appl.Softw.**26** (6), 161-163 (2009).
11. Li, Y., Li, P.: Research on improved model of stocks'portflio optimization based on hybrid genetic algorithm.J. Yanshan Univ.**32** (1), 65-69 (2008).
12. Du, Y., Zhou, Y.: Application of artificial glow worm swarm optimization algorithm to portfolio considering transaction cost.J. J.Comput.Appl.**34** (s2), 159-161 (2014).
13. Storn, R., Price, K.:Differential evolution a Simple and efficient heuristic for global optimization o ver continuous spaces.J. J.Glob. Optim.**11**, 341–359 (1997).
14. The editorial board of certification examination guidebook for security trading engaged persons. Sec. Inv.analys. Beijing: CHN. Comm.Publ.Co. (2002).

Solution of Media Risk and Social Responsibility Governance of Social Media

Yuan ZHANG[1,2,a], Ming-De LI[1] and Hong-Bang ZHANG[1]

[1]*School of Journalism and new media, Xi'an Jiao Tong University, Shaanxi, 710049, China*
[2]*Ciity College, Xi'an Jiao Tong University, Shaanxi, 710018, China*

Abstract. The rapid development of media technology makes the modern society become a "social media" or even "over social media", the rise of social media makes it beyond the tool attribute, and become an important force in the reconstruction of contemporary society, the risk of concomitant. The anomie and breach of Social media regularly staged, weakened its positive social function, forcing us to think about the social responsibility of social media,which are reflections on the lack of responsibility, but also positive response of resolving the media risk and ask for moral strength.

1 Introduction

Social media is widely used constructed on the Web 2.0, the modern society is a highly social media and even excessive. Almost everyone is affected by social media, the network technology is highly developed today, social media cognition, not only in the tool attribute angle, it should be noted that it is in fact the transformation, reconstruction of the world, for individuals, their way of thinking, behavior is a deep imprint. The risk of modern society is superimposed on social media, that most of the social risk by the dissemination of information on social media has caused, ordinary people feel the risk and not the actual risk, but the risk of social media by "Pseudo Environment". The issue of social responsibility and the risk of social media are closely related to the media, even the positive response to the moral demands of the age of social media.

2 The reality of media risk

As a social information exchange system, social and cultural system construction, social and psychological counseling system, social management and control system, the mass media has nothing comparable importance to social media in terms of the social function. In the Media Ecology theory, the media interacts with society symbioticly. A new media's advantages will lead to a new civilization. Similarly, a kind of new media's weaknesses, will also bring unique risks to civilization. From the diachronic perspective, with the development of media technology, now a variety of media integration stage with multiple functions has happened, if today's society is the power structure of knowledge, the deep structure is networked, so performance is in the social media. The media society, which is a full social life, social events and social relations can be exposed in the media society, on society the media

[a] Corresponding author: zhyuan223@sina.com

is full penetration. In essence, it is the media the relationship among people. In the 1980s, German sociologist Ulrich Beck in the book named "risk society" first mentioned the "risk society" concept and theory. He believes that after the industrial society it has entered a risk society. A medium risk is hard to ignore the reality of the problem.

Since 2004, as the representative of a new generation of social media began to appear such as Facebook, Twitter and the rapid growth of Chinese QQ, micro-blog, WeChat and other similar products followed in 2007, and occupied most of people's daily life time and space. According to the latest report of 2016 by Wc Arc Social revealed: at present, nearly 1/3 of the population using social media, an annual increase of 10%. North America is a social penetration rate in the region with the highest (59%), and more than half of the population in each month to visit Facebook in South America. East Asian social penetration rate reached 48% (not including Internet users under 13 years old). Social media has become an important force of the mass media. It should not be underestimated that social media's important force.

So we can say, the media risk, can be said to a social media risk. In theory, the difference of risk in the risk society and the traditional society lies in its inherent and man-made. The representative of social media as Micro-blog and WeChat, with its interaction, sharing, autonomy, dialogue characteristics become widespread communication platform. Lan PENG believes that the use of social media is the social relations dissemination of the "personal communication portal" mode[1].This respect for people and enhance the discourse space and behavior space release, Giving freedom a new meaning and attitude also means increasing risk and social responsibility is on the agenda.

3 Problems in social media's social responsibility practice

Social media is built up from Web concept and technology, a variety of emerging online media to give users in the great space, it gives users the ability to create and disseminate the content. Social media blog, micro-blog, forums, instant messaging as a representative. From the current situation of research about social responsibility, compared social media with traditional media, it shows the contents of a direct extension of the situation, that is to say the reason of the lack of responsibility, coping strategies is exactly the same. No matter what type of media, media properties are basically the same, the responsibility of related research content in common can be understood, but we cannot ignore the various types. In order to ensure the effective implementation of the responsibility behavior, therefore, the following issues should be paid attention to.

3.1 The complexity of responsibility's subject

Because the responsibility itself contains two aspects, one hand is to assume responsibility, on the other hand, to bear on the consequences of responsibility. To determine the main subject for responsibility is not easy. This problem doesn't only exist in the traditional media, more and more complex in social media. Generally speaking, social responsibility's subject of social media is social media. "media institutions cannot do without a single practitioner, at the same time perplexing partnership between single practitioners within the organization form a superindividual propagation, this behavior cannot be attributed to the reduction or any individual behavior unique properties, also has not the individual ability to bear a unique effect. "[2] that is to say, the social responsibility of the media is not only reflected in the media, at the same time journalist is every practitioner of communication activities, so the responsibility is reflected in each journalist. The dialectical relationship beyond the simple superposition of media organizations and journalist is difficult to operate. In addition, the social media for the audience release a great space to express. Ordinary people involved in news production and communication process, the behavior, has affected the communication process and public opinion situation. From a practical point of view, a reversal of public opinion of many events are caused by ordinary people publish information and comments, the original meaning of "audience" should be in the column, responsible for their own behavior. More scholars, from the legal perspective, think that the reason that the media's default in addition to the role of market mechanism, as well as a variety of power, interest group and social elite force clamp, more to "popularity, entertainment and even popular measure of film culture significance" by the majority[3].If possible, the main responsibility includes the majority of the audience, the broad range makes it fuzzy to ensure the responsibility, which is not conducive to fulfill responsibility, but also to increase the difficulty of the specific operational responsibility .

3.2 The homogeneity of the communication content

Providing information service is the first priority responsibility including traditional media. Social media, all kinds of media's social responsibility, provide true information of mass media is undoubted. Social media release information, fulfilling social responsibility will make it to win the public trust and social resource.Web2.0 technology makes the public influence the content of the information, spread and even results. Influence of ordinary people is the increase of the amount of information, the "information explosion" is supported by the Internet technology, and the power of the audience. Social media makes "grassroots truth" widespread, breaking the traditional sense of the media's information publishing monopoly. But from the quality of the information, the homogenization of serious problem of information is serious, information is blasted but lack. The content of homogenization performances in full of representation of information, from the formal point of view, this information only includes some basic time, place and simple description of fragmented information, from the type of view, such information is "new, strange, special" or even "strange" to attract the eye, even with bloody pictures, video. These superficial information is only a moment, lack of depth and innovation. We do not deny this kind of information, but if it's full of screen, we have to involve the responsibility problem of the media practitioners, can not help the media's professionalism, and querying oriented responsibility.

3.3 The single responsibility supervision

From the daily supervision of responsibility behavior, most is like this, first the public or the victim complaint to organization or association. After investigation, take administrative measures to supervise the rectification, or directly to the media, self-discipline to rectify completely rely on the media. But only rely on the media, self-discipline and restraint is not fundamentally to solve the problem, it is a kind of moral restraint means of social control which is soft, especially for people the lack of social responsibility and moral conscience, legal means is the rigid and support effective. Therefore, legislative norms are the key to the Internet management in China after decades of development, the network legislation has made some progress on social media. The performance of social supervision and regulation has a certain role in some aspects of the Internet, such as "Internet news information service management" "Provisional Regulations on Administration of Internet culture" "Information Network Transmission Right Protection Ordinance" "the National People's Congress Standing Committee's decision on safeguarding Internet Security", according to incomplete statistics, the number has reached 200. The Internet is not outside the law, the rule of law is necessary, social media's responsibility can be guaranteed. On the one hand, the legislative process on the one hand could not keep up with the rapid development of the Internet, on the other hand, due to the formulation of these rules' subjects are local governments and departments, legal order is limited on the legal effect, regulations on social media is low, the binding to the media or journalists misconduct cannot by timely corrected and punished, resulting in loss of responsibility anomie breeding.

4 How to urge social media to fulfill social responsibility

4.1 Develop a strong sense of social responsibility

The sense of social responsibility, in the rational thinking on the identity, is the deep feeling and understanding of the objective existence of social responsibility, and internalized in the heart, actively undertake the responsibility of psychological thought. Only the responsibility for sublimation role to "I want to do", rather than the external requirement of "I want to do", to fulfill the responsibility for the evolution of consciousness and self-discipline. Internalized sense of social responsibility is the foundation of social media's social responsibility, internalized in the heart can be of the line to the level of consciousness outside. The construction of social media's responsibility, includes the reasons of responsibility, the content of responsibility and the meaning of responsibility. In the 1940s, the western mass media monopoly control group, blindly pursues economic interests and abandon the media function, in the face of triggered a sharp criticism of the media and the public outcry, free with the responsibility of news once again become the focus of debate. In this context, Commission on freedom of the press published <a free and responsible press >, the report first advocated the media should assume social responsibility, the media is a social utility, should be for the public to provide information. The background and present of the theory of the media's social responsibility is very similar to social media era. This paper argues that social media's social responsibility should keep pace with the times in the social background and technical support of the content. Especially in the retention of information dissemination, media public opinion, the premise of cultural heritage and other basic responsibility content. In the social transformation into the deep water area, the excitation of social media's social responsibility should be further mining, such as mining depth and innovation in the content, the value of the media.

Have the strong sense of social responsibility, need to continue to fulfill its duty in practice gradually, also need to continue to receive professional education and training. The responsibility come from professional journalism education. "At least the following benefits: first is to promote a sense of professional responsibility; second is the occupation training concept; third is to grasp the advanced writing and management skills; fourth is to train the broad international perspective; fifth is to lay a solid foundation of deep humanities and social sciences."[4]On the whole, in China journalism education is in the growth stage, journalistic professionalism has not yet fully mature. The author believes that the talent training model of news should be adapt to the development of the media industry, change idea, adjust the content of education, train evaluation attitude and critical spirit. At present, based on network related research and education of social media, timely update the content of education, which will shorten the distance of talent from between the school to the social, in order to cultivate the media compound talents.

4.2 The identity and content reconstruction of Journalism

Journalism can be traced back to the United States in 1830s, when commercial newspapers oriented and Party newspapers lost living space. As the representative of penny press the commercial newspaper is neutral, advocating freedom and pursuiting independence, which make party newspapers be cast into the shade of traditional pattern, creating a new pattern of newspaper. Accordingly, the journalists are also gradually moving towards the professional. The concept of journalism advocacy journalism occupation and social public service. HANG Dan believes that journalism requires multiple conditions, including full-time work, training and professional associations, legal protection, self-discipline and so on. From the internal dimension, journalistic professionalism includes at least four aspects of professional news organizations, occupation news, news value and news ethics standard[5]. Thus, the journalistic professionalism is the requirements for professional journalists in the traditional media era occupation.

The era of social media, the traditional news production mode has been broken, citizen journalism form against the professional news, especially South Korea's pure citizen news website OH MY NEWS, creates a trend that citizen journalism will embezzle professional news. But this paper argues that it seems not possible, citizen journalism and professional news does not exist who eats who, only intertwined in the development of fusion, the final collapse of OH MY NEWS proved this point. The fundamental reason is the demand for information has never stopped. Similarly, journalism is not completely eliminated, only identity and content reconstruction in the social media era can play its due role, which is to do the social responsibility, thereby promote social media credibility.

The so-called *identity reconstruction*, refers not only to occupational journalists, "citizen journalists" of citizen journalism also should be included in the scope of journalism. From the practice of journalism, it is also necessary. "The news production has changed from the traditional professional production to socialized production. the form of social media that'everyone is a reporter could promote the organization of news production gradually to lose the center position. 'equal discourse rights become possible."[6]Depending on social media's low threshold technology, general public can participate in the news production process .As long as it is a member of the information dissemination process, should have professional ethics, because this is not just a personal behavior, but the behavior of public concerns the interests of the collective.

T*he content reconstruction*, is to improve and mine the quality and value of information. This puts forward more stringent requirements for the occupation. News is of the latest facts reported, but the news is in fact a multi-level concept. "The news is divided into three levels: the first level is the news facts now we generally think of, namely the dynamic appearance of the event, showing time, place, the basic situation, which exist in micro-blog, We Chat and another social media, because requirements of this level are the most basic to ordinary citizens of communication tools and pass showing capacity requirements , the journalistic professionalism in the levels of demand for "real"; the second level is digging through the in-depth investigation of the internal factors and the whole event model, which requires a certain amount of information technology and knowledge, generally difficult to reach; the level of third is to explore the deeper reason behind the secret, no more professional knowledge and occupation concept, a more scientific approach is not up to[7]. With a large number of first level news, or even false ones, with homogenization serious, "content is king" is still working in the era of social media. Occupational journalist is to do the second, third level news with their professional skill and deeply excavate, increase the value and quality of the content, it should be said that the updated communication technology broadens the journalistic world, can realize the ideal news from the more space, but to face the increasingly complex and severe challenges. More professional reports and performance, whether it is social media environment and future information environment, human's demand for information will not change.

4.3 Establish a sound mechanism of responsibility synergy

The synergy theory is proposed in the 1970s by German physicist Hermann Haken, "collaboration between the various factors caused the system coordinate collective effect, under the condition it's not only individual collaborative property enhancement, the overall effect will reach the maximum. In one word, order is synergetic, disorder chaotic. Then in a certain external force can be transformed into each other. In the collaborative theory, in order to enhance the credibility of social media, social media should establish a cooperative mechanism. The primary is the responsibility mechanism must be complete, Each element is complete, which can be coordinated. The author believes it can be reflected by training, performance management, evaluation, regulation, supervision and other aspects of the overall coordination. The training of responsibility is prior to the behavior, performance and management responsibility belongs to behavior, responsibility evaluation, regulation and supervision belong to afterwards behavior, through the responsibility process, enhance the credibility and form the benign circulation situation. The training of responsibility Mainly refers to cultivate the sense of responsibility, achieved through professional journalism education and practice, and fulfill the responsibility of management mainly refers to the content of innovation and mining production, which are discussed in detail in the above.

Here we mainly explain the evaluation, regulation and supervision of responsibility. Because of the social environment, improve the coordination mechanism of the responsibility may not happen overnight, it is necessary for social media's responsibility evaluation and timely diagnosis, which is the premise to adjust and perfect the responsibility, and a key part of the whole coordination mechanism. And the evaluation of social media's social responsibility is extremely lack. In December 7th, 2014,edited by information communication school of HUST and China network communication

DOI: 10.1051/itmconf/20171101007

society, <Report On the China's new media social responsibility (2014) > is released in Beijing, evaluates different types of new media's social responsibility, which is the first case in China, to fill the gaps in our country there's not new media social responsibility evaluation, at the same time, the new media social responsibility has aroused widespread concern. But the research associations universities and industry is limited in restraining the behavior of news communication, how to seek the cooperation with government departments, to maximize the value of evaluation, enhance the binding effect is worth pondering. The regulation of responsibility, as mentioned before, single means, imperfect legislation, "lack of coordination", the low rank of law to effect, the relevant government departments need to crack. Along with the deep influence of Internet, a suitable China Internet legislation has become particularly urgent. since 2014, to establish social responsibility report system strengthening the media to fulfill their social responsibilities, it's an effective measure and beneficial attempt. The supervision of responsibility at present mainly rely on social media and industry's self-discipline. Combine with ordinary people and play the power of encouragement ordinary users to support the spirit of criticism and supervision on social media information release, comments, communication.

The above is the discussion about synergy inside mechanism, finally specific behavior need organization or person to implement. The organizational structure of the collaborative refers to various departments, various organizational structure work together closely, rather than "each sweep the snow in front of their own. "Organization structure coordination is particularly important. Any part delay time will affect the global development. In China, social media has both the special status of the network and media, which determines the management mechanism and related are complex, resulting in Kowloon flood management structure. As the information reproduced and spread of media, it must first accept the examination of press and publication system; as the guidance and supervision of public opinion, it should be subject to the publicity department; as autonomous, self financing business organization, need to accept the license, such as the tax system management; as network technology and media industry, subject to the Internet News Information Service Committee. So bull management, bring a lot of action "inconvenience", directly or indirectly affect the validity of the behavior. So it should adhere to the active use, scientific development, according to management, to ensure the safety guidelines, and according to the management of large network efforts, to improve the leadership system of Internet governance. The author believes that the mechanism is simplified, clear function, formation of organization cooperation, improve the network behavior including regulation, supervision and validity of social responsibility, and promote the healthy development of the information network.

Summary

Social media break the traditional media production, mixed content production and social relations. The dissemination of information divergent as the core to the periphery, greatly affect the implementation of social responsibility and credibility. Social media strong business atmosphere take the initiative and consciousness of social responsibility decline sharply. Social responsibility must break the traditional thinking inertia, instead of a simple extension of the social responsibility from traditional media, should seek answers on the profound changes in social transformation.

References

1. Peng LAN, The first ten years of Chinese network media,Beijing: Tsinghua University press, 2005, pp. 4.
2. Tianding WANG, who is responsible- on the concept and characteristics of media social responsibility, Science, economics and society, 2007 (2), pp.126-128.
3. QingHe ZHU, Deconstruction and reconstruction of media "social responsibility", Journalism University, 2013 (1), pp.16-22.

4. Fei Wu ,ZhiYuan DING,Construction of journalism education and journalism theory ,Journal of Zhejiang University (SOCIAL SCIENCE EDITION), 2007,37 (6), pp. 128-137.
5. Dan HUANG, The construction and deconstruction journalistic professionalism one by one on the history of the Western Mass Communication,The study of Journalism and communication, 2002, pp.1-8.
6. GuoMing YU, Changes in the pattern of communication at this stage and the future development trend of the portal, News and collaboration, 2012 (12), pp.28.
7. Fei WU, New media reform of journalism? - citizen journalism and professional sports news the responsibility ,Press, 2013 (3), pp.11-19.

Forecast Model of Urban Stagnant Water Based on Logistic Regression

Pan LIU[1,a], Jian-Zhuo YAN[1], Miao-Wen JIANG[1], Mei LIU[2],Xiao-Lan YIN[2] and Xiao-Juan ZHANG[2]

[1]*Faculty of Information Technology, Beijing University of Technology, Beijing 100124, China*
[2]*Beijing Water Affairs Information Management Center, Beijing 100038, China*

Abstract. With the development of information technology, the construction of water resource system has been gradually carried out. In the background of big data, the work of water information needs to carry out the process of quantitative to qualitative change. Analyzing the correlation of data and exploring the deep value of data which are the key of water information's research. On the basis of the research on the water big data and the traditional data warehouse architecture, we try to find out the connection of different data source. According to the temporal and spatial correlation of stagnant water and rainfall, we use spatial interpolation to integrate data of stagnant water and rainfall which are from different data source and different sensors, then use logistic regression to find out the relationship between them.

1 Introduction

Big Data Analytics (BDA) is the core of big data concepts and methods. It analyzes the massive, diverse, fast-growing, and content-rich data (big data) to find out the hidden patterns, unknown correlation and other useful information [1]. But the very key of this whole process is to prepare the data which is suitable for data mining, which means we need to do the data fusion job to combine the data from different source.

Data fusion is different from the traditional data integration or knowledge database technology, it requires large span, deep and comprehensive research methods. Data fusion is the process of integrating two or more data. The purpose of the process is to generate an improved data set, which can be superior to the source dataset or the input dataset both in geospatial and attribute traits. Big Data is a complex set of data with large, diverse, high-speed variations [2-3], in these data, spatial data accounted for the vast majority, about 80% of the data has spatial location [4-5]. So in this paper we combine stagnant water data and rainfall data which are two kinds of data source into one dataset by their geographic Information Attributes and their time attribute, but then we may face a problem which is we cannot find these two properties on the same point at the same time. For example, we can get the data of stagnant water at one point and we assume its coordinate is (x,y), but we cannot find the rainfall data in database at the same point, but we can get other rainfall data around this point. So based on the geographical coordinates of the stagnant water, we calculate the value of the rainfall data of this point by the method of spatial interpolation.

[a] Corresponding author: 2795611970@qq.com

In this paper, we will use the method of Inverse Distance to a Power (IDW) to get the data of rainfall, then we use rainfall data as inputs, stagnant water data as output, and logistic regression as a method for machine learning to find the potential relationship between these two.

2 Data preparation

At present, the water data fusion between stagnant water and rainfall is only limited to transferring the data from each sensor into the data warehouse, because the different functions of the sensors are different, the correlation between the tables and the tables is transmitted, weak. However, because each sensor has its own unique spatial information, then I introduced IDW-based spatial interpolation method to integrate the data from different sensors, which means I calculate the rainfall data of this area which has stagnant water data. At last, we get a one point's data of stagnant water, while also be able to get this point's data of rainfall.

2.1 Preprocessing the data of rainfall

First of all, the current structure of the data itself which we can see it in table1.

Table 1. The current structure of data.

ID	Varchar(32)
Code	Varchar(16)
Time	Date
Z	Number(10,2)

The data stored in database comes with a unique code, and this code represents the spatial attribute of the data. In order to calculate the value by IDW, we need to change the structure of the table which is picking every code as a column and make Z as its value. For example, in a table we get 3 kinds of code which are "xxx", "yyy" and "zzz", then we change the structure of this table as Table2.

Table 2. The changed structure of data.

Time	Date
XXX-Z	Number(10,2)
YYY-Z	Number(10,2)
ZZZ-Z	Number(10,2)

Above all, the steps are:
(1) Make the raw data arranged by every hour per day;
(2) Change the table's structure to fit the IDW method just as we talked about above;
(3) Calculate the value by IDW.

2.1.1 Changing the structure of the table by SPSS Modeler

SPSS Modeler is a set of data mining tools that enable you to quickly build predictive models using business technology and apply them to business activities to improve your decision-making process. Designed with reference to the industry standard CRISP-DM model, SPSS Modeler supports the entire data mining process from data to better business results. Flow chart shown in Figure 1.

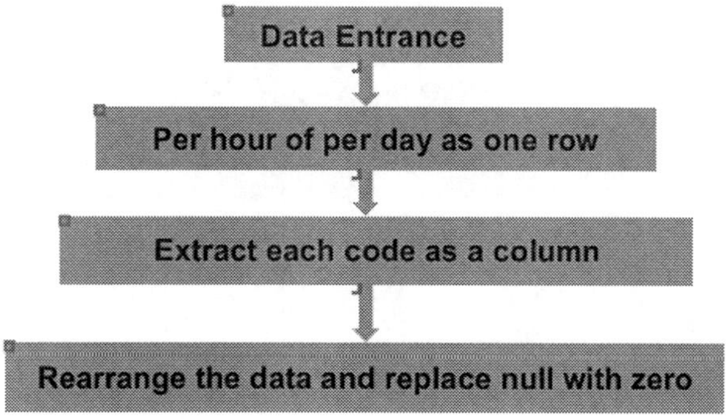

Figure 1. Flow chart of the rainfall data process by spss

SPSS provides "data disaggregation" components through which a given time field can be divided into two columns which are day and hour. At the meantime, SPSS also provides "data reconstruction" components through which each code can be extracted as one column. As shown in Figure 2 is the rainfall data processing flow chart.

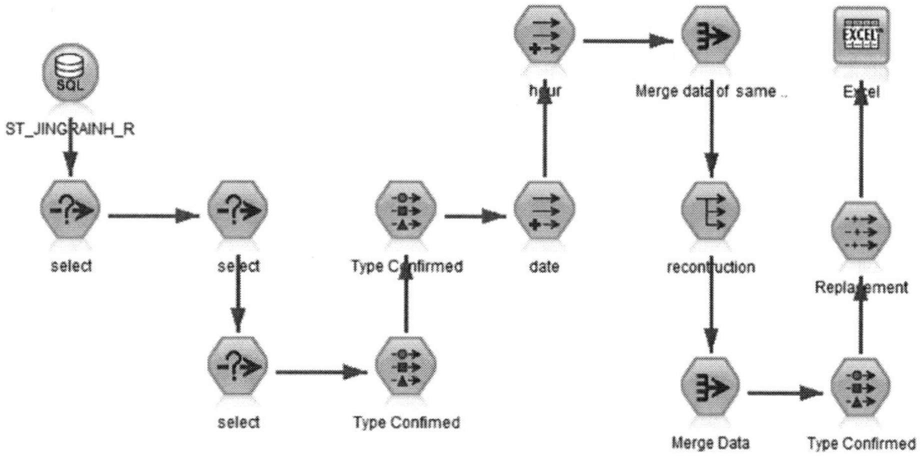

Figure 2. Flow chart of using SPSS to do data processing

As you can see, the flow chart upper there have components named date and hour of which used to change the time dimension to be hour, and the first merge data component is to get the average value of rainfall from same hour same day and record the total number of merge items, and the reason why we want to know how much rows we have merged is to determine the duration of the rainfall, part of the result is stored in excel which we can see in Figure 3. In Figure 3, each column in the first row represents the meaning of the data from this column. The first two columns are well understood, and we start with the third column. The third column represents the amount of rain collected for one hour, excluding the rainfall is zero, which is used to determine the length of time since data is collected every 15 minutes. After the third column represents the rainfall of each point at a certain time

DOI: 10.1051/itmconf/20171101008

DATE	HOUR	RECORD	30521900_	30522000_	30522850_	30523900_	30523960_	30524200_	30524300_	30526500_
2012/7/22	6	4	226	171	152	197	184	172	172	136
2012/7/22	4	4	226	171	151	197	184	172	171	136
2012/7/22	3	4	226	171	149	197	184	172	171	136
2012/7/22	2	4	226	170	147	195	182	168	170	136
2012/7/22	1	4	225	159	119	191	177	164	166	135
2012/7/22	0	4	222	151	119	188. 5	176	162	161	132
2012/7/21	23	1	222	151	119	184	170	152	152	121
2012/7/21	22	1	222	149	117	176	160	145	128. 5	109. 5
2012/7/21	21	1	220	146	101. 5	168	150	138	101	88. 5
2012/7/21	20	1	219	142. 5	71	154. 5	129	104. 5	36. 5	62
2012/7/21	19	3	212	135	42	104. 5	75	50	24. 5	43. 5
2012/7/21	18	1	208	126. 5	26. 5	42	30	21	21	24. 5
2012/6/25	6	1	34	51	20	67	52	51	28	39

Figure 3. The result set for IDW interpolation

2.1.2 Rainfall data interpolation based on IDW

Inverse Distance to a Power interpolation is first proposed by meteorologists and geologists. Inverse Distance to a Power is the earliest computer interpolation method and is still widely used. Its basic principle is to distribute a series of discrete points on the plane, if we know some point's position coordinates $(x_i, y_i)$and the attribute valueZ_i, according to the attribute values of the surrounding discrete points, the P-point attribute value is interpolated by the Inverse Distance to a Power[6,7]. If there are N data points around, the attribute value of point P is:

$$P(Z)=\sum_{i=1}^{N}\frac{z_i}{[d_i(x,y)]^u}/\left(\sum_{i=1}^{N}\frac{1}{[d_i(x,y)]^u}\right), i = 1,2, \dots N \tag{1}$$

And $d_i(x,y)=\sqrt{(x-x_i)^2+(y-y_i)^2}$ means the distance from the i-th data point to the p-point. In this paper, we only need to know the gis coordinates of all the rainfall points in the urban area and the targeted coordinates , so we can calculate the distance between each rainfall point and the targeted point. According to IDW interpolation method, we can get the influence factors of each rainfall point which we name it λ_i.

$$\lambda_i = \frac{\frac{1}{d_i}}{\left(\sum_{i=1}^{n}\frac{1}{d_i}\right)} \tag{2}$$

Then put each point's rainfall into the formula (3),we can get the value of targeted point.

$$\hat{Z}(x,y) = \sum_{i=1}^{n}\lambda_i Z(x_i,y_i) \tag{3}$$

According to figure 3, we can easily calculate the rainfall of targeted point at every hour every day.

2.2 Integrate the data of the stagnant water and the rainfall

We need to determine the possibility of stagnant water happened in this area according to its rainfall, so we plan to use the logistic regression to find out the relation between stagnant water data and rainfall data, we use rainfall data as input and stagnant water data as output. The accumulation area, ground structure, and drainage of the individual water points are different. Therefore, different models should be established for different water accumulation points, in this paper, we choose the point of the bridge of huaxiang as an example.

At first, we need to calculate the rainfall of one stagnant water point by IDW and change the value of stagnant water data into 0 or 1 based on whether stagnant water happened in this area, then we can combine the stagnant water data of this point with the rainfall data through the time dimension. There are three combinations of ways which are external connections, internal connections and partly external connections. In this paper, we choose partly external connection and take the time of stagnant water as reference. The result set are stored in excel which we can see in figure 4. And in figure 4, the first two columns are time which is based on the original stagnant water, the column called rainfall is calculated by the method of IDW.

A	B	C	D
DATE	HOUR	Rainfall	Stagnant water
2012/7/22	6	199.0206	1
2012/7/22	4	198.9362	1
2012/7/22	3	198.8662	1
2012/7/22	2	196.5751	1
2012/7/22	1	188.27075	1
2012/7/22	0	183.6454	1
2012/7/21	23	178.9515	1
2012/7/21	22	171.33905	1
2013/7/31	23	12.1026	0
2013/7/31	6	15.2719	0
2013/7/31	2	14.858	0
2013/7/31	1	12.4662	0
2013/7/16	6	26.2502	0
2013/7/8	12	15.8921	0

Figure 4. The result set for logistic regression

2.2.1 Filling in the vacancy value of the rainfall data

In this paper, we only fill the data of its stagnant water data is 1 and delete the rest unfilled data, because most of the data to be analyzed has a stagnant water property of zero, and in order to balance the data set, we need to reduce it. We choose the method of "linear regression" which is we consider the linear correlation between rainfall and time. The specific means is "if there are missing value in the same day, we calculate the data of the rainfall by the other data in the same day to fill, if not, we delete this row".

2.2.2 Data grouping based on the rainfall

Because the distribution of the entire dataset is not even, we cannot use single formula to describe the whole situation. By querying the Bureau of Meteorology on the definition of rainfall levels, we divide our data into five parts which we can see it in Table3.

Table 3. Data grouping based on rainfall levels.

Rainfall levels	Rainfall
Light rain	0.1-4.9mm
Medium rain	5.0-9.9mm
Heavy rain	10.0-29.9mm
Rainstorm	30.0-69.9mm
Super rainstorm	>70mm

3 Logistic regression analysis of rainfall and stagnant water

In the stagnant water analysis, rainfall can be used as independent variables, and the occurrence of stagnant water can be used as binary variables (0 on behalf of the stagnant water does not occur, and 1 represents stagnant does occur,). When a dependent variable is a bivariate variable, a multivariate logistic regression model is used to generate the regression coefficients for the respective variables based on the sample data and to discuss the relationship between the dependent and independent variables in the model. Let p be the probability of occurrence of the event, in the range of 0 to 1, then

1-p is the probability that the event does not occur, this probability can be calculated using logistic function, the expression is [8]:

$$p = \frac{1}{1+e^{-(\beta_0+\sum_{i=1}^{k}\beta_i x_i)}} \tag{4}$$

Logistic function is a nonlinear function of covariance, in order to obtain the regression coefficient, the logit transformation of (4), to obtain a linear formula :

$$ln\,({}^{p}/_{1-p}) = \beta_0 + \sum_{i=1}^{k}\beta_i \tag{5}$$

In this formula,X_i are the independent variables, and β are the coefficients for the variables, formula(5) is also called the odds ratio (OR). Since the OR has some good properties in measuring the association [9], it can be used to describe the effect of the independent variables on the event probability in the logistic regression model, Therefore, it is often used to interpret the regression coefficients of the logistic regression model [10].

3.1 Data preprocessing for logistic regression

3.1.1 Determine the data range based on the data distribution

Before data analysis, we need to look at the quality of the data of each group. We describe the quality of each group by stagnant water distribution ratio. Details can be seen in Table 4.

Table 4. Stagnant water distribution ratio of each data group.

Rainfall levels	Stagnant water(1)	Not stagnant water(0)
Light rain	3%	97%
Medium rain	14%	86%
Heavy rain	27%	73%
Rainstorm	72%	28%
Super rainstorm	92%	8%

As you can see, light rain only has the possibility of 3% to cause stagnant water and super rainstorm has the possibility of 92% to cause stagnant water, so we deem light rain with a very low possibility to cause stagnant water and rainstorm with a very high possibility to cause stagnant water.

As we know, not necessarily large rainfall will cause stagnant water, stagnant water is related with the duration of rain and urban drainage capacity. In all case, the urban drainage capacity is changeless and that makes the duration of rain to be our only concern. According to the data, almost 90% of the rainstorm lasts less than one hour so that we can take an hour as a unit analyse the relationship between the stagnant water and rainfall, and also we believe that the rainstorm can produce stagnant water more suddenly, and the other groups, we cannot simple assume the duration of the rainfall is less than one, so in this paper, we choose the group of rainstorm to analyse.

3.1.2 logistic regression between rainstorm and stagnant water

Before we put the group of rainstorm into logistic regression training, we only have the data of the average of the rainfall as one input and it's not enough, so we think about the length of the rainfall and we can get the number of the records of the rainfall through the section 2.1.1, and we can determine whether the duration of the rainfall is less than half hour through the record, if the record is less than 3 means the length of the rainfall is less than half hour, The data for logistic regression is below in Figure5.

Rainfall	rainfallPeriod	Stagnant water
69. 7047	0	1
63. 9312	1	1
61. 8981	0	1
57. 76515	1	1
54. 7541	1	1
54. 6983	0	1
54. 3044	1	1
54. 2553	1	1
53. 8186	0	1
53. 1894	1	1
53. 1522	1	1
53. 0445	0	1
52. 9581	1	1
52. 3235	1	1
51. 7775	1	1
50. 7895	0	1
50. 6901	1	1
50. 0265	1	1
49. 4876	1	1
48. 8222	1	1
48. 5478	1	0

Figure 5. The data set of rainstorm and stagnant water for logistic regression

In Figure 5, there are 3 columns, representing rainfall, the record of the rainfall, the existence of stagnant water, we use rainfall and continuous as input and stagnant water as output to perform logistic regression train.

After that, we find out the coefficient of the rainfall corresponding to the significant level of Sig less than 0.05, the regression results can be considered by 5% significance level test. So the formula of logistic regression is

$$p = \frac{1}{1+e^{-(-11.239+0.240x+0.761y_1)}} \tag{5}$$

In those formula, x stands for rainfall, y1 stands for the rainstorm whether lasts half an hour.

3.2 The test of regression equation

In order to test this model, we randomly selected some of the rainfall points which can be thought as rainstorm in the year of 2016 and the year of 2015, and the result is in Figure 6.

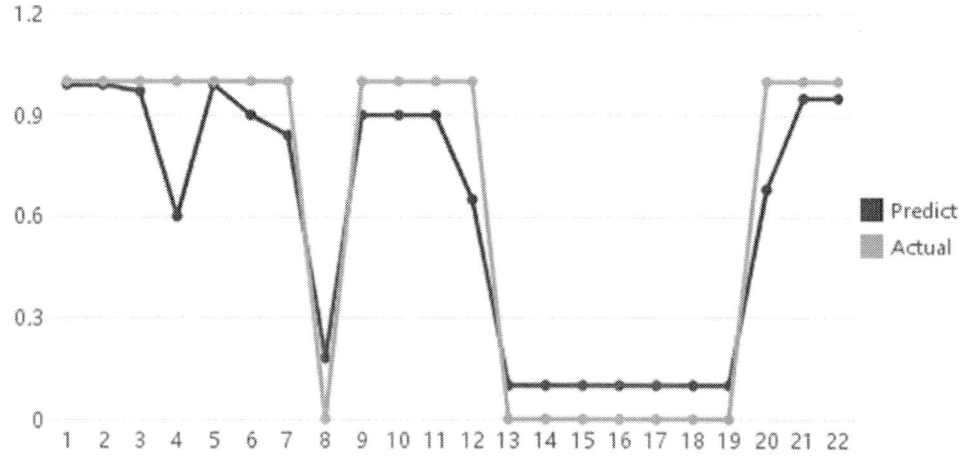

Figure 6. Comparison of Predictive Probability and Actual Value

As you can see, the green part represents the actual stagnant water status, and the blue part represents the predict stagnant water status. The value of 1 is the occurrence of water and the value of

DOI: 10.1051/itmconf/20171101008

0 represents no stagnant water occur. So according to this figure, we can see when there is actually stagnant water, the probability of the forecast mostly more than 80%, while there is no stagnant water, the probability of forecasts mostly less than 20%.

Conclusion

In this paper, we use the idea of big data analysis as the core, make the different sources of data together according to their spatial and temporal attributes by spatial interpolation, make the previous independent one-dimensional data into two-dimensional data. In the past studies, most of the scholars are through the analysis of drainage measures and other factors to determine whether the stagnant water exist, or according to the stagnant water to analyze the trend of stagnant water, but in this paper, we use logistic regression to get the relation of stagnant water and rainstorm. Through rainfall and rain duration to predict whether the water, which is based on a data mining ideas. With the formula we get we can get the possibility of the existence of stagnant water. In this paper, we only consider the amount of the rainfall and we hadn't considered the randomness of the rainfall, so if we want to predict stagnant water risk precisely, we may need to consider the randomness of rainfall on the basis of the logistic regression we established.

References

1. LAPKIN A. Hype Cycle for Big Data[R]. Gartner, Inc.G00235042,2002.
2. DENSHAMPJ, GOODCHILD M F. Spatial Decision Sup-port Systems: A Research Agenda [C]/ / Proceedings GIS / LIS 89, Orlando, FL, 1989: 707-716.
3. SHEKA R S, XIONG H(Eds). Encyclopedia of GIS[M]. New York: Springer,2007.
4. MILLER.H.J,HAN.J. Geographic-Data-Mining and Knowledge Discovery[M].2nd edition. London: Taylorand Francis, 2009.
5. ESTEM, et.al. Spatial Data Mining: Databases Primitives, algorithms and efficientDBMS support [J].Data-Mining and Knowledge Discovery,2000(4): 193-216.
6. Wu Lun, Liu Yu, Zhang Jin. Geographic Information System Principles and Applications[M]. Beijing Science Press, 2001:184-185.
7. Wu xincai. Geographic Information System[M] Electronic Industry Press,2002.172-173
8. Wang jichuan, Guo zhigang. The logistic regression model: methods and application.[M] Beijing: Higher Education Press,2001.
9. Bui D T, Lofman O, Revhaug I, et al. Landslide susceptibility analysis in the Hoa Binh province of Vietnam using statistical index and logistic regression[J].Natural Hazards, 2011, 59(3): 1413-1444.
10. Xie Hualin. Analysis of regionally ecological land useand its influencing factors based on a logistic regressionmodel in the Beijing-Tianjin-Hebei region, China[J].Resources Science, 33(11): 2063—2070. (in Chinese with English abstract)

The Research and Improvement of SDT Algorithm for Historical Data in SCADA

Xu-Dong XU[1] and Yan-Ping FU[1,a]

[1]*Faulty of Information Technology, Beijing University of Technology, Beijing, 100124, China*

Abstract. With the rapid development of Internet of things and big data technology, the amount of data collected by SCADA(Supervisory Control And Data Acquisition)system is growing exponentially, which the traditional SDT algorithm can not meet the requirements of SCADA system for historical data compression. In this paper, ASDT(Advanced SDT) algorithm based on SDT algorithm is proposed and implemented in the Java language, which is based on the deep research of the data compression method, especially the Swing Door Trending. ASDT algorithm through the sine curve fitting data to achieve data compression, compared with the performance of the traditional SDT algorithm, which it can achieve better compression results. The experimental results show that compared with the traditional SDT algorithm, the ASDT algorithm can improve the compression ratio in the case of no significant increase in the compression error, and the compression radio is increased by nearly 50%.

1 Introduction

SCADA system is one of the process industry system based on configuration software, through the real-time detection and control of industrial equipment to achieve real-time data acquisition and storage of process data, the parameters of the device settings, real-time display of warning signals, and other functions.

With the development of Internet of things and cloud storage technology, amount of data collected by RTU is more and more large which acquisition cycle is also getting shorter and shorter [1]. Historical database constantly storing the historical data is an important part of the SCADA system, which can predict and analyze the system fault in advance to ensure the safe and stable operation of the SCADA system. Because the massive historical data in SCADA system has caused great burden to data storage and data processing, the efficient data compression technology can save storage space and improve the utilization rate of storage space. In order to ensure the efficient storage of mass data, it is very useful to data compression technology in the process of historical data storage in SCADA system.

In industry, there are two methods for data compression --- lossless compression and lossy compression [2]. For lossless compression, it is that the data is totally the same after and before the compression; for lossy compression, it is that the compressed data will be uncompressed, by which the uncompressed data will be deviated from the original data, however, the deviation will not affect the variation trend [3]. For SCADA system, there are three methods for compressing historical data ---

[a] Corresponding author: 958591548@qq.com

DOI: 10.1051/itmconf/20171101009

piecewise linear method, vector quantization and signal conversion method. For piecewise linear method, it includes boxcar method, backward slope method, SDT method and PLOT method [4]. SDT method is used for industrial flow most because it is easy and simple to be operated, as well as that it can be executed quickly. Signal conversion includes lots of methods, such as DCT (discrete cosine transform) and WT (Wavelet Transform)[5]. Today, WT is being widely used. However, compared with SDT, WT is more complicated.

2 Strategy for SCADA historical data compressing

2.1 Compressing quantity of state

For quantity of state signal, there are only two values -- 0 and 1, which will be collected by the gathering module at a fixed interval. In real situation, the data related to quantity of state will not change within a while, that is the state signal collected right now is the same as the signal collected last time. For compressing quantity of state, the method that once the data changes, the data shall be collected and saved shall be followed. That is only when the data changes can it be saved. See Figure1, the time t0-t7 has the quantity of state 1,0,0,1,0,0,0,0. Then according to this method, only the quantity of state of t0, t3 will be saved while others will not.

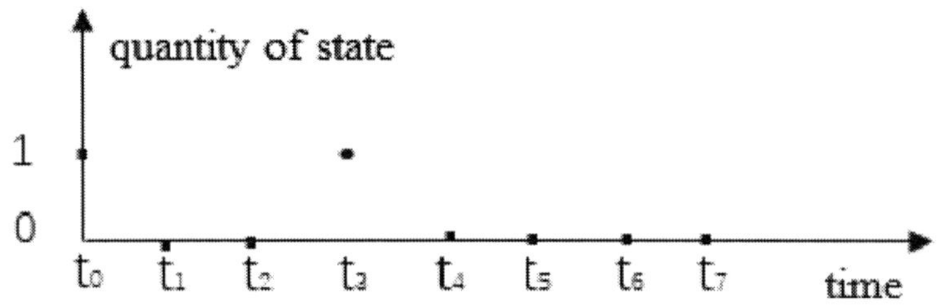

Figure 1. Compressing Quantity of State

2.2 Compressing analog quantity

2.1.1 SDT algorithm

SDT is a kind of data compression method based on linear fitting, which saves the data by establishing parallelogram while the data which is covered by the parallelogram will not be saved. That is only data out of the parallelogram will be saved [6]. See Figure2 for SDT steps. In Figure2, it is assumed that point a is the first data in the first compression duration, and the coordinate point (o, o') whose distance to point a is E, will be as the two supporting points for the revolving door. Once there is new data, the slope between o,o' and new data will be calculated. If there is only one data (a), o,o' and a is actually perpendicular to o,o'. The slope is 0, which means that the revolving door is closed; if there are more and more data, the revolving door will be gradually opened, whose slope will be changed at the same time, where we can find that the upper supporting point will have the maximal slope while the lower supporting point will have the minimal slope [7]. Within a while, once the door is opened, it cannot be closed until the slope of upper supporting point is the same as that of lower supporting point. As long as the two doors are not parallel to each other, or the sum of two interior angles is less than 180 degrees, t-he operation on revolving door will be continued. In Figure 2, the first compression duration is started from a to d, the straight line from a to d stands for data(a,b,c,d);Similarly, the second compression duration is started from e, the straigh line from e to h stands for the data (e, f, g, and h).

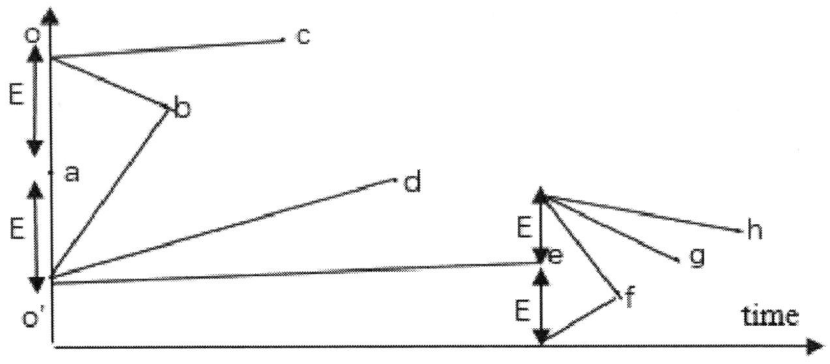

Figure 2. The basic steps of SDT algorithm

From what mentioned above (how SDT works), it can be found that there are some problems: first, the threshold value is the only controllable parameter, so E will directly affect the compression performance. Once E is defined, it cannot be changed during the compression. How to define E shall be realized via experimenting for a long time; if E is not proper, SDT performance will be greatly lowered. Second, if the data change is slow during a time, the time used by data compression will be long, which makes the instantaneity of linear trend lost [8].Third, in most situations, the data change is not linear. It is known that SDT is a method to fit data via linear trend.

3 Improved SDT

For the aforementioned problems, the researchers have proposed how to improve it. For example, Wang Ju [9], on the basis of the defect suffered by SDT -- E cannot be changed, proposed that E can be adjusted according to the initial threshold value; Yu Songtao [10] proposed an ideology --- dynamic regulation on allowance, that is the threshold value can be set dynamically according to the allowance. Qu Yilin,[11] depending on feedback control system, by which the allowance is able to have a dynamic change during the compression. Zhang Jingtao [12] proposed that the performance of data compression is largely determined by the compression deviation, so the compression deviation parameter shall be selected in a dynamic way. Duan Peiyong [13] proposed that a slope of a straight line cannot be used to show the change trend of several data, all the saved data shall be obtained by calculation but not by the compressed data. Ning Hainan [14] proposed that fitting of change trend shall be done via parabola, by which data compression can be realized; Zhang Jian [15] proposed that the abnormal points shall be inspected and removed, and the length of recording limit shall be set etc.

3.1 Basic principle of ASDT

For the improved SDT, the fitting is done between the straight line and compressed data; however, in real situation, the data change will not keep increasing or decreasing in a while. Even though there is fitting via curve, the change trend of data cannot be changed radically. It means that within a while, the data change is monotonous. Meanwhile, the improved SDT proposed that FSRL (Forced Storage-Recording Limit) can be set, which will make the calculation more complicated [16]. For ASDT, the data fitting is done via sine curve. So during a duration, the data will both increase and decrease, which is consistent with the change rule. The cycle of sine curve can be used to solve that how to set the recording limit.

DOI: 10.1051/itmconf/20171101009

3.2 Compression steps of ASDT

As for the setting of cycle of sine curve, it is required to consider the length of compression interval and compression ratio of process industry. For process industry, the compression ratio 10:1 is normally used. If the ratio exceeds this compression ratio, some useful details will be lost. Normally, one cycle of sine curve will be used as the compression interval. Therefore, the cycle shall be set as 10, which not only restricts the length of compression interval but also ensures the compression ratio. See Figure 3 for the flow diagram of ASDT, from which we can see that TL is the length of compression interval, E is the threshold, and the first data of each cycle is A_0. (A_0 shall be the benchmark of each sine cycle, which shall be fluctuated around A_0, for fluctuation, and the upper limit is toplimit as in (1) while the lower limit is lower limit as in (2)).

$$\text{toplimit} = A_0 + \max(\sin(\omega t + \phi) + E) \quad (1)$$

$$\text{lowerlimit} = A0 + \min(\sin(\omega t + \phi) - E) \quad (2)$$

Here below are the steps of ASDT:

Step1: initialization of parameters, TL and T shall be set as 10. $\omega = 2\pi/T = 2\pi/10 = \pi/5$.

Step2: judge that whether t is larger than TL, if not, move to step 4.

Step3: deal with the value of t, and t = t%TL.

Step4: judge that whether the first time point of sine cycle (that is t) is equal to 1, if yes, move to step 7.

Step5: get the value of current data, figure out Emax as in (3) and Emin as in (4). During one sine cycle (10), when t is 2.5 and 7.5, the maximal value and minimal vlaue will be obtained.

$$\text{Emax} = A0 + \sin(0.2\pi * 2.5 + \phi) + E \quad (3)$$

$$\text{Emin} = A0 + \sin(0.2\pi * 7.5 + \phi) - E \quad (4)$$

Step6: judge that whether data is no more than the maximal value and no less than the minimal value, if yes, save the data. If no, move to step8.

Step7: SaveA0, which shall be the data of the first time point of sine cycle.

Step8: an operation that t pluses 1 shall be done.

Step9: judge that whether there is a new data, if yes, move to step2.

Step10: the data compression is ended.

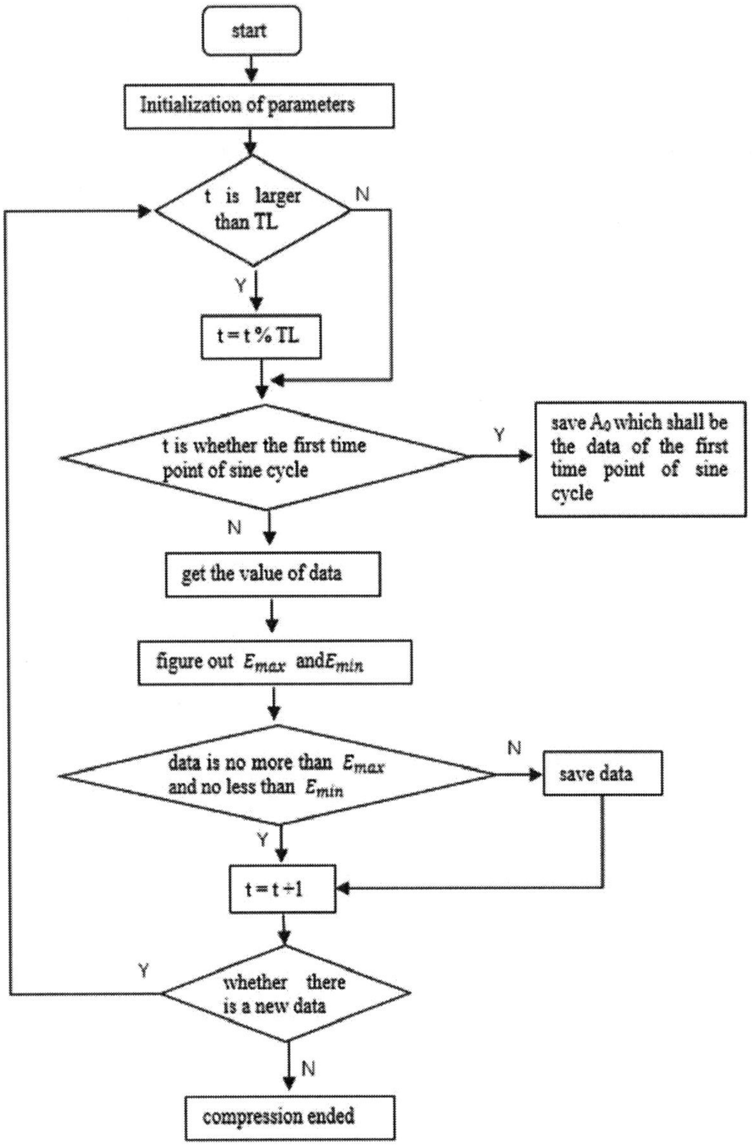

Figure 3. Algorithm flow chart of ASDT

4 Experiment result analysis

There are two indexes to evaluate the performance of data compression -- compression ratio and compression error. It is assumed that there is a group data (there are n values), which is recorded as $y_1 \sim y_n$; before compression, the number of data is m(m<=n); after compression, there are n values, which are recorded as $\hat{y}_1 \sim \hat{y}_n$ here below is the definition of MSE (mean square error) as in (5) :

DOI: 10.1051/itmconf/20171101009

$$MSE = \frac{1}{n}\sum_{i=1}^{n}(y_i - \hat{y}_i)^2 \tag{5}$$

For this experiment, the data is the remote temperature got by SCADA, 4 groups of data are selected. The digit quantity is 1000, 5000, 10000 and 50000 respectively. In Figure 4, there is a comparison on the compression ratio between SDT and ASDT. In Figure 5, there is a comparison on the compression error between SDT and ASDT. In Table 1, the data is about the experiment result; from the chart and the table, we can know that the compression error of SDT and ASDT almost the same; however, the compression ratio of ASDT is much higher than that of SDT.

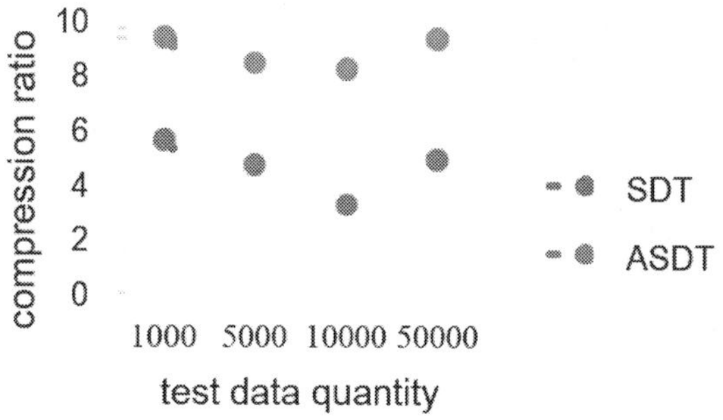

Figure 4. Comparison on the compression ratio between SDT and ASDT

Figure 4. Comparison on the compression error between SDT and ASDT

Table1. performance analysis and comparison between SDT and ASDT

Compression Algorithm	***Test Data Quantity***	***Compression Ratio***	***Compression Error***
SDT	1000	5.6	2.57
ASDT	1000	9.33	3.45
SDT	5000	4.67	2.35
ASDT	5000	8.40	3.94
SDT	10000	3.23	1.74
ASDT	10000	8.20	2.89
SDT	50000	4.89	1.77
ASDT	50000	9.30	2.76

Conclusion

In this thesis, it proposed an improved calculation based on the compression of revolving door, as well as an analog computation on the test data by compiling program. ASDT solves the problems suffered by traditional method, like fitting data via straight line does not consider the actual change happened during the data collection; most importantly, ASDT is no need to set the length of compression interval. By the experiments above, it compares SDT and ASDT, which concludes that ASDT can greatly enhance compression ratio without increasing error.

References

1. S.Sivalingam and M.Hovd, "Effect of data compression on controller performance monitoring, "in Control Automation(MED), 2011 19th Mediterranean Conference on, pp.594-599(2011).
2. H.Vedam, V.Venkatasubramanian, M.Bhalodia. A B-spline based method for data compression, process monitoring and diagnosis[J]. Computers & Chemical Engineering, **22**(12):S827–S830(1998).
3. J.Pettersson, P.O.Gutman. Automatic tuning of the window size in the Box Car Back Slope data compression algorithm[J]. Journal of Process Control, **14**(4):431-439(2004).
4. Li X, Qiu H, Zhu Y. Research and Design of Lossy Compression Algorithm in Embedded Real-Time Database[M]. Proceedings of the Second International Conference on Mechatronics and Automatic Control. Springer International Publishing, 1027-1034(2015).
5. R.S.H.Mah, A.C.Tamhane, S.H.Tung. Process trending with piecewise linear smoothing[J]. Computers & Chemical Engineering, **19**(2):129-137(1995).
6. E.H.Bristol. Swing Door Trending: Adaptive Trend Recording[C]. National Conference Proceeding. Sydey: ISA,749-753(1990).
7. Zhang Wang, Chen Xinchu, Lu Dingxing. Research and Application of Improved Process Data Compression Algorithm-SDT [J]. Industrial Control Computer,**08**:1-3+6(2009).
8. Zhao Xudong, Ding Jiexiong, Bian Zhiyuan, Guan Lichao, Xie Gang, Du Li, Wang W-ei. Application of improved SDT algorithm in CNC monitoring system[J]. Manufacturing T-echnology & Machine Tool, **10**:155-159(2014).
9. Wang Ju, Chen Xiaojiang, Xing Tianzhang, Fang Ding Yi, Yuan Chang, Data Compression of Wireless Sensor Networks in the Heritage Monitor [J]. Journal of Xidian University, **01**:157-162(2012).
10. Yu Songtao, Wang Xiaokun, Zhao Liqiang, Yu Tao, Wang Jianlin. The Improved Al-gorithm for SDT Based on the Dynamic Adjustment of Tolerance[J]. Journal of Beijing U-niversity of Chemical Technology (NATURAL SCIENCE), **03**:109-113(2013).
11. Qu Yilin, Wang Wenhai. Automatic Parameter Control SDT Algorithm for Process D-ata Compression[J]. Computer Engineering, **22**:40-42(2010).
12. Zhang Jingtao, Wang Hua, Wang Hongan. Accessing and Compressing of Real-time Data[J]. Control and Instruments in Chemical Industry, **03**:47-50(2003).
13. Duan Peiyong, Zhang Mei, Tang Tongkui. A Swing Door Trending(SDT) Algorithm and its Application to Compressing Process Data Received by Local Operation Network Nodes [J]. Information and Control, **02**:132-135(2002).
14. Ning Hainan. A New Process Data Compression Algorithm Based on SDT Algorithm[J]. Computer Technology and Development, **01**:25-28(2010).
15. Zhang Jian, Liu Guangbin. An New Data Compression Based on ISDT Algorithm an-d its Performance Analysis[J]. Fire Control and Command Control, **02**:80-82+86(2007).
16. Xing Rui, Qi Qi, Zheng Tao. Improved SDT Algorithm [J]. Computer Engineering a-nd Design,**02**:515-518+528(2013).

Development Situation, Trend and Countermeasure of Consumer-level UAV Market in China

Yu-Lei KANG[1] and Yang XI[2,a]

[1]*Beijing Institute of Fashion Technology, Business School, China*
[2]*Beijing Institute of Fashion Technology, Business School, China*

Abstract. This paper is based on the status of Chinese consumer-level UAV(Unmanned Aerial Vehicle) market. According to the main problems in Chinese consumer-level UAV market, the author analyses the trends of Chinese consumer-level UAV market. Then, the author put forward some suggestions to develop Chinese consumer-level UAV market. In 21st century, the research and development expenditure presents the explosive growth in Chinese consumer-level UAV market. From the year of 2012, DJI released their first consumer-level UAV product. Amazon, Facebook, Google and other companies have announced their entry into the UAV market. In 2016, Huawei also announced that it will enter the UAV market.

1 Introduction

With the continuous emergence of new technologies and the improvement of people's living standards, more and more consumers are beginning to pay attention to consumer-level UAV products. Today, the domestic superstar show have a quickly development. It is worth mentioning that the aerial shot in the program are mostly from consumer-level unmanned aerial vehicle. The introduction and development of the superstar show promote the development of consumer-level UAV. According to national customs statistics, China exported 891,000 unmanned aerial vehicles in 2015, increased 427.2% than 2014. The main export markets for the EU, Hong Kong and North America, the average export price equivalent to about 3670 yuan. Of these, 40% of exports to Hong Kong and re-exports to North America and the European Union. At the same time, China imported 14.5 million unmanned aerial vehicles, increased 1350% than 2014. The average import price is 4817 yuan. At present, China has about 400 UAV manufacturers, supply about 70% of the global demand for unmanned aerial vehicles market. This paper is based on the status of Chinese consumer-level UAV(Unmanned Aerial Vehicle) market. According to the main problems in Chinese consumer-level UAV market, the author analyses the trends of Chinese consumer-level UAV market. Then, the author put forward some suggestions to develop Chinese consumer-level UAV market.

Consumer-level UAVs are mainly used for aerial photography, delivery of gifts, mainly to meet the consumer's entertainment needs. And consumer-level UAV audience is mostly individual consumers. Relative to the professional UAV, consumer UAV to get started faster, lower prices, a wider audience.

[a] Corresponding author: 13407008@qq.com

2 Development status of consumer UAV market in china

2.1 Consumer UAV market is rapidly expanding

The KPCB (Internet Trends Research Institute) data shows that 2013-2015 global consumer UAV market size grow from 1.49 billion yuan to 11.05 billion yuan, the average annual compounded growth rate of 171.87%.China's civilian UAV market reached 2.33 billion yuan in 2015.According to DJI innovation company accounted for 70%-80%, we can estimated that China's consumer-level UAV market size is 1.75 billion yuan in 2015.

2.2 Upstream and downstream industry chain matures, production costs continue to decrease

Due to the success of DJI, Parrot, 3DR and other companies in the consumer UAV market, many manufacturers with unmanned aerial vehicle (UAV) related components manufacturing capacity rapidly enter the industry. What's more, the newly entered the market of UAV companies began to enter the UAV design and manufacturing industry.

With the explosive development of the consumer UAV market, due to the large increase, the manufacturers in the upstream industry chain have greatly expanded their production scale, and finally reduced the production cost of the upstream manufacturers. Because of declining parts prices, the UAV manufacturers' profits rising, shipments continue to grow. The UAV industrial chain enter a snowball-style outbreak period.

The Table 1 shows that the price of UAV related components have a significant reduction.

Table 1. The change of consumer-level UAV common components' price

The name of component	Model	The price in Apr.2015 (RMB)	The price in Oct.2016 (RMB)	Reduction (%)
lithium battery	5300mAh 14.8V	527	280	46.8%
Flight control	APM2.6 APM	470	399	15.1%
GPS	APM	369	348	12.2%
Frame	DJI-F450	188	169	10.1%
Forward and reverse oar	1047 carbon fiber (a pair)	30	20	33.3%

2.3 More industry giants to enter the consumer market

The global civil unmanned aerial vehicle market has entered the "civil unmanned aircraft first year" in 2016. With the DJI, 3DR, Parrot and other unmanned aerial vehicles innovation company in the consumer UAV market has achieved great success, consumer UAV market has become very popular. Amazon, Facebook, Google and other companies have announced their entry into the UAV industry. Amazon announced they would use the unmanned aircraft to delivery. It can greatly improve delivery speed and reduce labor costs.

In China, MI technology company announced they are starting the research of consumer-level UAV in 2016. What's more, they held a first flight live show by MI-UAV in May.2016. In addition to this, Jingdong announced the pace of keeping up with Amazon, plans to use UAV delivery. Tencent, Huawei and other technology companies have announced plans to enter the consumer UAV market.

3 The main problems of china's consumer - level UAV market

Some scholars pointed out that the prospect of consumer UAV market is excellent. However, the imperfect industry standard system, product safety, privacy and other issues cannot be avoided. At present, the management of consumer-level market is far behind the development speed in China.

3.1 Consumer UAV flight policy requirements and standard system need to be improved

In June.2009, the Civil Aviation Administration of China (CAAC) promulgated the Measures for Air Traffic Management of Civilian Unmanned Aerial Vehicles (UAVs), which stipulated that civil unmanned aerial vehicles (UAVs) should apply for and design airspace in accordance with relevant regulations and voluntarily accept flight management.

In November 2013, the Civil Aviation Administration of China promulgated the Provisional Regulations on Driver Pilot Management of Civil UAV Driving Aircraft Systems. The civil unmanned aerial vehicles (UAVs) were classified into micro unmanned aerial vehicles (UAVs), light unmanned aerial vehicles (UAVs), small UAVs and large unmanned aircrafts. machine. The Regulations require that these four unmanned aerial vehicles should be managed classified.

In April 2015, China Civil Aviation Authority awarded China AOPA (China Aircraft Owners and Pilots Association) UAV the access of driver qualification management. This is the second time China Civil Aviation Authority to give its authorization.

In December 2015, China Civil Aviation Administration issued a "light UAV operation requirements (Trial)", asked some unmanned aerial vehicles involved in cloud and the use of electronic fence.

In July 2016, the Civil Aviation Administration of China officially released "civil unmanned aerial vehicle pilot regulations", increase the new classification of UAVs, so that the provisions of the coverage more clearly.

Although the Chinese Civil Aviation Administration issued these regulations and standard system, but the illegal flight, UAVs crash caused by casualties still exist.

3.2 Some products have security risks

In China, the advanced consumer-level UAV technology are mostly concentrated in the DJI Innovation company, Beijing University of Aeronautics and Astronautics Institute and a small number of leading companies among the industry. At present, China has more than 400 unmanned aerial vehicles company, which means most of the consumer UAV technology is more backward. In addition, in order to obtain corporate profits, some UAV enterprises privately modified processing brand products. They can obtain the function of increased UAV load and extended battery life.

These privately changed unmanned aerial vehicle products which can not conform the requirements of scientific and security. If these products enter into the market, it will bring a huge security risk.

Due to UAV player's improper operation or violation of the provisions of the use of unmanned aerial vehicles, the number of UAV-accidents increase rapidly. US Federal Aviation Administration data show that from August 2015 to January 2016 period, only the record of the UAV security incidents there are about 600 cases. The most serious accident occurred in August 2015, an unmanned aerial vehicle UAVs will rise to the airport no-fly zone, a flight from the aircraft in just 20 feet, a great threat to the aircraft and passengers of the security.

3.3 The consumer-level UAV may infringe upon the privacy of people, and even facilitate the criminals committing the crime

In 2015, a US government intelligence officer in the use of four-rotor unmanned aerial vehicle without operational experience, so that the UAV disappeared into the night sky. In the next morning, the UAV was found crashed in the White House lawn. The US government attaches great importance to this matter. The presidential security affairs of the Secret Service has launched an investigation.

In the use of UAV aerial photography, whether it is fair use or improper use, there may be violations of other people's privacy and even national security, causing unnecessary misunderstanding. Moreover, there will be criminals using unmanned aerial vehicles to deliver drugs and other criminal acts, in addition to its received in pursuit, but also by the people used to continue to challenge the legal and social bottom line.

4 Development trend of consumer UAV market in china

4.1 Chinese consumer-level market will continue to grow

With the Chinese consumer-level unmanned aerial vehicle technology matures, the upstream and downstream industry chain is more mature, the popular development of consumer-level UAVs into the technical threshold of the market continue to decrease. It will attract more enterprises and manufacturers to participate in the entire industry, which will undoubtedly give China's consumer-level UAV market to bring greater opportunities for development and space.

According to IDC (United States International Data Corporation) predicted that China's civilian UAV product market size will reach RMB 20 billion. The Chinese consumer-level UAV shipments will reach 300 million units.

4.2 The gap between the consumer-level UAV company is likely to widen

According to the Internet public information, although the UAV flight control technology and the main components gradually began to generalize on the market, more and more advanced GPS navigation technology, advanced sensors, intelligent target recognition technology are created. The UAVs equipped with these new technology become more and more competitive.

With the continuous innovation and progress of consumer-level UAV technology, the gap between enterprises within the industry continues to expand, but the position of DJI innovation as a leader within the industry will not change in the short term. DJI have a large number of self-developed technology, including PTZ control, anti-collision technology, and through the vertical integration of management, will be assigned to a larger "cake" to get greater profits and create greater research and development of investment. And those who are not high technical capacity of enterprises will be eliminated or acquired. For example, the US leader in 3DR unmanned aerial vehicles in 2015 announced its withdrawal from the consumer UAV market.

4.3 Small-scale self-timer UAV will become the mainstream of the consumer-level UAV market

As technology continues to evolve and consumer demand increases, consumer-grade UAVs will be smaller, lighter, and easier to operate in the future.

In addition, along with the rapid development of social networking and smart phones, more and more people think the self-timer is a fashion. The self-timer will be became an essential element in life. A British newspaper made a survey about the time and frequency of self-timer from 2000 women. The survey data show that these women take the average self-timer 3 times a day. What's more, they take the average self-timer 5 hours per week. However, whether it is a smart phone self-timer or self-timer shot, there will be limited by viewing angle and position. Therefore, the small self-timer UAV is not only easy to carry, but also not subject to perspective and location constraints and can view the head of any angle.

5 Suggestions

5.1 Government should update and improve the small UAV flight management policies and regulations

With the rapid development of Chinese consumer-level UAV market, consumer-level UAV technology matures and simplifies, manufacturing costs are increasingly reduced, consumer-level UAV is no longer belongs to the professional-grade players' unique toys. More and more green hand join the queue of consumer-level UAV players, although consumer-level UAV mode of operation more and more simple, but still have some technical requirements for the players. So, these new players to join, it is easy to occur the situation of "bombing machine". We often see the news on "bombing machine" to hurt passers-by, invasion of privacy, the illegal flight and other hazards to social security News appears.

Therefore, the Chinese government should actively learn from the management experience of foreign small unmanned aerial vehicles, constantly update and improve the small UAV flight management policies and regulations for the consumption of UAV flight areas, flight distance and other flight control environment and strict management. Then, it will reduce the occurrence of unsafe events and make the whole consumer-level UAV market more healthy and safe development.

5.2 Enterprises should increase R & D investment, comply with the demand of market, improve independent innovation capability

China's consumer-level unmanned aerial vehicle products in the future development trend is based on small self-timer UAV-based, this UAV has a unique feature: easy to carry. At present, zero-degree intellectual control company launched the Dobby Pocket UAV, weighing only 199g, less than the US Federal Aviation Administration limit the registration of 0.55 pounds range.

With the development of consumer-level UAV market and consumer players are constantly updated, unmanned aerial vehicles enterprises should increase investment in research and development, improve the ability of independent innovation and accelerate the upgrading of products according to market demand.

5.3 Consumers should improve their operational skills and social safety awareness

At present, a large part of the consumer-level UAV accident is caused by the improper operation and inadequate awareness of owner. Of course, it can not be said that all accidents are due to this reason. With the continuous improvement of products and the strengthen management of government, consumers should also enhance our social security awareness. At the same time, consumers must show their own products in the prescribed security environment. What's more, consumers should consciously read the product operating instructions and continue to improve their operational skills, thereby reducing the consumption of UAV accidents.

References

1. Lianbo Wang, Science & Technology and Enterprise, Research on Development and Development Trend of Unmanned Aerial Vehicle, **14**,349(2013)
2. Qingyu Wang, New West (theoretical version), Research on the Development of Domestic Unmanned Aerial Vehicle (UAV) Technology Based on Patent Analysis - Taking "Shenzhen Dajiang Innovation & Technology Co., Ltd" as an Example, **14**,(2016)
3. Greiner L.E, Harvard Business Review, Evolution and Revolution as Organization Grow,37-46,(1972)

4. Miller, D., Friesen, Academy of Management Journal, P.H. Momentum and revolution in organizational adaptation,23,591-614,(1980)

ITM Web of Conferences **11**, 01011 (2017) DOI: 10.1051/itmconf/20171101011
IST2017

Multi-objective Virtual Machine Placement for Load Balancing

Feng FANG[1] and Bin-Bin Qu[1,a]

[1]*School of Computer Science & Technology, Huazhong University Of Science And Technology, Wuhan, China*

Abstract. The virtual machine placement is closely related to the efficient and balanced utilization of physical resources. In this paper, the influence of two scenarios about resource utilization on load balancing is analyzed. A multi-objective ant colony optimization algorithm is proposed to solve the virtual machine placement problem, which balances the load among physical machines and the internal load of physical machine simultaneously. The proposed algorithm is compared with two single objective ant colony optimization algorithms, first fit algorithm and greedy algorithm under some instances. The results show that the proposed algorithm can search and find solutions that exhibit good balance among objectives while others cannot. This demonstrates the proposed algorithm can balance the load in the process of mapping virtual machines to physical machines.

1. Introduction

Cloud computing [1] as a new service model can effectively cope with mass data processing and computing needs by integrating Internet resources. Cloud computing [2] can be roughly classified into three types according to the service type: Infrastructure as a Service (IaaS), Platform as a Service (PaaS) and Software as a Service (SaaS). The virtualization [3] technology can divide physical resources into isolated virtual machines, which meet the demand of users to improve the utilization of resources and reduce the investment in infrastructure. The isolated virtual machines make it possible for different applications to run on the single server. The high load will affect the performance of upper applications, and the low load will not make full use of the limited resources, so optimal virtual machine placement closely related to the balanced utilization of resources is very important.

A lot of research has been devoted to solve the virtual machine placement problem in a data center. Virtual machine placement is often modeled as bin packing problem [4], and some solutions combine the classic algorithms for bin packing problem, such as First Fit Decreasing (FFD) [5] and Best Fit Decreasing (BFD) [6]. In [7], the relationship among power consumption, resource utilization and performance has been studied. Power consumption optimization algorithm is proposed through modeling as bin packing problem. Beloglazov et al. [8] proposed Modified Best Fit Decreasing (MBFD) algorithm to solve the virtual machine placement problem based on CPU utilization. Virtual machine placement belongs to combinatorial optimization problem, so the improved algorithm can combine with genetic algorithm [9], ant colony algorithm [10] or particle swarm optimization algorithm [11] which is effective to the problem. In [12], a two-level control system is proposed to manage the mappings of workloads to virtual machines and virtual machines to physical resources. An improved multi-objective genetic algorithm is proposed to minimize total resource wastage, power

[a] Corresponding author: bbqu@hust.edu.cn

consumption and thermal dissipation costs. In [13], a prototype virtual machine packing optimization mechanism on Grivon is implemented. Genetic Algorithm (GA) method is employed to avoid SLA (Service level agreement) violation, reduce number of real nodes in use and reduce virtual machine migrations. Feller et al. [14] proposed Energy-Aware ACO-based Workload Consolidation algorithm minimizing the number of physical machines required. In [15], a multi-objective ant colony system algorithm for virtual machine placement in cloud computing is proposed to minimize resource wastage and power consumption. In [16], to reduce energy consumption in cloud data center, an energy efficient virtual machine allocation algorithm is proposed based on a proposed energy efficient multi-resource allocation model and the particle swarm optimization (PSO) algorithm.

Most research on virtual machine placement only considers the initial scenario that the resources of physical machines are all idle. In the real scenario, the load of physical machines being dynamic, the virtual machine would be deployed to the physical machine with low load preferentially. Under the condition of a certain number of virtual machine requests, minimizing the number of physical machines to achieve energy efficient goal will also affect the balanced utilization of resources. This paper will study the problem in the general situation, namely the part of physical machine resources is already used. The designed algorithm in this paper is to make the utilization of physical machine resources as balanced as possible, so more needs are met under the condition of limited resources.

This paper is organized as follows. The second part makes a brief introduction on the ant colony optimization algorithm and multi-objective optimization. The third part describes and formulates the virtual machine placement problem. In the fourth part, multi-objective ant colony algorithm for load balancing is proposed in detail to solve the problem. In the fifth part, the proposed algorithm is compared with two single objective ant colony optimization algorithms, first fit algorithm and greedy algorithm to verify the effectiveness of the algorithm. The sixth part is the conclusion of this paper.

2 Backgrounds

2.1 Ant colony optimization algorithm

Inspired by the collective behavior of real ant colony, Dorigo proposed ant colony optimization algorithm [10] systematically. The mechanism of ant colony optimization algorithm consists of two basic stages: adaptation phase and cooperation stage. In the adaptation phase, each candidate solution according to the accumulated pheromone adjusts the structure itself. On the one hand, the amount of pheromone will be greater if more ants pass through the path, and the probability of the path selected will be larger. On the other hand, the pheromone will evaporate over time. In the collaboration phase, candidate solutions communicate through pheromone to get the desired solution with better performance. The self-organization mechanism of the algorithm does not need to understand every aspect of the problem in detail, so it is effective to solve many combinatorial optimization problems.

2.2 Multi-objective optimization

Many scientific and engineering problems can be modeled as a multi-objective optimization problem [17] which is different from the single objective optimization problem. Performance improvement of one objective may result in performance degradation of other objectives, so it is very difficult or impossible to optimize multiple objectives simultaneously. The feasible solutions of multi-objective optimization problem form a Pareto [18] set. Generally speaking, the multi-objective optimization problem with n decision variables and m objective functions can be expressed as follows.

$$\begin{aligned} \min\ & y = f(x) = [f_1(x), f_2(x), \cdots, f_m(x)] \\ s.t.\ & g_i(x) \le 0, \quad i = 1,2,\cdots,p \\ & h_j(x) = 0, \quad j = 1,2,\cdots,q \end{aligned} \tag{1}$$

In expression (1), the decision vector is $x=(x_1,x_2,\cdots,x_n)\in X$, and the objective vector is $y=(f_1,f_2,\cdots,f_m)\in Y$. X is the decision space of decision vector, and Y is the objective space of objective vector. $g_i(x)\le 0(i=1,2,\cdots,p)$ defines p inequality constraints, and q equality constraints are defined by $h_j(x)=0(j=1,2,\cdots,q)$ .The following concepts [18, 19] is often used.

Pareto dominance: $\boldsymbol{x}^0$ dominates $\boldsymbol{x}^1$ ($\boldsymbol{x}^0\succ\boldsymbol{x}^1$), if and only if

$$
\begin{aligned}
&f_i(\boldsymbol{x}^0)\le f_i(\boldsymbol{x}^1), \quad \forall i\in\{1,2,\cdots,m\}\\
&f_j(\boldsymbol{x}^0)< f_j(\boldsymbol{x}^1), \quad \exists j\in\{1,2,\cdots,m\}
\end{aligned}
.
$$

Pareto optimality: $\boldsymbol{x}^0$ is Pareto optimal if and only if $\neg\exists\boldsymbol{x}^1:\boldsymbol{x}^1\succ\boldsymbol{x}^0$.

Pareto optimal set: The set of all Pareto optimal solutions is Pareto set $\mathrm{P}=\{\boldsymbol{x}^0|\neg\exists\boldsymbol{x}^1:\boldsymbol{x}^1\succ\boldsymbol{x}^0\}$.

3 Problem description and formulation

3.1 Problem description

Considering two scenarios about resource utilization, one scenario is that the utilization of one physical machine is far greater than the utilization of another for a long time, and the virtual machine migration [20] is usually used to balance load for such cases. The number of migrations should be reduced as much as possible because of the high costs. Such result is described as the load imbalance among physical machines. Another scenario is that the utilization of one certain resource is much larger than other resources' in a physical machine. This would lead to the fact that the physical machine cannot satisfy the virtual machine resource requirements, resulting in a waste of resources. Such result is described as internal imbalance load in a physical machine.

The virtual machine placement problem is actually to determine the mapping relationship between virtual machines and physical machines, and the mapping relationship between virtual machines and physical machines is multi-to-one. This paper will study that the multiple virtual machines are placed on a certain number of physical machines in the general situation. The goal is to make the load among physical machines and internal load as balanced as possible to achieve efficient and balanced utilization of physical resources so that more needs are met under the condition of limited resources.

3.2 Problem formulation

Virtual machine set is defined as $\mathrm{VM}=\{vm_1,vm_2,\cdots,vm_M\}$. Physical machine set is defined as $\mathrm{PM}=\{pm_1,pm_2,\cdots,pm_N\}$. M is the number of virtual machines and N is the number of physical machines. The types of resources include CPU, memory, storage and bandwidth. The resource request vector of virtual machine vm_i is defined as $R_i=(R_i^1,R_i^2,R_i^3,R_i^4)$. The available resource vector of physical machine pm_j is defined as $A_j=(A_j^1,A_j^2,A_j^3,A_j^4)$. The total resource vector of physical machine pm_j is defined as $S_j=(S_j^1,S_j^2,S_j^3,S_j^4)$. The resource utilization vector of physical machine pm_j is defined as $U_j=(U_j^1,U_j^2,U_j^3,U_j^4)$, where $U_j^d=(S_j^d-A_j^d)/S_j^d \quad (d\ \ 1,2,3,4)$.

When all virtual machines are placed on a certain number of physical machines, the resource utilization of each physical machine forms a matrix defined as $\mathrm{U}_{N\times4}=(U_1,U_2,\cdots,U_N)^{\mathrm{T}}$ .The average utilization of each dimension is defined as the Eq. (2), and d represents the dimension of resource.

$$Avg^d = \frac{1}{N}\sum_{j=1}^{N} U_j^d, \quad (d = 1,2,3,4) \tag{2}$$

The average resource utilization vector of all physical machines is defined as Eq. (3).

$$Avg = (Avg^1, Avg^2, Avg^3, Avg^4) \tag{3}$$

To measure the load balancing degree of physical machines in data center comprehensively, the load among physical machines and the internal load are considered. In order to reflect the degree of load balancing among the physical machines, the **O**uter load **B**alancing **D**egree(OBD) is defined as the average of Euclidean distance between each physical machine resource utilization vector and the average resource utilization vector of all physical machines. Details are shown in Eq. (4).

$$OBD = \frac{1}{N}\sum_{j=1}^{N}\sqrt{\sum_{d=1}^{4}(U_j^d - Avg^d)^2} \tag{4}$$

In order to reflect the load balancing degree of different resources in the physical machine, the **I**nternal load **B**alancing **D**egree(IBD) is defined as the average value of the standard deviation of the resource utilization of each physical machine. Details are shown in Eq. (5).

$$IBD = \frac{1}{N}\sum_{j=1}^{N}\sqrt{\frac{1}{4}\sum_{d=1}^{4}(U_j^d - \frac{1}{4}\sum_{d=1}^{4}U_j^d)^2} \tag{5}$$

Based on the above analysis and parameter definition, the problem can be formulated as follows.

Goals: $\min OBD \ and \min IBD$ (6)

Constrains: $\forall pm_j \in \mathrm{PM}, \sum_{i=1}^{M} R_i^d \delta_{ij} \leq A_j^d \quad (d = 1,2,3,4)$ (7)

$$\delta_{ij} = \begin{cases} 1, & \text{if } vm_i \text{ is placed on } pm_j \\ 0, & \text{else} \end{cases} \tag{8}$$

$$\forall vm_i \in \mathrm{VM}, \sum_{j=1}^{N} \delta_{ij} \quad 1 \tag{9}$$

$$R_i^d \leq A_j^d \quad (d = 1,2,3,4) \tag{10}$$

Expression (6) is to optimize two objectives simultaneously. Constraint (7) and (8) indicate that for each physical machine, the total resources of virtual machines placed on the physical machine do not exceed the available resources. Constraint (8) and (9) indicate that a virtual machine will eventually be placed on a physical machine. The virtual machine can be placed on the physical machine on condition that the Constraint (10) is satisfied. For each virtual machine, a corresponding set of candidate physical machines is established, and each physical machine in the set satisfies the constraint condition (10). Once a physical machine is selected, the available resource is updated until all virtual machines are placed. A feasible solution of the problem is the mapping of all virtual machines and their corresponding physical machine.

4 Multi-objective ant colony optimization algorithm

4.1 Heuristic function and selection strategy

In the process of virtual machine placement, the heuristic function can help the virtual machine select the appropriate physical machine. Eq. (11) defines the matching distance between the virtual machine and the physical machine, and Eq. (12) defines the heuristic function.

$$d_{ij} = \cos < R_i, A_j > \tag{11}$$

$$\eta_{ij}(t) = (1 - \frac{1}{4}\sum_{d=1}^{4} U_j^d) \cdot d_{ij} \tag{12}$$

There are two reasons about constructing the heuristic function. On the one hand, when the value of d_{ij} is greater, the proportion in all dimensions between R_i and A_j is more similar, so that can make the internal load more balanced, and the cosine of vectorial angle can eliminate the resource dimension. On the other hand, the heuristic function tends to choose the underloaded physical machine, so that can make the load among physical machines more balanced.

For virtual machine vm_i, ant k selects the physical machine pm_j with the probability p_{ij}^k in the set of candidate physical machines $Allowed_i$. p_{ij}^k is defined as Eq. (13).

$$p_{ij}^k(t) = \begin{cases} \dfrac{[\tau_{ij}(t)]^\alpha [\eta_{ij}(t)]^\beta}{\sum_{s \in Allowed_i} [\tau_{is}(t)]^\alpha [\eta_{is}(t)]^\beta}, & j \in Allowed_i \\ 0, & j \notin Allowed_i \end{cases} \tag{13}$$

In Eq. (13), $Allowed_i$ is the set of candidate physical machines of virtual machine vm_i. $\tau_{ij}(t)$ is the amount of pheromone between the virtual machine vm_i and the physical machine pm_j, and $\tau_{ij}(0) = C$ where C is a constant. $\eta_{ij}(t)$ is the heuristic function value between vm_i and pm_j. α is the pheromone heuristic factor, and β is the visibility heuristic factor, which indicate the relative importance of pheromone and heuristic function respectively. The virtual machine vm_i selects the physical machine pm_j by the roulette wheel algorithm. $r \in [0,1)$ is generated randomly, and physical machine pm_j is selected if the cumulative probability $\sum_s^j p_{is}^k(t), s \in Allowed_i$ is not less than r.

4.2 Maintenance of Pareto optimal set and pheromone updating

At the end of each cycle, the number of feasible solutions obtained is equal to the number of ants at most, and each feasible solution S_i should be judged by the following steps to obtain a temporary Pareto optimal set. For each element in the temporary Pareto optimal set, the same method is used to maintain the global Pareto optimal set. Figure 1 is the main process for maintaining Pareto optimal set.

DOI: 10.1051/itmconf/20171101011

```
boolean flag=false;
for S_j in P   /* P is a Pareto optimal set */
    if S_i dominates S_j
      Remove S_j from P;
    else if S_j dominates S_i
      flag=true;
      break;
    end if
end for
if(!flag)
    add S_i to P;
end if
```

Figure 1. The process for maintaining Pareto optimal set.

$\Delta\tau_{ij}^{k}(t)$ is the increment of pheromone between vm_i and pm_j defined as the Eq. (14) which considers the two objectives IBD and OBD .

$$\Delta\tau_{ij}^{k}(t)=\begin{cases}1/IBD+1/OBD, & \text{if the feasible solution is Pareto optimal}\\ 0, & \text{else}\end{cases} \tag{14}$$

$$\tau_{ij}(t+1)=(1-\rho)\tau_{ij}(t)+\sum_{k=1}^{A}\Delta\tau_{ij}^{k}(t) \tag{15}$$

The pheromone is updated after the completion of one cycle by Eq. (15). In Eq. (15), $\rho\in(0,1)$ is pheromone evaporation coefficient, and A is the total number of ants.

4.3 Deterministic virtual machine placement

For multi-objective optimization problems, the number of solutions is usually more than one. Considering the target weight is not easy to determine, this paper uses the stratified sequencing method to obtain the deterministic solution. The method is to rank all the objectives according to their importance, and then to obtain the set of optimal solutions for the most important objective, and to obtain the set of optimal solutions for the next objective on the basis of the previous set until the last objective. In the process of selecting the deterministic solution, the importance of the objective OBD is higher than that of the objective IBD, so the solution with minimum objective OBD is selected as the deterministic solution of the problem when the stratified sequencing method with two objectives is used. Figure 2 is the algorithm description. The deterministic solution is defined as S.

```
Input:  VM, PM, α, β, ρ, A, G, C
Output:  S
for i=1 to G
    for j=1 to A
        for vm in VM
            select pm according to Eq.(13)
            update available resources of pm
            maintain the set of candidate physical machines for virtual machines
        end for
        calculate the value of objective functions
    end for
    maintain global Pareto optimal set
    update the pheromone according to Eq.(14) and Eq.(15)
end for
return S    /* the deterministic solution*/
```

Figure 2. The algorithm for virtual machine placement.

VM is virtual machine set. PM is physical machine set. α is pheromone heuristic factor. β is visibility heuristic factor, ρ is the pheromone evaporation coefficient. A is the number of ants. G is cycle times for algorithm. C is the amount of initial pheromone. In each cycle, the complexity of each ant selects the physical machine for the virtual machine is O(N), and the complexity of maintaining the set of candidate physical machines is O(M), so the complexity of generating a feasible solution is O ($M(M+N)$). Because the number of solutions in Pareto optimal set is uncertain, the complexity of maintaining the Pareto optimal set is not analyzed. The algorithm will generate the number of $G*A$ feasible solutions at most, so the complexity of generating feasible solutions is O($GAM(M+N)$).

5 Experimental results

To verify the effectiveness of the proposed algorithm MOACO (Multi-Objective Optimization Based on Ant Colony Optimization), it is compared with two single objective ant colony optimization algorithms which are SACO-OBD and SACO-IBD, FF(First Fit algorithm) and GS(Greedy Scheduling) under some instances. The paper use java programming language to implement all algorithms. Because of the inherent parallelism of ant colony algorithm, the parallel computing framework Fork/Join in Java7 is used to reduce the running time of the algorithm.

(1) MOACO: The algorithm is a multi-objective ant colony optimization algorithm for OBD and IBD.
(2) SACO-OBD: The algorithm is a single objective ant colony algorithm for objective OBD, which is used to measure the optimization of MOACO for objective OBD.
(3) SACO-IBD: The algorithm is a single objective ant colony algorithm for objective IBD, which is used to measure the optimization of MOACO for objective IBD.
(4) GS: For each virtual machine, the physical machine with the maximum matching distance as Eq. (11) defined is selected.
(5) FF: For each virtual machine request, the physical machine for the first time to satisfy the resource constraints as Constraint (10) defined is selected.

5.1 Experiment parameters

In this paper, the virtual machine template and the physical machine template are set up in advance as shown in Table 1 and Table 2. The physical machines and virtual machines are generated randomly by the templates. The results of five algorithms are compared in the same scale. The parameters of ant colony algorithm are set by several experiments: $\alpha = 1$, $\beta = 5$, $\rho = 0.5$, $A = M$, $G = 50$, C=1.

Table 1. Virtual machine template

CPU/core	Memory/GB	Storage/GB	Bandwidth/Mbps
1	1	100	100
1	2	200	100
2	2	200	100
2	1	300	200
1	2	100	100
2	2	100	200

Table 2. Physical machine template

CPU/ core	Memory /GB	Storage/ GB	Bandwidth/ Mbps	available CPU/core	available Memory/GB	available Storage/GB	Available Bandwidth/Mbps
8	16	750	750	5	10	500	550
4	16	1000	1000	3	12	700	600
8	8	1000	750	4	6	650	400
4	8	750	1000	2	5	450	600

5.2 Comparison of different algorithms

Every test was repeated with 10 runs for each instance and the average result of MOACO is compared with other algorithms. Figure 3 shows the experimental results of two objectives in different scales.

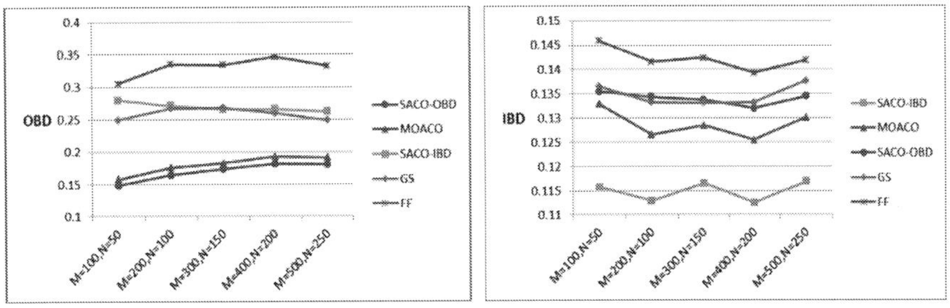

Figure 3. The results of different algorithms in different scales.

Figure 3 indicates that SACO-OBD performs best on the objective OBD, but it performs poor compared with MOACO and SACO-IBD on the objective IBD. SACO-IBD performs best on the objective IBD, but it performs poor compared with MOACO and SACO-OBD on the objective OBD. The experimental results of GS are similar to single objective ant colony algorithms on the objective OBD and IBD respectively, and that indicates the heuristic information is helpful for load balancing. The experimental results of MOACO are obviously better than GS and FF on the objective OBD and IBD. The results show that the proposed algorithm MOACO can search and find solutions that exhibit good balance among objectives while others cannot.

Conclusion

For the problem, this paper analyzes the influence of two scenarios about resource utilization on load balancing. Two objectives are proposed to measure the load balancing comprehensively as possible. A multi-objective ant colony optimization algorithm for virtual machine placement in the general situation is proposed to balance load by optimizing the proposed two objectives. The proposed algorithm is compared with two single objective ant colony optimization algorithms, first fit algorithm and greedy algorithm under some instances. The experimental results show that the algorithm can effectively optimize multiple objectives to achieve the goal of load balancing in different scales.

Acknowledgement

The work presented in this paper is supported by national ministries project which is the research on intelligent scheduling of cloud computing resources based on load balancing.

References

1. S. Yu, C. Wang, K. Ren ,W. Lou, *IEEE INFOCOM,* 1-9(2010)
2. M. Alhamad, T. Dillon, E. Chang, *IEEE International Conference on Digital Ecosystems and Technologies*, 606-610(2010)
3. P. Barham , B. Dragovic, K. Fraser, S. Hand, T. Harris, A. Ho, R. Neugebauer, I. Pratt, A.Warfield, *ACM SIGOPS Operating Systems Review*, **37(5)**, 164-177(2003)
4. S. Martello, D. Pisinger, D. Vigo, Operations Research, **48(2)**, 256-267(2000)
5. B. S. Baker, Journal of Algorithms, **6(1)**, 49-70(1985)
6. C. Kenyon, *Proceedings of the seventh annual ACM-SIAM symposium on Discrete algorithms. Society for Industrial and Applied Mathematics*, 359-364(1996)
7. S. Srikantaiah, A. Kansal, F. Zhao, *Proceedings of the 2008 conference on Power aware computing and systems*, **10**, 1-5(2008)
8. Beloglazov, J. Abawajy, R. Buyya, Future generation computer systems, **28(5)**, 755-768(2012)
9. P. C. Chu, J. E. Beasley, Computers & Operations Research, **24(1)**,17-23(1997)
10. M.Dorigo, M.Birattari, T.Stutzle, IEEE computational intelligence magazine, **1(4)**, 28-39(2006)
11. R. Poli, J. Kennedy, T. Blackwell, Swarm intelligence, **1(1)**, 33-57(2007)
12. J. Xu, J. Fortes, *IEEE/ACM International Conference on Green Computing and Communications & 2010 IEEE/ACM International Conference on Cyber, Physical and Social Computing*, 179–188(2010)
13. H. Nakada, T. Hirofuchi, *International Work Conference on Artificial Neural Networks: Part 2:Distributed Computing, Artificial Intelligence Bioinformatics Soft Computing and Ambient Assisted Living*, 651-654(2009)
14. E. Feller, L. Rilling, C. Morin, *IEEE/ACM International Conference on Grid Computing (GRID)*, 26–33(2011)
15. Y. Gao, H. Guan, Z. Qi, Y. Hou, L. Liu, Journal of Computer and System Sciences, **79(8)**, 1230-1242(2013)
16. A. Xiong, C. Xu , Mathematical Problems in Engineering, **2014**, 816518 (2014)
17. K. Deb, *Search methodologies*, 403-449(Springer US, 2014).
18. P. Ngatchou, A. Zarei, A. El-Sharkawi, *International Conference on Intelligent Systems Application to Power Systems*, 84-91(2005)
19. M. Gong, L. Jiao, D. Yang, W. Ma, Journal of Software,**20**,271-289(2009)
20. J. Zhao, L. Hu, Y. Ding, G. Xu, M. Hu, PloS one, **9(9)**, e108275 (2014)

The Study of Reservation Scheme for Managing Parking Cruising

Duo XU[a] and Tian-Chao GUAN

School of Traffic and Transportation, Beijing Jiaotong University, Beijing, China

Abstract. Cruising for parking is a main contributor to traffic jam while the related researches are few. Assume travelers are well-informed, this paper first analyses user equilibrium (UE) in no parking fee scheme with different scarcity of parking spaces. We get a conclusion that information fails to solve traffic problems effectively in absent of control. Followed by the principle of cape and trade, the paper proposes parking reservation scheme which combining guidance (information) with tolling (control). Example shows that system cost reduces significantly after the implementation of the parking reservation scheme.

1 Introduction

Parking is a growing problem in many large cities around world. Although the average parking time of a car is 23 hours a day [1], looking for vacant parking spaces accounts for about 30%-50% of the rest 1 hour and nearly 70% of the travel cost [2]. Study found that most drivers will spend 3.5 to 14 minutes before they get parked, and cruising for parking is a major contributor (30% on average) to traffic jam in downtown [3].

Demand management is an effective way to solve this problem. Vickrey first proposed that parking resources should be priced in accordance with the social marginal cost [4]. With the development of intelligent transportation systems, researches are focusing on time-varying toll, parking guidance and information, tradable credit, etc. [5]-[7]. However, the issue of searching has been less concerned about, and only information could not solve that problem. So we propose parking reservation scheme combining guidance (information) with tolling (control) to reduce system cost.

2 Basic settings

Consider a traffic corridor connecting residential area and central business district(CBD). Morning commuters drive from home to workplace everyday. The corridor contains an expressway with a bottleneck which has a finite capacity. Queue will emerge when traffic flow rate exceeds bottleneck capacity. Parking lots are near CBD. Cars can choose any free spot to park. After drives towards downtown, each commuter looks for an vacant parking spot, then walks to the workplace. All of the commuters are assumed to have a common work beginning time t^*, and both early and late arrival will be penalized.

[a] Corresponding author: ringloveyan1987@yahoo.com

The general cost of each traveler contains travel cost, searching cost and schedule delay cost. All commuters experience the same time on driving over the expressway and walking to the workplace. For simplicity, we ignore the free flow commute time and walk time [8].

Denote $T(t)$ be the travel time (the queuing time only). $T(t) = q(t)/s$, where $q(t)$ is the queue length at the bottleneck at time t, and s is the capacity of the bottleneck. The change of the queue can be express as

$$\frac{\mathrm{d}q(t)}{\mathrm{d}t} = \begin{cases} r(t) - s, r(t) > s \text{ or } q(t) > 0 \\ 0, r(t) \le s \text{ and } q(t) = 0 \end{cases} \tag{1}$$

Where $r(t)$ is the arriving rate of the traffic flow at bottleneck at time t (also can be seen as departure time). The queue will develop when traffic flow rate exceeds bottleneck capacity. Let α be the value of time of commuters. The travel cost of the commuter who departs at time t is

$$C_{\mathrm{q}}(t) = \alpha T(t) \tag{2}$$

Set the total number of parking spots is k and the total number of commuters is N. $n(t)$ is the occupied parking spots at time t, which satisfies $n(t) \leq N \leq k$. The probability that a randomly sampled spot is free is given by $[k - n(t)]/k$ [8]. Assume that a driver who checks whether or not a spot is free incurs a time cost λ, the expect time he will spend to get a free spot is $\lambda k/[k - n(t)]$. Therefore the expect searching cost to an individual is

$$C_{\mathrm{s}}(t) = \frac{\alpha\lambda k}{k - n(t)} \tag{3}$$

Let the β and γ be the marginal cost of early arrival and late arrival respectively, where $\gamma > \alpha > \beta$. The schedule delay cost of the driver who departs at time t is given by

$$C_{\mathrm{d}}(t) = \beta \max\{0, t^* - t - T(t)\} + \gamma \max\{0, T(t) + t - t^*\} \tag{4}$$

Denote $p(t)$ be the parking fee of the parking lot near CBD at time t. The generalized travel cost of the travelers who depart at t is given by

$$C(t) = C_{\mathrm{q}}(t) + C_{\mathrm{s}}(t + T(t)) + C_{\mathrm{d}}(t) + p(t + T(t)) \tag{5}$$

3 User equilibrium without parking fee

We suppose travelers are aware of parking information at any time via either online information system or sufficient experience. We first study on travelers' parking behaviors and corresponding parking flow pattern under no parking fee scheme. We define user equilibrium as, 1. All travelers' generalized travel costs are same. 2. No traveler can unilaterally change his parking choice and/or departure time choices to reduce his generalized travel cost.

3.1 Equilibrium analysis

Travelers are trying to minimize their cost. Let t_e and t_s be the departure time of the first and the last traveler. The first and the last traveler will not encounter queuing [9]. We assume that each of the searching cost and the queuing cost accounts for a certain part of the equilibrium cost. Therefore, the bottleneck will be at fully service capacity during the entire departure period which can be given as

$$t_e - t_s = N/s \tag{6}$$

The cost of the first and the last traveler, as well as the traveler without schedule delay are

$$C(t_s) = \beta(t^* - t_s - \lambda) + \alpha\lambda \tag{7}$$

$$C(t_e) = \gamma\left(t_e + \frac{\lambda k}{k - N + 1} - t^*\right) + \frac{\alpha\lambda k}{k - N + 1} \tag{8}$$

$$C(t_n) = \alpha(t^* - t_n) \tag{9}$$

Where t_n is the departing time of the traveler without schedule delay. Denote π is the equilibrium cost.

$$t_s = t^* + \frac{\alpha - \beta}{\beta}\lambda - \frac{\pi}{\beta} \tag{10}$$

$$t_e = t^* + \frac{\pi}{\gamma} - \frac{\alpha + \gamma}{\gamma}\frac{\lambda k}{k - N + 1} \tag{11}$$

$$t_n = t^* - \frac{\pi}{\alpha} \tag{12}$$

Combine (10) and (11) with (6), the equilibrium cost is

$$\pi = \frac{\beta\gamma}{\beta + \gamma}\frac{N}{s} + \frac{\beta(\alpha + \gamma)}{\beta + \gamma}\frac{\lambda k}{k - N + 1} + \frac{\gamma(\alpha - \beta)}{\beta + \gamma}\lambda \tag{13}$$

Accroding to (5), the queuing time is

$$T(t) = \begin{cases} \dfrac{\pi - \beta(t^* - t)}{\alpha - \beta} - \dfrac{\lambda k}{k - (t - t_s)s + 1} & t_s \le t \le t_n \\[2ex] \dfrac{\pi - \gamma(t - t^*)}{\alpha - \beta} - \dfrac{\lambda k}{k - (t - t_s)s + 1} & t_n \le t \le t_e \end{cases} \tag{14}$$

Combine (14) with (1), the departing rate of the travelers is given by

$$r(t) = \begin{cases} \dfrac{\alpha s}{\alpha - \beta} - \dfrac{\lambda k s^2}{[k - (t - t_s)s + 1]^2} & t_s \le t \le t_n \\[2ex] \dfrac{\alpha s}{\alpha + \gamma} - \dfrac{\lambda k s^2}{[k - (t - t_s)s + 1]^2} & t_n \le t \le t_e \end{cases} \tag{15}$$

3.2 Case study

In this subsection, we provide an example to illustrate commuters' travelling behavior and parking distribution under the influences of queuing cost and searching cost. Assuming the work beginning time is 9:00 and the total number of commuters N is 1000. Bottleneck capacity is 2000 per hour. The value of unit travel time α and the marginal schedule delay cost β and γ is 40 per hour, 20 per hour and 80 per hour, respectively. Searching time λ is set as 0.005 hour [10]. To reveal the characteristics of the system under different searching costs, we set the total number of parking spots k as a variable.

Figure.1 depicts the searching cost of the last traveler ($C_s\ (t_e) = \alpha\lambda k\ /\ (k - N + 1)$) with different occupancy rate ($N\ /\ k$). When the parking spaces are adequate (parking occupancy rate is lower than 0.8), searching cost is low, and its growth trend is slow. In contrast, the searching cost grows rapidly.

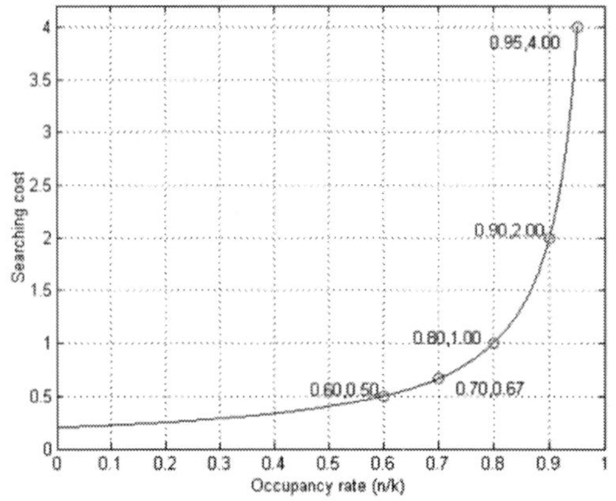

Figure 1. The relationship between occupancy rate and searching cost

In this example, the maximum parking occupancy rate that satisfies late arrivals is 0.94. Accroding to (15), the departure rate of early arrivals is greater than bottleneck capacity, the queue is accumlating and the travel time is on the rise. On the opposite, the departure rate of late arrivals is less than bottleneck capacity, the queue is dissipating and the travel time is declining.

Figure 2 shows the cumulative number of departure and arrival in the condition of parking spaces are adequate($N\ /\ k \rightarrow 0$, black dotted line) and inadequate($N\ /\ k = 0.94$, blue solid line), respectively. The ordinate represents the number of trips while the abscissa represents the time (30 to 65 represents 8: 30 to 9: 05). Points *A2* and *B2* are the traveler who arrives on time in both cases. Curve *A1A2* and line *B1B2* characterize the departure rate of the early traveler while curve *A2A3* and line *B2B3* depict the departure rate of the late traveler. Line *A1A3* and *B1B3* are the bottleneck capacity. The difference between curves *A1A2A3* and *B1B2B3* in vertical is the queue length at the bottleneck and the difference in the horizontal is queuing time.

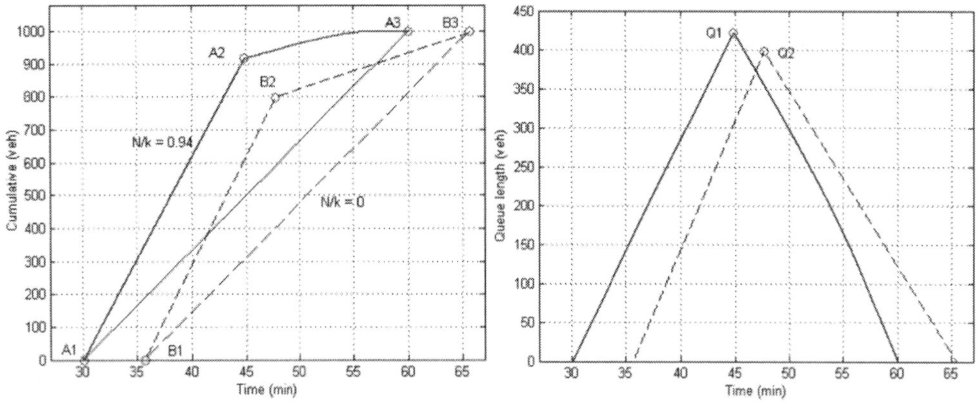

Figure 2. The departure (arrival) cumulative number and the queue length (queuing time) of in two cases

As can be easily seen, with the increase of the scarcity of parking spaces, 1. All the travelers depart earlier. The number of early arrivals increases while the number of late arrivals decreases. 2. The departure rate is on decreasing trend as the number of occupied parking spots increasing, and declines to zero when the parking lot approaches the full amount. 3. The maximum queuing length and the maximum queuing time at the bottleneck raises because of the more concentrated departing.

Figure 3 shows the departure time of the first (black solid line) and the last (blue solid line) traveler as well as the traveler with no schedule delay (red solid line) when N/k changes from 0 to 0.94. As we can see, 1. Three departure times change in a small range when N/k is lower than 0.8 and move ahead obviously when N/k is close to 0.94. It indicates the more scarce parking spaces are,the greater it impacts to travelers' departure time. 2. The departure time of the traveler with no schedule delay moves slowly compare with the first and the last traveler both. It reflects the departing order of that traveler is increasing when N/k grows.

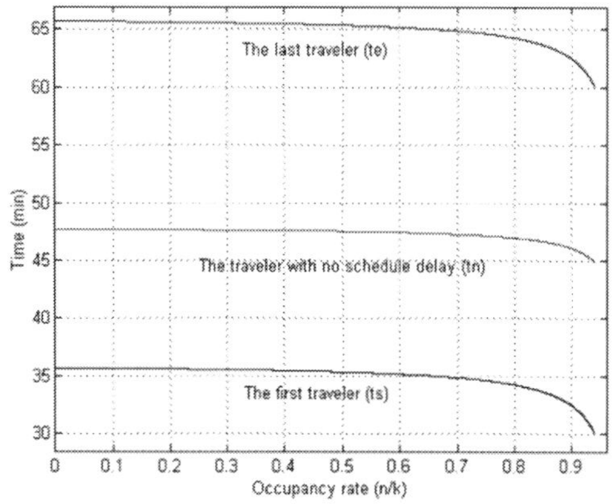

Figure 3. Departure time of the first (on time/ last) traveler in different N/k

4 System optimum in parking reservation scheme

Through subsection 3.4, we get the conclusion that travelers' behavior is affected by the scarcity of the parking spaces. The deadweight loss which contains queuing cost and searching cost grows obviously when commuters number is near to the number of spots in parking lot.

Tolling is an effective way to control the parking demand and distribution as well as minimizes the deadweight loss.Early researchs used to save the system cost by converting a portion of deadweight loss to the income of the parking lot through tolling, but they do not reduce the travelers' cost. Accroding to (3), searching cost becomes the main contributor as the parking lot is scarce which is consistent with the reality. Therefore, to further eliminate the searching cost so as to reduce the equilibrium cost is the goal of the traffic manager.

Parking reservation scheme, which establish a one-to-one link between parkers and parking spots before a trip, can effectively eliminates searching by avoiding the mutual influence among parkers. Reservations can also be designed according to the bottleneck capacity constraint so as to eliminate queuing [8].

The object of the system is on the premise of minimize travelers' equilibrium cost, parking managers should increase parking fees as much as possible.

$$\text{(U)} \quad \min . C(t) \tag{16}$$

$$\text{s.t. } t \geq 0$$

$$\text{(L)} \quad \max . p(t + T(t)) \tag{17}$$

$$\text{s.t. } t \geq 0$$

The equilibrium cost and the optimal parking fees are

$$\pi = \frac{\beta\gamma}{\beta+\gamma}\frac{N}{s} + \alpha\lambda \tag{18}$$

$$p(t) = \begin{cases} \dfrac{\beta\gamma}{\beta+\gamma}\dfrac{N}{s} + \alpha\lambda - \beta(t^* - t) & t_s \le t \le t^* \\ \dfrac{\beta\gamma}{\beta+\gamma}\dfrac{N}{s} + \alpha\lambda - \gamma(t - t^*) & t^* \le t \le t_e \end{cases} \tag{19}$$

Follow the example from the previous section. Let N/k equals to 0.94. We can see travelers' behavior before and after the implementation of parking reservation scheme from Figure 4.

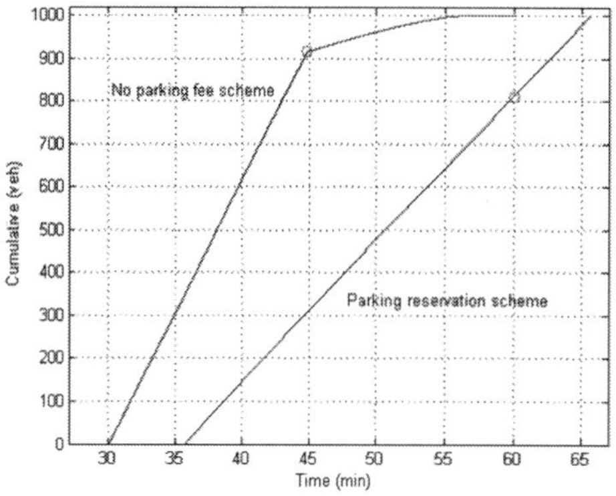

Figure 4. The cumulative number of departure and arrival in schemes

Compare with the no parking fees scheme, all travelers in parking reservation scheme can depart later on different extend. The equilibrium travel cost is decreased from 10.02 to 8.20, reduced by 18.16%. Parking fees is 4.10 per capita, and accounts for a half of the total cost. Because of the income of the parking fees, the system cost is 5.10, reduced by 59.08%.

Conclusion

In this paper, we analyze the process of how morning commuters choose their departure time under UE condition as well as how the searching cost influences their behavior and contributes to larger deadweight loss. Through an example, we found the system performance in parking reservation scheme is prior to in no parking fee scheme due to the significant reduction of both the cost of user and the deadweight loss of system.

References

1. Z. Qian, F. E. Zhang, Transportation Research Part A, **45 (9)**, 861-879 (2011)
2. R. Arnott, J. Rowse, Journal of Urban Economics, **45**, 97-124 (1999)
3. D. Shoup, *The high cost of free parking* (American Planning Association, 2005)
4. W. S. Vickrey, American Economic Review, **59 (2)**, 251-261 (1969)
5. H. Yang, X. Wang, Transportation Research Part B, **45 (3)**, 580-594 (2011)
6. Z. Qian, R. Rajagopal, Procedia - Social and Behavioral Sciences, **80**, 779-805 (2013)
7. G. S. Muller, M. Xu, Transport Reviews, **34 (2)** , 128-149 (2014)
8. W. Liu, H. Yang, Y. F. Yin, Transportation Research Part C, **44**, 185-201 (2014)

9. Z. X. Wu, H. J. Huang, System Engineering Theory and Practice, **1**, 130-135(2000)
10. S. Anderson, A. de Palma, Urban Economics, **55**, 1-20 (2004)

Realization of Signal Acquisition System in Seismoelectric Logging

Pan ZHOU[a] and Xiang-Yang SUN

University of Electronic Science and Technology of China, Chengdu 610054, China

Abstract. With the prosperous development of electronic science and technology, electrical logging technology has been widely used in the process of oil exploitation. Seismoelectric logging is one of the many electrical logging methods, which has some unique advantages compared with other logging methods. At present, there are a lot of theoretical research on the seismoelectric logging at home and abroad, but due to some engineering problems has not been solved, practical instrument is not yet come into being. The acquisition of seismoelectric signal is one of the most difficult problems in the practical application. In this paper, a set of seismoelectric signal acquisition system based on SPI bus is designed to solve this problem. Experiment show that the system basically meets the demand of signal acquisition in seismoelectric logging

1 Introduction

There are many kinds of oil logging methods, such as electric logging, acoustic logging, radioactive logging and so on[1]. Generally speaking, all kinds of logging methods can directly or indirectly reflect the characteristics of some aspects of the underground rock stratum, but it is necessary to use a variety of logging methods in order to fully evaluate the underground rock stratum. Seismoelectric logging is a kind of electrical logging, which based on the coupling mechanism of mechanical energy and electromagnetic energy, can directly detect the properties of formation, such as permeability, conductivity, porosity, and concentration of well liquid ion, with high resolution and excellent probing ability[2]. Compared with other logging methods, seismoelectric logging has its unique advantages and can serve as a useful complement to other logging methods. The research on seismoelectric logging has been started since the 90s of last century, but logging instrument based on this method is still not available. The reason is that there are still some key technical difficulties unsolved in engineering application, one of the major difficulties is the acquisition of underground seismoelectric signals.

Essentially, the seismoelectric signal is a electromagnetic signal, which is generated by the mechanical vibration in the fluid medium. In the process of seismoelectric logging, the logging system needs to coordinate the acquisition process of many measuring points underground.At the same time, a large number of data produced by each measurement point needs to be transmitted to the host computer in real time, which is the biggest difficulty for seismoelectric signal acquisition.

[a] Corresponding author: 15994237697@qq.com

2 Basic process of seismoelectric logging

The seismoelectric logging system usually uses acoustic wave as the source of vibration, which is easy to produce and also easy to adjust. A complete seismoelectric logging system, as shown in Figure 1, consists of three parts: acoustic emission system, seismoelectric signal acquisition system, host computer. In some cases, the seismoelectric logging device and acoustic logging device are integrated into one system, because the two logging methods have similarities in the principle of implementation, and can be complementary in function.

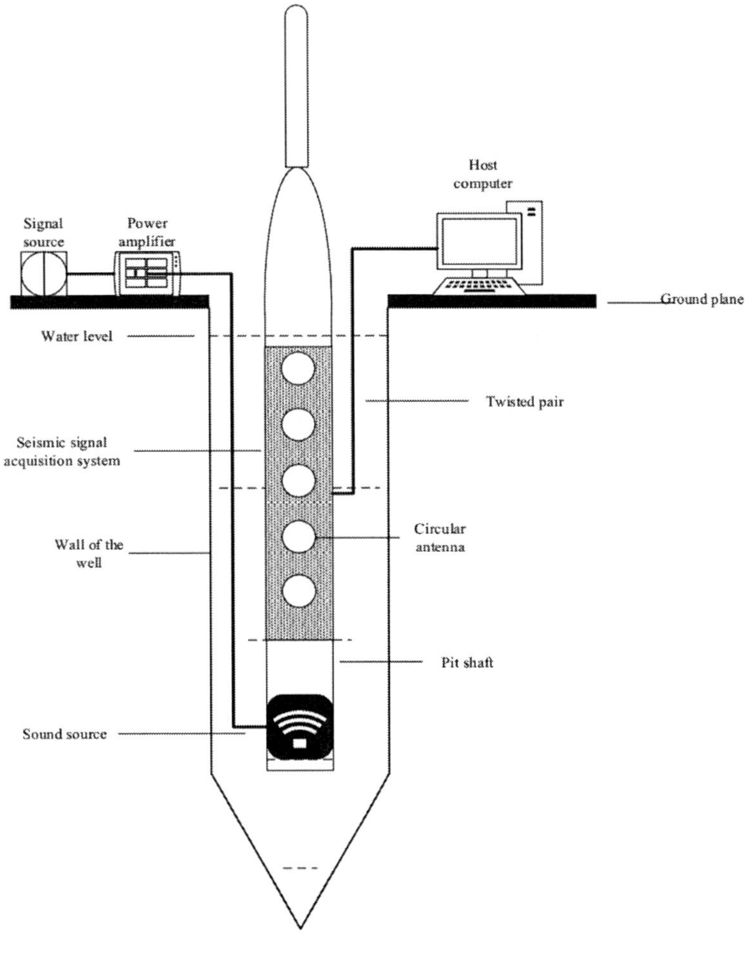

Figure 1. Basic frame of seismoelectric logging system

The acoustic emission system generates a square pulse signal to excite the sound source through the power amplifier,then the sound source generates a strong acoustic wave. Due to the existence of the seismoelectric effect, the acoustic wave will excite the seismoelectric signal in the porous medium when it propagates along the borehole wall.

The seismoelectric logging system is used to collect the electrical signals generated in different depths.Then,it will transfer the measurement data to the host computer immediately. In the host

DOI: 10.1051/itmconf/20171101013

computer, the parameters and properties of the the underground rock stratum are evaluated according to the collected data.

3 Design of seismoelectric signal acquisition system

In this paper, a SPI bus based seismoelectric signal acquisition system is presented. The system block diagram is shown in Figure 2, which includes two parts: data acquisition board and control board.

A total of eight data acquisition board, placed in the eight cavities of the pit shaft respectively, to collect seismoelectric signal of different depths. The trigger signal is generated by the acoustic emission system, which is a level pulse signal, and used to synchronize the data acquisition process of the eight acquisition board. When an effective trigger signal is sent out, the eight acquisition board starts to collect the seismoelectric signal synchronously. The data acquisition board receives the electrical signal by antennas, and then store the relevant data in storage space. The acquisition board will not send the data to the SPI bus until it dectect an effective control signal in the CS(Control Signal) line.

The control board sequentially selects the data acquisition board through the SPI bus in order to control the data transmission process. After the data acquisition board detects an effective CS signal, the data is transmitted from acqusition board to the control board through the SDI(Signal Data In) line in accordance with the timing of the SPI bus protocol. After receiving all the data of the current acquisition board, the control board will transfer the data to the host computer through the twisted pair cable.Then,control board switch to the next channel through CS line and repeat the data transfer operation above.

In the host computer, the data of seismoelectric signal will be used to evaluate the properties and parameters of underground formation[3].

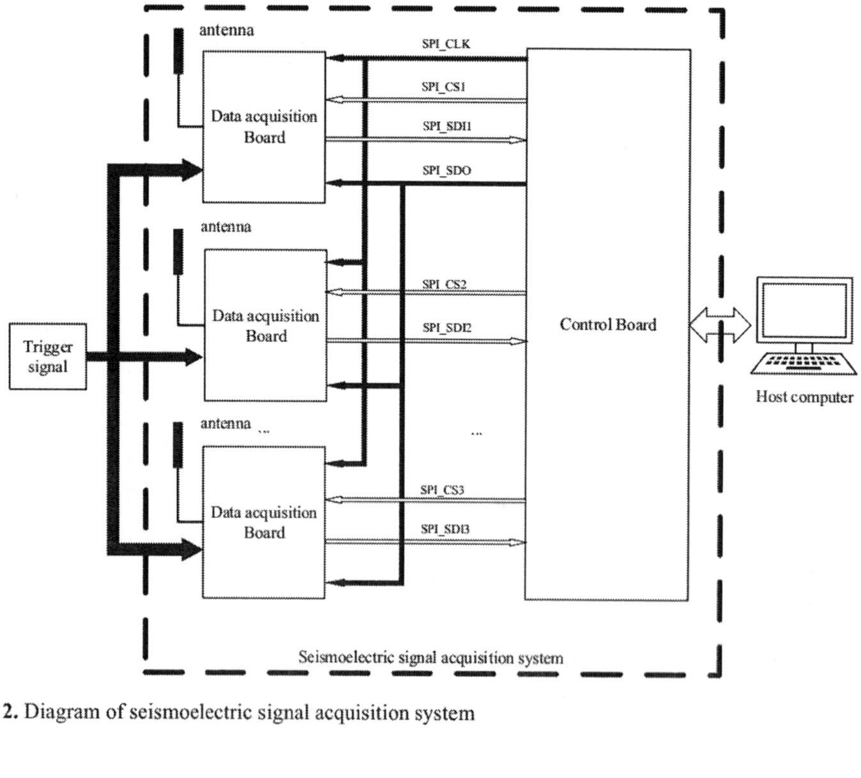

Figure 2. Diagram of seismoelectric signal acquisition system

DOI: 10.1051/itmconf/20171101013

4 Simulative well experiment

4.1 Experimental environment

Build an experimental environment to simulate the underground environment. The experimental facility comprises a water tank, grindstone, pit shaft.

Put the stone into the water tank, and then add enough water to drown the grindstone. Next, add a certain amount of salt to the water to change the ion concentration of the solution so that the seismoelectric signals are more easily detected.

Place the antennas, data acquisition boards ,control board and sound source in their right place of the pit shaft respectively, as shown in Figure 3. After taking waterproofing measures, put the shaft into the tank and close to the grindstone.

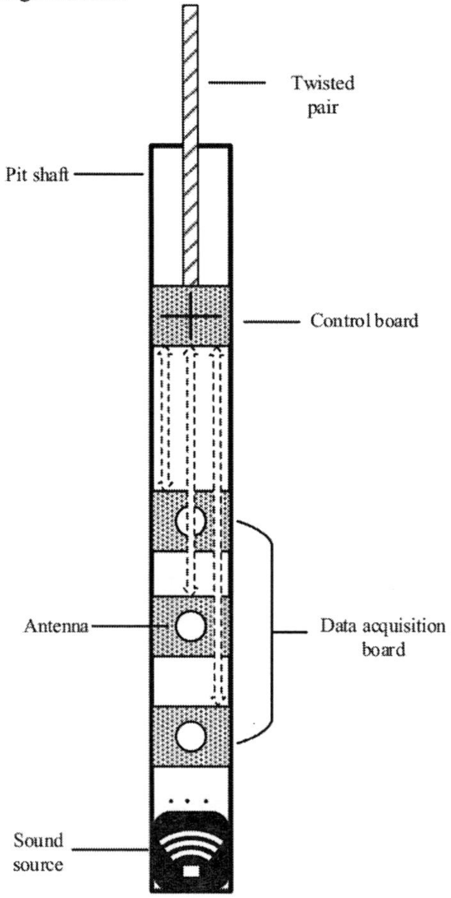

Figure 3. Installation diagram of the seismoelectric signal acquisition system

4.2 Experimental equipment

The experimental equipment includes signal source, power amplifier, sound source, oscilloscope, computer and so on.

4.3 Experimental principle

As can be seen from Figure 1,a complete seismoelectric logging system consists of three parts: the acoustic emission system, the seismoelectric signal acquisition system and the host computer.

A square wave pulse signal is generated by the signal source, and then amplified by the power amplifier. Amplified signal then is sent to the sound source,so the sound source will produce a strong sound wave. Because of the seismoelectric effect, acoustic shock will generate electrical signals in the surface of the grindstone. After the seismoelectric signal is received by the seismoelectric signal acquisition system, a series of processing will be carried out, and then related data will be transmitted to the host computer through the control board. At last,the host computer is used to analyze the data and judge the validity of the seismoelectric data.

4.4 Experimental conditions

•Excitation type to sound source: square pulse (voltage amplitude=600v,pulse width=65μv);
•Antenna type: helical antenna, as shown in Figure 4;
•Spacing of adjacent antennas: 0.15m;
•Sampling frequency of data acquisition board: 260KHz;

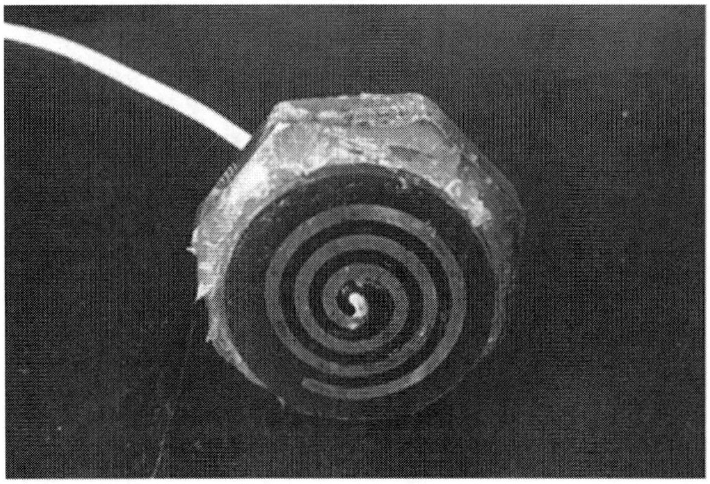

Figure 4. Waterproof helical antenna.

4.5 Experimental results

In actual measurement, there is a strong correlation bettwen the data of seven channel,while noise and seismoelectric signal are overlapped in the collected data of the remaining channel.Here we only analysis the seven channel that data has strong correlation.

Using origin to draw the seven channel data, as shown in Figure 5.

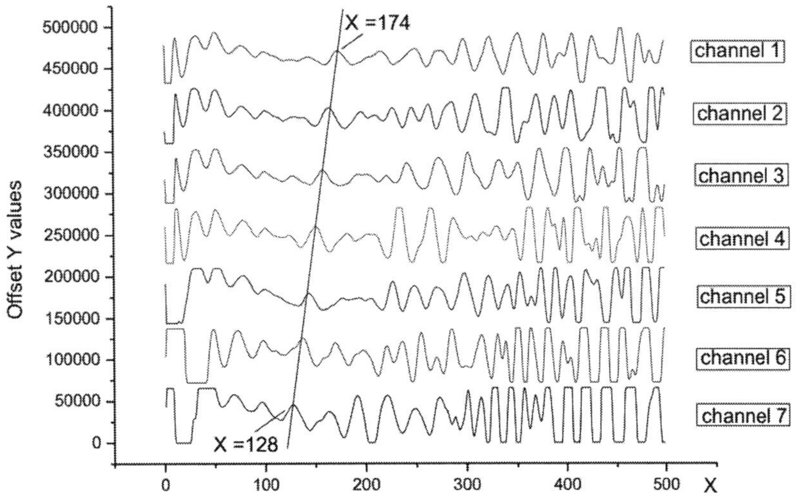

Figure 5. Experimental data waveform.

In Figure 5, the data of the channel 1 to the channel 7 is collected by data acqusition board from up to down respectively.The waveform of each channel not only include the seismoelectric signal, but also the noise. The main source of noise is the power amplifier. The power amplifier produces a very strong excitation,and the frequency of which is very close to the seismoelectric signal, so the electromagnetic wave of excitation will be received together with the seismoelectric signal by data acquisition board.

But we can distinguish the noise and the electrical signal from the waveform above .In Figure 4, the power amplifier is placed on the ground, and the noise signal is transmitted from the ground to underground. The sound source is placed at the bottom of the shaft, and the sound waves propagate along the wall from bottom to top. According to the analysis above, the waveform in front of the slash are mainly the noise,while the waveform behind the slash are mainly the seismoelectric signal.

According to the time interval between the seismoelectric signal waveform of different channel, it is also able to calculate the velocity of acoustic wave propagated along the borehole.

Figure 5 shows that the interval data points between channel 1 and the channel 7 is 46 in the abscissa . Known from 4.4 that the sampling frequency of the data acquisition board is 260KHz, so we can calculate that the time interval between adjacent data points is 3.85μs. Therefore, the time that sound spend to propagate from acquisition board 1 to acquisition board 7 is:

$$3.85\mu s*46=177.1\mu s \tag{1}$$

In addition, the distance between the acquisition board 1 and the acquisition board 7 is:

$$0.15m*6 = 0.9m \tag{2}$$

Therefore, it can be calculated that the velocity of sound wave propagated along the borehole wall:

$$0.9m \div 177.1\,\mu s \approx 5081m/s \tag{3}$$

This is consistent with the velocity of sound wave propagated in the rock (4500m/s to 7500m/s), which confirms that the seismoelectric signal acquired by acquisition board is arose from the acoustic wave[4].

Conclusion

Seismoelectric logging is a very promising oil logging technology, but the acquisition of seismoelectric signal is one of the most difficult problems in engineer application. This paper designs a set of signal acquisition system that is able to coordinate multiple measurement points to acquire underground seismoelectric signals of different depths underground. Simultaneously, the system can transmit all the data to the host computer in real time through SPI bus. It basically meets the demand of signal acquisition in seismoelectric logging and has certain application value in engineering.

Acknowledgements

This work was financially supported by the State's Key Project of Research and Development Plan(20 16YFC0303502), and supported by"the Fundamental Research Funds for the Central Universities" (Z YGX2015J019).

References

1. Segesman F F. Well-logging method[J]. *Geophysics*, **45**,1667-1684(2012)
2. Russell R D, Butler K E, Kepic A W, et al. Seismoelectric exploration[J]. *Leading Edge*, **16**,1611-1615(1997)
3. Zyserman F I, Monachesi L B, Jouniaux L. Dependence of shear wave seismoelectrics on soil textures: a numerical study in the vadose zone[J]. (2017)
4. Wang Shiguang,Sheng Yang,He Hanhan, Effect of petrophysical property on the propagation of ultrasonic in rocks. *Physics Experimentation*,**8**,9-13(2014)

Application of Data Smoothing Method in Signal Processing for Vortex Flow Meters

Jun ZHANG[1], Tian ZOU[2] and Chun-Lai TIAN[1,a]

[1]*School of Mechanical and Electronic Engineeing, Pingxiang University, 337055 Pingxiang, Jiangxi Province, China*
[2]*School of Law, Pingxiang University, 337055 Pingxiang, Jiangxi Province, China*

Abstract. Vortex flow meter is typical flow measure equipment. Its measurement output signals can easily be impaired by environmental conditions. In order to obtain an improved estimate of the time-averaged velocity from the vortex flow meter, a signal filter method is applied in this paper. The method is based on a simple Savitzky-Golay smoothing filter algorithm. According with the algorithm, a numerical program is developed in Python with the scientific library numerical Numpy. Two sample data sets are processed through the program. The results demonstrate that the processed data is available accepted compared with the original data. The improved data of the time-averaged velocity is obtained within smoothing curves. Finally the simple data smoothing program is useable and stable for this filter.

1 Introduction

As types of flow measurement equipments, vortex flow meters are commonly used to measure the flow velocity. According with the advanced development of the flow measurement technology, they play a major role in flow measurement business. The vortex flow meters are extensively used in industries and academic research. It is being currently applied extensively in the measurement of liquids, gases and steam [1].

The vortex flow meter is a device that works with based on the principle of shedding of vortices behind a bluff body placed in the flow. Disturbances in the flow called vortices are created while the fluid passes this bluff body. The vortices trail behind the cylinder, appearing alternatively from each side of the body. The frequency at which these vortices alternate sides is proportional to the fluid flow rate. The flow velocity can be obtained from this frequency. The accuracy and reliability of the meters keeps them ahead of other devices [2-5].

Vortex flow meters are commonly employed in a variety of industry applications. However their robustness and accuracy can easily be impaired by environmental conditions, such as inflow disturbances and pulsating conditions. Many works on the signal post-processing have been carried out [4-8]. Some of them were based on mathematical filter methods to establish the data filter. And others built the filter software in the embedded computer of the vortex flow meters.

In order to obtain an improved estimate of the velocity from the meter, we apply a classical simple smoothing filter for the signal data post-processing in this paper. It is based the Savitzky-Golay filter and is corrected to adjust the fluctuation of the gas and reduce the lag of the transition.

[a] Corresponding author: tianchunlai@bit.edu.cn

2 Methodologies

The Savitzky-Golay filter is a classical smoothing method for the signal processing [9]. It can be applied to a set of digital data points for the purpose of smoothing the data. And it helps to increase the signal-to-noise ratio without greatly distorting the signal. This is achieved, in a process known as convolution, by fitting successive sub-sets of adjacent data points with a low-degree polynomial by the method of linear least squares. The mathematic problem is described as the followings.

Assumed that there are the data consists of a set of $n\{x_j, y_j\}$ points (j=1, ..., n), where x is an independent variable and y_j is an observed value. They are treated with a set of m convolution coefficients, C_i according to the expression

$$Y_j = \sum_{i=-(m-1)/2}^{i=(m-1)/2} C_i y_{j+i} \tag{1}$$

The index j represents the running index of the ordinate data in the original data table. It is easy to apply this formula in numerical program. Selected convolution coefficients could be found in the Savitzky–Golay tables [9].

For example, for smoothing by a 5-point quadratic polynomial, m=5, i={−2,−1, 0, 1, 2} and Y_j is given by

$$Y_j = \frac{1}{35}\left(-3\times y_{j-2} + 12\times y_{j-1} + 17\times y_j + 12\times y_{j+1} - 3\times y_{j+2}\right) \tag{2}$$

where $C_{-2}=-3/35$, $C_{-1}=12/35$, $C_0=17/35$, $C_1=12/35$, $C_2=-3/35$.

Moreover such as another example, for smoothing by a 7-point quadratic polynomial, m=7, i={−3, −2, −1, 0, 1, 2, 3} and Y_j is given by

$$Y_j = \frac{1}{21}\left(-2\times y_{j-3} + 3\times y_{j-2} + 6\times y_{j-1} + 7\times y_j + 6\times y_{j+1} + 3\times y_{j+2} - 2\times y_{j+3}\right) \tag{3}$$

where $C_{-3}=-2/21$, $C_{-2}=3/21$, $C_{-1}=6/21$, $C_0=7/21$, $C_1=6/21$, $C_2=3/21$, $C_3=-2/21$.

3 Solutions

There is a simple application of data smoothing, which are performed primarily to make the data appear to be less noisy than it really is. According with above mathematic equations, the numerical solver is programmed within Numpy, a python scientific numerical library [10].

4 Results and discussion

Utilizing the solver, we obtain the processed data of two samples in normalized data. The original data of sample I are shown in Figure. 1. Its smoothed data processed by the filter with 5-point quadratic polynomial are shown in Figure. 2. And its smoothed data processed by the filter with 7-point quadratic polynomial are shown in Figure. 3. The other sample data set is shown in Figure. 4 (Original), Figure. 5 (filtered with 5-point quadratic polynomial) and Figure. 6 (filtered with 7-point quadratic polynomial).

Comparing these figures, it can be seen from Figure.1 that there are some noise signals in the original data. In the Figure. 2, the processed results are smoothed through the filter of the noise with 5-point quadratic polynomial. And in the Figure. 3, the data are demonstrated with fewer noise data. It looks like as same as that in Figure. 4 to Figure. 6 with simple data II. It shows that the proposed smoothing algorithm is feasible for the vortex flow meters in the fluctuation conditions. Moreover the lag of the transition is reduced here.

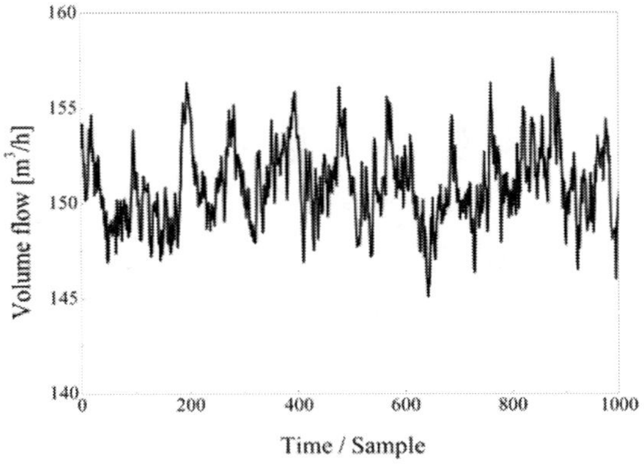

Figure 1. Original data I.

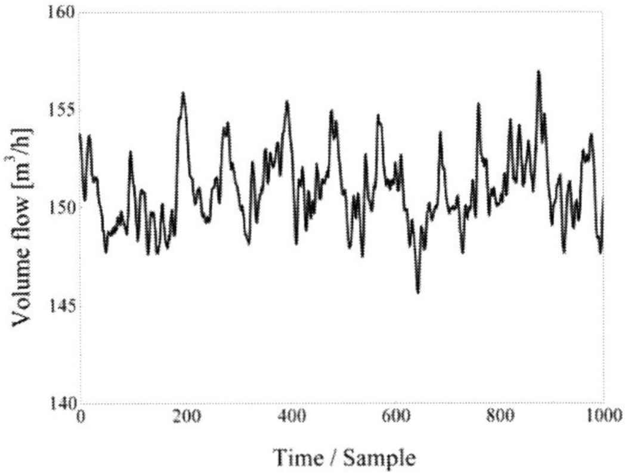

Figure 2. Processed data I by 5-point quadratic polynomial.

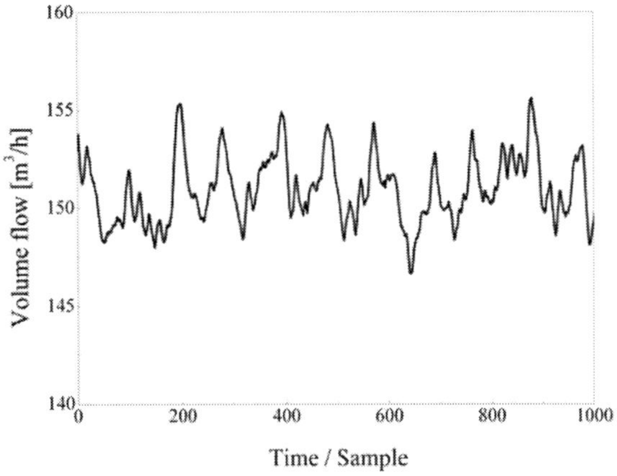

Figure 3. Processed data I by 7-point quadratic polynomial.

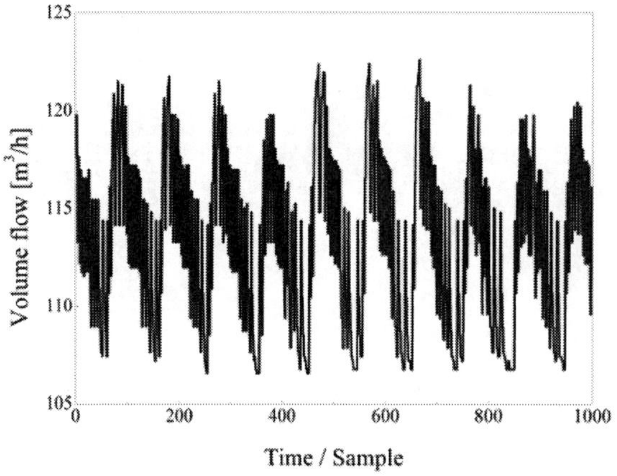

Figure 4. Original data II.

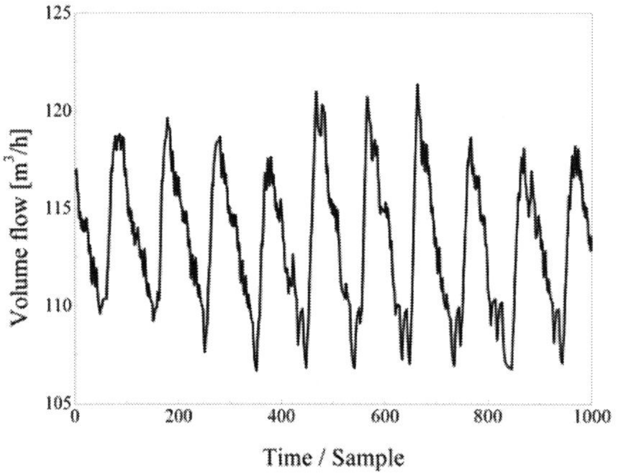

Figure 5. Processed data II by 5-point quadratic polynomial.

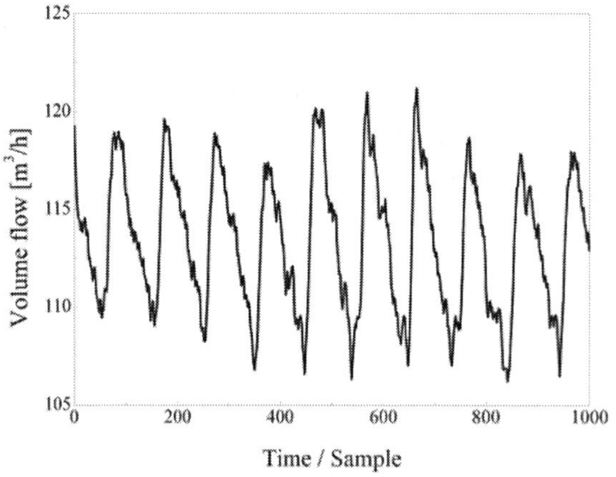

Figure 6. Processed data II by 7-point quadratic polynomial.

The data results, total average and standard deviation with maximal normalization, are listed in Table 1. The processed data has the same average as the original data. In terms of the data filter for Data I, its average of Processed by 5-point quadratic polynomial is a little more than the original results and a little less than the results processed by 7-point quadratic polynomial filter. The standard deviation of the results processed by 7-point quadratic polynomial filter is the smallest due to the filter mathematical method.

Table 1. Average and deviation of two sample data

Item		**Total average**	**Standard deviation**
Data I	Original	1.01060	0.01621
	Processed by 5-point quadratic polynomial	1.01020	0.01406
	Processed by 7-point quadratic polynomial	1.01030	0.01206
Data II	Original	0.98114	0.03712
	Processed by 5-point quadratic polynomial	0.98104	0.02966
	Processed by 7-point quadratic polynomial	0.98124	0.02238

Another data example with linear increase trend is shown in Figure. 7 with filtered results, which is shown in Figure. 8. In the Figure. 7 and Figure. 8, the dash lines display the linear increase trend. In the measurement, the trend of the gas or liquid flow would affect the meter data transition due to the system lag. The gradient of the linear fit for original data in Figure. 7 is 0.1505. And that gradient of the filter processed data in Figure. 8 is 0.1504, almost similarly with the original one. The little error is caused by some sample data changed by the filter.

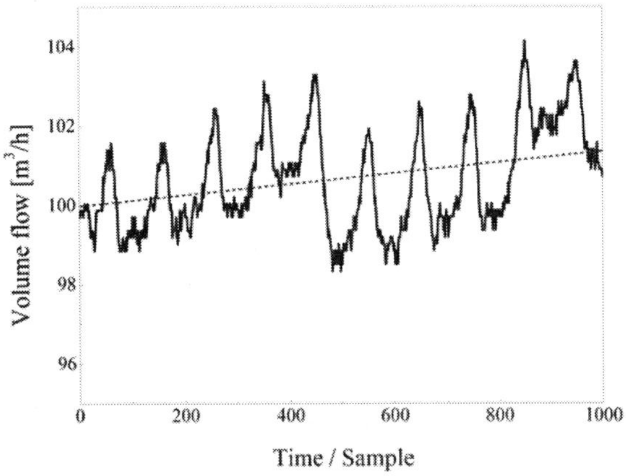

Figure 7. Original data III with linear increase trend.

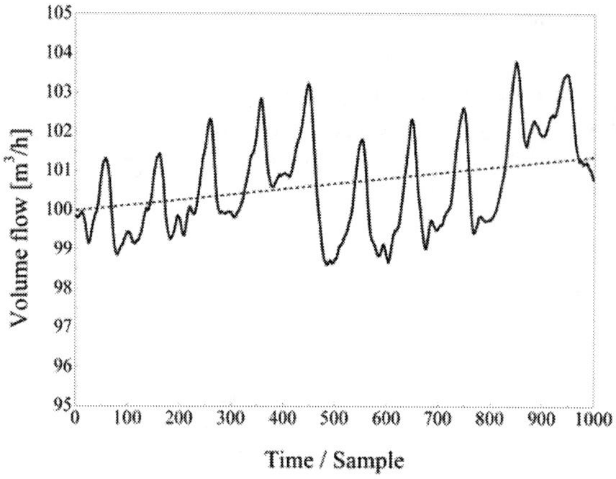

Figure 8. Processed data III by 7-point quadratic polynomial.

In all, it appears from comparing these results that there is a reasonable agreement between the original and processed signal data. However, the standard deviation of the processed data is much lower than the original one. It shows that this smoothing fitter method is efficient.

Conclusions

In order to obtain improved velocity data from the vortex flow meter, the signal filter method is applied here based on the simple Savitzky-Golay smoothing filter algorithm. The data is computed through the algorithm numerical program. Comparing the processed data between 5-point and 7-point quadratic polynomial filters, it shows that the similarly total average and standard deviation are obtained. The processed data is improved and could be accepted for the analysis. Moreover the filter is acceptable for the linear increase trend data and could prevent the lag error of the flow meter signals. However, due to the property of the vortex flow, the range of the suitable measurement in one meter is strictly limited. The filter for larger range of velocity fluid is under investigation.

Acknowledgements

The research work was supported by Science and Technology Research Project of Department of Education in Jiangxi Province under Grant No. GJJ151259.

References

1. A. Venugopal, A. Agrawal and S. V. Prabhu, SENSOR ACTUAT A-PHYS **170**, 8-23 (2011).
2. J. E. Amadi-Echendu and H. Zhu, IEEE T INSTRUM MEAS **41**, 1001-1006(1992).
3. H. Sato and K. Watanabe , IEEE T INSTRUM MEAS **49**, 2002-2005(2000).
4. T. Ghaoud and D. W. Clarke, FLOW MEAS INSTRUM **13**, 103-117 (2002).
5. A. G. Rossberg, P. Riegler, F. Buhl, J. Herwig and J. Timmer, FLOW MEAS INSTRUM **15**, 29-35 (2004).
6. J. J. Miau, C. F. Yeh, C. C. Hu and J. H. Chou, FLOW MEAS INSTRUM **16**, 397-404 (2005).
7. D. Zheng, T. Zhang, J. Xing and J. Mei, MEAS SCI TECHNOL **18**, 2769 (2007).
8. X. Lin, Y. Wang and Z. Pan, ADV INTE SOFT C **105**, 77-82(2011).
9. A. Savitzky and M. J. E. Golay, ANAL CHEM **36**, 1627-1639 (1964).
10. J. D. Hunter, F. Pérez and B. E. Granger, COMPUT SCI ENG **13**, 13-21(2010).

A Method of Information Fusion Based on Fuzzy Neural Network and Its Application

Ji-Pu GAO[1], Chang-Bao XU[1], Li ZHANG[1], Jun-Lin ZHENG[2], Huai SHU[2] and Xi YUAN[2]

[1]*Guizhou Electric Power Research Institute of Guizhou Power Grid Co., Ltd., Guiyang, 550002, Guizhou, China*
[2]*Wuhan Zhongyuan Huadian Science & Technology Co., Ltd, Wuhan 430074, China*

Abstract. In view of the limitation of fault diagnosis methods in substation intelligent patrol system, a fault diagnosis method based on multi-sensors information fusion is proposed. In the field of fault diagnosis, this method can deal with uncertain and imprecise information by using fuzzy theory, and has a high self-study capability based on neural network. Collecting samples of data through establishing many sensors in the scene of the intelligent patrol system, and then through the BP algorithm of fuzzy neural network training to achieve accurate fault diagnosis function of the intelligent patrol system. By comparing the result of an example, it shows that, compared with using single information, using multi-sensors information as the diagnosis method is more accurate and reliable in the intelligent patrol system.

1 Foreword

With the expansion of the system scale, the complexity of the increase, and the huge investment, it is urgent to improve the reliability and security of the system. Therefore, the establishment of a monitoring system to monitor the running of the whole system is necessary, constantly testing system changes and failures, and take the necessary measures to prevent damage and accidents. But because the system dynamic behaviour, function and the complex structure, nonlinear and uncertainty, a single information source fault diagnosis theory based on conventional or traditional methods, judging the fault by several major fault features, is difficult to achieve the corresponding goal [1-3]. So it is necessary to make full use of the detection method and status information obtained to form intelligent integration of intelligent diagnosis strategy.

Though the parallel processing network structure and strong learning function, neural network cannot make full use of the inspiring knowledge summarized by the domain expert [4, 5]. Fuzzy logic can better use the language knowledge, and knowledge of the form is easier to understand. But in fact, it has a weak learning ability and is difficult to use the value information.

Therefore, this paper combines neural network with fuzzy logic [6, 7], and puts forward a fault diagnosis method by using fuzzy neural network, which is more close to the human thinking [8-10]. The intelligent patrol system in the substation equipment in the resettlement of more than three different sources of the transformer sensors to detect the characteristics of the substation system, and using fuzzy neural network as the implementing agencies of information fusion to achieve substation intelligent patrol system fault diagnosis. At the same time, by comparing the result of fault diagnosis, it is demonstrated that using multi-sensors information fusion is more accurate and reliable in comparison to using single information.

2 Fuzzy neural network structure

FNN fault diagnosis is a combination of fuzzy logic and neural network technology. Through processing the tradition artificial neural networks by fuzzy method, retaining its results, the carrying on fuzzy processing in the neuron, fuzzy neural network can cause the neuron to evolve from processing the pure processing value data to can process the fuzzy information data.

2.1 FNN architecture

According to the actual situation of intelligent patrol system, the paper use a four-story fuzzy neural network structure, and the network consists of three parts: the first part is a fuzzy quantify function; the second part is the neural network; the third part is to get rid of the fuzzy. Its structure is shown in Figure 1.

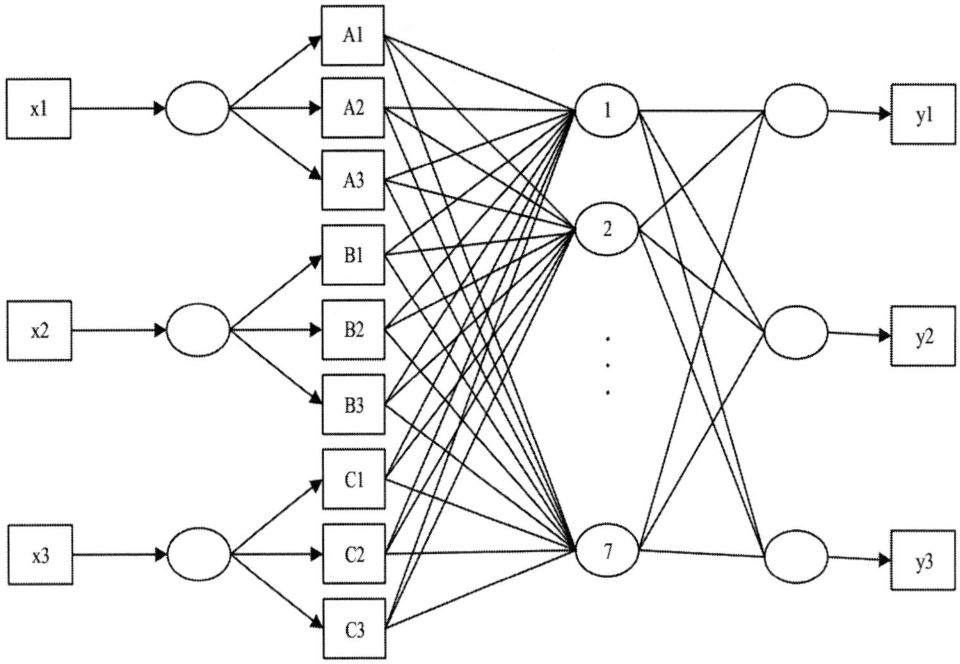

Figure 1. FNN architecture.

Network level 1 is the input layer, which the value of the neurons is 1, and the neurons directly transmit input data to the neurons of level 2. Each node responds to a variety of intelligent patrol system failure instructions. According to the analysis of the actual situation of intelligent patrol system and fault indication relationship, the main transformer fault indication is abnormal breathing light, abnormal cooler and abnormal disconnector and so on, corresponding to fuzzy neural Network x1, x2, x3 3 input variables.

Network 2 is a fuzzy quantified layer. According to the membership function defined in the fuzzy subset, it carries on fuzzy processing in the input continuous variable value, and transforms the serial number into the corresponding membership degree, to realize fuzzy processing.

Network level 3 is the implied layer. It maps the fuzzy input variables to the fuzzy output variables. The hidden nodes can be determined by the actual situation, and the general desirability is 2 N + 1 (n is the input layer node), the hidden activation function is Sigmoid function.

Network 4 is the output layer, and the output of each node responses to the substation fault in intelligent patrol system. The fuzzy value size of each output node represents the size of the probability of failure.

The four layer fuzzy neural network can be used to effectively implement the fuzzy input to the fuzzy output mapping, and through the neural network learning algorithm, and can enable the mapping to the method of fuzzy nonlinear function relations.

2.2 Membership function

The introduction of fuzzy mathematics transferred mathematical logic to value logic and shifted absolute "yes" and "no" to the relative "yes" and "no" in the appropriate feature space, thus promoted the logic relation of classical set theory.

The basic idea is that, in the general collection, the membership degree of elements to collection from the original value of the expansion can only take 0,1 to be admitted any value in the range of [0,1], so it is very suitable to descript and process the uncertain sensors information. In the application of multi-sensors data fusion, the fuzzy set theory expresses the uncertainty of various sensors information with the membership function. And in the field of fault diagnosis, the fault membership degree are generally obtained from the fault indication membership degree.

Supposing possible fault sign is m: $x_1, x_2, \ldots, x_m$, then the fault indicator fuzzy vector is $X = (\mu_1, \mu_2, \ldots, \mu_m)$, where μ_i is the target of the member, which have characteristics of x_i . Supposing the reason for the failure are n: $y_1, y_2, \ldots, y_n$, then the fault reason fuzzy vector is $Y = (\mu_1, \mu_2, \ldots, \mu_n)$, where μ_j is the membership of the target, which have faults y_j . So the fault diagnosis is function-mapping process, which acquired the reasons fuzzy vector from the corresponding indication fuzzy vector.

When the intelligent patrol system is working, the parameters of the substation should be kept in a stable range. When the substation system is in trouble, the state parameters, which are measured by the sensor, will deviate from the normal range, the larger departure from the normal the larger possibility of failure.

According to the actual situation of intelligent patrol system and the experience of experts establishes the fault indication membership function. The membership function has shown in Figure 2 and Figure 3.

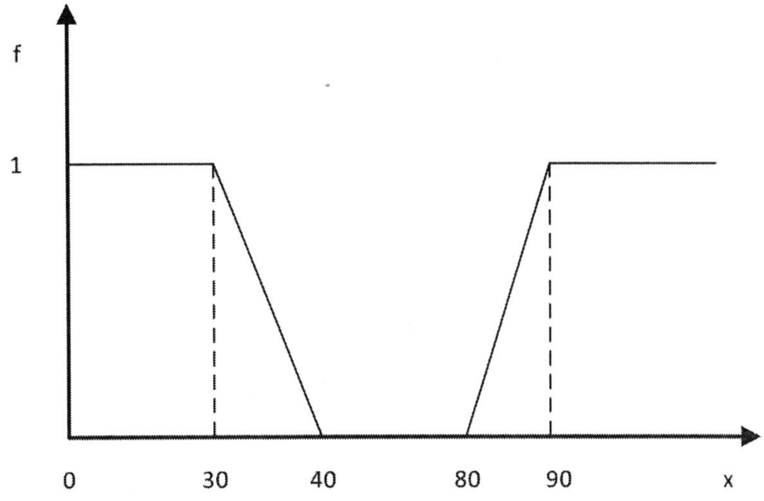

Figure 2. The membership function.

$$f(x)=\begin{cases} 1 & x\in[0,30] \\ -0.1x+4 & x\in[30,40] \\ 0 & x\in[40,80] \\ 0.1x-8 & x\in[80,90] \\ 1 & x\in[90,\infty] \end{cases}$$

Figure 3. The expression of the membership function.

2.3 FNN training algorithm

FNN learning algorithm uses a common BP algorithm which is often used in multilayer neural network. The nature of the algorithm modifies the threshold value by the error of the actual neural network output value $t_1,t_2,\ldots,t_n$ and the corresponding value of training samples $y_1,y_2,\ldots,y_n$, so the network structure will be more and more close to the real structure of the samples.

Supposing the output of m iterations is $y_i(m)$, and then the unit error will be $e(m)$, $e_i(m)=d_i(m)-y_i(m)$.

The calculation uses the gradient method. The revised value of ω_{ij} linked to the neurons m is: $\Delta\omega_{ij}=\eta\delta_i(m)y_i(m)$. In the formula, η means learning step, and $\delta_i(m)$ is the local gradient, the revised value of which declines in the direction of the gradient.

Because the traditional BP algorithm has the slow convergence rate, and has the local minimum problems in the objective function, a momentum α is increased to enhance the convergence rate, that is: $\Delta\omega_{ij}=a\Delta\omega_{ij}(n-1)+\eta\delta_i(n)y_j(n), a\in[0,1]$.

3 Applications

Because of the special working environment of substation equipment, safety is essential. According to the frequent fault phenomenon of substation equipment in practical work, three main reasons for failure were: (1) voltage transformer fault; (2) current transformer fault; (3) capacitor fault.

Three indication parameters by is detected by three sensors placed in substation system and the fault indication fuzzy vector is $X=(\mu_1,\mu_2,\mu_3)$, which is derived from the fuzzy sensors data, as fuzzy neural network training samples. And $\mu_i(i=1\sim3)$ is membership of fault indication i, and $Y=(\mu_1,\mu_2,\mu_3)$ is the fault reason fuzzy vector, and $\mu_j(j=1\sim3)$ is the membership of the fault reason j.

When the substation system is failure, the fault indication parameters will change significantly, and the sensors will get the parameters. This parameters are used as training samples, their fault membership degree were calculated by their respective membership functions. In this paper, the FNN has a three input nodes, seven hidden points, three output points, and the expected error is 0.001. Six group samples are selected for the network training, three groups as a network test samples, and the madab7 neural network toolbox was used to make the algorithm of the program, the network convergences after 2120 iterations. After entering the test samples of the three groups, the network can identify the failure of substation system, the fault diagnosis accuracy rate is high.

After the completion of the network training, enter the test samples to verify the accuracy and reliability of the FNN. After entering three groups test samples, the network can identify the failure in the hydraulic circuit brake system of mining equipment, and fault diagnosis accuracy rate is high, as shown in Table 1.

The output of FNN integration is the value of fault membership. The following principles can be used for the failure of the decision:

(1) The maximum membership principle: the fault component should have the maximum membership value.

(2) The minimum threshold principle: the value of the membership of fault component is greater than a certain threshold, and the threshold value is generally determined in the experiment.

Table 1. The results of single sensors information fault diagnosis and multi-sensors information fault diagnosis.

Fault	Sensors and Information Fusion	Failure membership			The result of Diagnosis
		μ_1	μ_2	μ_3	
1 Brake tank low level	A single sensor	0.650	0.210	0.600	Indefinite
	Multi-sensors fusion	0.956	0.093	0.003	1 Fault
2 Cooling pump failure	A single sensor	0.010	0.850	0.030	2 Fault
	Multi-sensors fusion	0.021	0.945	0.001	2 Fault
3 Brake valve fault	A single sensor	0.310	0.001	0.720	Indefinite
	Multi-sensors fusion	0.021	0.021	0.922	3 Fault

Conclusion

This paper make a full use of the advantages of fuzzy logic and neural network, and proposes the information fusion fault diagnosis method based on fuzzy neural network. This method is closer to human thinking. By using multiple sensors at the scene to collect data, express fuzzy rules and membership functions of fuzzy logic by using the neural network, and through the training of FNN by the BP algorithm, to achieve the precise fault diagnosis of intelligent petrol system. And then through the contrast of multi-sensors data fusion diagnostic identify methods and single sensors identify methods, multi-sensors fault diagnosis can effectively eliminate misjudgement due to lack of information and incomplete and not completely as well as identify the fault occurred reasons more reliably.

References

1. J. Zhang, X. P. Fan, C.L. Huang, T.F. Chen. Fusion monitoring system of locomotive wheelset state. *Journal of Traffic and Transportation Engineering*, **8(6)**, 13-19 (2008).
2. Zhu J, Zhang W, Zhang J, et al. An Improved Approach to Multi-Sensors Information Fusion Based on Evidence Theory [J]. *Computer Measurement & Control*, **21(2)**:547-549(2013).
3. L. Wei, S.C. Mukhopadhyay, R. Jidin, & C.P. Chen. Multi-source information fusion for drowsy driving detection based on wireless sensor networks. *Seventh International Conference on Sensing Technology*, pp.850-857(2013).
4. Ye Wang, & Lotfollah Najjar. Factor neural network theory and its applications. *International Journal of Information Technology & Decision Making*, **14(2)**, 239-251(2015).
5. D.Q. Zhu, S.L. Yu. Neural Networks Data Fusion Algorithm of Electronic Equipment Fault Diagnosis[C]. *Proceedings of the 5th world congress on intelligent control and Automation*, 5-19 (June, 2004).
6. Y.W. Li, X.D. Han, Z.Y. Wang. The temperature-variation fault diagnosis of high-voltage electric equipment based on information fusion. *ICMLC 2008*, 127-130 (July 2008).
7. Y. W. Li, W. Li, X. D. Han, J. Li. Application of multi-sensors information fusion technology in the power transformer fault diagnosis. *International Conference on Machine Learning and Cybernetics IEEE*, 29-33(2009).

8. B. Zeng, W. Wang, N. Wang, F. Li, F. Zhai, & L. Hu. Noninvasive blood glucose monitoring system based on distributed multi-sensors information fusion of multi-wavelength nir. *Engineering*, **05(10)**, 553-560(2013).
9. Bulac, C., Tristiu, I., Mandis, A., & Toma, L.. On-line power systems voltage stability monitoring using artificial neural networks. *International Symposium on Advanced Topics in Electrical Engineering* (pp.622-625). IEEE(2015).
10. Z. Yang, M. R. Chen, & W. Wu. Algorithm for wireless sensor network data fusion based on radial basis function neural networks. *Applied Mechanics & Materials*, 577(577), 873-878 (2014).

Attribute Reduction Algorithm Based on Structure Discernibility Matrix in Composite Information Systems

Mei-Jun GE[1], Nian-Bai FAN[1,a] and Tao SUN[2]

[1]*College of Information Science and Engineering, Hunan University, Changsha 410082, China*
[2]*College of Mathematics and Econometric, Hunan University, Changsha 410082, China*

Abstract. Attribute reduction, as an important preprocessing step for knowledge acquiring in data mining, is one of the key issues in rough set theory. It can only deal with attributes of a specific type in the information system by using a specific binary relation. However, there may be attributes of multiple different types in information systems in real-life applications. A composite relation is proposed to process attributes of multiple different types simultaneously in composite information systems. In order to solve the time-consuming problem of traditional heuristic attribute reduction algorithms, a novel attribute reduction algorithm based on structure discernibility matrix was proposed in this paper. The proposed algorithms can choose the same attribute reduction as its previous version, but it can be used to accelerate a heuristic process of attribute reduction by avoiding the process of intersection and adopting the forward greedy attribute reduction approach. The theoretical analysis and experimental results with UCI data sets show that the proposed algorithm can accelerate the heuristic process of attribute reduction.

1 Introduction

Pawlak proposed the Rough set theory in 1980s[1], this theory has become a powerful mathematical tool for analyzing one of various types of data[2,3]. It can be used in an attribute value representation model to describe the dependencies among attributes, evaluate the significance of attributes and derive reduction[4,5].

The classical rough set model can only be used to deal with categorical attributes, However, there may be attributes of multiple different types in real-life applications. many extended rough set models have been developed for attributes of multiple different types. A neighborhood relation was proposed by Hu to deal with numerical attributes[6]. Guan defined a tolerance relation and used the maximal tolerance classes to derive optimal decision rules from set-valued information systems[7]. Qian used a binary dominance relation to process set-valued data in set-valued ordered information systems[8]. Leung defined α-tolerance relations and employed the α-misclassification rate for rule acquisition from interval-valued information systems[9]. To deal with missing data, the toleration and similarity relations as well as the limited tolerance relation were proposed[10]. Grzymała-Busse combined the toleration and similarity relations and presented characteristic relations for missing data in information systems[11].

[a] Corresponding author: 398000862@qq.com

Most of the classical rough set methods fail to deal with more than attributes of two different types. Many scholars introduced the composite rough set model and proposed the basic idea to deal with attributes of multiple different types[12-14]. we introduced a structure discernibility matrix[15] to solve the time-consuming problem of traditional heuristic attribute reduction algorithms in this paper. The proposed algorithms can choose the same attribute reduction as its original version, but it can be used to accelerate a heuristic process of attribute reduction by avoiding the process of intersection and adopting the forward greedy attribute reduction approach. Extensive experiments on different data sets from UCI show that the proposed structure discernibility matrix-based method can process large data sets efficiently.

2 Composite rough set model

In many practical issues, there are attributes of multiple different types in the information system, we call it a composite information system. A composite information system can be written as $CIS=(U,A,V,f)$, where U is a non-empty finite set of objects; A is a non-empty finite set of attributes; $V=\bigcup_{a\in A}V_a$ and V_a is a domain of attribute a; $f:U\times A\rightarrow V$ is an information function such that $f(x,a)\in V_a$ for every $x\in U,a\in A$.

More specifically, a composite information system is also called a composite decision table if there are condition and decision attributes in the information system, which is denoted by $CDT=(U,A\cup D,V,f)$.

Definition 1[16]. Given $x,y\in U$ and $B\subseteq A$, the composite relation CR_B is defined as

$$CR_B=\{(x,y)\,|\,(x,y)\in\bigcap R_a,\forall a\in B\} \tag{1}$$

Where $R_a\subseteq U\times U$ is an indiscernibility relation defined by an attribute a on U.

When $(x,y)\in CR_B$, we call x and y are indiscernible on B. Let $CR_B(x)=\{y\,|\,y\in U,\forall a\in B,yR_ax\}$, we call $CR_B(x)$ the composite class for x on CR_B.

Definition 2[12]. Given a composite information system $CIS=(U,A,V,f)$, $\forall X\subseteq U,B\subseteq A$, the lower and upper approximations of X in terms of the composite relation CR_B are defined as

$$CR_B(X)=\{x\in U\,|\,CR_B(x)\subseteq X\} \tag{2}$$

$$CR^B(X)=\{x\in U\,|\,CR_B(x)\cap X\neq\emptyset\} \tag{3}$$

Here, the positive region $POS_{CR_B}(X)=CR_B(X)$ (4)

Definition 3[12]. Given a composite decision table $CDT=(U,A\cup D,V,f)$, $B\subseteq A$. Let $U/D=\{D_1,D_2,...,D_r\}$ be a partition over the decision D. Then the lower and upper approximations of the decision D with respect to attributes B are defined as

$$CR_B(D)=\bigcup_{j=1}^{r}CR_B(D_j) \tag{5}$$

$$CR^B(D)=\bigcup_{j=1}^{r}CR^B(D_j) \tag{6}$$

The positive region $POS_{CR_B}(D)=CR_B(D)$ (7)

Definition 4[17]. Let $S=(U,A\cup D,V,f)$ be a decision table, $B\subseteq A$ and $\forall a\in B$, if $POS_B(D)=POS_{B-\{a\}}(D)$, a is unnecessary in B relative to D, else a is necessary in B relative to D. If $\forall a\in B$ is necessary, B is independent relative to D.

Definition 5[18]. Let $S=(U,A\cup D,V,f)$ be a decision table, $B\subseteq A$. If $POS_B(D)=POS_A(D)$, and $\forall a\in B$ is necessary, B is the reduce of A relative to D.

Definition 6[18]. Let $S=(U,A\cup D,V,f)$ be a decision table, $B\subseteq A$ and $\forall a\in B$. The significance measure of a in B is defined as

$$Sig^{inner}(a,B,D)=(|POS_B(D)-POS_{B-\{a\}}(D)|)/U \tag{8}$$

If $Sig^{inner}(a,B,D)>0$, a is core attribute of B related to D.

Definition 7[18]. Let $S=(U,A\cup D,V,f)$ be a decision table, $B\subseteq A$ and $\forall a\in A-B$. The significance measure of a in B is defined as

$$Sig^{outer}(a,B,D)=(|POS_{B\cup\{a\}}(D)-POS_B(D)|)/U \tag{9}$$

Example 1. A composite decision table $CDT=(U,A\cup D,V,f)$ is presented in Table 1. Let $A=\bigcup_{k=1}^{5}a_k$. We set the neighborhood parameter $\delta=0.15$ and adopt Manhattan distance.

Table 1. A composite decision table

U	a_1	a_2	a_3	a_4	a_5	D
x_1	Y	{1,2}	0.2	0.1	*	Yes
x_2	Y	{1}	0.2	0.3	?	No
x_3	Y	{0}	0.1	0.1	Small	Yes
x_4	Y	{0,1,2}	0.1	0.2	Small	Yes
x_5	N	{1}	0.1	0.3	Large	Yes
x_6	N	{0,2}	0.2	0.2	Large	No

Table 2. Results of composite classes

U	$R_{a_1}(x)$	$R_{a_2}(x)$	$R_{a_3}(x)$	$R_{a_4}(x)$	$R_{a_5}(x)$	$CR_B(x)$
x_1	$\{x_1,x_2,x_3,x_4\}$	$\{x_1,x_2,x_4,x_5,x_6\}$	U	$\{x_1,x_3,x_4,x_6\}$	U	$\{x_1,x_4\}$
x_2	$\{x_1,x_2,x_3,x_4\}$	$\{x_1,x_2,x_4,x_5\}$	U	$\{x_2,x_4,x_5,x_6\}$	U	$\{x_2,x_4\}$
x_3	$\{x_1,x_2,x_3,x_4\}$	$\{x_3,x_4,x_6\}$	U	$\{x_1,x_3,x_4,x_6\}$	$\{x_1,x_3,x_4\}$	$\{x_3,x_4\}$
x_4	$\{x_1,x_2,x_3,x_4\}$	U	U	U	$\{x_1,x_3,x_4\}$	$\{x_1,x_3,x_4\}$
x_5	$\{x_5,x_6\}$	$\{x_1,x_2,x_4,x_5\}$	U	$\{x_2,x_4,x_5,x_6\}$	$\{x_1,x_5,x_6\}$	$\{x_5\}$
x_6	$\{x_5,x_6\}$	$\{x_1,x_3,x_4,x_6\}$	U	U	$\{x_1,x_5,x_6\}$	$\{x_6\}$

According to the introduction in Section 2, it is easy to know that $R_{a_1},R_{a_2},R_{a_3},R_{a_4},R_{a_5}$ are equivalence relation, tolerance relation, neighborhood relation, neighborhood relation and characteristic relation respectively. By Definition 4, $CR_B(x)=\{y\mid y\in U,\forall B_k\in B,yR_{B_k}x\}$, the results are listed in Table 2.

It is easy to obtain that $U/D=\{D_1,D_2\}$, where $D_1=\{x_1,x_3,x_4,x_5\}$, $D_2=\{x_2,x_6\}$.

Since $CR_A(x_1)=\{x_1,x_4\}$, $CR_A(x_2)=\{x_2,x_4\}$, $CR_A(x_3)=\{x_3,x_4\}$,

$CR_A(x_4)=\{x_1,x_3,x_4\}$, $CR_A(x_5)=\{x_5\}$, $CR_A(x_6)=\{x_6\}$.

$POS_A(D)=\{x_1,x_3,x_4,x_5,x_6\}$.

$CR_{(a_2\cup a_3\cup a_4\cup a_5)}(x_1)=\{x_1,x_4,x_6\}$, $CR_{(a_2\cup a_3\cup a_4\cup a_5)}(x_2)=\{x_2,x_4,x_5\}$,

$CR_{(a_2\cup a_3\cup a_4\cup a_5)}(x_3)=\{x_3,x_4\}$, $CR_{(a_2\cup a_3\cup a_4\cup a_5)}(x_4)=\{x_1,x_3,x_4\}$,

$CR_{(a_2\cup a_3\cup a_4\cup a_5)}(x_5)=\{x_5\}$, $CR_{(a_2\cup a_3\cup a_4\cup a_5)}(x_6)=\{x_6\}$.

$POS_{(a_2\cup a_3\cup a_4\cup a_5)}(D)=\{x_3,x_4,x_5,x_6\}\neq POS_A(D)$.

So a_1 is necessary in A relative to D. Use the same method to calculate every attribute in A, for simplicity, just think a_1, finally the core is$\{a_1,a_2,a_4,a_5\}$.Then use the same method we obtain that

$CR_{(a_1\cup a_2\cup a_4\cup a_5)}(x_1)=\{x_1,x_4\}$, $CR_{(a_1\cup a_2\cup a_4\cup a_5)}(x_2)=\{x_2,x_4\}$,

$CR_{(a_1\cup a_2\cup a_4\cup a_5)}(x_3)=\{x_3,x_4\}$, $CR_{(a_1\cup a_2\cup a_4\cup a_5)}(x_4)=\{x_1,x_3,x_4\}$,

$CR_{(a_1\cup a_2\cup a_4\cup a_5)}(x_5)=\{x_5\}$, $CR_{(a_1\cup a_2\cup a_4\cup a_5)}(x_6)=\{x_6\}$.

$POS_{(a_1\cup a_2\cup a_4\cup a_5)}(D)=\{x_1,x_3,x_4,x_5,x_6\}=POS_A(D)$.

According Definition 5, $\{a_1,a_2,a_4,a_5\}$is the reduction of attribute sets A relative to D.

The traditional heuristic attribute reduction algorithms is time-consuming, section 3 gives structure discernibility matrix-based heuristic attribute reduction algorithms, which can accelerate a heuristic process of attribute reduction by avoiding the process of intersection and adopting the forward greedy attribute reduction approach.

3 Structure discernibility matrix-based attribute reduction algorithm

In this section, the attribute reduction algorithm based on structure discernibility matrix in complex information system is presented and the sample is listed.

3.1 The sample analysis of attribute reduction algorithm based on structure discernibility matrix

Definition 8[12]. Given an composite information system $CIS=(U,A,V,f)$. Let $a\in A$ and R_a be an discernibility relation on U, $M^{R_a}_{n\times n}=(\xi_{ij})_{n\times n}$ be an $n\times n$ matrix representing R_a, called the relation matrix on a. Then

$$\xi^a_{ij}=\begin{cases}1,(x_i,x_j)\in R_a\\0,(x_i,x_j)\notin R_a\end{cases}\tag{10}$$

Definition 9[15]. Given an composite information system $CIS=(U,A,V,f)$. Let $B\subseteq A$ and R_B be an discernibility relation on U, $M^{R_B}_{n\times n}=(\xi_{ij})_{n\times n}$ be an $n\times n$ matrix representing R_B, called the relation matrix on B. Then

$$\xi^B_{ij}=\begin{cases}|B|,(x_i,x_j)\in R_B\\\sum_{k=1}^{|B|}\xi^k_{ij},(x_i,x_j)\notin R_B\end{cases}\tag{11}$$

ξ^k_{ij} is the value of the kth attribute in B.

Proposition 1 A composite decision table $CDT=(U,A\cup D,V,f)$, Let $B\subseteq A$ and R_B be an discernibility relation on U, $M^{R_B}_{n\times n}=(\xi_{ij})_{n\times n}$ is a relation matrix on B, $M^{R_D}_{n\times n}=(\xi_{ij})_{n\times n}$ is a relation matrix on

D, If the value is $|B|$ in the ith row of $M^{R_B}_{n\times n}$, corresponding location is 1 in $M^{R_D}_{n\times n}$, then x_i is in $POS_{CR_B}(D)$.

Proof: $\exists X \subseteq U/D, R_B(X)=\{x_i \in U \mid CR_B(x_i)\subseteq X\}$,

$CR_B(x_i)\subseteq R_B(X)$, so $x_i \in POS_{CR_B}(D)$.

$POS_{CR_A}(D)$ can be calculated by proposition 1.

Let $B\subseteq A, a\in B$ and R_a be an discernibility relation on U, let $M'_{sum} = M_{sum} - M^{R_a}_{n\times n} = (\xi'_{ij})_{n\times n}$, $B' = B - \{a\}$, then $POS_{B'}(D)$ can be calculated by the same method.

Propositon 2 A composite decision table $CDT=(U, A\cup D, V, f)$, $B\subseteq A$. If $POS_{B'}(D)\neq POS_B(D)$, then $a\in B$ is a core attribute of B related D. The proof of proposition 2 is easy by definition 6.

Example 2. A composite decision table $CDT=(U, A\cup D, V, f)$ is presented in Table 1. Let $A=\bigcup_{k=1,2,3,4,5} a_k$. We set the neighborhood parameter $\delta = 0.15$ and adopt Manhattan distance. The process of get one attribute reduction usually includes three steps.

Step1 The construction of the relation matrix

According to Definition 8, we have

$$M^{R_{a_1}}_{6\times 6}=\begin{bmatrix}1&1&1&1&0&0\\1&1&1&1&0&0\\1&1&1&1&0&0\\1&1&1&1&0&0\\0&0&0&0&1&1\\0&0&0&0&1&1\end{bmatrix} M^{R_{a_2}}_{6\times 6}=\begin{bmatrix}1&1&0&1&1&1\\1&1&0&1&1&0\\0&0&1&1&0&1\\1&1&1&1&1&1\\1&1&0&1&1&0\\1&0&1&1&0&1\end{bmatrix} M^{R_{a_3}}_{6\times 6}=\begin{bmatrix}1&1&1&1&1&1\\1&1&1&1&1&1\\1&1&1&1&1&1\\1&1&1&1&1&1\\1&1&1&1&1&1\\1&1&1&1&1&1\end{bmatrix}$$

$$M^{R_{a_4}}_{6\times 6}=\begin{bmatrix}1&0&1&1&0&1\\0&1&0&1&1&1\\1&0&1&1&0&1\\1&1&1&1&1&1\\0&1&0&1&1&1\\1&1&1&1&1&1\end{bmatrix} M^{R_{a_5}}_{6\times 6}=\begin{bmatrix}1&1&1&1&1&1\\1&1&1&1&1&1\\1&0&1&1&0&0\\1&0&1&1&0&0\\1&0&0&0&1&1\\1&0&0&0&1&1\end{bmatrix} M^{R_D}_{6\times 6}=\begin{bmatrix}1&0&1&1&1&0\\0&1&0&0&0&1\\1&0&1&1&1&0\\1&0&1&1&1&0\\1&0&1&1&1&0\\0&1&0&0&0&1\end{bmatrix}$$

Step2 The calculation of core attributes

First we add the structure discernibility matrix of all the condition attributes, namely

$$M_{sum}=\sum_{k=1}^{5} M^{R_{a_k}}_{6\times 6}=\begin{bmatrix}5&4&4&5&3&4\\4&5&3&5&4&3\\4&2&5&5&1&3\\5&4&5&5&3&3\\3&3&1&3&5&4\\4&3&3&3&4&5\end{bmatrix}$$

If $\xi_{ij}=k$, it illustrated that i and j are in the same class on k attributes. in this example, there are 5 conditional attributes, so if $\xi_{ij}=5$, i and j are in the same class on the conditional attributes. If all of the location is 5 in the i row, corresponding location in the $M^{R_D}_{6\times 6}$ is 1, x_i is in $POS_{CR_A}(D)$, so we have $POS_{CR_A}(D)=\{x_1, x_3, x_4, x_5, x_6\}$.

According to M_{sum}, we have

$CR_A(x_1)=\{x_1, x_4\}$, $CR_A(x_2)=\{x_2, x_4\}$, $CR_A(x_3)=\{x_3, x_4\}$,

$CR_A(x_4)=\{x_1, x_3, x_4\}$, $CR_A(x_5)=\{x_5\}$, $CR_A(x_6)=\{x_6\}$.

$CR_D(x_1)=\{x_1, x_3, x_4, x_5\}$, $CR_D(x_2)=\{x_2, x_6\}$, $CR_D(x_3)=\{x_1, x_3, x_4, x_5\}$,

$CR_D(x_4)=\{x_1, x_3, x_4, x_5\}$, $CR_D(x_5)=\{x_1, x_3, x_4, x_5\}$, $CR_D(x_6)=\{x_2, x_6\}$.

According to Definition 3, we have $POS_{CR_A}(D)=\{x_1, x_3, x_4, x_5, x_6\}$.

$$M_{(A-a_1)} = M_{sum} - M_{6x6}^{R_{a_1}} = \begin{bmatrix} 4 & 3 & 3 & 4 & 3 & 4 \\ 3 & 4 & 2 & 4 & 4 & 3 \\ 3 & 1 & 4 & 4 & 1 & 3 \\ 4 & 3 & 4 & 4 & 3 & 3 \\ 3 & 3 & 1 & 3 & 4 & 3 \\ 4 & 3 & 3 & 3 & 3 & 4 \end{bmatrix}$$

In order to save the storage space, we use char to Store the matrix. If $g_{ij}^{(A-a_1)} = 4$, i and j are in the same class, we use 1 to represent it ,else we use 0 to represent it.

If all of the location is 1 in the i row, corresponding location in the $M_{6x6}^{R_D}$ is 1, x_i is in $POS_{CR_{(A-a_1)}}(D)$, so we have $POS_{CR_{(A-a_1)}}(D) = \{x_3, x_4, x_5\}$.

According to $M_{(A-a_1)}$, we have

$CR_{(A-a_1)}(x_1) = \{x_1, x_4, x_6\}$, $CR_{(A-a_1)}(x_2) = \{x_2, x_4, x_5\}$, $CR_{(A-a_1)}(x_3) = \{x_3, x_4\}$,

$CR_{(A-a_1)}(x_4) = \{x_1, x_3, x_4\}$, $CR_{(A-a_1)}(x_5) = \{x_5\}$, $CR_{(A-a_1)}(x_6) = \{x_1, x_6\}$.

$POS_{CR_{(A-a_1)}}(D) = \{x_3, x_4, x_5\} \neq POS_{CR_A}(D)$.

According to Definition 4, we have a_1 is necessary of A relative to D.

The method of determining whether a_2, a_3, a_4, a_5 is core is same as the method of determining a_1, no longer list here. After calculation, we know that $\{a_1, a_2, a_4, a_5\}$ is the core attributes of A relative to D.

Step3 The calculation of attribute significance

After calculated core attributes, we with the core attributes as the opening of attribute reduction. First we add the structure discernibility matrix of the core attributes, namely

$$M_{core} = M_{6x6}^{R_{a_1}} + M_{6x6}^{R_{a_2}} + M_{6x6}^{R_{a_4}} + M_{6x6}^{R_{a_5}} = \begin{bmatrix} 4 & 3 & 3 & 4 & 2 & 3 \\ 3 & 4 & 2 & 4 & 3 & 2 \\ 3 & 1 & 4 & 4 & 0 & 2 \\ 4 & 3 & 4 & 4 & 2 & 2 \\ 2 & 2 & 0 & 2 & 4 & 3 \\ 3 & 2 & 2 & 2 & 3 & 4 \end{bmatrix}$$

If all of the location is 4 in the ith row, corresponding location in $M_{6x6}^{R_D}$ is 1, x_i is in $POS_{CR_{core}}(D)$, so we have $POS_{CR_{core}}(D) = \{x_1, x_3, x_4, x_5, x_6\} = POS_{CR_A}(D)$. According to definition 5, we have $\{a_1, a_2, a_4, a_5\}$ is the reduce of A relative to D. If the core attributes set is not the reduce of A relative to D, we will calculate the significance of the attribute in $\{A - core\}$ according definition 7. Then add the attribute whose significance is the biggest in order until find the reduce of A relative to D.

3.2 Attribute reduction algorithm based on structure discernibility matrix

In this section, we design attribute reduction algorithm based on structure discernibility matrix in the composite decision table. MRPR algorithm is a structure discernibility matrix reduction algorithm based on positive region.

Step 1 is to construct the relation matrix and its key steps are to compute the equivalence relation, the neighborhood relation, the tolerance relation, the characteristic relation. Suppose $A = \bigcup_{k=1,2,3,4} a_k$ and a_1, a_2, a_3, a_4 generate the equivalence relation, the neighborhood relation, the tolerance relation, the characteristic relation on the universe. The time complexity of computing the equivalence relation is $O(|U|)$ [19]; The time complexity of computing the neighborhood relation is $O(|U|\log|U|)$[6]; The time complexity of computing the tolerance relation is about $O(|U|)$ [20]; The time complexity of computing the characteristic relation is about $O(|U|)$ [18].

Step 2 is calculate the sum of the structure discernibility matrix of all the condition attributes and its time complexity is $O(|A||U|^2)$.

Step 3 is calculation core attributes of the condition attributes A relative to D and its time consume is $2|A||U|^2$. This step is the key step outperform previous heuristic attribute reduction algorithms by avoid the process of intersection.

Step 4 is calculation significance of attribute in A but not in core, its time complexity is $O(|A||U|^2)$.

Step 5 is add the attribute whose significance is the biggest in order until find the reduce of A relative to D. we adopt greedy and forward search algorithms. These search algorithms start with a nonempty set, and keep adding one attribute of highest significance into a pool each time until the dependence has not been increased. its time complexity is $O(|A||U|)$ [18].

Algorithm. A structure discernibility matrix reduction algorithm based on positive region (MRPR)

Input: A composite decision table $CDT = (U, A \cup D, V, f)$.
Output: A reduce of the composite decision table.
begin
1 Construct the relation matrix: $M^{R_a}_{|U|\times|U|} = (\xi^a_{ij})_{|U|\times|U|}$. // According to Definition 8
2 Calculate the sum of the structure discernibility matrix of all the condition attributes. // According to Definition 9
3 Calculation core attributes of the condition attributes A relative to D. // According to Definition 6
4 Calculation significance of attribute in A but not in core. // According to Definition 7
5 Add the attribute whose significance is the biggest in order until find the reduce of A relative to D. // According to Definition 5
end

4 Experimental analysis

The experiments are carried out on a PC with the operation system win7 (64-bit), which has 4 GB main memory and uses Inter Core (TM) i3-3240 CPU with a clock frequency of 3.40 GHz. All the algorithms are coded in C++ and complied with Dev-C++.

To test and compare the performances of the MRPR algorithms and traditional heuristic attribute reduction algorithms based on positive region (RPR)[17] and A general improved feature selection algorithm based on the positive region (FSPR)[18], we download six data sets from UCI[21]. All these data sets are outlined in Table 3.

Table 3. A description of data sets.

Data sets	Sam-ples	Attri-butes	Cla-sses
Lenses	24	4	3
Lung	32	56	3
Zoo	101	16	7
Vehicle	846	18	4
Car	1728	6	4
Chess	3196	36	2

Table 4. The time-consuming of different attribute reduction algorithms.

Data sets	Core attribute	Reduction result	MRPR time(s)	FSPR time(s)	RPR time(s)
Lenses	4	4	0.002	0.003	0.003
Lung	0	20	0.012	0.025	0.035
Zoo	2	6	0.011	0.020	0.026
Vehicle	0	4	0.747	1.665	2.419
Car	6	6	0.670	0.735	0.739
Chess	27	30	19.590	96.542	119.479

Table 4 shows the experimental result, the time is average value of 10 times reduction time-consuming. Figure 1-6 can express the results more clearly.

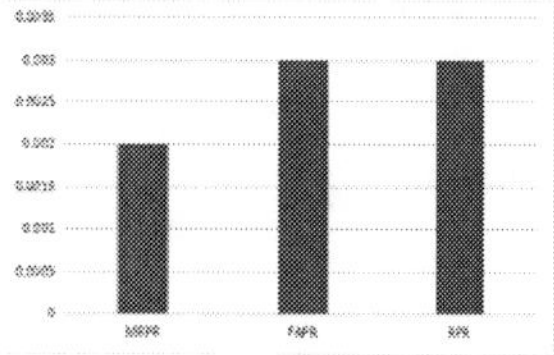

Figure 1. Lenses database

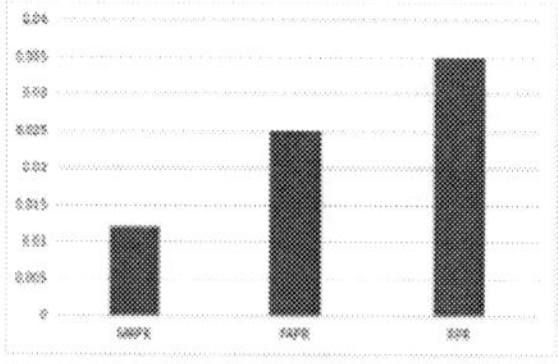

Figure 2. Lung database

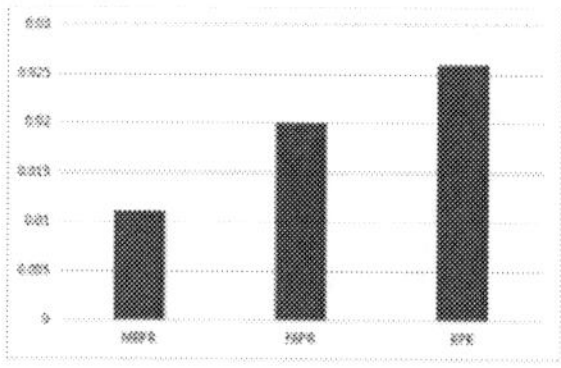

Figure 3. Zoo database

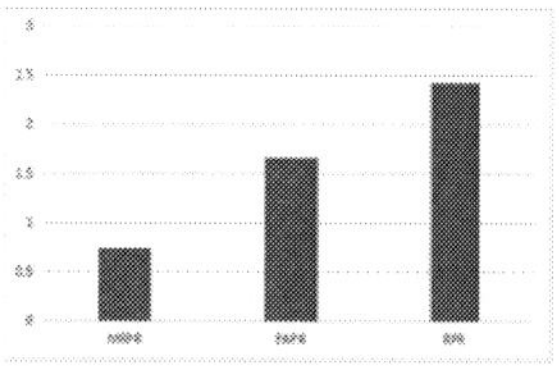

Figure 4. Vehicle database

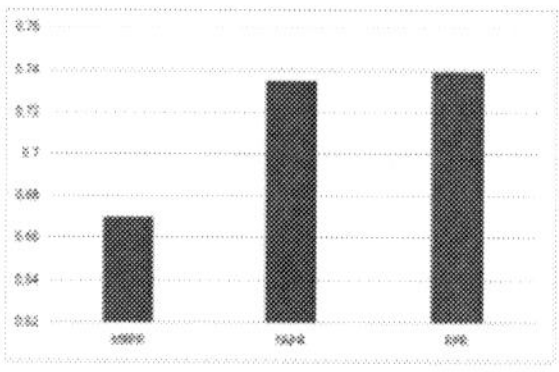

Figure 5. Car database

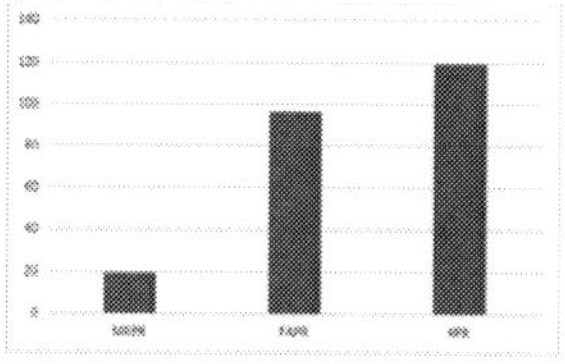

Figure 6. Chess database

We can see that the modified algorithms are faster than their original counterparts on these six data sets, which shows that the proposed structure discernibility matrix-based method can process data sets more efficiently. Sometimes, the effect of this reduction can reduce over half the computational time and even more. For example, the MRPR algorithm reduced time achieves 0.012 seconds on the data set Lung, while the reduced time is 0.025 seconds of FSPR algorithm and the reduced time is 0.035 seconds of RPR algorithm. The result on large data sets is more outstanding, For example, the MRPR algorithm reduced time achieves 19.590 seconds on the data set Chess, while the reduced time is 96.542 seconds of FSPR algorithm and the reduced time is 119.479 seconds of RPR algorithm. So the proposed structure discernibility matrix-based method can accelerate the heuristic process of attribute reduction and process large data sets more efficiently.

Conclusions

To overcome the time limitations of the existing heuristic attribute reduction schemes, in this paper, a theoretic framework based on rough set theory have been proposed, called attribute reduction algorithm based on structure discernibility matrix, which can be used to accelerate algorithms of heuristic attribute reduction. Based on this framework, a structure discernibility matrix reduction algorithm based on positive region (MRPR) has been presented. Note that the MRPR algorithm can choose the same feature subset as the previous attribute reduction algorithm. Experiment on six UCI data sets show that the modified algorithms can significantly reduce computing time of attribute reduction while producing the same attribute reductions and classification accuracy as those coming from the previous methods. The results show that the attribute reduction algorithm based on structure discernibility matrix is an effective accelerator and can efficiently obtain an attribute reduction. We will develop a parallel method to process attribute reduction in future work.

Acknowledgment

This paper was supported by the key program of Hunan Provincial Department of Science and Technology support (Project Number: 2016JC2014).

References

1. Z. Pawlak,Rough Sets[J].International Journal of Information Computer Science,1982,11(5):341-356.
2. Z. Pawlak, Rough Sets: Theoretical Aspects of Reasoning about Data, System Theory, Knowledge Engineering and Problem Solving, vol. 9, Kluwer Academic Publishers, Dordrecht, 1991.
3. Z. Pawlak, A. Skowron, Rudiments of rough sets, Information Sciences 177 (2007) 3–27.
4. D. Liu, T.R. Li, D. Ruan, J.B. Zhang, Incremental learning optimization on knowledge discovery in dynamic business intelligent systems, Journal of Global Optimization 51 (2011) 325–344, http://dx.doi.org/10.1007/s10898-010-9607-8.
5. J. Qian, D.Q. Miao, Z.H. Zhang, W. Li, Hybrid approaches to attribute reduction based on indiscernibility and discernibility relation, International Journal of Approximate Reasoning 52 (2011) 212–230.
6. Q.H. Hu, D.R. Yu, J.F. Liu, C.X. Wu, Neighborhood rough set based heterogeneous feature subset selection, Information Sciences 178 (2008) 3577–3594.
7. Y. Guan, H. Wang, Set-valued information systems, Information Sciences 176 (2006) 2507–2525.
8. Y.H. Qian, C.Y. Dang, J.Y. Liang, D.W. Tang, Set-valued ordered information systems, Information Sciences 179 (2009) 2809–2832.
9. Y. Leung, M.M. Fischer, W.Z. Wu, J.S. Mi, A rough set approach for the discovery of classification rules in interval-valued information systems,International Journal of Approximate Reasoning 47 (2008) 233–246.
10. G.Y. Wang, Extension of rough set under incomplete information systems, in: Proceedings of the 2002 IEEE International Conference on Fuzzy Systems,vol. 2, pp. 1098–1103.
11. J. Grzymala-Busse, Characteristic relations for incomplete data: a generalization of the indiscernibility relation, in: S. Tsumoto, R. Slowinski, J.Komorowski, J. Grzymala-Busse (Eds.), Rough Sets and Current Trends in Computing, Lecture Notes in Computer Science, vol. 3066, Springer, Berlin/Heidelberg, 2004, pp. 244–253.
12. J.B. Zhang, T.R. Li, H.M. Chen, Composite rough sets for dynamic data mining, Information Sciences, 2014, 257(2):81-100.
13. J.B. Zhang, T.R. Li, H.M. Chen, Composite rough sets, in: J. Lei, F. Wang, H. Deng, D. Miao (Eds.), Artificial Intelligence and Computational Intelligence, Lecture Notes in Computer Science, vol. 7530, Springer, Berlin/ Heidelberg, 2012, pp. 150–159.
14. H.M. Abu-Donia, Multi knowledge based rough approximations and applications, Knowledge-Based Systems 26 (2012) 20–29.
15. GE Hao, LI Longshu, YANG Chuanjian. Discernibility matrix-based reduct representation and quick algorithms [J]. Control and Decision, 2016, 31(1):12-20.
16. Z. Pawlak, A. Skowron, Rough sets: some extensions, Information Sciences 177 (2007) 28–40.
17. Zhang Wenxiu,Wu Weizhi,liang Jiye, The theory and method of rough set.Science Publishing Company.2003.1.
18. Y.H. Qian, J.Y. Liang, W. Pedrycz, C.Y. Dang, Positive approximation: an accelerator for attribute reduction in rough set theory, Artificial Intelligence 174 (2010) 597–618.
19. Z.Y. Xu, Z.P. Liu, B.R. Yang, W. Song, A quick attribute reduction algorithm with complexity of max(O(jCjjUj), O(jCj2jU/Cj)), Chinese Journal of Computers 29 (2006) 391–398.

20. Y.H. Qian, J.Y. Liang, F. Wang, A positive-approximation based accelerated algorithm to feature selection from incomplete decision tables, Chinese Journal of Computers 34 (2011) 435–442.
21. J. Stefanowski, A. Tsoukias, Incomplete information tables and rough classification, Computational Intelligence 17 (2001) 545–566.

Android Based GIS Terminal Design in Tobacco Distribution

Hao-Bo LI[a], Hao-Liang LI, Ming-Yuan YANG and Na WANG

Zhengzhou University, School of Information Engineering, 450001 Zhengzhou, China

Abstract. With the development of intelligent devices, Android smart device is widely used in daily life. Based on android smart device, this paper aims to implement a multifunctional GIS mobile terminal which integrates Internet communication, bar-code scanning, and LBS (Location Based Service) technologies. The GIS terminal, based on Android application designing, make it possible to optimize the management in tobacco distribution. At last, test results prove that the design of the application development can meet the expected functional requirements of the GIS system.

1 Introduction

With the development of intelligent devices, a variety of portable intellectual equipment has been applied to various industries, especially Android based intelligent terminals. Since the open source of Android system, it has been widely used and further developed. The lower cost and easy operation advantages of the Android device make it possible for integrating Android based device into the tobacco distribution GIS system.

Based on Android platform, GIS mobile terminal can extend many function modules, and provides unique functions integrated with real-time positioning, route navigation, network communication, and bar-code scanning [1]. All the functions, as is described above, depend on the wireless network technology, especially 3G or 4G network.

In conclusion, this paper designs a GIS terminal software on Android platform. The main content of this paper is summarized in the following three sections. The section two introduces mobile positioning, wireless network, bar-code recognition, and database technology. The section three presents the software application designing. In section four, it introduces the potential problem and challenge in the design.

2 The key technology

2.1 Mobile positioning technology

Mobile positioning technology uses satellite and wireless network techniques to calculate current position, by receiving signals of the satellite or base-station [1,2,3]. It's an indispensable part of the GIS system. Mobile GPS technology needs multiple satellites to get device location. Via at least four

[a] Corresponding author: ielihaobo@163.com

DOI: 10.1051/itmconf/20171101017

satellites signal, it can calculate the target's location information by a specific algorithm [4]. Similarly, wireless network positioning uses the destination between client and base-station, computing the target location.

Compared with the traditional GPS positioning technology, Baidu Map could provide a more precise location service. Using Baidu Map service, the terminal can combine GPS and GPRS to get location. It can not only improve the positioning accuracy, but also reduce the power waste of the device. Using the Baidu Map can design a comprehensive, real-time monitoring program for GIS system. As shown in Figure.1, the Baidu Map can provide multiple features for user.

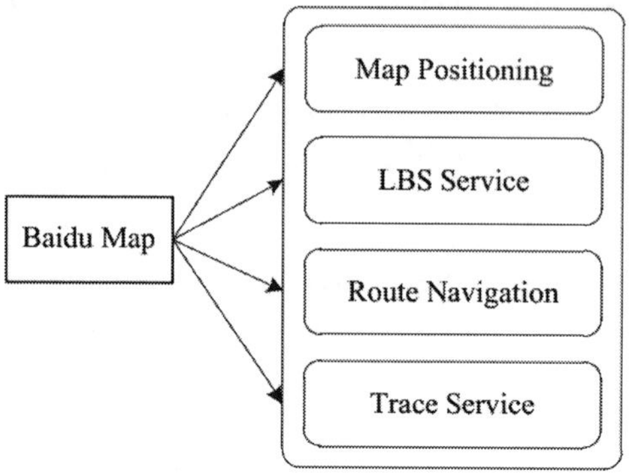

Figure 1. Some features of Baidu Map

2.2 Wireless network technology

Mobile terminal usually utilizes wireless network connect to the Internet [5]. The digital cellular network is the mainstream technology of mobile network.

Mature 3G and 4G network have been quite popular, especially 4G wireless network. With the development of network speed and signal quality, the wireless network technology can provide a very good environment for using of mobile GIS terminal.

2.3 Image processing technology

Camera equipment, providing photograph function, is usually integrated into Android devices. Native Android system contains camera software, which can open the camera to capture image or video information.

To start a camera hardware, software application calls camera interfaces in the Android system, and calls the camera driver to start the camera device, realizing image capture capability. Combined with image processing technology, the Android device enables to realize image recognition feature, identifying information from bar-codes or QR codes.

2.4 Database technology

Database technology uses a lightweight database to cache network data and geographical information data. Database cache technology will speed up data reload, and resolve the problem that data cannot be accessed from the Internet under the condition of network broken. Database designing in this paper will help improve work efficiency, facilitating data access for the user [1,3].

In this design, the terminal software uses the database operation method add data to the database, after converting network data into a special data model. To read and upload data, the terminal will query data from database and package the data into special format, then using mobile network send data to the server.

3 Software specification of GIS

3.1 Basic map service

Based on Android system, the GIS terminal can realize basic map service by using Baidu Map API. Baidu Map SDK offers rich functions such as map display and positioning, route planning, etc. Meanwhile, it provides query and playback method of historical data, that includes geographical information and customization data.

By combining GPS, GPRS, and Wi-Fi technology, the Baidu Map can obtain location information of the device. Based on this function, GIS terminal can get real-time location data of the device, then upload those data to the supervision and management system [5].

3.2 Route navigation

Traditional vehicle navigation system depends on the GPS technology. And the navigation software can analyze route data, providing route planning and guidance between current location and destination address.

Combined with basic road information and real-time traffic condition, Baidu Map navigation, depending on cloud computing, can provide users with various navigation plans under different constraints [6,7]. Using the Baidu Map navigation function, GIS terminal can recalculate navigation route under the condition of avoiding traffic congestion [8,9]. In the design of GIS software, a detection method is implemented to estimate whether the vehicle needs to recalculate navigation route. In Figure.2, it briefly shows the process of Baidu Map navigation.

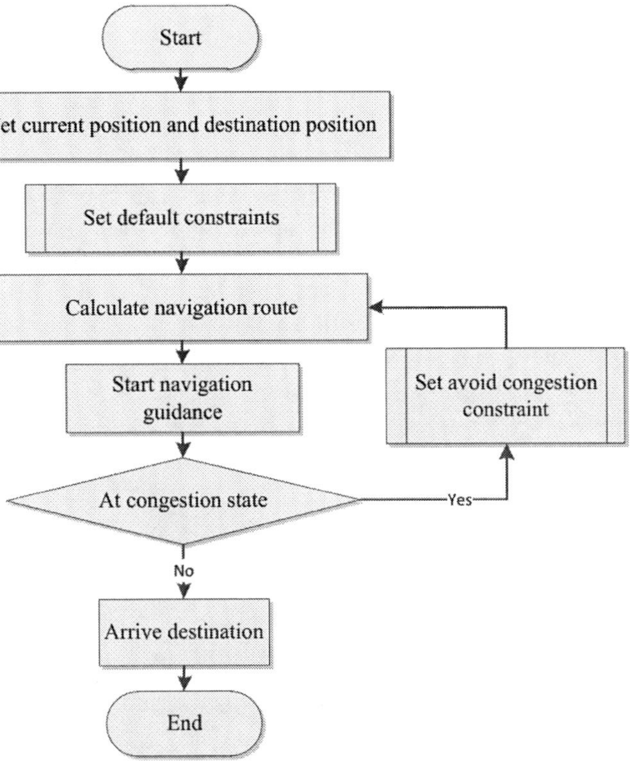

Figure 2. The process of Baidu Map Navigation

In order to test the efficiency of the terminal, we made a comparison about the cost of the time and distance, delivering from Shop A to Shop B. In Table 1, we could see a clear cut down, compared with previous condition.

Table 1. The comparison of time and distance.

	Time Cost	**Traveling Distance**
Previous	35min	13.3km
Now	25min	12.8km

3.3 Wireless network communication

Utilizing Android wireless network module and the Http network protocol, delivery personnel could transmit personal information to the supervision and management system [10,11]. Meanwhile, the terminal will start background service process to upload vehicle location information.

GIS terminal calls map positioning function to get current position information of the vehicle, and applies database operation method get local delivery state data. This information will be packaged into Json data format, and uploaded to the system server. To meet the requirement of real-time monitoring, GIS terminal device needs uninterrupted send data to the back-end server.

The terminal design uses the Http protocol to access the network data. The application software would package related information, and add working condition, geographical location and other information to the Http request. With wireless network data transmission technology, the terminal can transmit various information to the system, which will help back-end system get real-time distribution state and manage distribution process.

3.4 Bar-code scanning

Bar-code scanning technology is widely used in the logistics system to facilitate receipting of the order form. In this design, using the camera model, the terminal can parse digital information from bar-code image, that is taken by the terminal [12].

Utilizing digital image analysis technology, bar-code scanning device based on Android is different from traditional bar-code scanner. First, camera model of the device get the bar-code image. And then scanner passes over the image to produce a special stream. Through several steps decoding the stream, it will produce a stream of completely decoded symbol data. The decoded data result is extracted from the image. And finally, the result is passed to the user interface display. According to the result data, terminal can query database to get detail information of order form. The Figure.3 shows the process of bar-code decoding.

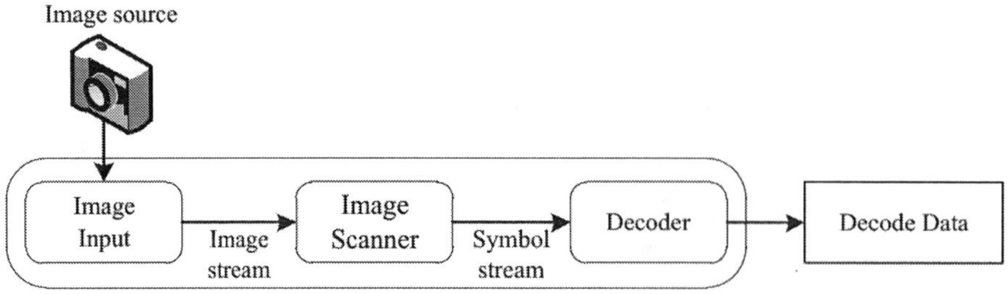

Figure 3. The process of bar-code decoding

When signing for the order, it usually spends about half an hour to completely confirm the order from. By using the function of bar-code scanning, it can be more easier and faster to finish this process. In Table 2, it shows a decrease of average time cost, during checking an order.

Table 2. An average decrease of time cost.

	Check Order	Sign for Order From
Previous	10min	5min
Now	5min	2min

4 The challenge for GIS technology on android device

GIS terminal applies wireless network to access to the back-end system, which will bring some network security risks. During data transmission, vehicle location and customer information could be leaked, that may cause huge economic losses to the operators and customers. In addition, the GIS terminals need uninterruptedly access to the network, leading to power consumption increase of the device. In summary, it requires application designers to optimize program design to overcome these challenges.

Conclusion

The conclusion of this paper can be summarized as following points. Using Baidu Map development tools, the terminal can provide positioning, route navigation and real-time guidance of route planning. Based on wireless network technology, this design implements real-time information interacting with the back-end system. And a local database is designed to cache the network data. It also integrates bar-code scanning technique to get order number from images. After completed and tested the terminal functions, the results show that the Android based GIS terminal is able to meet the expected requirements of GIS system.

References

1. Jingsong. Ge, Fang. Wang and Hui. Deng, *2013 6th International Conference on Intelligent Networks and Intelligent Systems (ICINIS)*, "An Investigation on GIS Technology for Android Embedded System", pp.312-315(2013).
2. J. Huang, Y. Zhan, W. Cui, Y. Yuan and P. Qi, *2010 International Conference on Computer Design and Applications*, "Development of a campus information navigation system based on GIS", pp.491- 494(2010).
3. S. Exauty, H. Gao, X. Wang and X. Yu, *2016 International Conference on Logistics, Informatics and Service Sciences (LISS)*, "Design of navigation system and transmitter based on GPS and GSM", pp.1-4(2016).
4. H. Guan, L. Li and X. Jia, *2013 IEEE Third International Conference on Information Science and Technology (ICIST)*, "Multi-sensor fusion vehicle positioning based on Kalman Filter", pp.296-299(2013).
5. E. D'Andrea and F. Marcelloni, *2016 IEEE International Conference on Smart Computing (SMARTCOMP)*, "Incident Detection by Spatiotemporal Analysis of GPS Data", pp.1-5(2016).
6. P. Jeefoo, *2014 International Conference on Information Science & Applications (ICISA)*, "Real-Time Field Survey Using Android-Based Interface of Mobile GIS", pp.1-3 (2014).
7. E. K. Hashi, M. R. Hasan and M. S. U. Zaman, *2016 19th International Conference on Computer and Information Technology (ICCIT)*, "GIS based heuristic solution of the vehicle routing problem to optimize the school bus routing and scheduling", pp.56-60(2016).
8. K. Yamamoto and T. Ikeda, *2016 IEEE 18th International Conference on High Performance Computing and Communications; IEEE 14th International Conference on Smart City; IEEE 2nd International Conference on Data Science and Systems (HPCC/SmartCity/DSS)*, "Social Recommendation GIS for Urban Tourist Spots", pp.50-57(2016).

9. M. Fu, W. Song, Y. Yi and M. Wang, *2015 IEEE 18th International Conference on Intelligent Transportation Systems*, "Path Planning and Decision Making for Autonomous Vehicle in Urban Environment", pp.686-692(2015).
10. A. Hrazdira, A. Cela, etc, *2012 15th International IEEE Conference on Intelligent Transportation Systems*, "Optimal Real-Time Navigation System: Application to a Hybrid Electrical Vehicle", pp.409-414(2012).
11. P. K. Arora, R. Bhatia, S. Parkash and B. J. S. Sekhon, *2015 4th International Conference on Reliability, Infocom Technologies and Optimization (ICRITO) (Trends and Future Directions)*, "Web based GPS and GIS model for rural areas", pp.1-5(2015).
12. S. F. A. Razak, C. L. Liew, C. P. Lee and K. M. Lim, *2015 IEEE Student Conference on Research and Development*, "Interactive android-based indoor parking lot vehicle locator using QR-code", pp.261-265(2015).

ITM Web of Conferences **11**, 01018 (2017) DOI: 10.1051/itmconf/20171101018
IST2017

Lung Lesion Segmentation Using Gaussian Filter and Discrete Wavelet Transform

Kamil Dimililer[1], Ali Hesri[1] and Yoney Kirsal Ever[2]

[1]*Electric and Electronic Engineering Department, Near East University, North Cyprus, Mersin 10 Turkey*
[2]*Software Engineering Department, Near East University, North Cyprus, Mersin 10 Turkey*

Abstract. Lung cancer is the growth of a tumour, referred to as a nodule that arises from cells covering the airways of the respiratory arrangement. Effective detection of lung cancer at premature stages enables any cure options, and reduce risk of insidious surgery and increased continued existence rate. Recently, image processing techniques are extensively used in different medical areas for lung tumour image improvement in early detection and cure stages. This is due to the importance of the time factor of discovering the abnormality issues in target images. The developed system is mainly an algorithm combining different image processing techniques such as filtering, erosion, discrete wavelets transform, and thresholding. However, the main aim of this work is to investigate the effectiveness of different filters along with different types of discrete wavelets toward an accurate segmentation of a lung tumour in a CT image. The experimental results of the developed system show that the use of Gaussian filter with the Haar wavelets is the best for such segmentation task.

1 Introduction

Lung cancer is thought to be the fundamental driver of cancer death around the world, and in its initial stages it is hard to identify considering the fact, that lone in the propelled organize side effects show up bringing about the death rate to be the most astounding among every single other sort of cancer [1]. In the event of lung knobs can be distinguished precisely at an early stage, the patient's survival rate can be expanded by a noteworthy rate. The rank request of cancers for both guys and females among Jordanians in 2008 demonstrated that there were 356 instances of lung cancer representing (7.7 %) of all recently analysed cancer cases in 2008 [14]. Lung cancer influenced 297 (13.1 %) guys and 59 (2.5%) females with a male to female proportion of 5:1 where lung cancer positioned second among males and tenth among females [20], [23].

The humankind pace of lung cancer is the most extreme among every single other kind of cancer. Lung cancer is one of the grimmest cancers on the planet, with the littlest proceeded with presence rate after the judgement, with a moderate yet beyond any doubt increment in the quantity of passing consistently. Writing has an extensive variety of segmentation strategies utilized as a part of lung cancer conclusion. Picture processing has wide extension in medicinal picture processing for diagnosing the lung cancer [1], [23]. The reason for this paper is to audit related work on programmed conclusion of lung cancer and run-down different segmentation and characterization methods for discovery of lung nodules. The detection of lung cancer should be possible in various routes, for example, Computed Tomography (CT), Magnetic Resonance Imaging (MRI), X-rays and sputum cytology [21], [22].

Utilizing image processing methods like pre-processing and highlight extraction, area of interest is isolated. Building up the algorithm, features like area, limit, intensity and entropy are computed from every one of the images. Tumours are characterized into two sorts. Benign tumour: Benign tumours are non-cancerous. They have a propensity to grow slowly and stay in one place, not spreading into other parts of the body. Benign tumours usually stay non-cancerous, except in very rare cases. Malignant tumour: Malignant tumours are cancerous. Cancer can commence in any one of the trillions of cells in our body. Frequently in our body new cells are generated and old cells or damaged cell will die.

2 Methodology

The developed system is to segment the lung tumour in CT images. Different image processing techniques are used to reach that goal. The images first were filtered to reduce the noise found in them and to increase their intensity pixels. In later stages, the enhanced images undergo wavelets transform techniques to extract 4 different output images that represent the horizontal, vertical, approximation, and the diagonal images. These 4 images are then summed to the reconstructed image which is the image inverse wavelet image.

The last stage is when the summed image is eroded, thresholded and then the subtraction operation takes place so that the tumour is segmented. As can be seen in figure 1 the developed segmentation system consists of different techniques that eventually lead to the lung tumour segmentation. For this purpose, two types of filters are used in addition to many types of wavelets transform as well. The results of each version of the system are different and they will be discussed in next chapters.

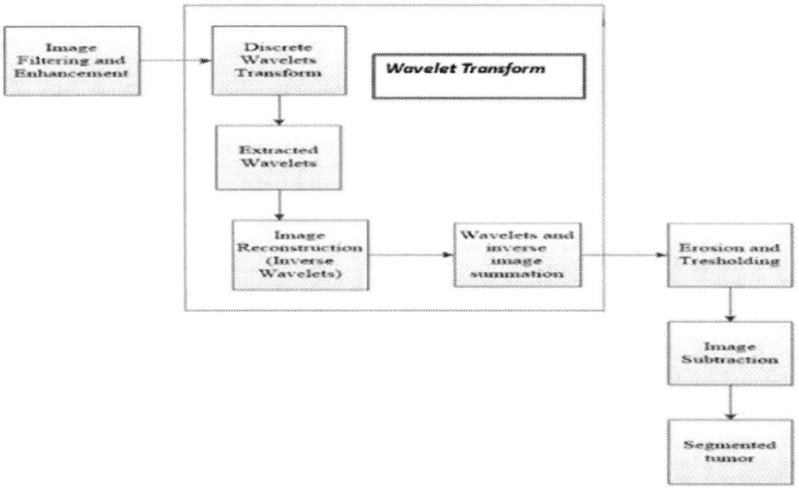

Figure 1. Proposed system flowchart.

2.1 Stage 1: Filtering of images and results

Median Filter: Median filter is utilized to lessen in-discreet commotion or the salt-and pepper noise in an image with keeping the helpful component and the edges of the image [1].

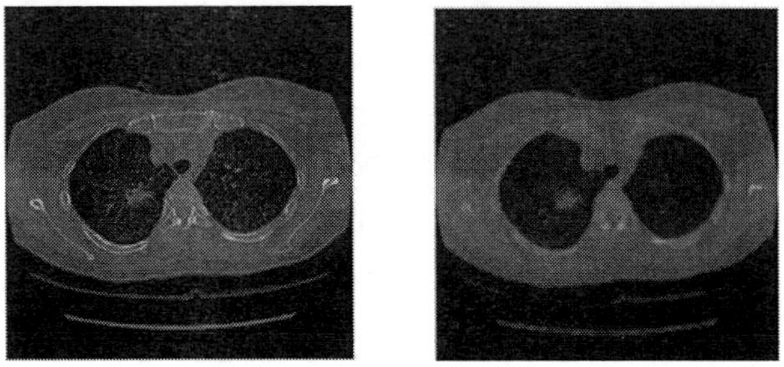

Figure 2. Median filtering.

Gaussian filter: The Gaussian filter is good when standard deviation is high since it blurring all parts which allows to the removal of the unwanted. However, applying high standard deviation is not always good for this segmentation task because the high blurring effect may also blur and the remove the tumour which is the region of interest which will lead to a low accuracy system. Therefore, the standard was selected to be 0.8 which showed good results.

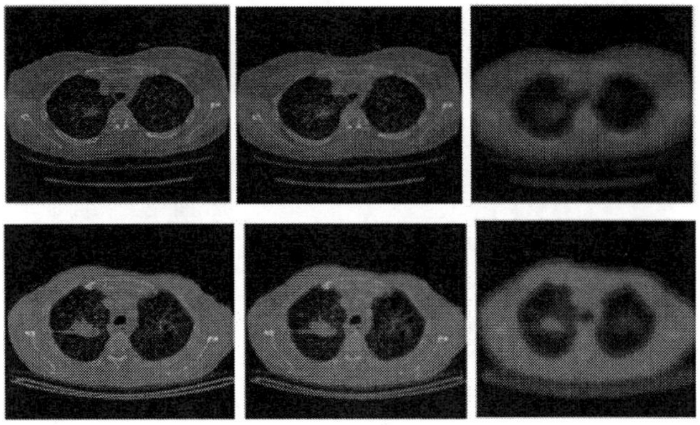

Figure 3. Gaussian filtering.

2.2 Stage 2: Transformation Wavelet transform

The wavelet transform is like the Fourier transform (or considerably more to the windowed Fourier transform) with a totally unique legitimacy function. The wavelet transformation of the image is shown below:

$$F(a,b) = \int_{-\infty}^{\infty} f(x)\, \psi^{*}_{(a,b)}(x)\, \mathrm{d}x \tag{1}$$

Discrete wavelet transform: The discrete wavelet transform (DWT) is a utilization of the wavelet transform using a discrete course of action of the wavelet scales and interpretations agreeing to some described guidelines. All things considered, this transform separates the banner into generally orthogonal course of action of wavelet, which is the essential difference from the consistent wavelet transform (CWT), or its execution for the discrete time game plan now and again called discrete-time constant wavelet transform (DT-CWT) [4].

DOI: 10.1051/itmconf/20171101018

$$\phi(x) = \sum_{k=-\infty}^{\infty} a_k \phi(Sx - k) \tag{2}$$

where S is a scaling factor (which is usually selected to be 2).

$$\int_{-\infty}^{\infty} \emptyset(x)\emptyset(x+l)\mathrm{d}x = \delta_{0,l} \tag{3}$$

Haar Wavelet: The Haar wavelet is likewise the easiest conceivable wavelet. The specialized drawback of the Haar wavelet is that it is not continuous, and subsequently not differentiable.

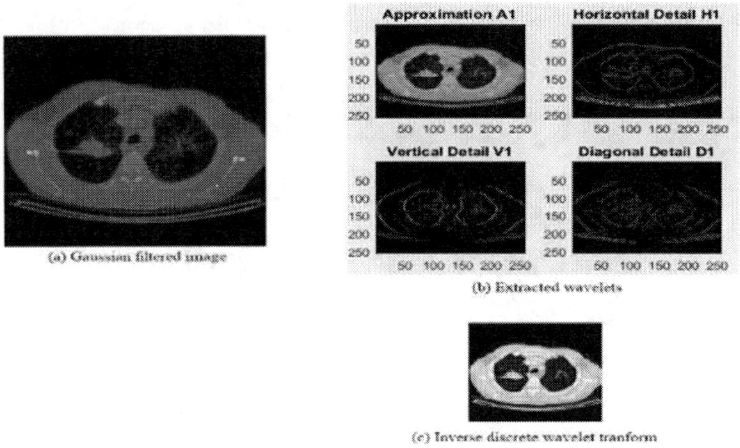

Figure 4. Haar wavelet transform with Gaussian filter.

The Haar wavelet's wavelet function $\psi(t)$ can be depicted as:

$$\psi(t) = \begin{cases} 1 & 0 \le t < \frac{1}{2}, \\ -1 & \frac{1}{2} \le t < 1, \\ 0 & \text{otherwise.} \end{cases} \tag{4}$$

Bi-orthogonal discrete wavelet: Bi-orthogonal wavelets highlight a couple of scaling functions and related scaling channels one for examination and one for union.

It can be utilized the wavelet with the more noteworthy number of vanishing minutes for examination bringing about a meagre representation, while the smoother wavelet for recreation is utilized.

Inverse discrete wavelet transform: The Haar transform *yn* of an n-input function *xn* is

$$y_n = H_n x_n \tag{5}$$

The Haar transform matrix is real and orthogonal. Thus, the inverse Haar transform can be derived [19].

2.3 Stage 3: Summation of enhanced images

After getting the 4 different wavelets from the image, the image is reconstructed using the inverse discrete wavelets transform. Then, these images are summed together to obtain a clearer and enhanced image where the tumour is well defined and separated from the other parts of the image. This addition operation helps to segment the tumour in later [12].

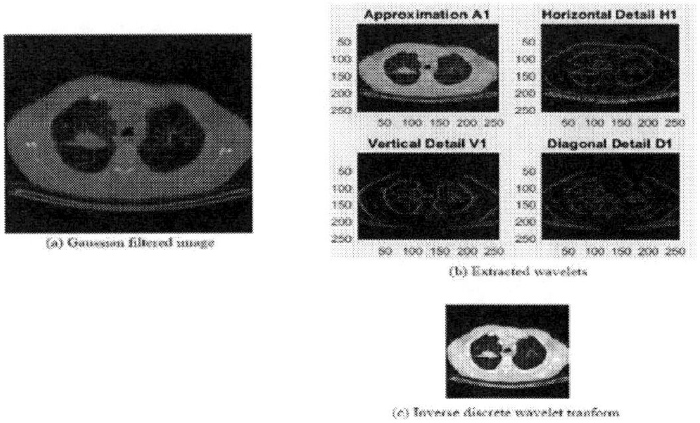

Figure 5. Biorthogonal discrete wavelet transform with Gaussian filter.

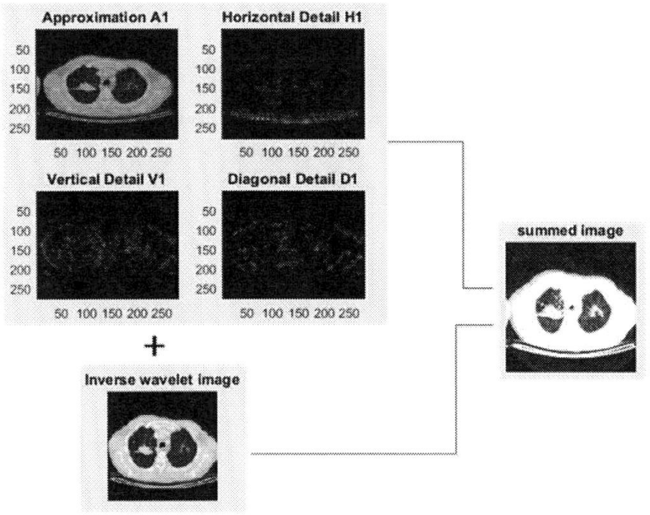

Figure 6. Summation of Haar wavelet and reconstructed image.

The filter used here is the Gaussian filter.

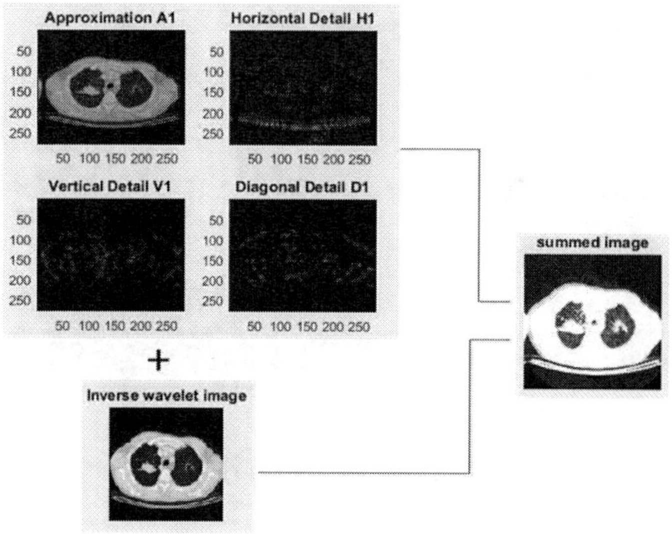

Figure 7. Summation of "Bior 3.7" wavelets and reconstructed image.

The filter used here is the median filter.

2.4 Stage 4: Erosion

Morphology technique can be de-fined as a group of image processing operations that process images based on shapes. These morphological operations depend on applying an organizing component to an input image with a specific end goal to make a yield image of a similar size [15].

2.5 Stage 5: Thresholding

Thresholding is the detachment of district of images into two areas. One district compares to the frontal area locale, in which it contains the articles that we are keen on. The other area is the foundation, compares to the un-needed items [14].

Amid thresholding, every pixel is contrasted with that edge value. On the off chance that the pixel value is more prominent than that edge, then this pixel is considered as frontal area pixel (white). In the event, that the pixel value is lower than that limit value, then the pixel is considered as foundation pixel (black) [1].

2.6 Stage 6: Image subtraction

Image subtraction is a basic tool for the analysis, processing, and interpreting of medical images.

3 Results and discussions

The developed system was tested on 70 images. Among them, 50 are lung images with tumour, and 20 are non-tumour images. The same images were used for testing the different versions of the developed system to investigate the effectiveness of each. For each version of the developed system the accuracy of the tumour and non-tumour lungs were calculated. Then the total accuracy was calculated.

The accuracy was defined as the number of the correctly segmented tumours divided by the total number of images.

$$ACC=P/N$$

where P is the number correctly segmented images, and N is the total number of images. The tables below show the accuracies of the system developed.

- Table 1 shows the accuracy of the system when the Gaussian filters and Haar wavelet type used
- Table 2 shows the accuracy of the system when the Median filter and Haar wavelet type is used.
- The table 3 shows the Bi-orthogonal 3.7 wavelets along with the median filter.
- Table 4 shows the same wavelets type but within the Gaussian filter.
- The table 5 and 6 show the median filter and Gaussian filter with the Bi-orthogonal 3.5 wavelets
- The table 7 shows the use of median filter together with the Db7 wavelets.

Table 1. Gaussian filter and Haar wavelet.

Dataset	Filter type	Discrete Wavelet transform type	Correctly segmented images	Total Recognition
Abnormal images (50)	Gaussian filter	Haar wavelet	46/50	96%
Normal images (20)	Gaussian filter	Haar wavelet	20/20	100%
System Performance	96%			

Table 2. Median filter and Haar wavelet.

Dataset	Filter type	Discrete Wavelet transform type	Correctly segmented images	Total Recognition
Abnormal images (50)	Median filter	Haar wavelet	39/50	78%
Normal images (20)	Median filter	Haar wavelet	20/20	100%
System Performance	89%			

Table 3. Gaussian filter and Bi-orthogonal 3.7 wavelet.

Dataset	Filter type	Discrete Wavelet transform type	Correctly segmented images	Total Recognition
Abnormal images (50)	Gaussian filter	Bi-orthogonal 3.7	43/50	86%
Normal images (20)	Gaussian filter	Bi-orthogonal 3.7	20/20	100%
System Performance	93%			

Table 4. Median filter and Bi-orthogonal 3.7 wavelet.

Dataset	Filter type	Discrete Wavelet transform type	Correctly segmented images	Total Recognition
Abnormal images (50)	Median filter	Bi-orthogonal 3.7	44/50	88%
Normal images (20)	Median filter	Bi-orthogonal 3.7	20/20	100%
System Performance	94%			

Table 5. Median filter and Bi-orthogonal 3.5 wavelet.

Dataset	Filter type	Discrete Wavelet transform type	Correctly segmented images	Total Recognition
Abnormal images (50)	Median filter	Bi-orthogonal 3.5	42/50	84%
Normal images (20)	Median filter	Bi-orthogonal 3.5	20/20	100%
System Performance	92%			

Table 6. Median filter and Db7 wavelet.

Dataset	Filter type	Discrete Wavelet transform type	Correctly segmented images	Total Recognition
Abnormal images (50)	Median filter	Db7 wavelet.	38/50	76%
Normal images (20)	Median filter	Db7 wavelet.	17/20	85%
System Performance	80.5%			

Table 7. Median filter and Db4 wavelet.

Dataset	Filter type	Discrete Wavelet transform type	Correctly segmented images	Total Recognition
Abnormal images (50)	Median filter	Db4 wavelet	41/50	82%
Normal images (20)	Median filter	Db4 wavelet	18/20	90%
System Performance	91%			

The experimental results of the developed system show that the use of Gaussian filter with the Haar wavelet is the best for such segmentation task. This is shows in table 1 where the accuracy is the highest 96%. It can be seen that, the use of median filter with Haar wavelet lead to less effectiveness in segmenting the tumour where the accuracy is 89% shown in table 2. The table 3 shows the use of Gaussian filter along with the Bi-orthogonal wavelet (Bior 3.7). this table shows an 93% accuracy which is good but still less than the results shows in table 1 where Haar wavelet and Gaussian filter are used. The median filter was then used with the Bi-orthogonal wavelets (Bior 3.7), but the results were different here. The accuracy was 94% which is higher than the previous one where the Gaussian filter is used. This shows that Gaussian is not always good for getting higher accuracy. It depends on the type of wavelets transform used also. A different type of Bi-orthogonal wavelet was used (Bior 3.5) in table 5 with the median filter and the accuracy was 92% which is less than the Bior 3.7 accuracy although the same filter was used. In contrast, the median filter was also used with the Db4 wavelet transform in table 7 and it showed good segmentation results of 91% which is better than the results of table 6 where the Db7 is used. Thus, the results were always better when Haar wavelet type was used.

4 Conclusions and future work

This paper proposed method de-scribes a method for the segmentation lung tumour in CT scan images Thus it can be concluded that the proposed system performs fine and is robust against anatomical variations of the lungs. During the experiment, different discrete wavelet transforms were used with two types of filtering. After which, the Haar and Gaussian filtering with 96% accuracy was found to be the best. Thus, this algorithm showed an efficient and accurate result for segmenting the lung tumour in CT medical images and it will help radio-gist as second opinion for the better diagnosis of lung cancer.

References

1. Eng, H. L., and Ma, K. K. (2001).Noise adaptive soft-switching median filter, IEEE Transactions on Image Processing, 10(2), 242251.
2. Yujin, Z., (2006). Image Engineering (I): Image Processing. Second Edition. Japan: Tsinghua University Press.
3. Calderbank A. R., Daubechies I., Sweldens W., Yeo B. L.: Wavelet transforms that map integers to integers. Applied and Computational Harmonics Analysis, 5(3), 332369.
4. Daubechies, I. Recent results in wavelet applications. Journal of Electronic Imaging 7.4 (1998): 719-724.
5. Daubechies, I., & Sweldens, W. (1998). Factoring wavelet transforms into lifting steps. Journal of Fourier analysis and applications, 4(3), 247-269.
6. Davis, G. M., & Nosratinia, A. (1999). Wavelet-based image coding: an overview. In Applied and computational control, signals, and circuits (pp. 369-434). Birkhuser Boston.
7. Sonka M., Hlavac V., Boyle R.: Image processing, Analysis and Machine Vision. Brooks/Cole Publishing Comp.1999.
8. Haar, A. "Zur Theorie der orthogonalen Funktionen systeme", Math. Ann. 69, 331- 371, 1910.
9. Strang, G. "Wavelet Transforms Ver-sus Fourier Transforms", Bull. Amer. Math. Soc. 28, 288-305, 1993.
10. Davis G., Strela V., Turcajova R.; Multi wavelet Construction via the Lifting Scheme. Wavelet Analysis and Multi resolution Methods, T. X. He (editor), Lecture Notes in Pure and Applied Mathematics, Marcel Dekker.
11. Kim, Y. T. (1997). Contrast enhancement using brightness preserving bi-histogram equalization. IEEE transactions on Consumer Electronics, 43(1), 1-8.
12. Wang, Y., Chen, Q., & Zhang, B. (1999). Image enhancement based on equal area dualistic sub-image histogram equalization method. IEEE Transactions on Consumer Electronics, 45(1), 68-75.
13. Seil, M., Obuz, F., Altay, C., Gencel, Igci, E., Sagol, ., & Dicle, O. (2008). The role of dynamic subtraction MRI in detection of hypocellular carcinoma. Diagnostic and Interventional Radiology, 14(4), 2004.
14. Sezgin, M. (2004). Survey over image thresholding techniques and quantitative performance evaluation. Journal of Electronic imaging, 13(1), 146-168.

15. Lim, Y. W., & Lee, S. U. (1990). On the colour image segmentation algorithm based on the thresholding and the fuzzy c-means techniques. Pattern recognition, 23(9), 935-952.
16. Dimililer, K. (2013). Back propagation Neural Network Implementation for Medical Image Compression. Journal of Applied Mathematics.
17. Dimililer K (2012) "Neural network implementation for image compression of X- rays", Electronic World 118 (1911):26-29.
18. Khashman A., Dimililer K (2005) "Compression criteria for optimum Image compression", The International Conference on Computer as a Tool, 2005, dx.doi.rog/10.1109/EURCON. 2005.1630100.
19. Sonka M., Hlavac V., Boyle R.: Image processing, Analysis and Ma-chine Vision. Brooks/Cole Publishing Comp.1999.
20. Adnan Khashman, Boran Sekeroglu, Kamil Dimililer, "Intelligent Coin Identification System", Proceedings of the 2006 IEEE International Symposium on Intelligent Control Munich, Germany, (2006).
21. Dimililer, K., & Ilhan A., Effect of image enhancement on mri brain images with neural networks, Proc Comp Sci, 102, 39-44 (2016)
22. Dimililer, K., Kirsal Ever, Y., & Ratemi H., Intelligent eye tumour detection system, Proc Comp Sci, 102, 325-332 (2016)
23. Dimililer, K., Kirsal Ever, Y., & Ugur B., ILTDS: Intelligent lung tumor detection system on ct images. Int J Intell Syst, 530, 225-235 (2016)

DOI: 10.1051/itmconf/20171101019

Discrimination of Different Types Damage of Tomato Seedling by Electronic Nose

Shao-Ming CHENG, Jun WANG[a], Yong-Wei WANG and Zhen-Bo WEI

College of Bio-systems Engineering and Food Science, Zhejiang University, Hangzhou, 310058, PR. China

Abstract: The profiles of volatile compounds emitted by plants varies in response to different damage.The potential of electronic nose technology to monitor such changes,with the aim of diagnosing plant health was investingted.An electronic nose(E-nose)was used to analyse tomato seedlings that were subjected to differnent types of damage(infection by Early blight disease, infection by Gray mold disease, mechanically damage, and undamaged). Principal component analysis(PCA),linear discrimination analysis(LDA),back-propagation neural network(BPNN),and support vector machine (SVM) network were used to evaluate the E-nose data.The results indicated that the E-nose can successfully discriminate between tomato seedling with different types of damage. The results of PCA and LDA showed that clusters of data were divided into 3 groups (ZP, HP, and CP/MP). Samples from groups CP and MP overlapped partially. Back-propagation neural network (BPNN) and support vector machine (SVM) network were used to evaluate the E-nose data. Good discrimination results were obtained using SVM and BPNN. The results demonstrate that it is plausible to use E-nose technology as a method for monitoring damage in tomato seedling.

1 Introduction

Plants increase the amount of volatile compounds that they release when they were damaged by insects or diseases. A number of studies have demonstrated that plants respond to damage with releasing a variety of volatiles [1-3]. Over the past decade, there has been significant progress in plant volatile research as a result of the increasing sensitivity of analytical instrumentation and improvements in molecular and biochemical analyses. However, this method involves several stages which makes it time consuming, especially at the stage of volatile-compound trapping and sample preparation. In addition, the technology is very expensive, the equipment is bulky, and the analysis requires skilled analysts. Therefore, it is not suitable for use in a warning system for plant insects and disease attacks in a commercial plant-growing setting.

An electronic nose (E-nose) system is sensor-based technology that measures total headspace volatiles and creates a unique smell print. An E-nose does not resolve the sample's volatiles into individual components but rather responds to the whole set of volatiles in a unique digital pattern. This pattern is the signature of a particular set of aromatic compounds. For each process or application of interest, a database of such digitized patterns is created, called the training set. When an unknown sample is exposed to the E-nose sensors, the E-nose first digitizes the sample's volatiles, and then

[a] Corresponding author: jwang@zju.edu.cn

DOI: 10.1051/itmconf/20171101019

compares the resulting pattern with the existing training set. Its principle is different from that of chemical analysis methods such as gas and liquid chromatography, mass spectrometry, nuclear magnetic resonance, and spectrophotometry. The E-nose does not resolve the sample's volatiles into its individual components but responds to the whole set of volatiles in a unique digital pattern. E-nose technology has been successfully used in a variety of applications, including food quality and control [5,6,14], environmental monitoring [7,17,18], micro-organism identification (Magan et al., 2000), medical and health detection [15,16] and plant monitoring [9-13]. Recently, more research has been directed towards early detection of insect and disease attack. This technology has been used to differentiate volatile profiles from tomato, cucumber, and pepper leaves damaged by spider mites and beet armyworm [4,8]. The E-nose technology is rapid, sensitive, specific, non-destructive, and easy to use. Unlike GC-MS, the E-nose does not require prolonged pre-concentration intervals and is appealing as a potential technology for monitoring changes in disease-induced plant volatiles signatures. However, little information about E-nose monitoring of damaged tomato seedlings has been reported.

The objective of the present study was to determine the feasibility of detecting tomato seedling damage caused by the Early blight disease, the Gray mold disease, mechanical means damage and undamaged control seedlings utilizing an E-nose (PEN2). The aim was to develop discrimination models of E-nose signals for different types of damage. Principal component analysis (PCA), linear discrimination analysis (LDA), back-propagation neural network (BPNN) and support vector machine (SVM) network were used to verify the classification capacity of the proposed methods.

2 Materials and Methods

2.1 Electronic nose

In this study, a PEN2 (Airsense Analytics, Germany) E-nose, equipped with 10 different metal oxide semiconductor (MOS) sensors was used. The PEN2 system consists of a sampling apparatus, a detector unit containing the array of sensors, and pattern recognition software (WinMuster v.1.6) for data recording. The sensor array is composed of positioned in a small chamber. Each sensor has a certain degree of affinity towards specific chemicals or volatile compounds. Table 1 lists all the sensors used and their main application.

Table 1. Sensors used and their main application in PEN2

Number in array	Sensor-name	General description	Reference
S1	W1C	Aromatic compounds	Toluene,10 ppm
S2	W5S	Very sensitive, broad range sensitivity, react on nitrogene oxides, very sensitive with negative signal	NO_2, 1ppm
S3	W3C	Ammonia, used as sensor for aromatic compounds	Propane, 1ppm
S4	W6C	Mainly hydrogen, selectively(breath gases)	H_2, 100ppb
S5	W5C	Alkanes, aromatic compounds, less polar compounds	Propane, 1ppm
S6	W1S	Sensitive to methane (environment)ca.10ppm. Broad rang, similar to No.8	CH_3,100ppm
S7	W1W	Reacts on sulfur compounds, H_2S 0.1ppm. Otherwise sensitive to many terpenes and sulfur organic compounds, with are important for smell, limonene, pyrazine	H_2S, 1ppm
S8	W2S	Detects alcohol's, partially aromatic compounds, broad range	CO, 100ppm
S9	W2W	Aromatic compounds, sulfur organic compounds	H_2S, 1ppm
S10	W3S	Reacts on high concentrations>100ppm,sometime very selective(methane)	H_2S, 1ppm CH_3,10 CH_3,100ppm

DOI: 10.1051/itmconf/20171101019

Figure.1 shows a schematic diagram of the PEN2 E-nose measurements during the experiments.Each tomato seedling was enclosed in a cylindrical stainless steel support(400 mm high×100mm internal diameter) covered with a plastic bag over the top.The plastic bag was a colourless and odourless food-grade polyethylene bag(0.08mm thick).The plant was sealed at the lower stem by 2 hermetic boards with a hole in the middle.This excluded the ordour coming from the medium.The plant was kept at room temperature (28±2℃) for 20 min before static headspace sampling was begun.

Before each measurement, the E-nose system was cleaned with zero-air(air filtered on active carbon).The main purpose of this was to clean the circuit and to return the sensors to their baselines.During the measurement,the headspace gas of a plant was pumped into the sensor chamber at a constantrate of 200 ml min-1 through a Teflon tube (3mm) connected to a needle.When the headspace gas that had accumulated in the bag was pumped into the sensor chamber,the ratio of conductance of each sensor changed.The response of each sensor was expressed as a ratio of conductance(G/G0;G and G0 are the respective conductivities of the sensors when the seedling gas and the zero gas pass over).The measuement procedure was controlled by a computer program.The measurement time was 65s,which was sufficient for the sensors to reach stable values.The interval for data collection was 1s.A computer recorded the response of the E-nose every second.The fulsh time was set to 40s.When the measurement was completed,the acquered data was stored for later use.

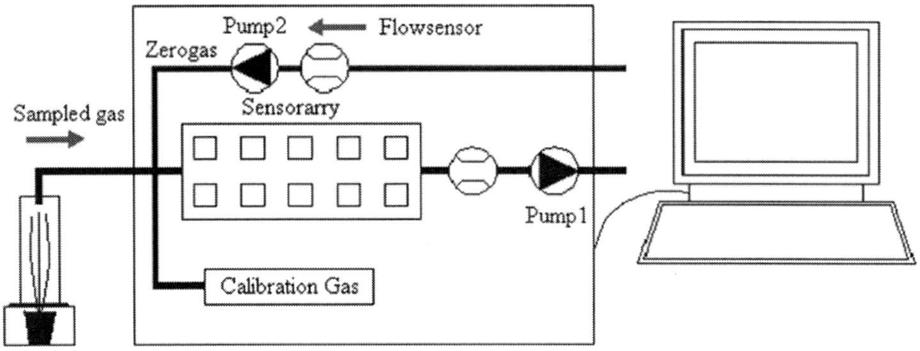

Figure 1. Schematic diagram of the electronic nose measurements of PEN2

2.2 Tomato seedlings

The variety of tomato seedling was ZheZa 809. Pre-germinated seeds were sown at common clay pots (80 mm diameter and 100 mm high) in greenhouse where the temperature was maintained at 28±2℃ and relative humidity (RH) was 70-80%. Plants were managed daily. After 35 days, uniform-tomato seedlings were selected for the experiment.

2.3 Plant treatment

In this study,4 treatments were tested: (1)damage caused by Early blight disease(EP),(2)damage caused by Gray mold disease(GP),(3)mechanically damage(MP), and(4)undamaged(CP).

First the Pathogenic bacteria of Early blight disease and Gray mold disease were training at laboratory, and then the diseases were vaccinated to 35 day tomaot seedlings, respectively. The vaccinated tomato seedlings were kept with high temperature and high RH for 48h.

For the Early blight disease treatment, 4 leaves disease infection were used per tomato seedling. For the Gray mold disease, also 4 leaves disease infection were used per tomato seedling. For the mechanical damage treatment, a single tomato seedling was punched 90 times with a

DOI: 10.1051/itmconf/20171101019

needle(0.8x26mm).Sixty-four plants were sellected for the experiment,and there were 16 replicates for each treatment.

2.4 Data analysis

In this study,the data was subjected to different statistical analyses,including Principal component analysis (PCA), linear discrimination analysis(LDA),back-propagation neural network(BPNN),and support vector machine (SVM) network.All statistical analyses were conducted with SAS v.8 and Matlab 7.0.

3 Results and discussion

3.1 Electronic nose responses to tomato seedling volatiles

Figure. 2 shows the typical responses of 10 sensors during measurements on a tomato seedling. Each curve represents the variation in conductivity of each sensor with time. Electro-value changes when the volatiles from the tomato seedling reach the measurement chamber. The response signal was measured and expressed as, where G and G0 are the resistance of a sensor in clean air and in a detecting gas, respectively. It is clear that the ratio of G/G0 was close to 1.0 at the initial period, then increased or decreased gradually,and stabilized after about 60s.The signals of each sensor at response 60s were used in the subsequent analyses.

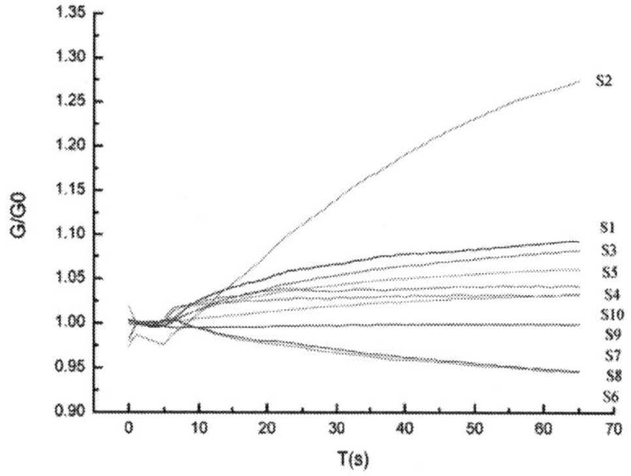

(a) Control tomato seedling

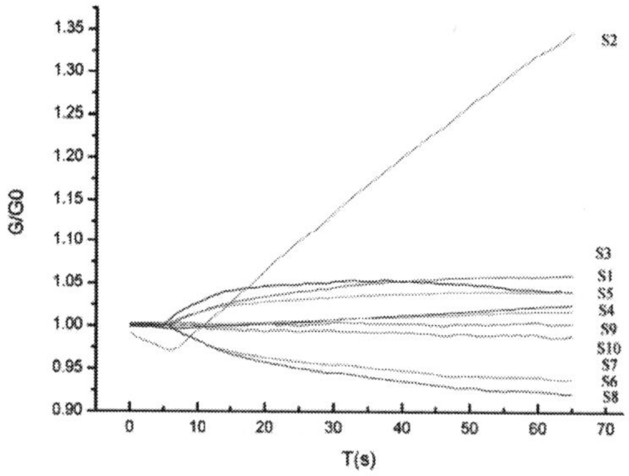

(b) mechanical damage tomato seedling

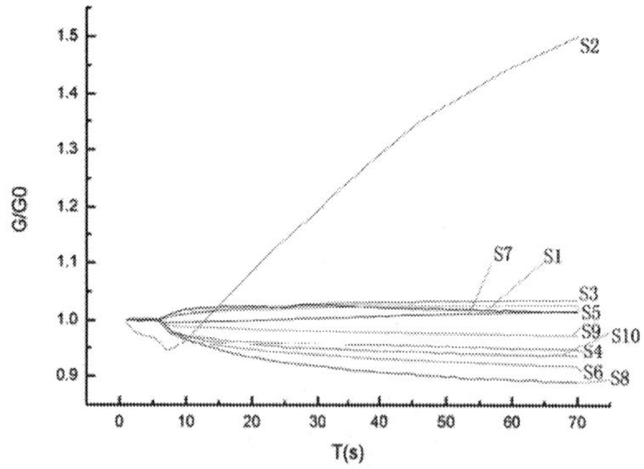

(c) Early blight disease damage tomato seedling

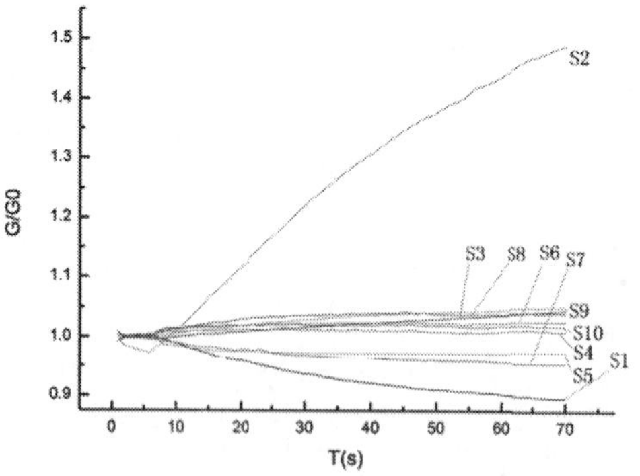

(d) Gray mold disease damage tomato seedling

Figure 2. Response curve of 10 sensors to tomato seedling volatiles

DOI: 10.1051/itmconf/20171101019

3.2 Signal analysis

Figure.3 shows the changes of the sensor signals in response to tomato seedling with different types of damage. Each point represents the mean value of each sensor's response signal to tomato seedlings,linked to the measurements of conductantce increases or decreases experienced by the sensors.The E-nose sensor response changed by tomato seedling with 4 different types of treatments.The values of the sensor response singnals differed with the different types of damange.The variation in the sensor responses in the CP was small compared to the 3 groups of damaged tomato seedlings(Figure.3).This result is due to the specific changes in the chemical composition in tomato seedlings after the damage.

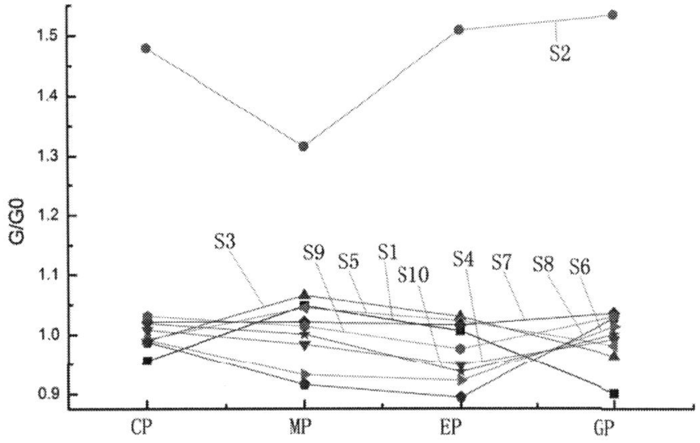

Figure 3. Value of each sensor's response to tomato seedling with different types of damage (CP, control seedlings; MP, mechanically damaged seedlings; EP, seedlings infected by Early blight disease; GP,seedlings infected by Gray mold disease)

3.3 PCA and LDA analysis

PCA and LDA are commonly used techniques for data classification and dimensionality reduction. The data from 64 samples (16 samples from each group) obtained by the E-nose for 4 tomato seedling groups were used for the PCA.Fig.4 shows the results of the PCA. The first component contributed 59.93% of the total variance; the second component, 33.01%.This added up to 92.94% in total. In Fig.4, clusters of data were divided into 3 groups (CP/MP, EP and GP).Samples from groups EP and GP were easily discriminated, whereas samples from groups CP and MP overlapped partially. PCA did not clearly discriminate between these different types of tomato seedlings. Therefore, LDA was used for further separation of the tomato seedling samples.

The results of the LDA are shown in Figure.5. Function1(LD1) contributed 85.83% of the total variance; Fuction2(LD2),10.52%,adding up to a total of 96.35%.In the LDA plot, 4 groups of tomato seedling samples could be clearly distinguished. The separation of the samples was better using LDA than using PCA.

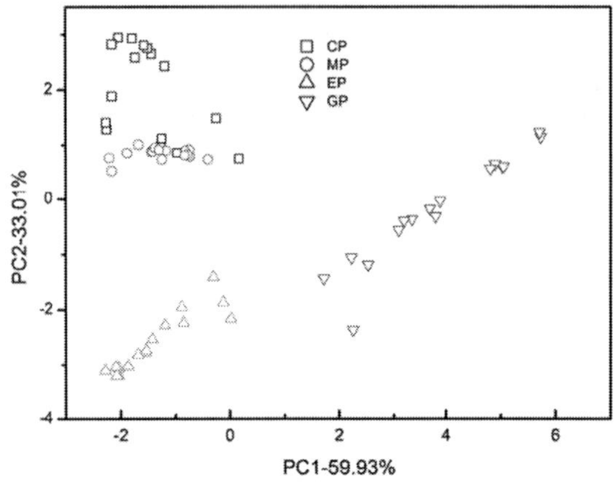

Figure 4. PCA plot for tomato seedlings with different types of damage (CP, control seedlings; MP, mechanically damaged seedlings; EP, seedlings infected by Early blight disease; GP,seedlings infected by Gray mold disease)

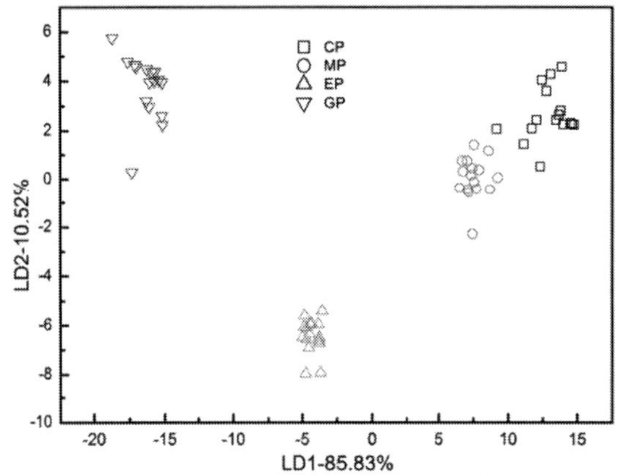

Figure 5. LDA plot for tomato seedlings with different types of damage (CP, control seedlings; MP, mechanically damaged seedlings; EP, seedlings infected by Early blight disease; GP,seedlings infected by Gray mold disease)

3.4 BPNN and SVM

In this study, sixty-four samples (16 duplicates for each of the 4 groups) were divided into 2 groups: 40 samples (10 samples of each group) for the training set and 24 samples (6 samples of each group) for testing set.

For the BPNN, the chosen architecture of the artificial neural network was a 10-15-1 three-layer back-propagation according to Kolmogorov's theorem. The 10 input neurons correspond to the data obtained by 10 sensors, while the 1 output is the different types of damage. The training function is 'traingda' and the training epoch is 2000.The training parameters were chosen a epoch of 0.01 and a goal of 0.001.The result is shown in Table 2.The correct rate of the training set was 100%.The correct rates of the testing set for the CP, MP, EP and GP groups were 100%, 100%, 83.3%, and 100%, respectively.

The SVM network also had 10 and 1 neurons in the input and output layers, respectively. The kernel function used in this paper was 'radial basis kernel function'. The SVM analysis showed an overall classification success of 100% for the training sets and 95.8% for the testing sets. The result is shown in Table 2.The results indicate that it is possible to use E-nose signals to discriminate between tomato seedlings with different types of damage.

Table 2. Results of BPNN and SVM analyses for tomato seedling with different types of damage

Network style	Correct rate of training set	Correct rate of testing set			
		CP	MP	EP	GP
BPNN	100%	100%	100%	83.3%	100%
SVM	100%	100%	100%	83.3%	100%

Conclusions

To sum up, the results prove that the E-nose PEN 2 can successfully distinguish between tomato seedlings with different types of damage (infection by Early blight disease, infection by Gray mold disease, mechanically damage, and undamaged). The LDA discriminates more effectively between the different groups than the PCA. Good discrimination results are obtained in BPNN and SVM. The results demonstrate that it is plausible to use E-nose technology as a method for monitoring damage in tomato seedling.

Acknowledgement

The first author acknowledges the financial grant from the National Natural Science Foundation of China (Grant No. 31370555).

References

1. Kessler, I.T.Baldwin.Defensive function of herbivore-induced plant volatile emissions in nature. Science, **291**(2001):2141-2144
2. Y.J.Lu,X.Wang,Y.G.Lou,J.A.Cheng.Role of ethylene signaling in the production of rice volatiles induced by the rice brown planthopper Nilaparvata lugens, Chines Science Bulletin, **51**(2006):2457-2465
3. Y.G. Lou, X.Y. Hua, T.C.J.Turlings, J.A.Cheng, X.X.Chen, G.Y.Ye.Differences in induced volatile emissions among rice varieties result in differential attraction and parasitism of Nilaparvata lugens eggs by the parasitoid Anagrus nilaparvatae in the field, Journal of Chemical Ecology,**32**(2006):2375-2387
4. J.Laothawornkitkul,J.P.Moore,J.E.Taylor,M.Possell,T.D.Gibson,C.N.Hewitt,N.D.Paul.Discrimina tion of plant volatile signatures by an electronic nose: a potential technology for plant pest and disease monitoring, Environmental Science and Technology, **42**(2008):8433-8439
5. A.H.Gomez,J.Wang,G.X.Hu,A.G.Perira.Discrimination of storage shelf-life for mandarin by electronic nose technique, LWT-Food Science and Technology,**40**(2007):681-689
6. L.Pang,J.Wang,X.Lu,H.Yu.Discrimination of storage age for wheat by E-nose, Transactions of the ASABE,**51**(2008):1707-1712
7. A.C. Bastos,N.Magan.Potential of an electronic nose for the early detection and differentiation between Stretomyces in potable water, Sensors and Actuators B:Chemical,**116**(2006):151-155
8. N.Magan,P.Evans.Volatiles as indicator of fungal activity and differentiation between species, and the potential use of electronic nose technology for early detection of grain spoilage, Journal of Stored Products Research,**36**(2000):319-340

9. M. Kunert,A.Biedermann,T.Koch,W.Boland.Ultrafast sampling and analysis of plant volatiles by a hand-held miniaturized GC with pre-concentration unit: kinetic and quantitative aspects of plant volatile production, Journal of Separation Science,**25**(2002):677-684
10. R.M.Jansen,J.W.Hofstee,J.Wildt,F.W.Verstappen,H.J.Bouwmeester,E.J.vahenten.Induced plant volatiles allow sensitive monitoring of plant health status in greenhouse, Plant Signal Behav.,**4**(2009):824-829
11. H.M.Zhang,J.Wang.Detection of age and insect damage incurred by wheat with an electronic nose, Journal of Stored Products Research,**43**(2007):489-495
12. W.G.Henderson,A.Khalilian,Y.J.Han,J.K.Greeme,D.C.Degemjardt.Detecting stink bugs/damage in cotton utilizing a portable electronic nose, Computers and Electronics in Agriculture,**70**(2010):157-162
13. B.Zhou,J.Wang.Use of electronic nose technology for identifying rice infestation by Nilaparvata lugens, Sensors and Actuators B:Chemical,**160**(2011):15-21
14. S.Cheng,Y.Wang,J.Wang,Z.Wei,Q.Lu.Detection of eggshell crack using electronic nose[J]. Transactions of the ASABE, **53**(2010):789-794
15. J.Dummer,M.Storer,M.Swanney,M.McEwan,A.S.Thomas,S.Bhandari,S.Chambers,R.Dweik,M.E pton.Analysis of biogenic volatile organic compounds in human health and disease,Trends in Analytical Chemistry,**30**(2011):960-967
16. M.Bernabei,G.Pennazza,M.Santonico,C.Corsi,C.Roscioni,R.Paoeesse,C.DiNatale,A.D'Amico.A preliminary study on the possibility to diagnose urinary tract cancers by an electronic nose, Sensors and Actuators B:Chemical,**131**(2008):1-4
17. J.H.Sohn,N.Hudson,E.Gallagher,M.Dunlop,L.Zeller,M.Atzeni.Implementation of an electronic nose for continuous odour monitoring in a poultry shed, Sensors and Actuators B:Chemical, **133**(2008):60-69
18. S.DeVito,E.Massera,M.Piga,L.Martinotto,G.DiFrancia.On field calibration of an electronic nose for benzene estimation in an urban pollution monitoring scenario, Sensors and Actuators B:Chemical, **129**(2008):750-757

Calibration of Abnormal Brightness Area on the LED Display

Xin-Yue MAO[1], Rui-Guang WANG[1], Hong-Bin CHENG[1,a], Jing MIAO[1], Yu CHEN[1] and Hui CAO[1]

[1]*CIOMP, Cedar Electronics, Research Department, China*

Abstract. Due to the collection method, the acquisition environment and the LED's own light-emitting characteristics, the effect of LED point-by-point brightness correction will be affected, which results in the abnormal brightness area on the display. In this paper, a calibration method based on the brightness correction coefficient map is presented, which uses the step-by-step weighted shrinkage algorithm to post-process the correction coefficient in order to eliminate the abnormal area on the screen. The result showes that uniformity of the entire LED display is greatly improved and the deviation decreases from 12.86% before correction to the present 2.39%.

1 Introduction

The display quality is a critical indicator for the LED screen as an important multimedia display terminal, which is often affected by pitting and mosaic phenomenon due to brightness and chromatic dispersion of the light-emitting diodes[1-5]. In recent years, the industrial camera_(CCD/CMOS) or SLR camera has been generally used to collect the brightness of red, green and blue LED chip of each pixel on the screen in order to realize the point-by-point calibration to improve the uniformity of the whole display[6-10]. However, some abnormal area will occur during the correction process in term of LED light-emitting characteristics, acquisition equipment, acquisition methods and acquisition environment. As a result, there were large brightness deviations for red, green and blue three primaries for each pixel in the abnormal area which impaired the display uniformity after calibration. Currently many methods such as vignetting correction [11-12], deviation of LED brightness with temperature[13] and calibration angle[14] have been explored to improve the result of the LED display calibration. But the above methods can only solve some kinds of phenomenons, and are not suitable for correction of abnormal regions caused by multiple factors.

In this paper, brightness calibration coefficient map was constructed combining with the generated calibration coefficients after analyzing the brightness calibration method of point-by-point. A step-by-step weighted shrinkage algorithm was proposed to post-process the abnormal area on the calibration coefficient maps and the display quality was greatly improved.

[a] Corresponding author:chenghb@ccxida.com

2 Point-by-point brightness calibration model and calibration coefficient map with abnormal regions

The method of point-by-point brightness calibration is based on the theory of chromaticity. The procedure of the calibration is shown in Figure 1.

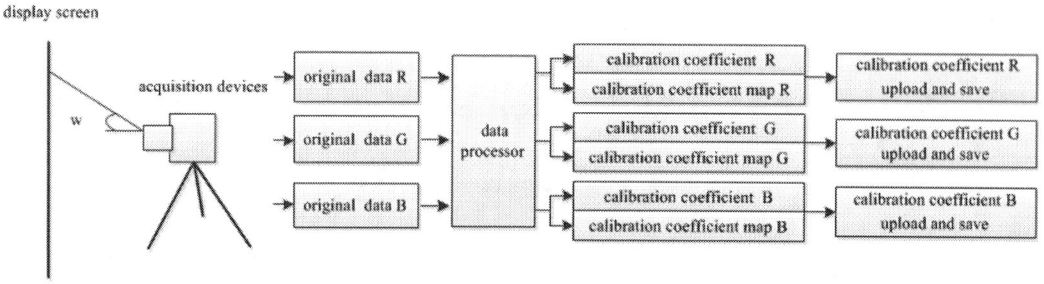

Figure 1. Diagram of point-by-point brightness calibration.

In Figure 1, R, G, B means the red, green and blue three primary colors of the LED display. First, the brightness of three primaries red, green and blue for each pixel on the screen is collected point-by-point by the acquisition devices in front of the LED display. Then, the calibration coefficient is calculated through data processing to generate the calibration coefficient map. After that, the calibration coefficient is uploaded to the LED display to calibrate the display quality of the whole panel. However, wrong brightness values of red, green and blue for some regions are gathered in the above process due to the unreasonable acquisition mode, the abrupt change of the calibration environment or the drift of R, G and B with temperature, which indirectly leads to the generation of wrong calibration coefficients and calibration coefficient maps.The figure shows the calibration coefficients map with shadows on the display screen in a uniform illumination environment during the calibration process.

Figure 2. A, B, C and D are calibration coefficient maps of R, G, B and W, respectively.

3 Selection and location of abnormal areas

A. The R, G, B calibration coefficient map was transferred into 8-bit gray scale diagram and the gray scale histogram of R, G, B was plotted respectively as shown in Figure 3. Here diagram R was taken as an example for analysis in this section. The three-dimensional graph of calibration coefficient is shown in Figure 4.

B. Calibration coefficient deviation ratio Δ_i for each pixel is expressed as in Eq. (1), where I_i is the gray scale value of the i-th pixel and I_n is the maximum gray scale value in the calibration coefficient map. As the theoretical luminance value L_i and the luminance limit error value L' from the same batch LED chips have been provided by the manufacturer, the maximum luminance deviation value ΔL is defined as $\Delta L = 2 \times \max(L' - L_i)$. The maximum brightness deviation ratio Δ' is equal to $\Delta L / L_i$ and the maximum calibration coefficient deviation ratio Δm is equal to Δ'. Then, the difference between Δ_i and Δm is used as the physical coordinates of the pixel on the calibration coefficient map if it is greater than zero.

 DOI: 10.1051/itmconf/20171102001

$$\Delta_i = \frac{|(I_i - I_n)|}{I_n} \quad i=0,1,2.....N \tag{1}$$

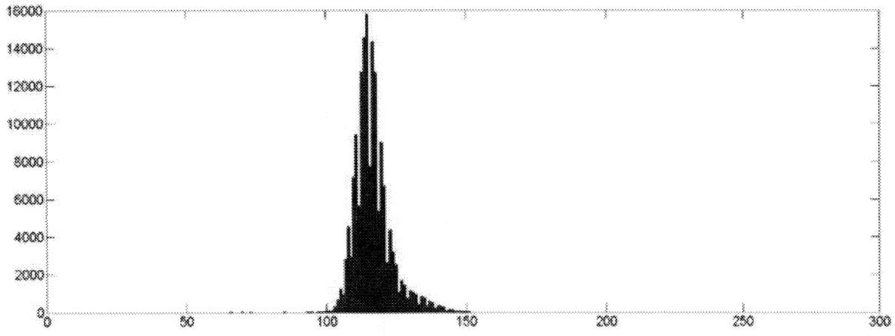

Figure 3. Gray scale histogram of calibration coefficient map.

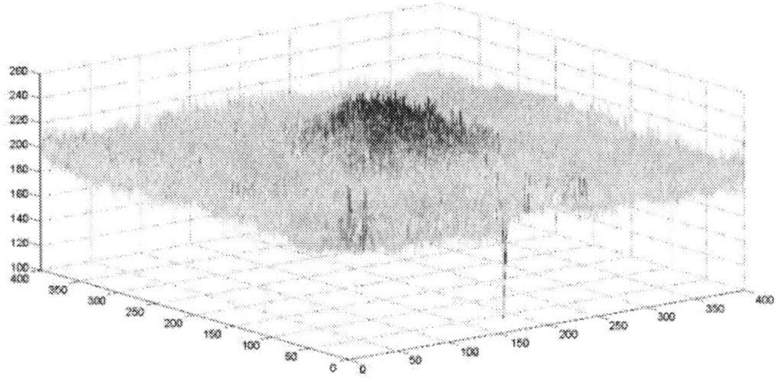

Figure 4. 3D graph of calibration coefficient for R.

C.The connectivity of the recorded coordinates is judged, and the connected area including those points is called the virtual abnormal region G_0 where the virtual curved surface region G_0 is diffused X pixels to the surroundings to ensure that there is no significant transition between the modified anomaly and non-anomaly boundaries. Here $X = \frac{1}{2}(H'+W')$ and H' and W' are row and column variables respectively which are progressively weighted to the center of the anomaly area in a stepwise manner at each level, as shown in section 4. G_1 is the true abnormal region and G_2 is the non-abnormal region.

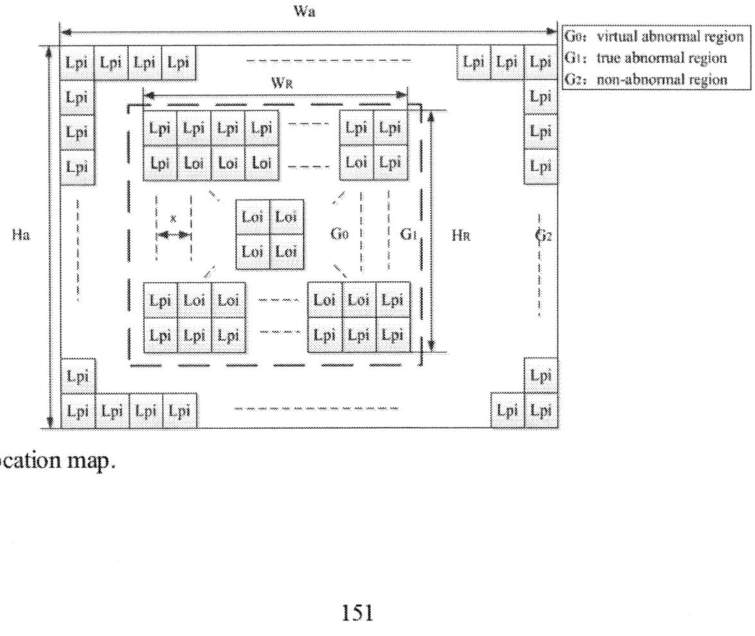

Figure 5. Surface location map.

As indicated in Figure 5, W_R and H_R are the number of columns and rows of pixels respectively in the area of G_1 for the calibration coefficient map R. L_{pi} is the point within the non-abnormal region, L_{oi} is the point within the virtual anomaly region, W_a is the number of pixel columns of the calibration coefficient map, H_a is the number of pixel rows of the calibration coefficient map.

4 Stepwise weighted shrinkage algorithm and correction of coefficient Map

The gray value of R, G and B of the pixel in the abnormal region are denoted as $L_{oqr}(x_i,y_i)$, $L_{oqg}(x_i,y_i)$ and $L_{oqb}(x_i,y_i)$ respectively, where $x_i \in W_{(r/g/b)}$, $y_i \in H_{(r/g/b)}$,$W_{(r/g/b)}$ is the number of pixel columns in the abnormal region of the calibration coefficient map, and $H_{(r/g/b)}$ is the number of pixel rows in the abnormal region of the calibration coefficient map. The gray value of R, G and B of the pixel in the non-abnormal region are denoted as $L_{pr}(x_i,y_i)$, $L_{pg}(x_i,y_i)$ and $L_{pb}(x_i,y_i)$ respectively, where $x_i \in W_a$, $y_i \in H_a$, $x_i \notin W$, and $y_i \notin H$. The gray values of R, G, and B for all pixels in the abnormal and non-abnormal regions are sorted from small to large respectively, and 1% of the total pixels at two ends is discarded to eliminate the influence of the distortion point. The average gray-scale values L_{pr}', L_{pg}', L_{pb}' in the non-abnormal region and the gray-scale average values L_{oqr}', L_{oqg}', L_{oqb}' in the abnormal region are calculated according to Eq. (2)

$$\begin{aligned}
L_{pr}' &= \sum_{i\in Wa, j\in Ha, i\notin Wr, j\notin Hr} L_{pr}(x_i, y_j)/[(W_a - W_r)\times(H_a - H_r)] \\
L_{pg}' &= \sum_{i\in Wa, j\in Ha, i\notin Wg, j\notin Hg} L_{pg}(x_i, y_j)/[(W_a - W_g)*(H_a - H_g)] \\
L_{pb}' &= \sum_{i\in Wa, j\in Ha, i\notin Wb, j\notin Hb} L_{pb}(x_i, y_j)/[(W_a - W_b)*(H_a - H_b)] \\
L_{oqr}' &= \sum_{i\in Wr, j\in Hr} L_{oqr}(x_i, y_j)/(W_r\times H_r) \\
L_{oqg}' &= \sum_{i\in Wg, j\in Hg} L_{oqg}(x_i, y_j)/(W_g\times H_g) \\
L_{oqb}' &= \sum_{i\in Wb, j\in Hg} L_{oqb}(x_i, y_j)/(W_b\times H_b)
\end{aligned} \quad (2)$$

The maximum correction weights W_{maxr}, W_{maxg}, W_{maxb} are expressed as in Eq. (3)

$$\begin{cases} W_{\max r} = L_{oqr}'/L_{pr}' \\ W_{\max g} = L_{oqg}'/L_{pg}' \\ W_{\max b} = L_{oqb}'/L_{pb}' \end{cases} \quad (3)$$

When $L_{pr}'=L_{oqr}'$, $L_{pg}'=L_{oqg}'$ and $L_{pb}'=L_{oqb}'$, the average calibration coefficients for both normal and abnormal regions are same without any correction, and the minimum correction weight is 1. The brightness changes more than 3%, can be significantly perceived according to the human visual characteristics. Thus, the white color correction value of adjacent points in the abnormal area cannot exceed the brightness by 3% in order to ensure that the obvious demarcation phenomenon does not appear. As white color is made by R, G, B in accordance with the ratio 1: 1: 1 mixture of superposition, the correction value of R, G, B for adjacent points cannot exceed by 1%.

Based on the above analysis, it can be seen that the maximum weight change of each level is 0.01 when the calibration coefficients of R, G, and B are gradually changed from the minimum weight 1 to the maximum weight. In this paper, only 0.01 is used as an example for analysis. The weighting grade X_r, X_g and X_b for color R, G, B are given as in Eq. (4)

$$\begin{cases} X_r = \left|(\mathrm{W}_{\max r} - 1) / 0.01\right| \\ X_g = \left|(\mathrm{W}_{\max g} - 1) / 0.01\right| \\ X_b = \left|(\mathrm{W}_{\max b} - 1) / 0.01\right| \end{cases} \tag{4}$$

According to the weighting grade X_r, X_g, X_b and the total row and column number of pixels in the abnormal region $H_{(r/g/b)}$ and $W_{(r/g/b)}$, the amount for the row weighting grade H_r',H_g',H_b' and the column weighting grade W_r', W_g', W_b' is calculated as in Eq. (5)

$$\begin{cases} H_r' = \dfrac{1}{2}\dfrac{H}{X_r} \\ H_g' = \dfrac{1}{2}\dfrac{H}{X_g} \\ H_b' = \dfrac{1}{2}\dfrac{H}{X_b} \end{cases} \qquad \begin{cases} W_r' = \dfrac{1}{2}\dfrac{W}{X_r} \\ W_g' = \dfrac{1}{2}\dfrac{W}{X_g} \\ W_b' = \dfrac{1}{2}\dfrac{W}{X_b} \end{cases} \tag{5}$$

After that, the step-by-step weighted shrinkage algorithm is applied to correct the anomaly area, and the contraction mode is shown in Figure 6.

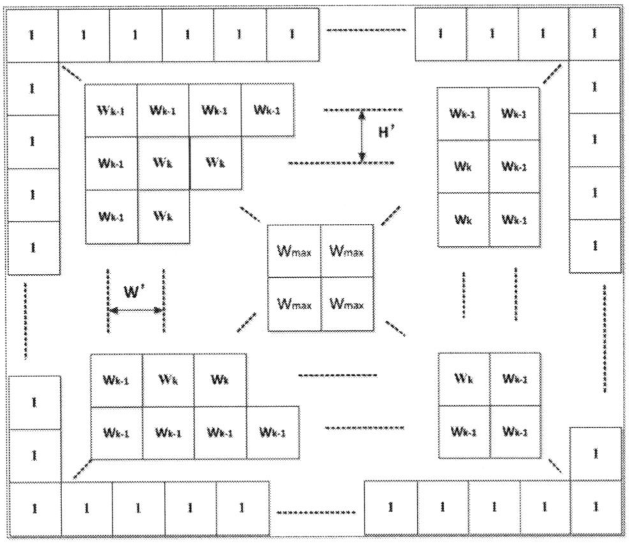

Figure 6. Shrinking mode of gradual weighted contraction algorithm.

In Figure 6, W_k is the k-level weight of any color of R, G, B, and H' and W' are the value of row and column weighting grades respectively, the shrinkage formula is expressed as below:

$$L_r''(m,n) = L_r'(m,n) \times (1 \pm k_r \times 0.01) \tag{7-1}$$

$$L_g''(m,n) = L_g'(m,n) \times (1 \pm k_g \times 0.01) \tag{7-2}$$

$$L_b''(m,n) = L_b'(m,n) \times (1 \pm k_b \times 0.01) \tag{7-3}$$

where $m = (0,1,2.....W)$ and $n = (0,1,2.....H)$ are the physical coordinate of each pixel point in the abnormal region $W_{(r/g/b)} \times H_{(r/g/b)}$. With the gradual change of k_r, k_g, k_b, m and n contract following Eq. (7-4), (7-5), (7-6).

$$(k_r - 1) \times W_r' \leq m \leq W - (k_r - 1) \times W_r', (k_r - 1) \times H_r' \leq n \leq H - (k_r - 1) \times H_r'$$
$$k_r = 1, 2 ...... X_r; \tag{7-4}$$

$$(k_g-1)\times W_g'\leq m\leq W-(k_g-1)\times W_g',(k_g-1)\times H_g'\leq n\leq H-(k_g-1)\times H_g'$$
$$k_g=1,2......X_g; \quad (7\text{-}5)$$
$$(k_b-1)\times W_b'\leq m\leq W-(k_b-1)\times W_b',(k_b-1)\times H_b'\leq n\leq H-(k_b-1)\times H_b'$$
$$k_b=1,2......X_b; \quad (7\text{-}6)$$

In Eq. (7-4), (7-5), (7-6), a minus sign is taken when W_{max}-1≥0, a plus sign is taken when W_{max}-1≤0. $L_r''(m, n)$, $L_g''(m, n)$ and $L_b''(m, n)$ are calibration coefficients of R, G and B respectively for pixel points in the abnormal region after calibration. $L_r'(m, n)$, $L_g'(m, n)$ and $L_b'(m, n)$ are the original calibration coefficients of R, G and B respectively for pixel points in the abnormal region.

5 Modified effects and uniformity verification

The effect of the calibration coefficient map after correction is shown in Figure 7.

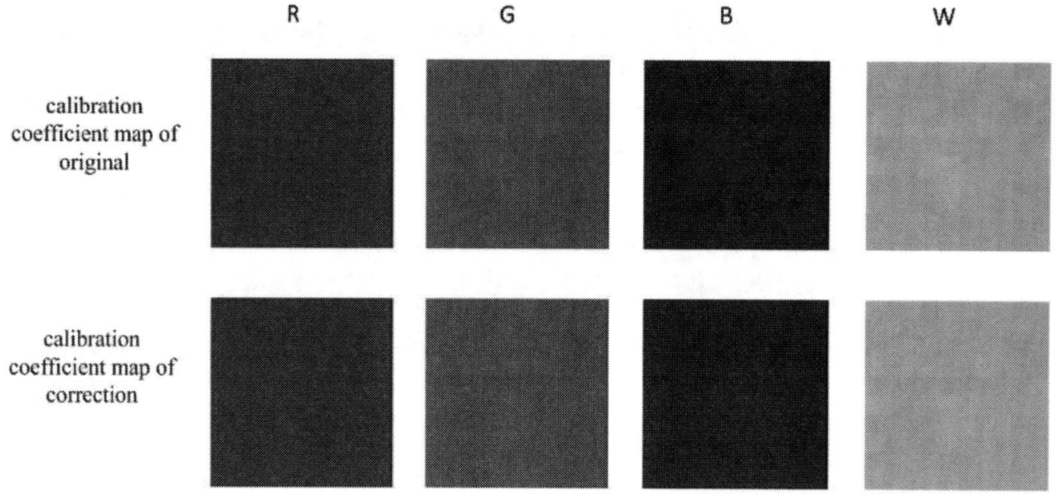

Figure 7. Effect of calibration coefficient map after correction.

The 3D diagram of correction coefficient map R after calibration is shown in Figure 8.

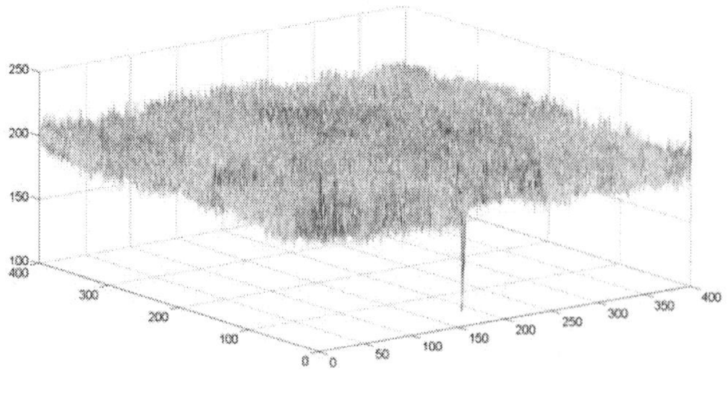

Figure 8. 3D diagram of calibration coefficient map R after correction.

In this paper, the correction coefficient map of 400×400 was used for verification and the correction coefficients of R, G, B after calibration were uploaded to the LED display. Through the test method of homogeneity in 4.2.7.2 module of industry standard SJ / T 11281-2007, 80 samples were taken before and after correction to make a quantitative comparison of the uniformity of the display screen. The experimental results are shown in Table 1(color temperature 9300K).

Table 1 Comparison of uniformity

uniformity	I_j
Before calibration	12.86%
After calibration	2.39%

The uniformity I_j is given as in Eq. (8) where $i = 1,2,...,80$, $\bar{I}$ is the average of all samples.

$$I_j = \frac{\left|I_i - \bar{I}\right|_{\max}}{\bar{I}} \times 100\% \tag{8}$$

Conclusions

Currently the requirement for the calibration is becoming more and more critical as the super large LED displays are applied widely. At the same time the correction process is easily affected by multiple factors of the outside conditions. Thus in this paper, a calibration method based on the brightness calibration coefficient map is proposed, which used a step-by-step weighted shrinkage algorithm to post-process the correction coefficient in order to eliminate the abnormal area on the screen. The result showed that uniformity of the entire LED display was greatly improved and the deviation decreased from 12.86% before correction to the present 2.39%. This method has greatly improved the display uniformity and will be suitable for many engineering applications in the future.

References

1. G.S. Liang, Q. Qin, S.H. Chen,et al, Chinese Journal of Liquid Crystals and Displays,**29**(5):850-855(2014).(in Chinese)
2. Y.R. Hao, Z.Q. Deng, C.J. Deng, Chinese Journal of Liquid Crystals and Displays,**31**(5):470-476(2016).(in Chinese)
3. J.Y. Liu, S.F. He, B. Cao, China Illuminating Engineering Journal, **26**(1):104-107(2015). (in Chinese)
4. J.Q. Cai, F. Yang, P. Du, et al, China Illuminating Engineering Journal, **26**(1):94-98(2015). (in Chinese)
5. F. Yan, R.G. Wang, Y.C. Deng,et al, Opt. Precision Eng,**21**(12):3248-3254(2013).(in Chinese)
6. H.G. Deng, Z.J. Li, M.W. Guo,et al, Chin.J.Lumin,**34**(4):529-534(2013).(in Chinese)
7. J. Parzych, Proc. of SPIE Vol. **6937**,69371M, (2007).
8. S. Yokoi, T. Horiuchi, T. Ejaz, Y. Shimodaira, IIEEJ Technical Report,vol.**208**, pp.15–19, (2004).
9. Zhao. Z.Q, Wang R.G, Zheng. X.F,et al, Opt. Precision Eng,**21**(3):575-582(2013).(in Chinese)
10. D. Travis, Displays,**19**(18):29-36(1998).
11. X. Zhang, R.G. Wang, Y. Chen,et al, Opt. Precision Eng,**18**(11):2332-2338(2010).(in Chinese)
12. Z.H. Tian, J. Miao, X.Y. Mao, H.B. Cheng,et al,Chin.J.Lumin,**37**(8):1008-1013(2016).(in Chinese)
13. Y. Piao, R.G. Wang, T.F. Ding, Journal of Optoelectronics.Laser,**19**(1):125-127(2008).(in Chinese)
14. B.X. Ding, X.F. Zheng, Y. Chen,et al, Opt. Precision Eng,**21**(5):1318-1325(2013).(in Chinese)

Research on Infrared and Visible Images Registration Algorithm Based on Graph

Xiao-Lin ZHU[1,a], Ying-Guang HAO[1], and Hong-Yu WANG[1]

[1]*Dalian University of Technology, School of Information and Communication Engineering, Dalian, China*

Abstract. In this paper, we proposed a registration algorithm based on the combination of pyramid hierarchical idea and graph theory. It can solve the challenging problem of extracting consistent characteristics and matching the infrared and visible images. First, extracting the maximally stable extremal regions (MSERs) in the determining maximum down-sampling images and each MSER is represented by a polygon. Then constructing the gragh features and the mapping relationship of MSERs between the infrared and visible images are determined by the graph matching method. Next we can construct the initial point set for matching according to the mapping relationship. Finally, using the random sample consensus (RANSAC) algorithm to obtain the optimal parameters and determine the error evaluation parameters. According to the idea of pyramid stratification, the above process is repeated in the high resolution images under the constraint condition of current matching error. The experiment results show that the algorithm can make full use of the visual similarity structures between images, and can achieve a smaller matching error under the premise of ensuring the robustness of the matching.

1 Introduction

Image registration is the process of aligning two or more images in the same scene of different times, different angles and different sensors. It has been widely used in military, medical, remote sensing, pattern recognition, computer vision and other fields [1-3]. The registration of infrared (IR) and visible images (VI) is an important branch in the field of multi-sensor registration. At present, the IR and VI registration algorithms mentioned in the literature can be divided into two categories: the method based on image gray and the method based on feature [4-5]. The gray level registration algorithm is to calculate the spatial transformation relation of the images using the gray information under certain similarity measure criteria. This method does not need to extract image features, but use the gray information of the image directly. The advantages of it are no need for image preprocessing and good versatility. And the disadvantages include the large amount of calculation and sensitivity to the change of image gray. Besides, it only reflects the statistical information of gray value about each pixel in the image while ignoring the image spatial structure information, so it is easy to cause false matches [6]. The registration method based on the image features is implemented by extracting the invariant features (such as corners, lines, contours, etc.) to obtain the transformation relation. However, because the IR and VI are in different bands, there is little relevance between them, making registration method based on feature points easily lead to a large amount of false matches. Since

[a] Corresponding author: zxlcheer@163.com

registration method based on line features puts forward more stringent requirements on image content and deformation, it limits the application scope of the algorithm [7]. And the validity of the registration method based on contour features is largely dependent on the quality of extracted contour features, while stable and effective contour extraction is a classical problem in the field of computer vision [8].

In this paper, we proposed a registration algorithm which combines pyramid hierarchical idea and graph theory. First, extracting the maximally stable extremal regions (MSER) in the determining maximum down-sampling images and constructing the graph feature for each region. Then the regional mapping relationship between the IR and VI is determined by the graph matching method. Finally, we can construct the initial set of matching points based on the regional mapping and obtain the optimum matching parameters using the random sample consensus (RANSAC) algorithm and determine the error evaluation parameters. According to the idea of pyramid stratification, the exact matching in local range in the high resolution images is carried out under the constraint condition of current matching error. Good performance can be achieved under the premise of ensuring the robustness of matching.

2 Registration definition and transformation model

Image registration is to make two images $f_1(x,y)$ and $f_2(x,y)$ achieve the consistency on geometric position and gray level. The relationship between them can be expressed as follows:

$$f_2(x,y) = g(f_1(h(x,y))) \tag{1}$$

where g represents a one-dimensional gray transform function, and h represents a two-dimensional spatial position transform function. Image registration is to find the ideal transformation parameters. Before the registration, it is necessary to determine the transformation model. The commonly used models are rigid body transformation, similarity transformation, affine transformation, perspective transformation, etc. In this paper, we consider affine transformation, that is, there are not only existing translation, rotation and scaling between images, but also inversion and shear [9]. The form of the transformation matrix $\mathbf{H}$ is as follows:

$$\mathbf{H} = \begin{pmatrix} m_0 & m_1 & m_2 \\ m_3 & m_4 & m_5 \\ 0 & 0 & 1 \end{pmatrix} \tag{2}$$

where m_0, m_1, m_2, m_3, m_4, m_5 represent six independent degrees of freedom, an affine transformation can be expressed as follows:

$$\begin{bmatrix} x_2 \\ y_2 \end{bmatrix} = \begin{bmatrix} m_0 & m_1 \\ m_3 & m_4 \end{bmatrix} \begin{bmatrix} x_1 \\ y_1 \end{bmatrix} + \begin{bmatrix} m_2 \\ m_5 \end{bmatrix} \tag{3}$$

3 Algorithm

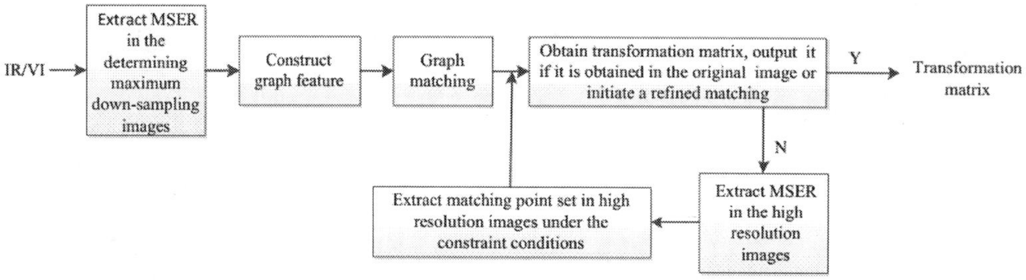

Figure 1. Algorithm block diagram of image registration.

3.1 Extraction of MSER

It is difficult to extract the common features for IR and VI due to the different imaging mechanisms. For the IR and VI, the same target may have different contrast and gray level; on the other hand, the same contrast and gray level may not belong to the same target. The purpose of extracting MSER is to solve the above difficulties, as many as possible to extract the common targets in IR and VI. And MSER is a kind of regional feature extraction operator which has characteristic of affine invariant. Firstly, the original images need to be converted into the gray images, and then the connected pixel sequences are obtained according to the pixel gray value. Finally, detecting the stability of connected regions according to the maximum rate of change V_{max} and the region area to obtain the MSERs [10-11]. For region Q and its border ∂Q, if gray value $\mathrm{I}(\mathrm{p})<\mathrm{I}(\mathrm{q})$ for $\forall p \in Q$ and $\forall q \in \partial Q$, then Q is called a minimum region; conversely, if $\mathrm{I}(\mathrm{p})>\mathrm{I}(\mathrm{q})$, then Q is called a maximum region. $Q_1, Q_2, \ldots, Q_{i-1}, Q_i, \ldots$ represent extremal regions that are nested with each other, that is $Q_{i-1} \subset Q_i$, the change rate on area Q_i is shown as follows:

$$q(i)=\frac{|Q_{i+\Delta}-Q_{i-\Delta}|}{Q_i} \tag{4}$$

if $q(i) \le V_{max}$, then Q_i is called the most stable extremal region, Δ represents the change of gray value, $|\bullet|$ represents the region area, that is the number of pixels covered by the region. The gray values of the most stable extremal regions are less than (MSER-) or larger than (MSER+) the gray values of the pixels on the boundary. As shown in Figure 2, (a) is part of MSERs marked in VI, and (b) is the MSER extraction results of marked regions in (a). Because the connectivity is used in the extraction process and the constraint of region size, so the second word only retains the lower part. The goodness of MSER comes from its extraction process which is in accordance with human visual system, that is, the human eyes are more sensitive to the saliency regions (corresponding to the MSERs).

(a) MSER annotation (b) MSER extraction

Figure 2. The extraction of MSER.

3.2 Construction of graph features

In order to describe the structure characteristics of the extracted MSERs, we make a polygon approximation for each MSER, and then construct the attribute graph [12-15]. For the matching of two polygons, let us consider two attribute graphs G_1 and G_2, where $G_1 = (V_1, \varepsilon_1, A_1^V, A_1^\varepsilon)$ with n_1 nodes and $G_2 = (V_2, \varepsilon_2, A_2^V, A_2^\varepsilon)$ with n_2 nodes. $V, \varepsilon, A^V, A^\varepsilon$ represent a set of nodes, edges, node attributes and edge attributes, respectively. We only consider the edge attributes and they are expressed by 1×19 vectors. The first component represents the normalized distance, and the remaining 18 components represent the angle information of the edge and its adjacent edges. For the edge e_{ij} of point v_i to v_j, its first component represents the normalized length L_{ij}, and we use cyclic Gauss histogram for angle information, as shown in Figure 3.

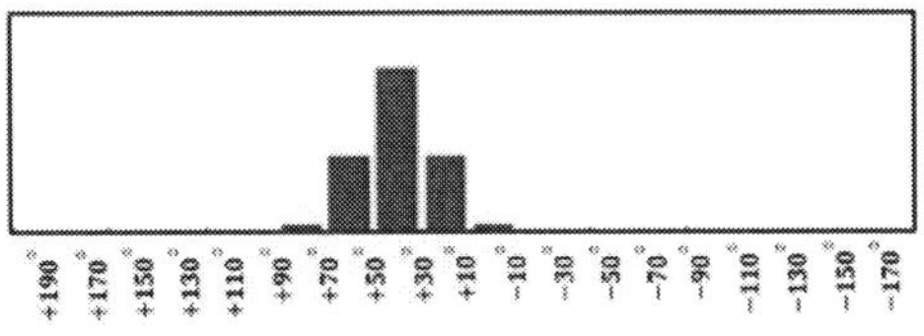

Figure 3. The representation of angle information.

We use uniform bins of size $\frac{2\pi}{n_P}$, where $n_P = 18$, that is, each interval represents 20 degrees. For angle θ_{ij}, the angle information $\mathbf{P}_{ij}$ is shown as follows:

$$\mathbf{P}_{ij}(k) = f_P(k - m),$$

$$\text{s.t. } f_P(x) = N(0, \sigma_P) + N(\pm n_P, \sigma_P),\ \theta_{ij} \in bin_\theta(m) \tag{5}$$

where $N(\mu, \sigma)$ represents a discrete Gaussian window of size σ centered on μ, additional Gaussian terms in $f_P(x)$ induce the circular bins for angle. The final edge attribute $\mathbf{a}_{ij}$ is composed by concatenating the normalized distance L_{ij} and angle information $\mathbf{P}_{ij}$. For edge e_{ij} : $\mathbf{a}_{ij} = [L_{ij}; \mathbf{P}_{ij}]$, which is asymmetric ($\mathbf{a}_{ij} \neq \mathbf{a}_{ji}$). In this work, we used a window size $\sigma_P = 5$, so that $N(0,5) = 1.0$, $N(\pm 1,5) = 0.4578$, $N(\pm 2,5) = 0.0439$, and 0 otherwise.

3.3 Graph matching

3.3.1 Graph matching model

In this paper, one-to-one matching constraints are adopted so that every node in G_1 is mapped to at most one node in G_2 and vice versa. Graph matching identifies the subset of node correspondences between G_1 and G_2 among all of the possible correspondences, which best preserve the attribute relations under the matching constraints. We use binary indicator vector $\mathbf{y} = \{0,1\}^{n_1 n_2}$ which has $n_1 \times n_2$ components to represent the correspondence between G_1 and G_2, where n_1 and n_2 are the numbers of nodes in G_1 and G_2 respectively. If $v_i \in V_1$ matches $v_a \in V_2$, so that $y_{i,a} = 1$, and $y_{i,a} = 0$ otherwise. Affinity matrix M consists of the affinity values between edges and nodes. The compatibility of two edge attributes $\mathbf{a}_{ij} \in A_1^e$ and $\mathbf{a}_{ab} \in A_2^e$ is encoded in the non-diagonal component $M_{ia;jb}$, and the compatibility of two node attributes $a_i \in A_1^V$ and $a_a \in A_2^V$ is encoded in the diagonal component $M_{ia;ia}$. $M_{ia;jb}$ can be expressed as follows:

$$M_{ia;jb} = \exp(-\|\mathbf{a}_{ij} - \mathbf{a}_{ab}\| / \sigma_s^2) \tag{6}$$

where scaling factor σ_s^2 is chosen to be 0.1. In this paper, the diagonal components of M are set to zero, because no node attributes are used. The graph matching problem is to find the best matching relation $\mathbf{y}^*$ between two graphs.

3.3.2 Construction of objective function

We can find the corresponding affinity values of edge attributes in M according to the components whose values are equal to 1 in match result $\mathbf{y}$. Then the affinity values are calculated as matching score, and the matching score is used to evaluate the matching result of the two graphs. Graph matching can be expressed as follows:

$$\begin{aligned} &\mathbf{y}^* = \arg max_{\mathbf{y}} \mathbf{y}^T \cdot M \cdot \mathbf{y} \\ &\text{s.t. } \mathbf{y} \in C_{int} \cap C_{one} \end{aligned} \tag{7}$$

where $C_{int} = \{\mathbf{y} \mid \mathbf{y} \in \{0,1\}^{n_1 n_2}\}$ enforces the integer constraint for the $n_1 \times n_2$ components in $\mathbf{y}$, namely the component in $\mathbf{y}$ only can be 0 or 1. And $C_{one} = \{\mathbf{y} \mid \forall i, \sum_a y_{ia} \le 1\} \cap \{\mathbf{y} \mid \forall a, \sum_i y_{ia} \le 1\}$ enforces the one-to-one constraint. The affinity measure is typically restricted to be nonnegative, therefore the number of matches in the final solution is implicitly determined to the maximum possible number of matches under one-to-one constraint. The underlying assumption is that the solution that contains true matches would have a higher objective value than those which do not. However, this assumption poorly holds even with few outliers. The matching score S is composed of two parts, $S = S_{in} + S_{out} = \mathbf{y}^T \cdot M \cdot \mathbf{y}$, where S_{in} represents the matching score of the correct matching point pairs, and S_{out} represents the matching score of the outliers. The existence of the outliers will increase the matching score, so in this paper, we consider not only the matching score but also the number of matching points. By changing the objective function of formula (7) to the following:

$$\begin{aligned} &\mathbf{y}^* = \arg max_{\mathbf{y}} \mathbf{y}^T \cdot M \cdot \mathbf{y} - \boldsymbol{\lambda}^T \Omega(\|\mathbf{y}\|) \\ &\text{s.t. } \mathbf{y} \in C_{int} \cap C_{one} \end{aligned} \tag{8}$$

where $\Omega(\|\mathbf{y}\|) = [\|\mathbf{y}\|, \|\mathbf{y}\|^2]$, we approximate $\boldsymbol{\lambda}$ as $\boldsymbol{\lambda} = [0, 0.7]$ in all the experiments. We adopt the Markov chain Monte Carlo (MCMC) sampling technique proposed in literature [16] to solve the optimization problem in formula (8).

3.4 Solve transformation matrix

We adopt the coarse-to-fine strategy, so the transform matrix needs to be obtained at each level of resolution, and the transformation matrix is obtained at low resolution plays a guiding role on the high resolution matching; finally using the matrix obtained in the original images to achieve registration. In this paper, the original images are processed by three times of down-sampling and the initial matching point set is obtained on the maximum down-sampling images, and then the matching point set is used as the input of the RANSAC algorithm. According to the idea of Pyramid stratification, the above process is repeated in high resolution images to realize the precise matching in local area until the original resolution images according to the transformation matrix obtained in low resolution and with the constraint of current matching error.

3.5 Evaluation criteria

In this paper, we adopt the root mean square error (RMSE) as the basis for testing the accuracy of registration algorithms. The smaller the RMSE is, the higher is the accuracy of registration. The calculation formula for RMSE is defined as:

$$\mathrm{RMSE} = \sqrt{\frac{1}{m}\sum_{i=1}^{m}(x_i - x_i')^2 \quad (y_i + y_i')^2} \tag{9}$$

where m is the number of matching points, x_i , y_i are the coordinates of reference image, x_i' , y_i' are the transformed coordinates in the image to be registered. At the same time, we also consider the subjective evaluation, if the registration accuracy is high, the common visual sensitive structure information in IR and VI can completely align, so it does not appear significant dislocation in the fused image and we can obtain the good visual effect.

4 Experiments

In this section we evaluate our method using real images of three scenes, and the scene 1 contains a building background, as shown in Figure 4 (a) and (b). There is a tiny deformation between images in scene 2, as shown in Figure 5 (a) and (b). And the image quality is poor in scene 3, as shown in Figure 6 (a) and (b). For each scene, we compare the result with two matching methods, namely, the registration method based on mutual information and the registration method based on line features. In the experiment, the VI is the image to be registered and the IR is the reference image. For scene 3, the registration method based on mutual information cannot be implemented due to the difference between VI and IR. Therefore, we only give the experimental results based on line features and the method proposed in this paper. The experimental results are shown as follows:

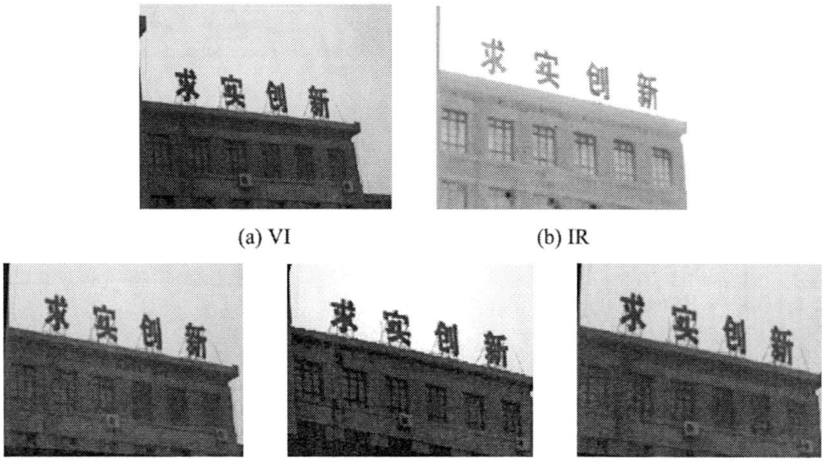

(a) VI (b) IR

(c) mutual information method (d) line features method (e) proposed method

Figure 4. Comparison of results for the first scene.

(a) VI (b) IR

(c) mutual information method (d) line features method (e) proposed method

Figure 5. Comparison of results for the second scene.

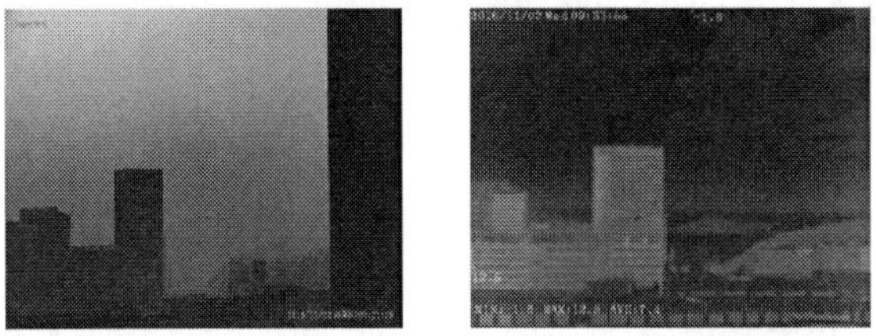

(a) VI (b) IR

(c) line features method (d) proposed method

Figure 6. Comparison of results for the third scene.

4.1 Objective evaluation

In order to quantitatively evaluate the effect of registration, we calculate the RMSE of the registration method based on mutual information, the registration method based on line features and the proposed method respectively. The results are shown in Table 1:

Table 1. The RMSE of three registration methods.

Methods	RMSE (scene 1)	RMSE (scene 2)	RMSE (scene 3)
Mutual information	8.4524	11.462	---
Line features	4.769	2.769	4.683
Proposed	1.8797	1.536	2.320

It can be seen from Table 1 that our method achieves the best performance on three scenes compared with the registration methods based on mutual information and line features.

4.2 Subjective evaluation

In order to facilitate the observation of the effect of registration, we fuse the visible reference image and infrared image which has been registered, and the fusion results as shown in the following figures:

(a) mutual information method (b) line features method (c) proposed method

Figure 7. Comparison of fusion results for the first scene.

(a) mutual information method (b) line features method (c) proposed method

Figure 8. Comparison of fusion results for the second scene.

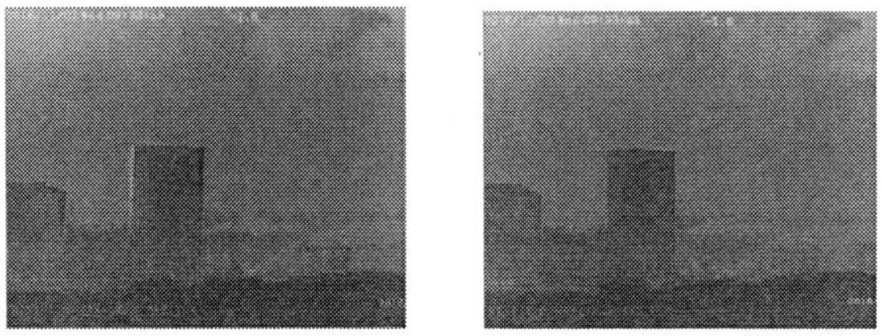

(a) line features method (b) proposed method

Figure 9. Comparison of fusion results for the third scene.

From the fusion results, we can see that the registration result based on mutual information method exhibits serious dislocation phenomenon for scene 1 and scene 2, and the mutual information method is not able to achieve the registration for scene 3 due to too poor quality, while there is a slight dislocation for registration method based on line features. After applying the registration algorithm proposed in this paper, the common visual sensitive structure information completed the alignment, and compared with the other two methods, there is no significant dislocation phenomenon and visual effect is good enough.

Conclusion

The gray characteristics are different for infrared image and visible images in the same scene due to different imaging mechanisms. Thus it causes the difference of extracted corners, lines and contours, especially for images of poor quality. So some of the existing registration algorithms are not ideal. In order to solve this problem, we proposed a registration algorithm based on the pyramid hierarchical idea and graph theory, and we consider the structure information of the graphs in the coarse-to-fine matching process. Experimental results show that the proposed method has a good adaptability to the image content and image deformation. Compared with other methods, the proposed algorithm can achieve state-of-the-art performance, merely with a small matching error under the premise of ensuring the robustness of the matching.

References

1. S.E. A Raza, Registration of thermal and visible light images of diseased plants using silhouette extraction in the wavelet domain, *Pattern Recognition*, **48** 7 2119-2128 (2015).
2. T. Chakravorty, G.A. Bilodeau, E. Granger, Automatic Image Registration in Infrared-Visible Videos using Polygon Vertices, *print arxiv* (2014).
3. H.R. Su, S.H. Lai, Non-rigid registration of images with geometric and photometric deformation by using local affine Fourier-moment matching, *CVPR*, 861-866 (2015).
4. Y.Y. Peng, W.J. He, G.H. Gu, Infrared and visible images registration based on feature points, *Laser and infrared*, **42** 6 713-717 (2012).
5. L. Lian, G.H. Li, J. Zhang, Automatic registration algorithm of infrared and visible images based on parameter estimation, *Electronic journal*, **40** 9 1829-1838 (2012).
6. J.L. Zhang, X. Jin, L. Hao, Infrared and visible images registration based on alignment and mutual information, *Modern electronic technology*, **12** 5-8 (2013).
7. C.L. Lu, L.H. Ma, M. Yu, Visible and infrared images registration algorithm based on parallel line group, *Journal of PLA University of Science and Technology Natural Science Edition*, **5** 439-446 (2015).
8. L. Lian, G.H. Li, J. Zhang, Automatic registration algorithm of infrared and visible images based on edge optimal mapping, *Acta Automatica Sinica*, **38** 4 570-581 (2012).
9. J. Zhang, J.S. Li, Y.W. Yang, Image distortion correction based on affine transformation and multilayer B spline registration, *Optics and precision engineering*, **23** 3 846-854 (2015).
10. M.M. Manafzade, A. Harati, Point cloud registration using MSSIR: Maximally stable shape index regions, *Electrical Engineering*, 1-6 (2013).
11. L. Liu, H. Tuo, T. Xu, Multi-sensor image registration using edge-enhanced maximally stable extremal region, (2012).
12. Y. Suh, K. Adamczewski, K.M. Lee, Subgraph matching using compactness prior for robust feature correspondence, *CVPR*, 5070-5078 (2015).
13. M. Cho, J. Lee, K.M. Lee, Reweighted Random Walks for Graph Matching, *ECCV*, **9** 492-505 (2010).
14. M. Cho, K. Alahari, J. Ponce, Learning Graphs to Match, *ICCV*, 25 – 32 (2013).
15. F. Zhou, F.D. L Torre, Deformable Graph Matching, **9** 4 2922-2929 (2013).
16. W.R. Gilks, Markov chain monte carlo, *Wiley Online Library*, (2005).

Application of Alternate Iterative Algorithm to Image Restoration

Xu-Chao LI[1,a], Song-Yan MA[1] and Wen-Juan LI[2]

[1]*College of Computer and Information Engineering, Chifeng University, Chifeng, Inner Mongolia, 024000, China*
[2]*College of Mathematics and Statistics, Chifeng University, Chifeng, Inner Mongolia, 024000, China*

Abstract. For overcoming the disadvantage of total variation for regularization, which easily produces stair effect, an improved weight energy functional regularization model and alternate algorithm is proposed. Because of non-smooth property of total variation semi-norm regularization model, it is impossible to solve primal model directly. For solving the problem, taking advantage of Fenchel transform, the primal model is converted into dual model, resorting to variable splitting technology, the alternating iterative algorithm is deduced. Moreover, the step length updating principle of primal-dual variable is given. Finally, using Camera image blurred by Gaussian noise, Telescope image blurred by system and Poisson noise for image restoration, simulations show the proposed can achieve smaller relative error, deviation error, higher peak of signal-to-noise ratio, and better visual effect.

1 Introduction

In remote sensing, microscopic imaging, computed tomography imaging etc. The imaging processing can be described by first kind of Fredholm integral equation[1], which is written as

$$f(X)=\int_{R^2} a(X,Y)u(Y)dY \tag{1}$$

Where $f(X)$ and $u(Y)$ represent sample signal and ideal signal respectively, $a(X,Y)$ represents point spread function (PSF). Discretizing formula (1), we get the following model

$$f = Au + \varepsilon \tag{2}$$

Where ε is noise, A is linear tight operator with a large condition number, and it is impossible to get effective solution of (2). Moreover, transformation error of imaging device, atmospheric turbulence and random impulse,etc, all of them can make image blurry. For obtaining high quality and meaning image, at present, it is widely accepted to establish reasonable energy functional regularization model (EFRM)[2], which can be described as

$$E(u)=E_0(u)+\alpha\Phi_0(Bu) \tag{3}$$

[a] Corresponding author: bsx7096@sohu.com

Where $E_0(u)$ is fitting term, $\Phi_0(Bu)$ is regularization term, B is first or second order differential operator, and α is regularization parameter.

For fitting term, the model is established according to noise statistical distribution of imaging processing[3]. Such as, if ε is Gaussian noise, fitting term is described by L_2 norm, if ε obeys Poisson distribution, fitting term is measured by Kullback-Leiber function, if ε is salt and pepper noise, fitting term is approximated by L_1 norm[4]. For regularization term, in academic field, it is widely accepted that the model is described by total variation semi-norm, which can accurately describe singular and jump property of solution. Taking advantage of the property, Rudin et al establish ROF model for image restoration[5], which can effectively protect image edges, however, which easily produces stair effect in steady area, moreover, because of the non-smooth property of total variation semi-norm, it is difficult to design effective algorithm for primal EFRM.

For the shortcomings of total variation semi-norm, scholars mainly carry out three aspect researches: 1) Converting the primal EFRM into smooth EFRM. For example, using smooth square root function approximating total variation semi-norm, taking advantage of EFRM differential property, many classic algorithms can be used. Such as the steepest descent iterative algorithm, fixed point iterative algorithm, Newton and quasi-Newton iterative algorithm[6], etc. However, if the gradient magnitude of EFRM is too small, the convergence speed of algorithm is very slow. Moreover, generally speaking, the descriptive question of EFRM is always large scale, and it is difficult to compute the inverse Hessian matrix for Newton iterative algorithm. For overcoming these shortcomings, a lot of scholars divide the integrated EFRM into several sub-problems. For example, differential fitting term forms predictive sub-problem, non-differential regularization term forms proximal sub-problem, two sub-problem alternate iterations form iterative soft threshold algorithm(ISTA)[7], which doesn't need to compute the inverse Hessian matrix, but the convergence speed of algorithm is slower. To accelerate the convergence speed of algorithm, resorting to ISTA idea, reference [8] proposed a fast ISTA (FISTA). Although the convergence speed of FISTA is faster than that of ISTA, the convergence speed of FISTA depends on the characteristic value of $A^{T}A$. 2) Using Fenchel transform, converting the primal EFRM into dual EFRM. Based on the idea, reference [9] proposed half implicit gradient descent algorithm, which initiated the application landmark of dual EFRM to image restoration. Simulation shows that the quality of image restoration of dual EFRM is better than that of primal EFRM[10]. 3) Converting the primal EFRM into primal-dual EFRM. Such as primal-dual iterative algorithm[11] with constant, adaptive, and variable step length updating[12]. The image restoration quality of primal-dual EFRM is better than that of dual EFRM. However, if without good initialization, the primal-dual EFRM easily makes the image edge blurry.

This paper is structured as follows: In Section 2, in order to protect image edges, we establish an EFRM with adaptive edge detection weight function. Then, the EFRM is converted into dual EFRM, using variable splitting technology, dividing dual EFRM into primal and dual sub-problems, then, an alternate iterative algorithm with adaptive step length updating scheme is proposed. In Section 3, we focus on the implementation of the proposed algorithm, using blurred image by Gaussian, system and Poisson noise for quantitative and qualitative numerical experiments, and comparing with previous state-of-the-art algorithms. Conclusion about the proposed algorithm is drawn in Section 4.

2 Establishment EFRM for image restoration

2.1 Primal EFRM

Suppose that the fitting term of (3) is second order differential convex function with Lipschitz continuous condition[13]. For accurately describing the singular and jump characteristics of image, an improved regularization term with adaptive edge detection weight function can be rewritten as

$$\Phi(Bu) = \alpha\int_{\Omega} g(x)|Bu|dx \tag{4}$$

Where $\int_\Omega |Bu| dx$ is total variation function semi-norm, and it is defined as

$$\int_\Omega |Bu| dx = \sup\left\{\int_\Omega u \operatorname{div}\phi dx\right\} \tag{5}$$

Where $x \in \Omega$, $\phi \in C_0^1(\Omega, \ R^2)$ and $|\phi(x)| < 1$. div is divergent, $g(x)$ is adaptive weight function, which is defined as

$$g(x) = \frac{1}{1 + K|\nabla G_\sigma * u|^2} \tag{6}$$

Where $K \geq 0$, $G_\sigma = \frac{1}{2\pi\sigma^2}\exp\left(-\frac{x^2}{2\sigma^2}\right)$, ∇ is gradient and $*$ is convolution. In steady area of image, the magnitude of $|\nabla G_\sigma * u|$ is bigger, the diffusion coefficient of $g(x)$ is smaller, which is advantageous to image edge. On the contrary, the magnitude of $|\nabla G_\sigma * u|$ is smaller, the diffusion coefficient of $g(x)$ is bigger, which can prevent from producing stair effect in unsteady area. So $g(x)$ can adaptively embody image property. Substituing (4) into (3), we establish an improved primal EFRM, which is formulated as

$$E(u) = E_0(u) + \alpha\Phi(Bu) \tag{7}$$

Expression (7) about u is coercive, according to direct variation principle, the solution of (7) exists. Becaus fitting term and regularization term about u are both convex, the solution of (7) is unique.

2.2 Converting primal EFRM into primal-dual EFRM

Expression (7) is non-differential, it is difficult to solve directly. For solving the problem, taking advantage of Fenchel transform, primal EFRM is converted into dual EFRM. Suppose $\Omega \subset H$, H is Hilbert space, the map φ: $X \to Y$ is proper, convex function, $Y = R \cup \{\infty\}$, Fenchel transform of $\varphi(x)$ is defined as

$$\varphi^*(\xi) = \sup_{\omega \in X}\{\langle \xi, \omega\rangle - \varphi(\omega)\} \tag{8}$$

Where $\langle \bullet, \bullet \rangle$ is inner product, φ^*: $\xi \to R \cup \{\infty\}$ is proper function, if $\varphi^*(\xi)$ is lower semicontinuous, then $\varphi^{**}(\xi) = \varphi$.

$\Phi(Bu)$ of (7) is proper, convex, semicontinuous convex function, let $z = Bu$, then

$$\Phi(z) = \alpha\int_\Omega g(x)|z| dx \tag{9}$$

Suppose the dual variable of z is z^*, according to (8), the dual expression of (9) is expressed as

$$\Phi^*(z^*) = \max_z\{\langle z^*, z\rangle - \Phi(z)\} = \max_z\left\{\langle z^*, z\rangle - \alpha\int_\Omega g(x)|z| dx\right\} = \begin{cases} 0 & if\ |z^*| \leq \alpha g(x) \\ +\infty & otherwise \end{cases} \tag{10}$$

Because $\Phi^*(z^*)$ is proper, lower semicontinuous convex function, $\Phi^{**}(z)$ is the conjugation of conjugation of $\Phi(z)$, according to (8), then $\Phi^{**}(z) = \Phi(z)$. Let $q = z^*$, according to (10), then

$$\Phi(z) = \max_{q}\{\langle q, z\rangle - \Phi^*(z)\} \tag{11}$$

z Replaced by Bu in (11), substituing (11) into (7), the primal-dual EFRM is expressed as

$$\min_{u}\max_{q}\{E_0(u) + \alpha[\langle q, Bu\rangle] - \Phi^*(q)\} \tag{12}$$

Where $q = \{(q_1, q_2)^T \mid |q(x)| \leq \alpha g(x)\}$.

2.3 Alternate iterative algorithm for primal-dual EFRM

Expression (12) is Min-Maximum problem, by performing the maximization over q in (12), and we get the dual variable sub-problem

$$\max_{q}\{\alpha[\langle q, Bu\rangle] - \Phi^*(q)\} \tag{13}$$

Similary, performing the minimization over u in (12), we get the primal variable sub-problem

$$\min_{u}\{E_0(u) + \alpha[\langle q, Bu\rangle]\} \tag{14}$$

The iterative algorithm is described as
Initialization: δ_0 , τ_0 , u_0 , q_0 , k , maximum iterative number $num = 1000$.
Loop iteration:
1)The dual sequences $\{q_k\}$is updated as follows

$$q_{k+1} = (1 + \delta_k \alpha \partial \Phi^*)^{-1}(q_k + \delta_k \alpha B \bar{u}_k) \tag{15}$$

Where δ is step length of dual variable, $(1 + \delta_k \alpha \partial \Phi^*)^{-1}$ is proximal operator, $\partial \Phi^*$ is sub-gradient.
2)The primal sequences $\{u_k\}$is updated as follows

$$u_{k+1} = P_X(u_k - \tau_k B^T q_k) \tag{16}$$

Where τ is step length of primal variable, $P_X(r)$is projection operator, which is defined as

$$P_X(r) = \underset{x \in X}{\operatorname{argmin}} \frac{1}{2}\|x - r\|^2 \tag{17}$$

3)The auxiliary sequences $\{\bar{u}_k\}$is updated as follows

$$\bar{u}_{k+1} = \bar{u}_k + \theta(u_{k+1} - \bar{u}_k) \tag{18}$$

Where $\theta \in [0,1]$.
Termination conditions:
If $k > num$ or $\|E(u_{k+1}, q_{k+1}) - E(u_k, q_k)\| \leq t$, output u_k . Otherwise, $k = k + 1$, updating δ_k , τ_k .

2.4 Step length updating principle

According to (15) and (16), Step length updating principle produces profound influence on alternate iterative algorithm convergence. Supposed the fitting term satisfies Lipschitz continuous condition, step length series of $\{\delta_k\}$, $\{\tau_k\}$ must satisfy the following conditions

$$\lim_{k\to\infty}\tau_k = 0,\ \sum_{k=0}^{\infty}\tau_k = \infty,\ \lim_{k\to\infty}\delta_k = \infty \tag{19}$$

$$\sum_{k=0}^{\infty}\frac{\tau_k}{\sigma_k} < +\infty,\ \sum_{k=0}^{\infty}\tau_k^2 < +\infty \tag{20}$$

If alternate iterative algorithm satisfies (19) and (20), the iterative series (u_k, q_k) of (15)-(18) will converge to the optimum solution (u^*, q^*) of (12).

3 Experiment results and analysis

In order to measure image restoration quality, three kinds of performance index, mean absolute error (MAE), peak signal-to-noise ratio (PSNR) and relative error (RE), are respectively defined as

$$\mathrm{MAE} = \frac{1}{mn}\sum_{i=1}^{m}\sum_{j=1}^{n}\left|u_{ij}^{(k)} - u_{ij}\right| \tag{21}$$

$$\mathrm{PSNR} = 10\log_{10}\left(\left\|max(u_{ij})\right\|_2^2\right)/\,mn\left\|u_{ij}^{(k)} - u_{ij}\right\|_2^2 \tag{22}$$

$$\mathrm{RE} = \left\|u_{ij}^{(k)} - u_{ij}\right\|_2^2 / \left\|u_{ij}\right\|_2^2 \tag{23}$$

Where u is original image, u_k is restoration image, $m \times n$ is image size. Generally, if PSNR is larger, MAE and RE is smaller, the restoration quality of image is better. On the contrary, the quality is worse.

Experiment 1: For image blurred by Gaussian noise, set $A = I$, the fitting term of (12) is described by $E_0(u) = \|u - g\|_2$, according to (17)-(18), the step length sequences of primal and dual are updated as follows

$$\tau_k = \frac{\eta_k}{1-\eta_k},\ \delta_k = 0.2 + 0.08k \tag{24}$$

Where $\eta_k = \left(0.5 - \dfrac{5}{15+k}\right)/\delta_k$.

The image is Camera of size 256×256, and the grey level is 0-255. The blurred version of Camera is shown in Figure 1(b) with PSNR=22.081db. To assess the relative merit of the proposed, we compare the restored results by the proposed strategy with those of classical Landweber iterative algorithm[6], ROF model[5], Chambolle dual model[9].

The qualitative results are shown in Figure 1. In Figure 1(c), the restored image of Landweber algorithm is more smoother than original image, and makes a lot of edges lost. Figure 1(d), the restored image of ROF model produces a lot of staircasing artificts in smooth regions. Figure 1(e), using Chambolle dual model for restoration image, the visual effect is improved, but in smooth regions, a lot of pseudo-trances are produced. Figure 1(f), using the proposed for restoration image, the visual effect is better than that of previous three algorithms.

 DOI: 10.1051/itmconf/20171102003

(a) original image

(b) blurry image

(c) Landweber algorithm

(d) ROF model

(e) Chambolle dual model

(f) the proposed algorithm

Figure 1. Restoration comparison of different algorithms

According to the quantitative performance index of Table 1, Landweber algorithm obtains the lowest PSNR, the highest RE and MAE, which shows that the quality of image restoration is worse. PSNR of Chambolle dual model is higher than that of ROF model, RE is lower than that of ROF model, but MAE is higher than that of ROF model. The proposed obtains the highest PSNR, the smallest RE and MAE, which show that the quality of image restoration is best.

Table 1. comparison of different restoration algorithms for blurred image by Gaussian noise

original image	index	Blurry Fig.1(b)	Landweber Fig.1(c)	ROF model Fig.1(d)	Chambolle Fig.1(e)	The propose Fig.1(f)
	RE	0.1485	0.0918	0.0754	0.0701	0.0657
Fig.1	MAE	15.909	6.6955	5.8901	5.9578	5.4845
	PSNR	22.081	26.258	27.972	28.595	2.9168

Experiment 2: For image blurred by Poisson noise, the fitting term of (12) is described by $E_0(u)=\|Au-g\log Au\|_1$, according to (19)-(20), the step length sequences of primal and dual are updated as follows

$$\tau_k = 0.5/\delta_k\text{,}\quad \delta_k = 0.2+0.08k \tag{25}$$

The image is Telescope of size 256×256, and the grey level is 0-255. According to the Poisson property, the PSF of size 128×128 and 256×256 are constructed respectively. We compare the restoration results of the proposed algorithm with quasi-Newton algorithm.

Taking advantage of psfGaussian function[14] for producing PSF of size 128×128 and 256×256, they are shown in Figure 2(a) and 2(b), respectively. Figure 3 is singular value decomposition (SVD) of PSF, circle and solid line represent matrix SVD of Figure 2(a) and Figure 2(b), respectively. Figure 3 shows the condition number of marix A is ill-posed, which satisfies the condition of (1) and (2).

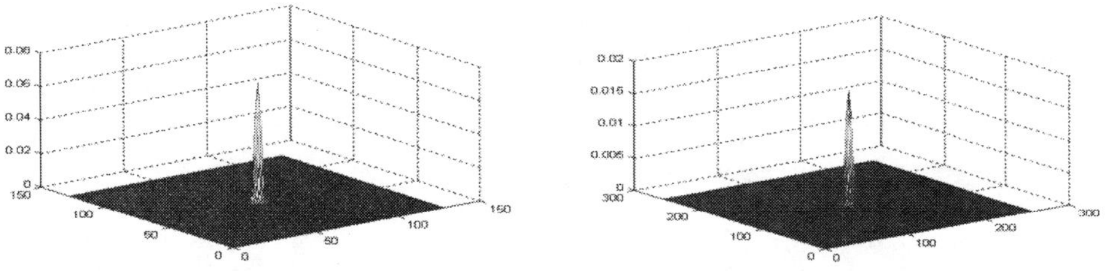

(a)PSF of size 128×128 (b)PSF of size 256×256

Figure 2. PSF with different size

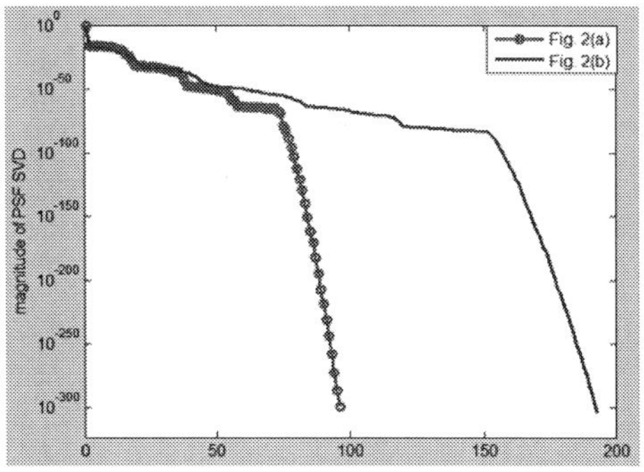

Figure 3. SVD of PSF

Figure 4(a) is original telescope image, Figure 4(b) is blurred by Figure 2(a) of PSF and Poisson noise. According to qualitative results, reference [10] algorithm produces a lot of pseudo-trances, as shown in Figure 4(c). in Figure 4(d),the visual effect of the proposed is better than that of reference [10].

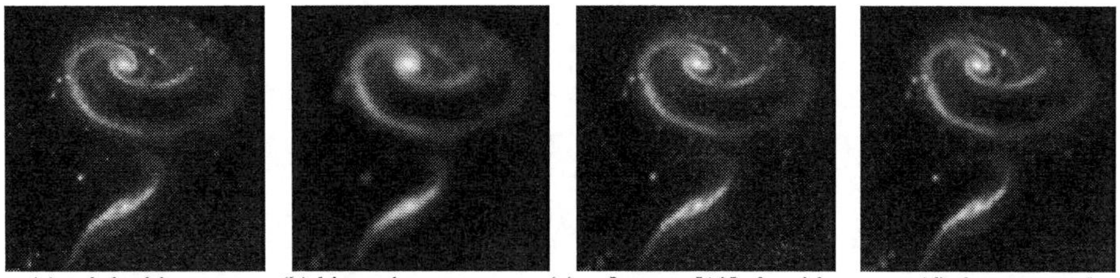

(a) original image (b) blurry image (c) reference [10] algorithm (d) the proposed

Figure 4. Restoration comparison of different algorithms(128×128)

According to the quantitative performance index of table 2, PSNR of the proposed is higher than that of reference [10] algorithm, and RE and MAE of the proposed are lower than that of reference [10] algorithm. The quantitative results shows that image restoration quality of the proposed is better than that of reference [10] algorithm.

Table 2. comparison of restoration image blurred by Poisson noise

Original image	index	Blurry image Figure 4(b)	Reference [10] Figure 4(c)	The proposed Figure 4(d)
4(a)	RE	0.1228	0.0755	0.0691
Telescope	MAE	0.0113	0.0116	0.0098
128×128	PSNR	31.443	35.668	36.433

Figure 5(a) is original telescope image, Figure 5(b) is blurred by Figure 2(b) of PSF and Poisson noise, it is blurred more serious than figure 4(b). According to qualitative results, reference [10] algorithm produces lots of pseudo-trances in Figure 5(c), it is more serious than Figure 4(c). Visual effect of restoration of Figure 5(d) is better than that of Figure 5(c).

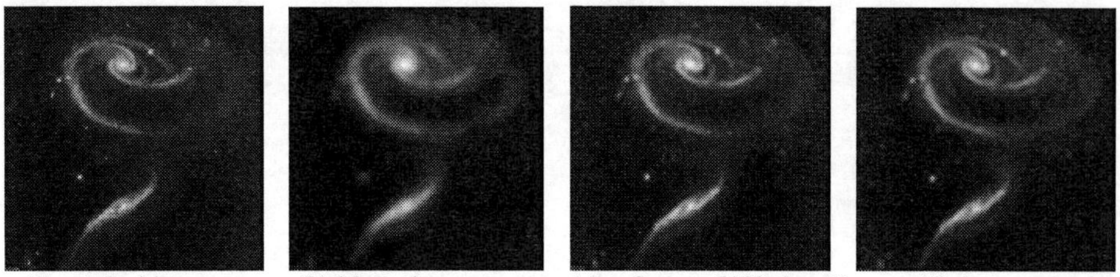

(a) original image (b) blurry image (c) reference [10] algorithm (d) the proposed

Figure 5. Restoration comparison of different algorithms(256×256)

According to the quantitative performance index of table 3, PSNR of the proposed is higher than that of reference [10] algorithm, and it is improved about 0.3db. RE and MAE of the proposed are lower than that of reference [10] algorithm.

Table 3. comparison of restoration image blurred by Poisson noise

Original image	index	Blurry image Figure 5(b)	Reference [10] Figure 5(c)	The proposed Figure 5(d)
5(a)	RE	0.1370	0.0849	0.0825
Telescope	MAE	0.0123	0.0109	0.0090
256×256	PSNR	30.760	34.917	35.164

Conclusion

The paper proposes an improved weight EFRM, taking advantage of Fenchel transform, converting the primal model into dual model, resorting to splitting technology, and deducing an alternate iterative algorithm. Experiment results show the algorithm can effectively restore image blurred by Gaussian noise, system and Poisson noise, and obtain smaller RE and MAE, the larger PSNR.

Acknowledgement

This work was supported by Higher Educational Scientific Research Projects of Inner Mongolia Autonomous Region, China (NJZY16254), and project supported by the Natural Science Foundation of Inner Mongolia Autonomous Region, China (2016MS0602).

References

1. Bai zhengjian, Donatelli Marco, Capizzano Stefano Serra, Fast preconditioners for total variation deblurring with anti-reflective boundary conditions, SIAM Journal on matrix analysis and applications, **32**, 3(2011)
2. Serafini Thomas, Zanghirati Gaetano, Zanni Luca, Gradient projection methods for large quadratic programs and applications in training support vector machines, Optimization Methods and Software, **20**, 2-3(2004)
3. Du Z M, Li H A, Kang B S, Ye F Y, Recovery method of compressed sensing signals based on quadratic convergence regularization with a smooth functional[J], Journal of Image and Graphics, **21**, 4(2016).

4. Li X C, Bian S X, Li Y Y, Survey of convex energy functional regularization model of image restoration[J], Journal of Image and Graphics, **21**, 4(2016).
5. Leonid I. Rudin, Stanley Osher, Emad Fatemi, Nonlinear total variation based noise removal algorithms, Physical D: Nonlinear Phenomena, **60**, 1(1992)
6. Curtis R. Vogel, *Computational methods for inverse problems*(SIAM: Society for Industrial and Applied Mathematics, 2002)
7. Combettes P. L, V. Wajs, Signal recovery by proximal forward-backward splitting, SIAM Journal on Multiscale Modeling and Simulation, **4**, 4(2005)
8. Beck Amir, Teboulle Marc, A fast dual proximal gradient algorithm for convex minimization and applications, Operations Research Letters, **42**, 1(2014)
9. Antonin Chambolle, An algorithm for total variation minimization and applications, Journal of Mathematical Imaging and Vision, **20**, 1-2(2004)
10. Duran Joan, Coll Bartomeu, Sbert Catalina, Chambolle's projection algorithm for total variation denoising, Image Processing on Line, **3**, (2013)
11. Antonin Chambolle, Thomas Pock, A first-order primal-dual algorithm for convex problems with applications to imaging, Journal of Mathematical Imaging and Vision,**40**,1(2011)
12. Goldstein Tom, Esser Ernie, Baraniuk Richard, Adaptive primal-dual hybrid gradient methods for saddle- point problems, http://arxiv.org/abs/1305. 0546 (2013)
13. Gilles Aubert, Pierre Kornprobst, *Mathematical problems in image processing, partial differential equations and the calculus of variations, second edition* (Springer-Verlag, New York, USA, 2006)
14. Katrina Palmer Lee, James G. Nagy, Lisa Perrone, Iterative methods for image deblurring: a matlab object- oriented approach, Numerical Algorithms, **36**, 1(2004)

Non-smooth Hybrid Energy Functional Regularization Model for Image Reconstruction

Xu-Chao LI[1,a], Song-Yan MA[1] and Wen-Juan LI[2]

[1] *College of Computer and Information Engineering, Chifeng University, Chifeng, Inner Mongolia, 024000, China*
[2] *College of Mathematics and Statistics, Chifeng University, Chifeng, Inner Mongolia, 024000, China*

Abstract. For overcoming the shortcomings of total variation for image reconstruction, which easily smooth image texture, and produce lots of artificial edges, a non-smooth hybrid energy functional regularization model and iterative algorithm is proposed. Firstly, fitting term is described by L_1 norm for blurred image by system and salt and pepper noise, regularization terms are described by fractional order bounded variation function semi-norm and L_1 norm. Secondly, resorting to introduce auxiliary variables, the primal non-smooth energy functional regularization model without condition constraints is converted into energy functional regularization model with condition constraints, which is split into six easily computing sub-problems by the alternating direction method of multipliers (ADMM). Finally, alternating iterative six sub-problems, an improved image reconstruction algorithm is proposed. Numerical experiments show that the proposed model has advantages over several state-of-art approaches in terms of the reconstruction visual effect.

1 Introduction

In recent years, reconstruction blurred image by system and noise, the widespread acceptance is how to establish hybrid energy functional regularization model, which is composed of fitting term and regularization term [1]. For blurry image by salt and pepper noise, the image statistical distribution is described by L_1 norm, the solution singularity property is described by bounded variation (BV) function [2]. However, BV easily leads to texture information of image lost, and produces artificial edges in steady area. For overcoming the disadvantages, reference [3] proposed adaptive energy functional regularization model, but the parameters of weight coefficient are difficult to determine. For reducing the stair effect of steady area of BV, reference [4] used the second BV for regularization term of image reconstruction model. However, the four order elliptic equation is obtained by energy functional regularization model of calculus of variation, which easily smears image edge.

First order BV is advantage of image edges [5], second order BV is advantage of image steady area [6], which shows the complex image characteristics, it is difficult to describe solution properties by a special functional space, hence, hybrid functional space is adopted for description of image properties [7]. Recent research show the image is composed of cartoon and texture information [2], which can be described by different function spaces, and establishment hybrid energy functional regularization model based on image decomposition, which is widely applied in image reconstruction

[a] Corresponding author: bsx7096@sohu.com

and compress sensing [8]. For overcoming the image over smooth caused by higher order model, image cartoon part is described by fractional BV [9]. For embodying the sparse property of solution, using tight frame transform [10] for image texture part sparse property, the transform coefficients is described by L_1 norm [11].

The rest of this paper is organized as follows : In section 2, we review the tight frame theory and establish hybrid energy functional regularization model for reconstruction image blurred by system and salt and pepper noise. In section 3, taking advantage of the alternative direction method of multiplier (ADMM), we split the hybrid energy functional regularization into six sub-problems, which form alternative iterative algorithm. In section 4, we carry out several numerical experiments to show that the reconstruction model and algorithm are effective. In section 5, some remarks and future works are discussed.

2 Hybrid regularization model for image restoration

2.1 Tight frame transform for image sparse representation

Using a cluster of framelet functions for basic function of tight frame, image can be represented by multi-resolution analysis, and the transform coefficients in tight frame domain are sparse, which can embody image singular characteristics, the details about tight frame theory are presented in reference[12, 13]. Suppose that the countable set $\boldsymbol{W} \subset \boldsymbol{L}_2(\boldsymbol{R})$, $\forall \boldsymbol{u} \subset \boldsymbol{L}_2(\boldsymbol{R})$, the tight frame must satisfy

$$\boldsymbol{u} = \sum_{\psi \in W} \langle \boldsymbol{u}, \psi \rangle \psi \tag{1}$$

Where $\langle \bullet, \bullet \rangle$ represents the inner product of $\boldsymbol{L}_2(\boldsymbol{R})$, $\boldsymbol{W}$ represents the tight frame. The element of framelet system $\boldsymbol{\psi} = \{\psi_1, \psi_2, \cdots, \psi_M\}$ is dilated and shifted, and get tight frame $\boldsymbol{W}(\boldsymbol{\psi}) \subset \boldsymbol{L}_2(\boldsymbol{R})$ $\boldsymbol{W}(\boldsymbol{\psi}) = \{2^{l/2}\psi_m(2^l \bullet - n)\}$, $\psi_m \in \boldsymbol{\psi}$, ψ_m is called framelet, $m = 1, \cdots, M$. The refinable function ϕ and framelet function of tight frame satisfy the following expression

$$\hat{\phi}(2\omega) = \hat{h}_0(\omega)\hat{\phi}(\omega),\ \hat{\psi}_m(2\omega) = \hat{h}_m(\omega)\hat{\phi}(\omega) \tag{2}$$

Where $\hat{\phi}, \hat{h}_0, \hat{h}_m$ is the Fourier transform of ϕ, h_0, h_m. According to unitary extension principle [14], the filter coefficients of tight frame $\boldsymbol{W}(\boldsymbol{\psi})$ satisfy the following expression

$$\hat{h}_0(\omega)\overline{\hat{h}_0(\omega + \gamma\pi)} + \sum_{m=1}^{M} \hat{h}_m(\omega)\overline{\hat{h}_m(\omega + \gamma\pi)} = \chi_{\gamma,0} \tag{3}$$

Where $\gamma = 0,1$, $\chi_{\gamma,0}$ is sample function.

2.2 Using Bayesian principle for hybrid image reconstruction model

Suppose expectation image $\boldsymbol{f}$ and observation image $\boldsymbol{g}$ obey independent statistical distribution, the imaging system is described by matrix A that is produced by point spread function (PSF). The sample image is blurred by salt and pepper noise, then the conditional probability of sample image is defined as

$$p(g \mid f) = \|Af - g\|_{L_1} \tag{4}$$

Where, Given ideal image, $p(g \mid f)$ represents the conditional probability of observation image. In practical application, it is impossible for user to get the ideal image. To obtain physical variables with practical meaning, supposed that the priori probability of ideal image is $p(f)$, using Bayesian principle[15], the maximum posterior probability of ideal image is written as

$$p(f \mid g) \propto p(g \mid f) \bullet p(f) \tag{5}$$

If the transform coefficients of ideal image is sparse, and ideal image belongs to some kinds of function space, such as variable exponent function space, fractional BV function space and L_1 function space, etc. Supposed the image properties of different function space is independent, we can describe these properties by the following probability distribution function

$$p(f) = \prod_{\tau} p(T_\tau f) \tag{6}$$

Where T_τ represents function space, and τ is integer, which represents the number of function space. Substituting (4) and (6) into (5), using ln likelihood function for both sides of equation, the hybrid energy functional regularization model is written as

$$\hat{f} = \underset{f}{\operatorname{argmin}}\{E(f)\} \tag{7}$$

Where $E(f) = \|Af - g\|_{L_1} + \sum_{\tau} \ln p(T_\tau f)$.

In order to using the explicit physical meaning of priori probability, at the same time, the problem of (7) is not too complex, using the cartoon and texture for describing the image properties, which are characterized by fractional order BV function space and L_1 norm of tight frame domain, and the priori probabilities of expectation solution are respectively written as

$$-\ln p(T_1 f) = |Wx|_{L_1} \tag{8}$$

$$-\ln p(T_2 f) = |\nabla^{\alpha} u|_1 \tag{9}$$

Where x and u respectively represent texture and cartoon. Substituting (8) and (9) into (7), the hybrid energy functional regularization model for image reconstruction is written as

$$\underset{f,\ x,\ u}{\operatorname{argmin}}\{E(f,\ x,\ u)\} \tag{10}$$

Where $E(f,\ x,\ u) = \|Af - g\|_{L_1} + \alpha|Wx|_{L_1} + \beta|\nabla^{\alpha} u|_{L_1}$, α and β are non-negative constant. If $\alpha = 0$, formula (10) is image deblurry model of tight frame domain.

3 Splitting principle and algorithm of image reconstruction model

3.1 ADMM algorithm

Formula (10) is composed of fitting term and regularization term, it is non-smooth and -differential, the fixed point iterative algorithm based on first order gradient and Newton iterative algorithm[16] based on second order gradient can not be applied to (10). According to non-smooth convex optimization theory, the most effective method to compute non-smooth convex function that is composed of two terms is variable splitting technology. The variable splitting technology divide the object function that is composed of two terms into two easy to deal with sub-problems, alternating iterative sub-problems form ADMM algorithm[17]. Supposed the optimization object function can be formulated as

$$\underset{h}{\operatorname{argmin}}\{E_1(h)+E_2(Gh)\} \tag{11}$$

Where, non-smooth convex function E_1: $R^r \to R$ and E_2: $R^s \to R, G \in R^{s\times r}$. Taking advantage of variable splitting technology, formula (11) splits into two sub-problems that are expressed as follows

$$h^{k+1} = \underset{h}{\operatorname{argmin}}\left\{E_1(h)+\frac{\mu}{2}\left\|\gamma^k + Gh - z^k\right\|_2^2\right\} \tag{12}$$

$$z^{k+1} = \underset{z}{\operatorname{argmin}}\left\{E_2(z)+\frac{\mu}{2}\left\|\gamma^k + Gh^{k+1} - z\right\|_2^2\right\} \tag{13}$$

$$\gamma^{k+1} = \gamma^k + \left(Gh^{k+1} - z^{k+1}\right) \tag{14}$$

Supposed $\hat{h}$ is optimal solution of (11), if the cluster point $\{h^k\}$ is produced by alternating iterative (12)-(14), then $\lim_{k\to\infty}\left\|h^k - \hat{h}\right\|_2^2 = 0$.

However, image reconstruction model of (10) is composed of three terms, it is impossible to apply ADMM algorithm directly. Hence, the formula (10) must be improved.

3.2 Transformation of image reconstruction model

In order to apply ADMM algorithm to (10), we must transform (10) into similar to standard form formula of (11). Introducing auxiliary variables of $Af = \theta$, $Af - g = z$, $f = u + x$, the formula (10) is written as

$$E(f,\ x,\ u) = \|z\|_{L_1} + \alpha|Wx|_{L_1} + \beta\left|\nabla^\alpha u\right|_{L_1} \tag{15}$$

Set $h_1(x) = \alpha\|Wx\|$, $h_2(z) = \|z\|$, $h_3(\theta) = \sigma_{R^*}(\theta)$, $g_1(y) = \beta\left\|\nabla^\alpha u\right\|$, $g_2(Dy) = \sum_{j=1}^{3} h_j(D_j y)$, formula (15) is converted into standard form, which is written as

$$\underset{y}{\operatorname{argmin}}\{g_1(y)+g_2(Dy)\} \tag{16}$$

Where $y = [u \quad g \quad f]^T$, $D = \begin{bmatrix} -I & 0 & I \\ 0 & -I & A \\ 0 & 0 & A \end{bmatrix}$, set $b = [x \quad z \quad \theta]^T$, then $b = Dy$. Applying (12)-(14), formula (16) split into two bigger sub-problems, which are written as

$$y^{k+1} = \underset{y}{\operatorname{argmin}}\left\{g_1(y)+\frac{\mu}{2}\left\|d^k + Dy - b^k\right\|_2^2\right\} \tag{17}$$

$$b^{k+1} = \underset{b}{\operatorname{argmin}}\left\{g_2(z)+\frac{\mu}{2}\left\|d^k + Dy^{k+1} - b\right\|_2^2\right\} \tag{18}$$

$$d^{k+1} = d^k + \left(Dy^{k+1} - b^{k+1}\right) \tag{19}$$

1) according to sub-problem of (17), optimization about y is expressed as

$$\left(u^{k+1}, g^{k+1}, f^{k+1}\right) = \underset{u,g,f}{\operatorname{argmin}} \left\{ \beta \left|\nabla^{\alpha} u\right|_{\mathrm{TV}} + \frac{\mu}{2}\left(\left\| d_1^k + f - u - x^k \right\|_2^2 + \left\| d_2^k + Af - g - z^k \right\|_2^2 + \left\| d_3^k + Af - \theta^k \right\|_2^2 \right) \right\} \tag{20}$$

Optimization (20) about f, u and g, respectively, they form the following three sub-problems
(1) optimization (20) about f sub-problem

$$f^{k+1} = \underset{f}{\operatorname{argmin}} \frac{\mu}{2} \left\{ \left\| d_1^k + f - u - x^k \right\|_2^2 + \left\| d_2^k + Af - g - z^k \right\|_2^2 + \left\| d_3^k + Af - \theta^k \right\|_2^2 \right\} \tag{21}$$

Formula (21) is quadratic equation, according to first order Karush-Kuhn-Tucker (KKT) conditions [16], the first order variation of (21) about f is written as

$$\left(2A^{\mathrm{T}}A + I\right)f = u + x^k - d_1^k + A^{\mathrm{T}}\left(g + z^k - d_2^k + \theta^k - d_3^k\right) \tag{22}$$

Imposing periodic boundary condition on image, carrying out Fourier transform and inverse Fourier transform, we can get the following formula

$$f^{k+1} = F^{-1}\left(\frac{F\left(u^k + x^k - d_1^k + A^{\mathrm{T}}\left(g^k + z^k - d_2^k + \theta^k - d_3^k\right)\right)}{F\left(2A^{\mathrm{T}}A + I\right)} \right) \tag{23}$$

Where F and F^{-1} respectively represent Fourier transform and inverse Fourier transform.
(2) optimization (20) about u sub-problem

$$u^{k+1} = \underset{u}{\operatorname{argmin}} \left\{ \beta \left|\nabla^{\alpha} u\right|_{\mathrm{TV}} + \frac{\mu}{2} \left\| d_1^k + f - u - x^k \right\|_2^2 \right\} \tag{24}$$

In order to obtain the solution of (24), taking advantage of Fenchel transform for converting (24) into dual model [18], and using fixed point iterative theory, we get the following expression

$$u^{k+1} = \left(d_1^k + f^{k+1} - u^k - x^k\right) - \frac{\beta}{\mu}\overline{(-1)^{\alpha}}\operatorname{div}^{\alpha} p^{k+1} \tag{25}$$

where p^{k+1} is expressed as

$$p^{k+1} = \frac{p^k + \tau\left[\nabla^{\alpha}\overline{(-1)^{\alpha}}\operatorname{div}^{\alpha} p^k - \frac{\beta}{\mu}\left(d_1^k + f^{k+1} - u^k - x^k\right)\right]}{1 + \tau\left|\nabla^{\alpha}\overline{(-1)^{\alpha}}\operatorname{div}^{\alpha} p^k - \frac{\beta}{\mu}\left(d_1^k + f^{k+1} - u^k - x^k\right)\right|} \tag{26}$$

(3) optimization (20) about g sub-problem

$$g^{k+1} = \underset{g}{\operatorname{argmin}} \frac{\mu}{2}\left(\left\| d_2^k + Af - g - z^k \right\|_2^2 \right) \tag{27}$$

According to first order KKT conditions, the first order variation of (21) about g is written as

$$g^{k+1} = Af^{k+1} - z^k + d_2^k \tag{28}$$

2)according to sub-problem of (18), optimization about b is expressed as

$$\left(z^{k+1}, x^{k+1}, \theta^{k+1}\right) = \underset{z,\theta,x}{\operatorname{argmin}}\left\{\|z\|_1 + \alpha\|Wx\|_1 + \sigma_{R^+}(\theta) + \frac{\mu}{2}\left(\left\|d_1^k + f^{k+1} - u^{k+1} - x\right\|_2^2 + \right.\right.$$

$$\left.\left.\left\|d_2^k + Af^{k+1} - g^{k+1} - z\right\|_2^2 + \left\|d_3^k + Af^{k+1} - \theta\right\|_2^2\right)\right\} \tag{29}$$

Optimization (29) about z, x and θ, respectively, they form the following three sub-problems
(4) optimization (20) about z sub-problem

$$z^{k+1} = \underset{z}{\operatorname{argmin}}\left\{\|z\|_1 + \frac{\mu}{2}\left\|d_2^k + Af^{k+1} - g^{k+1} - z\right\|_2^2\right\} \tag{30}$$

Formula (30) is standard L2-L1 type, we can get

$$z^{k+1} = \operatorname{Soft}_{1/\mu}\left\{g^{k+1} - \left(d_2^k + Af^{k+1}\right)\right\} \tag{31}$$

Where $\operatorname{Soft}_{\xi}[\pi] = \max\{0, |\pi| - \xi\}\operatorname{sgn}(\pi)$, $\operatorname{sgn}(\bullet)$ is sign function.
(5) optimization (29) about x sub-problem

$$x^{k+1} = \underset{x}{\operatorname{argmin}}\left\{\alpha\|Wx\|_1 + \frac{\mu}{2}\left\|d_1^k + f^{k+1} - u^{k+1} - x\right\|_2^2\right\} \tag{32}$$

Similar to (30), we get the following formula

$$x^{k+1} = W^{\mathrm{T}} \operatorname{Soft}_{\alpha/\mu}\left[W\left(d_1^k + f^{k+1} - u^{k+1}\right)\right] \tag{33}$$

Where W^{T} is inverse transform of W ,and $W^{\mathrm{T}}W = I$, T represents transpose.
(6) optimization (29) about θ sub-problem

$$\theta^{k+1} = \underset{\theta}{\operatorname{argmin}}\left\{\sigma_{R^+}(\theta) + \frac{\mu}{2}\left\|d_3^k + Af^{k+1} - \theta\right\|_2^2\right\} \tag{34}$$

$$\theta^{k+1} = \max\left(0, d_3^k + Af^{k+1}\right) \tag{35}$$

3)according to formula of (19), auxiliary variable d is updated as following

$$d_1^{k+1} = d_1^k + f^{k+1} - u^{k+1} - x^{k+1} \tag{36}$$

$$d_2^{k+1} = d_2^k + Af^{k+1} - g^{k+1} - z^{k+1} \tag{37}$$

$$d_3^{k+1} = d_3^k + Af^{k+1} - \theta^{k+1} \tag{38}$$

3.3 ADMM algorithm for image reconstruction

1) set $k = 0$, u^0, g^0, f^0, and the maximum iterative number N.
2) compute (23) for f^{k+1}, compute (26) for p^{k+1}, compute (25) for u^{k+1}, compute (28) for g^{k+1}.

3) compute (31)for z^{k+1} ,compute (35) for x^{k+1}, compute (36) for θ^{k+1}, compute auxiliary variables d_1^{k+1}, d_2^{k+1} and d_3^{k+1} by (36), (37) and (38), respectively.

4) if $\left\|E\left(f^{k+1},x^{k+1},u^{k+1}\right)-E\left(f^{k},x^{k},u^{k}\right)\right\|\le t$ or $k>N$, jump 5), otherwise, set $k=k+1$, jump 2).

5) output the reconstruction image f^{k+1}.

4 Experiment results and analysis

Using refinable functon and tight frame with two generators for image sparse, they are shown in Figure 1. Taking advantage of Matlab fspecial function for producing PSF of size 9×9 and 13×13, they are shown in figure 2(a) and 2(b), respectively. The figure 3(a) and 4(a) is original Barbara image of size 256×256 and 512×512, respectively, and grey level is 0-255. The relative merits of the algorithm assessed by visual quality and quantitative peak signal-to-noise ratio (PSNR), we compare the restored results of the proposed with those of fast iterative soft threshold algorithm (FISTA) [5], dual model [19] and fast total variation deconvolution (FTVd) [20].

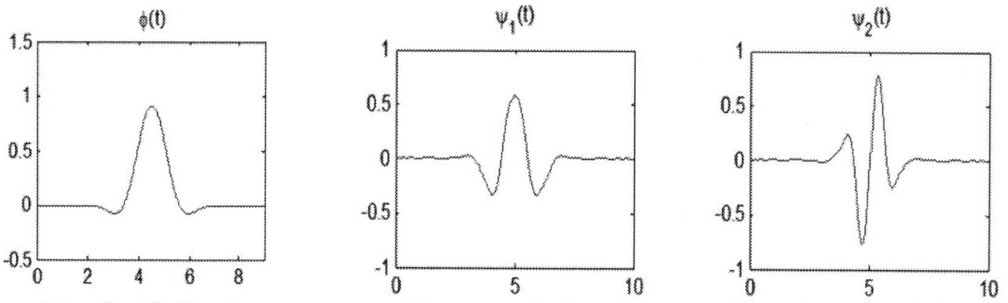

(a) refinable function (b) symmetric framelet (b) anti-symmetric framelet

Figure 1. refinable function and framelet with two generators

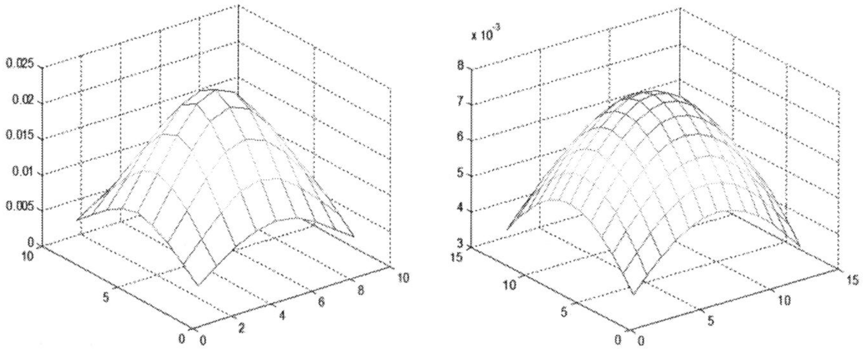

(a) PSF of size 9×9 (b) PSF of size 13×13

Figure 2. PSF with different size

In Figure 3, Camera image is blurred by Figure 2(a), and and 30% salt and pepper noise, it is difficult to distinguish the texture and cartoon information. In Figure 3(c), FISTA makes restored image become cartoon, texture information is completely lost. Dual model and FTVd produce a lot of staircases in steady regions, but restoration image of Figure 3(d) is more smoother than that of Figure 3(e). Figure 3(f), using the proposed for restoration image, the visual effect is better than that of other algorithms. According to qualitative index, PSNR of the proposed is higher that that of other algorithms, which shows image restoration quality is better that of other algorithms.

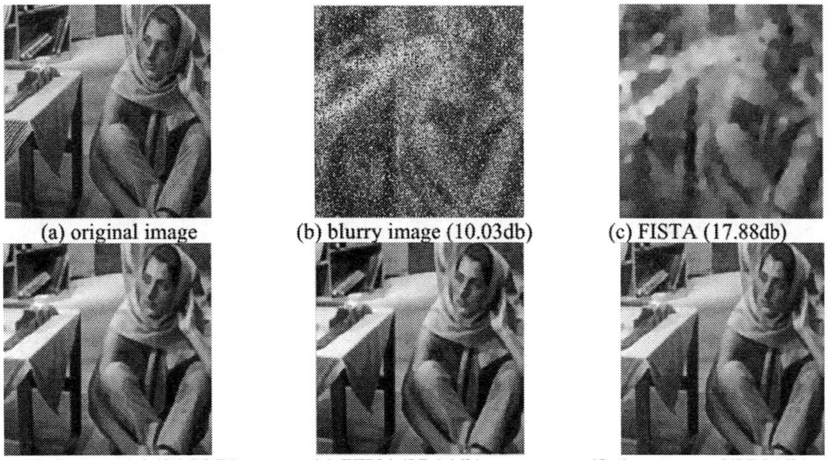

(a) original image (b) blurry image (10.03db) (c) FISTA (17.88db)

(d) dual model (26.85db) (e) FTVd (27.16db) (f) the proposed(27.34db)

Figure 3. Restoration comparison of different algorithms(256×256)

Figure 4(b) is is blurred by figure 2(b) of PSF, and 40% salt and pepper noise, and is more blurry than figure 3(b). According to visual quality, FISTA produces a lot of cartoon, the image texture information is thoroughly lost in figure 4(c). In figure 4(d) and figure 4(e), the visual effect of dual model and FTVd is better than that of FISTA, In figure 4(f), the visual effect is the best in these algorithms.

According to the quantitative performance, FISTA obtains the lowest PSNR, which shows the quality of image restoration is worse. PSNR of dual model is lower than that of FTVd, the proposed obtains the highest PSNR, which show that the quality of image restoration is best.

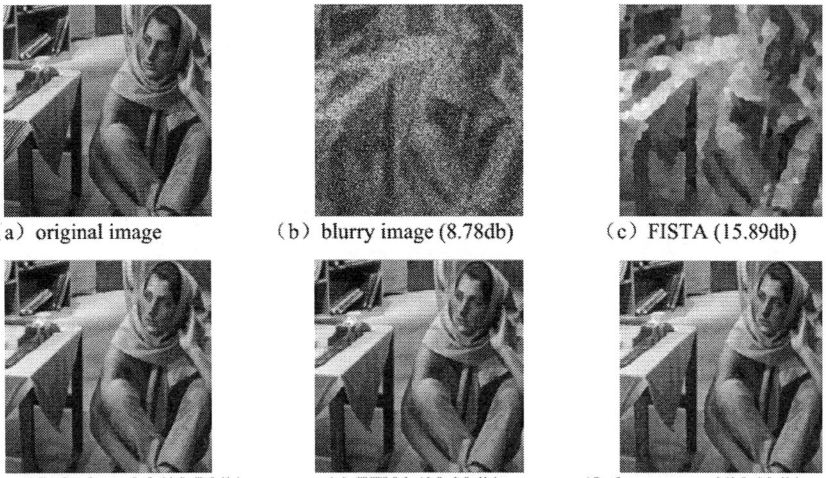

(a) original image (b) blurry image (8.78db) (c) FISTA (15.89db)

(d) dual model (22.76db) (e) FTVd (22.99db) (f) the proposed(23.03db)

Figure 4. Restoration comparison of different algorithms(512×512)

Conclusion

In this paper, a new hybrid energy function regularization model is proposed, by introducing auxiliary variables, image reconstruction model is converted into standard convex optimization model, using ADMM algorithm, standard model is split into six sub-problems, and every sub-problem has simple closed expression, which form a fast alternate iterative algorithm. Experiment results show the proposed algorithm can effectively reconstruct image blurred by salt and pepper noise, and obtain better visual quality than that of other methods. In the future work, we will carry out research on the parameters of regularization terms for image restoration performance influence.

Acknowledgement

This work was supported by Higher Educational Scientific Research Projects of Inner Mongolia Autonomous Region, China (NJZY16254), and project supported by the Natural Science Foundation of Inner Mongolia Autonomous Region, China (2016MS0602).

References

1. Li X C, Bian S X, Li Y Y, Survey of convex energy functional regularization model of image restoration[J], Journal of Image and Graphics, **21**, 4(2016)
2. Zhang Zhengrong, Zhang Jun, Wei Zhihui, Cartoon-texture composite regularization based non-blind deblurring method for partly-textured blurred images with Poisson noise [J], Signal Processing, **116**, 11(2015)
3. Li X C, Ma S Y, Bian S X, Application of dual algorithm to TV-L1 deblurring model of frame domain[J], Journal of Image and Graphics, **20**, 11(2015)
4. Li Fang, Shen Chaomin, Fan Jingsong, Image restoration combining a total variational filter and a fourth-order filter [J], Journal of Visual Communication and Image Representation, **18**, 4(2007)
5. Beck Amir, Teboulle Marc, A fast dual proximal gradient algorithm for convex minimization and applications, Operations Research Letters, **42**, 1(2014)
6. Jiang Le, Huang Jin, Lv Xiaoguang, Alternating direction method for the high-order total variation-based Poisson noise removal problem [J], Numerical Algorithms, **69**, 3(2015)
7. Fan Qibin, Jiang Dandan, Jiao Yuling. A multi-parameter regularization model for image restoration [J], Signal Processing, **114**, 9(2015)
8. Becker Stephen, Bobin Jerome, Candes Emmanuel J, NESTA: a fast and accurate first-order method for sparse recovery [J], SIAM Journal on Imaging Sciences, **4**, 1(2011)
9. Yang Z Z, Zhou J L, Lang F N, Noise detection and image de-noising based on fractional calculus [J], Journal of Image and Graphics, **19**, 10(2014)
10. Fan W, Cai G G, Zhu Z K, Sparse representation of transients in wavelet basis and its application in gearbox fault feature extraction [J], Mechanical Systems and Signal Processing, **56-57**, 5(2015)
11. Cai Jian-Feng, Ji Hui, Shen Zuowei, Data-driven tight frame construction and image denoising [J], Applied and Computational Harmonic Analysis, **37**, 1(2014)
12. Daubechies I, Han B, Ron A, Framelets : mra-based constructions of wavelet frames [J], Applied and Computational Harmonic Analysis, **14**, 1(2003)
13. Cai J F, Chan R, Shen Z W, A framelet-based image inpainting algorithm [J], Applied and Computational Harmonic Analysis, **24**, 2(2008)
14. Selesnick Ivan W, Abdelnour, Symmetric wavelet tight frames with two generators [J], Applied and Computational Harmonic Analysis, **17**, 2(2004)
15. Li X C, Expectation maximization method for parameter estimation of image statistical model[J], Journal of Image and Graphics, **17**, 6(2012)
16. Curtis R. Vogel, *Computational methods for inverse problems*(SIAM: Society for Industrial and Applied Mathematics, 2002)
17. Eckstein J, Bertsekas D P, On the Douglas-Rachford splitting method and the proximal algorithm for maximal monotone operators [J]. Mathematical Programming, **55**, 1(1992)
18. Antonin Chambolle, An algorithm for total variation minimization and applications, Journal of Mathematical Imaging and Vision, **20**, 1-2(2004)

19. Clason Christian, Jin Bangti, Kunisch Kral, A duality-based splitting method for l1-tv image restoration with automatic regularization parameter choice, SIAM Journal on Scientific Computing, **32**, 3(2010)
20. Yang J, Zhang Y, Yin W, An efficient tv-l1 algorithm for deblurring multichannel images corrupted by impulsive noise, SIAM Journal on Scientific Computing, **31**, 4(2009)

The Indoor Personnel Inertial Positioning Based on Image Recognition Technology in Substation Depth

Min XU[a], Lin PENG, Hai-Yun HAN, Ni-Ge LI, Zhan-Sheng HOU, Gang WANG, Xing-Chuan BAO, He WANG and Hai YU

Global Energy Interconnection Research Institute, China

Abstract. A kind of inertial positioning technology personnel indoor substation depth based on image recognition, scene modeling using 3D scanning depth camera for image acquisition of fast; key position of image recognition front-end uses image recognition software algorithm, the image information is converted to dot matrix data, connect the background server to obtain accurate positioning coordinates, greatly reduce the direct image transmission to the identification of the amount of data in the deployment of additional equipment to achieve precise positioning of field personnel without the aid, effectively solve the traditional Bluetooth, millimeter wave and laser positioning need in the site layout a lot of equipment problems, eliminate safety hazards in the substation; finally, the inertial navigation algorithm, field personnel positioning using gyroscope and accelerometer do the positioning of the auxiliary, smooth, real-time and accurate, have The utility model solves the problem of poor positioning accuracy of the electric field operation, and improves the working efficiency of the field operators.

1 Introduction

With the development of electric power industry in our country is increasingly expanding and new equipment put into operation, operation and maintenance of power equipment maintenance information, facing complicated procedures, complicated equipment disassembly and high precision and the staff level is not a problem, the type and size of equipment in the substation is also increasing, fully enclosed substation is currently the most advanced, more profound changes in the original open substation deployment mode, all devices are placed in the substation of large and small size ranging from relatively independent closed room, operation and maintenance personnel to accurately find the target device only through experience in the field, can not accurately know its location information location and the target device, need to spend a lot of time to find the equipment, seriously affecting work the efficiency, especially in emergency situations, facing the emergency situation of substation unprepared, on-site personnel can quickly It is very important to find the location of the fault equipment quickly for the repair process, the traditional operating mode can not meet the requirements of the development of the power grid, so it is urgent to solve the problem of indoor positioning.

The substation network communication environment is more complex, often plagued by high voltage equipment electromagnetic interference and substation remote area information intensity is

[a] Corresponding author: xumin1@geiri.sgcc.com.cn

weak and other issues, but the field of power equipment variety, modeling workload, and the model takes up more resources, all from the terminal identification is too large for the terminal pressure, therefore must by the background server real-time online image recognition. But by the communication technology, real-time live streaming video transmission to the background recognition efficiency is low, so it is necessary to study a set of front image preprocessing technology, image recognition for dot matrix information, dot matrix data transmission compression to the background recognition, greatly reduce the amount of data transmission, improve the bandwidth utilization rate.

Secondly, because of the special environment of substation and high risk equipment, determine its application in indoor positioning technology requirements as much as possible to build less auxiliary equipment, but the indoor positioning and navigation technology to traditional coordinate positioning by building auxiliary equipment, build environment is more complex and high cost, including Bluetooth positioning method, millimeter wave localization method, infrared positioning method, GPS positioning method, for the special environment of substation, cannot build various types of equipment in the field, so the traditional indoor positioning technology in substation environment not suitable.

2 Indoor inertial positioning technology in substation depth based on image recognition

Due to the rapid development of power equipment, including the full closed type substation, the on-site personnel demand for location information is more and more urgent, but because of the special environment of substation and high risk equipment, determine its application in indoor positioning technology requirements as much as possible to build less auxiliary equipment, this paper put forward to solve the above problems effective method for processing, using three-dimensional modeling scene scanning depth camera quickly and effectively solve the three-dimensional modeling [1] requires a lot of manual operation and operating personnel with professional knowledge of the operating problems; secondly, image acquisition of the key position of online image recognition using image recognition software algorithm, connecting the backend server to get accurate coordinate positioning, to achieve precise positioning of the auxiliary equipment on-site personnel without additional arrangement, Effectively solve the traditional Bluetooth, millimeter wave and laser positioning method [2] in the site layout a lot of equipment problems, eliminate safety hazards in the substation; finally, the inertial navigation algorithm, field personnel positioning using gyroscope and accelerometer assisted, do the personnel positioning of the smooth, real-time and accurate operation, effectively solve the positioning accuracy the electric field difference problem, improve the work efficiency of on-site personnel. Including the following steps:

Step one: using the scene modeling for 3D scanning depth camera fast, according to the modeling method of image, video and depth vision sensor data driven, 3D geometry of the two-dimensional images to restore the scene, or the use of depth vision sensor RGB-D, the three-dimensional point of continuous data frame mosaic to obtain scene cloud, realize Panorama modeling the scene in a rapid manner. The 3D depth camera using two camera while shooting photos, according to the geometrical relationship of the relationship between two images and camera image space, the actual location information of feature points, imaging principle as shown in Figure 1. If the camera projection model, image point position corresponding to determine (p_1, p_2 and known), between the two outside the parameters of the camera (C_1, C_2 and determine the position of known) case, only to determine the spatial position in world coordinates, the three-dimensional P coordinate of the reconstruction.

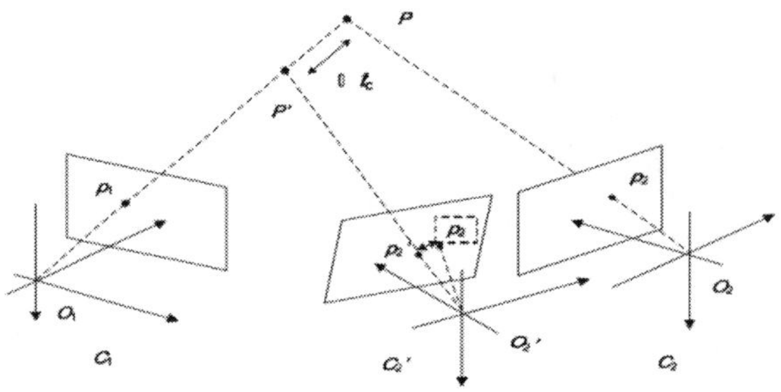

Figure 1

Step two: in the substation site selecting feature image points different as standard template matching, using feature block template matching algorithm for on-line identification of images, in front of the equipment deployment image preprocessing module [3], for each frame of the collected images were preprocessed as the sample template, the feature of template matching, the first is the transformation of the standard template and template, according to the number of feature block template is divided into a plurality of same size blocks, such as the real-time video frame has 10 feature blocks, the video frame image is divided into 64 squares average size the same, the assumption that the 10 the average distribution of feature blocks in one of the 8 boxes, the remaining 56 squares abandon feature points statistics only the remaining 8 squares, the final image is cut into dot matrix information. Through the transmission of the lattice data, the amount of data transmitted directly to a large number of video images is greatly reduced, the transmission efficiency is improved, and the bandwidth utilization rate is reduced.

Step three: terminal dot data to the backend server, the server receives the lattice data, using lattice data feature block and standard template block by block matching, then don't is small, it is not matching. As the sample $D(k)$ template and template matching in block comparison $(i,\ j)$ results (results for 0, 1, the results do not match), $N(i,\ j)$ as the sample feature block template, $N_k^T(i,j)$ as a standard feature block matching template, the difference between the size of the threshold T, according to the threshold to identify the corresponding image model, block matching (i,j) results:

$$D(k) = \begin{cases} 0 & N(i,j)-N_k^T(i,j) \le T \\ 1 & N(i,j)-N_k^T(i,j) > T \end{cases}$$

Finally, the result is compared with the standard image feature block template $C = \min_{k=1}^{A}[\sum_{i=1}^{\frac{h}{2}} \sum_{j=1}^{\frac{w}{2}} D(k)]$, Where h is the height of the lattice, w is the width of the lattice, A is the number of standard image lattice set.

Step four: through the background data to identify the current location of the image lattice number, query the database to obtain precise location coordinates, encrypted transmission to the terminal for analysis by using the SM1 cryptographic algorithm, terminal server to receive encrypted, decrypted by using the SM1 cryptographic algorithm, obtaining user coordinates where information, dynamic real-time correction of terminal guide map marker the position, to achieve precise positioning of field personnel without additional auxiliary equipment layout, the specific architecture is shown in Figure 2.

DOI: 10.1051/itmconf/20171102005

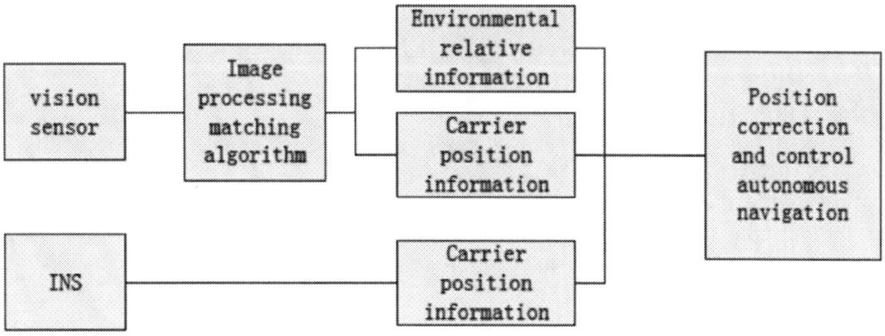

Figure 2

Step five: image recognition and localization algorithm using mathematical description of image features, in addition to the accuracy of the image error introduced by the image will show similar characteristics, so in the computer matching process, according to the characteristics of mathematical description, there will be mistakes and errors, matching, there will have an impact on the whole, the reliability of the result. The accuracy and therefore, there must be the image matching results were determined by determining the appropriate method, eliminating the false matching, to ensure the reliability of matching results; and for a certain time, can not use the image matching technology, you need to consider additional auxiliary navigation information to maintain visual navigation algorithm operation. The strapdown inertial navigation algorithm, the positioning of gyroscope and accelerometer assisted site personnel, auxiliary image recognition and positioning technology, inertial orientation modification without image marks or image recognition errors, where the smooth movement of personnel in the mobile map to mark the location of the. According to the characteristics of the substation in the power grid, a simple inertial navigation algorithm is designed to meet the needs of fast navigation.

Inertial navigation algorithm [4] is mainly divided into three parts: attitude update, speed update and location update. Its core is based on a correct attitude, so the most important impact on the accuracy of strapdown inertial navigation algorithm is the attitude update algorithm, followed by the speed update algorithm.

The attitude update algorithm is as follows:

$C_{b(k)}^{n} = C_{b(k-1)}^{n} C_{b(k)}^{b(k-1)}$, among, $C_{b(k)}^{b(k-1)}$ When the n system is used as the reference coordinate system, b is t_{k-1} to t_k transform direction cosine, $C_{b(k)}^{n}$ is t_k attitude direction cosine, $C_{b(k-1)}^{n}$ is t_{k-1} attitude direction cosine. If make $w_{nb}^{b}(t)$ the rotational angular velocity of the carrier coordinate system relative to the navigation coordinate system, Φ_k is t_{m-1} to t_m moment coordinate system b equivalent rotation vector relative to navigation coordinate system, the final rotation vector is $\Phi_k = \int_{t_{k-1}}^{t_k} w_{nb}^{n}(t)dt = \int_{t_{k-1}}^{t_k} w_{ib}^{b}(t) \quad (C_b^n(t))^T w_{in}^{n}(t)dt$.

Speed update algorithm is as follows:

$$V_k^n = V_{k-1}^n + \int_{t_{k-1}}^{t_k} C_b^n f_{ib}^b dt + \int_{t_{k-1}}^{t_k} [g_l^n \quad [2w_{ie}^n \quad \times w_{en}^n] \quad v^n]dt$$

, v_k^n is t_k velocity of a time carrier; v_{k-1}^n is t_{k-1} velocity of a time carrier; $\int_{t_{k-1}}^{t_k} C_b^n f_{ib}^b dt$ is t_{k-1} to t_k velocity increment of time ; $\int_{t_{k-1}}^{t_k} [g_l^n - [2w_{ie}^n + w_{en}^n] \times v^n]dt$ is t_{k-1} to t_k gravity and velocity increment.

Step six: calculate the coordinates of inertial navigation based on real-time strapdown inertial navigation algorithm and terminal acceleration and gyro sensor, real-time correction of the client map marks the position, to achieve a smooth navigation in the feature image between the blank area features make navigation between images, the auxiliary field personnel for precise navigation [5].

Summary

This paper presents an indoor positioning method of substation personnel inertial depth based on image recognition, scene modeling using 3D scanning depth camera for image acquisition of fast; key position of image recognition front-end uses image recognition software algorithm, the image information is converted to dot matrix data, connect the background server to obtain accurate positioning coordinates, greatly reduce the direct the background image is transmitted to the identification data, and deployment of additional equipment to achieve precise positioning of field personnel without the aid, effectively solve the traditional Bluetooth, millimeter wave and laser positioning need in the site layout a lot of equipment problems, eliminate safety hazards in the substation; finally, the inertial navigation algorithm, field personnel positioning by using gyroscope and the acceleration sensor, do smooth, real-time positioning And accurately and effectively solve the problem of poor positioning accuracy of electric field operation, and improve the working efficiency of field workers.

References

1. Infinite reality avatars, eternal life, new worlds, and the dawn of the virtual revolution. J. Blascovich,J. B. Bailenson. . 2011
2. Power,madness and immortality:the future of virtual reality. Mychilo Stephenson Cline. . 2005
3. Exodus to the Virtual World:How Online Fun is Changing Reality. Castronova,Edward. . 2007
4. An introduction to the finite element method. J. N. Reddy. . 1993
5. The CMS experiment at the CERN LHC. J.?Instrum. 2008

Random Access Preamble Generation with Low Storage for LTE Networks

Pei-Zhe XIN[1], Yu-Qi LV[2,a], Lan SU[3] and Yu-Dong WANG

[1]*State Power Economic Research Institute, Beijing 100052, China, 10653224309@qq.com*
[2]*University of Electronic Science and Technology of China, Chengdu, China*
[3]*State Power Economic Research Institute, Beijing 100052, China*

Abstract. Long Term Evolution (LTE) random access preambles are generated from cyclically shifted Zadoff-Chu(ZC) sequences of prime length by using so-called Discrete Fourier Transformation-Spread-Orthogonal Frequency Division Multiplexing (DFT-S-OFDM) modulation. In this paper we propose a novel preamble generation to reduce the storage and complexity of cyclically shifted ZC sequences' Discrete Fourier Transformation (DFT). The proposed preamble generation allows the DFT of cyclically shifted ZC sequences to rely only on several constant factors and the elements of non-cyclically shifted ZC sequences which have already been generated. This preamble generation merely requires the storage of several constant factors, while avoids large storage and complex computation of complex exponential function.

1 Introduction

As the rapid development of the communication technology and the microelectronic technology, the electronic power system develops gradually towards informatization and intellectualization. The electric energy data acquire system is an important part of smart grid which covers the power users and electrical information. Stable and reliable communication network are the guarantee of energy data acquisition. Compared with the optical fiber network, wireless communication network has a lower cost, and can directly use of the existing mobile communication network to establish connections quickly.

Electric energy data acquire system consists of three parts: master station, communication network and collectors. Its structure is shown in Fig. 1. Master station is the center of electric energy data acquire system, which is responsible for controlling the data acquire terminals, processing and sharing the information of electric energy, and offering the data interface to the services of electric power department and the marketing applications. Communication network provides a communication channel to connect data acquire terminals and master station.

Next taking the LTE communication system for an example, the paper illustrates the advantage of the electric energy data acquire system. The random access channel (RACH) is a common uplink channel in LTE communication systems used by the mobile user equipment (UE) to establish the initial access and uplink synchronization to a base station (Node B) [1]–[4]. The random access (RA) preambles transmitted from the UE are generated from cyclically shifted Zadoff-Chu sequences,

[a] Corresponding author: lyq-tiantian@139.com

owing to their good correlation properties [5]. In the generation of the random access preambles, first we need to perform an N-point discrete fourier transform of a cyclically shifted ZC sequences defined by the root index u and the cyclic shift C_v. However, large storage and complex computation of complex exponential function in DFT cannot meet the mobile transceivers' storage and computational requirements.

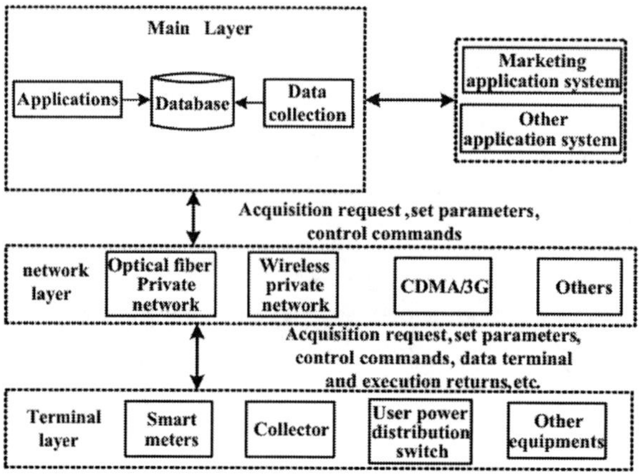

Figure 1. Structure of electric energy data acquire system

To reduce the storage and complexity of cyclically shifted ZC sequences' discrete fourier transform, several effective work has been done. CHARLES M. RADER expressed a fast fourier transform (FFT) algorithm of prime length M as a fast convolution [6-7]. But the computation of three FFTs of highly composite length $N>M$ is still required. Then the efficient discrete fourier transform structures more suitable for applications of ZC sequences have been derived [8]. Nevertheless, the discrete fourier transform structures in [8] cannot always be used to reduce the number of operations in the transmitter of long term evolution user equipment, as the transmitted random access (RA) preamble can be a cyclically shifted version of the basic ZC sequences. In addition, this discrete fourier transform structures cannot avoid large storage and complex computation of complex exponential function.

In this paper, we propose the discrete fourier transform of cyclically shifted ZC sequences of prime length depends only on several constant factors and the elements of the non-cyclically-shifted ZC sequence which has already been generated. The fact allows us to reduce the number of arithmetic operations and the storage of complex exponential function for computing the discrete fourier transform of a cyclically shifted ZC sequence of prime length.

2 Definition and previous DFT of preamble sequences

In this paper, we propose the discrete

2.1 Definition

The uth root Zadoff-Chu sequence of prime length N_{ZC} is defined as [5]

$$x_u(n) = e^{-j\frac{\pi u n(n+1)}{N_{ZC}}}, \quad 0 \le n \le N_{ZC}-1 \tag{1}$$

where the root index u is an integer less than the prime N_{ZC}. From the uth root Zadoff-Chu sequence, random access preambles with zero correlation zones of length $N_{CS}-1$ are defined by cyclic shifts according to [5]

$$x_{u,v}(n) = x_u((n+C_v) \bmod N_{ZC}) \tag{2}$$

where the cyclic shift C_v is equal to vN_{CS}, for unrestricted sets.

In LTE, the uplink random access preamble is defined by a complex baseband signal of the form [8]:

$$s(k) = \sum_{m=0}^{N_{ZC}-1} \sum_{n=0}^{N_{ZC}-1} x_{u,v}(n) e^{-j\frac{2\pi nm}{N_{ZC}}} \cdot e^{j\frac{2\pi(m+m_0)k}{L}} \tag{3}$$

where $-N_{CP} \leq k < L$ and $N_{ZC}=839$, $L=24576$. N_{CP} is the variable cyclic prefix length. The above formula is the discrete time expression of the formula given in [5] where a number of random access protocol parameters have been condensed into a single m_0 for brevity. In the generation of such RA preambles, the first step is to perform a N-point discrete Fourier transform of a cyclically shifted ZC sequence by the root index u and the cyclic shift C_v.

2.2 Previous DFT of preamble sequences

In practice, the DFT is almost always implemented as a FFT, which allows a reduction in the number of arithmetic operations from approximately N^2 to $N\log_2 N$ [9]. Considering the special properties of ZC sequences, an attempt to reduce the computation complexity of ZC sequences' DFT has been done in [8]. The DFT of the uth root ZC sequence $x_u(n)$ of prime length N_{ZC} is equal to a conjugated and time-scaled version of $x_u(n)$, up to a constant factor:

$$X_u(k) = x_u^*[u^{-1}k] X_u(0) \tag{4}$$

where '*' denotes complex conjugation, and $u^{-1}=1/u$ is the modular multiplicative inverse of u, i.e. an integer such that $uu^{-1}=1 \bmod N_{ZC}$.

By using the DFT properties of cyclically shifted sequences, the DFT $X_{u,v}(k)$ of cyclically shifted ZC sequence $x_{u,v}(n)$ can be expressed as

$$X_{u,v}(k) = X_u(k) e^{j\frac{2\pi k C_v}{N_{zc}}} \tag{5}$$

By applying (4) to (5), we obtain

$$X_{u,v}(k) = x_u^*(u^{-1}k) X_u(0) e^{j\frac{2\pi k C_v}{N_{zc}}} \tag{6}$$

It is obvious that (6) cannot avoids complex computation of complex exponential function in computing the DFT of cyclically shifted ZC sequences. In addition, (N_{ZC}-1) complex values of $X_u(0)$ should be prestored in memory, since there are (N_{ZC}-1) root Zadoff-Chu sequences that can be transmitted from the mobile transceivers [5].

3 Proposed preamble generation

To avoid complex computation of complex exponential function and obtain the structure of an efficient DFT of a cyclically shifted ZC sequence, (6) should be transformed into another form that includes no extra complex exponential functions.

By utilizing the definition of the uth root Zadoff-Chu sequence of prime length N_{ZC}, we obtain that

$$\begin{aligned} x_u^*(u^{-1}k)e^{j\frac{2\pi kC_v}{N_{zc}}} &= e^{j\frac{\pi u[u^{-1}k(u^{-1}k+1)]}{N_{zc}}} e^{j\frac{\pi u(2u^{-1}kC_v)}{N_{zc}}} \\ &= e^{j\frac{\pi u[(u^{-1}k+C_v)(u^{-1}k+C_v+1)-C_v(C_v+1)]}{N_{zc}}} \\ &= e^{j\frac{\pi u[(u^{-1}k+C_v)(u^{-1}k+C_v+1)]}{N_{zc}}} e^{-j\frac{\pi uC_v(C_v+1)}{N_{zc}}} \\ &= x_u^*(u^{-1}k+C_v)x_u(C_v) \end{aligned} \tag{7}$$

In the derivation of (7), the periodicity of the root ZC sequences has been applied. It is easily verified that $x_u(n)$ is periodic with prime N_{ZC}. After substituting (7) into (6), it can be seen that

$$X_{u,v}(k) = x_u^*(u^{-1}k+C_v)x_u(C_v)X_u(0) \tag{8}$$

Through observing the form of $X_u(0)$, we find that $X_u(0)$ can be expressed as

$$\begin{aligned} X_u(0) &= \sum_{n=0}^{N_{ZC}-1} e^{-j\frac{\pi un(n+1)(N_{ZC}+1)}{N_{ZC}}} \\ &= \sum_{n=0}^{N_{ZC}-1} e^{-j\frac{2\pi u\alpha n(n+1)(N_{ZC}+1)}{N_{ZC}}} \\ &= \sum_{n=0}^{N_{ZC}-1} e^{-j\frac{2\pi u\alpha[(n+\alpha)^2-\alpha^2]}{N_{ZC}}} \\ &= e^{j\frac{2\pi u\alpha^3}{N_{ZC}}} \sum_{n=0}^{N_{ZC}-1} e^{-j\frac{2\pi u\alpha(n+\alpha)^2}{N_{ZC}}} \\ &= e^{j\frac{2\pi u\alpha^3}{N_{ZC}}} G(u\alpha, N_{ZC})^* \end{aligned} \tag{9}$$

where $G(m, L)^*$ is the complex conjugate of the quadratic Gauss sum [9]

$$G(m,L) = \sum_{k=0}^{L-1} e^{j\frac{2\pi mk^2}{L}} \tag{10}$$

and $\alpha=(N_{ZC}+1)/2$ is an integer for odd prime N_{ZC}. Considering prime N_{ZC} and $(u\alpha, N_{ZC})=1$, $G(u\alpha, N_{ZC})^*$ can be expressed as

$$\begin{aligned} G(u\alpha, N_{ZC})^* &= (\frac{u\alpha}{N_{ZC}})G(1, N_{ZC})^* \\ &= (\frac{u}{N_{ZC}})(\frac{\alpha}{N_{ZC}})G(1, N_{ZC})^* \end{aligned} \tag{11}$$

where (u/N_{ZC}) and (α/N_{ZC}) denote Legendre symbols [10]. And if $u \neq 0$ mod N_{ZC}, then the values of the Legendre symbol (u/N_{ZC}) are 1 or -1. From (10) and (11), it can be seen that

$$X_1(0) = e^{j\frac{2\pi\alpha^3}{N_{ZC}}} (\frac{\alpha}{N_{ZC}})G(1, N_{ZC})^* \tag{12}$$

Thus by applying (11) and (12) to (10), we obtain

$$X_u(0) = e^{j\frac{2\pi(u-1)\alpha^3}{N_{ZC}}} (\frac{u}{N_{ZC}}) X_1(0) \tag{13}$$

To avoid complex computation of the complex exponential function $e^{j\frac{2\pi(u-1)\alpha^3}{N_{ZC}}}$, (13) should be simplified further as

$$\begin{aligned} e^{j\frac{2\pi(u-1)\alpha^3}{N_{ZC}}} &= e^{j\frac{\pi(u-1)(1-N_{ZC})\alpha^2}{N_{ZC}}} \\ &= e^{-j\frac{2\pi(u-1)\beta\alpha}{N_{ZC}}(\frac{N_{ZC}}{2}+\frac{1}{2})} \\ &= e^{-j\frac{\pi(u-1)\beta\alpha}{N_{ZC}}} \\ &= x_{u-1}(\beta) \end{aligned} \tag{14}$$

where β=(N_{ZC}-1)/2. And then substituting (13) and (14) into (8), the DFT of cyclically shifted ZC sequences can be expressed as

$$X_{u,v}(k) = (\frac{u}{N_{ZC}}) x_u^*(u^{-1}k + C_v) x_u(C_v) x_{u-1}(\beta) X_1(0) \tag{15}$$

To simplify the computation of (15), the constant factors can be prestored in memory. (N_{ZC}-1) and 2M bits are needed to prestore the Legendre symbol (u/ N_{ZC}) and the complex value $X_1(0)$ respectively if real and imaginary parts art M bits. Therefore (N_{ZC}-1+2M) bits are needed to prestore the constant factors in memory.

4 Storage and complexity analysis

From (15) it follows that, for a given root u and the cyclic shift C_v of the ZC sequence of prime length N_{ZC}, the corresponding DFT is cyclically delayed and then cyclically sampled complex conjugated version of already generated basic ZC sequences, multiplied by a constant, which consists of four factors: the $(C_v+1)^{th}$ element of the uth root ZC sequence, the $(\beta+1)^{th}$ element of the $(u\text{-}1)^{th}$ root ZC sequence, the sum of all the elements of the 1th root ZC sequence, and the Legendre symbol. Some constant factors, like the sum and the Legendre symbol, can be prestored in memory to accelerate the generation of LTE random access preambles. For the previous DFT of preamble sequences, (N_{ZC}-1) complex values of $X_u(0)$ and N_{ZC} complex values of exp($j2\pi kC_v/N_{ZC}$) should be prestored, while the proposed DFT merely requires the storage of (N_{ZC}-1) binary values of the Legendre symbol and one complex values $X_1(0)$.

The table of storage and complexity analysis between the previous and proposed DFT of preamble sequences goes as follows.

Table 1. Storage and Complexity Analysis

	Storage (bit)	Complexity (complex multiplication)
Previous DFT	(N_{ZC}-1) ·2M+N_{ZC}·2M	N_{ZC}+1
Proposed DFT	N_{ZC}-1+2M	N_{ZC}+3

Suppose M bits are required for storing the real or imaginary of one complex.

In the generation of random access preambles for LTE systems, the random access preamble sequence length N_{ZC} is 839 when preamble formats 0~3 are in application [5]. And suppose M is equal to 12. The different storage requirement of the above two kinds of preamble generation is showed in the following Fig.2.

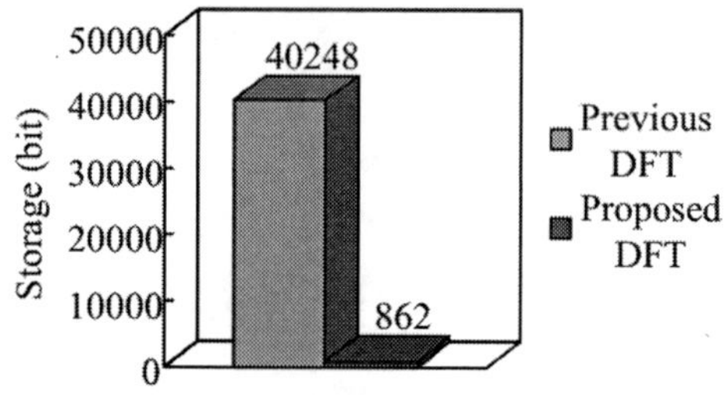

Figure 2. The storage requirement of the previous and proposed DFT of preamble sequences

From the above table and figure it follows that, although proposed DFT of preambles requires two more complex multiplications than the previous one, it reduces $(N_{ZC}-1)\cdot 2M + (N_{ZC}-1)\cdot(2M-1)$ bits storage, which is very helpful for hardware implementation of preamble generation.

Conclusion

Random access preamble generation of low storage for LTE systems is presented. This preamble generation allows the DFT of cyclically shifted ZC sequences to depend only on several constant factors and the elements of already generated non-cyclically-shifted ZC sequences. In addition, large storage and complex computation of complex exponential function are replaced by prestoring several constant factors, which is significant for hardware implementation of LTE RA preamble generation.

Acknowledgment

The paper is sponsored by the science and technology program of the State Grid Corporation of China (No. SGTYHT/15-JS-191).

References

1. Mohammad M. Mansour, "Optimized Architecture for Computing Zadoff-Chu Sequences with Application to LTE," in *Global Telecommunications Conference*, 2009, pp. 1-6.
2. Yang Wen, Wei Huang, and Zhongpei Zhang, "CAZAC sequence and its application in LTE random access," in *Information Theory Workshop*, Oct. 2006, pp. 544-547.
3. B. M. Popovic, and O. Mauritz, "Random Access Preambles for Evolved UTRA Cellular System," *Spread Spectrum Techniques and Applications, 2006 IEEE Ninth International Symposium on*. Aug. 2006, pp. 488-492
4. Mehdi Aminjoo, Fredrik Gunnarsson, and Filip Andren, "3GPP LTE Random Access Channel Self-Optimization", *Proc. IEEE*, pp.2784-2793, January 2014.
5. 3GPP TS 36.211, "Evolved Universal Terrestrial Radio Access (E-UTRA); Physical Channels and Modulation," Mar. 2010.
6. Charles M. Rader, "Discrete Fourier transforms when the number of data samples is prime," *Proc. IEEE*, vol. 56, no. 6, pp. 1107-1108, June 1968.
7. Arun C.A. , P. Prakasam, "Design of high speed FFT algorithm For OFDM technique", *Proc. IEEE*, October 2016.
8. S. Beyme and C. Leung, "Efficient computation of DFT of Zadoff-Chu sequences," Electron. Lett., vol. 45, no. 9, pp. 461-463, Apr. 2009

9. John G. Proakis, and Dimitris G. Manolakis, Digital Signal Processing: Principles, Algorithms and Applications, Fourth Edition. June 2007, pp. 379-399.
10. B. C. Berndt, R. J. Evans, and K. S. Willias, *Gauss and Jacobi sums*. 1998, pp. 7-28.
11. Godfey Harold Hardy, Edward Maitland Wright, and Joseph H. Silvevman, *An introduction to the theory of numbers*. Mar. 2007, pp. 79-85.
12. Min Hua, Mao Wang, and Kristo Wenjie Yang, "Analysis of the Frequency Offset Effect on Zadoff-Chu Sequence Timing Performance", *Proc. IEEE*, pp. 4024-4039, October 2014.

Communication Base Station Log Analysis Based on Hierarchical Clustering

Shao-Hua ZHANG and Chang-Hua LIU[a]

School of Mathematics & Computer Science, Wuhan Polytechnic University, Wuhan, Hubei, China

Abstract. Communication base stations generate massive data every day, these base station logs play an important value in mining of the business circles. This paper use data mining technology and hierarchical clustering algorithm to group the scope of business circle for the base station by recording the data of these base stations. Through analyzing the data of different business circle based on feature extraction and comparing different business circle category characteristics, which can choose a suitable area for operators of commercial marketing.

1 Introduction

Today mobile terminal penetration and usage occupy a high proportion in People's Daily life. With the development of the Internet, the mobile network in urban and rural areas in our country basically achieves the all-weather and full coverage[1]. The study found that although mobile phone positioning data is discrete and sparse, but the mobile phone data can still be people's activities for high-precision prediction[2]. This conclusion provides a theoretical basis for the study of people's activities. The user's mobile phone positioning data to some extent can also reflect the user's habits. Real-time communication between the mobile terminal and the base station will generate the base station cell number information of the mass-tagged mobile terminal time series, which will be uploaded to the server terminal for storage[3]. Business circle represents the gathering area of the people's production and consumption. According to the coverage of mobile phone signal in real geographical space, the real-time location data of mobile phone users can be mapped to the corresponding real geospatial location, which can restore the realistic trajectory of users realistically and objectively. Differentiating the business scope of the current area and pushing for accurate business activities by excavated the link between regional population distribution and activity characteristics. The analysis of mining high-value information log has an important practical value[4]. Through precision marketing, businesses can get huge profits. So more and more researchers have devoted to the studying of the base station log.

Data mining is to extract the hidden information from the massive existing data by the algorithms[5]. Nowadays, data mining is applied in many fields. Data mining is one of the most important applications in the field of data mining. Domestic and foreign scholars have done a lot of research in this field. The log information in the communication base station covers a wide range of people, high real-time data and long acquisition period. It can record the spatial and temporal

[a]Corresponding author: liuch@whpu.edu.cn

characteristics of urban residents' activities for a long time, and there is no pressure on the respondents, so the academics think that it can dig out the characteristics of resident activities on the current area efficiently[6].

From the mass mobile phone positioning data of base station to obtain the characteristics of the stream of people, which can lock the current area of population activities effectively and found a high value area quickly to target business promotion. In the existing literatures, they analyze the population flow types according to the log of base station to find out the region type. For example, Zhigang Zhang and others through the design of two kinds of distributed mining algorithms(GPMA and SPMA) to dig out the important position[7]. A general framework is proposed to improve the usability of trajectory data in his paper, including a filter to improve data usability and a model to get the mining results. Xin yang Kong, etc. analysis the population movements through the using of SD-JUPF decision algorithm for the mobile phone log[8]. In their paper, a Movement Features-based Judging Urban population Flow(MF-JUPF) algorithm utiliziing cellphone trajectory data was proposed to deal with the is sure about the population flow. Jia Chen, etc. using the DBSCAN method to carry on the extraction to the mobile phone location data and identify the characteristics of the users[9]. In order to acquire personal profiles they propose a resonable technical route that first extracts the geographic regions from personal mobile phone location data based on a density-based clustering algorithm.

In this paper, the calculation model of the human flow characteristic index is established, and the calculated index value is clustered by the hierarchical clustering algorithm. To analyze the experiment data through part of the base station provided by the local mobile operators. The results show that the algorithm can achieve good clustering effect, and can be divided into different types of business district, which shows the feasibility and effectiveness of the algorithm in data mining. This provides a reference for accurate business marketing. Therefore, this paper studies the base station log, proposes the use of hierarchical clustering algorithm to find out the important information, which can provide a new idea for future research work.

2 Business circle division method

The use of mobile phones' related services such as text messages, browsing the Web, switching machines, etc. will generate log records. The current mobile phone users connected by the base station number, connection time, and the information such as user EMASI number[10] can identified by these records. The activities of the corresponding mobile phone users are reflected in log records. Each of base stations' service area on behalf of the different business circle type. Clustering analysis of mobile phone users within the coverage area of the base station, summarizing their demo graphic characteristics, and identifying different types of base station coverage areas, is equivalent to identifying the different types of business circle.

2.1 Analysis of activity area category

This paper extracts the characteristics of people flow in the coverage area of the base station and then finds out the high-value business circle by the base station. Due to the coarse-time and coarse-grained limits of mobile phone base station data, The active areas are identified by the users' activity time[11]. High-value business circles has the characteristics of large flow and long percapita residence time. However, due to office workers working in the base station during the day in which the location is fixed and the residence time is relatively long. At the same time, residential area residents in the base station range is basically fixed, residence time is relatively long. It is difficult to distinguish the high-value shopping district, residence and work area only through the retention time as a flow characteristics. Therefore, the extracted features of the flow must be able to more clearly distinguish between these base stations coverage. The following assumptions also needed to divided the flow characteristics in this paper:

1)Only one active area is the users' residence

2)The user has at least one workspace

3)The user can only work in the region and can not appear in other regions in working hours.

According to the above suppose, we can use the residence time per person in working hours, percapita residence time in the early morning, percapita residence time at the weekend and daily traffic as the base station coverage area of the flow characteristics. The users' activities are divided into the following: early morning hours (00:00~07:00), work hours (09:00~18:00).On the other hand, due to the fact that the working time and the daily life of some people are different, the premise of this paper may not be applicabled to all users in real life, and the corresponding rules need to be reformulated for special activities. After analysis and discussion, we divided four types of active regions. There are four flow characteristics as follows:

1)residence time per person in working hours: All users during working time (09:00 ~ 18:00) in average time within the scope of the base station. This indicator can be used to characterize the flow characteristics near the base station during the working period.

2)percapita residence time in the early morning: It represents the average residence time of people in the base station service area in the morning(00:00 to 07:00).Generally in this time period, the users are in the rest, through this indicator can be excavated pedestrian flow characteristics of residential base stations.

3)percapita residence time at the weekend: It stands for people around the base station per capita residence time at the weekend. High value business circle the number of shopping at the weekend and time will be greatly increased. With this indicator can indicate the flow characteristics of high-value shopping district.

4)daily traffic: It represents the number of people in the service area of the base station everyday. The more people, the greater the possibility of consumption. So it can reflect the characteristics of the high value business circle of people.

2.2 Construction of the flow characteristics of the calculation model

Supposed the total length of the user's date in the raw data is S days. The total number of base stations that all users pass through are X, the number of users are Y. The m on behalf of a day and n represents a user. Determine the current user's residence time by calculating the time difference between the two records. Then for a base station x, the time that the user y stays on the day of the week is w_t_{xy} . A user's retention time is n_t_{xy} in the morning and his(her) retention time is z_t_{xy} over the weekend. A user retention time is d_t_{xy} a day. If a user is not in service area for the base station, the four indicators of 0. For a base station, the base station coverage area of the flow characteristics of the formulas are as follows:

1)residence time per person in working hours

$$w = \frac{1}{SY}\sum_{m=1}^{S}\sum_{y=1}^{Y} w\_t_{xy} \tag{1}$$

2)percapita residence time in the early morning

$$n = \frac{1}{SY}\sum_{m=1}^{S}\sum_{y=1}^{Y} n\_t_{xy} \tag{2}$$

3)percapita residence time at the weekend

$$z = \frac{1}{SY}\sum_{m=1}^{S}\sum_{y=1}^{Y} z\_t_{xy} \tag{3}$$

4)daily traffic

$$d = \frac{1}{S}\sum_{m=1}^{S}\sum_{y=1}^{Y} d\_t_{xy} \tag{4}$$

2.3 Hierarchical clustering algorithm

Clustering is the process of grouping physical or abstract collections into multiple classes of similar objects. Clustering analysis is a group of data according to the similarity and differences into several categories. The purpose is to make the similarity between the data of the same category as large as possible, and the similarity between the data in different categories is as small as possible[12, 13]. Hierarchical clustering algorithm for a given level of decomposition of the data until a certain condition is met, can be divided into specific types of cohesion and split. Cohesive hierarchical clustering is a bottom-up strategy. At first, each object is used as a cluster and then the cluster is combined into more and more large clusters, until all the objects in a cluster or a condition is terminated. The split level clustering is just the opposite of the hierarchical clustering. Split hierarchical clustering uses a top-down strategy. First, it puts all objects in a cluster and then subdivides them into smaller and smaller clusters until each object becomes a cluster or to a termination condition[14]. The basic idea of hierarchical clustering algorithm is to calculate the distance between each object, and the closer object merged into a class. Loop execution until merged into one large class[15]. In this paper, a hierarchical clustering algorithm is used. Hierarchical clustering algorithm includes the following four steps:

Step1: Each object is classified as a class, so the total number of categories is N. Each category contains only one object. We should calculate all the categories of the distance between each other.
Step2: Find the two categories with the smallest distance and merge it into one class.
Step3: Recompute the distance between the new category and all the old categories.
Step4: Repeat Step2 and Step3 until the last merge into one class.

3 Experiment and analysis

3.1 Experiment environment

In this paper, the Matlab R2014b is useded to realize programming. Experiment environment as follows:

Processor: Inter (R) Core(TM)
CPU: i3-2330M
Frequency: 2.20GHz
Memory: 4G
Operating System: Windows 7-64 bit

3.2 Experimental data preprocessing

In this paper, the positioning data obtained from the analysis of the specific interface provided by the local mobile communication operators. Select the base station data from 2014-1-1 to 2014-6-30 as the observation window for analysis. Selecting the base station data from 2014-1-1 to 2014-6-30 as the observation window of the analysis and extracting the location data of the city to form the modeling data. The partial position data of the base station of the period is shown in Table 3-1. There are two types of network: 2G and 3G in the table. The LOC number represents the base station location number. The EMASI represents the base station location number.

Table 3-1 Part of the base station location data

Date	Time	Base Station Number	EMASI Number
2014-1-1	02:21:32	36983	55555
2014-1-1	02:25:43	36981	55555
2014-1-1	02:35:13	36981	55555
2014-1-1	02:55:23	36981	55555

By analyzing the base station mobile log found that part of the log records incomplete, we call these data "noise"[16]. On the one hand, due to the huge amount of data, and the log contains a lot of "noise" data, which is needed to denoising. On the other hand, there are many attributes of the positioning data, which need to filter out the useless attributes. So we need to clean the data in the first step. There are three types of network type. The LOC number and signaling type are useless for the purpose of this paper, and the three kinds of redundant attributes are eliminated by word segmentation tools. Measuring the user's retention time does not need to be accurate to the millisecond, so the time will be removed in the same way. After the above steps on the collation of the log, we get the log after the pretreatment. As we can see, the Table 3-2 shows the format of data pre-processing.

Table 3-2 Preprocessing data

Date	Time	Network Type	LOC Number	Station Number	EMASI Number	Signaling Ty pe
2014-1-1	02:21:32:45	2	99598990383092	36983	55555	334109CA
2014-1-1	02:25:43:23	3	93592190333561	36981	55555	334204CA
2014-1-1	02:35:13:03	2	93592190333561	36981	55555	334204CA
2014-1-1	02:55:23:00	3	93592190333561	36981	55555	334204CA

3.3 Experimental results

By calculating the switching time between successive two base stations (by subtracting the last release time of the last base station from the initial connection time of the next base station) to represent the dwell time of the user at a single base station. However, the first thing we need to make a reasonable assumption. The assumption is that there are no consideration of the time error between base stations. The collected data is calculated according to the calculation formula of the flow characteristics of the prior defined base station coverage area, and the sample data of each base station can be obtained. Some sample data are calculated as shown in Table 3-3. The time unit is minute.

Table 3-3 Part of the calculation results

residence time per person in working hours	percapita residence time in the early morning	percapita residence time at the weekend	daily traffic
36902	78	521	602
36903	144	600	521
36904	95	457	468
36905	69	596	695

In order to eliminate the influence of the difference of the magnitude of each attribute data, this paper carries out the standard deviation treatment on the collected statistical data. This division is based on that the more close to 1, the greater the original data before the standardization processed, the longer the residence time. The processed result is shown in Table 3-4. The results of normalization of variance are plotted by using the Matlab software.

DOI: 10.1051/itmconf/20171103002

Table 3-4 Deviation Normalization Results

residence time per person in working hours	percapita residence time in the early morning	percapita residence time at the weekend	daily traffic
36902	0.103865	0.856364	0.850539
36903	0.263285	1	0.725732
36904	0.144928	0.74	0.644068
36905	0.082126	0.992772	0.993837

A dendrogram consists of many U-shaped lines that connect data points in a hierarchical tree. The height of each U represents the distance between the two data points being connected. The measure unit is minute. The image is shown in Figure 1.In order to facilitate the study of this paper, we will enlarge the clustering map in order to clearly observe the characteristics. The image is partially enlarged as shown in Figure 2.

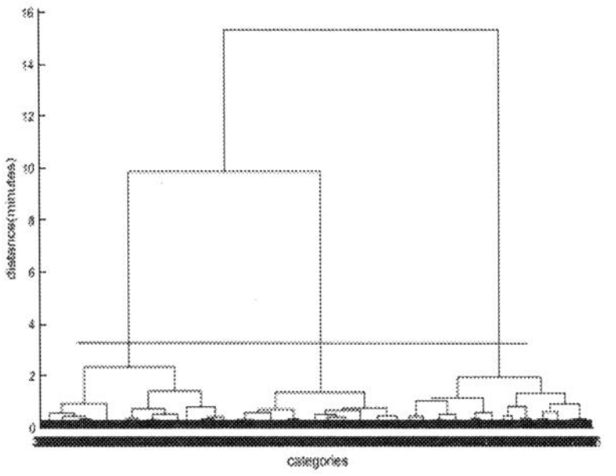

Figure 1 Clustering of Pedigrees

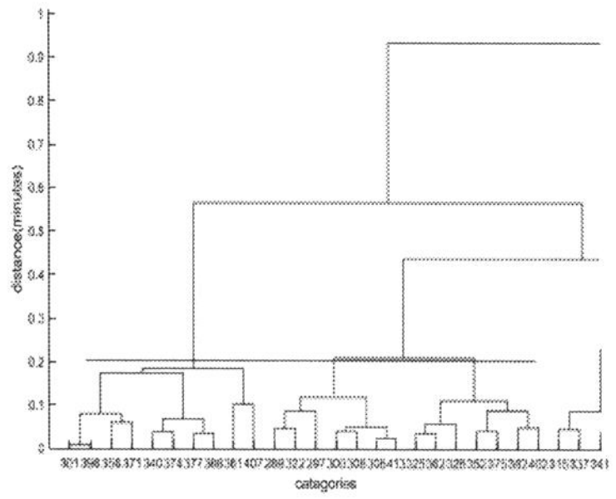

Figure 2 Partially Enlarged

The hierarchical clustering algorithm is implemented in the Matlab. Hierarchical clustering algorithm execution flow chart as follows:

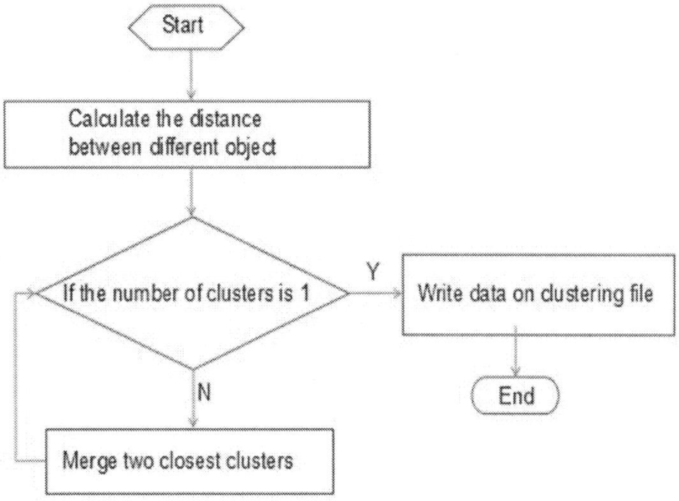

Figure 3 Hierarchical clustering algorithm

We can clearly see that in the Figure1-1 in the U tree, horizontal line in the node is divided into three parts, which is achieved the best clustering effect. So as it can be seen in Figure 1,the standardized data are best classified into three Categories[16,17]. The number of the clusters is set to three. After performing the above four steps, we can draw a cluster diagram with four indexes for the clustering results, as shown in Figure 4, 5, 6.The vertical coordinates represent the residence time after the standardized treatment. There are four abscissa and they are "working hours", "early morning", "weekend", "daily". They represent the "residence time per person in working hours", "percapita residence time in the early morning", "percapita residence time at the weekend" and "daily traffic".

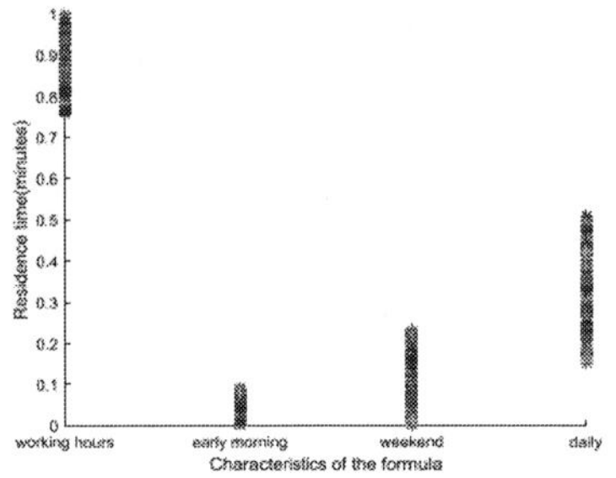

Figure 4 Business Circle Category 1

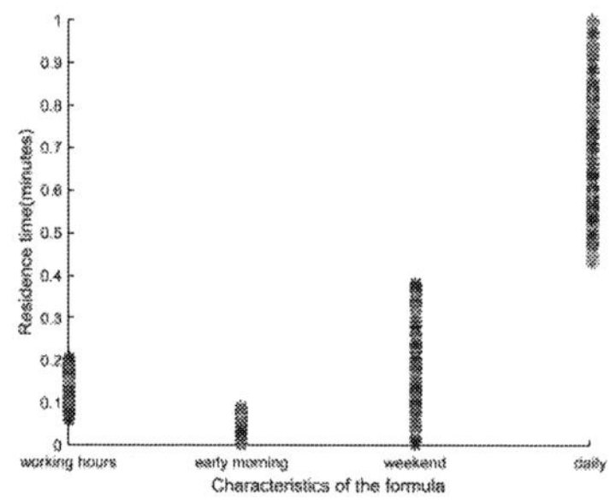

Figure 5 Business Circle Category 2

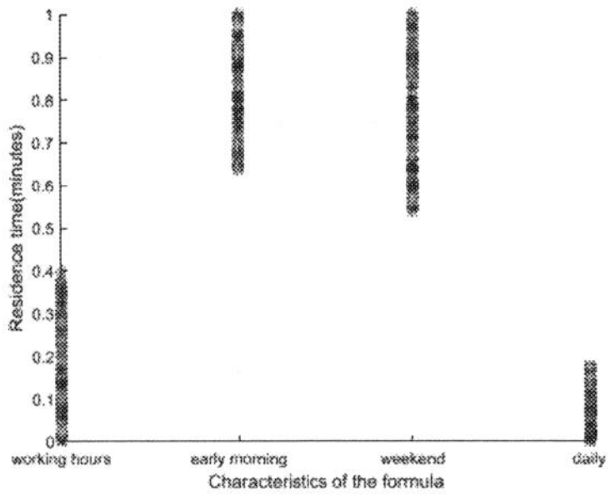

Figure 6 Business Circle Category 3

3.4 Results analysis

In a set of experiments, we have analyzed the results. The contrasts of Figures 4, 5, 6 make it clear that the value of the different business circles is quite different. For Business Circle Category1, we can see that the abscissa is marked as "working hours percapita residence time" and the axis coordinate value is higher, then the user staying time in the coverage area of the first clustering result is longer. At the same time in the morning, the weekend percapita residence time and the average daily traffic volume corresponding to the axis of the coordinate value is relatively low, which is represented the morning and weekend coverage within the user residence time is relatively short in the two time base station. This can be inferred that the region is similar to the white-collar family work area, which is more in line with white-collar workers working area time flow changes. For the Business Circle Category 2, it can be clearly seen from the figure that the first three indicators have a shorter residence time, while the average daily traffic volume has a longer residence time. This can be inferred that the region is similar to the white-collar workers. As it can be seen from the Business Circle Category 3, for all levels, the abscissa is marked as "working hours percapita residence time" and the axis coordinate value is lower. However, the axis coordinate value of "percapita residence time in the early

DOI: 10.1051/itmconf/20171103002

morning" and "percapita residence time at the weekend" are higher than the others. We can get the conclusion that this region are similar to the residential district .

As a result of a huge business area every day, and in the early hours of the morning is generally closed, so Figure 4 more in line with the business district. So this paper can be inferred for the second kinds of cluster base station coverage area belong to the business district. Analysis of Figure 5,we can see in the working day and the average daily traffic volume of the two coordinates of the corresponding coordinate axis value Y is relatively small and the morning and the weekend corresponds to a relatively large axis coordinates, you can see in the observation window during this period of time people stay in the early hours of the morning and a longer time, we can infer a third cluster type base station service area in residential areas.

In summary, based on the analysis of base station log data, the cluster analysis shows that the average daily traffic volume of Business Circle Category1 and Business Circle Category 3 is relatively small, while white-collar workers are concentrated in eating time and commuting time, such areas are not suitable for commercial marketing. For Business Circle Category2, due to its large daily traffic volume, and this part of the base station coverage within the crowd stay relatively long, so it is suitable for commercial marketing.

Conclusion

With the development of mobile communication technology, the use of mobile terminals such as mobile phones are becoming more common, the growth of the mobile phone positioning data for the analysis of the individual activities or understanding urban development provides a powerful data support. In order to increase the business to business circle and carry out the precise marketing business, in this paper, the calculation model of the flow characteristics index is established. By using the hierarchical clustering algorithm, the coverage of the business circle, residential area and work area near the base station is analyzed. The experiments results show that the hierarchical clustering algorithm has good clustering effect and can distinguish the residential area, the work area and the commercial area. It shows the feasibility and effectiveness of the algorithm in data mining. Digging out the high-value information to make recommendations to businesses and to rationalize the promotion of commercial marketing activities. However, this paper does not optimize the distance calculation of the first step data of the hierarchical clustering algorithm, which will inevitably lead to the high time complexity of the algorithm. So my future research work is mainly on the level of clustering algorithm to improve, to further improve the efficiency of the implementation of clustering computing time. Secondly, the hierarchical clustering algorithm is applied to other research fields, extending the use of hierarchical clustering algorithm to study its feasibility in other areas, this is bound to promote the development and application of clustering algorithm.

Acknowledgement

This research was in part supported by grands from the Natural Science Foundation of China (No.61502438), the Hubei Provincial Department of Education Science and Technology Project (No.2014-47).

References

1. T.F. Bao. A Study On Context Recognition and Mining of Mobile User data. University of Science and Technology of China(2012).
2. C. Song, Z. Qu, N. Blumm, et al. Limits of Predictability in Human Mobility. Science, **327**(5968), 1018-1021(2010).
3. X.F. Zhu.Research on Rapid Mining Algorithm for Massive Data.Nanjing University of Posts and Telecommunications(2012).

4. Z.A. Dong, X.Q. Lu. User Behaviour Analyses Based on Baidu Search Logs. Computer Applications and Software, **30**(7), 18-20(2013).
5. Z.G. Z, C.Q. J, X.L. Wang, A.Y. Zhou. etc. Discovering Import Locations from Massiveand Low-Quality Cell Phone Trajectory Data. Journal of Software, **27**(7), 1-14(2016).
6. Y.X. Kong, C.Q.Jin, X.L. Wang. etc. Population Flow Analysis Based on Cellphone Trajectory Data. Journal of Computer Applications, **36** (1), 44-51(2016).
7. J. Chen, B. Hu, X.Q. Z, Y. Yang.Personal Profile Mining Based on Mobile Phone Location Data. Geomatics and Information Science of Wuhan University, **39**(6), 734-738(2014).
8. S.F. Gong, W.L. Chen, P.T. Jia.Surver on Algorithms of Community Detection. Application Research of Computers, **30**(11), 3216-3227(2013).
9. T. Bao, Z.G. Zhang, C.Q. Jin.An Urban Population Flow Analysis System Based on Mobile Big Data[J]. Journal of East China Normal University(Nature Science), **9**(5), 162-170(2015).
10. Z.C. An. Mining User Mobility Behavior Based on Base Station. Harbin Institute of Technology(2011).
11. N. X, L. Y, J.X. Hu. Identifying Home-Work LocationsFromShort-Term,Large-Scale, and Regularly Sampled Mobile Phone Tracking Data. Geomatics and Information Science of Wuhan University,**39**(6), 750-755(2014).
12. J. Shen, L. Z, J.W. Yang, R. Li. Archical Clustering Algorithm Based onPartion. Computer Engineering and Applications, **43**(31), 175-177(2007).
13. Y.Miu. The Analysis of Data Based on TheHierarchical Clustering.Anhui University (2013).
14. H. Ying, K.J. Xia, Data preprocessing method based on user characteristic of interests for web log mining. Proceedings-2014 4th International Conference on Instrumentation and Measurement, Computer, Communication and Control, 867-872(2014).
15. Montoliu R, GaticaPerez D. Discovering human places of interest from multimodalmobile phone data.Proceedings of the 9th International Conference on Mobile andUbiquitous Multimedia. ACM, **12**(2010).
16. Blumenstock J E. Using mobile phone data to measure the ties betweennations. Proceedings of the 2011IConference. ACM, 195-202(2011).
17. Park M, Lee T. Understanding science and technology information users through Iransaction loganalysis. LibraryHi Tech, **31**(1), 123-140(2013).

Energy Efficiency Comparison between Co-located and Distributed Antenna Systems with D2D Communication

Xing-Quan LI[1,a], Chun-Long HE[1], Ce ZHANG[1] and Zi-Hao LI[1]

[1]*Shenzhen Key Lab of Multi-dimensional Signal Processing, College of Information Engineering, Shenzhen University, China*

Abstract. In this paper, we investigate energy efficiency (EE) of co-located antenna system (CAS) and the distributed antenna system (DAS) with and without device-to-device (D2D) communications, respectively. We derive an approximate EE expression for both the idealistic and the realistic power consumption models in CAS and DAS with D2D communication. Numerical results show that the D2D communication is exactly benefited to improve the EE, especially in the DAS.

1 Introduction

Device-to-device (D2D) communication has been widely used to increase the cellular capacity, improve the energy efficiency (EE) of communication systems and extend the battery using time of UEs [1]–[3] because it can short the communication distances and reusing the channel resources with existing cellular users. It allows a user to communicate with another close user directly through D2D communication without extra communication through base stations. However, there are still many challenges when adding D2D links into the communication systems, which is mainly caused by the interference between cellular and the D2D users.

In fact, D2D underlaying cellular networks have attracted some research attention to improve the communication system performances [4]–[6]. Mode selection is an important part in D2D communication systems to further improve the performance of communication systems. In [7], the authors considered the mode selection problem for spectrum sharing between D2D links and cellular users in the cellular network. In [8], in order to prevent the excessive interference, the authors considered the transmission power control for D2D communications. To improve the scalability of D2D communications, authors of [9] discussed a distributed resource allocation method for D2D communications. Improving the reliability by interference management of D2D communications are considered in [10], [11].

Energy efficiency (EE) is becoming more and more important role for future communication systems due to the amount of energy consumption increasing dramatically with the exponential growth of service requirements [12]. In [13], three energy efficient modes switching scheme for single D2D pair has been considered to maximize energy efficiency under different conditions. For a multi-input multi-output (MIMO) architecture [14], [15] with multi-antenna base station is also an useful research area in design D2D communications underlaying such network models, which has not been

[a] Corresponding author: bedynamic@sina.com

fully studied yet. What's more, the systems considered above mainly discussing contain D2D communications in the co-located antenna systems (CAS). However, to the best of the authors' knowledge, there is little investigation about D2D communications in the distributed antenna systems (DAS).

In this paper, we consider a cellular network with single UE and one D2D pair underlaying communications with base station antennas, which are located in different distributions, i.e., co-located antenna system (CAS) and distributed antenna system (DAS). We use the orthogonal frequency division multiple access (OFDMA) scheme [16] to study the effectiveness of the cellular energy efficiency by adding D2D communication into these two different models. Two different power consumptions models are considered. The first case only contains the overall transmit power. In the second case, beyond overall transmit power, we still consider the systems' dynamic power and static power consumptions. Numerical results show that the performance of DAS with D2D communication is much better than CAS.

The rest of this paper is organized as follows. Two different system models and two total power consumption models are presented, and the energy efficiency expression of the cellular are shown in section II. In Section III, numerical results are presented to demonstrated the effectiveness of DAS with D2D communication. In Section IV, concludes the paper and indications for future works directions are given.

2 System models

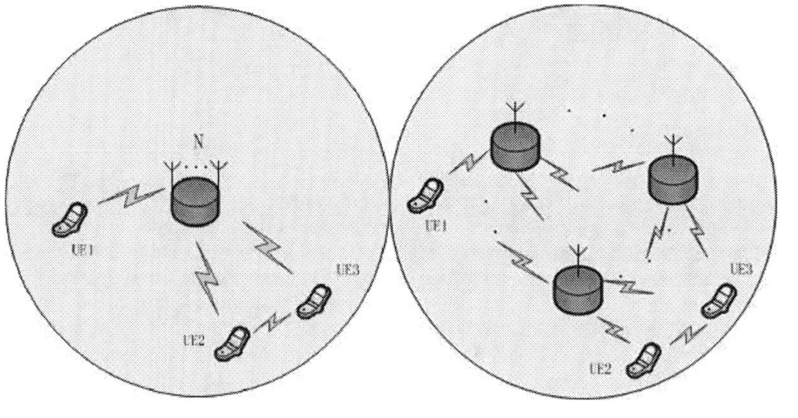

(a) (b)

Figure 1. Two BS antenna layouts are considered in this paper: (a) With the CA system, all the BS antennas are located in the center of the cellular. (b) With the DA system, the BS antennas are uniformly distributed in the cellular.

We consider a downlink cellular network with three cellular user equipments (UEs), which are randomly distributed in the cellular. The cellular radius is R. N base station (BS) antennas in the cellular are distributed in two different scenarios. The first scenario is all the base station antennas are co-located in the center of the cellular (CAS) and the other scenario is uniformly distributed in the cellular (DAS), which can be illustrated in the Figure 1. For simplicity, we assume that each UEs are equipped with single antenna and also assume that the total bandwidth is equally divided to each link between BSs and UEs so each UE is allocated with an orthogonal channel. We focus on the downlink performance of the *k*th user. The received signal of user $k, k \in \{1,2,3\}$ can be represented as

$$y_k = \mathbf{h}_k \mathbf{x}_k + n_k \tag{1}$$

where $n_k \sim \mathrm{CN}\ (0, N_0)$ is the additive white Gaussian noise (AWGN) at UE k. $\mathbf{x}_k$ is $N \times 1$ dimensional and $\mathbf{x}_k \sim \mathrm{CN}\ (0, P_k)$. $\mathbf{h}_k$ is $1 \times N$ dimensional vector, as the transmission signal vector and the channel gain vector from the BS to UE k, respectively. $\mathbf{h}_k$ denotes small scale and large scale fading channel, which can be modeled as

$$\mathbf{h}_k = \gamma_k \circ \mathbf{g}_k \tag{2}$$

where $\mathbf{g}_k$ denotes the $1 \times N$ small scale fading vector that can be modeled as independent and identically distributed complex Gaussian random variables with zero mean and unit variance and γ_k is the $1 \times N$ dimensional large scale fading vector [17]. For simplification, we ignore the shadowing effect and model the large scale fading coefficient as

$$\gamma_{k,i} = \left\| p_i^B - p_k^U \right\|^{-\alpha/2} \tag{3}$$

where p_i^B is the position of the i th BS antenna and p_k^U is the position of UE k. α is the pathloss factor and is typically between 3 and 5. Moreover, we assume that the channel state information (CSI) of all the involved links is perfectly known at BSs. The total transmission power of the BS is assumed to be fixed at P_t, and it is equally allocated to all the UEs, which is modeled as

$$P_i = \frac{P_t}{3}, 1 \le i \le 3 \tag{4}$$

3 Systems Analysis

3.1 Systems Rate Calculations

In this paper, we normalize the total system bandwidth into unit. Orthogonal frequency division multiple access (OFDMA) is the access scheme for the downlink of the systems, i.e. the links between BS antennas and UEs use orthogonal channel to communicate with each other. The achievable rate of user k can be represented as

$$R_k = \frac{1}{3N} \log_2 \left(1 \quad \frac{P_k \left\| \gamma_k \right\|^2}{N_0} \right) \tag{5}$$

So the total downlink achievable rate of the cellular can be written as

$$R_{total} = \sum_{k=1}^{3} R_k \tag{6}$$

DOI: 10.1051/itmconf/20171103003

3.2 Systems Rate Calculations with D2D

We add D2D communication into the systems. Device-to-Device users are those who do not communicate through the BS antennas but communicate with each other directly. We assume that UE2 and UE3 are chosen as D2D user. We consider UE2 as D2D transmitter (Tx) has data to send to UE3 as D2D receiver (Rx) and the distance between Tx and Rx is fixed as $L, L \ll R$, which D2D communication takes half of the bandwidth from the other UE and there is no interference between D2D and cellular communication. The achievable data rate at D2D Rx can be expressed as

$$R_{D2D\_k} = \frac{1}{2N}\log_2\left(1+\frac{P_d L^{-\alpha}}{N_0}\right) \tag{7}$$

where P_d is the transmitter power of Tx and $P_d \ll P_k$. So the data rate of UE1 can be expressed as

$$R_1 = \frac{1}{2N}\log_2\left(1+\frac{P_k\|\gamma_1\|^2}{N_0}\right) \tag{8}$$

It's easy to get the total achievable rate of the cellular with D2D communication, which can be written as

$$R_{D2D\_total} = R_1 + R_{D2D\_k} \tag{9}$$

3.3 Total Power Consumption Model

As the related work discussed in [18], the realistic power consumption in the DAS contains three parts which can be written as

$$P_{real} = \frac{P_t}{\tau} + LP_{dy} + P_{st} \tag{10}$$

where τ is the radio frequency power amplifier efficiency, P_{dy} and P_{st} are the dynamic and the static power consumption, respectively. In the ideal condition, which means the circuit power is zeros. The idealistic power consumption can be expressed as

$$P_{ideal} = \frac{P_t}{\tau} \tag{11}$$

3.4 EE Model

As in [19], the EE model of the communication systems can be expressed as the ratio of the sum capacity and the total power consumption, which can be written as

$$\eta_{EE}(R) = \frac{R}{P_{Total}} \tag{12}$$

where R is the sum capacity of the systems, which R is equal to (6) when the systems without adding D2D communication, otherwise it can be expressed as (9). P_{total} is equal to (10) when discussing the realistic power consumption model, otherwise P_{total} is equal to (11).

4 Simulation Results

In this section, We present the different simulation results by comparing different scenarios, which are listed in the Table 1. Scenario 1 and 2 correspond to the traditional co-located antenna system model (CAS) and distributed antenna system model (DAS) without the D2D communications. Scenario 3 and 4 correspond to these different system models with green communications, i.e. with D2D communications. The system parameters in the simulations are listed in the Table 2. We average over 1000 randomly generated UEs locations and present the average results.

Table 1. Different investigated scenarios.

	System Model	**D2D communication**
Scenario 1	CAS	NO
Scenario 2	DAS	NO
Scenario 3	CAS	YES
Scenario 4	DAS	YES

Table 2. Simulation parameters.

Parameters	**Value**
The cellular radius R	1000 m
The D2D distance L	100 m
The BS antenna number N	5
The noise power N0	-104 dBm
The dynamic power consumption Pdy	30 dBm
The static power consumption Pst	40 dBm
The maximum transmit power Pt	5~46 dBm
Path loss exponent α	4
Drain efficiency τ	38%

From Figure 2., we show the total achievable rate of the overall cellular network with the four scenarios listed in the Table 2. It is obviously shows that the total achievable rate of DAS is much better than CAS under different maximum transmit power. After adding D2D communications, the total achievable rates of these two systems are apparently better than the original systems, which means D2D communication is a better way to increase the systems' total achievable rate.

From Figure 3., we present the results of EE of CAS and DAS in the ideal power consumption, with and without D2D communications under different maximum transmit power, respectively. We can easily find that in the condition of lower maximum transmit power, after adding D2D communications in the systems, since they can communicate with each other directly and save the energy consumption to communicate through BSs, EE of the systems will slightly increase. What's more, from the general view, it's easy to find that the systems EE decreases with the growth of the maximum transmit power in the idealistic power consumption model. And EE in the realistic power consumption model of these two systems under the same condition with Figure 3. are presented in the Fig 4., which apparently shows EE first increases and then decreases with the growth of the maximum transmit power. We can find the optimal transmit power to maximize EE is about 33 dBm. The results of these two figure is consistent with the theorems concluded in [20].

From Figure 5., we demonstrate the influence of systems EE when the D2D communications distance is changing under the maximum transmit power is set as 46dBm. It's apparently that EE decreases with the growth of the D2D communication distance. The reason is, when the D2D communications distance growth, the achievable rate of D2D communications will slightly decrease, which causes the total achievable rate decreasing.

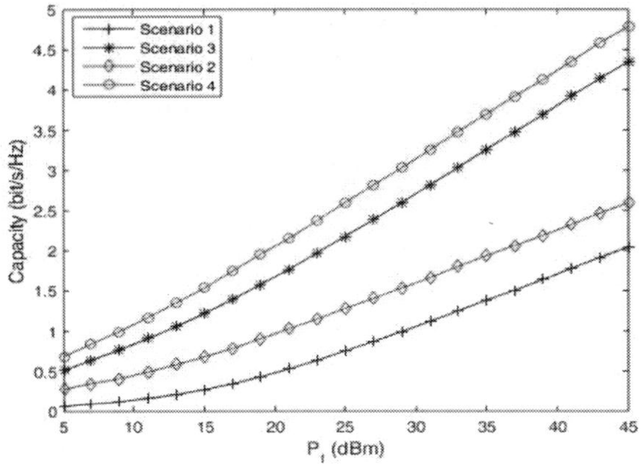

Figure 2. Capacity versus the maximum transmit power.

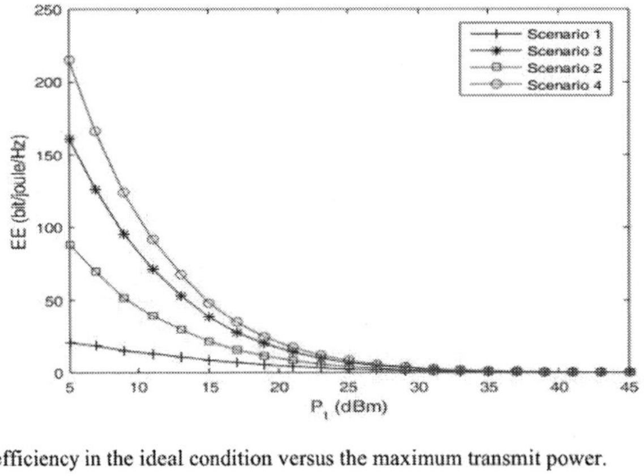

Figure 3. Energy efficiency in the ideal condition versus the maximum transmit power.

DOI: 10.1051/itmconf/20171103003

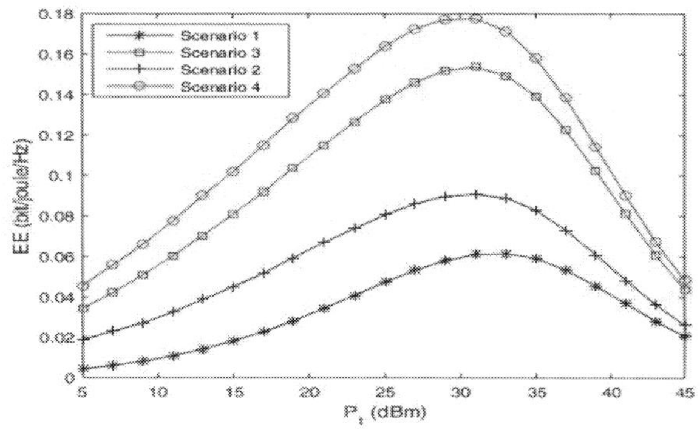

Figure 4. Energy efficiency in the real condition versus the maximum transmit power.

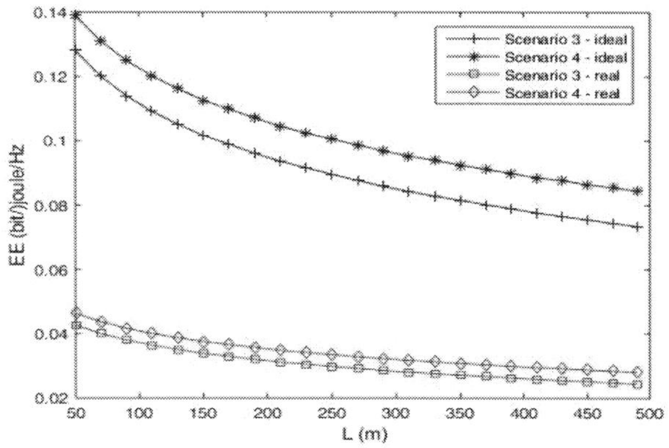

Figure 5. Energy efficiency in the ideal and real conditions versus the different D2D distances.

Conclusion

In this paper, we investigated the EE of the CAS and DAS, with and without D2D communications, respectively. We also find that when the systems adding D2D communications, the systems' total achievable rate remarkably increased and the same as the systems' EE, which is depended on the distance of D2D users. Simulation results also confirm it's correctness. What's more, adding D2D communications to the CAS and DAS is very useful to reduce energy efficiency consumption. Since all the scenarios only contain one D2D pair and a cellular user in a single cellular, we will extend it to multi-cells with more D2D pairs and cellular users in the future works.

Acknowledgment

This work is partially supported by the Natural Science Foundation of China under grants 61601300, the Science and Technology Innovation Commission of Shenzhen under Grants JCYJ20150324140036835, the Open Research Fund through the National Mobile Communications Research Laboratory, Southeast University, Nanjing, China, under Grant 2017D10, Shenzhen University start-up funding No. 2016053.

References

1. K. Doppler, M. Rinne, C. Wijting, IEEE Commun. Mag., **47**, 12(2009)
2. G. Fodor, E. Dahlman, G. Mildh, IEEE Commun. Mag., **50**, 3(2012)
3. C. H. Yu, K. Doppler, C. B. Ribeiro, IEEE Trans. Wireless Commun., **10**, 8(2011)
4. Z. Zhou, M. Dong, K. Ota, IEEE Commun. Lett., **3**, 5(2014)
5. F. W. F, C. X. C, L. Song, Proc. WCSP, 2012
6. T. D. Hoang, B. L, T. Le-Ngoc, Proc. IEEE ICC, 2015
7. M. Zulhasnine, C. Huang, and A. Srinivasan, Proc. IEEE WiMob'2010, 2010
8. C. H. Yu, O. Tirkkonen, K. Doppler, Proc. IEEE VTC, 2009
9. N. Reider, G. Fodor, EURASIP Journal on Wireless Commun.and Networking, **2012**, 1(2012)
10. H. Min, W. Seo, J. Lee, IEEE Trans. Wireless Commun., **10**, 2(2011)
11. Y. Xu, R. Yin, T. Han, Proc. IEEE ICCC, 2012
12. G. Fettweis, E. Zimmermann, Proc. WPM Commun., **4**(2008)
13. D. Feng, G. Yu, C. Xiong, IEEE Trans. Wireless Commun., **14**, 12(2015)
14. Q. H. Spencer, C. Peel, A. L. Swindlehurst, IEEE Commun. Mag., **42**, 10(2004)
15. D. Gesbert, M. Kountouris, R. W. H. Jr., C. Chae, T. Salzer, IEEE Signal Proc. Mag., **4**, 5(2007)
16. C. He, G. Y. Li, F Zheng, IEEE Trans. Vehicular Technology, **63**, 3(2014)
17. C. He, B. Sheng, P. Zhu, IEEE J. Sel. Areas Commun., **31**, 5(2013)
18. D. W. K. Ng, E. S. Lo, IEEE Trans. Wireless Commun., **11**, 9(2012)
19. Y. Rui, Q. T. Zhang, L. Deng, IEEE J. Sel. Areas Commun., **31**,5(2013)
20. C. L. He, J. Yin, Y. He, Journal of Commun. and Networks, **18**, 4, (2016)

Research on Matrix-type Packet Loss Compensation Scheme for Wireless Video Transmission on Subway

Qing-Wu FAN[1,a], Shu-Ting DONG[1], Shu-Kai ZHANG[2] and Bin HE[2]

[1]*Faculty of Information Technology, Beijing University of Technology, No.100 Pingleyuan, Chaoyang District, Beijing,100124, China*
[2]*Beijing Yuxing Electronic Technology Co., Ltd, No.2 Xin Feng Street, Xicheng District, Beijing,100088, China*

Abstract. As the mainstream wireless LAN technology, Wi-Fi can achieve fast data transfer. With the subway moving in a high speed, video data transmission between the metro and the ground is achieved through Wi-Fi technology. This paper aims at solving the Caton problem caused by switching packet loss in the process of playing real-time video on the train terminal, and proposes matrix-type packet loss compensation scheme. Finally, the feasibility of the scheme is verified by experiments.

1 Introduction

In recent years, the problem of traffic congestion has seriously affected and restricted the cities' development in China [1]. Rail transit has become the primary choice for most urban trips [2]. The subway plays as an important form of rail transportation, its fast, security, environmental protection, large capacity, which makes it play an irreplaceable role in people's work and life. With the subway construction going to a high-speed development period, Subway has now entered a period of comprehensive network operations. Passengers' needs for the Metro to play real-time video information are also increasing [3].

This paper is just in this background and proposes a real-time wireless video transmission scheme. As the subway is always in a state of motion, it is unrealistic to transmit video data by cable. This article uses the mainstream Wi-Fi technology for real-time video data transmission. However, Wi-Fi technology, although able to meet the requirements of moving data transmission for the terminal, the technology itself also has some limitations, such as, a single Wi-Fi has a limited coverage, Wi-Fi's signal strength is not stable and so on. Limited coverage cannot meet the needs of continuous receiving video data in the process of subway moving. Now is to deploy multiple wireless AP next to the subway lines to cover the entire range of traffic section.

With the train moving at a high speed, the train terminal undergoes the process of switching from the coverage of one AP to the coverage of another AP. As the switch takes some time, it means that there will be switching loss inevitably during the switching process. It is due to the existence of the switch packet loss, which results in the train terminal appearing Caton phenomenon in the process of playing real-time video. In order to improve the users' satisfaction for the public transport, the video

[a] Corresponding author: 609048854@qq.com

playback fluency should be improved. As a result, packet loss has become an urgent problem to be solved.

As the previous investigators, Jiang Lei, who proposed a WLAN based on the prediction of switching technology (WHFT). WHFT allowed the on-board AP to establish a connection with a new AP (such as APn+1) before disengaging from the old AP (such as APn), that was, connection before interruption. In addition, the adjacent Aps overlap each other with a sufficient area, a zero switching time can be realized [4]. Cheng Hanlin evaluated the effect of packet size on video quality and presented the concept of maximum packet size. If there was no video transmission recovery protection (such as FEC), the video transmission quality of the larger packet size was better than the smaller packet size. This approach only took into account the impact of a single factor on the quality of video transmission, without considering the actual transmission environment [5]. Jiang Xueyuan proposed a study based on the Gilbert model, simulated of the real wireless transmission environment. The packet loss mode with the specified packet loss feature was obtained by reverse modelling [6]. However, the proposed solutions for the packet loss were just used in a single scene, and there were no specific measures for real-time video data transmission. They were not suitable for improving packet loss in complex transmission environment. This article is based on the subway, such a complex and volatile transmission environment, a matrix packet loss compensation scheme is proposed. Aiming at solving the Caton problem due to the switching packet loss in the process of real-time video data transmission through the Wi-Fi way [7] [8] [9] [10].

2 Analysis of wireless video transmission system between subway cars and ground

2.1 The overall structure diagram of the subway communication system

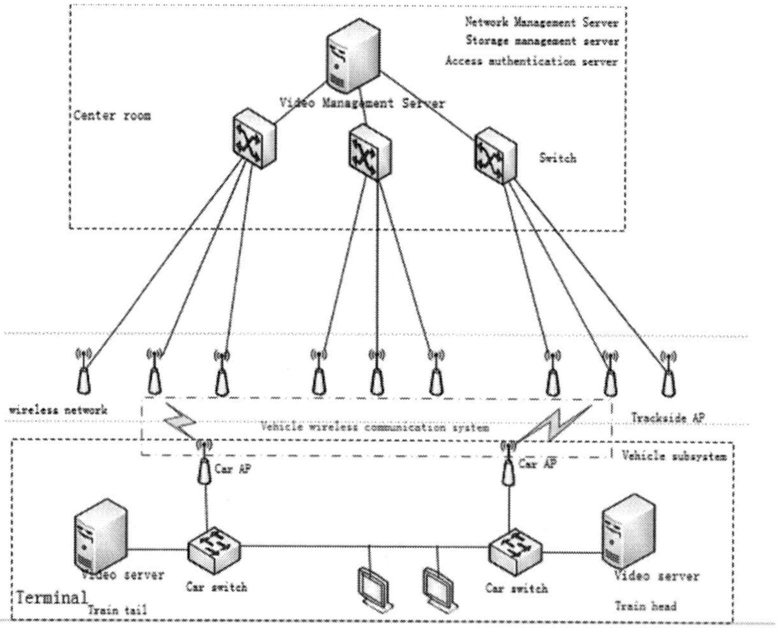

Figure 1. The overall structure diagram of the subway communication system

Figure 1 shows the overall structure diagram of the subway communication system. Each subway line has a central machine room. Switches and various types of servers are deployed in the center room. The switches in the center room are connected to the trackside APs by fiber. Trackside APs transmit the real-time video data to the vehicle Aps. However, a single wireless AP has a limited coverage, in order to allow the moving train to receive continuous data, multiple wireless APs should be deployed along the track. In general, a wireless AP is deployed every 300-500 meters. So as to cover the whole range of vehicles, and there is a certain overlap between adjacent APs.

2.2 Analysis of Wireless Communication System between subway cars and ground

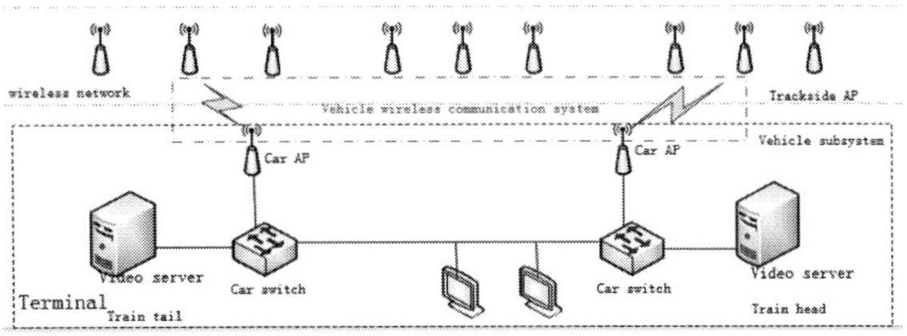

Figure 2. Wireless communication system between subway cars and ground

Wireless communication system between subway and the ground in figure 2 is the focus of this paper. Real-time video data is transmitted wirelessly between the rails and the train terminals. In the figure, the trackside AP is the sender and the on-board AP is the receiver. There are multiple APs along the subway line. With the train moving at a high speed, the video data received by the on-board AP comes from different trackside APs, that is, switching between different trackside APs.

3 Design of matrix packet loss compensation program

3.1 Working principle

As shown in Figure 3 is the principle diagram of matrix packet loss compensation, three data streams are now defined: the fast stream, the slow stream and the combined stream. The fast stream is sent five seconds earlier than the slow stream. The combined stream is the final video stream that needs to be played.

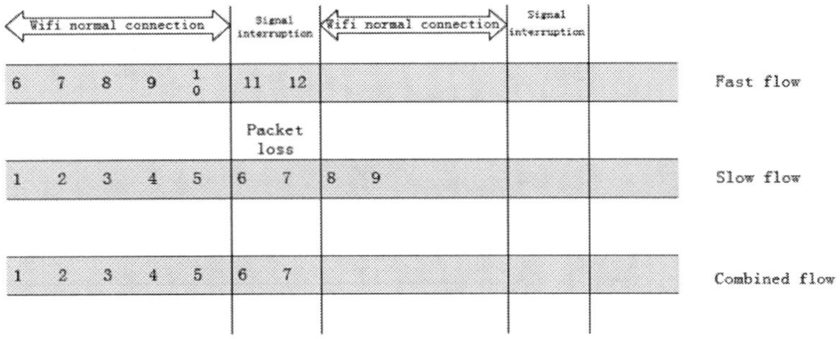

Figure 3. Schematic diagram of matrix packet loss compensation

There are three buffers in the system, to receive fast flow, slow flow and combined flow respectively. The source of the combined stream is the data from the slow flow, when the data packet loss occurs in the slow flow, the missing data in the slow flow will be found from the fast flow and then stored in the combined stream. So that the combined stream is a complete data stream.

As the fast flow is sent five seconds earlier than the slow flow, when the slow flow appears data loss, this lost part of the data has been cached in the fast flow in advance, so the lost part of the slow stream can be found directly from the fast stream. In Figure 3, when the signal is interrupted for two seconds, slow flow of data loss is the number 6 and 7. At this time, this part of the data existed in the fast flow normally. When the combined stream cannot find the data labeled 6 and 7 in the slow flow, they can be just obtained in the fast flow. Thereby a complete one-way data is formed to send to the terminal. Through this compensation way which deal with the packet loss can effectively improve the Caton phenomenon in the process of playing real-time video on the train terminal.

Figure 4. Real-time video transmission process

Figure 4 is the concrete realization of the proposed matrix packet loss compensation scheme in subway. The encoder outputs the original video stream. And then the set-top box transforms one stream to two streams through the internal programming. Two video streams are output from the set-top box (STB1). The data are sent to the directional antenna through the switch. Directional antenna sends the two video streams to the receiving end through wireless way. The location labeled 3 is two streams. The two-way video streams are restored to one way by the set-top box, the location labeled 4 is the final restored combination stream. The end of the one-way video stream is received and played on the train terminal player.

3.2 AP switching flow chart

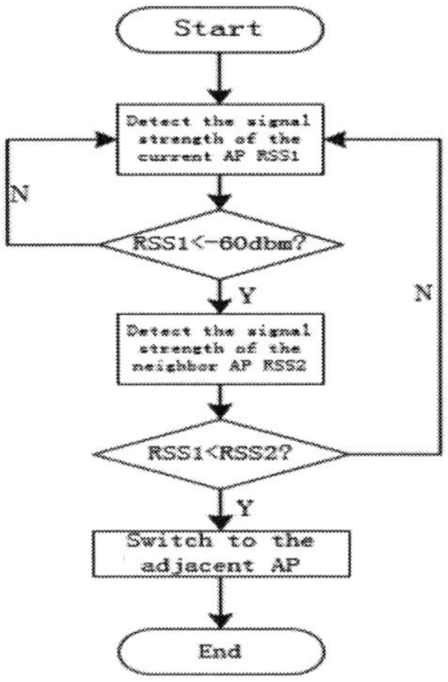

Figure 5. AP switch flow chart

In the flow chart of Figure 5, the signal strength value is detected by a customized Wi-Fi module. This Wi-Fi module is different from the generic Wi-Fi module, it is designed specifically for switching. The normal Wi-Fi module cannot switch, unless the original AP signal is completely gone. However, in the practical application of subway, there must be some overlap between neighboring APs, instead of waiting for the signal to be completely lost and then switching to another AP.

The Wi-Fi signal strength indicator is represented by the signal power absolute value dbm (negative value). From the flow chart can be seen that with the train moving at a high-speed, if the signal strength of the serving AP is less than a certain threshold (-60dbm) and the currently serving AP's signal strength is smaller than the signal strength of the neighboring AP, the on-board AP will switch from the current AP to the next neighboring AP.

3.3 Critical code

(1) SubwayServerDemux.c file is to send the data stream. One-way stream is transformed into two streams through the function subwayDemuxSend and then sent out. Define static void subwayDemuxSend (SubwayServerDemux* subway) as a static function;
(2) SubwayClient.c is the receiver. Two streams are received through the function subway_recv. Define static void subway_recv (SubwayClient* subway) as a static function;
(3) SubwayServer.c file is to add RTP head. The function subway_recv adds the RTP head to the transmitted TS stream. Define static void subway_recv (SubwayServer* subway) as a static function;
(4) SubwayClientMux.c parses the head and restores the stream. The function SubwayClientMuxPush analyzes the two received data and is defined as void SubwayClientMuxPush (SubwayClientMux* subway, StrmBuffer **psb). The function subwayMuxSend is to restore two video streams to one way stream. Define static void subwayMuxSend (SubwayClientMux* subway) as a static function.

4 Experimental verification

4.1 Parameter configuration

First of all, setting up the PC and input set-top box connection through the ping command. And then setting the parameters of the set-top box configuration. The multicast address configured at the input set-top box output must be the same as the multicast address configured at the input of the output set-top box, in order to establish the correct connection between two such set-top boxes. The specific parameters of the configuration are shown in Table 1and Table 2.

Table 1. Configuration parameters of the send packages

Parameter configuration		
	Type	Send packets
	Delay	five seconds
Input Configuration		
	Multicast	igmp://239.255.0.3:5003
	IP	112.1.1.153
	Mask	255.255.255.0
Output Configuration		
	Multicast	igmp://239.255.0.2:5002
	IP	10.0.0.199
	Mask	255.255.255.0
	Gateway	10.0.0.88

 DOI: 10.1051/itmconf/20171103004

Table 2. Configuration parameters of the receive packages

Parameter configuration		
	Type	Receive packets
	Delay	five seconds
Input Configuration		
	Multicast	igmp://239.255.0.2:5002
	IP	112.1.1.111
	Mask	255.255.255.0
	Gateway	112.1.1.1
Output Configuration		
	Multicast	igmp://239.255.0.3:5003
	IP	192.168.100.112
	Mask	255.255.255.0

(1) Simulation platform building

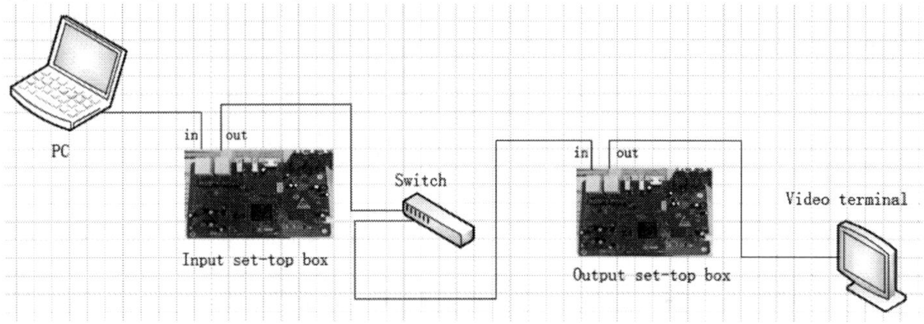

Figure 6. Experimental platform building

The experimental platform is divided into five parts: PC, input set-top box (encoding device), switch, output set-top box (decoding equipment), and video terminal.

Functional analysis of each part:

1) The PC side is the sending end, send the original one-way video stream to the first set-top box;

2) The input set-top box has two network ports. The left side is in and the right side is out. The in port is connected with the PC side and receive the one-way video stream from the PC. This input set-top box transforms the one video stream data into two identical content, but different transmission time point video streams through the internal programming (fast stream and slow stream).

3) The switch is the transmission medium. It transmits the two-way video stream from the output of the input set-top box to the output set-top box.

4) The in port of output set-top box is connected to the switch and receive the two-way video stream. Two receiving video streams are restored to one stream through the internal programming. The final output to the video playback terminal is a complete video stream data.

5) Video terminal receives the video stream data from output set-top box and plays the multicast stream.

4.2 Experimental design

In the laboratory experiment platform, in order to simulate the real environment of the packet loss. The measure is now taken by unplug the network between the out port of the input set-top box and the switch. The packet loss time setting in the program is five seconds. In the absence of taking any measures, unplug the network will appear Caton phenomenon on the video terminal. And when a packet loss compensation scheme is adopted, in the five seconds packet loss time, even unplug the network, the video terminal can still play the video smoothly.

4.3 Experimental results

The final experimental results are reflected by the smoothness f of video playback. The smoothness of video playback is obtained by testing in some subway lines. The test here is the mosaic time t1 statistics in the process of video playback. The smoothness of video playback means the ratio of the time t2 of the mosaic does not occur during video playback to the total video playing time t. And finally through a large number of experiments calculated that after the implementation of matrix packet loss compensation scheme, relative to the original system without taking any measures, video playback smoothness from less than the original degree of 50% to the current 90%. Thereby greatly improving the fluency of video playback.

$$f = t2/t \tag{1}$$

$$t2 = t - t1 \tag{2}$$

Conclusion

In this paper, the subject is wireless transmission system between the subway and the ground. Using Wi-Fi technology to transmit video data. Starting from the principle of Wi-Fi access, the paper analyzes the principle and procedure of AP switch and the packet loss during switch. A matrix packet loss compensation scheme is proposed to deal with packet loss. It compares before and after the program implementation of video playback quality through the experimental way. After using the packet loss compensation scheme, the Caton phenomenon caused by switching loss is significantly improved. Even if there is a short packet loss, the train terminal can still be able to playback video data smoothly, without giving users a poor visual experience due to packet loss. But although the Caton phenomenon has been largely improved, in the real experimental environment, video playback fluency cannot reach 100%. This is due to the subway running in the real environment, in addition to switching packet loss that effecting the video playback fluency, there may be a certain number of transmission packet loss. The problem of transmission packet loss is also the focus and direction of the next research.

References

1. X. Zheng , W. Chen , P. Wang , D. Shen , S. Chen , X. Wang , Q. Zhang , and L. Yang , " Big data for social transportation ," IEEE Transactions on Iotekxjdqtntelligent Transportation Systems , vol. 17 , no. 3 , pp. 620 – 630 , March 2016 .
2. Xiaoxuan Wang; Hailin Jiang; Wenzhe Sun; Tao Tang. Efficient dual-association resource allocation model of train-ground communication system based on TD-LTE in urban rail transit [J]. Intelligent Transportation Systems (ITSC), 2016 IEEE 19th International Conference on, 1-4 Nov. 2016.
3. Ana Vallejo-Mora; Matias Toril; Salvador Luna-Ramirez; Adriano Mendo; Salvador Pedraza. Congestion Relief in Subway Areas by tuning Uplink Power Control in LTE [J]. IEEE Transactions on Vehicular Technology, 24 November 2016.

4. Jiang Lei. Research on Wireless Video Transmission System of Tianjin Metro Line 1[J].Information Technology, 2013 NO.06.
5. Cheng-Han Lin; Chih-Heng Ke; Ce-Kuen Shieh; Chilamkurti, N.K. The Packet Loss Effect on MPEG Video Transmission in Wireless Networks [J]. Advanced Information Networking and Applications, 2006. AINA 2006. 20th International Conference on, **18-20** April 2006.
6. Jiang Xueyuan; Shi Zhiyuan; Huang LianFen. A new scheme of establishing packet loss patterns for wireless video transmission based on Gilbert model [J].Wireless, Mobile and Sensor Networks, 2007. (CCWMSN07). IET Conference on, **12-14** Dec.2007.
7. Z. He, and C. W. Chen, "End-to-End Quality Analysis and Modeling for Video Streaming over IP Network", Proc. IEEE International Conference on Multimedia and Expo, ICME 2002.
8. V. Parthasarathy, J. W. Modestino, K. S. Vastola, "Reliable Transmission of High-Quality Video over ATM Networks", IEEE Trans. on Image Proc., vol. 8, no. 3, pp. 361-374, March 1999.
9. I. Cidon, A. Khamisy, M. Sidi, "Analysis of Packet Loss Processes in High-Speed Networks", IEEE Transactions on Information Theory, vol. 39, pp. 98-108, Jan. 1993.
10. Yutaka Uchimura; Tooru Suhara; Hiromu Noritsuki. Model-error feedback control for compensating packet loss and time delay. Industrial Electronics Society, IECON 2016 - 42nd Annual Conference of the IEEE, 23-26 Oct. 2016.

ITM Web of Conferences **11**, 03005 (2017) DOI: 10.1051/itmconf/20171103005
IST2017

Optimization of Resource Allocation in Multihop HARQ Relay Networks with a Delay Constraint

Jun-Mei HAN[a], Xu LIU, Yong XI and Ji-Bo WEI

School of Electronic Science and Computer Engineering, National University of Defence Technology, Changsha, 410073 China

Abstract. By minimizing the outage probability, optimization is carried out in this paper to find joint optimal power allocation (OPA) and relay placement (ORP) for multihop relay networks adopting Hybrid Automatic Repeat reQuest (HARQ). Different from previous works, the joint OPA and ORP is analysed under generalized fading channels with the constraint on total transmit power, end-to-end relaying distance and maximum transmission number (delay). The simulation results demonstrate that for different fixed number of nodes and fading models, there are preferred deployments depending on path loss exponent and power retransmission strategy. By employing multiple retransmission round which can improve the reliability and energy efficiency without significant overhead, the end-to-end outage probability is no longer bounded by that of the weaker hop, i.e., the hop with a poor channel condition. The proposed strategy provides a dramatic improvement for the end-to-end outage probability by compensating the channel difference.

1 Introduction

Multihop Hybrid-automatic repeat request (HARQ) relay networks, which combined the advantage of multihop relay and HARQ techniques, have great potential to improve the performance of wireless networks due to their ability to improve the reliability and efficiency of transmission. In particular, the presence of multiple users between source and destination enables the division of long links into multiple shorter links which reduce signal attenuation, extends battery life, and provides broader and cheaper coverage along with high efficiency. On the other hand, HARQ protocols are widely employed to increase the reliability of packet transmissions by combining forward error-correcting coding (FEC) technique with ARQ technique. Because multiple retransmission rounds can improve the transmission reliability and efficiency without significant overhead, the performance of multihop relay networks can be improved by adopting HARQ schemes. Although various schemes have been proposed to analyze the performance of multihop relay networks and HARQ schemes, optimization of these two techniques are usually investigated separately.

The end-to-end (e2e) performances of the multihop relay networks have been extensively studied in the literature where most of them consider only one transmission round. In particular, the joint optimization of power allocation (OPA) and relay placement (ORP) is presented for multihop communication in a Rayleigh-fading environment in [1]. The distance-dependent route selection

[a] Corresponding author: hjm.han@163.com

problem is approached from the viewpoint of energy efficiency in [2]. By minimizing the outage probability of a decode-and-forward (DF) MIMO relay system with orthogonal space-time block coding, [3] shows that relay position optimization improves the finite-SNR (signal-to-noise ratio) diversity gain of a relay system whose adjacent hops have different diversity orders (unbalanced system). These studies show that joint optimization outperforms separate optimization significantly by improving the coding gain and diversity order.

By assuming fixed relay placement, optimal rate and power allocation problems have been addressed for truncated HARQ based multihop systems in several literatures. For instance, [4] proposed a joint power and rate optimization scheme to maximize the long-term average transmission rate of the multihop HARQ relay networks under Rayleigh-fading channels. Likewise, the e2e outage probability was studied in [5] by using a Markov chain model. However, these studies are limited to the Rayleigh-fading channels and have only analysed the e2e performance without attempting to optimize the system parameters for further performance enhancement.

In this paper, by modeling the retransmission number of a packet from source to destination as delay, the e2e outage probability is derived under generalized fading channels and will be employed as the performance metric in the system optimization. For the power and delay limited applications, we consider the following two constraints: 1) The maximum retransmission number should no more than L; 2) The sum of the power for all retransmission rounds for one packet should be less than or equal to P_T. We focus on two issues in multihop HARQ relay networks, i.e., how to allocate power and relay position for each relay and how to allocate retransmission times for each hop to minimize the outage probability under power consumption constraint. Note that the two issues are closely correlated and should be jointly optimized. Moreover, due to the versatile and flexible features of generalized fading, it is worthy to note that the generalized fading channel has the advantage of including various fading models such as Hoyt, Nakagami-m, and Rician fading as special cases [6].

2 System model and outage probability

We consider a linear M-hop network consisting of $M+1$ nodes under block-fading channel, where relays are serially connected from the source to the destination and the channel gain is constant during a single HARQ round, but the channel gains of different HARQ rounds are independent and identically distributed (i.i.d.). Each node has a single antenna and uses half-duplex transmission and performs with maximal-ratio combining (MRC). For different hops $R_i \neq R_j$, the channel gains h_i and h_j are mutually independent and may assume different fading models. We use the fixed and normalized source-to-destination distance $\left(d_{SD}=\sum_{m=1}^{M} d_m = 1,\ 0<d_m<1\right)$, where d_m is the distance between any two terminals. Without loss of generality, we assume $\varepsilon\left[|h_m|^2\right]=d_m^{-\alpha}$, where $\varepsilon[\cdot]$ denotes the expectation and α is the path-loss exponent. Assuming that the transmission power keeps constant in each (re)transmission round (i.e., $P_{l_i}=P_m$ for $i=1,2,\ldots,m$.), SNR of the i-th hop is denoted as $\gamma_m=(P_m/N_0)|h_m|^2$ with $\varepsilon[\gamma_m]=\bar{\gamma}_m=P_m\big/\left(N_0 d_m^{\alpha}\right)$, where N_0 denotes the AWGN power spectral density.

We first analysis the approximate outage probability for the m-th hop after l_m retransmission with the moment generating function (MGF)-based approach [6]. By adopting the results in [7], the probability density function (PDF) of $\bar{\gamma}_m$ is approximated by:

$$f_{\gamma_m}(x) \approx \frac{a_m}{t_m}\left(\frac{x}{\bar{\gamma}_m}\right)^{t_m} \tag{1}$$

where t_m is related to the diversity order of the channel, and a_m is related to the SNR gain of the i-th hop. The parameter pairs $\{t_m, a_m\}$ for Nakagami- m , Rician, and Hoyt fading channels are provided in Table I of [8]. Accordingly, the MGF of γ_m can be written as:

$$M_{\gamma_m}(s)=\int_0^{\infty} f_{\gamma_m}(x)e^{-sx}dx=\frac{a_m}{t_m}\left(\frac{1}{\bar{\gamma}_m}\right)^{t_m}\left(\frac{\Gamma(1+t_m)}{s^{1+t_m}}\right) \tag{2}$$

where $\Gamma(m)=\int_0^{\infty} t^{m-1}e^{-t}dt$ is the Gamma function. We define $Z \triangleq \sum_{i=1}^{l_m}\gamma_i$, then the MGF of Z is given by: $M_Z(s)=\left(a_m\Gamma(1+t_m)/\left(t_m\bar{\gamma}_m^{t_m}s^{t_m+1}\right)\right)^{l_m}$ The PDF of Z can be written as :

$$f_Z(z)=L^{-1}(M_Z(s))=\left(\frac{a_m\Gamma(1+t_m)}{t_m\bar{\gamma}_m^{t_m}}\right)^{l_m}\frac{z^{(1+t_m)l_m-1}}{\Gamma(l_m+l_m t_m)} \tag{3}$$

Accordingly, the approximate outage probability of the m th hop can be calculated as

$$\Pr\left\{\sum_{i=1}^{l_m}\bar{\gamma}_m<\gamma_{th}\right\}=F_Z(\gamma_{th})=\int_0^{\gamma_{th}} f_Z(t)dt=\left(\frac{a_m\Gamma(1+t_m)}{t_m\bar{\gamma}_m^{t_m}}\right)^{l_m}\frac{\gamma_{th}^{l_m(1+t_m)}}{l_m(1+t_m)\Gamma(l_m+l_m t_m)} \tag{4}$$

where F_Z is the cumulative distribution function (CDF) of Z , γ_{th} is the SNR threshold and l_m is the maximum retransmission number for m th hop.

Now we investigate the multihop case. The e2e outage probability of multihop HARQ relay network is given by

$$P_{e2e}=\Pr\left\{\min\left(\sum_{l_1=1}^{l_1}\gamma_{l_1},\sum_{l_2=1}^{l_2}\gamma_{l_2},...,\sum_{l_m=1}^{l_m}\gamma_{l_m}\right)\le\gamma_{th}\right\}=1-\prod_{m=1}^{M}\Pr\{\gamma_m>\gamma_{th}\}\approx\sum_{i=1}^{M}F_{\gamma_i}(\gamma_{th}) \tag{5}$$

Since the integration term is much smaller than the sum term, we ignore it approximately. Thus, the e2e outage probability is given by:

$$P_{e2e}\approx\sum_{m=1}^{M}\Pr\left\{\sum_{i=1}^{l_m}\bar{\gamma}_m<\gamma_{th}\right\}=\sum_{m=1}^{M}\left(\frac{a_m\gamma_{th}^{(1+t_m)}N_0^{t_m}\Gamma(1+t_m)}{t_m l_m(1+t_m)\Gamma(l_m+l_m t_m)}\left(\frac{d_m^{\alpha t_m}}{P_m^{t_m}}\right)\right)^{l_m} \tag{6}$$

In the following, by assuming the retransmission number of each hop to be an constant, we first formulate the joint optimizations of power allocation $\mathbf{P}=[P_1,P_2,...,P_N]$ and relay placement $\mathbf{d}=[d_1,d_2,...,d_N]$ which minimizes P_{e2e} in (5). Then, the retransmission allocation strategy are studied based on the joint OPA and ORP optimization strategy.

3 Joint optimization of PA and RP

With the definition of the e2e outage probability, the joint OPA and ORP optimization problem is given by:

$$\min P_{e2e} = \sum_{m=1}^{M} \mathrm{F}\left(\mathbf{P},\mathbf{d}\right)$$
$$s.t. \quad \sum_{m=1}^{M} P_m l_m \le P_T ; \sum_{m=1}^{M} l_m = L \quad \text{and} \quad \sum_{m=1}^{M} d_m = 1 \tag{7}$$

where $\mathrm{F}\left(\mathbf{P},\mathbf{d}\right) = \mathrm{A}\left(m\right)\left(d_m^{\alpha} P_m^{-1}\right)^{l_m t_m}$ and $\mathrm{A}\left(m\right) = \left(\frac{a_m \gamma_{th}^{(1+t_m)} N_0^{t_m} \Gamma\left(1+t_m\right)}{t_m l_m \left(1+t_m\right) \Gamma\left(l_m + l_m t_m\right)}\right)^{l_m}$. The optimization problem in (7) is not always convex with respect to the optimization variables. In particular, the non-convexity arises from the objective function and is related to the distance d_m, the retransmission round l_m and the pathloss factor α . In order to obtain tractable solution for the optimization problem, we first recast optimization problem (7) as a convex optimization problem and then study the relationship of d_m, l_m and α .

Theorem 1: *The problem in (7) is a convex optimization problem if* $\alpha\left(t_m l_m \left(\alpha-1\right)-1\right) > 0$ *for* $m = 1,2,\ldots,M$.

Proof: Taking the first-order derivative of function $\mathrm{F}\left(\mathbf{P},\mathbf{d}\right)$ with respect to P_m, we can obtain that $\frac{\partial \mathrm{F}}{\partial P_m} = -\frac{t_m l_m d_m^{\alpha l_m t_m} \mathrm{A}\left(m\right)}{P_m^{t_m l_m + 1}}$ Then we check the second-order derivative of function $\mathrm{F}\left(\mathbf{P},\mathbf{d}\right)$ with respect to $P_m \cdot \frac{\partial^2 \mathrm{F}}{\partial P_m^2} = \frac{t_m l_m d_m^{\alpha l_m t_m} \left(t_m l_m + 1\right) \mathrm{A}\left(m\right)}{P_m^{t_m l_m + 2}}$ .Similarly, we can get the first-order and second-order derivatives of function $\mathrm{F}\left(P,d\right)$ with respect to d_m as $\frac{\partial \mathrm{F}}{\partial d_m} = \frac{\alpha t_m l_m d_m^{\alpha_m l_m t_m - 1} \mathrm{A}\left(m\right)}{P_m^{t_m l_m}}$ and $\frac{\partial^2 \mathrm{F}}{\partial d_m^2} = \frac{\alpha t_m l_m \left(\alpha t_m l_m - 1\right) d_m^{\alpha_m l_m t_m - 2} \mathrm{A}\left(m\right)}{P_m^{t_m l_m}}$, respectively.

The Hessian matrix of F is given by

$$H\left(F\right) = \begin{bmatrix} \frac{\partial^2 \mathrm{F}}{\partial P_m^2} & \frac{\partial^2 \mathrm{F}}{\partial P_m \partial d_m} \\ \frac{\partial^2 \mathrm{F}}{\partial d_m \partial P_m} & \frac{\partial^2 \mathrm{F}}{\partial d_m^2} \end{bmatrix} \tag{8}$$

where $\frac{\partial^2 \mathrm{F}}{\partial d_m \partial P_m} = \frac{\partial^2 \mathrm{F}}{\partial P_m \partial d_m} = -\frac{\alpha \left(t_m l_m\right)^2 d_m^{\alpha_m l_m t_m - 1} A\left(m\right)}{P_m^{t_m l_m + 1}}$ The determinant of the Hessian matrix can be evaluated as :

$$\det\left[H\left(\mathrm{F}\right)\right] = \alpha\left(t_m l_m \left(\alpha-1\right)-1\right)\left(\frac{d_m^{\alpha l_m t_m - 2} t_m l_m A\left(m\right)}{P_m^{t_m l_m + 2}}\right)^2 \tag{9}$$

Obviously, if $\alpha\left(t_m l_m \left(\alpha-1\right)-1\right) > 0$, then (9) is always positive, which is equivalent to that F is jointly convex. Since the constraints are linear and the non-negative summation of convex functions is convex, Theorem 1 is proved. □

Note that $l_m > 1$ and $\alpha > 0$ always hold true, moreover, α is normally in the range of 2-6 and t_m is normally no less than 1 [6], accordingly, $\alpha\left(t_m l_m \left(\alpha-1\right)-1\right) > 0$ holds true for most typical fading channel models. In the rare case, i.e., in buildings and stores when $\alpha\left(t_m l_m \left(\alpha-1\right)-1\right) < 0$, geometric programming (GP) approximation [9] can be adopt to obtain the solution. The parameters for the approximation are similar with that in [8].

To solve this problem, we introduce nonzero Lagrange multipliers λ and μ , the Lagrange function for joint optimization problem of PA and RP can be formulated as:

$$\Gamma = \sum_{m=1}^{M} A(m)\left(\frac{d_m^{\alpha}}{P_m}\right)^{l_m t_m} + \lambda\left(\sum_{m=1}^{M} l_m P_m - P_T\right) + \mu\left(\sum_{m=1}^{M} d_m - 1\right) \tag{10}$$

Take the first derivatives of $\mathrm{F}\left(\mathbf{P},\mathbf{d}\right)$ with respect to P_m and d_m to zero, we can obtain the optimal solution $\left(\mathbf{P},\mathbf{d}\right)$:

$$\frac{\partial \Gamma}{\partial P_m} = -\frac{t_m l_m}{P_m}\frac{d_m^{\alpha l_m t_m}\mathrm{A}(m)}{P_m^{t_m l_m}} + \lambda l_m = 0 \tag{11}$$

$$\frac{\partial \Gamma}{\partial d_m} = \frac{\alpha t_m l_m}{d_m}\frac{d_m^{\alpha l_m t_m}\mathrm{A}(m)}{P_m^{t_m l_m}} + \mu = 0 \tag{12}$$

The relationship of P_m and d_m for $m = 1,2,...,M$ can be written as: $P_m = -\mu d_m / (\alpha \lambda l_m)$. Accordingly, we have $P_T = -\mu/\alpha\lambda l_m$ and $P_m = d_m P_T$. By substituting them into (11) and (12), we have: $P_m^* = \left(\frac{\lambda^* P_T^{\alpha l_m t_m}}{t_m \mathrm{A}(m)}\right)^{\frac{1}{(\alpha-1)l_m t_m - 1}}$ and $d_m^* = \left(\frac{\lambda^* P_T^{t_m l_m + 1}}{t_m \mathrm{A}(m)}\right)^{\frac{1}{(\alpha-1)l_m t_m - 1}}$, where λ^* satisfies $\sum_{m=1}^{M}\left(\frac{\lambda^* P_T^{t_m l_m + 1}}{t_m \mathrm{A}(m)}\right)^{\frac{1}{(\alpha-1)l_m t_m - 1}} = D$.

Note that the solution of the joint optimization is a special case of a separate optimization resulting in the best performance. Apparently, the joint optimization of PA and RP provides the best performance.

The mathematical analysis shows that the e2e outage probability performance of the proposed joint optimization scheme is related to the number of transmissions in relays. Unfortunately, a closed-form expression for l_m appears to be hard to find. In this paper, we shed some light on the performance analysis by proposing a retransmission allocation strategy based on the joint OPA and ORP strategy. The retransmission allocation strategy is done in two steps. In the first step, we set retransmission number as $l_m = \lfloor L/M \rfloor$, m=1,2,...M . In the second step, if L is not a multiple of M , use the retransmission time on the weak link. Otherwise, we allocate one retransmission chance from the strongest hop to the weakest hop. As a consequence, more retransmission chance is allocated to the weaker hop to leverage the performance of weaker hops. Since the channel difference can be compensated by the joint optimization, the proposed scheme achieves equivalent or better e2e outage probability.

4 Analytical and simulation results

In this section, the simulation and analytical results are presented to verify the performance of optimized multihop relay networks in various fading channels. The performance is evaluated with normalized distance , three hop ($M = 3$) relay networks with pathloss exponent $\alpha = 3$, and SNR threshold $\gamma_{th} = 5dB$, unless stated otherwise. The total SNR constraint is denoted by $\rho_T = P_T / N_0$. The analysis results are compared with the Monte-Carlo simulation results. In the following figures the analysis results are denoted with lines while the simulation results are denoted with marks.

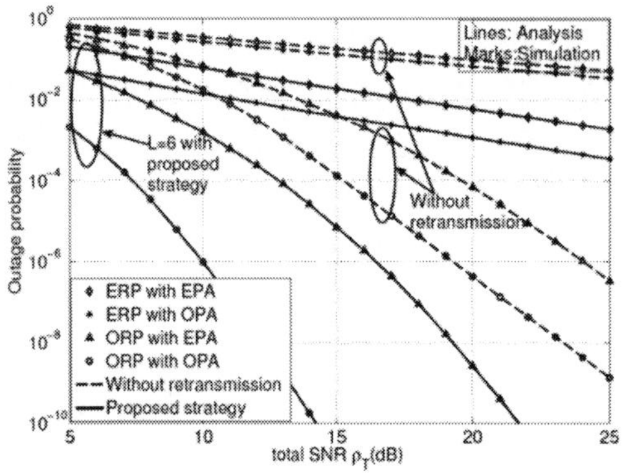

Figure 1. The P_{e2e} of three hop relay networks versus total SNR ρ_T in Nakagami-m fading channels with $(m1, m2, m3) = (0.5, 1, 5)$.

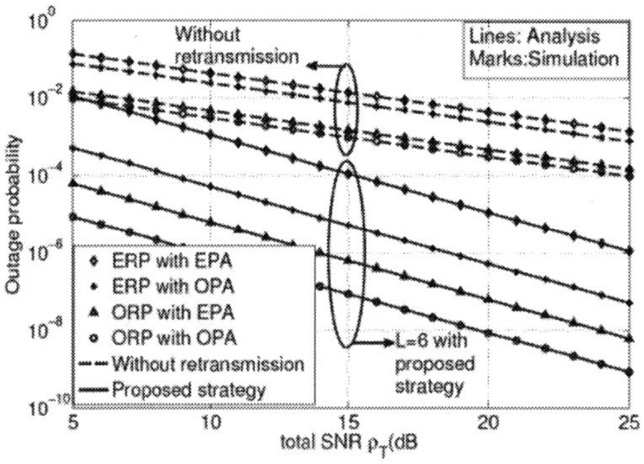

Figure 2. The P_{e2e} of three hop relay networks versus total SNR ρ_T in Rician fading channels with $(K1, K2, K3) = (1, 5, 7)$.

Fig. 1 and Fig. 2 compare the e2e outage probability P_{e2e} of three hop relay networks versus SNR ρ_T in unbalanced channel parameters for Nakagami fading channel with $(m1, m2, m3) = (0.5, 1, 5)$ and Rician fading channels with $(K1, K2, K3) = (1, 5, 7)$. It can be observed that the analytical results match the simulation results nicely for a wide range of SNR, which verify the accuracy of the algorithm. Although ORP with equal PA (EPA) scheme outperform OPA with equal RP (ERP) schemes, the separate optimization of PA and RP are suboptimal to the joint optimization of PA and RP as expected. It should be noticed that the performance gains come form the compensation of the channel difference. In the meantime, the HARQ schemes with retransmission number $L = 6$ are compared with the scheme without retransmission. According to the results, the outage probability is significantly improved by the use of HARQ techniques. An important observation is that the joint optimization scheme is more sensitive to retransmission. This implies that the gain from optimization gets better as the channel condition gets more favourable.

To evaluate the effect of retransmission on different RP and PA strategy, the P_{e2e} of three hop relay networks versus retransmission number L in Nakagami-m fading channel with $(m1, m2, m3) = (1, 1, 5)$ and total SNR $\rho_T = 10$ are shown in Fig.3. Three power and relay optimization strategies are compared for two retransmission strategies, i.e., the average retransmission strategy which is denoted by the dash-dot lines and the proposed retransmission strategy which is denoted by soiled lines. For comparison, we also include in the figures the transmission power level of the equal-retransmission assignment strategy. We observe that the proposed retransmission strategy achieves significant performance improvement within the first few retransmission rounds. The proposed retransmission strategy shows better performance compared to the equal-retransmission strategy. The reason is that with the increase of the total power, the outage probability of the hops with better channel condition will decrease much faster than that of the weaker hop due to the channel difference. By allocating more retransmission chance to the weaker hop, the proposed retransmission strategy eventually improves the e2e performance. Moreover, the e2e outage performance improves with increasing number of retransmission numbers and the performance gains in the outage probability do not increase linearly.

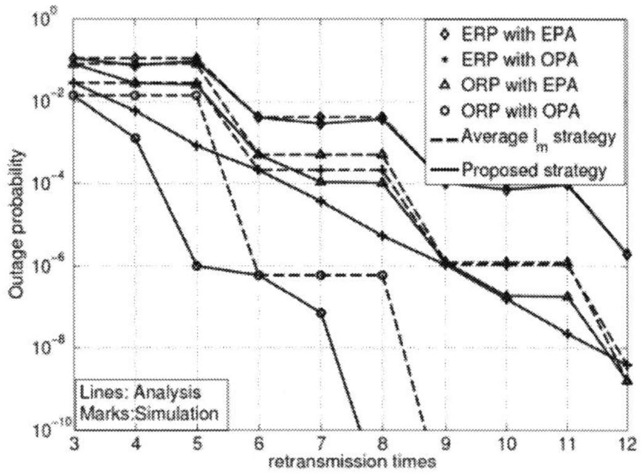

Figure 3. The P_{e2e} of three hop relay networks versus retransmission number L in Nakagami-m fading channel with $(m1,m2,m3)=(1,1,5)$ and total SNR $\rho_T=10$.

Conclusion

This paper has addressed the problem of joint optimization of OPA and ORP of a multihop relay networks adopting HARQ. The expression for the e2e outage probability is derived under generalized fading channels and optimization is carried out to find joint optimal power allocation (OPA) and relay placement optimal (ORP) for multihop relay networks. The result demonstrates that the equidistant relay placement with equal power allocation strategy is not the optimal way of power apportionment for unbalanced channel conditions, and the proposed strategy can improve the e2e outage probability significantly by dramatic compensating the channel difference. As future work, the proposed policy can be extended to systems employing practical coding and modulation schemes. Furthermore it is interesting to consider the range expansion and power allocation problem when the end-to-end retransmission constraint is enforced on the whole HARQ process.

References

1. K. Dhaka, R. K. Mallik, R. Schober. : 'Optimisation of power allocation for asymmetric relay placement in multi-hop relay systems ', *IET Commun.*, **7**, 2, pp. 128-136.(2013).
2. Caleb K. Lo, S. Vishwanath, and R. W. Heath, Jr. 'An Energy-Based Comparison of Long-Hop and Short-Hop Routing in MIMO Networks', *IEEE Trans. Veh. Technol.*, **59**, 1, pp. 394-405 (2010).
3. X. Chen, S. H. Song and K. B. Letaief. : 'Relay Position Optimization Improves Finite-SNR Diversity Gain of Decode-and-Forward MIMO Relay Systems', *IEEE Trans. Commun.*, **60**, 11, pp. 3311-3321, (2012).
4. S. H. Kim, S. J. Lee, and D. K. Sung. 'HARQ Rate Selection Schemes in a Multihop Relay Network With a Delay Constraint ', *IEEE Trans. Veh. Technol.*, **64**, 6, pp. 2333-2348, (2015).

5. A. A. Haghighi and K. Navaie. : `Truncated HARQ-Based Multi-Hop Systems:Outage and Related Performance Metrics `, *IEEE Trans. Wireless Commun.*, **63**, 10, pp. 303-313, (2015).
6. M. K. Simon, M. S. Alouini,: *Digital Communication over Fading Channels.* (John Wiley and Sons, second edition, 2005.)
7. Z.Wang and G. Giannakis. : `A simple and general parameterization quantifying performance in fading channels `, *IEEE Trans. Commun.,* **51**, 8, pp. 1389-1398, (2003).
8. T. P. Do, I. Song and Y. H. Kim. : `Optimization of Power Allocation and Relay Position in Multihop Relay Networks Over Generalized Fading Channels `, *IEEE Trans.Wireless Commun.*, **64**, 11, pp. 5031-5041, (2015).
9. *GGPLAB: A Simple MATLAB Toolbox for Geometric Programming.* Available: http://www.stanford.edu/~boyd/ggplab/.

DOI: 10.1051/itmconf/20171103006

Subspace Method-based Blind SNR Estimation for Communication between Orbiters in Mars Exploration

Ze-Zhou SUN[1, 2], Cheng-Hua WANG[1] and Xiao-Fei ZHANG[1,a]

[1]*College of Electronic and Information Engineering, Nanjing University of Aeronautics and Astronautics, Nanjing, 210016, China*
[2]*Department of overall design, the China Academy of space technology, Beijing, China*

Abstract. In Mars exploration the effective time of communication between orbiters is short, and the relative distance and gesture between them change fast. The signal to noise ratio (SNR) estimation is required in receiver to change adaptively the data rate in the communication system. Therefore, SNR estimation is a key technique in adaptive data transmission. We propose a blind SNR estimation for communication between orbiters in Mars exploration via subspace method. The subspace method has better SNR estimation than some conventional SNR estimation algorithms. Numerical simulations demonstrate the effectiveness and improvement of the proposed algorithm.

1 Introduction

The long distance between Mars and Earth causes long transmission time delay and signal attenuation. In Mars exploration the effective time of communication between orbiters is short, and the relative distance and gesture between them change fast [1, 2, 3]. The signal to noise ratio (SNR) estimation is required in receiver to change adaptively the data rate of the communication system. SNR estimation approach contains frequency domain method and time domain method. Time domain method contains data aided (DA) method and non-data aided (NDA) method [4]. DA method has higher estimation accuracy than NDA method, but it needs the insertion of the training sequence, which lowers the transmission efficiency. In time domain method, SNR estimation algorithms based on DA contain maximum likelihood (ML), minimum mean square error (MMSE) [5, 6], split symbol moments estimator (SSME) [7, 8], and the separation of signal and noise using higher-order cumulants [9]. SNR estimation algorithms based on NDA are second- and fourth-order moments (M2M4) [10, 11], signal-to-variation ratio (SVR) [12], squared signal-to-noise variance (SNV) [13], and data fitting (DF) [14]. Classic frequency domain method is based on the flat character of power spectrum of white noise, which is suitable for SNR estimation of AWGN channel, but not for colored-noise environment.

This paper intends to develop a blind SNR estimation for communication between orbiters in Mars exploration via subspace method, which not only achieves accurate estimate result. The subspace method has better SNR estimation than some conventional SNR estimation algorithms including DF, SVR, SNV and M2M4.

[a] Corresponding author: fei_zxf@163.com

 DOI: 10.1051/itmconf/20171103006

The reminder of this paper is structured as follows. The data model is given in Section 2. Section 3 introduces the blind SNR estimation algorithm via subspace method. Section 4 presents the simulation results, and the conclusions are drawn in Section 5.

2 Data model

In complex additive white Gaussian noise (AWGN) channel, the received signals can be represented as follows:

$$r_k = x_k + n_k \tag{1}$$

where n_k is a zero-mean complex AWGN sample with a variance of σ_n^2. When the sampling time is t, the noise column vector consisting of L samples is $\mathbf{n}(t) = [n_t, n_{t-1}, \cdots, n_{t-L+1}]^T$, where $(\bullet)^T$ denotes the transpose. The second-order moment of the noise vector can be written as

$$E[\mathbf{n}(t)\mathbf{n}^{\mathrm{H}}(l)] = \sigma_n^2 I \, \delta_{tl} \tag{2}$$

where $E[\bullet]$ denotes the mathematical expectation, the upper-case symbol H is the Hermitian transpose, and I is the $L \times L$ identity matrix. Function δ_{tl} has the value of 1 only when $t = l$, while under other circumstances it has the value of 0. x_k is the bandpass signal at the carrier frequency f_c, i.e.,

$$x_k = \tilde{x}e^{-j(2\pi f_c k/f_s + \theta)} \tag{3}$$

$\tilde{x}_k$ is the complex equivalent baseband signal. In terms of MPSK signal. In terms of MQAM signal, $\tilde{x}_k = A_l e^{j2\pi l/M}$ ($l = 0, \ldots, M-1$), $A_l \in C$ represents the corresponding amplitude. θ is the initial phase of the carrier, and f_s is the sampling rate. Let the signal power and the noise power be P_x and P_n, respectively, so the SNR can be written as [14]

$$\rho = 10\lg(P_x / P_n) \tag{4}$$

3 Blind SNR estimation algorithm via subspace method

Assume that the receiving signal has N numbers of symbols. We sample L times for each symbol, then the nth symbol after sampling can be expressed as $\mathbf{r}_n(t) = [r_n(t), r_n(t-1), \cdots, r_n(t-L+1)]^T$. The receiving signal is a $L \times N$ matrix

$$\mathbf{R} = \begin{bmatrix} \mathbf{r}_1(t) & \mathbf{r}_2(t) & \mathrm{L} & \mathbf{r}_N(t) \\ \mathbf{r}_1(t-1) & \mathbf{r}_2(t-1) & \mathrm{L} & \mathbf{r}_N(t-1) \\ \mathrm{L} & \mathrm{L} & \mathrm{L} & \mathrm{L} \\ \mathbf{r}_1(t-L+1) & \mathbf{r}_2(t-L+1) & \mathrm{L} & \mathbf{r}_N(t-L+1) \end{bmatrix}.$$

The covariance matrix of it is $\mathbf{R}_{rr} = E[\mathbf{r}_n(t)\mathbf{r}_n^H(t)]$. Assume the signal and the noise are uncorrelated. $\mathbf{R}_{rr}$ can be expressed as

$$\mathbf{R}_{rr} = \mathbf{R}_{xx} + \mathbf{R}_{nn} \tag{5}$$

According to the eigenvalue decomposition theorem, R_{rr} can be denoted by[15]

$$\mathbf{R}_{rr} = \mathbf{A}\Sigma\mathbf{A}^H \tag{6}$$

where $\mathbf{A}$ consists of the eigenvectors. The diagonal matrix $\Sigma = \mathrm{diag}(b_1, b_2, \cdots, b_L)$ represents the eigenvalues of $\mathbf{R}_{rr}$, where $b_1 \geq b_2 \geq \cdots b_L$. From Eq. 2 we know that the autocorrelation matrix of white noise $\mathbf{R}_{nn}$ satisfies

$$\mathbf{R}_{nn} = \sigma_n^2 \mathbf{I} \tag{7}$$

Then the eigenvalues of $\mathbf{R}_{rr}$ is in the form of

$$b_i = \begin{cases} \sigma_{x_i}^2 + \sigma_n^2, & 1 \leq i \leq p \\ \sigma_n^2, & p+1 \leq i \leq L \end{cases} \tag{8}$$

where $\sigma_{x_i}^2$ denotes the signal power of the i th eigenvector. The signal subspace is the subspace spanned by the first p eigenvectors, while the noise subspace is the subspace spanned by the last $L-p$ eigenvectors. And the noise power P_n is L times of σ_n^2. When the signal subspace dimension p is fixed, the SNR estimates could be obtained via calculation of σ_n^2 and P_n.

The noise power can be obtained by

$$\hat{P}_n = \sum_{i=p+1}^{L} b_i \Big/ (L-p) \tag{9}$$

Then, the source signal power is

$$\hat{P}_s = \sum_{i=1}^{p} (b_i - P_n) \tag{10}$$

We can adopt the Minimum Description Length (MDL) criterion [16] to estimate the signal subspace dimension p, while p is known as the number of source signal in this paper. Actually it is hard to get the perfect value of correlated matrix $\mathbf{R}_{rr}$, since we can only estimate it via the limited-length received signals. Assume there are N observation vectors, and the sampled covariance matrix is

$$\hat{\mathbf{R}}_{rr} = \frac{1}{N}\sum_{n=1}^{N}\mathbf{r}_n(t)\mathbf{r}_n^H(t) \tag{11}$$

It is proven that the eigenvalues of $\hat{\mathbf{R}}_{rr}$ defined by Eq. 11 are the maximum likelihood of eigenvalues of $\mathbf{R}_{rr}$.

The steps of blind SNR estimation algorithm via subspace method are as follows:

Step1: Obtain the covariance matrix estimate $\hat{\mathbf{R}}_{rr}$ from the received signal.

Step2: Compute the ED of $\hat{\mathbf{R}}_{rr}$ according to Eq. 6.

Step3: Sort the eigenvalues b_i in descending orders.

Step4: Estimate the noise power and the signal power according to Eq. 9 and Eq. 10, respectively;
Step5: Obtain the SNR estimate according to Eq. 4.

4 Simulation results

We use Monte Carlo simulations to assess the performance of the proposed algorithms. Use ρ to represent the actual value of SNR, and $\hat{\rho}_k$ is the estimate of ρ in the lth Monte Carlo trial, so the RMSE can be written as

$$RMSE\{\hat{\rho}\} = \sqrt{\frac{1}{M}\sum_{k=1}^{M}(\hat{\rho}_k - \rho)^2} \tag{12}$$

where M is the number of Monte Carlo simulations.

In simulations, we choose QPSK signal over AWGN channel. The roll-off root of the raised cosine filter factor is 0.5 and tap number is 65. The number of samples L is 16, the number of symbols N is 300, and the number of Monte Carlo simulations M is 500.

Figure.1 demonstrates the SNR estimate of subspace method. SNR estimate gradually approaches to real SNR as the real SNR increasing.

The RMSE of SNR estimate via subspace method under different numbers of symbols is shown in Figure. 2. Under the same SNR, the greater the number of the symbols is, the smaller the RMSE of SNR estimate is.

We compare our proposed algorithm against the DF, M2M4, SVR and SNV, which is shown in Figure.3. It is shown in Figure.3 that the SNR estimation performance of subspace tracking method is the best among the algorithms.

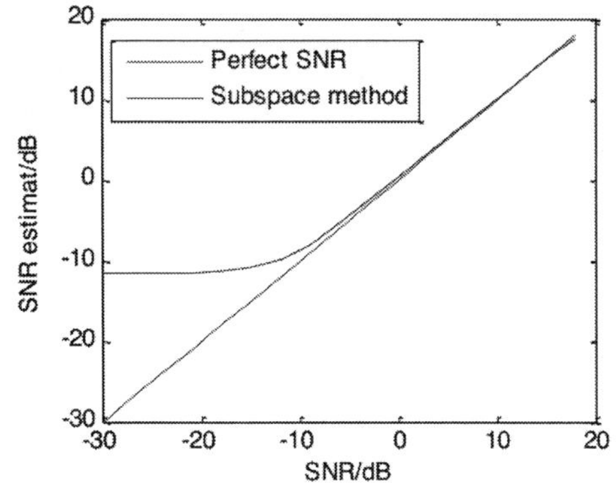

Figure. 1 SNR estimate of subspace method

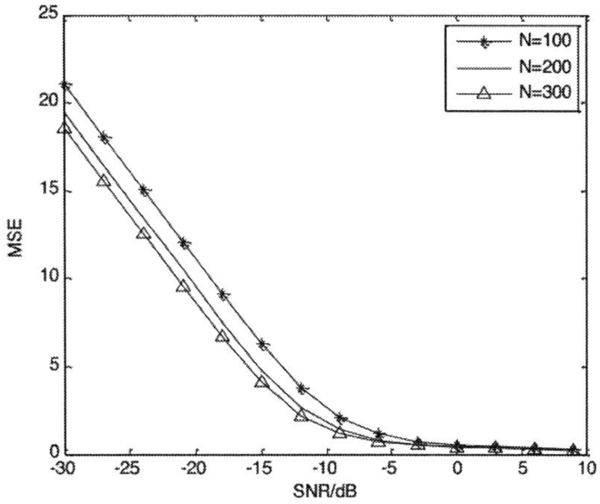

Figure. 2 RMSE of SNR estimate under different numbers of symbols

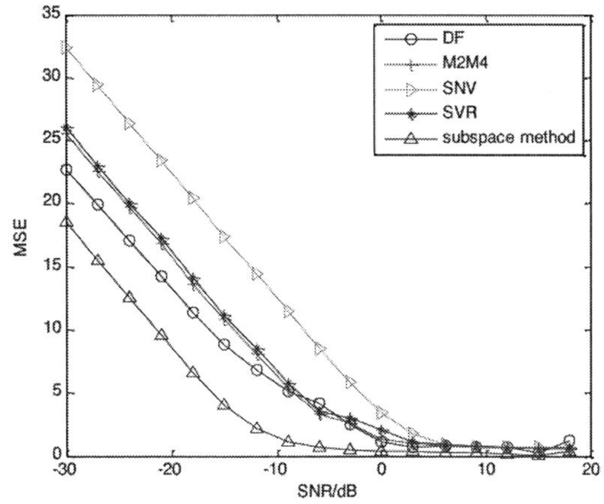

Figure. 3 Estimation performance comparison of different algorithms (N=300)

Conclusions

A blind SNR estimation for communication between orbiters in Mars exploration via subspace method is proposed in this paper. The subspace method has better SNR estimation than some conventional SNR estimation algorithms.

Acknowledgement

This work is supported by China NSF Grants (61371169), Qing Lan Project, and priority academic program development of Jiangsu high education institutions.

References

1. Ru J X. Numerical analysis of Mars exploration orbit[J]. Science in China (Series E: Technological Sciences), **39**(03): 528-534. (2009)
2. Guo H L, Wang Z S, Qu G J. Flight principle of Mars exploration and launch timing analysis [J]. Science in China (Series E: Technological Sciences), **39**(03): 535-543. (2009)
3. Zhang X H, Liu Z S. Trajectory Design and Optimization of Mars Satellite. MISSILEAND SPACE VEHCILE. **NO.2.** 15-23. (2008)
4. Fu W J, Jiang J S, Wang X R, Liu S Y. New SNR Estimation Methods in Digital QPSK Receiver [J]. Journal of Electronics & Information Technology, **29**, No.2, 255-258. (2007)
5. Wiesel A, Goldberg J, Messer H. Non-Data-Aided Signal-to-Noise-Ratio Estimation[C]// *2002 IEEE International Conference on Communications*, 197-201. (2002)
6. Li B, Difazio R, Zeira A. A low bias algorithm to estimate negative SNRs in an AWGN channel [J]. IEEE Communications Letters, **6(11)**:469-471. (2002)
7. Shah B, Hinedi S. The split symbol moments SNR estimator in narrow-band channels [J]. IEEE Transactions on Aerospace & Electronic Systems, **26(5)**:737-747. (1990)
8. M. K. Simon and S. Dolinar. Signal-to-noise ratio estimation for autonomous receiver operation [J]. IEEE GLOBECOM **04**:pp: 282-287 Dallas, TX. (2004)
9. Tugnait J K, Gummadavelli U. Blind channel estimation and deconvolution in colored noise using higher-order cumulants [C]// Advanced Signal Processing: Algorithms, Architectures, and *Implementations*, 106-125. (1994)
10. Ren G L, Chang Y L, Zhang H. A new SNR estimator for QPSK Modulation in an AWGN channel [J]. IEEE Transactions Circuits and Systems II: Express Briefs, **52(6)**: 336-338. (2005)
11. Matzner R, Englberger F. An SNR estimation algorithm using fourth-order moments [C]// 1994 *IEEE International Symposium on Information Theory,* IEEE. (1994)
12. Salman T, Badawy A, Elfouly T.M, Khattab T. Non-data-aided SNR Estimation for QPSK Modulation in AWGN Channel [C]. *IEEE Wireless and Mobile Computing, Networking and Communications Conference,* Larnaca, 611-616. (2014)
13. Gilchriest C E. Signal-to-noise monitoring [J]. JPL Space Programs Summary, **4**: 169-184. (1966)
14. Hua Xu, Zupeng Li, Hui Zheng. A non-data-aided SNR estimation algorithm for QAM signals [C]. *IEEE Circuits and Systems, International Conference on Communications,* Chengdu,999-1003. (2004)
15. Ramakrishna D, Mandayam N B, Yates R D. Subspace-based SIR estimation for CDMA cellular systems [J]. IEEE Transactions on Vehicular Technology, **49**(5):1732-1742. (2000)
16. Wax M. and Kailath T. Detection of signals by information theoretical criteria. IEEE Trans. on ASSP, **33**(2): 387-392. (1985)

Research on Algorithm of Indoor Positioning System Based on Low Energy Bluetooth 4.0

De-Yi ZHANG[1], Wen-Yue WANG[2] and Lian-Rong LV[1,a]

[1]*College of Electrical and Electronic Engineering, 300384 Tianjing University of Technology, China*
[2]*College of computer and Communication Engineering, 300384 Tianjing University of Technology, China*

Abstract This paper mainly analyzes and compares several well-known algorithms for indoor positioning. By many nodes jump tests, relation between RSSI and distance and relation between LQI and packet error rate can be obtained. Then based on the relations, LQI confidence coefficient is classified. By comparing these different kinds of algorithms, this paper perfects the algorithm of fuzzy fingerprint indoor positioning, which can shorten the time required to process off-line data. At last, this algorithm was verified by indoor and outdoor experiments, by which we can know that this algorithm greatly lower RSSI error. And it is concluded that this algorithm has a better positioning accuracy.

1 Introduction

1.1 Research background and significance

Wireless location is an important technology belonging to Things of Internet, which is also a development trend of science and technology in the future. Fuzzy fingerprint positioning algorithm in this paper is based on RSSI (received signal strength indication) and LQI (link quality indicator). which through a certain algorithm to eliminate the signal propagation in the process of loss and error to achieve our desired accuracy, and as far as possible the fingerprint database to reduce the difficulty.

2 Research of technology concerning indoor positioning system

2.1 Several classical indoor positioning technologies

At present, the mainstream indoor positioning technology is as follows:

(1) Infrared ray positioning: transmission distance is short and the penetrating power is weak; however, it is easily affected by the indoor lighting. Thus, the equipment consumption and the unit price cost will be high.

(2) Ultrasonic wave positioning: being greatly affected by multipath effect, ultrasonic wave will have a positioning error. What's worse, the receiving device will cost a lot.

(3) RFID (radio frequency identification) positioning: propagation distance is short and the devices

[a] Corresponding author: 163lvlianrong@163.com

DOI: 10.1051/itmconf/20171103007

are difficult to be integrated with general equipment, so it is hard to have a wide popularization.

(4) Ultra-wide band positioning: the equipment costs a lot so it is difficult to be widely used.

(5) BLE(Bluetooth Low Energy) 4.0 positioning: a battery with the same size as a button can provide enough power for the BLE device for one year. The signals from the area which is 100m around the BLE can be received. We all know that now almost all cell phones have the newest BLE4.0 module available. Therefore, the mobile terminal with tiny BLE module can be smaller and lighter. In this case, the indoor positioning system based on BLE will have advantages and application values which cannot be available by other indoor positioning technologies.

2.2 Algorithm for several classical indoor positioning technologies

2.2.1 AOA positioning

The accuracy of AOA positioning will be affected by the sensitivity and 3D resolution of the antenna array. As a result, the places in a city or the indoor places where the arrangement is too crowded, accuracy of AOA positioning will be greatly affected.

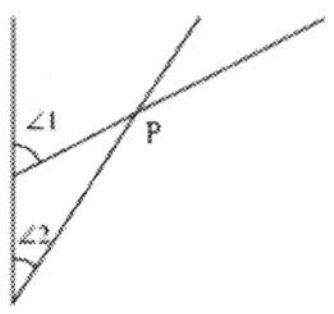

Figure. 1 AOA Positioning Schematic diagram

2.2.2 TOA positioning

Time of Arrival positioning is a method to figure out the location of the mobile terminals by three known AP points. TOA greatly depends on the time and the signal transmission has an obvious multipath effect because of the barriers indoor, so TOA is difficult to be widely used for indoor positioning if there is a high requirement on accuracy.

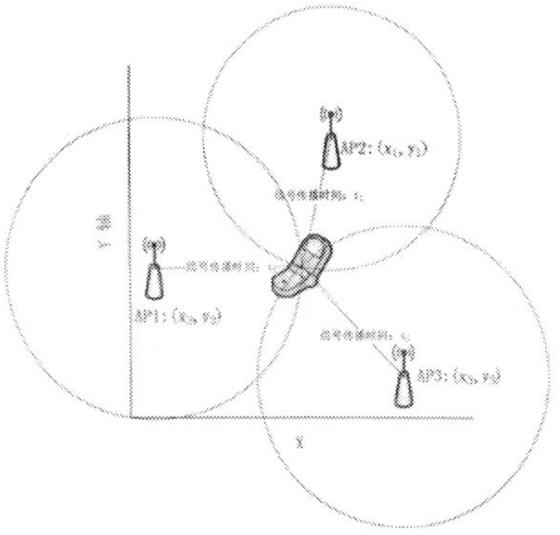

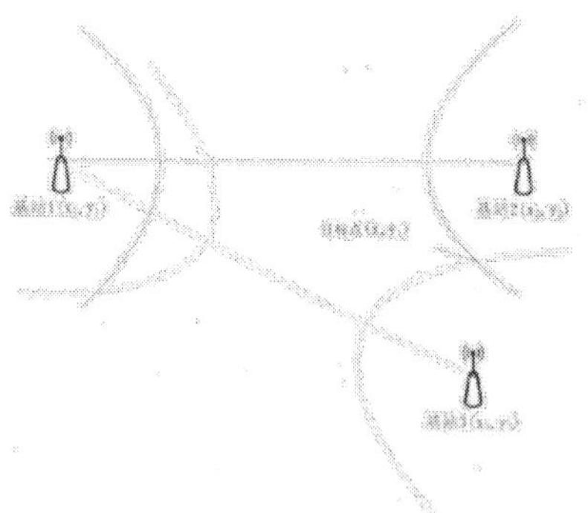

Figure.2 TOA Positioning Schematic Diagram

Figure.3 TDOA Positioning Schematic Diagram

2.2.3 TDOA positioning

Unlike TOA positioning, TDOA positioning is a method to define the location of mobile terminal by the time gap of signals arriving at the two base stations but not the absolute time of arrival. That is TDOA does not need to have a high accurate clock synchronization between the base station and the

 DOI: 10.1051/itmconf/20171103007

mobile terminal. In this way, the cost will be lowered. However, it is impossible to fully overcome the adverse affect caused by the complicated indoor environment. That is the signals cannot be transmitted long and the multipath effect is quite obvious, which will seriously affect the accuracy of indoor positioning.

2.2.4 Fingerprint location positioning

Compared with other methods, fingerprint positioning is able to fully overcome the problems caused by complicated indoor environment (signals cannot be transmitted far and multipath effect is obvious), which will perfect the allocation of AP points. Because of the complicated indoor environment, multipath transmission of the signals will be much more obvious compared with the signals transmitted at flat outdoor environment. Even though some methods can have a highly accurate positioning outdoor, they cannot be as accurate as fingerprint positioning. The fingerprint location method is just to match the characteristics of multipath propagation, and to a large extent, reduce the error of indoor positioning.

3 System-based RSSI indoor propagation model

3.1 Impact on BLE distribution by distance

Samples shall be taken from the points which are differently far from the BLE launcher. Each point shall have 100 samples taken. The sampling interval shall be one second. After all the samples are taken, figure out the average value of each BLE sample. See the figure here below for the relationship between RSSI and distance.

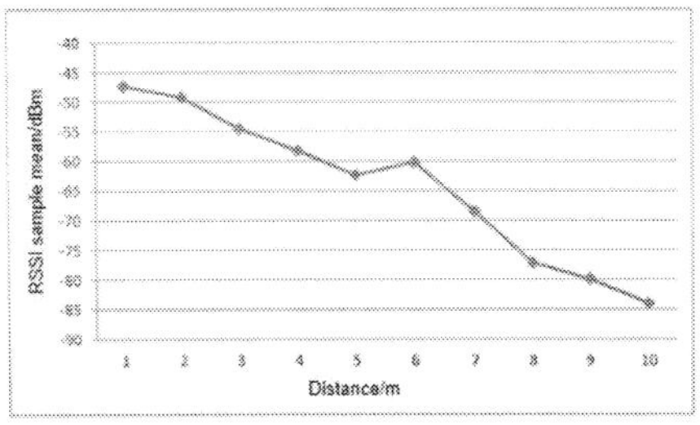

Figure.4 Relationship between RSSI and Distance

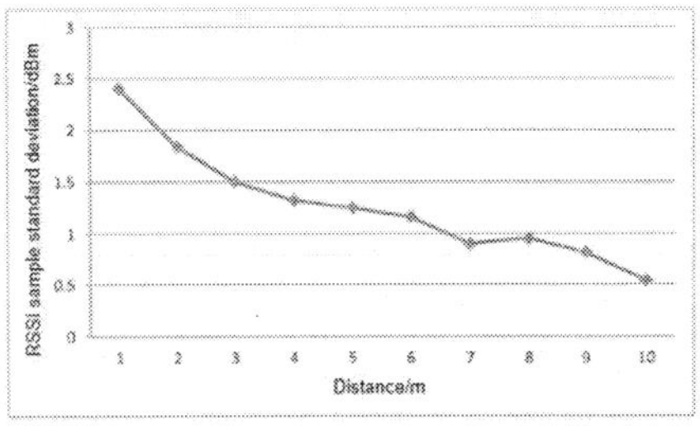

Figure.5 Relationship between Sample Point RSSI and Distance

From Figure 4 (relationship between RSSI and distance), we can see that the signal strength from BLE will be decreased if the distance is increased. However, the decreasing range is getting smaller and smaller. When the signal strength is decreasing, we can see that there is a signal fluctuation. In my opinion, the fluctuation is resulted in by signal diffraction, signal reflection, signal refraction, signal scattering or multipath effect. This proves that if signal loss model is used to figure out the distance between sample points indoor, a big error will be caused.

From Figure 5 (Relationship between sample point standard deviation and distance), we can see that as the distance increases, the standard deviation is decreased. That is fluctuation of the samples becomes smaller and smaller when the distance is increasing. Theoretically, the smaller sample fluctuation is, the better fingerprinting positioning will be[2]. This is because that the smaller fluctuation is, the possibility for several sample points to have the same value will be smaller. Thus, combing with Figure 6, I think the places where the standard deviation is small and the average value is higher, it will be much better for fingerprint positioning. Based on my conclusion, here gets the figure showing the relationship between sample point standard deviation and average value. From the figure, we can see that the places which are more than 5m away from BLE will have a more correct positioning. The places which are too close to or too far from the BLE, a correct positioning will be difficult. What's more, we can also see that when the distance is about 5m, the values shown on RSSI will have a regular curvature. Therefore, we can reduce the time to get data by using Lagrange interpolation polynomial formula. When we use the existing positioning algorithm, the standard deviation of sample signals can be applied. That is we can use different algorithms or fingerprint database to adapt to the demands of different positioning. Therefore, this research selects fuzzy fingerprint for the positioning.

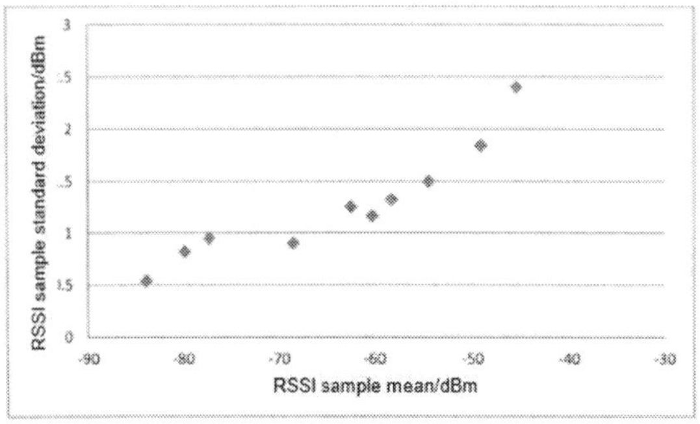

Figure. 6 Relationship between Average Value I and Standard Deviation

4 Research on BLE 4.0-based fingerprint positioning algorithm

4.1 Principle of BLE 4.0-based fingerprint positioning algorithm

Normally, fingerprint positioning is divided into 2 stages --- offline stage and online real-time positioning stage.

At offline stage, at the designated place whose area is already known, several reference points shall be set. The location of these reference points shall be determined by the environment and the equipment. Then get the signal from these reference points (AP). For example, in this paper, the featured signal that we collect are the BLE RSSI value and LQI value. Combining the signals from these reference points and the Lagrange interpolation polynomial formula, a complete fingerprint offline network for the designated place will be set up. This network is the vector space of these signals. Each signal point will be the location of offline fingerprint existed in the offline fingerprint database. At offline stage, AP points shall be set properly. So if more signals needed to be collected, our workload will be increased[3]. When Matlab simulation, if the algorithm can pass the RSSI value and LQI value, the accuracy of positioning can be as high as 90%; what's more, the algorithm will be much easier (with 1/c decreased, c is the coefficient of fuzzy clustering). Here below is the figure showing the procedures of classification:

DOI: 10.1051/itmconf/20171103007

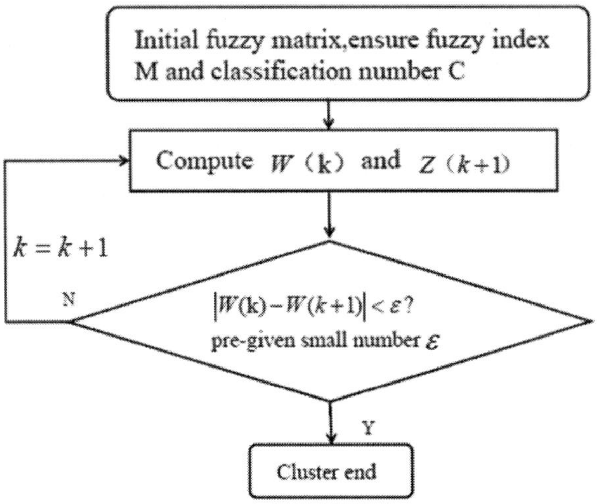

Depending on the iterative process shown above, we can classify the space of data sampled at offline stage: the data space is C, and each data space has K samples, k and z are the center of the fourth space. All the data from space C form the fingerprint database of offline space.

When the fingerprint database is set up at the offline stage, real-time matching stage shall be started. This stage is to compare and sort out the data and offline fingerprint database. For traditional fingerprint positioning, if the deterministic algorithm is used for positioning, the signals received from designated reference points will be fluctuated (this has been proved aforementioned), so deterministic algorithm cannot well handle this situation. If probabilistic synchronization algorithm, the possibility of signals received at offline stage shall be used as the fingerprint database, and Bayes rule shall be used to judge the location. Since probabilistic synchronization algorithm is based on Bayes rule, which also uses the probability of gaussian distribution, and we can easily proved that the BLE signal strength does not strictly follow gaussian distribution according to the data we got, so it will result in a great error. Therefore, in order to enhance the correctness, fuzzy theory is added into deterministic algorithm.

Online real-time positioning: this is the time when matching the fingerprint. Just like the fuzzy decision, fingerprint matching shall have a modeling via fuzzy decision theory in order to get a more correct positioning. First of all, match the categories and transfer the data at unknown points at the designated places where 4 BLE anchor nodes are measured to the upper computer. Then figure out the fuzzy membership of centers (quantity: C) which have been confirmed by fuzzy clustering. After that, choose the category j where the maximal fuzzy membership is, do a fuzzy decision. In this case, the location of the unknown point can be defined[3].

4.2 Simulation verification of positioning algorithm

At the stage to verify the fuzzy fingerprint algorithm, matlab simulation is used. First of all, the empty place in front of the gate of school of Electronic Engineering, Tianjing University of Technology was selected to collect the offline data. This place is also the one to be positioned by us. Around this empty place,4 BLE 4.0 models were located, which are to be used as the AP points. See the Figure 7 here below for the layout of the 4 models (at the 4 corners of this place). The 4 AP points forms a square with an area of 10m*10m. Then, inside the square, points whose interval is 0.5m are considered as the supervision. There are 441 points for supervision in total. Then use a BLE 4.0 model with a display to collect the eigenvalue of signals from the 4 AP points, then we can get RSSI and LQI.

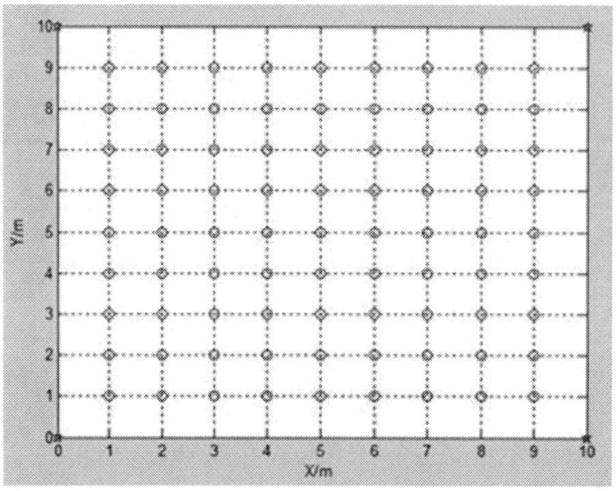

Figure 7. Map of simulation experiment

At the place where we have selected, well set AP points and reference points and then we can start to collect data. We collect 441 groups of data in total (3528 data). They are the RSSI values and LQ values in this paper. Input all the data into Excel so that we can easily read them when matlab simulation. See the figure here below for the save format of part of data.

	A	B	C	D	E	F	G	H	I	J	K
1	33	49.8	55.7	61.3	65.5	68.2	70.6	75.7	80.6	80.5	81.5
2	52.6	50	59.2	59.3	67.1	70.9	70.9	74.2	80.3	77.3	83.7
3	59.5	63.4	61.2	68.3	70	71.9	77.5	78.9	77.6	78.4	81.2
4	62.4	63.7	71.8	68	76.7	68.9	77	80.2	81	80.3	77.5
5	71.9	70.2	70.9	71.7	74.8	73.7	72.8	80.6	75	82.5	80.5
6	72.9	76.7	78.8	71.7	75.6	73.5	78.1	81.7	78.3	81	80.6
7	71.5	76.4	78.9	79.2	76.5	74.5	77.5	82.7	79.4	85	81.4
8	74.8	81	81.5	76.5	81.7	75.2	78.4	81	81.3	83.1	80.8
9	78.3	82.5	77.6	79.3	82.8	79.4	79.4	81.8	79.3	84.8	86.4
10	76.6	77.4	84.5	78.6	79.2	78.7	84.3	83.5	84.2	84.7	85.1
11	81.5	83.7	81.2	77.5	80.5	80.6	81.4	80.8	86.4	85.1	84.7
12	80.4	80.6	79.3	78.3	82.4	85.4	79.9	85	85.1	84.4	87.5
13	79.5	84.4	87	86.3	83.1	81.2	84.8	85.3	84.6	85.1	84.1
14	83	80.2	83.1	86.8	82	82.3	85.1	86.1	87.4	84.9	88
15	83.6	83.4	87.3	85.3	87.5	83.6	88.3	87.6	88.7	85.1	86.3
16	84.3	82.6	86	86.6	87.3	84.3	86.4	87.5	87.7	84.9	86
17	87.8	85.5	85.7	85.4	86.1	85.2	86.2	86.2	86.3	86.4	83.8
18	84.3	84.1	85.5	87.6	88.1	87.9	88.1	85.1	86.7	85.7	85.6
19	87.1	85	82.7	85.9	88	86.4	88	86.1	84	86.4	86.5
20	86.8	85	85.1	87.9	86.1	87.1	88.6	88.3	86.6	86.2	86.3
21	87.4	88.3	87.6	85.7	87.7	87.5	87.4	88.4	87.4	86.4	86.5

From the output result, we can see that at the AP points, the coordinate of a point can be accurately figured out by RSSI value and LQ value if fizzy fingerprint positioning is used.

On the simulated drawing, if the reference points on the actual coordinate (6.3, 2.7) are used as the simulation targets, we can get the estimated coordinate (6.1,2.9).

By formula $\Delta = \sqrt{(x'-x)^2 + (y'-y)^2}$

We can figure out that Δ is 0.3. That is the error between the estimated value and the actual value is 0.3. Therefore, from the data obtained via simulation, the fingerprint positioning algorithm based on fuzzy theory can greatly enhance the positioning accuracy. If we can make sure that the eigenvalue of the signals from mobile terminal will not fluctuate a lot, the gap between the estimated coordinate and the actual coordinate can ensure that the positioning system based on BLE4.0 is able to be widely used for our daily life. At offline stage, the Lagrange interpolation polynomial formula is added, which reduce the collection halfway. Therefore, the calculation workload is greatly lowered. In this way, only one second is needed to figure out the coordinate of the unknown point (3 seconds is required by other algorithms).

Conclusion

This paper compares and analyzes several well-known indoor positioning algorithms, by which it introduces the advantages and disadvantages of indoor positioning algorithm based on BLE 4.0. After a comprehensive analysis on the requirements of indoor positioning and signal propagation loss, BLE4.0 model is selected as the hardware to establish indoor positioning system. This paper studies several algorithms (AOA, TDOA) which are maturely used by indoor positioning system, and fingerprint positioning algorithm is finally selected as the foundation of our research. After discussing the advantages and disadvantages of fingerprint positioning algorithm, and combining the features of signal transmission, this paper perfects the fuzzy fingerprint positioning algorithm based on the fingerprint positioning algorithm. Fuzzy fingerprint positioning algorithm depends on fuzzy theory. From the results got by simulation, we can know that it greatly simply the calculation and enhance the accuracy and error tolerance of the positioning.

References

1. ZHANGHao .ZHA0Qian.chuan., JournalofComputerApplicatlons, **31**. (2011)
2. Caozhe, *Research and implementation of indoor positioning system based on Bluetooth and location fingerprint* (2014)
3. LI Juan-juan, Journal of Shanghai University(Natural Science). *Fuzzy Fingerprint Location for Bluetooth Specification Version 4.0*, **19** (2013)
4. R.W.Jeffre y Hightower, and Gaetano Borrielo, UW Cse,*SpotON: An Indoor 3D Location Sensing Technology Based on RD Signal Strengt h.*(2000)
5. R.Want, A Hopper,J Gibbons, veronica Falcao and Jonathan Gibbons, Acm, *The Active Badge Location Syste m.*(2000)
6. Specification of the Bluetooth Core System, www.bluetooth.org
7. Kegen Yu, *Ground wireless location technology*, 2012
8. Robin Heydon, *Bluetooth Low Energy The Developer's Handbook*, 2014

A Novel Frequency Communication Technology in Power Distribution Communication Network

Ying-Jun LI[1,a]

[1]*State Grid Shangrao Electric Power Supply Company, Shangrao Jiangxi, 334000, China*

Abstract. With the expansion of the power terminal access network scale, the main road corridor resources, branch line cable Laying difficulties has become an important factor restricting the construction of the network. In this paper, we focus on the frequency communication technology in power distribution communication network, and design a novel technology in communication mode, error correcting coding and data transfer frame format. We also discuss the influence of voltage phase difference on power frequency communication. Meanwhile, we present the application scenario Electricity information collection, electricity remote control and other power business in smart grid with the novel frequency communication technology.

1 Introduction

As of December 2015, the distribution automation communication network of State Grid of China Company has deployed about 22.2 million power terminal devices, and covered about 28,000 lines of 10kV lines, about 300 million courts, about 12 million concentrators and other types of terminals and covered about 311 million smart energy meters[1]. The communication network met the basic business needs.

With the expansion of the power terminal access network scale, the main road corridor resources, branch line cable Laying difficulties has become an important factor restricting the construction of the network. Power line carrier communication (hereinafter referred to as: power line) And wireless communication with no wiring, covering a wide area, flexible networking and other characteristics, is to achieve the use of low power station Cost, wide coverage of the important means of communication access, optical fiber communication is an important complement and extension[2]. But head Before the power line and wireless communication two technical standards are relatively independent, failed to form an organic whole, there is coverage And network redundancy and other issues; at the same time in some remote areas is still a lack of effective means of communication, Letter blind area, the urgent need for effective communication to meet the basic needs of business, such as small hydropower / small thermal power station information collection, remote mountain meter reading and so on.

In this paper, we focus on the frequency communication technology in power distribution communication network, and design a novel technology in communication mode, error correcting coding and data transfer frame format. We also discuss the influence of voltage phase difference on

[a] Corresponding author: lyj730@sina.com

power frequency communication. Meanwhile, we present the application scenario Electricity information collection, electricity remote control and other power business in smart grid with the novel frequency communication technology.

The rest of this paper is organized as follows: in section 2, we present related works. Section 3 shows the system model including the communication model, the transmission framework, error correction and the influence of voltage phase difference on power frequency communication. And section 4 describes applications of new power frequency communication technology. Finally, we end the paper with a conclusion.

2 Related works

Foreign mainly in North America on the frequency of communications technology research, Mak, S.T. will supply lines, transformers and Load are equivalent to impedance, as a basis for the establishment of frequency communication signal modulation and transmission model, through simulation[3]. It is shown that when the modulation is made at 30 before the zero crossing of the voltage, the main component of the distortion signal is in the vicinity of the voltage zero to about 3ms, the frequency between 200Hz to 600Hz, the amplitude of the distortion signal and the modulation transformer Capacity and modulation device parameters, when the distribution network load is heavy, the modulation signal will exist residual oscillation section[3,4].

The setting of the distortion signal and the threshold is related to the magnitude of the voltage distortion signal and the noise of the grid. Traditional upside Data demodulation is achieved by judging the difference between the positive and negative values of the current signal in the zero crossing of the voltage [5]. The receiver only set the detection window near the voltage zero crossing. Therefore, the reception of frequency communication includes synchronization detection and data solution Adjust the two links, the traditional synchronous detection method is based on the voltage zero-crossing time to determine whether the threshold Distortion signal to achieve, the downlink data demodulation is based on the power frequency cycle voltage zero-crossing time to change the situation[6].

In the frequency of communication signal transmission characteristics of the study, some simulation results show that the transmission frequency of the power frequency communication signal in China is close to that of the model simulation[7]. Meanwhile, the modulation signal is analyzed, and the modulation signal is analyzed by the field test and transmission simulation. The effect of residual oscillation on the signal detection is also proposed, and the method of reducing the residual oscillation signal by wavelet analysis is also proposed. Among them, there is a system voltage phase difference between the secondary winding wires of the Dy11 transformer, and the frequency attenuation is affected by the frequency communication signal crossing the type of transformer[7,8].

3 The novel frequency communication technology in power distribution network

In order to make the power line frequency communication technology can reliably transmit data, as a smart grid construction feasible Information transmission options, this paper to carry out the new power line frequency communication technology research, including multi-feeder, Three-phase, multi-channel signal transmission model research, multi-channel power frequency signal modulation and demodulation technology research, communication agreement research[9].

3.1 Research model

The protocol of the frequency communication needs to adapt the multi-channel parallel transmission, including three aspects: the research of communication mode, the research of data transmission frame format and the study of error correction coding as shown in Figure 1.

 DOI: 10.1051/itmconf/20171103008

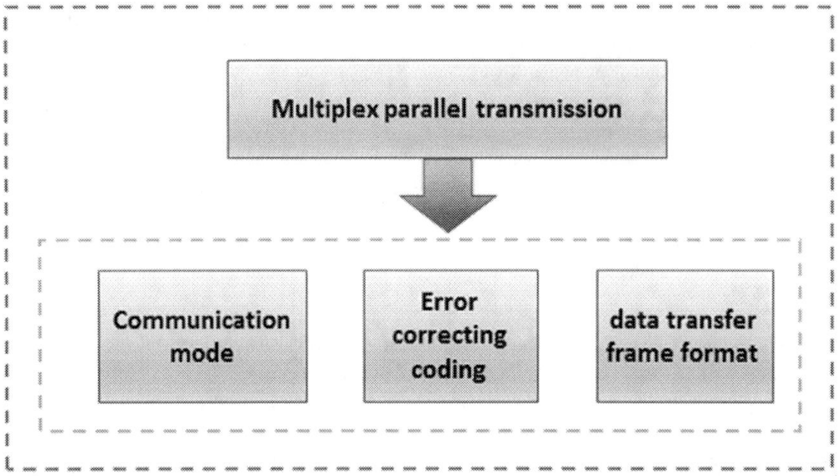

Figure 1. The research model.

3.2 Communication model

The traditional frequency communication system usually adopts master-slave communication model. In this model, the user terminal must receive sub-site broadcast and then send the ACK information. Meanwhile, each downlink data indicated by two position of voltage distortion signal of the two frequency cycle, and each uplink information indicated by the four frequency cycle current distortion signal position. Assume T denotes the frequency cycle, the downlink data occupies the M-bit, the uplink data for the N-bit, the data structure is shown as Figure 2.

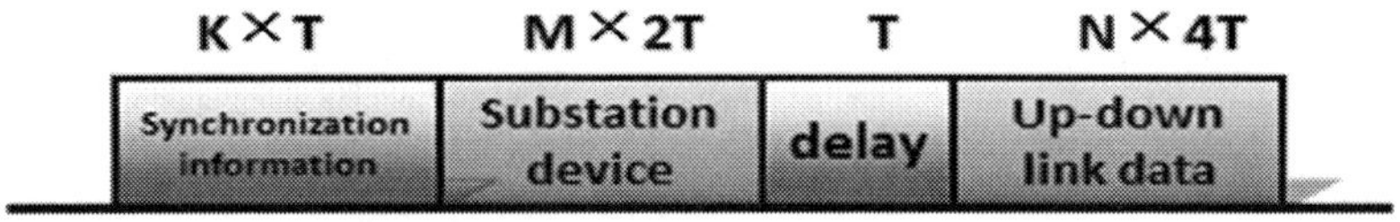

Figure 2. The data structure in the master-slave communication model.

However, there are some weaknesses in this model. When the fault occurs, the communication terminal can only wait for the sub-station inspection to be able to upload alarm information. And due to the low frequency of communication frequency, sub-station equipment inspection time is too long for the inspections of all user terminals, which is very difficult to obtain real-time fault alarm information. Therefore, we design a novel model: the active uplink communication model shown as figure 3. In this model, we proposed a positive uplink communication as a supplement, when the terminal detects an electrical fault, it can send the alarm to the sub-station information actively.

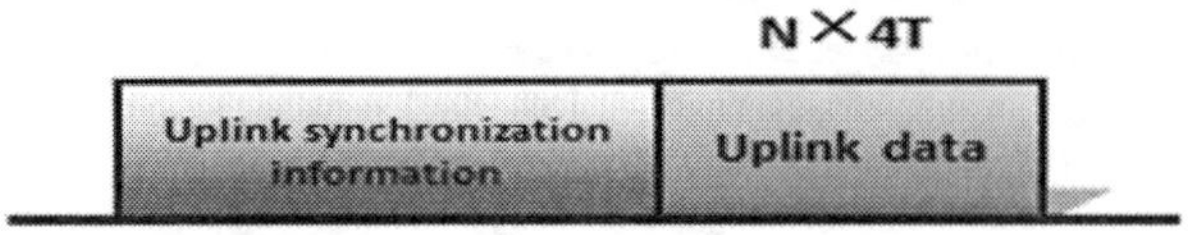

Figure 3. The data structure in the active uplink communication model.

In the active model, the uplink synchronization information provides the basis for determining the start time of the data encoding for the sub-station device, and the uplink data encoding is consistent with the master-slave mode.

3.3 Transmission frame

The uplink synchronization information is modulated by pseudo-random coding combined with Manchester coding. And the sub-station device determines the starting time of the uplink data by signal synthesis and time-frequency analysis, and determines the modulation time domain of the signal, so that the burst of the uplink alarm data. Thus, we present a new downlink frequency communication frame format as shown in Figure 4.

Synchronize	Frame Header	Address information	Function code	Control domain	Error correction	Frame tail

Figure 4. The downlink frequency communication frame format.

As shown in Figure 4, the synchronization information is the basis for the signal detection of the physical layer. The address information reflects the location of the user terminal in the distribution network. The control domain information may have control type, parameter setting and so on. The error correction coding can reduce the system SNR demand. Down the contents of the instructions more simple, you can use a fixed frame length mode.

As a result of multi-channel frequency communication parallel transmission, address information, including: 10KV branch number, distribution transformer number, phase number, low side user number. According to the same substation 10KV branch number, in the same branch on the distribution of the number of phase number 3 (A, B, C), each distribution single-phase power supply terminal number of features, address information using 2 to 3 words Section is suitable.

In the functional code, control domain, should meet the functional requirements of the case, as short as possible. In the case of error correction coding, the coding gain and the coding efficiency should be balanced.

The structure of the upstream coding is similar to the downstream coding as shown in figure 5. The difference is that the response data field is long and the situation is complicated. Therefore, the variable frame length is used. The frame length information needs to be included in the function code, and the error correction coding needs to be treated differently.

When the frequency communication technology is used in FTU, meter reading terminal information transmission, it also need those areas of communication protocol adapter, in particular, to consider the frequency of communication frequency situation.

Leading	Frame Header	Address information	Function code	Data domain	Error correction	Frame tail

Figure 5. The uplink frequency communication frame format.

3.4 Error correction

According to the research situation of the research group, the downlink frequency communication data adopts the fixed frame length, and the BCH error correction coding can get the better effect, and the uplink and the traffic frequency communication data can be used to improve the communication performance. Power frequency data is using RS error correction coding more appropriate. In this group has been carried out in the transmission test, the use of error correction coding, the uplink and downlink communication data success rate can be improved.

In the case of three-phase transmission combined with single-phase multiplexing, the interference noise will be further serious, so there are

It is necessary to strengthen research in this area.

3.5 Influence of voltage phase difference on power frequency communication

Due to the presence of the voltage phase difference between the transmission and output terminals of the power frequency communication signal, the traditional signal demodulation method based on the local voltage zero crossing will appear in the time domain deviation. In the industrial distribution network, due to the large reactive power in the line current, The phase difference is large, which will cause serious impact on the signal demodulation, the subject of cross-correlation demodulation of the next line of data as an example to analyze the impact of the situation.

In the voltage signal sense output, the noise has a large randomness, and for the sake of convenience, we assume the noise is the Gaussian white noise with zero mean. The reference signal and noise related output $N(\lambda)$, the mean and variance are as shown in Eq(1):

$$\begin{gathered} E[N(\lambda)]=0 \\ \delta_{\mathrm{n}}^{2}=E[N^{2}(\lambda)]=\frac{K^{2}}{2}N_{0}E_{s} \end{gathered} \tag{1}$$

Where N_0 indicates Noise power. Eq(1) shows the noise variance σ_n^2 is not affected by the correlation delay.

4. Applications of new power frequency communication technology

Power frequency communication technology utilizes the weak low frequency distortion signal (200Hz to 600Hz) of the voltage and current waveform in the power grid to realize the information transmission. Because the distortion signal can cross the transformer, the power frequency communication technology has the unique advantage that can cross the transformer long distance communication; In the field of electricity information collection, user side intelligent power equipment remote control, distributed generation island detection and other fields

4.1 Electricity information collection

Remote automatic meter reading technology AMR is a no need to reach the first check function can complete the automatic meter reading of the new meter reading. It is through the public telephone network, load control channel or low-voltage distribution line carrier and other communication links, the power of the data automatically transmitted to the computer power management center for processing. The meter reading scheme based on power line frequency communication technology is shown in Figure 6.

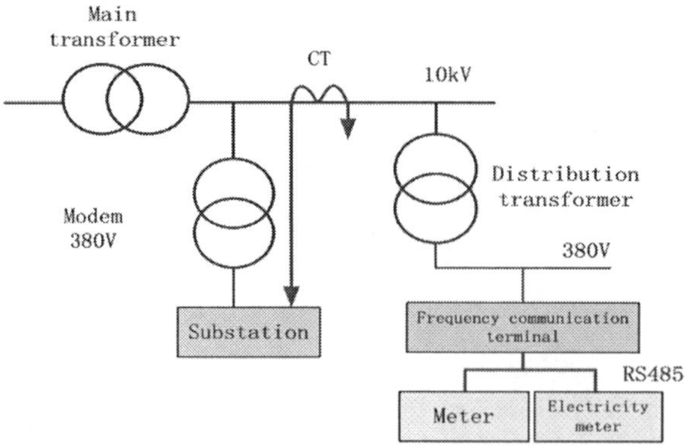

Figure 6. Remote meter reading based on power frequency communication.

DOI: 10.1051/itmconf/20171103008

After the electricity information is sent through the frequency communication technology to the substation, the internal enterprise networks forward these data to the management through the power system.

When using multi-channel frequency communication signal transmission technology, the single-phase user's downlink rate of 25b / s, the uplink rate up to 75b / s, lower than the current GPRS with PLC way, but the power line frequency communication technology has the ability to cross Transformer, no need to install the coupling device in the 10KV line characteristics, you can in the distribution of small number of users and scattered areas, such as rural areas or grassland on the long-range meter reading.

4.2 User side intelligent power equipment remote control

Intelligent electricity is an important part of building a strong smart grid, which means the use of advanced measurement, efficient control, high-speed communications, fast energy storage and other technologies to achieve rapid market response, fair and accurate measurement, real-time data collection, Efficient and convenient to build a grid and customer energy flow, information flow, real-time interactive business flow for the new relationship.

In the smart electricity, in particular, emphasizing the exchange of information between smart meters and power grid, in order to achieve intelligent power control, based on power line frequency communication technology user side intelligent power remote control as shown in Figure 7.

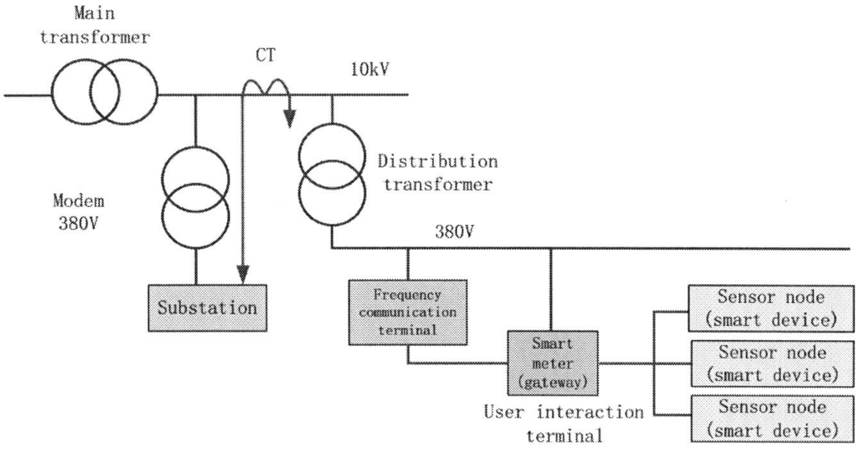

Figure7. Remote control of intelligent power consumption for power line based on power line communication

In the structure of Figure 7, according to the characteristics of frequency communication, most of the processing in the local, the key data upload, for the location of the three-phase users scattered, the downlink rate of 75b / s, the maximum uplink rate of up 225b / s, although the rate is low, the power line frequency communication technology does not need to install the coupling equipment in the 10KV line, and there is no communication operation cost, in the local processing to reduce the amount of transmission information, the way has a good price.

Conclusion

Power Line Carrier (PLC) communication and wireless communication are important communication means in the distribution communication network. The power line is susceptible to the influence of line load and interference. In this paper, we focus on the frequency communication technology in power distribution communication network, and design a novel technology in communication mode,

DOI: 10.1051/itmconf/20171103008

error correcting coding and data transfer frame format. We also discuss the influence of voltage phase difference on power frequency communication. Power line frequency communication is in the zero to add a weak distortion to achieve the signal modulation. The research of the new power line frequency communication technology includes multi-feeder, three-phase, multi-channel signal transmission model research, multi-channel frequency signal modulation and demodulation technology research, communication protocol research, etc. Meanwhile, we present the application scenario Electricity information collection, electricity remote control and other power business in smart grid with the novel frequency communication technology.

References

1. Yu Q, Huang H, Yu Y, et al. Research on Heterogeneous Communication Network for Power Distribution Automation, International Conference on Material, Mechanical and Manufacturing Engineering. 2015.
2. Razani M. Power Line Carrier Communication. Journal of Chongqing Institute of Technology, 2011.
3. Varadarajan B, Kim I, Dabak A, et al. Empirical measurements of the low-frequency power-line communications channel in rural North America, IEEE International Symposium on Power Line Communications and ITS Applications. IEEE, 2011:463-467.
4. Chervenkov A, Chervenkova T. Investigation of the Influence of the Electromagnetic Field in the Vicinity of High Voltage Overhead Line[C]// Materials Science Forum. 2016:190-195.
5. Wu F, Li X, Duan J. Improved Elimination Scheme of Current Zero-Crossing Distortion in Unipolar Hysteresis Current Controlled Grid-Connected Inverter. Industrial Informatics IEEE Transactions on, 2015, 11(5):1111-1118.
6. López-Colino F, Sanchez A, Castro A D, et al. Handling input voltage frequency variations in power factor correctors with pre-calculated duty cycles. Electrical Engineering, 2016:1-12.
7. Facina M S P, Ribeiro M V. The influence of transmission power and frequency bandwidth on in-home cooperative power line communication, International Symposium on Power Line Communications and ITS Applications. IEEE, 2015:239-244.
8. Ebenezer M, Ramachandralal R M. Study and Analysis of the Effect of Harmonics on the Hot Spot Temperature of a Distribution Transformer Using Finite-Volume Method. Electric Power Components & Systems, 2015, 43(20):1-11.
9. Yong L I, Zuo H U. Fault analysis of Dy11 connection mode of distribution transformers parallel. Power System Protection & Control, 2009.
10. Jian-Qi L I, Huang B Y, Wang Z H. Application of power frequency communication technology in power distribution network. Telecommunications for Electric Power System, 2009.
11. Mastellone S, Lee D, Spong M W. Master-slave synchronization with switching communication through passive model-based control design, American Control Conference. IEEE Xplore, 2006:6 pp.
12. Tujkovic D. Mobile subscriber information transmission over multiple uplink frames. 2016.

DOI: 10.1051/itmconf/20171103009

A RFID-based JIT Application for Least Waiting Time for Dynamic Smart Diet Customers

Long-Fei CHEN[a] and Shu-Jun CHEN

[1]*Department of Management Engineering, Business College, NanFang College of Sun Yat-Sen University, GuangZhou, China, 510970*

Abstract. Waiting in queue is part of everyone's life. A day may include several different waiting in queue. Waiting in line is always a bit of phenomena for a prosperous restaurant at dinner time. How to manage the queues and keep their feet into customers is the operating challenge facing everyone manager. In addition, rising energy costs and growing demand for protection of the environment call for a shorter waiting queue. Thus, we devise a dynamic smart diet App manager to reduce customer waiting time through radio frequency identification (RFID) and just in time (JIT) principle to reduce inventory of restaurant food materials, thereby increasing customer satisfaction and loyalty, and improving revenue and social responsibility.

1 Introduction

How to manage the waiting queues and keep customers feet is the operating challenge facing everyone manager. A devised dynamic smart diet app manager can reduce customer waiting time and inventory of restaurant food materials, thereby increasing customer satisfaction and loyalty, and improving revenue and social responsibility[1].

Dynamic smart diet serves for customers who have ever come to the restaurant and have its membership cards. When customers arrived at the parking lots of the restaurant, their membership cards will be recognized by the RFID and then the recipe of the restaurant will be sent to the customer's cellphone automatically by the system[3,4]. What's more, some dishes will also be recommended by the system according to the customer's consumed menu. All of these can spend less time than sitting in the chair or waiting in queue to order.

Besides the use of RFID, JIT production is also adopted in the dynamic smart diet whose aim is to achieve zero-inventory or reduce inventory. The reason why JIT production, which comes from logistics management, can be introduced to catering services is that it's too difficult to predict each day's ingredients. All the ingredients are purchased in the morning, but not all of them in the menu are included. If what customer-needs are in shortage, the restaurant will recommend other dishes instead of restocking.

[a] Corresponding author: y2kmorg@yahoo.com

Figure 1. Smart diet recipe (Source : Microsoft Word)

Figure 2. Smart diet recipe can be forwarded at parking yard after sensing RFID card (Source : Microsoft Word)

2 Literature review

As waiting lines have been associated with reduced service evaluations, negative perception of service quality, and reduced satisfaction, having to wait makes a customer's first experience of a service a negative one[1]. So, effectively manage queues is important.

In coming chaotic future of wearable electronics, devices can promise to connect real to digital lives seamlessly. These gadgets are rapidly multiplying, and within five years there could be half a billion devices strapped onto, or even embedded in, human bodies [2]. Internet of things (IOT) are constantly developing; the impact on traffic, medical, military has greatly increased. In this paper, we want to introduce IOT into the restaurant, which through RFID and app. RFID is a technology that has attracted considerable attention in the realm of information systems during recent years[3]. Thus, RFID technology is more widely accepted. Digitization, networking and information are the era characteristics of the 21st century. With the rapid increasing number of mobile users, e-commerce has been in worldwide popularity and development. It provides the world with a good environment of trades and greatly facilitates the communication, saves the costs of management as well as the enterprise costs[4]. With the popularity of mobile phones, various apps also came into being, which brings opportunities for our vision of smart recipes.

There is an excessive consumption which may lead to 7 trends of crises, including destruction of the atmosphere, energy crisis, social decline and conflicts and so on [5,8]. Now climate change is really great, global warming is getting worse. As part of the planet citizenship is the responsibility of hours from his side to start. If restaurant can control their food storage by JIT principle, it can reduce waste of perish food due to over duration time. In fact, it can save raw materials down from dining with less waste and protect our environment.

Security is always a problem for wireless networks. Although encryption is becoming more pervasive and advanced, it is not always fully used in low-cost wearable devices. California-based information-management company Symantec revealed that the location of many health monitors can be easily tracked. And some of their passwords are vulnerable to hacking in clear text in wireless communication. Either because of unnecessarily broad permissions or because of malware, the smartphone or hub device that links it to the Internet could also be a weak point, even if a health monitor is encrypted[2].

As the coming advance of new wireless sensor networks, restaurants can adopt new technology like references to enhance their app recipe with ZigBee-based RFID system in a longer distance before their customers reach their parking yard [6,7]. If the smart diet recipe can integrated with werable devices, it may suggest suitable recepie to fit customers' current physical health after comparing the status of pressure, heartbeat rate and sleep hours[9].

3 Research method

3.1 Methodology

Firstly, some terminologies related to our method will be introduced.

JIT production is the production pattern of producing something in time as well as on time based on the demand. Its aim is to accelerate the circulation of semi-manufactured products, which can minimize the overstocked products and then enhance the production efficiency of enterprises.

RFID (Radio Frequency Identification) technology is a communication technology, which can identify specific targets and then record some related data without the help of the identification of the mechanical and optical contacts between the system and specific targets.

MRP (Material Requirement Planning) is a system designed to be used in information processing of inventory management in manufacturing. It solves the problem of the inventory management towards manufacturing, especially about how to get the needed products on time.

Green Logistics (Environmental logistics) is to stop the environment from being destroyed during the process of logistic, which can help to achieve the goal of purifying the logistic environment and make the best of logistics resources. It includes the whole greening process of logistics operation and management. Logistics operation consists of green transportation, green packaging, and green circulating processing and so on. As for the logistics management, it gives priority to the environmental protection and resource saving to improve logistics system. It is necessary to consider the positive aspects of green logistics. The ultimate goal is the sustainable development of green logistics, whose criterion is the unification of economic interests, social interests and environmental interests.

3.2 Design features

The dynamic smart diet is considered to make the use of JIT production, RFID, materials management and some other knowledge from the major of logistics management. The idea may have the following three advantages :

Saving customers' time is the most basic advantage of all. What dynamic smart diet wants to achieve is saving customer's waiting time, which can help them to have enough time to enjoy their food, take a break after their busy work, listen to some music, think about life and so on, which help a lot in their physical and spiritual health. For restaurants, more customers will be attracted because of the less waiting time and their satisfaction and loyalty towards restaurants will be enhanced.

Secondly, it can increase profits of restaurants. To apply RFID to hotels or restaurants can combine logistics management with hotel management: customers will receive membership cards with electronic tags after their first consumption, and when they come to the restaurant again, their cards will be recognized by the reader when they arrived at the parking lots of the restaurant. Although it costs much on RFID, the advanced satisfaction and loyalty of customers will make big profits. With RFID technology, customers' waiting time are less than before and more customers can be received in given time.

Finally, it follows the principle of green logistics. Green Logistics aims to achieve environmental protection and resource conservation. To apply dynamic smart diet to restaurants, restaurants can check the adequacy of the ingredients they need according to the customers' orders, if not; they'll give a feedback to the customer and recommend other dishes for them through the system. There are two advantages from doing these: one is cost saving from restocking; the other is the reduction of the restaurant's inventory. The goal of JIT is just the reduction of inventory, which can reduce waste and ensure the quality of ingredients, especially fruit and vegetables.

3.3 Questionnaire

Questionnaire is the most widely used method for data collection, which is feasible and effective. It is economical and timesaving. In order to testify the hypothesis effectively, the study will base on the general principles and methods of empirical research, using questionnaires to testify the theoretical construction [8]. This paper is the use of questionnaires, they were investigating RFID and smart approach to customer recipes, restaurant managers.

There is a questionnaire is for customers, researching for their frequency and reasons of dining out and their attitudes towards membership cards with RFID.

3.4 Hypotheses and t-test

Observation will also be adopted during the research because of the subjectivity and limitations of questionnaires. It will be used to verify hypotheses with t-test.

4 Results

The questionnaire is used for data collection in the the study, but because of the limited time and capability, only 152 of them have responses. Table 1 shows the listed primary results.

4.1 Sample description

Table 1. Personal Information of Sample 1

Variable	Sort	Frequency	Percent (%)	Cumulative Percent (%)
Gender	Male	67	44.08	44.08
	Female	85	55.92	100
Age	Under 20	2	1.32	1.32
	20-29	70	46.05	47.37
	30-39	50	32.89	80.26
	40-49	27	17.76	98.02
	Above 50	3	1.97	100
Occupation	Student	68	44.74	44.74
	Office worker	50	32.89	77.63
	Private business employer	18	11.84	89.47
	Free profession	11	7.24	96.71
	Others	5	3.29	100

There are 67 males (44.08% of all) and 85 females (55.92% of all) in the sample whose age ranges mainly from 20 to 29 years old while participants in 30-39 years old are in the second place. And most of them are students or office workers.

As for the education background, 30% of the participants have college degree and 40% of all have undergraduate degree. 85% of the participants have used smart-phones for more than 3 years. 75% of the participants dine out for more than fifth a month. Among those who dine out, 32.9% of them are office workers without time to cook while 50% of them dine out for parties of social activities. 86.27% of participants said that there are many customers in the restaurants where there have their meals. And 88.4% of all the participants have ever been in the trouble that they still had to wait for long time even though they had ordered. From the above information, it can be easily concluded that most of the participants are highly educated, and maybe it's easier for them to be open to trying new things. And the popularity of smart-phones makes the idea of using RFID possible. Faced with the problem of long waiting time in the restaurants, customers may be highly desired to use RFID and JIT technology to reduce their waiting time.

In the survey, 92.16% of the people are willing to use the following membership cards with RFID identification; 82.35% of people are willing to order a meal by app remotely, and have it after parking their car and reach the restaurant immediately; there are 74.51% of people are willing to pay for online ordering remotely.

Table 1. Key surveyed items with formatted responses

	App functions in survey	Response	Percentage (%)
1	willing to own membership cards with RFID	140	92.16
2	willing to order a meal by app	125	82.35
3	willing to pay for online ordering	113	74.51

4.2 Hypotheses and t-test

Let U_1-the duration time of customers waiting time for the queue who do not use RFID, and
U_2- the duration time of customers waiting time for the queue who use RFID
Hypothesis H_0: $U_1 = U_2$
Hypothesis H_1: $U_1 > U_2$

T-test formula of statistics is used to analyze these two data sets in the EXCEL, and the result is that P value is very close to zero, which means that after the use of RFID, the time spent on waiting for the queue is remarkably reduced. It means $U_1 > U_2$. Thus H_0 is rejected, and H_1 is accepted.

4.3 Limitations

Because of the limited time and incapability, available questionnaires that were returned are not enough to exactly represent all customers' opinions.

Besides, the recorded average duration time 100 sets of customers spending on waiting for the queue is around 11minutes with the normal distribution, and it has a standard deviation of 3.8. From the data of simulated experiment, after the use of RFID, time can be reduced from 11 minutes to5.5 minutes with a normal distribution and a standard deviation of 1.7. And using t-test to analyze these two data sets in the EXCEL, and the result shows that P value is very close to zero, which means that after the use of RFID, the time spent on waiting for the queue is remarkably reduced. If there exists membership cards with RFID for coming into use, the results will be more persuasive.

The cost of RFID is a little too high for restaurants to apply it to their service. If the cost can be analyzed to work out the time when they can recover the cost or make profits, restaurants will be more eager to use it.

5 Conclusions

With the popularity of smart phones, various apps have emerged, but RFID technology has become increasingly mature, dynamic and intelligent recipe we want to conceive can be combined with RFID, JIT and MRP, to have three major advantages: the first reducing customer waiting time, and secondly, increase revenue, and more importantly, in favor of green logistics. We designed a questionnaire to the customer and the result shows most customers are willing to use this dynamic management of intelligent recipe. The simulation experiments have come to use RFID can significantly decrease the waiting time for dynamic smart diet customers with RFID. In real practice, security for customers' data needs to pay attention for special care.

References

1. Alinda Kokkinoua, David A. Cranageb, Using self-service technology to reduce customer waiting times, International Journal of Hospitality Management 33, 435–445. (2013)
2. KAT AUSTEN, the Trouble with Wearables, September, VOL 525, Nature, 23-24. (2015)
3. Henning Baars, Daniel Gille and Jens Stru¨ker, Evaluation of RFID applications for logistics: a framework for identifying, forecasting and assessing benefits, European Journal of Information Systems, 18, 578–591. (2009)
4. Peng Gegang, Song Zhixing, Feng Zhanbo, Xiang Lisheng, Shen Jing, Li Renfa, Mobile client application for mobile electronic commerce research, The 2015 International Conference on Electronic Business, HongKong, December 6-10, (2015).
5. LongFei Chen, Book Review: The Little Green Handbook: Seven Trends Shaping the Future of Our Planet, Ron Nielsen, St. Martin's Press, New York, USA, ISBN 0-312-42581-3, Ecological Economics, 89, 202-203. (2013)
6. Cho, H., Kim, J., Baek, Y. Large-scale active RFID system utilizing ZigBee networks, IEEE Transactions on Consumer Electronics, 57 (2), 379-385. (2011)
7. Nellore, K.; Hancke, G.P., A Survey on Urban Traffic Management System Using Wireless Sensor Networks, *Sensors*, *16*, 157. (2016)
8. Si-Ting Lee, Long-Fei Chen, Hui-Guo Zhu, A New Innovative IOT Watch Reduces Excessive Consumption and Its Implications to Green Logistics, The 2015 International Conference on Electronic Business, HongKong, December 6-10, (2015).
9. Kenry, Yeo, J. C., & Lim, C. T. Emerging flexible and wearable physical sensing platforms for healthcare and biomedical applications, Microsystems & Nanoengineering, *2*, 16043, (2016).

Research on Intelligent Agriculture Greenhouses Based on Internet of Things Technology

Ying SHANG[a] and An-Ying FU

Shaanxi Institute of International Trade & Commerce, Xi'an 712046, China

Abstract. Internet of things is a hot topic in the field of research, get a lot of attention, On behalf of the future development trend of the network, Internet of Things has a wide range of applications, because of the efficient and reliable information transmission in modern agriculture. In the greenhouse, the conditions of the Greenhouse determine the quality of crops, high yield and many other aspects. Research on Intelligent Agriculture Greenhouses based on Internet of Things, mainly Research on how to control the conditions of the greenhouses, So that the indoor conditions suitable for crop growth. In the pater, we study of Zigbee technology, Designed the solar power supply module, greenhouse hardware and software part, And the system was tested by experiment, The analysis of the experimental data shows that the system can provide good conditions for the growth of crops to achieve the high yield and high quality of crops.

Introduction

In modern agricultural production, the control of the surroundings of crops is an important part of improving crop quality. Greenhouse environment and biological growth are closely related, Environmental monitoring is assurance, achieve the greenhouse automation, scientific, In system study, we can analyze the testing data, Combined with crop growth regular pattern, Control environmental conditions, So that achieve the purposes of crops high quality, high yield and efficient cultivation. Intelligent Agriculture Greenhouses Based on Internet of Things Technology, Combined with the current emerging Internet of Things technology, which can achieve the goals, efficient and reasonable use of various agricultural resources and improve the environment of this sustainable development. Can maximize the agricultural real productivity, Is an effective way to achieve high quality, high yield, low consumption and environmental protection of sustainable development of agriculture[1].

1 System composition

The system includes data acquisition sensor terminal, heating equipment, ventilation equipment, control terminal, Zigbee wireless communication network terminal, monitoring center and other components, System block diagram shown in Figure 1.

[a] Corresponding author: 81593866@qq.com

DOI: 10.1051/itmconf/20171103010

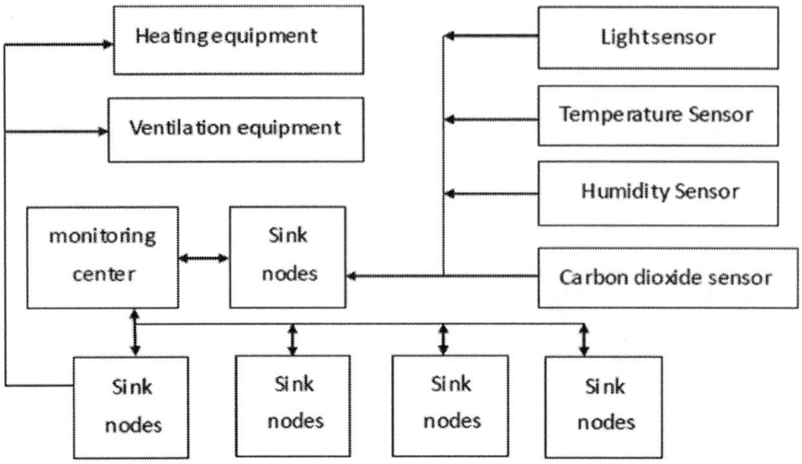

Figure 1. System block diagram

2 System hardware design

2.1 Zigbee technology

In the system, the acquisition node and the sink node processor adopt the Zigbee technology chip cc2530. The CC2530 is a true system-on-chip solution for IEEE 802.15.4, Zigbee and RF4CE applications. It enables robust network nodes to be built with very low total bill-of-material costs. The C2530 combines the excellent performance of a leading RF transceiver with an industry-standard enhanced 8051 MCU, in-system programmable flash memory, 8-KB RAM, and many other powerful features. The CC2530 comes in four different flash versions: C2530F32/64/128/256, with 32/64/128/256 KB of flash memory, respectively. The CC2530 has various operating modes, making it highly suited for systems where ultralow power consumption is required. Short transition times between operating modes further ensure low energy consumption[2].

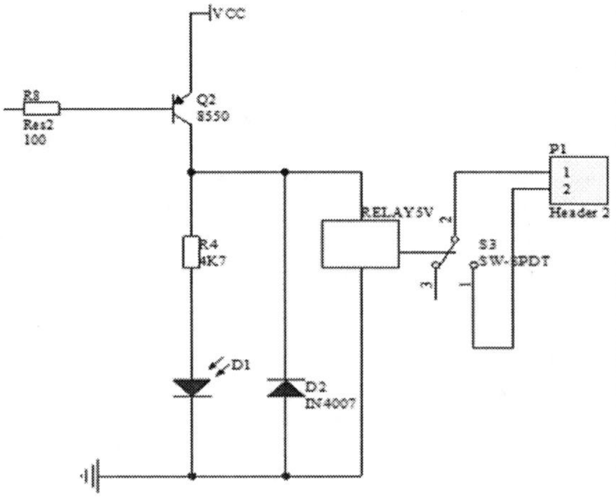

Figure 2. CC2530 Application Circuit

DOI: 10.1051/itmconf/20171103010

2.2 System power supply

Based on the Internet of Things intelligent agricultural greenhouses use dual supply that power supply system solar and electric power. Green is an advantage of the design; Greenhouses are usually located in relatively open fields, there is no shelter around, Very suitable for solar power supply. The designing of the solar power supply system use ST-150P solar panels, About two square feet, The system can automatically rotate and capture sunlight according to the sun's light intensity, To maximize the use of sunlight, The overall block diagram of the power supply system is shown in Figure 3.

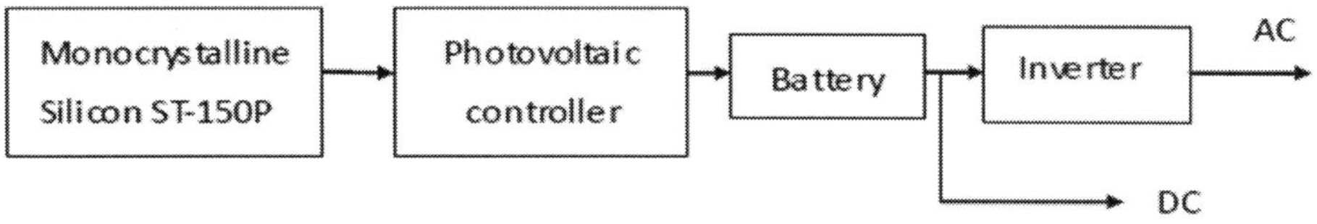

Figure 3. Solar power supply system block diagram

There are four photosensitive resistors around the center of the installation in the electromagnetic plate, Divided into two groups, The photoresistor is used to collect light intensity, And then the light intensity signal into a voltage signal for comparison, According to the size of the voltage signal, The motor determines the direction of rotation and the angle of rotation[3].

2.3 Temperature and humidity control

The temperature and humidity control section mainly monitors the temperature and humidity. First set the normal temperature threshold of the temperature and humidity, When the current temperature or humidity is not in the normal threshold range, The sink node will send the data to the monitoring center, According to the instruction, the monitoring center makes the corresponding processing. When the temperature is higher than the normal threshold, Start fan exhausting function; When the temperature is below the normal threshold, Start heating equipment for heating, A constant temperature is maintained after reaching the normal threshold. When the humidity is higher than the normal threshold, Start the exhaust fan; when the humidity is below the normal threshold, Start the watering equipment to water[4]. The circuit is shown in Figure 4.

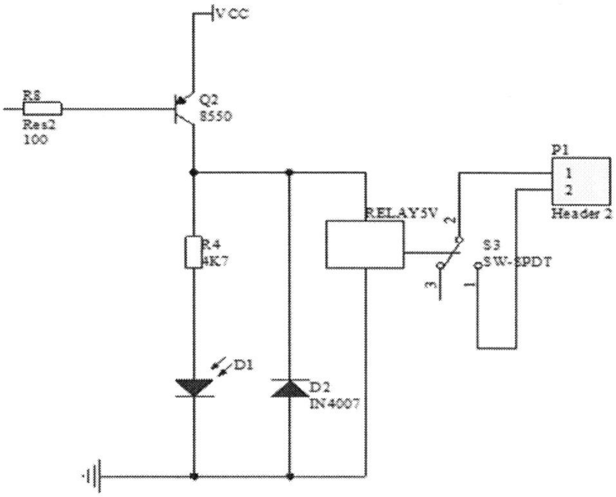

Figure 4. Temperature and humidity control circuit

2.4 Switch ventilation window

In the system, In addition to has a temperature and humidity control circuit there are also contains a photosensitive sensor, In real time, the light sensor can detect the intensity of light in the greenhouse, So that the signal through the AD conversion and the signal will be collected to the CPU,CPU to do processing, Thereby controlling the actuator to open and close the ventilation window[5-7]. The circuit is shown in Figure 5.

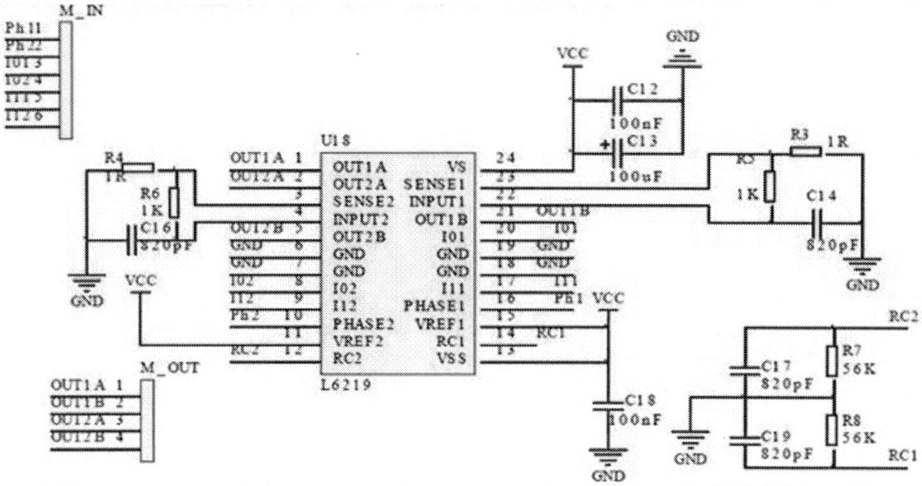

Figure 5. Switch ventilation window circuit

3 System software design

In the greenhouse the temperature and humidity sensors to collect temperature and humidity data at various points, The data is recorded at regular intervals. And converted into analog data, the date transfer to the CUP for processing, The supervisory control is controlled according to the received data status, And then record and transfer[8-9].

When the temperature and humidity is not in the normal region，System startup related processing scheme. Power on and to initialize each variable, set the parameters by pressing the key, Then compares the data that the temperature and humidity sensor collected with the value set by the key, In order to achieve the corresponding action[10-11]. The acquisition data and control flow chart are shown in Figure 5 and Figure 6.

 DOI: 10.1051/itmconf/20171103010

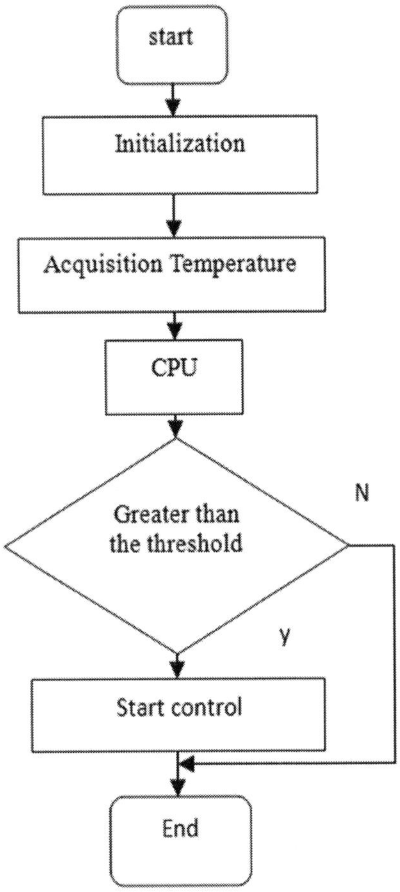

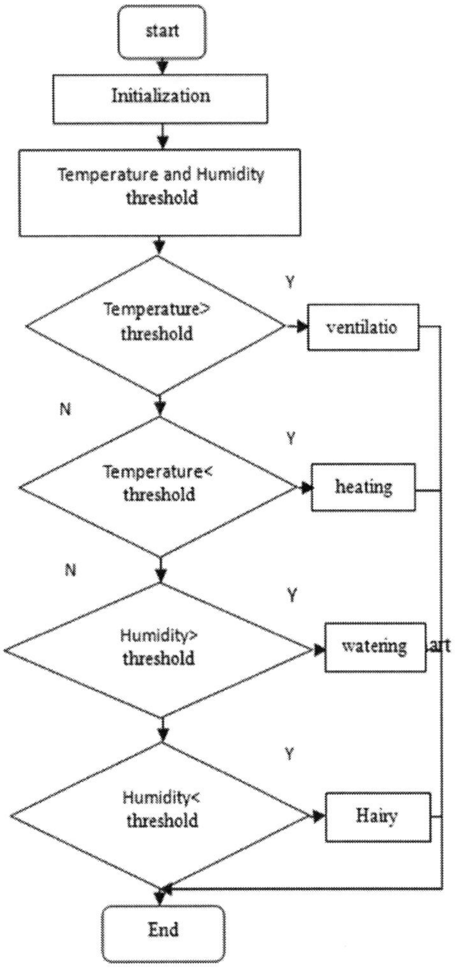

Figure 5. A flow chart for collecting data

Figure 6. Temperature and humidity control flow chart

4 Test results and analysis

In the system testing phase, Selected a farmhouse measure, the farmhouse in Yulin, At the same time, In the measurement process use a special measurement instrument measurement, Each set of measurement data is spaced 10 minutes, The measurement results are shown in Table 1 and Table 2.

Table 1. The testing results of the Study system

number	Air temperature	Air humidity %	Soil temperature	Soil moisture %	CO2 concentration (PPM)
1	21.3℃	29.1	25.5	3000.1	441
2	21.6℃	29.1	25.6	3000.2	444
3	21.6℃	29.3	25.7	3000.2	449
4	21.7℃	30.0	25.8	2999.2	455
5	21.9℃	30.1	26.9	2999.1	459
6	21.9℃	30.1	27.1	3000.2	467
7	22.1℃	29.1	29.5	3001.2	471
8	22.2℃	29.2	27.8	3005.1	473
9	23.1℃	30.1	28.2	3010.1	482
10	23.5℃	30.0	28.9	3011.2	491

Table 2. The testing results of the Dedicated testing tools

number	Air temperature	Air humidity %	Soil temperature	Soil moisture %	CO2 concentration (PPM)
1	20.3℃	28.1	25.2	2999.1	439
2	20.5℃	28.1	25.2	2995.2	442
3	20.6℃	28.2	25.3	2991.2	448
4	20.5℃	29.0	25.5	2988.2	452
5	20.6℃	29.0	26.1	2995.1	458
6	20.7℃	29.0	26.5	2999.2	465
7	21.3℃	28.0	26.9	3000.2	469
8	21.8℃	29.0	27.1	3004.1	472
9	22.1℃	29.2	27.9	3009.1	480
10	22.5℃	29.3	28.2	3010.2	489

Through the above data analysis, the data results that using a dedicated test tool to measure are higher than the testing value that test in the research system. The comprehensive analysis shows that the system under study has a certain delay in the actual measurement, The measured data is measured after the actual time. But the overall measurement results are close to the actual value, the error is very small.

Conclusions

In this paper, intelligent agriculture greenhouses were studied, The Zigbee technology can be used in the system design, The system can collect the temperature and humidity data, CO2 concentration, etc. Intelligent agriculture greenhouses have heating function, Can be heat to the greenhouse, as same as the human warm, So that the temperature inside the greenhouse is more suitable for crop growth, to achieve high yield, high quality to the purpose. Furthermore, the dual power supply used in the system, Power and solar dual power supply. Through analysis the testing data, The system test error is very small, Can be applied in practice. In the follow-up study, Will continue to study the system, Further reducing the measurement error.

Acknowledgment

This work is supported by the Scientific Research Project of Education Department of Shaanxi Province Government (2016JK2038).

References

1. Ya-Di LI, MIAO Teng, ZHU Chao, JI Jianwei. J. Agric Sci Tech China18,94(2016)
2. Lin-Li Guo. D. HLJU.(2015)
3. Shi-Hong LI. J. E World,66(2016)
4. Zhi-Bo Lin. J. Autom Inf Eng, 36,19(2015)
5. Hong-Ye Yang.J. JS Agricultural Sciences,44,401(2016)
6. Xiao-Tao Zhang. J. New Technology & New Process,10,20(2016)
7. Jie-Rong Zhao.J. Journal of Dalian Polytechnic University,35,373(2016)
8. Li-Ying Han.J. Journal of Chinese Agricultural Mechanization,37,65(2016)
9. Hua Ren.J. Intelligent Processing and Application,6,66,(2014)
10. Kai-Sheng Zhang.J. Journal of xi'an university of science and technology,35,805(2015)
11. Xin-Hao Zhu. Comput Eng Appl,11,244,(2015)

Design and Research of Intelligent Remote Control Fan Based on Single Chip Microcomputer and Bluetooth Technology

Xue-Xia Zhang[1,a], You-Yun DANG[2] and An-Ying FU[1]

[1]*Shaanxi Institute of International Trade & Commerce, Xi'an, Shaanxi, China*
[2]*XiAn Polytechnic University, Xi'an, Shaanxi, China*

Abstract. This paper is designed for intelligent remote control fans. The design of the microcontroller as the core, the sensor, Bluetooth and Andrews system applied to the design of intelligent remote control fan. According to the temperature sensor to achieve the indoor temperature collection, to achieve and set the temperature comparison, thus affecting the fan speed. At the same time, the system according to the infrared sensor components to detect external factors, in order to achieve the running or stopping of the fan, that is, to achieve intelligent control of the fan. In addition, the system achieve the Bluetooth and mobile phone Andrews system of effective combination, and through the software program to complete the fan remote operation and wind speed control.

Introduction

With the rapid development of society, the fan as a common household appliances, also often applied to the elevator system. Most of the common fans use manual operation to control speed or control switch, only according to the actual operation of the fan to complete the control, the indoor temperature cannot be detected, appear frequently where is empty, the fan is still open, this not only wastes resources, but also reduces the fan's life. If the fan can be based on the presence or absence of timely operation or stop, and can detect the Elevator interior temperature, according to set temperature to adjust the fan speed, will make the fan more humane. These assumptions are applied to the control system of the fan, thus realizing the intelligent fan[1-3].

1 Overall design

In view of the shortcomings of the current control system of the fan, the design idea of the intelligent fan is proposed to achieve the fan speed control of the refinement and humanization. When the room temperature reaches or exceeds artificially set temperature and detects someone, then the fan is automatically opened, And change the size of the wind speed according to the change of the temperature; when the temperature is lower than the artificial temperature or when nobody exists, the fan will automatically stop.

[a] Corresponding author:187383930@qq.com

Through the analysis of the fan control system, the overall design method of intelligent fan is put forward. This design mainly implements the following functions:

(1) Wind speed control function: According to the set temperature to achieve the motor speed control, adjust the wind speed of the fan, to achieve better cooling effect.

(2) Remote control function: through the mobile phone Andrews client and Bluetooth technology for remote control of the fan speed, operation, stop and other operational status.

(3) Real-time temperature display function: real-time monitoring of the current ambient temperature through the sensor, and through the display terminal shows the current indoor temperature and the set temperature, according to reference the indoor temperature, user-friendly set the temperature at which the fan is on[4-7].

System overall design block diagram shown in Figure 1, the hardware consist of the STC15F2K61S2 microcontroller, infrared temperature sensor and Bluetooth devices. Through the infrared temperature sensor to detect the existence of people, and the STC15F2K61S2 microcontroller get the person's information, then control fan to start or stop, while the fan starts to detect the current room temperature and display on the monitor. Through the Bluetooth module connected Andrews client to the fan, transmit the corresponding information to control the fan, to achieve remote control of the fan.

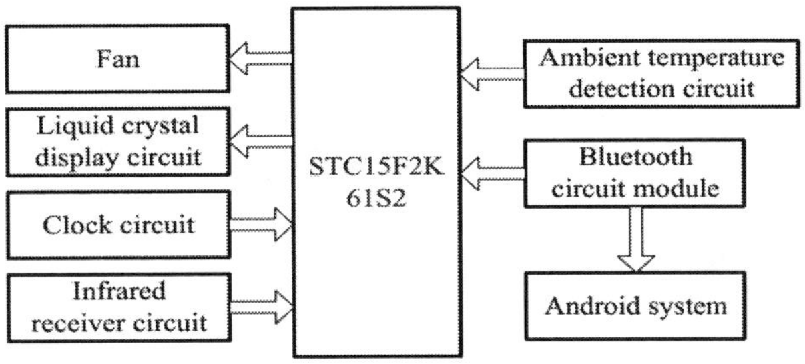

Figure 1. System design block diagram

2 Hardware circuit design

2.1 SCM control module

Intelligent remote control fan use STC15F2K61S2 microcontroller as the core controller to control and coordinate the normal operation of the entire system. DS1302 clock real-time module to achieve real-time display temperature and timing function, STC15F2K61S2 microcontroller receiving the accurate time information through the DS1302 to control timing program, and complete the remote control intelligent fan timing system.

The pins of X2 and X1 of the DS1302 external crystal oscillator circuit to generate the reference clock signal, through the frequency to get accurate second signal, to achieve the timing function, thereby improving the stability and efficiency.

2.2 Temperature detection feedback and display module

Select the DS18B20 temperature sensor to achieve real-time temperature detection. By shielding or detecting the reflected beam, the photoelectric sensor cycle scan to collect human infrared information, when detect the information of the human and reach the set temperature, the external information is transmitted to the STC15F2K61S2 single chip microcomputer, and which control to open the fan instructions. When a person's presence is detected and the state lasts for a long period of time, the fan automatically turns off to conserve energy.

Through an input line DQ achieve to information transfer between DS18B20 and the microcomputer, a 10K ohm resistor in series, then connect the input to the P13 port of the microcontroller and transmit the temperature information. The OUT pin of the photoelectric switch connect to P32 pin of microprocessor. The reset pin RST of LCD5110 connect to the P14 port, DIN pin as the data input connect to P17 port [8-13].

2.3 Motor control module

Controlling the motor is an important aspect of the overall control system. which achieves the control of the fan speed. STC15F2K61S2 chip contains PWM module, obtain temperature information from the DS18B20, according to the different set temperature, output different PWM to L298N, the driver module L298N will have a different PWM and speed corresponding to it, then change the terminal voltage, in other words, the fan drive voltage changes, which will be transmitted to the fan can control the fan speed, obtain to the set temperature, the fan speed is almost close to the infinitely variable speed.

OUT1 and OUT2 of L298N, as the fan data input and output, IN + and IN- are connected to the power and ground, and the EN pin connect to the microcontroller P13 port, by receiving the microcontroller output PWM signal to control the motor speed[14].

2.4 Bluetooth technology control module

Implant Bluetooth module and Andrews client in the design, so that people can remotely remote control the fan. The TXD side of the Bluetooth module is connected to the RXD terminal in the microcontroller, and the RXD terminal in the Bluetooth module is connected to the TXD terminal in the microcontroller. The Bluetooth module is operated by two-way communication to the chip and the handset, and transmitted to the microcontroller via Bluetooth Of the data, and receive feedback from the Bluetooth phone[15].

The Bluetooth module is operated by both hardware and software, you can control the fan through the mobile phone operation, Not only can achieve the timing of fan work, you can also set the temperature control fan speed.

3 Design of the software program

In order to realize the intelligent control of the fan, the main program of the system consists of module initialization program, infrared photoelectric display program, Bluetooth control program, temperature detection program and LCD display program and so on. The main program flow chart shown in Figure 2.

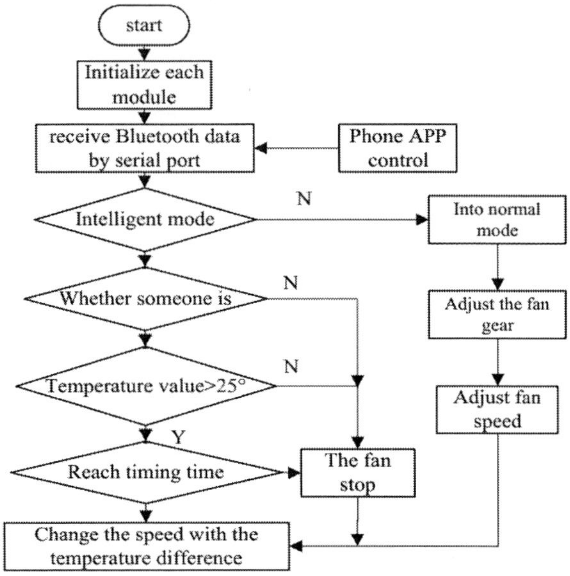

Figure 2. Main program flow chart

After the DS18B20 has initialized the data, it starts to measure the temperature and set the corresponding parameters. The internal temperature processing system calls the corresponding control program to make internal judgment, output the data and display it through the LCD. Digital temperature sensor module program flow chart shown in Figure 3.

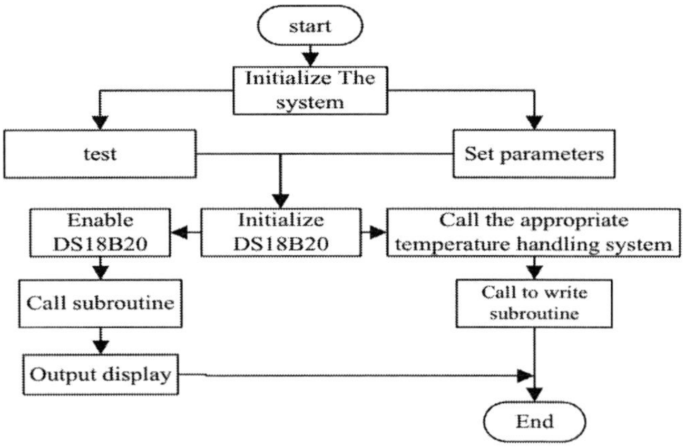

Figure 3. Digital temperature sensor module program flow chart

The microcontroller STC15F2K61S2 controls the DS1302 by calling the corresponding driver programs. The program completes the definition of the address of the DS1302 register and writes the control words, and reads the data in the DS1302 register. Initialization of DS1302 causes SCLK to be low, and when set to high, data transfer begins. I / O line data on the rising edge of SCLK is sent to the DS1302, write DS1302 program flow chart shown in Figure4.

DOI: 10.1051/itmconf/20171103011

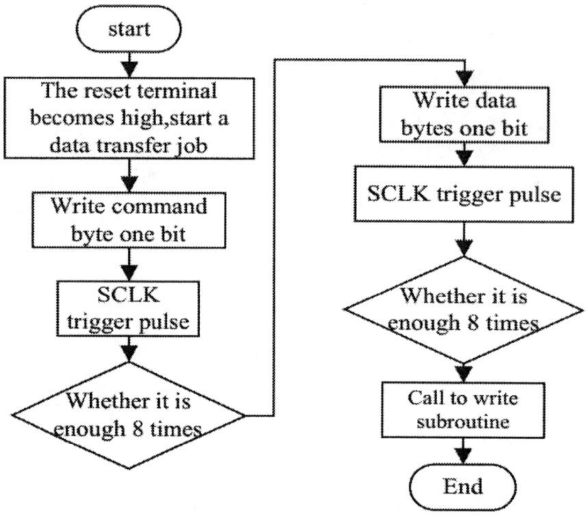

Figure 4. Write DS1302 program flow chart

The protocol of host control interface is the interface between the host's HCI driver and the control host located between the firmware of the Bluetooth communication module, which is included in the Bluetooth protocol stack and used in the hardware part of the Bluetooth communication module. RTS / CTS is used to prevent temporary UART buffer overflow. Bluetooth data transceiver system program flow shown in Figure 5.

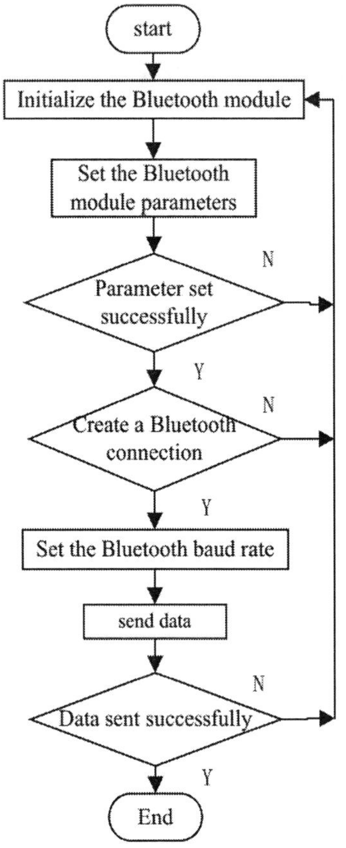

Figure 5. Bluetooth data transceiver system program flow chart

4 System debugging

According to the system circuit schematic manual welding circuit, and implante the program into system. Turn on the power, start the fan switch, adjust the fan running mode, so that it works in the general mode that is the normal fan of the manual speed mode, by adjusting the fan gear, change the fan speed. Start the second mode of operation that is intelligent mode, through the Bluetooth technology for remote control, the monitor shows the current room temperature of 25□, set the temperature abover than the room temperature, the sensor detected the information of pepole , turn on the fan. If the room temperature is belower than the set temperature, the fan stops rotating, which plays a very good temperature control.

5 Summary

The intelligent fan in the system can be adjusted speed according to the temperature changes, but also according to the presence of room to the conver the switch; Combined with Bluetooth technology, install Andrews client that specially designed for this fan, you can achieve the remote control. The microcontroller process the data, and compare set temperature and indoor temperature, determine whether the fan is turned on, in order to determine the fan speed corresponding self-set temperature. Will be applied to the elevator design process, can play a ventilation, cooling and energy saving role.

Acknowledgment

Shaanxi Provincial Department of Education research funding, Project Fund Number: 15JK2020.

References

1. XueLong. Li, EP,*The use of single-chip microcomputer control of intelligent remote controller.* J,**9**(2003)
2. QingMei. Li ,TAA, *The design of intelligent electric fan speed based on AT89C51.***7**(2008) J, AT89C51 automation technology.2014
3. JinShan. Liu, Guangzhou EQ ,*Design of Intelligent Governor of Fan Based on MCS – 51.*J, **71** (2004)
4. YiGang. Zhang ,EIP,*MCS-51 MCU application design* .M(2004)
5. Hao. Dou,CSA, *Design of intelligent fan control system.*J, **10**(2012)
6. LiGong.Zhou, Beijing university ASP,*microcontroller experiment and practice.*M(2004)
7. HanCai.Hu, Beijing tsinghua university press ,*Single-chip microcomputer principle and interface technology.*M(2004)
8. YunFeng.Ma,CMAC , *Single-chip microcomputer and interface design of digital temperature sensor DS18B20.*J,4(2007)
9. HuiQing. Jin, coal technology, *Principle and application of pyroelectric infrared sensor.*J,**4**(2011)
10. Gang. Li, modern electronic technology ,*1-Wire digital temperature sensor DSI8B20 principle and application* .J,**21**(2005)
11. ZhiJun. Han, *Journal of Nanjing Institute of Technology, Digital temperature sensor DS18B20 and its applicati*on .J,**5**(2010)
12. DiDa.Li, Modern Electronic Technology,*A simple design of the control system of intelligent temperature control fan.*J,**35**(2012)
13. Long. Chen, Wuhan University of Technology, *Research on human target recognition based on wireless pyroelectric infrared sensor.*A(2013)
14. HouRong.Lan, Industrial control computer, *MCU PWM control technology.* J, 3(2010)
15. XiaoQun. Liu, science and technology information, *Application of Bluetooth technology.* J,**7** (2010)

An Improved K-means Clustering Algorithm Applicable to Massive High-dimensional Matrix Datasets

Dong-Yuan LI[1] and Cai-Feng CAO[1,a]

[1]*Wuyi University, School of Computer, 529020 Jiangmen, China*

Abstract. Since K-means clustering algorithm is easy to implement and high efficient, it has been widely used in cluster analysis of massive datasets. The value of k is difficult to determine in advance and the randomness of choosing initial centers leads to a series of social problems, such as instability, local optimal solution sensitivity to outliers. Results from hierarchical clustering are more natural than those from K-means clustering, but its high time complexity and space complexity makes it difficult to be applied to a large data set. In this paper, through combination of hierarchical clustering and K-means clustering, we have proposed an improved K-means clustering algorithm, and have done experiments using datasets provided by MovieLens.

1 Introduction

As a method of unsupervised learning, clustering analysis is an important means of data mining. Without knowledge of the data distribution beforehand, clustering is to classified data into groups which are driven by data [1].

In all cluster analysis methods, K-means clustering algorithm has application usability, fast convergence and ability to handle large datasets [2]. However, K-means clustering algorithm also has some disadvantages: 1) Because of data distribution, the value of K is difficult to estimate; 2) Randomness of initial centers cause the clustering results often fall into local optimum which is not stable, but not the global optimum; 3) Sensitivity to outliers; 4) Unable to deal with non-spherical clusters and clusters of different sizes and densities.

Results from hierarchical clustering can reflect the hierarchical structure of the dataset. But the time complexity and the space complexity of hierarchical clustering are so high that hierarchical clustering is unsuited for high-dimensional massive dataset.

In this paper, we have integrated principal component analysis and sampling into combination of hierarchical clustering and K-Means clustering, and have proposed a new clustering algorithm named SPHK-means clustering algorithm.

[a] Corresponding author: cfcao@126.com

2 Associated knowledge and working

2.1 K-means clustering algorithm

K-means is a clustering algorithm based on partition.

2.1.1 Basic algorithm

Basic steps of K-means clustering algorithm are as follows:

1) Selecting initial cluster centers: randomly select k data objects from dataset containing m data objects;
2) Cluster object classification: calculate similarities between every data object and every center, and divide each data object into the group whose center is most similar to it;
3) Calculate new centers: for each group, calculate new center which is mean value of all member data objects in the group;
4) Determine whether the process is to terminate: if continuously twice iteration results in equality, the process stop, or else, proceed to the next iteration and go to step 2).

Space complexity of K-means clustering algorithm is $O((m+k)\cdot n)$ [4], and time complexity of it is $O(t\cdot k\cdot m\cdot n)$ [4], m is the number of data objects, n is the number of properties each data object has, t is the number of iterations.

2.1.2 Shortcoming and solutions

There are four main disadvantage of K - Means clustering algorithm: 1) How to determine the optimal value of K; 2) Randomness of initial centers; 3) Sensitivity to outliers; 4) It is difficult to process clusters which is aspherical or with uneven density and size. According to the fact, "the distance from the sample points in the most unlikely point to the same cluster ", D.H.Zhai, etc, used the maximum distance method [5] to select initial cluster centers. Y.Qin, etc [6], generated initial centers on the basis of detecting populated area. J.P.Zhang, etc [7], optimally partitioned data sample space basing on histogram method, and determined value of k and initial centers for k-mean algorithm according to the characteristic distribution of the data sample.

2.2 Agglomerative hierarchical clustering

Hierarchical clustering whose results are closer to the natural classification of the data object is an old clustering technology. It include two basic approaches-- cohesion and splitting, the latter is more commonly used.

2.2.1 Basic algorithm

Agglomerative hierarchical clustering begins from the initial state that each data point individually becomes a cluster. In each iteration, it merge two clusters between which the distance is shortest as a new cluster. It controls the number of result clusters by setting the threshold of inter-cluster distance, once distances between all pairs of clusters are larger than the threshold set, it stop the process of merging. There are three methods of measuring the distance between clusters: 1) single-linkage; 2) Complete-linkage; 3) Group average. In this paper, we have used the last. Let $\mathbf{u}$ and $\mathbf{v}$ are respectively two clusters, $\mathbf{u}$ and $\mathbf{v}$ are respectively the ith member of $\mathbf{u}$ and the jth member of $\mathbf{v}$, then Distance between clusters using group average is:

$$d(\mathbf{u},\mathbf{v}) = \sum_{i,j} \frac{d(\mathbf{u}_i, \mathbf{v}_j)}{(|\mathbf{u}| * |\mathbf{v}|)} \tag{1}$$

2.2.2 Shortcoming and solutions

As P.N. Tan, etc[4] mentioned, the space complexity of agglomerative hierarchical clustering algorithm is $O(m^2)$ [4], and the time complexity of it is $O(m^2 \log m)$ [4], m is the number of data points. Relatively high time complexity and space complexity makes it difficult for hierarchical clustering algorithm to process datasets whose volume is very large.

2.3 Principal component analysis

PCA can reduce dimensionality of highly dimensional data and to some extent remove the noise. Supposing there are p characteristics: $X_1, X_2, \ldots, X_p$. PCA transform original characteristics into new characteristics which is linear combinations of original ones: $F_1, F_2, \ldots, F_k, (k \le p)$ [8],

$$\begin{cases} F_1 = \mu_{11} X_1 + \mu_{21} X_2 + \cdots + \mu_{p1} X_p \\ F_2 = \mu_{12} X_1 + \mu_{22} X_2 + \cdots + \mu_{p2} X_p \\ \cdots \\ F_p = \mu_{1p} X_1 + \mu_{2p} X_2 + \cdots + \mu_{pp} X_p \end{cases} \tag{2}$$

Meeting these conditions: 1) For each principal component, sum of squares of its factor is 1; 2) all principal components are independent of each other; 3) Variances of principal components must be in descending order, namely, their importance must be in descending order [8]:

$$\begin{cases} \mu_{1i}^2 + \mu_{2i}^2 + \cdots + \mu_{pi}^2 = 1 \\ Cov(F_i, F_j) = 0, i \ne j, i, j = 1, 2, \ldots, p \\ Var(F_1) \ge Var(F_2) \ge \cdots \ge Var(F_p) \end{cases} \tag{3}$$

3 Model design of sphk-means clustering algorithm

Let row coordinates represent the objects to be scored, and column coordinates represent users. We have built a scoring matrix Mo :

DOI: 10.1051/itmconf/20171104001

$$Mo = \begin{bmatrix} p_{0,0} & p_{0,1} & \cdots & p_{0,M-2} & p_{0,M-1} \\ p_{1,0} & \ddots & & & \vdots \\ \vdots & & \ddots & & \vdots \\ p_{N-2,0} & & & \ddots & \vdots \\ p_{N-1,0} & p_{N-1,1} & \cdots & \cdots & p_{N-1,M-1} \end{bmatrix} \tag{4}$$

The jth user scored the ith object $p_{i,j}$ points, $p_{i,j}$ is float, $i \in \{0,1,\ldots,N-1\}$, $j \in \{0,1,\ldots,M-1\}$. According to the above analysis, when N and M are large enough, either K-means clustering or agglomerative hierarchical clustering is unfavorable to solve the problem. Model of SPHK-means clustering algorithm summarily proceed in two phases: 1) Pre-cluster by means of integration of sampling, principal component analysis and hierarchical clustering to determine the value of and the initial centers; 2) K-means clustering with and initial centers determined in phase 1) get the final result. Its working process is shown in Figure. 1.

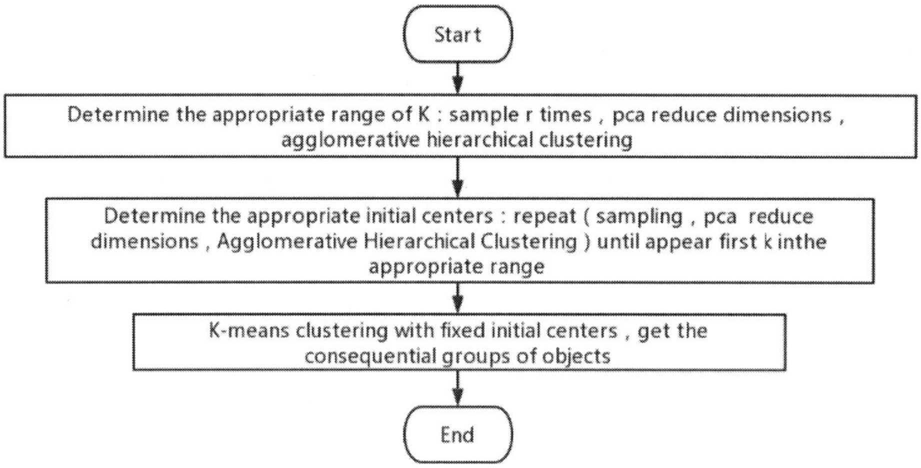

Figure 1. The process of SPHK-means clustering algorithm.

3.1 Sampling PCA hierarchical clustering

As pre- cluster, this stage in order to determine the value of and the initial centers.

3.1.1 Determine the appropriate value of K

Totally r samples is extracted. The process of dealing with the ith $(i = 1,2,\ldots,r)$ sample is as follow:

$\frac{1}{5}N$ objects is extracted as sample from the whole including N objects. PCA reduces dimensions of sample to $\frac{1}{6}M$. Scoring matrix of sample after dimensional reduction is as follow:

$$Mp(i)=\begin{bmatrix} P_{0,0}(i) & P_{0,1}(i) & \cdots & P_{0,\frac{1}{6}M-1}(i) \\ P_{1,0}(i) & \ddots & & \vdots \\ \vdots & & \ddots & \vdots \\ P_{\frac{1}{5}N-1,0}(i) & P_{\frac{1}{5}N-1,1}(i) & \cdots & P_{\frac{1}{5}N-1,\frac{1}{6}M-1}(i) \end{bmatrix} \tag{5}$$

Use formula (1) to cluster $\frac{1}{5}N$ objects by means of agglomerative hierarchical clustering algorithm. Record the numbers of consequential groups as $k(i)$. Calculate average $\bar{k}$ and standard deviation $\sigma(k)$ of $k(i)(i=1,2,\ldots,r)$:

$$\begin{cases} \bar{k}=\frac{1}{n}\sum_{i=1}^{n}k(i) \\ \sigma(k)=\frac{1}{n}\sqrt{\sum_{i=1}^{n}\left(k(i)-\bar{k}\right)^2} \end{cases} \tag{6}$$

Let $\left(\bar{k}-\frac{\sigma(k)}{2},\bar{k}+\frac{\sigma(k)}{2}\right)$ be appropriate range of K.

3.1.2 Determine the appropriate Initial centers

Repeat the above process of "sampling--reducing dimensions--hierarchical clustering", until first appear a k_0 in $\left(\bar{k}-\frac{\sigma(k)}{2},\bar{k}+\frac{\sigma(k)}{2}\right)$, then, the same time, the ultimate centers $\{v_1,v_2,\ldots,v_{k_0}\}$ are the appropriate initial centers.

3.2 K-means clustering

After reduce dimensions of N objects to $\frac{1}{6}M$ using PCA, cluster N objects by means of K-means clustering algorithm with initial centers $\{v_1,v_2,\ldots,v_{k_0}\}$, get consequential groups.

3.3 Analysis of time complexity and space complexity

In the phase of sampling PCA hierarchical clustering, samples n times, its space complexity is $O\left(10\cdot(m/5)^2\right)$. Supposing the first k in appropriate range in the Cth sampling, its time complexity is $O\left((10+C)\cdot(m/5)^2\log(m/5)\right)$. In the phase of K-means clustering, the space complexity is $O\left((m+k)\ n/6\right)$, the time complexity is $O\left(t\cdot k\cdot m\cdot n/6\right)$.

When finish pre-clustering, memory of all variables except for the appropriate initial centers is cleared. So if m ≫ n, space complexity of SPHK-means clustering algorithm is:

$$\max\left(O\left(10\cdot(m/5)^2\right),O\left((m+k)\cdot n/6\right)\right)=O\left(10\cdot(m/5)^2\right)=O\left(\frac{2}{5}\cdot m^2\right) \quad (7)$$

However, space complexity of classical agglomerative hierarchical clustering algorithm is $O\left(m^2\right)$. Space complexity of SPHK-means clustering algorithm is lower than that of classical agglomerative hierarchical clustering algorithm.

Time complexity of SPHK-means clustering algorithm is:

$$O\left((10+C)\cdot(m/5)^2\log(m/5)+t\cdot k\cdot m\cdot n/6\right)=O\left(((10+C)/25)\cdot m^2\log(m/5)\right) \quad (8)$$

However, time complexity of classical agglomerative hierarchical clustering algorithm is $O\left(m^2\log m\right)$, If C is small enough, time complexity of SPHK-means clustering algorithm is lower than that of classical agglomerative hierarchical clustering algorithm.

4 Experiments

Due to restriction of article length, we have put experimental process and results analysis in another paper for this conference, *Discovering Movie Categories Based on SPHK-means Clustering Algorithm*, which has proved that SPHK-means clustering algorithm has better classification accuracy and find more movie categories than classical K-means clustering algorithm.

Conclusion

We have synthetically applied sampling, principal component analysis and agglomerative hierarchical clustering to proposing an improved clustering algorithm named SPHK-means clustering algorithm, and have analyzed that it is better than classical K-means clustering algorithm in aspect of classification accuracy and number of categories found, and that it is better than classical agglomerative hierarchical clustering algorithm in aspect of time complexity and space complexity.

MovieLens[9] provides rating data involving sufficiently large number of pairs of movie and user and category labels of movies. We have designed experiments which has been described in another paper for this conference in detail to verify the superiority of SPHK-means clustering algorithm compared to classical K-means clustering algorithm on performance.

Recommendation algorithm based on neighbourhood uses KNN algorithm which is with high time complexity and high space complexity looking for neighbours, facing the problem of low classification accuracy. Next, we could apply SPHK-means clustering algorithm to improving recommendation algorithm based on neighbourhood.

Acknowledgment

This paper is supported by the Features Innovative Project in Guangdong Province "Research and Application of Mass Media Data Mining Technology" (2015KTSCX145).

References

1. Y. Zhang, L. He, H.D. Zhu, J. Chongqing Normal Uni(Nat Sci), **33**, 97-101 (2016)
2. Z. Y.Xiong,R.T.Chen, Y.F. Zhang, Appl. Res.Comput, **28**, 4188-4190 (2011)
3. J. Gong, J. Hunan. Uni. Technol, **22**, 52-54 (2008)
4. P. N. Tan, M. Steinbach, V. Kumar, *Introduction to Data Mining* (Posts &Telecom Press, Beijing, 2011)
5. D.H.Zhai, J.Yu, F Gao, L.Yu, F Ding, Appl. Res.Comput, **31**, 713-719 (2014)
6. Y.Qin, J.W.Jing, J.Xiang, J.Grad.Sch.Chin. Acad.Sci, **24**, 771-777 (2007)
7. J.P.Zhang, Y.Yang, J.Yang, J. Sys.Sim, **21**, 2586-2590 (2009)
8. Shlens, Jonathon, *A Tutorial on Principal Component Analysis*, CoRR abs/1404.1100 (2005): n. pag.
9. http://grouplens.org/datasets/movielens/

Discovering Movie Categories Based on SPHK-means Clustering Algorithm

Dong-Yuan LI[1] and Cai-Feng CAO[1,a]

[1]*Wuyi University, School of Computer, 529020 Jiangmen, China*

Abstract. Basing on SPHK-means, an improved K-means clustering algorithm, we have used dataset provided by MovieLens to design experiment. First, we have reduced dimensions of movie-user scoring matrix. Then, we have multiply sampled movies to conduct agglomerative hierarchical clustering in order to determine the appropriate value of k and initial centers. Finally, according to fixed k and initial centers, we have divided movies into groups through K-means clustering. With evaluation indicators as precision, recall and number of groups found, experiment in this paper has indicated that result of SPHK-means clustering algorithm is better than that of classical K-means clustering algorithm.

1 Introduction

Our anther paper for this conference, *An Improved K-means Clustering Algorithm Applicable to Massive High-dimensional Matrix Datasets*(IST1810), has proposed SPHK-means clustering algorithm, and has analyzed in theory that it may be better than classical K-means clustering algorithm in aspect of classification accuracy and number of categories found, and that it was better than classical agglomerative hierarchical clustering algorithm in aspect of time complexity and space complexity. SPHK-means clustering algorithm further integrates sampling and principal component analysis, which makes it more applicable for massive high-dimensional datasets.

Due to restriction of article length, in this paper, we would not describe the model of SPHK-means clustering algorithm in detail. Instead, we herein have designed experiment using datasets provided by MovieLens [1] to verify that SPHK-means clustering algorithm is better than classical K-means clustering algorithm in aspect of classification accuracy and number of categories found.

2 Introduction of datasets

MovieLens, a movie recommendation system, has recommended MovieLens Latest Datasets for education and development. Our experiment has used MovieLens Latest Datasets (small) updated at January 16th 2016.

Ratings that 668 users scored 10325 movies have been used as training dataset, a fraction of training dataset are showed in Table 1. Style tags of 10325 movies have been used as testing dataset, a fraction of testing dataset are showed in Table 2.

[a] Corresponding author: cfcao@126.com

Table 1. A fraction of training dataset.

userId	movieId	rating
1	16	4
1	24	1.5
2	17	5
2	784	2
⋮	⋮	⋮
668	144976	2.5
668	148626	4.5

Table 2. A fraction of testing dataset.

movieId	genres
5	Comedy
9	Action
14	Drama
⋮	⋮
148238	Comedy
148626	Drama

3 Implementation of SPHK-means clustering algorithm

Experiment environment is Windows 10. We have used python 2.7 and modules including 'csv', 'numpy', 'scipy', 'math' and 'matplotlib'. The process of our experiment is showed in Figure 1.

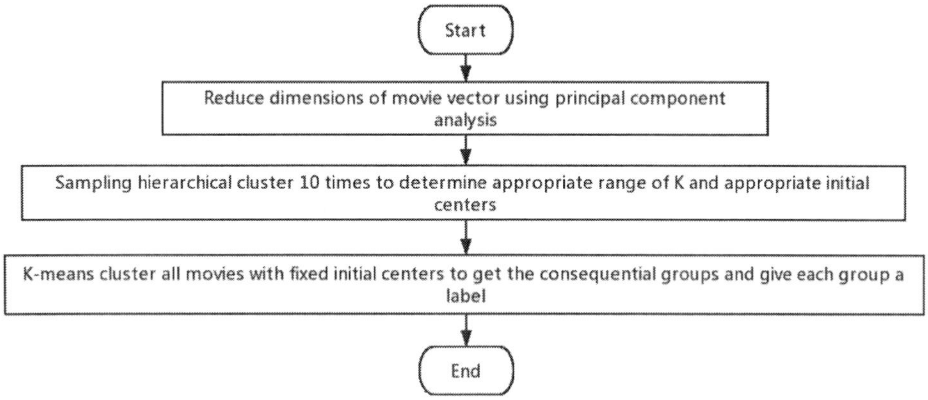

Figure 1. The process of our experiment.

Major portion of functional codes are specifically as follows.

3.1 Reduce dimensions of movie vector using principal component analysis[2]

Function pca(dataMat, topNfeat=999999) realize principal component analysis and reducing dimensions, dataMat is dataset that PCA deals with, topNfeat, number of features extracted, is optional. Its codes are as follows:

```
def pca(dataMat, topNfeat=999999):
meanVals = mean(dataMat, axis=0)
meanRemoved = dataMat - meanVals # Subtract the mean value
covMat = cov(meanRemoved, rowvar=0)
eigVals,eigVects = linalg.eig(mat(covMat))
eigValInd = argsort(eigVals)          # Sort from smallest to largest
eigValInd = eigValInd[:-(topNfeat+1):-1] # Remove unneeded dimensions
redEigVects = eigVects[:,eigValInd]      # From large to small restructure characteristic vector
lowDDataMat = meanRemoved * redEigVects # Transform the data into the new space
reconMat = (lowDDataMat * redEigVects.T) + meanVals
return lowDDataMat, reconMat
```

3.2 Sampling hierarchical clustering determines appropriate range of K and appropriate Initial centers

Codes are as follows:

```
sampsize =2000 # sample capacity
samp = random.randint(len(mId1), size=(10,sampsize)) # independently sample 10 times
ncH = []
print '--------- Sampling PCA hierarchical clustering determine the appropriatevalue of K ----------'
for sampi in samp:
  radR = []
  radC = []
  radD = []
  iR = -1
  for j in sampi:
    iR += 1
    for k in range(len(uid)):
      if M[j,k]!=0 :
        radR.append(iR)
        radC.append(k)
        radD.append(M[j,k])
  rR = np.array(radR)
  rC = np.array(radC)
  rD = np.array(radD)
  m = sparse.coo_matrix((rD,(rR,rC)), shape=(sampsize,len(uid))).todense()
  mp = pca(m,100)[0] #PCA, reduce dimensions
  Z = linkage(mp.real,'average','correlation')
  cluH = fcluster(Z+abs(Z.min()), 1.1547)
  print cluH.max()#number of groups of sampling hierarchical clustering
  ncH.append(cluH.max())
print '-----------------------------'
k1 = np.mean(ncH)-np.std(ncH)/2
k2 = np.mean(ncH)+np.std(ncH)/2
print ' Upper limit of appropriate range: %d' % k1
print ' Lower limit of appropriate range: %d' % k2
print '-----------------------------'
print '----------------results of SPHK-means clustering algorithm ---------------'
k = -1000
while (k<k1)|(k>k2) : # until k in appropriate range
  samp1 = random.randint(len(mId1), size=(1,sampsize))
  radR = []
```

DOI: 10.1051/itmconf/20171104002

```
    radC = []
    radD = []
    iR = -1
    for i in samp1[0]:
        iR += 1
        for j in range(len(uid)):
            if M[i,j]!=0 :
                radR.append(iR)
                radC.append(j)
                radD.append(M[i,j])
    rR = np.array(radR)
    rC = np.array(radC)
    rD = np.array(radD)
    m = sparse.coo_matrix((rD,(rR,rC)), shape=(sampsize,len(uid))).todense()
    mp = pca(m,100)[0]
    Z = linkage(mp.real,'average','correlation')
    cluH1 = fcluster(Z+abs(Z.min()), 1.1547)
    print cluH1.max()
    k = cluH1.max()
print ' divide all movies into %d categories (repeated): ' % k
code = []
for i in range(k) :
    sumC = np.zeros(len(uid))
    numC = 0
    for j in range(sampsize):
        if cluH1[j] == i+1 :
            sumC = sumC+np.array(m[j].tolist()[0])
            numC += 1
    code.append((sumC/numC).tolist())
code_book = np.array(code) #appropriate initial centers
```

3.3 K-means clustering according to fixed K and initial centers

Function kmeans1(M, k, code_book, iter=10, thresh=1e-05) realize 3) K-means clustering with fixed k and initial centers, M is matrix to deal with, code_book is initial centers. Its codes is as follows:

```
def kmeans1(M, k, code_book, iter=10, thresh=1e-05):
    ii = 0
    while ii<iter :
        kind = vq(M,code_book)[0].tolist() #groups each movie belong to
        kind1 = []
        kind1.extend(kind)
        kindex = [] # index of movies in every group in 'kind'
        for i in range(k) :
            iindex = []
            while i in kind1 :
                iindex.append(kind1.index(i))
                kind1[kind1.index(i)] = k
            kindex.append(iindex)
        code = []
        lastCode = code_book.tolist()
        for i in range(k) :
            sumC = np.zeros(len(uid))
```

```
            numC = 0
            for j in range(M.shape[0]):
                if kind[j] == i :
                    sumC = sumC+np.array(M[j].tolist()[0])
                    numC += 1
            with np.errstate(invalid='ignore'):
                code.append((sumC/numC).tolist())
        for i in range(k) :
            if np.sqrt(((np.array(code[i])-np.array(lastCode[i]))**2).sum()) >= thresh :
                lastCode = code
                break
            if i == k-1 :
                code_book = np.array(code)
                return code_book
        ii += 1
    code_book = np.array(code)
return code_book, kindex
```

4 Experimental results

4.1 Evaluation indexes

In statistics, precision, recall and F-score are typical evaluation indexes for classification problem. If result of classification is as Figure 2[3], precision and recall are defined as formula (1) and formula (2).

$$\text{Precision}=\frac{|\text{true positives}|}{|\text{true positives}|+|\text{false positives}|} \tag{1}$$

$$\text{Recall}=\frac{|\text{true positives}|}{|\text{true positives}|+|\text{false negatives}|} \tag{2}$$

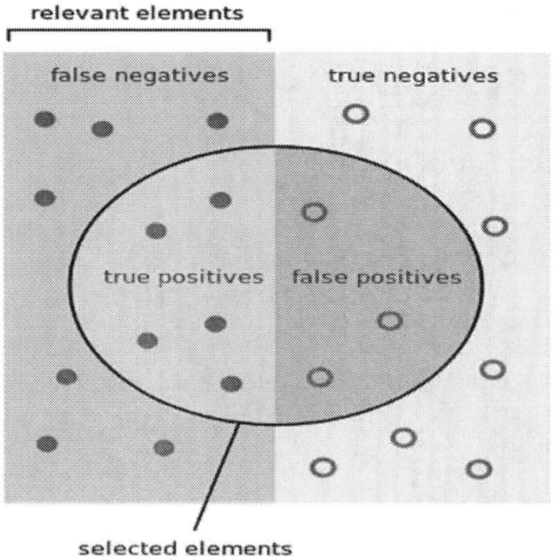

Figure 2[3]. Description precision and recall.

 DOI: 10.1051/itmconf/20171104002

F-score, defined as formula (3), is a measure that combines precision and recall.

$$F=2\cdot\frac{\text{Precision}\cdot\text{Recall}}{\text{Precision+Recall}} \tag{3}$$

The higher the evaluation indexes (precision, recall and F-score) are, the better classification accuracy is.

4.2 Data analysis of experimental results

At the same ambient conditions, we have repetitive repeatedly experimented in accordance with SPHK-means clustering algorithm and classical K-means clustering algorithm respectively. Data of experimental results is showed in Table 3 and Table 4.

Table 3. Comparison of evaluation indexes of SPHK-means and classical K-means.

Order	Algorithm	precision	recall	F-score
1	SPHK-means	53.3837%	56.3688%	54.8357%
	Classical K-means	50.5373%	53.3633%	51.9119%
2	SPHK-means	55.0198%	58.0965%	56.5163%
	Classical K-means	50.5373%	53.3633%	51.9119%
3	SPHK-means	54.5842%	57.6365%	56.0688%
	Classical K-means	50.5276%	53.3531%	51.9019%

Table 4. Comparison of movie categories found of SPHK-means and classical K-means.

No.	Algorithm	Movie categories found and amount of each category	Diagram: Pie Chart
1	SPHK-means	12 categories found: Action: 51; Adventure: 13; Animation: 5; Comedy: 1365; Crime: 1; Documentary: 1; Drama: 8789; Horror: 25; Mystery: 1; Romance: 18; Sci-Fi: 24; Thriller: 33.	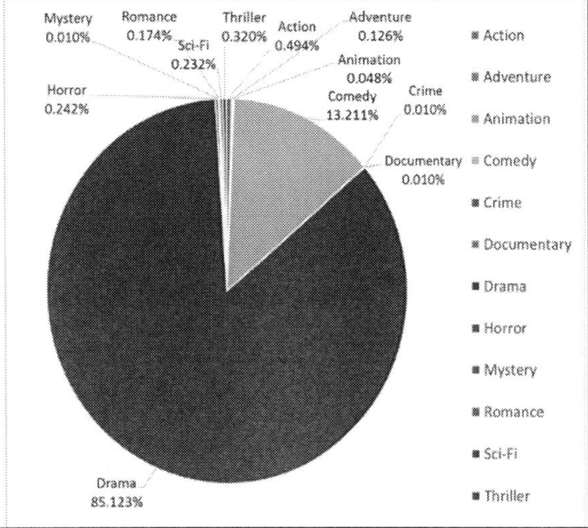

	Classical K-means	3 categories found: Animation: 1; Drama: 10322; Musical: 2.	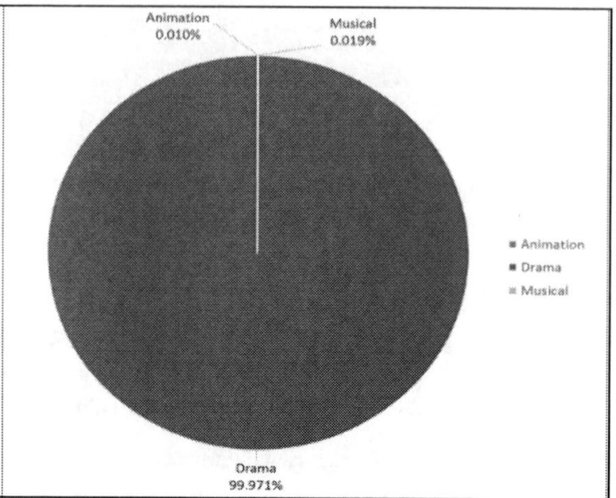
2	SPHK-means	15 categories found: Action: 84; Adventure: 47; Animation: 4; Comedy: 1583; Crime: 12; Documentary: 7; Drama: 8336; Fantasy: 3; Film-Noir: 14; Horror: 59; Musical: 3; Romance: 20; Sci-Fi: 103; Thriller: 48; Western: 2.	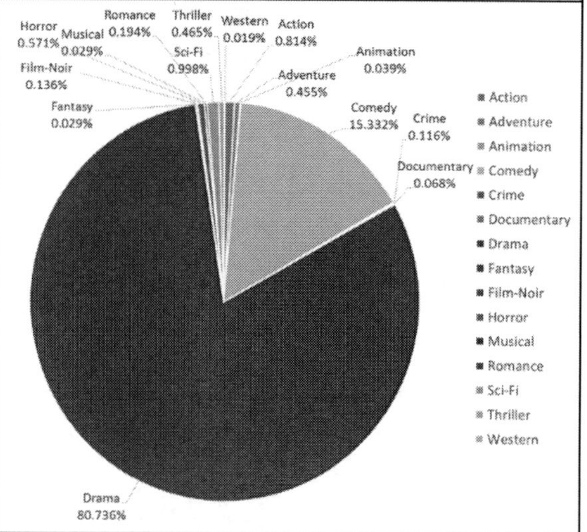
	Classical K-means	2 categories found: Crime: 1; Drama: 10324.	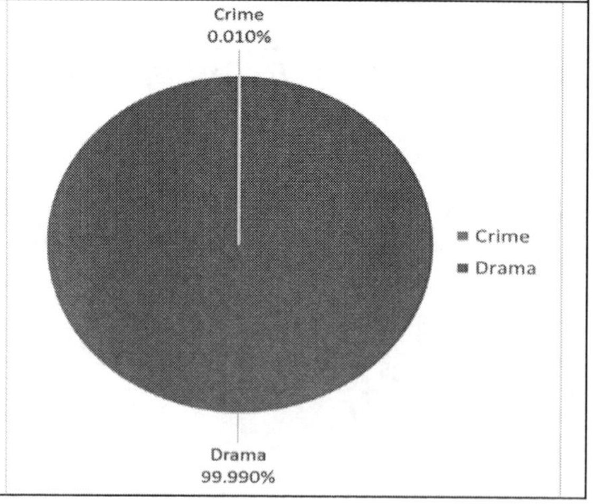

In contrast, we can find it from Table 3 that precision and recall of SPHK-means clustering algorithm are both higher than those of K-means clustering algorithm.

In the test data set, movies are actually divided into 19 categories: Action, Adventure, Animation, Children, Comedy, Crime, Documentary, Drama, Fantasy, Film-Noir, Horror, IMAX, Musical, Mystery, Romance, Sci-Fi, Thriller, War and Western. Table 4 has shown that movie categories found by SPHK-means clustering algorithm are greatly more than those found by classical K-means clustering algorithm.

Conclusion

In this paper, through experiment, we have verified that SPHK-means clustering algorithm is better than classical K-means clustering algorithm in aspect of classification accuracy and number of categories found.

Next, in order to adapt SPHK-means clustering algorithm to more scenarios, we will consider situation that one object may belong to two or more categories which require us to integrate membership degree[4] mentioned in fuzzy mathematics into it.

Acknowledgment

This paper is supported by the Features Innovative Project in Guangdong Province "Research and Application of Mass Media Data Mining Technology" (2015KTSCX145).

References

1. http://grouplens.org/datasets/movielens/ (Jan.16th 2016)
2. P. Harrington, Machine Learning (Posts &Telecom Press, Beijing,2013)
3. https://en.wikipedia.org/wiki/Precision_and_recall
4. C. M.Zhang, Sw.G, **15**, 41-43 (2016)

A Massive Structured Data Storage Technology for Commodity Screening Applications

Feng XU[1,a] and Wei ZHANG[1]

[1]*School of Computer Science, Beijing Information Science &Technology University, Beijing 100101, China*

Abstract. With the rapid development of e-commerce, the number of goods has become more and more. When commodity screening system is used to store and process mass information, the existing models require all nodes in the distributed system to work in parallel, then the results of each node are integrated to get the final results, the process produces a lot of invalid queries. In order to solve this problem, proposed a new distributed structured data storage method. It statistics the history search results and chooses the high frequency or core columns to be key columns. The data can be stored based key columns and distribute system architecture. Then in the searching stage, only some nodes work when the search refer to key columns. The results show that this method can reduce the tasks and improve the throughout without extra storage consumption.

1 Introduction

With the development of cloud computing and Internet of things, more and more people choose online shopping. According to the thirty-seventh CNNIC China Internet Statistics report shows that as of December 2015, a total of 413 million Internet users online shopping. With the increasing of commodity information, the electronic commerce system needs to store large amount of commodity information, the rapid growth of access requirements and product data has brought great pressure on data query and storage.

At present, the electronic commerce system usually uses the massive data processing model based on Hadoop[1-4] to process the data. In Hadoop processing model, HDFS[5-6] is used to store data and MapReduce[7-9] for distributed computing. However, with the wide application of Hadoop in e-commerce system, the common problems are becoming more and more serious. For example, it is easy to produce invalid query and so on, which reduces the overall throughput of the system and increases the system load. So how to store data and reduce the invalid query is a very worthy of inquiry.

To solve the above problems, this paper presents a distributed structured data storage technology for commodity screening applications. This technique makes the statistical analysis of the history table query, use the field of high frequency or core as a key column, in accordance with the key column data partition. For the query with key columns, the query task can be generated only for the region containing the result information, which can greatly reduce the query data and the number of working nodes, thus effectively improve the throughput of the system.

[a] Corresponding author: fenng.xu@foxmail.com

2 Related research

In the research of Chinese scholars, literature [10] proposed a two-stage data placement strategy based on relevancy, The strategy will be closely related data as much as possible into the same data center, Relatively loose data will be placed in different data center, Ensuring high cohesion between data sets in the same data center and low coupling between data sets in different data center, the task scheduling policy schedules tasks to the largest data dependence of the data center. literature [11] presents a data placement strategy for data intensive applications in a cloud computing environment, This strategy models based on the data dependencies between datasets, The data dependencies between datasets are expressed as clustering matrix, then the clustering matrix is used to classify the data sets, and allocates a storage location for each partition. An improved Hadoop data placement strategy is proposed in [12], the strategy considers both node distance and load, improve the overall performance of the system and balance the node load. The clustering index of the database is described in [13]. The clustering index, the difference between the clustered index and the non-clustered index, and how to select the clustered index are described.

In the research of foreign scholars, literature [14] proposed CoHadoop, modified the underlying HDFS data placement strategy, allowing applications to control the data storage location, as far as possible the relevant data placed in the same group of nodes. In [15], a dynamic data placement strategy is proposed based on the characteristics of actual data, such as the interdependence of data, the actual application and the change of user location. In [16], the processing capacity of each node is taken into account during the data placement, and then the data blocks are allocated according to the node processing capacity, the load is balanced and the throughput of the system is improved.

Based on the above analysis, the domestic and foreign scholars have optimized the default data placement strategy from the aspects of node performance, system performance, data characteristics and data dependency. In this paper, from the data dependency point of view, a data storage strategy based on key column pre-processing is proposed, which can significantly reduce the number of invalid queries and reduce the overall system query times and improve the system throughput.

3 Based on pre-processing key columns distributed data storage technology

In this section, the basic idea and the specific design of the distributed data storage technology based on the key column pre-processing are proposed, reduces the invalid query and improves the throughput of the system effectively.

3.1 The basic idea of distributed data storage technology based on key column pre-processing

In order to solve the problem that the existing e-commerce website is easy to generate invalid query, this paper proposes a distributed structured data storage technology. The technology statistics table query through history, the data in the table in accordance with the query frequency in descending order, then select the core or higher frequency field as the key column. In Figure 1, in the data storage phase, the data is partitioned into multiple storage areas according to the data dependency of the key columns. In the query processing stage, when dealing with the query with key columns, through the key column pre-processing, can only query for some storage area, reduce the invalid query. The experiment results show that this technique can reduce the total number of tasks in each node of the distributed system without the extra storage overhead, and improve the system throughput.

In the data storage phase, the technology divides all data nodes into multiple storage areas according to the specific application requirements. As shown in Figure 1, the original data is preprocessed and the data with the relevant attributes is stored in the same area. For example, in Figure 1, after the historical query data statistics, the key column number N is 3, the number of storage area M is 3, assuming that the original data table has nine records, through the key column pre-processing, these nine records divided into three storage areas. Area 1 is an area having the same shape, Area 2 is an area having the same gray, and Area M is an area having the same shading.

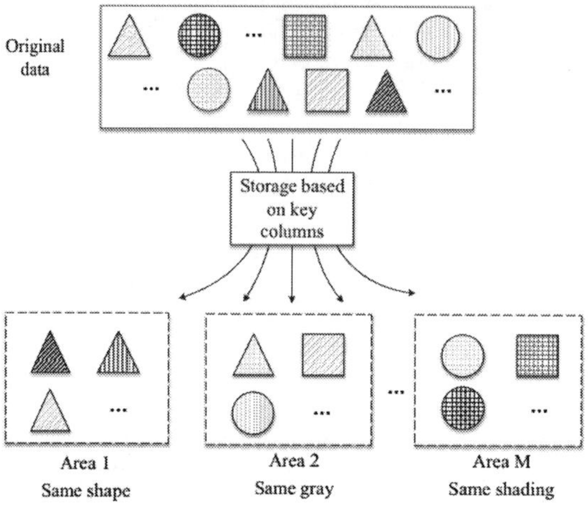

Figure 1. Storage model based on key column pre-processing

In the query processing phase, the query request can generate query tasks only for the region containing the result information by key column pre-processing. When an existing model processes a query request, it traverses all the storage nodes, but some nodes do not contain the result information, resulting in many invalid queries. In the key column pre-processing model, when the query containing the key columns is processed, After the pre-processing phase, the query request condition can be judged, which can only generate valid query task for some nodes and reduce invalid query. For example, in Figure 1, Area2 stores gray-level data. When performing gray-level data query, the existing model will query all the nodes, while the query request can only query Area2 after pre-processing based on key columns.

After the historical query data statistics, this paper assumes that the number of key columns is N, the number of storage areas is M, the data after the key column pretreatment, and then processing the query request, through theoretical analysis and experimental verification of the following rules: When a query request, the query conditions as long as any storage area to meet more than N/2 (down rounding) key columns, you only need to query the storage area, Otherwise, query all storage areas.

Therefore, when there are a large number of query requests, this technology can reduce the number of tasks in the distributed system, reduce the system load and improve the throughput of the system.

3.2 The design of distributed data storage based on key column pre-processing

This section mainly describes the design of the distributed storage technology based on the key column pre-processing.

3.2.1 The design of data storage based on Key Column pre-processing

In the existing storage model, the request for the query requires all nodes in the system all work in parallel, the process will produce a lot of invalid queries. To solve the above problem, this section divides the data into the corresponding storage area according to the data attributes of the key columns, and then the subsequent query request for pretreatment. The results show that the method can effectively reduce the number of nodes query and improve the system throughput.

In this paper, we assume that the number of key columns is N and the data nodes are divided into M storage areas according to the statistics of historical query records, where N and M are not less than

1. Through this design, the original data in the data table through the key column pre-processing, all the original data according to the value of N key columns, re-partitioned into M storage area, any record in the data table will be assigned to a specific region. The newly added data is also partitioned according to the key column data partitioning strategy. In Figure 2, the raw data is divided into each region by the key column pre-processing. There are N possibilities for data in each region. Through the above process the original data through the key column data partitioning strategy to re-partition the regional storage.

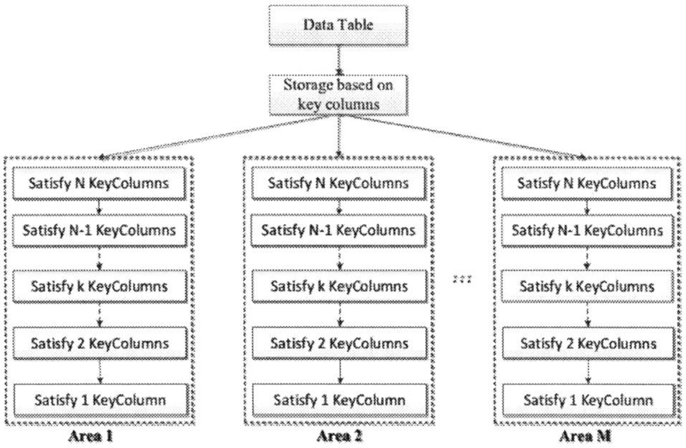

Figure 2. The design of data storage based on Key Column pre-processing

The following is a detailed description of the data storage method based on the key column pre-processing.

First, get the number of key columns N and the number of storage area M. Key column collection based on history query of data table, and sorted according to the key column heat, using TopK algorithm to solve the problem of selecting key columns, thereby determining the key column and its number N and the storage area and its number M, where M, N are not less than 1. For example, the statistical analysis of the notebook product information table, using TopK algorithm to obtain the table column Top3: brand, price and size. Then the number of key columns N is 3, the brand is the first key column, the price for the second key column, the size of the third key column. Assuming the number of data nodes is greater than 3, and after research found that commodity prices need to be divided into three files to sell, then the number of storage area M 3.

Then, the value of each key column is divided into the storage area. According to different data types, there are two kinds of specific partitioning strategies: data partitioning strategy for continuous fields and data partitioning strategy for discrete fields.

The data partitioning strategy for continuous fields is mainly applicable to the key column for continuous values, and has a certain range of values. When the data of the key columns are continuous values, the strategy divides the values of the key columns into different ranges and assigns them to M storage areas. For example, the price in the data table is the key column, and the value of the price is continuous from 0 to 999, the number of storage area M is 2, then the price in the range of 1 is [0-499], the price in the range of 2 is [500-999].

The data partitioning strategy of the discrete field is mainly applied to the discrete value of the key column, and the value does not have certain regularity. When the data of the key column is not continuous or does not have a certain range of values, the strategy according to the hash algorithm to assign the value of the key column to the storage area. For example, the size of the commodity information table is the key column, and the size of the value of 6, 9, 10, 11, 14 and 16, the number of storage area M is 3, then according to the hash algorithm, the size of the range of values in the region 1 Is [6, 9], the size in the range 2 is [10, 16], the size in the range 3 is [11, 14].

Finally, the data in the data table is divided into various storage areas. For any record in the data table, after all the key column points are judged, the record is divided into the area with the highest drop point, as shown in Figure 3, the specific strategy is as follows:

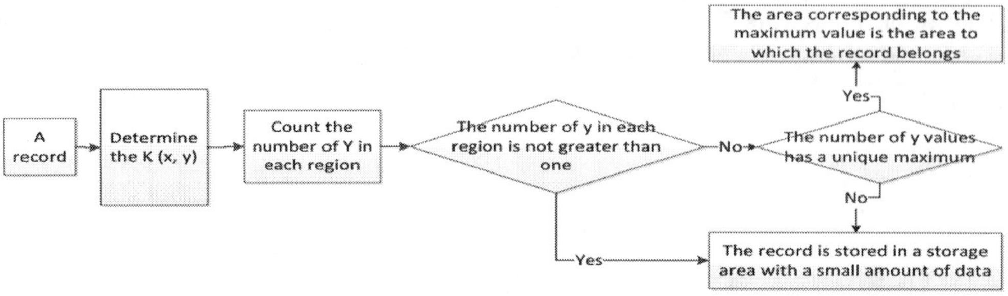

Figure 3. The data placement strategy based on key columns

1. Determine the K (x, y) for all the key columns in the record. K (x, y) indicates that the value of the x-th key column in a data record belongs to the y-th region, For example, K (1, 2) of a record, then the value of the first key column of the record belongs to the second region.
2. Statistics the number of y in each area, that is, the number of key columns in the same area.
3. If the number of y in each region is not greater than 1, it means that each key column in the record belongs to a different region. Then, according to the storage load balancing, the record is stored in a storage area with a small amount of data
4. If a region or a number of regions within the y is greater than 1, that there are a number of key columns belong to the same region. If the number of y within a region has a unique maximum value, which means that the key column in the region is the largest, then the record will be divided into the region; If the number of y in each region does not have a unique maximum value, which means that the number of y in the plurality of regions is the same and maximized, the record is stored in the storage region with a small amount of data according to the storage load balancing. For example, the number of key columns N is 4, assuming that all the key columns K (x, y) of a record are K (1, 3), K (2, 3), K (3, 4),K(4, 4), That is, the first and second key columns belong to the region 3, the third and fourth key columns belong to the region 4, the region 3 and the region 4 have two key columns, the number of all regions y does not have a unique maximum value, And the number of the key columns of the regions 3 and 4 is the largest, the record is stored in a storage area with a small amount of data according to the storage load balancing.

3.2.2 The design of data query based on key column pre-processing

This section describes the data query strategy based on key column pre-processing. In this strategy, all the query requests through the key column pre-processing, can only contain the results of the storage area to generate query tasks, the specific strategy shown in Figure 4.

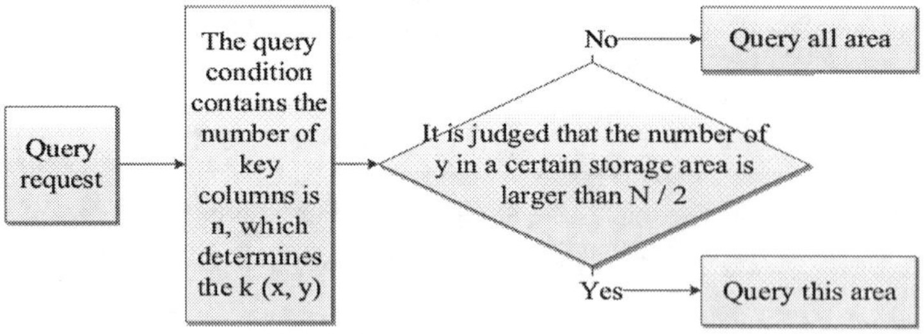

Figure 4. The data query strategy based on key column

Assuming that the total number of key columns is N and the total number of storage areas is M, the query condition of a query task contains n key columns, and n is not greater than N. Specific strategies are as follows:

1. Determine K (x, y) for all the key columns in the query condition;
2. Statistics of the number of y in each storage area, that is, Statistics the number of key columns in the same area;
3. It is judged in each storage area that if the number of y in a storage area is larger than N/2 (rounding down), the storage area is directly inquired, otherwise, all the storage areas are queried.

4 Case verification

In order to verify the performance of the distributed data storage technology based on the key column pre-processing, the verification experiment is carried out on Hadoop and Hive, and compared with the existing system. The experimental platform is CDH version Hadoop and Hive, the data transmission tool is Sqoop. There are 4 nodes in the cluster, including 1 NameNode and 3 DataNodes, so the number of memory area is M is 3 and the number of key columns N is 3 in this experiment. Memory area 0 corresponds to DataNode0, memory area 1 corresponds to DataNode1, and storage area 2 corresponds to DataNode2, as shown in Figure 5.

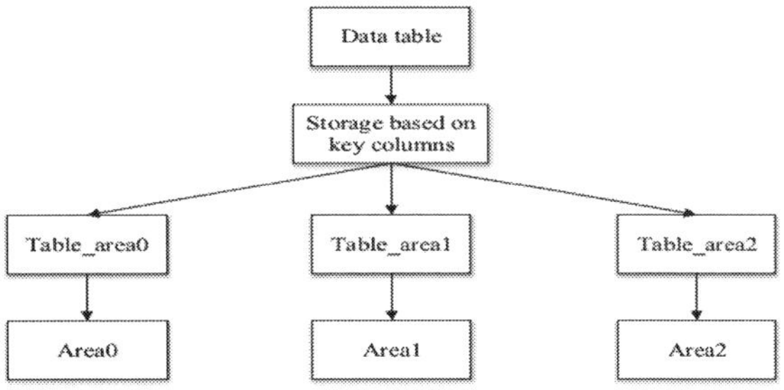

Figure 5. The experiment process

Experiment the first step to get the key columns. The key columns are collected for the historical query log of the data table. The MapReduce program is programmed to calculate the number of occurrences of each column in the query condition. The TopK algorithm is used to get the most K columns, which are the key columns. Because K = N = 3, so find Top 3, the highest occurrence of the three columns, these three columns is the key column.

The second step of the experiment divides the value of three key columns into three storage areas, and obtains the range of the key columns in each storage area. After inspection and analysis, the test data are discrete integer data, through the key column in section 3.2.1 value division method, the value of the three key columns are divided into three storage areas.

In the third step of the experiment, the data in the original data table is divided into the sub tables corresponding to each storage area. According to the data division strategy in 3.2.1 section, the original data table is divided into 3 sub tables: table_area0, table_area1, table_area2. The 3 sub tables correspond to 3 storage areas: area0, area1, area2.

In the fourth step, the 3 sub data tables are transmitted to the corresponding storage area in HDFS. In the Hadoop cluster, through the configuration of the hdfs-site.xml file, the configuration file to add the dfs.hosts.exclude blacklist of DataNode, dynamic control delete/add DataNode. When the sub table Area0 is transferred to area0, the Host1 and Host2 are added to the blacklist, and then sqoop is used to import the data sheet table_area0 into area0, which in turn introduces the other sub tables into the corresponding storage area.

Step 5 of the experiment data query test. In turn, 1000 random data queries, each query request through the pre-processing module processing, data query strategy is as follows pseudo-code:

DOI: 10.1051/itmconf/20171104003

```
for each area in areas{
  flag←false;
  n←k(x, y);
  if n > N/2 then
        flag←true;
        query(area);
  else
        continue;
  end if
  if flag != true then
        query(areas);
  end if
  }
```

As shown in Figure 6, the abscissa indicates the type of query and the ordinate indicates the time required for the query. And then 1000 queries are carried out, and the key column query is compared with the full table query. When 1000 queries satisfy 3 key columns, the query time is shortened by 13.86% compared with the full table query time. When 1000 queries satisfy 2 key columns, the time is shortened by 14.02%. When the query satisfies 1 key column Query conditions, the query time is not much change. The experimental results are in agreement with the conclusion. The three key columns and the two key columns are larger than N/2 (rounded down), so only one storage area is queried; one key column does not satisfy the condition, so query all areas.

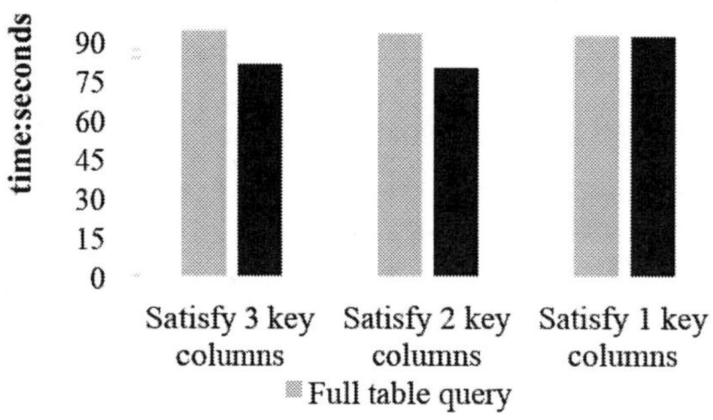

Figure 6. The Four groups of query test results

As shown in Figure 7, the abscissa represents the ratio of three or two key columns in the query request, and the ordinate represents the time required for the query. The experiments were carried out 1000 queries in turn, and the queries consisted of three key columns, two key columns, and one key column. The higher the proportion of three key columns or two key columns in a hybrid query, the shorter the query time. In the experiment, seven experiments were conducted. When the proportion is 30%, the query time is 92.5 seconds; when the ratio is 40%, the query time is 90.8 seconds; when the proportion is 50%, the query time is 88.3 seconds; when the proportion is 60%, the query time is 86.1 Seconds; when the ratio is 70%, the query time is 84.3 seconds, when the ratio is 90%, the query time is 80.9 seconds. The experimental results are in agreement with the conclusion. The higher the ratio of N/2 key columns in the query request, the shorter the query time, and the less the number of tasks and the number of working nodes, the higher the throughput of the system.

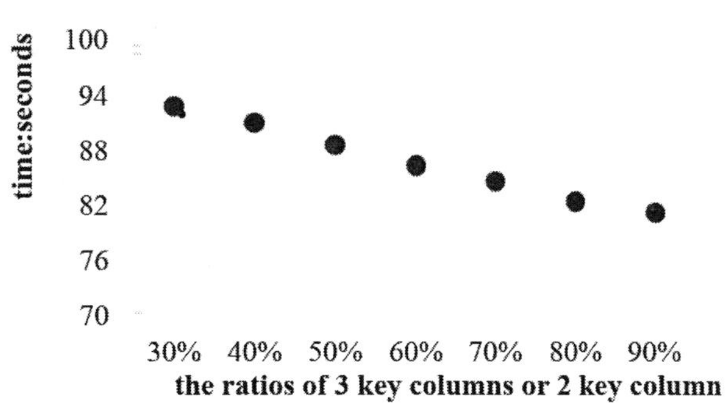

Figure 7. The Mixed query test results

In summary, the data storage technology based on the key column pre-processing can effectively reduce the invalid query and improve the system throughput, but when the query request contains less than or equal to N/2 (rounded down) key column, the query results are the same as the original system.

Conclusion

In this paper, we present a distributed structured data storage and query technology for commodity selection applications. In the data storage stage, the data is partitioned and stored by key column pre-processing. In the data query phase, when a query request containing a key column is processed, the query task can be generated only for the storage region containing the result information, reducing the number of full table queries and the number of query nodes. The technology is mainly applied to the application of commodity screening category, In the case of key column requirements unchanged, can significantly improve system throughput, it has obvious effect on reducing the latency and high workload of the existing e-commerce system in the high concurrent query.

Acknowledgements

Funding for this research was provided by the Program for Beijing Top Young Talents Cultivation Project(CIT&TCD201504057). We like to thank anonymous reviewers for their valuable comments.

References

1. Aysan Rasooli, Douglas G. Down. High Performance Computing, Networking, Storage and Analysis (SCC), 2012 SC Companion. IEEE **2012**:1284-1291 (2012)
2. Yazd S A, Venkatesan S, Mittal N. Proceedings of the IEEE Symposium on Reliable Distributed Systems, **34(1)**:457-462 (2012)
3. Lu J, Guting R H. Proceedings of the IEEE International Conference on Parallel & Distributed Systems, **90(1)**:738-743 (2012)
4. Lu H, Hai-Shan C, Ting-Ting H. International Conference on NETWORKING & Distributed Computing, **2012**:59-63 (2012)
5. Kala Karun A, Chitharanjan K. Information & Communication Technologies, **2013**:132-137 (2013)
6. Farag Azzedin. International Conference on Collaboration Technologies and Systems. **2013**:155-161 (2013)
7. Kalavri V, Brundza V, Vlassov V. IEEE International Conference on Cloud Computing Technology and Science. IEEE Computer Society, **2013**:250-257 (2013)
8. Kurazumi S, Tsumura T, Saito S, et al. 2012 Third International Conference on Networking and Computing. IEEE Computer Society, **2012**:288-292 (2012)

9. He Y, Lee R, Yin H, et al. Data Engineering (ICDE), 2011 IEEE 27th International Conference on. IEEE, **2011**:1199-1208 (2011)
10. Liu SW, Kong LM, Ren KJ, et al. Chinese Journal of Computers, **34(11)**:2121–2130 (2011).
11. Zheng P. Chinese Journal of Computers, **33(8)**:1472-1480 (2010).
12. Lin W W. Journal of South China University of Technology, **40(1)**:152-158 (2012).
13. Zhou S. Nonferrous Metals Processing **41(6)**:53-55 (2012)
14. Eltabakh M Y, Tian Y, Zcan F, et al. Proceedings of the Vldb Endowment, **4(9)**:575-585 (2011)
15. Agarwal S, Dunagan J, Jain N, et al. Usenix Nsdi, **2010**:17-32 (2010)
16. Xie J, Yin S, Ruan X, et al. IEEE International Symposium on Parallel and Distributed Processing, IPDPS 2010, **2010**:1-9 (2010)

ITM Web of Conferences **11**, 05001 (2017) DOI: 10.1051/itmconf/20171105001
IST2017

Research on Multi-sensor Image Matching Algorithm Based on Improved Line Segments Feature

Hui YUAN[1,a], Ying-Guang HAO[1] and Jun-Min LIU[1]

[1]*Dalian University of Technology School of Information and Communication Engineering, 116024, Dalian, China*

Abstract. In this paper, an improved multi-sensor image matching algorithm based on line segments feature is proposed. Firstly, the line segments in the image are extracted and optimized. And the virtual feature points are constructed by the line segments. Then a set of affine transformation matrices of two images is obtained by different combinations of virtual feature points. And then the matching function is constructed, by which the relationship of affine transform between the two images are preliminarily determined. And the matching point set is obtained. Finally, false matching points are eliminated based on RANSAC algorithm and the final transformation matrix to accomplish accurate matching is achieved. The experimental results show that the matching accuracy of this proposed algorithm can reach up to 80%. At the same time, the speed of the algorithm is significantly improved.

1 Introduction

The technology of multi-sensor image matching is a new technology developed on the basis of multi-discipline, and it has important application value in civil, military, medical, and some other fields[1]. In the scene matching aided navigation system, the matching reference image and real-time image are used to determine the real-time position of the UAV, and to correct the errors of inertial navigation system in order that the UAV can fly at a predetermined track [2]. The difficulties the multi-sensor image matching algorithm to overcome are that the imaging mechanism is different, the gray correlation is small, and there are many differences between the images, such as scale, view angle, brightness, resolution, and so on [3]. In recent years, many scholars at home and abroad have done a lot of research on the field of multi-sensor image matching [4,5,6]. At present, the commonly used scene matching algorithm is divided into three parts: region based image matching algorithm, image matching method based on transform domain and image matching algorithm based on feature [10]. Region based image matching methods mainly include region similarity matching method and mutual information matching method. In this kind of method, the pixels of the image are involved in the matching operation. It is difficult to achieve a high success rate of matching because the gray difference between the multi-sensor images is too large. The image matching method based on transform domain mainly includes Fourier-Mellin algorithm (FMT) and phase congruency algorithm. This kind of algorithm is not suitable for the image with a larger scale and translation, and is sensitive to the deformation of the image. In addition, the ability to adapt to the distortion of the image or the change of some content is poor [7]. Feature based image matching algorithm mainly includes point

[a] Corresponding author: 919147463@qq.com

feature matching algorithm [8], edge feature matching algorithm [9] and line segments feature matching algorithm [10,11,12]. The algorithm based on point feature has a higher precision in the image gray difference, but it is invalid for the image with large gray difference. Edge based matching algorithm has high matching accuracy, but the time complexity is too high. Based on the line segments feature matching algorithm, the feature is easy to extract and the time complexity is low, but it is difficult to ensure the accuracy of the matching in the case of the large gray difference.

The single image feature is difficult to be applied in the field of image matching, and the main method is the combination of line segment features and point features. In the literature [11], the control points are constructed by the extracted line features, and the matching degree function is established to get the matched control points. In literature [10], the line pairs are constructed by using the extracted line segments, and the similarity measure function is established to get the matching line pairs. However, when the two methods are used to construct the objective function, the length and angle information of the line segments are directly used. Therefore, there will be an match error when there is a scaling or rotation transformation between the images. In the literature [12], the control points are constructed by the extracted line features, and the affine transformation relation between the images is obtained by the control points, so that the two images to be matched are first aligned in the geometric space, which eliminates the influence of the affine transformation between the images. And then the matching line pairs are obtained. However, this method is to obtain the optimal affine transformation matrix by cyclic traversal and it result in high time complexity.

Aiming at the problems in the literature [12], this paper presents a matching algorithm based on the improved line segments feature, and it is based on the visible image and SAR image of typical artificial target. In this paper, the algorithm mainly includes line segments extraction, line segments optimization, construction of virtual feature points and feature matching. First of all, the line segments in the image are extracted and optimized. On line optimization, some short line segments and collinear line segments are removed. And the virtual feature points are constructed by the reserved line segments. Then a set of to be elected affine transformation matrices of two images is obtained by different combinations of virtual feature points. And then we construct the matching function, by which the relationship of affine transform between the two images are preliminarily determined. And the matching point set is obtained. Finally, we eliminate false matching points based on RANSAC algorithm and get the final transformation matrix to achieve accurate matching.

2 Algorithm introduction

2.1 Line segments extraction

The existing line segments extraction algorithms mainly include Hough transform [13], line detection method based on edge detection operator [15] and LSD line extraction algorithm [14]. Due to the influence of the application background, the matching algorithm applied to the aerial scene must be able to meet the requirements in terms of time complexity. In the above three algorithms, the time complexity of Hough transform is too high, so it is not suitable to be used in real time. The algorithm based on edge detection operator has low detection accuracy. It is difficult to extract the complete line segment. The LSD algorithm can be used to obtain the sub-pixel accuracy results in linear time. In this paper, LSD algorithm is used to extract the line segments in the image.

The LSD algorithm is based on the gradient value and direction of each pixel in the image, excluding the influence of pixels whose gradient values are too small. It combines pixels of similar gradient direction and adjacent pixel position to get line segments to be screened. The final line segments are determined by calculating the similarity of line segments to be screened. In this paper, the visible image is taken as the reference image, and the SAR image is used as the measured image. The line segments set extracted from the reference image and the measured image are respectively recorded as S_1 and S_1'. The result of using the LSD to extract line segments is shown in Figure 1.

DOI: 10.1051/itmconf/20171105001

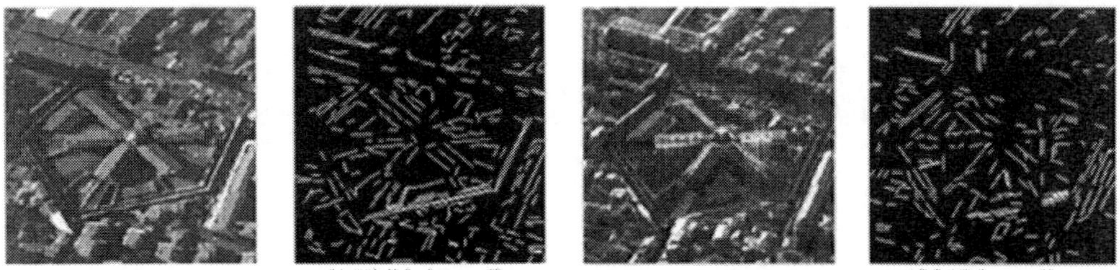

(a) Visible image　(b) Visible image line segment detection results　(c)SAR image　(d)SAR image line segment detection results

Figure 1. LSD line segments extraction

2.2 Line segments optimization

The method proposed by literature [12] can get a good matching result, but the method has a high time complexity. Therefore, the extracted line segments are optimized in this paper, and this will greatly reduce the time complexity of the algorithm. First of all, since the line segments extracted by LSD method do not intersect each other, it will result in some complete long segments being divided into several shorter segments. In order to preserve the original segment information in the image, we need to merge these short segments. At the same time, the image feature of this paper is obtained by the intersection points of the straight lines of the extracted line segments. The intersection of two collinear line segments and other segments are overlapped, and multiple collinear segments will lead to many repeated calculations. So we remove collinear segments before the feature is constructed.

2.2.1 line segments merging

For two given line segments s and s', the distance function $D_{\rho\theta}\left(s,s'\right)$ is defined according to the literature [16]. As shown in Figure 2, the angle $\Delta\theta$ and vertical distance Δd of two line segments are calculated. The vertical distance Δd of the two lines is defined as:

$$\Delta d = \max(d, d') \tag{1}$$

Where d is the distance from the midpoint of the line segment s to the line segment s', d' is the distance from the midpoint of the line segment s' to the line segment s.

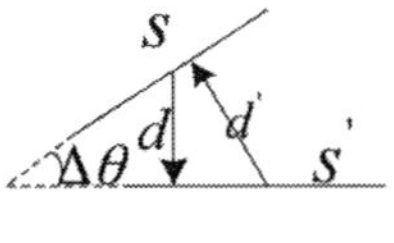

Figure 2. The angle and the vertical distance

Then the distance between the two line segments is defined as:

$$D_{\rho\theta}\left(s,s'\right) = \frac{1}{\sqrt{2}}\left(\left(\frac{\Delta\theta}{d_{\theta\max}}\right)^2 + \left(\frac{\Delta d}{d_{\rho\max}}\right)^2\right)^{1/2} \tag{2}$$

Where $d_{\rho\max}$ and $d_{\theta\max}$ are thresholds for angle and vertical distance, respectively. We set $d_{\rho\max} = 5pixels$, $d_{\theta\max} = 5°$. If two line segments are collinear, then $\Delta d = 0$ and $\Delta\theta = 0$, so $D_{\rho\theta}(s,s') = 0$. If $\Delta d = d_{\rho\max}$, $\Delta\theta = d_{\theta\max}$, then $D_{\rho\theta}(s,s') = 1$. Thus, we get the collinear condition of two line segments:

$$D_{\rho\theta}(s,s') \in [0,1] \tag{3}$$

At the same time, for two collinear line segments l_1 and l_2 that meet the above condition, if they don't have overlap region, and the distance between two most recent endpoints in the four endpoints of the two line segments is greater the threshold, which is set to 3 in this paper, the two line segments will not be merged. As shown in Figure 3, for three collinear line segments $\{l_1, l_2, l_3\}$, only l_1 and l_2 should be merged, l_2 and l_3 should not be merged.

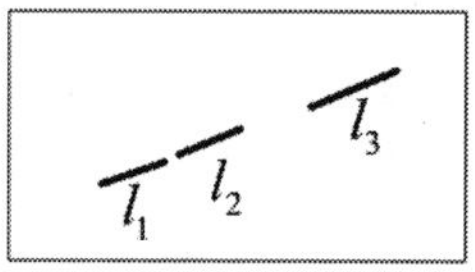

Figure 3. Collinear line segments

Thus, the merging rule of two line segments is obtained: the two lines are collinear, and the distance between the two most recent endpoints in the four endpoints of two line segments is less than the threshold. After merging, the set of line segments in the reference and measured image are recorded as S_2 and S_2', respectively, as shown in Figure 4 (a) (b).

2.2.2 Collinear segments elimination

The image feature of this paper is obtained by the intersection points of the straight lines of the extracted line segments. The intersection of two collinear line segments and other segments are overlapped, and multiple collinear segments will lead to many repeated calculations. So we eliminate the collinear line segments of merged line segment set. Specific methods are as follows: for any two line segments in the image, we determine whether they are collinear according to the formula (2). If they are collinear, then we calculate the length of each line segment, and retain the longer one. After excluding collinear line segments, the set of line segments in the reference and measured image are recorded as S_3 and S_3', respectively, as shown in Figure 4 (c) (d).

2.2.3 Line segment reservation

After the collinear line segments are removed, there are still a large number of line segments in the image. And the time complexity is still unable to meet the requirements. Therefore, for the above obtained line segments, we select the first 8% line segments with the longest length to construct features. After reservation, the set of line segments in the reference and measured image are recorded as S_4 and S_4', respectively, as shown in Figure 4 (e) (f).

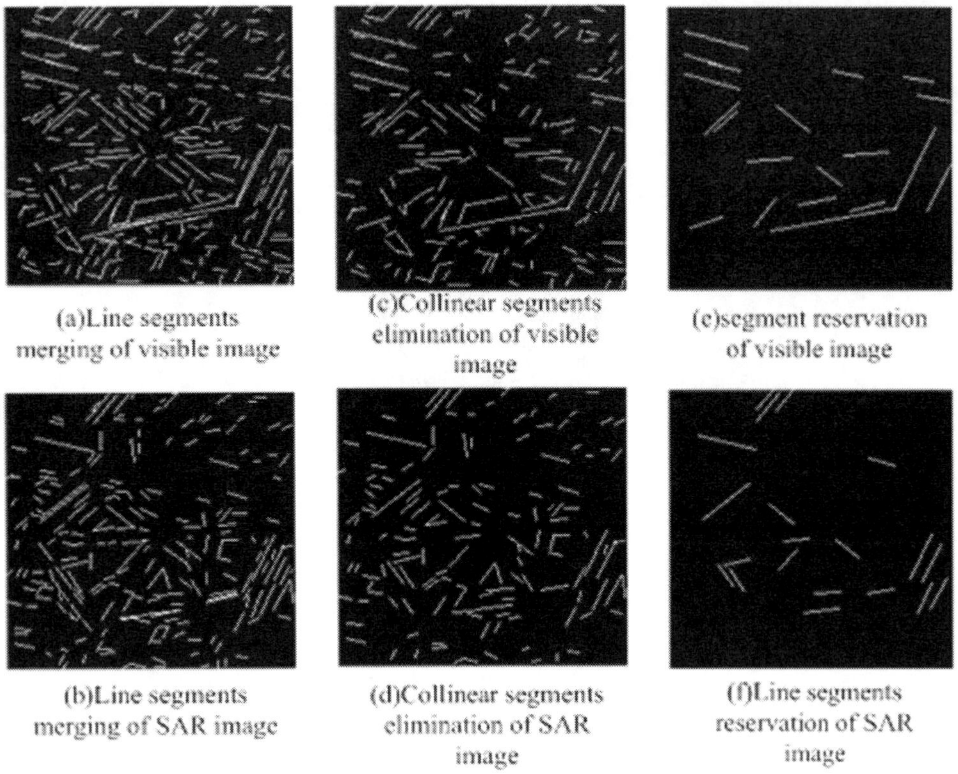

Figure 4. Line segment optimization results

2.3 Constructing virtual feature points

Visible images and SAR images have the same stable line segment features, but their location and length are often inconsistent. It is difficult to match directly. However, these line segments show stable geometric properties in the two kinds of images, such as parallel and intersection of lines. We therefore construct the virtual feature points by using the geometric properties of the line segments, and establish the matching function based on the virtual feature points.

If three non-collinear line segments or their extension lines don't intersect at the same point, they can form a triangle, as shown in Figure 5. A group of three line segments $\{a,b,c\}$ intersect at point $\{P_0,P_1,P_2\}$. Taking these three points as a set of virtual feature points, the virtual feature points do not necessarily correspond to an actual corner of the image, but can reflect the geometric properties of the line segments. In this paper, a set of triangles are constructed by S_4 and $S_4^{'}$, respectively. At the same time, we screen out the triangles which do not meet the requirements, and finally get the triangle set G_1 and $G_1^{'}$. Screening rules are to remove the triangles whose area is less than 20 and angle is less than 5 degrees. The area threshold 20 and angle threshold 5 degree are empirical values.

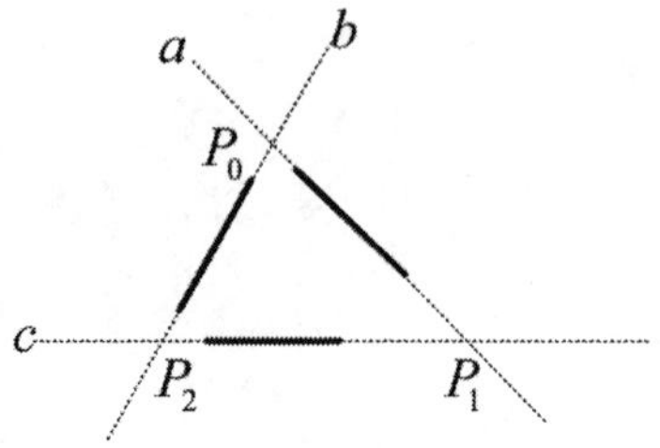

Figure 5. Three line segments or their extension form a triangle

After getting the triangle set, we match each of two triangles. According to clockwise order, there are three kinds of corresponding relations between the three vertices of a triangle $P_0P_1P_2$ in the line segment set G_1 and the three vertices of a triangle $P_0^{'}P_1^{'}P_2^{'}$ in the set $G_1^{'}$, as shown in Figure 6. And an affine transformation matrix can be obtained according to each corresponding relation.

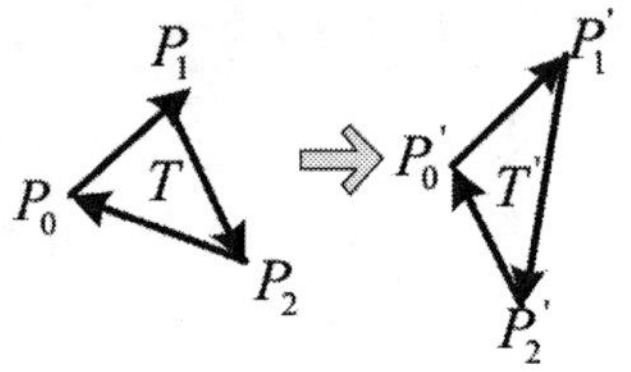

Figure 6. Correspondence of the three groups of two triangles

$$\{p_0, p_1, p_2\} \rightarrow \begin{cases} \{p_0^{'}, p_1^{'}, p_2^{'}\} \\ \{p_1^{'}, p_2^{'}, p_0^{'}\} \\ \{p_2^{'}, p_0^{'}, p_1^{'}\} \end{cases} \tag{4}$$

If M_1 and M_2 triangles are obtained in the triangle set G_1 and $G_1^{'}$, respectively, the number of candidate affine transformation matrices can be obtained: $N = 3 * M_1 * M_2$.

For the assignation $\{p_0, p_1, p_2\} \rightarrow \{p_0^{'}, p_1^{'}, p_2^{'}\}$, equations are:

$$p_i = T_1 \cdot p_i^{'} \forall i \quad 0,1,2 \tag{5}$$

Where $p_i = (x_i, y_i), p_i^{'} = (x_i^{'}, y_i^{'})$ are the coordinates of the points in the reference image and the measured image, and T_1 is the affine transformation.

2.4 Constructing matching degree function

After obtaining an affine transformation matrix, we use the related attributes of the extracted line segments to construct the matching function, so that we can measure the matching degree of the two images in the affine transformation. Finally, the affine transformation matrix with the maximum value of the matching function is chosen as the initial matching result.

Because the line segments in the $S_4^{'}$ are few, it is not possible to ensure that each line segment in S_4 can find line segments that meet the requirements in the $S_4^{'}$. So we select the line segment set $S_1^{'}$. The line segment set S_1^{*} are obtained by transforming $S_1^{'}$ using matrix T. And the reference image and measured image are aligned in the geometric space. Then, for each segment in S_4, we find line segments of the closest matching degree in S_1^*, and get the matching degree between the measured and the reference image under the affine transformation.

Firstly, the distance $D_{\rho\theta}(l_i,l_j)$ between the line segment l_i in S_4 and the line segment l_j in S_1^* is obtained by formula (2):

$$D_{\rho\theta}(l_i,l_j)=\frac{1}{\sqrt{2}}\left(\left(\frac{d_\rho(l_i,l_j)}{d_{\rho\max}}\right)^2+\left(\frac{d_\theta(l_i,l_j)}{d_{\theta\max}}\right)^2\right)^{1/2} \quad (6)$$

Where, the definition $d_\rho(l_i,l_j)$ is the same as $d_{\rho\max}$, and the definition $d_\theta(l_i,l_j)$ is the same as $d_{\theta\max}$.

According to the distance function, the matching degree of two line segments $Q(l_i,l_j)$ is defined as :

$$Q(l_i,l_j)=\begin{cases}1-D_{\rho\theta}(l_i,l_j) & D_{\rho\theta}(l_i,l_j)\le 1\\ 0 & D_{\rho\theta}(l_i,l_j)>1\end{cases} \quad (7)$$

The smaller the distance between the two lines is, the higher is the degree of matching.

Furthermore, the matching degree $Q(S_4,S_1^*)$ between the reference image and the measured image is defined as: the sum of the matching degree of each line segment in S_4 with line segments in S_1^*.

$$Q(S_4,S_1^*)=\sum_{s_i\in S_4}Q(l_i,S_1^*) \quad (8)$$

Where $Q(l_i,S_1^*)=MAX\left(\left\{Q(l_i,l_j)\middle|l_j\in S_1^*\right\}\right)$

After getting the affine transformation matrix T, which makes the objective function to get the maximum value, we can obtain the line segment set matching with S_4. In this paper, we use the midpoint of each line segment to represent the line segment. In this way, we get the candidate matching points set. Because the candidate matching points may be mismatched points, we use RANSAC algorithm to get the final matching points set.

3 Experimental results and analysis

In order to verify the effectiveness of the matching algorithm proposed in this paper, a large number of visible images and SAR images are used in simulation experiments. Due to limited space, only two groups of experimental results are given, as shown in Figure 7.

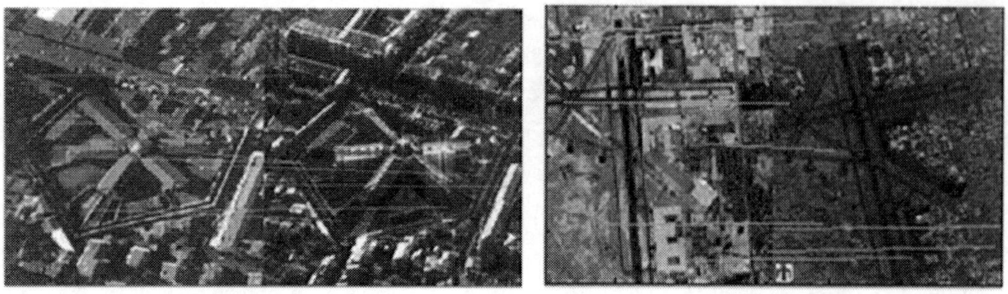

Experiment 1 Experiment 2

Figure 7. Matching results

In addition, in order to objectively evaluate this method, the method of this paper, the SIFT matching method, the mutual information method and the matching method proposed in literature [12] are quantitatively compared in two groups of experiments. As shown in Table 1.

Table 1. Performance comparison of the four algorithms

	Method	Matching time /s	Correct matching rate/%
Experiment 1	SIFT	3	0
	Mutual information	4120	32
	The method of [12]	754	87
	Algorithm in this paper	121	84
Experiment 2	SIFT	1	0
	Mutual information	2807	29
	The method of [12]	514	83
	Algorithm in this paper	83	87

It can be seen from the table that the matching time of this method is greatly shorter than that of the method in literature [12] under the premise of keeping high accuracy.

Conclusion

In this paper, we propose an improved matching algorithm for multi-sensor image based on line segments feature in order to solve the problem that there exist the large gray difference of multi-sensor image caused by different imaging mechanism. The experimental results show that the proposed algorithm has a good adaptability to image rotation and scaling, and the matching speed is greatly improved compared with the method in literature [12]. In addition, since the algorithm is based on line segments, and there are a large number of line segments in the artificial scene. However, in some natural scenes where line segments are difficult to extract, such as oceans and grasslands, the performance of the algorithm will be greatly affected.

References

1. Z. Lei, J. Longxu, H. Shuangli. Infrared and visible image fusion based on Nonsubsampled Contourlet transform and region classification, *Optics and precision engineering,* **23**, 810-818. (2015)
2. L. Xuefei. Research on Key Technologies of scene matching aided navigation system based on image features, *Nanjing University of Aeronautics & Astronautics* (2007)
3. W. Jianming, J. Zhongliang, W. Zheng. Study on an improved Hausdorff distance for

multi-sensor image matching, *Communications in Nonlinear Science & Numerical Simulation,* **17**, 513-520 (2012)
4. W. Yingdan, Y. Ming. A Multi-sensor Remote Sensing Image Matching Method Based on SIFT Operator and CRA Similarity Measure, *ISIE,* 115-118 (2011)
5. J. Son, S. Kim, K. Sohn. A Multi-vision Sensor-based Fast Localization System with Image Matching for Challenging Outdoor Environments, *Expert Systems with Applications,* **42**, 8830-8839 (2015)
6. Y. Luo, S. Juan, M. Qingxun. Multi-sensor Image Matching Method Based on Block Shape Features, *Infrared,* (2013)
7. S. Tongsheng, Z. Jian, et al. Accurate registration of spatial observation images for object detection, *Optics and precision engineering,* **22**, 2205- 2213 (2014)
8. D. Lowe. Distinctive Image Features from Scale-Invariant Keypoints, *International Journal of Computer Vision,* **60**, 91-110 (2004)
9. L. Zhuang, Z. Xianwei. Image matching based on edge similarity, *Journal of aircraft measurement and control,* **30**, 37-41 (2011)
10. L. Wang, P. Jia, Y. Zhang, et al. Multi-sensor image matching based on line features under complex object conditions, *Chinese Optics,* **9** (2016)
11. L. Ying, C. Yangyang, H. Xiaoyu, et al. Visible and SAR image registration based on line features and control points, *Journal of automation,* **38**, 1968-1974 (2012)
12. C. Enrique, S. Javier, M. Carlos. Segment-based registration technique for visual-infrared images, *Optical Engineering,* **39**, 282–289 (2000)
13. P. Hart. Use of the Hough transformation to detect lines and curves in pictures, *ACM,* 11-15 (1972)
14. R. Gioi, J. Jakubowicz, J. Morel, et al. LSD: A line segment detector, *Image Processing on Line*, **2**, 35-55 (2012)
15. J. Chengli. Study on road and airport extraction methods of SAR images, *National Defense Science and Technology University* (2006)
16. L. Yong, S. Robert, G. Jiading, Line segment based image registration, *Proc Spie*, 6822 (2008)

Classification for Motion Game Based on EEG Sensing

Ran WEI[1,3,4], Xing-Hua ZHANG[1,4], Xin DANG[2,3,4,a] and Guo-Hui LI[3]

[1]*School of Electronics and Information Engineering, Tianjin Polytechnic University, Tianjin, China*
[2]*School of Computer Science and Software Engineering, Tianjin Polytechnic University, Tianjin, China*
[3]*TEDA Orking Hi-Tech Company Limited, Tianjin, China*
[4]*Tianjin Key Laboratory of Optoelectronic Detection Technology and System, Tianjin, China*

Abstract. Due to the sensor technology and classification algorithm, the accuracy of the EEG and the motion signal based classification system are limited. And the motion sensor based interface system cannot show user's mental activity such as engagement situation, tiredness state and so on, which are very important in education and medical care situations. In this paper, an openBCI and a Kinect sensor based motion classification system are proposed. The experiments results shown that the proposed method are out form the traditional motion or EEG based activity classification systems, and it is expected to develop a novel interactive device for the children and elders based on the integration algorithm.

1 Introduction

Brain-computer interfaces (BCI) technology enable users to control a device according to his or her neural activity. An important part of the BCI motion features have been used in many motion games by using body surface sensors, such as Microsoft Kinect, Leapmotion, Nintendo Wii and so on. However, the accuracy of the electroencephalography (EEG) and the motion signal based classification system are limited, due to the sensor technology and classification algorithm. Moreover, the motion sensor based interface system cannot show user's mental activity such as engagement situation (positive or negative), tiredness state and so on, which are very important in education and medical care situations. The motions also couldn't be always performed well for the children and elders [1]. To settle this problem, BCI and motion technologies are both integrated together with follow two devices: (1) OpenBCI, which is an open source software framework for brain-computer interfaces. It is reported that the OpenBCI board could indeed be an effective alternative to traditional EEG amplifiers [2]. (2) Microsoft Kinect, which is a motion sensing input device for video game of the Xbox 360 and windows PC. The infrared projector and camera and a special microchip are used to track the movement of objects and individuals in three dimensions, and interpret specific gestures.

In this paper, an openBCI and a Microsoft Kinect sensor based motion classification system are proposed. Moreover, the motion and EEG features are applied to train and test the SVM classifiers.

[a] Corresponding author: xindang_tjpu@126.com

DOI: 10.1051/itmconf/20171105002

2 Activities Classification

Using Kinect, the users need not be bothered with body sensors and that the system can save the users from wearing sensors that can be intrusive [3, 4]. The Application Programmer's Interface (API) was used to interface with the Kinect sensor. Its skeletal tracking software provides an estimate for the position of 20 anatomical landmarks (30 Hz, 640*480 pixels). The skeleton is described by the following joints: head, neck, right shoulder, left shoulder, right elbow, left elbow, right hand, left hand, torso, right hip, left hip, right knee, left knee, right foot, and left foot. The Kinect has the capacity to determine the position of the center of specific joints by using a fixed and rather simple human skeleton, which can be measured for joint motion.

To uniquely identify a vector, two angles are calculated for each of these vectors.

$$\theta_Y = \cos^{-1}\left(\frac{v_{iy}}{|v_i|}\right) \qquad \theta_{XZ} = \cos^{-1}\left(\frac{v_{ix}}{|v_i|}\right) \tag{1}$$

where θ Y is the angle between joint vector vi and positive X-axis and viy denotes the Y component of vi. θ YZ is the angle between the projection of the vector on XZ- plane and X-axis. A set of fourteen vectors from the twenty joint points are calculated for the input of the feature extraction of the motion signals. Some parts of the body are not considered in calculation (head, wrists, and feet) as they contribute little to classifier the movement.

The OpenBCI board can be used to collect 8 lead EEG signals by standard electrodes. Data were recorded from 3 children (5±1.5 years old) and 3 elders (60±5). Our prototype application on a desktop computers and set it up to project the activities on the whiteboard. The Kinect is mounted at the top of the whiteboard. Five movement massages are conducted in all experiment which include "left", "right", "up", "down", "rest". In order to record user's motions and faces in all the activities, a HD camera was mounted near the Kinect. The openBCI board is fixed on the back of the Electro-Cap and transmits data to the windows PC by Bluetooth module.

2.1 Overall structure

The raw signals of skeleton and EEG are processed following the proposed classification system shown in Figure 1. The overall system structure is composed of the following steps. Firstly, removing the noise from the raw signals of the skeleton and EEG by using the 1€ Filter [5], which use a first order low-pass filter with an adaptive cut-off frequency and suitable for a high precision and responsiveness task of the event-driven system. Secondly, filtered signals are segmented at a constant size by framing. Furthermore, the motion/EEG features are obtained from the segmented signals. In the training stage, the SVM training produces support vectors for 4 classes of movement, NG movement, positive engagement, and negative engagement. During the testing stage, the SVM classifier classifies the input feature vectors into the different movement or engagement modes. The training and classification system are shown in Figure 2.

 DOI: 10.1051/itmconf/20171105002

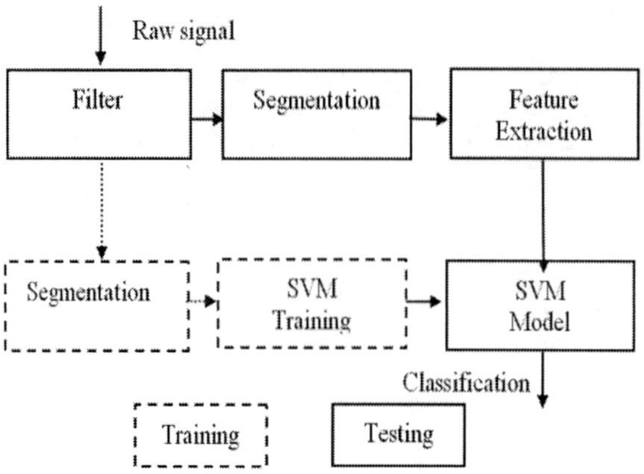

Figure 1. Block diagram of the event classification system.

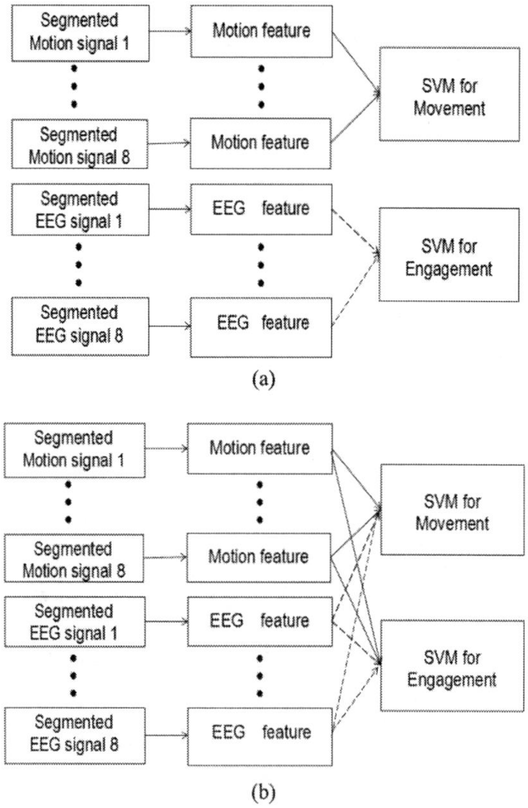

Figure 2. The training and classifying system

2.2 Feature extraction

For the movement and engagement classifier task, follow motion based features are considered:

1) Mean differentiation of joint angle;

 DOI: 10.1051/itmconf/20171105002

2) Median differentiation of joint angle;
3) Standard deviation of differentiation of joint angle.

EEG based features are considered as:
1) Mean of each lead EEG waves;
2) Median of each lead EEG waves;
3) Standard deviation of each lead EEG waves.

As the Motion and EEG recording was annotated per second, each feature vector was computed based on one second of motion and EEG signals. Each second-wise annotation indicates both the movement situation (Good or NG) and engagement situation (positive or negative). Each one-second period are divided into 8 equal epochs. For each epoch there are 14*3 corresponding motion feature vectors and 7*3*8 corresponding EEG feature vectors are calculated. Concatenated the results to form 336-dimensional and 1344-dimensional feature vectors for each second considered. These feature vectors were then collected, along with their corresponding annotations, to train our classier.

Two frameworks are considered in our experiments: I. The motion and EEG features are used for the training and classification of movement and engagement, respectively (Figure 2a); II. The motion and EEG features are both used for the SVM training and classification of movement and engagement (Figure 2b). For the framework I, we consider that the motion and EEG features are suitable for the movement and engagement classifier task; Furthermore, a classification model considered integrating the motion and EEG features are built in framework II.

In evaluation scheme, the classification was performed independently on the snoring sounds recorded by microphones, and its performance was compared in terms of sensitivity, specificity and accuracy:

$$\begin{aligned} Sen &= \frac{TP}{TP+FN} \times 100\% \\ Spe &= \frac{TN}{TN+FP} \times 100\% \\ Acc &= \frac{TP+TN}{TP+FN+FP+FN} \times 100\% \end{aligned} \tag{2}$$

where TP, TN, FP and FN are the number of true positive, true negative, false positive and false negative classified segments, respectively. Note that TP and TN refer to the number of correctly classification movement segments and the number of correctly classified positive engagement segments, respectively.

3 Results

In order to gain adequate results from the data of 3 children and 3 elders, proposed system is tested using four independent experiments, which include good movement, NG movement, positive engagement, and negative engagement tests. For the testing data, episodes of these four kinds of events were randomly extracted and manually annotated by using each of the recordings, and the data from the other subjects were used for training.

The proposed approaches were conducted using the datasets shown in Table 1. The data length for each class is given in the table, and the length in each cell was converted into frames using a frame size of 256ms, with a 50% overlap. The four experiments were performed independently. In addition, the training and testing data for each experiment were non-overlapped. The motion and EEG features for the experimental datasets were produced and applied to the SVM for training and classification.

Table 1. The information of experimental datasets (seconds)

Movement	Total	A	B	C	D	E	F
Good	1692	256	275	286	250	260	365
NG	2789	119	88	270	190	170	260
Positive	2667	256	245	239	264	246	320
Negative	2789	119	118	317	176	184	305

Motion has been recommended as the best feature for gesture detection [6, 7]. Therefore, several related works have used motion feature, and were able to obtain good performance. On the other hand, EEG feature shown the mental activity of the user. The confusion matrix is shown in Table 2.

Furthermore, the integrated features are applied to the movement and engagement SVM for training and classification according to the framework II. The confusion matrix is shown in Table 3.

For two frameworks, the most errors occurred between NG-Positive and Good-Negative. Integrated features achieved 97.4% and 94.4% accuracy for the Good-Positive, NG-Positive classification, while the accuracies for Good-Negative, and NG-Negative were 95.21% and 98.60%, respectively. Moreover, it can be seen from Tables 2 and 3 that the integrated features outperformed in movement and engagement classification task. Specifically, the motion and EEG based classification rates were 92.2%, 87.1%, 83.74% and 91.35%, for the Good-Positive, NG-Positive, Good-Negative, and NG-Negative, respectively.

Table 2. The results using the Framework I

	Good-Positive	NG-Positive	Good-Negative	NG-Negative
Good-Positive	**92.20%**	6.20%	1.50%	0.10%
NG-Positive	2.50%	**87.10%**	1.56%	8.84%
Good-Negative	5.41%	2.81%	**83.74%**	8.04%
NG-Negative	2.10%	6.40%	0.15%	**91.35%**

Table 3. The results using the Framework II

	Good-Positive	*NG-Positive*	*Good-Negative*	*NG-Negative*
Good-Positive	**97.40%**	1.25%	2.40%	-1.05%
NG-Positive	1.02%	**94.40%**	0.28%	4.30%
Good-Negative	3.41%	0.17%	**95.21%**	1.21%
NG-Negative	0.18%	1.09%	0.13%	**98.60%**

The classification results of three frameworks are shown in Table 4. Comparing the classifier performances for motion and EEG based features, it is evident that the performance of the framework II with the integrated features is superior in all experiments.

Table4. The classification results of 3 features

Feature-task	*Accuracy*	*Sensitivity*	*Specificity*
Motion-Movement	95.5±4.0%	98.2±0.1%	95.2±2.1%
EEG-Engagement	88.3±2.1%	98.5±0.6%	98.7±0.6%
Integrated-Movement	97.8±0.1%	99.6±0.1%	97.15±1.5%
Integrated-Engagement	97.1±1.2%	99.7±0.1%	99.4±0.3%

Conclusions

In this study, a simple and efficient movement and engagement classification system is present. Based on the motion and EEG feature and two SVM classifiers, proposed system outperforms the motion-based system. By using a low cost of the hardware platform, which can be installed in a children's home, nursing home, or clubs, the proposed system can be convenient to implement and allow the natural interface for the children. The motion features to guide automatic analysis and game designing. Moreover, other kinds of interactive technologies, such as speech recognition, will also be explored in the training system.

Acknowledgments

This work is supported by the National Natural Science Foundation of China (61403276), Tianjin Research Program of Application Foundation and Advanced Technology (14JCYBJC42400), Ministry of Education Returned Overseas Students to Start Research Fund(the 49th), Tianjin Key Laboratory of Cognitive Computing and Application.

References

1. Bartoli, L., Garzotto, F., Gelsomini, M., et al: Designing and evaluating touchless playful interaction for ASD children. In: Proceedings of the 2014 conference on Interaction design and children, pp. 17-26. (2014)
2. Frey, J.: Comparison of a consumer grade EEG amplifier with medical grade equipment in BCI applications. In: International BCI meeting, pp. 5442 - 5445. (2016)
3. Parry, I., Carbullido, C., Kawada, J., et al: Keeping up with video game technology: objective analysis of Xbox Kinect and PlayStation 3 Move for use in burn rehabilitation. Journal of the International Society for Burn Injuries, vol. 40(5), pp. 852-859. (2014)
4. Chang, Y. J., Han, W. Y., Tsai, Y. C.: A Kinect-based upper limb rehabilitation system to assist people with cerebral palsy. Research in Developmental Disabilities, vol. 34(11), pp. 3654-3659. (2013)
5. Casiez, G., Roussel, N., Vogel, D.: 1 € filter: a simple speed-based low-pass filter for noisy input in interactive systems. In: Proceedings of the SIGCHI Conference on Human Factors in Computing Systems. pp. 2527-2530. (2012)
6. Monir, S., Rubya, S., Ferdous, H. S.: Rotation and scale invariant posture recognition using Microsoft Kinect skeletal tracking feature. In: Intelligent Systems Design and Applications (ISDA), 12th International Conference on. IEEE, pp. 404-409. (2012)
7. Nguyen, D. D., Le, H. S.: Kinect Gesture Recognition: SVM vs. RVM. In: Knowledge and Systems Engineering (KSE), Seventh International Conference on. IEEE, pp. 395 - 400. (2015)

Application of Multi-sensor Information Fusion Technology on Fault Diagnosis of Electrical System

Ling-Wen MENG[1,a], Ji-Pu GAO[1], Ming-Yong XIN[1], Jin-Mei XIONG[2] and Rui GUO[2]

[1]*Guizhou Electric Power Research Institute of Guizhou Power Grid Co., Ltd., Guiyang, 550002, Guizhou, China*
[2] *Wuhan Zhongyuan Huadian Science & Technology Co., Ltd, Wuhan 430074, China*

Abstract. This paper presents a multi-sensor information fusion technology based on electrical system fault diagnosis model, analysis the multi-sensor information fusion technology of several structure layer and realization method, and discusses its application in fault diagnosis of electrical system. Select and implement appropriate methods for the information fusion, the different error characteristic parameters in electrical system can be fused and calculated by this model, and a more valuable conclusion for the fault diagnosis of electrical system can be provided.

1 Introduction

Electricity plays a vital role in human life. Fault diagnosis need to ensure that the electrical system is safe and reliable, without any potential accidents. However, in practice, whether the system is faulty can't be determined by diagnosis based on one parameter. But different angles of the electrical system operating parameters can be gotten by the multi-sensor information fusion technology, Thereby effectively integrating and merging all the parameters. Not only Fault diagnosis of electrical system can be guaranteed, but also identify and locate the electrical system failure accurately. This paper analyzes the multi-sensor information fusion technology and its application in the electrical system.

2 Technology of multi-sensor Information Fusion

Multi-sensor information fusion is a comprehensive multi-layer processing program. In order to realize the state estimation, including the situation estimation of the system and the risk estimation of the system, the system has the functions of detecting, predicting, merging and combining all the parameters measured in the electrical system.[1,2] The fault diagnosis system which is designed for the power system using multi-sensor information fusion technology, this technology including data fusion and knowledge fusion, moreover, data-knowledge fusion, namely data mining.

2.1 Layers of multi-sensor information fusion

As shown in Figure 1, information fusion can be divided into 3 layers [3].

[a] Corresponding author: 1205954738@qq.com

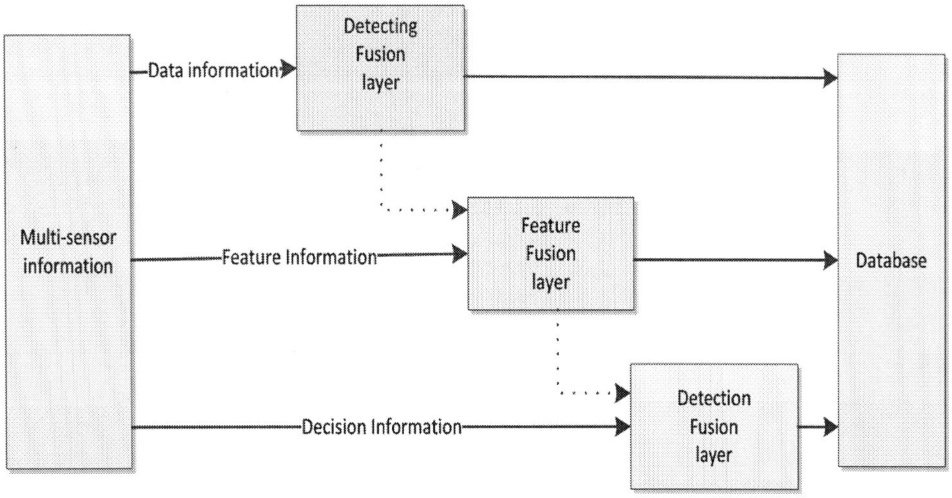

Figure 1. Caption of the Figure 1. Below the figure.

• Detection Layer: Primarily responsible for the fusion of the original information measured by the same type of sensor before preprocessing. So in the shortest time, the system operating conditions can be intuitively and sensitively detect the information. At the same time all the information is entered into the database for data mining. This is the prerequisite for fault diagnosis.

• Feature layer: Mainly responsible for the integration of the original information and related theoretical knowledge measured various sensors. In this way, it can accurately identify and locate faults in the electrical system. Thus, to ensure that when the system fails, the staff can know the cause of the malfunction in the shortest time. [4, 5]

• Decision layer: This is the highest layer in the system. System fuse all the information and related theoretical knowledge which is measured by different kinds of sensors, in order to achieve including fault isolation, redundant control for specific methods and techniques of fault diagnosis. And if the final countermeasure is feasible, the experience of such fault will be entered into the database for use at a certain time.

2.2 Methods of multi-sensor information fusion

In the variety of sensor information fusion methods, such as Bayesian theory, Damper Shafer (D-S) theory, neural network technology and some estimation theory and so on, as a modification theory of Bayes' theorem, D-S theory has more extensive application in multi-sensor information fusion technology. The method is able to display the determined probabilities and the uncertain probabilities of the information, and eliminates the simple assumptions about the unknown probabilities.

The evidence is set into mutually independent parts by the basic way of D-S theory. Every evidence part has a belief function which means probability distribution function to the related theoretical diagnosis. The total belief degree of comprehensive evidence based on related theoretical knowledge is obtained by fusion based on different clues and diagnosis of related theoretical knowledge.[6-8] Figure 2 shows the course of reasoning of D-S theory.

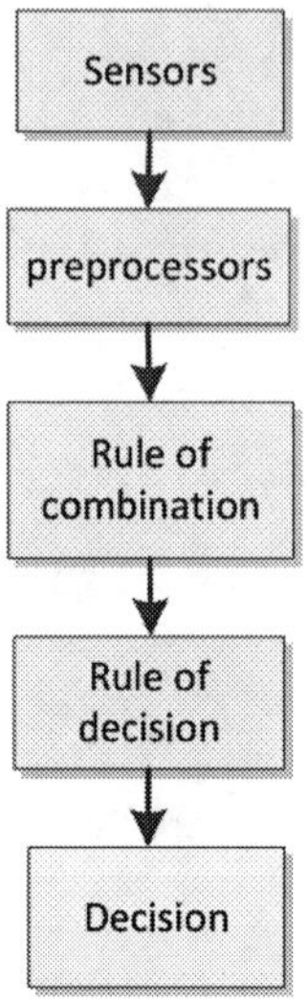

Figure 2. Schematic diagram of the course of reasoning of D-S theory

3 Application of multi-sensor information fusion technology on fault diagnosis of hydraulic system

3.1 Structure and principle of the fault diagnosis system

The electrical system common failure consist of include leakage, wire wear, corrosion, equipment fatigue and so on. The electrical system based on multi-sensor information fusion technology should monitor parameters which include power system voltage, current flow, equipment temperature, oil spills and so on. Detection and diagnosis system mainly includes two functional modules: data acquisition module and central process module. The data acquisition module includes sensors, signal conditioning circuits, A / D converters and bus interfaces, which are installed in each important part to collect and transmit each status signal of the power system. Central processing module Implement data analysis, fault diagnosis, integration and give response methods and other functions. It is mainly composed of CPU and computer software. The fault data of the electrical system is stored in the database[9].

Figure 3 shows the block diagram of the model of fault diagnosis system. Figure 4 shows the flow chart of the diagnostic program.

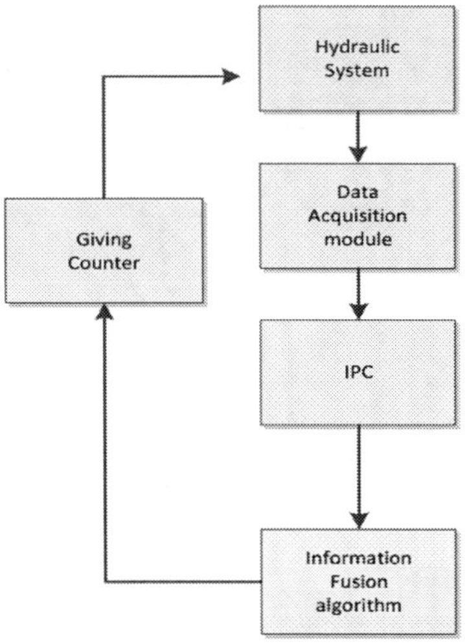

Figure 3. Block diagram of the model of fault diagnosis

3.2 Characteristics of the fault diagnosis system

• The system can monitor all the operating parameters at any time, including voltage, current, temperature, oil leakage.

• All operational parameters measured by the sensor are fused by the D-S theory .Not only can successfully achieve state recognition, but also for some typical failure to make a diagnosis and security protection.

3.3 Key technology of the fault diagnosis system

• Getting accurate signals id very important. It is critical to select the type of sensor reasonably and preprocess all available signals.

• The method of selecting and realizing information fusion is the guarantee of fault diagnosis. The D-S theory approach may not achieve the desired results under certain conditions, thus affecting the stability of the system. So neural network technology may be a better choice.

 DOI: 10.1051/itmconf/20171105003

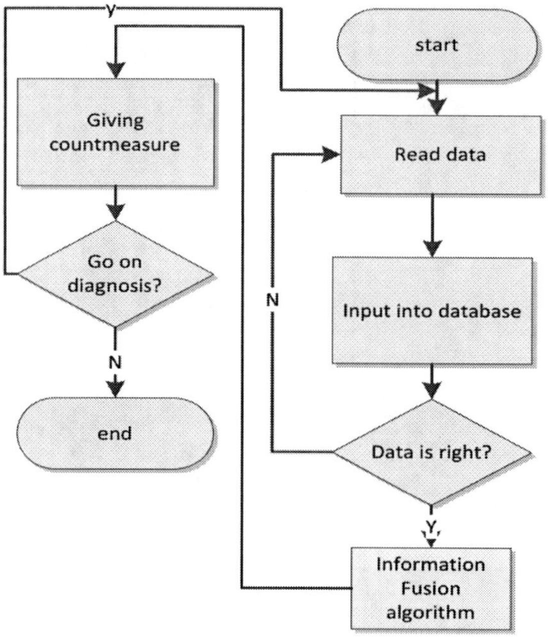

Figure 4. Flow chart of the diagnostic program

Conclusions

This paper presents a fault diagnosis system based on multi-sensor information fusion technology. The system realizes the status alarm and diagnosis of the electrical system. By making full use of a plurality of signals that can be measured from the power system, information fusion is realized, and the system is diagnosed in time. This can improve the efficiency and safety of the power system. This fault diagnosis system model based on electrical system described in this paper is a generalized model. In practice, for different power systems, fault diagnosis system monitoring parameters and the actual structure is different.

References

1. Jun Han, Jianzhong Zhang, Ming Cheng. Fault diagnosis of wind turbine based on multi- sensors information fusion technology, *IET renewable power generation. 8(3)* (2014)
2. Fengyong Lang,Xiaogang Li . Multi-Sensors Information Fusion Based on Momentis Method and Euclid Distance, *International Conference on Manufacturing Science and Technology*. (2011)
3. Fengyong Lang,Xiaogang Li. Multi-Sensors Information Fusion Based on Momentis Method and Euclid Distance. *International Conference on Manufacturing Science and Technology (ICMST)* (2012)
4. Halld L. Mathematical technique in multi-sensor data fusion Artech House 15–21 (2000)
5. H F. Durrant Whyte Sensor models and multi-sensor integration. *The Int. J. of Robotics Research* **7**(6) 87–92(2011)
6. Mourad O. Some notes on fusion of uncertainty information. *Int. J. of Intelligent Systems* **19**(6) 457–471(2012)
7. Richard T. Principles of effective multisensor data fusion, *Military Technology* **27**(5) 29–37.(2013)

8. An F Y, Lu H W, Liu C J, et al. Research and application of information fusion technology on machinery fault diagnosis *Chinese Journal of Chongqing University* **29**(1) 15–18 (2006)
9. Ge Bing, Yu Yi. Application of Multi-Sensors Data Fusion Technology in the Theodolite Tracking system. *International Conference on Mechanical and Electrical Technology 5th*. (2013)

Analysis of Environment Monitoring Platform Based on Wireless Sensor Network

Zhi-Jun YANG[1,2], Yang SU[1,a], Hong-Wei DING[1] and Yang-Yang DING[1]

[1]*School of Information Science and Engineering, Yunnan University, Kunming, 650091, China.*
[2]*The Academy for Educational Science Research, Educational Department of Yunnan Province, Kunming, 650223, China.*

Abstract. This paper established a TinyOS operating system for wireless sensor network of temperature and humidity monitoring system. It introduces the basic structure of the monitoring system, sensor nodes, the TinyOS operating system, and the NesC language. Besides, it preliminary design the application of temperature and humidity monitoring. This paper choose cc2538cb as the sensor nodes in the design of system, and introduce the design method of environmental monitoring mobile phone software.

1 Introduction

Wireless sensor network (WSN)[1] is the new generation of sensor network, has a very broad application prospect, and its development will have a profound impact on the various areas of human life and production. By arranging a large number of sensor nodes in the environment, we can collect a lot of physical data such as temperature and humidity to digitize the simulation environment of the physical world, giving people an intuitive understanding of the subtle changes that are happening in the environment in which we live. As people increasingly concern for the environment, environmental science is becoming more and more extensive. The sensor network can be used to monitor crop irrigation, environmental conditions, granary storage, etc. in environmental studies. With the development of the wireless sensor network technology, the wireless sensor network applications to the needs of environmental monitoring system is becoming more and more urgent[2].

In the aspect of environmental monitoring, temperature and humidity are two important parameters[5], this paper mainly analyzes the temperature and humidity collection method, using TinyOS as the embedded operating system, and writing the underlying driver to realize the collection of environmental data.

2 The structure of wireless sensor network

As shown in Figure 1, a typical sensor network system structure, including sensor nodes (groups), sink nodes, infrastructure networks (Internet or satellite) and management nodes (users)[5]. A large number of sensor nodes are randomly distributed within the monitoring area. The data collection through the sensor nodes are transmitted along the other sensor nodes hop-by-hop, and after the

[a] Corresponding author: 2402600114@qq.com

multi-hop route arrives at the sink node, the sink node passes the collected information to the user[3,5]. When the sink node is far away from the management node, it can converge to the network server through GSM, GPRS, and satellite. So the user can through the browser, mobile phone and other methods, observe the changes of environmental monitoring whenever and wherever possible.

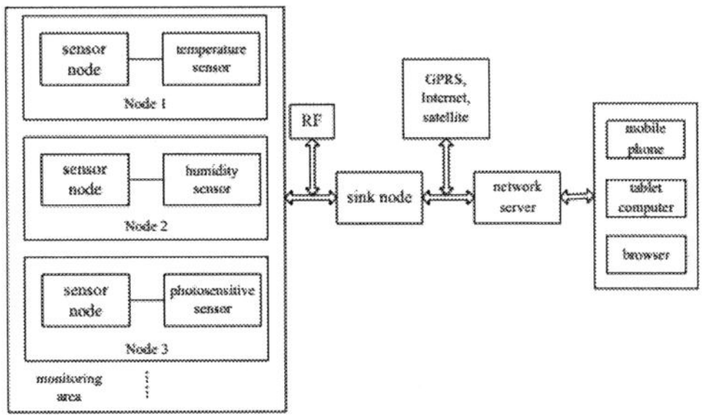

Figure 1. Sensor network architecture.

3 Software platform and hardware platform of the system

3.1 Implementation of system software platform

TinyOS is a modular wireless sensor network operating system developed by UC Berkeley (University of California, Berkeley) based on the US Department of Defense's "Smart Dust" project[8]. It depend on the event driven mechanism, with less code, low energy consumption, high concurrency, fast response characteristics, and can better meet the specific application. TinyOS is actually the standard for sensor network node operating system, which provides a component-based software framework for the integration of application-oriented wireless sensor network operating system[3,4]. The operating system does not distinguish between the user and kernel mode, and does not provide memory protection mechanism, but it can provide concurrent processing capability, under the condition of limited resources.

3.1.1 Component structure of TinyOS

Component technology in the embedded system has been widely used. The hardware and underlying software in the system are abstracted as a component, thus enabling external shielding. When the users are programming, only need to pay attention to the interfaces of the components, they are not necessary to understand the specific implementation process of the components, so as to improve the reusability and development efficiency of the software.

The TinyOS operating system provides a set of components for user invocation, including the main components, application components, execution components, sensor components, communication components and underlying hardware components[4], as shown in Table 1. Components from top to bottom can usually be divided into three categories: high-level software components, composite components and hardware abstract components. High-level software components achieve control, routing, data transmission and other application layer functions. Composite components simulate advanced hardware behavior, such as sensor components, communication components, etc.. Hardware abstract components map the physical hardware to TinyOS component model.

Table 1. TinyOS application structure.

main components		
application components		
communication components	execution components	sensor components
underlying hardware components		

3.1.2 NesC language

TinyOS was originally written in C language and assembly language, but researchers further study finds C language can not effectively and easily support the development of applications and operating systems of sensor network. So the researchers carried out some extensions on the basis of C language, combined component-based thinking with event-driven execution models, and developed nesC languages that support component programming[6,7].

The main features of the nesC language are as follows:

(1)Separation of structure and entity;

(2)Components can use or provide interfaces;

(3)The interface has bidirectional, for the same interface of the same component;

(4)Components are statically linked through interfaces;

(5)The nesC compiler can automatically mark the potential data competition caused by preemptive interrupts.

3.2 The design of system hardware platform

In the introduction of the sensor network system, the wireless sensor network mainly involves the hardware: sensor node, sink node, management platform. For the management platform, we can choose the computer, this article will not repeat them. The main difference between the sensor node and the sink node is whether the serial communication can be carried out, but now the mainstream sensor nodes have these two functions. At present, there are many kinds of sensor nodes and sink nodes, many research institutions have developed their own hardware platform, but the main difference between these hardware platforms is used in the processor, wireless communication, the discrepancy sensor configuration. Including CrossBow's TelosB series of nodes, Intel's Intel Mote (iMote) nodes[2].

3.2.1 Cc2538cb node

In the essay, the cc2538cb node is selected as the sensor node and the sink node. You choose what kind of hardware platform to run the prepared nesC code, then the most famous platform of TinyOS is TelosB node. TelosB is an open source, low-power wireless sensor node produced by Crossbow. TelosB node in line with IEEE802.15.4 protocol specification, the use of low-ultra power antenna templates. In order to meet the requirements of easy development and high fault tolerance in wireless sensor network. The onboard USB interface can modify and update the node program, also can collect information.

Cc2538cb node compared to the TelosB node is slightly less than in the low power consumption , but in the *RAM* memory, TelosB node use the cc2420 chip, the *RAM* memory only has 10K size, but cc2538cb node *RAM* memory has reached 32K.So the use of cc2538cb node do not have to worry about *RAM* storage space is not enough. Similarly, cc2420 *RF* characteristics compared with the cc2538 is still a bit stretched, in addition, cc2538cb node price is much cheaper, and very suitable for beginners to use, when they learn TinyOS.

DOI: 10.1051/itmconf/20171105004

3.2.2 Cc2538cb node structure

This article uses the cc2538cb node part of the design as shown in Figure 2.

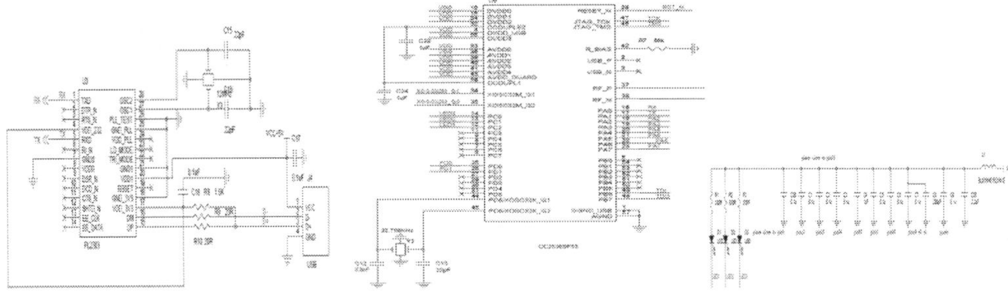

Figure 2. Cc2538cb node structure.

Cc2538cb node in the design process reserved ten IO port, from left to right are: GND,PD1,PD0,PA7, PA6, PA5,PA4,PA3,PA2,VDD,the distance is 2.00mm.Cc2538cb IO port can specify the function according to the software programming, such as UART, SPI, I2C, SSI, ADC, input, output, etc.Cc2538cb node doesn't weld sensor, but in the process we can use the reserved IO port to complete the sensor access or other chip bus communication.Cc2538cb node use PL2303 USB converter chip instead of using the 2538 USB function directly .Because the PL2303 driver for the virtual machine Linux/Ubuntu, Android etc. are driver-free, it can be more simple and fast use of Linux/Android.

4 Wireless transmission and data reception

4.1 Data transmission

The node program uses six components in the design process, including the *MainC* component, the time component *TimerMillliC*, the *AMSendC* component that controls the transmission, the *AMReceiverC* component that controls the reception, and the *LedsC* component. The relationship between the component and the interface as shown in the following Figure 3.

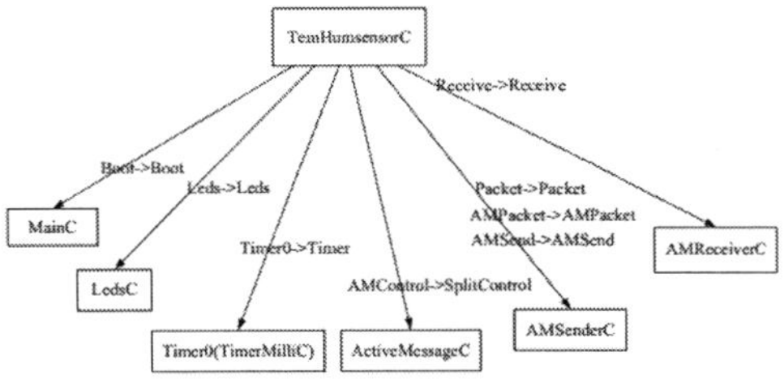

Figure 3. Relationship between components and interfaces.

We through the cc2538cb node reserved IO port to connect the sensor, this paper uses thedht11 sensor to measure the temperature and humidity in the environment, the sensor pin is connected with the IO port according to the corresponding relation. Next, in the TinyOS compiler environment to join the dht11 driver, the dht11 directory will be copied to the *tinyos-main-release_tinyos_2_1_2\tos\chips\cc2538*, where the dht11 directory contains *dht11.c* and *dht11.h* files. Then modify the *.Platform* file under the *tinyos-main-release_tinyos_2_1_2\tos\ platforms\cc2538cb* directory, increase the path *%T/chips/cc2538/dht11*. Finally, modify the*cc2538cb.rules* file under *tinyos-main-release_tinyos_2_1_2\support\make\cc2538cb* and add *EXTRA_MODULES + = $ (CHIP_DIR) /dht11/dht11.c* after *EXTRA_MODULES + =* ..... So, in the node programming we will add the program to read the sensor data, start the event, read the sensor data every 2 seconds, and the data will be stored in the packet. We use the *AMSend* interface to send packets, it can send data to the specified AM address, then the *Packet* and *AMPacket* interface into the *message_t* abstract data type. These interfaces are provided with the component *AMSendC*, although they can also be provided by *ActiveMessageC*, but *AMSendC* providesa virtual abstraction. Because the transceiver is the public resource, different components canbe used, so it needs to be virtualized to avoid mutual interference between different components. Next, add the program logic to ensure that no packets are sent, and finally through the *send* command send packets to all nodes within the scope of acceptance, according to SUCCESS command, interpretation of data has been successfully transmitted.

4.2 Data reception

Receive information through the *receive* interface to achieve, *receive* interface provide basic information to receive and forward information function, which is achieved by the *ActiveMessageC* component. In this way, it is possible to transfer information through the AM to the sink node. The sink node directly connected with the computer, then use computer to observe the data that is collected by sensor nodes, and achieve the environmental data monitoring and collection.

As shown in the following Figure 4.

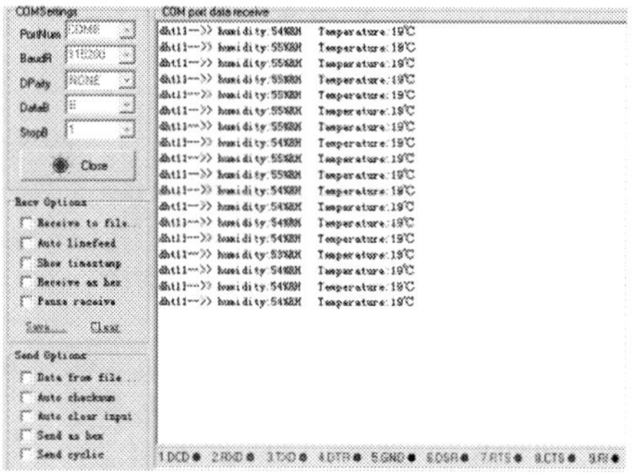

Figure 4. Data reception

5 Design of remote environment monitoring

5.1 Cloud server and database design

The Figure 5 shows the process of collecting data from sensor nodes to observe data through a computer or Android client. Since the database cannot be directly connected to the Android client, the server is used as a bridge between the two designs. We can use ECS (Elastic Compute Service). If we purchase it, we can deploy a virtual machine in the background, and will provide users with a public network IP, as the design system IP number. The client can communicate with the server through this IP connection. As the monitoring area contains multiple sensor nodes, this will produce a lot of data, so the system can be used in the design of MySQL database to store data. After ECS (Elastic Compute Service) build a good server environment and install the MySQL database, the code can be written with the Android client communication.

DOI: 10.1051/itmconf/20171105004

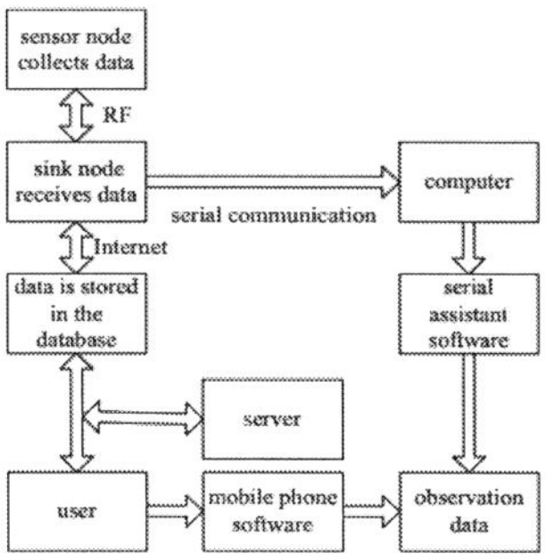

Figure 5. Data acquisition and observation process.

5.2 The design of android mobile phone software

The control interface of mobile phone software is the main way of interaction between the user and the device, the interface will affect the design of your environment monitoring system to promote. So a good interface design is essential, the design interface is considered an important factor in the operation is simple, free and convenient. Mobile phone software design mainly includes the following parts: user login interface, the main interface, function interface and the message of the push part. As shown below.

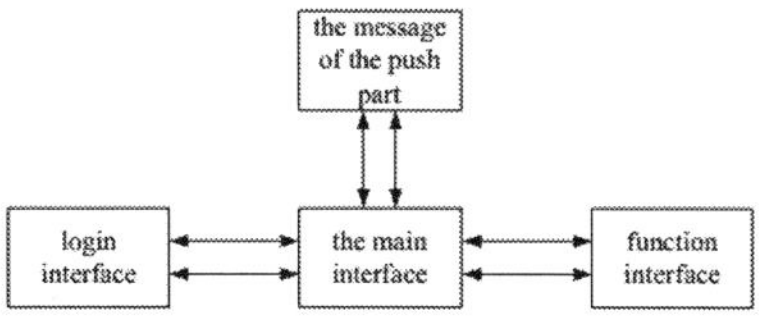

Figure 6. The main structure of Mobile phone software.

If the users enter the IP address assigned by the server in the login interface, as shown in Figure 7, they will enter the main interface. In the main interface, we can according to the needs of environmental monitoring choose to observe the main parameters, such as: temperature, humidity, light intensity and so on, as shown in Figure 8. Then, the waveforms and data changes of the environmental monitoring parameters can be displayed through the function interface. If the monitoring environment changes dramatically, or when a fire occurs, you can use message push technology, it can timely convey the message to the user, and cause people's attention.

Figure 7. The login interface.

Figure 8. The main interface.

Conclusions

Wireless sensor network[9,10] has a wide range of application prospects, this paper specifically analyzes the temperature and humidity data from the acquisition to the monitoring process, and make full use of the flexibility and scalability of wireless sensor network[4]. The introduction of TinyOS has a great impact on the development of wireless sensor network. TinyOS has a great advantage from simplifying the development and reduction of functions. It provides a basis for wireless sensor network environment data acquisition system. The wireless sensor network platform designed in this paper can be easily extended to other applications, which provides a good solution for the design of environmental monitoring and alarm subsystem in smart home.

Acknowledgements

This work was supported by the National Natural Science Foundation of China under Grant Nos.61461054 and 61461053.

References

1. Z.J.Yang,H.W.Ding,Z.Guan,L.Z.Zhu, A New Transportation Control System Based On Priority Differentiated Polling Strategy, *Proceedings of 2015 World Conference on Control, Electronics and Electrical Engineering*,vol.**116**,38-44,(2015).
2. T.Peng, The research and implementation of wireless sensor network environment monitorsystem based on TinyOS, Master thesis, *Beijing University Of Posts And Telecommunications*.(2010).
3. X.W.Zhai,M.Wu, Wireless Sensor Network Node Design and Implementation Based on TinyOS, *idea technology*,vol.**39**,no.3,57-60,(2015).
4. P.Y.Duan,C.G.Ning,L.P.Xu,C.X.Duan,Wireless Sensor Networks for Temperature and Humidity Acquisition System Based on TinyOS, *Computer system&application*,vol.**23**,no.8,53-58,(2014).
5. K.G.Qian,N.Sang,H.Ma, Design and Implement Wireless Sensor Network for Monitoring Temperature and Humidity Based of Tinyos, *Journal of Kunming University*,vol.**30**,no.4, (2008).
6. L.H.Yang,Y.Z.Li,J.Zhou, Design and implementation of smart home control system based on TinyOS, *Electronic Design Engineering*,vol.**23**,no.15,109-114,(2015).
7. C.P.Li,X.Chen, Intelligent Home Control System Based on TinyOS and Embedded Technology, *Microcontrollers & Embedded Systems*,no.1,22-25,(2016).
8. D.F.Chen,Z.S.Tao,D.Zhou,Design of point to point communication on CC2430 based on TinyOS, Electronic Design Engineering,vol.**18**,no.3,94-95,(2010).
9. Z.J.Yang,H.W.Ding, Characteristics of a Two-Class Polling System Model, TSINGHUA SCIENCE AND TECHNOLOGY, vol.**19**,no.5,516-520,(2014).
10. Z.J.Yang,H.W.Ding,C.L.Chen, Research on E(x) Characteristics of Two-Class Polling System of Exhaustive-Gated Service, *Acta Electronica Sinica,* no.4,775-778,(2014)

Game Equilibrium of False Information Diffusion in Public Crisis on Interpersonal Network

Kai LI[1,a] and Jia-Jia HAO[2]

[1]*Foreign Affairs Center of Ministry Industry and Information Technology Beijing, China*
[2]*School of Economics and management Yanshan University Qinghuangdao, China*

Abstract. The public crisis evolution will make a variety of impact on society, the public and the mass media will also focus on public crisis. In the evolution of public crisis, objective and non-objective information about the crisis will arise. Such harmful but not objective information is "false information". Various factors working together lead to the false information diffusion in public crisis. We will identify eight factors inducing false information in public crisis, and study the game equilibrium process of false information diffusion in public crisis on interpersonal network, and determine the equilibrium which was looked for. When the public identify that their interests are lower than the equilibrium, the false information is accepted, then false information on this node begins diffusing; When the public identify that their interests are higher than the equilibrium, the false information is identified, then diffusion on this node ends.

1. Introduction

With the rapid development of economic, the social and economic environment will become more complex and difficult to predict. By this time, the probability of public crisis occurring closely together will be enhanced greatly. When the public crisis happens, people tend to express their views of the event. But in the process of information diffusion, the content of the information may conflict with true information due to some artificial and inevitable factors. The false information such as rumor, gossip, hearsay, which is not in accordance with real information will surely contribute to the fear and anxiety of the public create more factors that lead to social instability. This is an main source of secondary damage of public crisis.

So what is the connotation of the "false information" in public crisis? What are the factors that led to the false information in public crisis? What kind of role did the inducing factors play in the spreading of false information in public crisis of game equilibrium? The research of these propositions has great importance in the scientific definition of the false information in public crisis. Meanwhile, to specify the inducing factors of false information in public crisis and their roles in the spread of game equilibrium is critical for us to grasp the development direction of the false information in public crisis and the factors that public care about in the event development .

[a] Corresponding author: likaigary@163.com

2 The connotation of the false information in public crisis

The evolution of the public crisis is actually a series of diffusion effects of crisis information[1]. With the appearing of an huge amounts of information, some discordant voices will arise. It will raise the possibility of public who lack recognition to echo it. At this time "false information" will appear. What is "false information"? "False information" is not the information in a real sense, it's the information that is "untruthfulness or unrealistic"[2]. False information has some other appellations, such as dummy message, inferior information, expanding information, the selfish information[3]. False information in public crisis is the information that looks like the real but actually not[4]. False information is the information transmitted in the non-public media channels. It is a kind of harmful information that is not true, not objective, not conductive to social stability and easy to mislead the public[5].

In addition to the research on the definition of false information, some scholars have studied the process of false information diffusion. They suggest that the essence of false information diffusion in public crisis is a class of complex nonlinear evolution process[6]. Thompson et al. established the rumor model which is similar to the Daley-Kendall model. Considering the effect of the population's diversity in the rumor spreading, they found that people's activity is the most sensitive parameter that will influence the spread of rumors. They also found that increasing activity can control the size of the rumor spreading[7]. Kawachi developed the dynamics model in finite and infinite dimensional with considering varying accepting degrees of different populations, and then derived the rumor diffusion threshold[8]. Based on the influence of different contact for eventually diffusion. Seki et al. discussed the results through mathematical simulation[9]. Huo et al. studied the interactive model between rumors spreading and the government's emergency utility and drew the phase diagram of the system through data simulation . On the basis of these, they put forward strategies and policy recommendations about emergency management[10]. Zhong et al. divided the information into real information and false information and discussed the process of crisis information diffusion from the perspective of ecology. They built the model of social crisis information diffusion which is based on Lotka-Volterra model. Then carried out simulation and empirical analysis for social crisis information diffusion and found that the diffusion of crisis information is closely related to the diffusion coefficient and diffusion rate[11].

Some of the researchers think that crisis information only has two states: Absolute truth and totally untrue. However, in our real life there is some information which seems real but actually not. There is also some which seems far from objective truth, but is the real information in fact. The reason of information become seemingly far from objective truth is that the partial distortion of strictly true objective information leads to the qualitative change of a small part information. Its essence is real and less harmful to the society. We define information with characters above as virtual information in this paper. The information that seems objectively true is false information as a whole with a part of the true appearance. We defined the information as the false information in this paper. The purpose of this study is to reveal the game equilibrium of false information diffusion. As long as the information is related to the public crisis, whether rumors or gossip or rumors are included in this paper.

3 Assumptions of false information Diffusion in public crisis

The process of false information diffusion in public crisis is a process of decision-making in two sides. There are utility values for people to evaluate what decisions should be made, which means the value of maximum satisfaction. So the diffusion of false information in public crisis is a process of game equilibrium. But in real life, the public are restrained by attention, emotion, ability and personal psychological, so the decisions they made are limited. The decision-making process is not complete and accurate under the interference of each external environment, which means that it is an incomplete and imperfect decision-making process.

When the false information in public crisis generated, individuals try to express their views from the aspects of the false information inducing factors in public crisis and to persuade other individuals to judge the fairness and security of the environment from these perspectives as well. Therefore, the process of false information diffusion in public crisis is the result from interactions of the eight factors which are mentioned above. Next, we will study the game equilibrium of false information diffusion in public crisis from the eight aspects.

Assumption1: Information of different aspects which the recipients try to express is independent, which means that the eight factors: culture, personal life needs, interpersonal relationship, group attitude, profit distribution, the sanity of legal system, the government credibility and development coordination are not related to each other. One of the intentions that contained in the comments is represented by i , the total information of type i is represented by $I_i = x_i + \varepsilon_i$. Where I_i represent the amounts of i , ε_i is the amount of uncertainty of the intention. ε_i is one of the normal distribution random variables. Then, we have $E(\varepsilon_i) = 0, \mathrm{var}(\varepsilon_i) = \delta_i^2$. The total intention of a particular aspect that individuals express is: $I = \Sigma x_i + \Sigma \varepsilon_i$.

Hypothesis2: The individuals who haven't accept the false information in public crisis will identify the information of their surrounding environment in all aspects which are independent. It means that they can judge fairness and security from the eight factors of culture, personal life needs, interpersonal relationship, group attitude, profit distribution, the sanity of legal system, the government credibility, and development coordination are not related to each other. The intention of a particular aspect distinguished in the comments of the individual who accepted false information can be represented by i in public crisis. The total information of type i is represented by $D_i = x_i + \varepsilon_{di}$. D_i represent the amounts of i . ε_{di} is a normal distribution random variable which represents the amount of uncertainty intention. We can derive the formula: $E(\varepsilon_{di}) = 0, \mathrm{var}(\varepsilon_{di}) = \delta_{di}^2$. The relevance between ε_i and ε_{di} is ρ_i . spreaders' intention from eight aspects are represented by i . The total intention of a particular aspect that individuals express is $D = \Sigma x_i + \Sigma \varepsilon_{di}$.

Hypothesis3: When the false information recipient express their intentions, the more information they express the more satisfied they are. In this article, we assume that this kind of satisfaction is π . It is proportional to the total amount of information they express. When the individuals who haven't accept false information distinguish the information, the more information they identify, the more satisfied they are. In this article, we assume that this kind of satisfaction is P , which is proportional to the total information that they identify. For the sake of simplicity, we assume:

$$\pi = \Sigma \pi_i = I = \Sigma I_i = \Sigma x_i + \Sigma \varepsilon_i \quad (1)$$

$$P = \Sigma P_i = D = \Sigma D_i = \Sigma x_i + \Sigma \varepsilon_{di} \quad (2)$$

In the formula (1).(2), i represents the eight kinds of intention contained in the false information in public crisis.

Hypothesis4: The utility of individual who haven't accepted the false information is the sense of achievement after judging the fairness of their surroundings and security. We set it as $u(w, x_i) = \ e^{r(w \ \ (x_i))}$. When the recipient expresses false information, the utility of is the satisfaction after resonate with other individuals. We set it as: $u(t_i, f_i, s_i) = E(\pi \ \ w)$. Where $(x_i) = \frac{1}{2} \Sigma c_i x_i^2$ is the emotional cost that the individuals who haven't accepted the false information spend on distinguishing the environment. $w = \Sigma w_i$ represents the satisfaction that the individuals who won't accept the false information have after identifying the false information(It also can be called the emotional cost that false information recipients paid). It is the linear combination of i , $w_i = t_i + f_i \ \pi_i + s_i p_i$. t_i represents the identity amount of the existing fixed environmental fairness and security. f_i represents the rate of being persuaded, s_i represents the rate of self-persuasion. $\pi \;\; w$ represents the false information recipients' sense of accomplishment after they persuaded others. i represents the eight aspects of the intention that the individuals want to express.

Hypothesis5: The model of false information diffusion in public crisis assume that the recipients of false information in public crisis want to achieve their own maximization of satisfaction by spreading false information. Meanwhile the individual who does not accept false information in public crisis will not spread the false information in public crisis and make themselves the most satisfaction in participation utility condition.

4 The equilibrium of the model

The decision model that the recipients in public crisis spread false information and individuals who haven't accepted false information in public crisis identify the information is following:

$$\begin{gathered}\max_{t_i,f_i,s_i} u(t_i,f_i,s_i)=E(\pi \;\; w)\\ S.t\\ x_i\in\arg\max E\left[\;e^{\;r(w\;\;(x_i))}\right]\\ E[\;e^{\;r(w\;\;(x_i))}]\geqslant E\left[\;e^{\;rw_0}\right]\end{gathered} \tag{3}$$

Where, w_0 represents the satisfaction before they identify the false information.

The process of false information diffusion in public crisis is a incomplete process. Which has a variety of combinations. To solve the balance of many combinations is very complicated and unnecessary. While the complete false information diffusion model in public crisis are comprehensive and representative, we solve the equilibrium in the process of the complete diffusion in this paper.

A complete diffusion process of the model for certainty equivalent equation is following:

$$\begin{gathered}\max_{x_i,t_i,f_i,si}\Sigma[(1\;\; f_i\;\; s_i)x_i\;\; t_i]\\ S.t\;\; x\in\arg\max_{x_i}\{\Sigma[(f_i+s_i)x_i\;\; t_i\;\; \frac{c_ix_i^2}{2}]\;\frac{1}{2}\Sigma(f_i^2\delta_i^2+2\rho_is_if\delta_{di}+s_i^2\delta_{di}^2)\}\\ \Sigma[(f_i+s_i)x_i\;\; t_i\;\; \frac{c_ix_i^2}{2}]\;\frac{r}{2}\Sigma(f_i^2\delta_i^2+2\rho_is_if\delta_{di}+s_i^2\delta_{di}^2)\geqslant w_0\end{gathered} \tag{4}$$

The equilibrium of formula (4) is following:

$$f_i^*=\frac{\delta_i^{\,2}\;\;\rho_i\delta_i\delta_{di}}{\delta_i^2\;\;2\rho_i\delta_i\delta_{di}+\delta_{di}^{\,2}}\frac{1}{1++rc_i\Omega_i} \tag{5}$$

$$s_i^*=\frac{\delta_{di}^{\,2}\;\;\rho_i\delta_i\delta_{di}}{\delta_i^2\;\;2\rho_i\delta_i\delta_{di}+\delta_{di}^{\,2}}\frac{1}{1++rc_i\Omega_i} \tag{6}$$

$$x_i^*=\frac{f_i^*+s_i^*}{c_i}=\frac{1}{c_i(1++rc_i\Omega_i)} \tag{7}$$

$$I^*=D^*=\Sigma x_i^*=\Sigma\frac{1}{c_i(1++rc_i\Omega_i)} \tag{8}$$

$$w^*=\Sigma w_i^*=\Sigma[t_i+\frac{1}{c_i(1++rc_i\Omega_i)^2}] \tag{9}$$

In the formula of (5).(6).(7).(8).(9), $\Omega_i=\dfrac{\delta_i^2\delta_{di}^2(1\;\;\rho_i)}{\delta_i^2+\delta_{di}^2\;\;2\rho_i\delta_i\delta_{di}}$, i represents eight kinds of intention that contained in false information in public crisis.

5 The game equilibrium rule of false information diffusion in public crisis on interpersonal network

(1) The equilibrium of false information diffusion in public crisis is determined by the following factors:

When the recipients of false information in public crisis spread information, the attitude stability is δ_i^2. The certainty of individuals who haven't accepted false information for fairness and security of the environment they lived is δ_{di}^2;

The fairness and safety factor that the individuals who haven't accepted false information in public crisis avoid the misjudgment for environment is r;

The emotional cost that individuals who haven't accepted false information in public crisis will pay to identify the environmental fairness and security is c_i;

The relevance between recipients spreading information and individuals who haven't accepted the false information identifying it is represented by ρ_i.

Through the analysis above ,we can know that the process of false information diffusion in public crisis is the communication between the spreader and the which is a result of interaction between subjective and objective factors.

The objective factors refer to the fairness and security of realistic environment. The subjective factors refer to the tendency that both of them express and identify information, psychological reactions and avoiding miscalculation. These factors will affect the transmission and the recognition of information, and make fluctuations in information diffusion process, which form the main reason for information difficult to control.

(2) The diffusion process of false information in public crisis is the process that the public judge the nature of the environment from multiple aspects and make a decision. The public is emotional complex, so the decision-making process is also the outcome of various complicated factors interaction. According to the analysis on the result of game equilibrium, the game equilibrium of false information diffusion process in public crisis is that intentions, the rate of being persuaded, the rate of self-persuasion change according to deciding factors' changes. The differences of marginal changes are shown in Table 1.

Table 1. The game equilibrium of false information diffusion in public crisis varies with each factor

Factors	f_i^*	s_i^*
δ_i	$\frac{\partial M}{\partial \delta_i}\frac{1}{G}\quad\frac{rc_iM}{G^2}\frac{\partial\Omega_i}{\partial\delta_i}$	$\frac{\partial N}{\partial \delta_i}\frac{1}{G}\quad\frac{rc_iN}{G^2}\frac{\partial\Omega_i}{\partial\delta_i}$
δ_{di}	$\frac{\partial M}{\partial \delta_{di}}\frac{1}{G}\quad\frac{rc_iM}{G^2}\frac{\partial\Omega_i}{\partial\delta_{di}}$	$\frac{\partial N}{\partial \delta_{di}}\frac{1}{G}\quad\frac{rc_iN}{G^2}\frac{\partial\Omega_i}{\partial\delta_{di}}$
c_i	$\frac{rc_iM}{G^2}\frac{\partial\Omega_i}{c_i}$	$\frac{rc_iN}{G^2}\frac{\partial\Omega_i}{c_i}$
ρ_i	$\frac{\partial M}{\partial \rho}\frac{1}{G}\quad\frac{rc_iM}{G^2}\frac{\partial\Omega_i}{\rho_i}$	$\frac{\partial N}{\partial \rho}\frac{1}{G}\quad\frac{rc_iN}{G^2}\frac{\partial\Omega_i}{\rho_i}$
r	$\frac{c_iM\Omega_i}{G^2}$	$\frac{c_iN\Omega_i}{G^2}$

In Table 1, $M = \frac{\delta_i^{\ 2} \quad \rho_i\delta_i\delta_{di}}{\delta_i^2 \quad 2\rho_i\delta_i\delta_{di} + \delta_{di}^{\ 2}}$,

$$N = \frac{\delta_{di}^{\ 2} \quad \rho_i\delta_i\delta_{di}}{\delta_i^2 \quad 2\rho_i\delta_i\delta_{di} + \delta_{di}^{\ 2}},$$

$$G = 1 + +rc_i\Omega_i,$$

$$\Omega_i = \frac{\delta_i^2\delta_{di}^2(1 \quad \rho_i)}{\delta_i^2 + \delta_{di}^2 \quad 2\rho_i\delta_i\delta_{di}}$$

The higher δ_i^2 (the attitude stability of false information recipient in public crisis when express information) is, the higher the rate of self-persuasion is. At the same time, the possibility of the individuals who haven't accepted the false information in public crisis being persuaded is higher; The higher δ_{di}^2 (the certainty the individuals have in environment fairness and security)is, the lower the rate of being persuaded and the rate of self-persuasion are.

The higher$r$(The factors that the individual who haven't accepted false information in public crisis) avoid the misjudgment for the environmental fairness and safety is, the lower the possibility of being persuaded and self-persuasion are. The more clearly that public can understand the environment around, the less willingly they want to waste time and effort to identify environmental justice and security. The result is that the probability to accept false information in public crisis is low.

When $\rho = 0$, the behavior of the individuals who spread the false information in public crisis is not related to the intention of the individuals who haven't accepted the false information in public crisis. When the false information recipients in public crisis express the false information, the uncertainty of expression will decline the probability of being persuaded. Meanwhile the ability of them to identify false information in public crisis will decrease and the satisfaction after identification will also fall. At this time, this information will only be accepted by a few people. The reason for this phenomenon is that the information is strictly false information and has small correlations with other individuals. It shows that the false information that can be diffused is a kind of information which is related to people's satisfaction in many aspects, which means the false information in public crisis that can be diffused is the information that is related to people's vital interests and life desires. This is in accordance with the definition in this paper.

When c_i (the emotional cost that individual who haven't accepted false information in public crisis will pay to identify the environmental fairness and security.)increases, the rate of being persuaded and the rate of self-persuasion will fall.

(3) When the spreaders spread false information or the individuals who haven't accepted the information recognize it, the most fundamental motivating factors are different. It means that the reasons that different individuals accept or refuse false information are different. It's not single factor, but the interaction of various objective and subjective factors. The false information spreader will enrich the content of false information according to their own circumstances. At the same time, the individuals will identify the false information according to the information provided by the spreaders and their own conditions, which will add to the complexity in game process of spreading and recognizing false information.

(4) The satisfaction after recognizing false information changes according to the fluctuation of certainty for each inducing factors in all aspects. It means that the certainty attitude of environmental fairness and security that the individual who haven't accepted the false information in public crisis is associated with the satisfaction after they identify it. The emotion cost that the recipient in public crisis paid is related to the attitude stability of environmental fairness and security.

(5) When $\frac{\delta_{di}^{\ 2} \quad \rho_i\delta_i\delta_{di}}{\delta_i^2 \quad 2\rho_i\delta_i\delta_{di} + \delta_{di}^{\ 2}}\frac{1}{1 + +rc_i\Omega_i} > \frac{\delta_{dj}^{\ 2} \quad \rho_i\delta_j\delta_{dj}}{\delta_i^2 \quad 2\rho_i\delta_j\delta_{dj} + \delta_{dj}^{\ 2}}\frac{1}{1 + +rc_j\Omega_j}$, the rate of self-persuasion though intention i is higher than the intention j for the individuals who haven't identified

DOI: 10.1051/itmconf/20171106001

the false information in public crisis, $s_i^* > s_j^*$. It means that we can identify the false information in public crisis easier according to the intention of i.

whe $\dfrac{\delta_i^2 \quad \rho_i\delta_i\delta_{di}}{\delta_i^2 \quad 2\rho_i\delta_i\delta_{di}+\delta_{di}^2}\dfrac{1}{1++rc_i\Omega_i} > \dfrac{\delta_j^2 \quad \rho_i\delta_j\delta_{dj}}{\delta_i^2 \quad 2\rho_i\delta_j\delta_{dj}+\delta_{dj}^2}\dfrac{1}{1++rc_j\Omega_j}$, the rate of being persuaded through intention i is higher than the intention j for the individual who haven't accepted the false information in public crisis, $f_i^* > f_j^*$. It means that the spreaders and individuals who haven't accepted information resonate on the intention i. In this case, the individuals who haven't accepted the false information in public crisis will accept false information easily. The individuals who haven't accepted the false information in public crisis should distinguish the intention selectively. Sometimes they cannot obtain the greatest satisfaction even exhausted all intentions. It can also lead to excessive information identification and increase dissatisfaction.

6 Diffusion process of false information in public crisis on interpersonal network

The thought of liberty and democracy spur people to continually judge the fairness of the surroundings, especially when public crisis happens. With the increasing frequency of judgment, the of social development and the imbalance of the profit distribution lead to dissatisfaction with their surroundings. At this time, people want to express their dissatisfaction by proper channels and they expect the dissatisfaction can be solved. But some evasive and laissez faire behaviors of some departments have intensified people's sense of injustice. So people will express their views in the range of their communication, which can't show the real facts completely. The information with part of distortion mingles with the citizen's personal feelings of events and it is biased. But the unfairness and security of their surrounding environment let them believe that their views of the event are correct. Thus the false information in public crisis will be inspired. The process is shown in Figure 1.

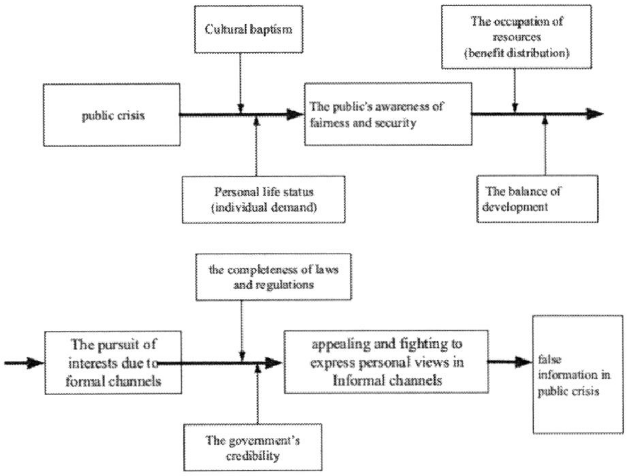

Figure 1. The emerging process of false information in public crisis

When false information in public crisis generates, the public will judge the fairness according to the resources they occupied, the culture they accepted, their personal status, etc. If the public's decision results are that the public environment is fair, then the false information in public crisis does not involve the public interest. The enthusiasms of the public to express false information will disappear. This is the phenomenon that "we don't care the thing that has nothing to do with us". They just take the event or situation as the topic of communication rather than take it as a way of expressing social discontent. So the false information in public crisis is identified successfully and will stop spreading. And when the public's decision results are that they are not treated fairly or they feel the environment around them isn't safe, they want to express their dissatisfaction in some ways. If they get the deserved interests from normal complaint channels, it will stop spreading. If the complaint through formal channels is not successful, people will choose to accept false information and diffuse it in their interpersonal network. The process is shown in Figure 2.

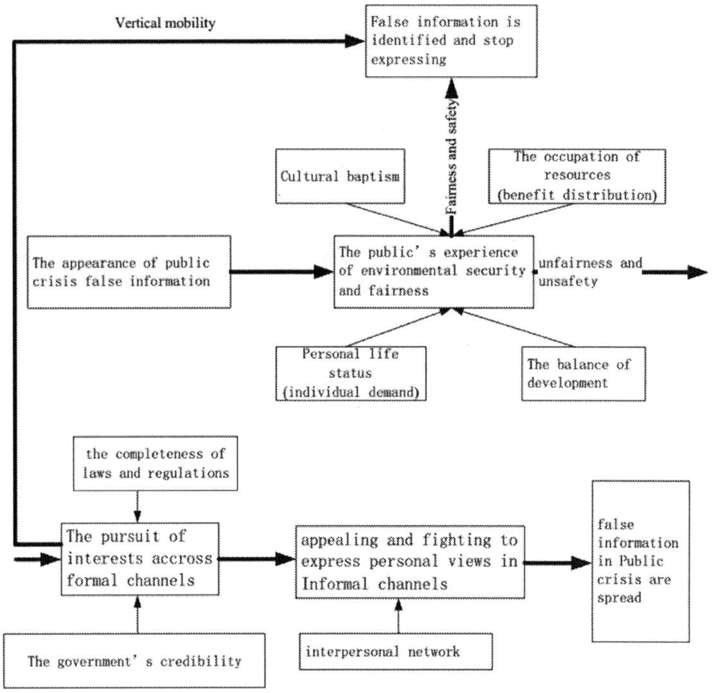

Figure 2. The spread process of false information in Public crisis

7 The interventions of false information diffusion in public crisis

(1) When public crisis generates, some objective and subjective factors, which contain the fairness and safety of the real environment, the tendency of different individual to spread and identify the false information, psychological reaction, avoiding mistakes, will affect the process of false information diffusion. They will lead to false information spreading or stopping spreading. At the same time, the interaction of subjective and objective factors increase supervision difficulties of false information in public crisis. When we want to intervene the process of false information diffusion in public crisis, we can begin from two aspects.

From the aspects of the external soft environment, the relevant departments should plan as a whole, increase the balance of social development, reduce the phenomenon of distribution unequally and increase public's satisfaction of their surroundings. Beyond that, the relevant departments should also increase the degree of supervision and regulation from the environment for living. For example, they can meet the public's needs of safe environment from the aspect of environmental enhancement, improving medical level, improving the quality of education, raising employment rate, etc. They should complete the corresponding laws and regulations, and specify the responsibility scope of the relevant departments. When the public interests are violated and complain to the relevant departments, the departments should resolved it in time. The phenomenon of shirking responsibility and omission should be put an end in order to increase the public's sense of security.

From the aspects of the public themselves, the stability of attitude, the emotion cost of identifying false information in public crisis and the part authenticity of the false information's kernel are the factors that can affect individuals to accept false information. That is the instability of external environment can make the public to suspect their safety. The relevant departments should establish feasible crisis guarantee system and implement it in order to reduce the doubts of the public. They should do a good job of crisis aftermath, eliminate the motion of unfair and insecurity, enhance the public's certainty degree of environmental fairness and safety, which means they should reduce the cost of identification of the false information and the attitude stability. Thus when public crisis happens, the public are not willing to and also have no need to spread false information.

(2)When the spreaders spread false information or the individuals who haven't accepted the information recognize it, the most fundamental motivating factors are different. It means that the reasons that different individuals accept or refuse false information are different. The individuals will distinguish the intention selectively. Sometimes they cannot obtain the greatest satisfaction even exhausted all intentions. It can also lead to excessive information identification and increase dissatisfaction. If they resonate on intentions, the individuals will accept the crisis information. So when the false information generates, the relevant departments should intervene it according to different principal contradictions in different areas, which requires the apartments to do well in crisis management and specify the principal contradictions that will dissatisfy the public in different areas.

(3) False information in public crisis is concerned more by the public. If force to stop its spreading, we will infuriate the spreaders and make matters worse. Indirect measures should be taken in the relevant departments, rather than deny part of the authenticity .At the same time in the process of resource allocation, we should insist on human-oriented principle, the principle of high efficiency, sustainability, fairness principle and reduce the degree of public's complaint and dissatisfaction about the social system and decrease the number of inducing factors about false information diffusion in public crisis

References

1. Z. Gang, X. Q. Yang, Info. J, 22-25 (2006)
2. X. Feng, tech. Phil, *People's Publishing House,* (2007)
3. W. d. Cheng, Jinggangshan University. J, (Social Sciences),54-59(2012)
4. L. Tuo, Journal of Information, 155-157 (2008)
5. L. Tuo, F. W. Yu, Z.g. Fa, Info. Stud:Theo& Appl, 825-828 (2008)
6. F. W. Yu, L. Tuo, Z. g. Fa, Journal of Information, 8(2007)
7. K. Thompson, Tech. Repo BU-1642-M,(2003)
8. K. Kawachi, *Nonlinear Analysis: Real World Applications* , 1989 -2028(2008)
9. K. Kawachi, M. Seki, Theo Biol. J, **253**, 55-60(2008)
10. L. A. Huo, P. Q. Huang, X .Fang, Phys A: Stat. Mech. Appl, **1**, 3267-3274(2011)
11. Q. Zhong, W. Qi, L. Zhang. Syst. Engi-Theo&Prac, **32**, 104-110(2012)

ITM Web of Conferences **11**, 06002 (2017) DOI: 10.1051/itmconf/20171106002
IST2017

A Self-adaptive Bit-level Color Image Encryption Algorithm Based on Generalized Arnold Map

Rui-Song YE[1,a], Hui-Qing HUANG[2], Yu-Cheng LI[1], Chang WANG[1] and Min-Yu LIAO[1]

[1]*Department of Mathematics, Shantou University, Shantou, Guangdong, 515063, China*
[2]*School of Mathematics, Jiaying University, Meizhou, Guangdong, 514015, China*

Abstract. A self-adaptive bit-level color image encryption algorithm based on generalized Arnold map is proposed. The red, green, blue components of the plain-image with height H and width W are decomposed into 8-bit planes and one three-dimensional bit matrix with size $H \times W \times 24$ is obtained. The generalized Arnold map is used to generate pseudo-random sequences to scramble the resulted three-dimensional bit matrix by sort-based approach. The scrambled 3D bit matrix is then rearranged to be one scrambled color image. Chaotic sequences produced by another generalized Arnold map are used to diffuse the resulted red, green, blue components in a cross way to get more encryption effects. Self-adaptive strategy is adopted in both the scrambling stage and diffusion stage, meaning that the key streams are all related to the content of the plain-image and therefore the encryption algorithm show strong robustness against known/chosen plaintext attacks. Some other performances are carried out, including key space, key sensitivity, histogram, correlation coefficients between adjacent pixels, information entropy and difference attack analysis, etc. All the experimental results show that the proposed image encryption algorithm is secure and effective for practical application.

1 Introduction

With the rapid development of computer network and multimedia processing technology, large amounts of information like audio, image and video transmitted by the network. More than 70% of the information transmitting in the network is related to image information. The security transmission and storage of image information attract more and more attention. Image encryption is usually adopted to handle the security issue. Image with large data volume, strong correlation and high redundancy, makes the traditional encryption algorithms like the International Data Encryption Algorithm (IDEA) and Advanced Encryption Standard (AES) reduce encryption efficiency, which cannot meet the requirements of real-time applications. Therefore, the traditional encryption algorithms cannot be suitable for encrypting digital images [1]. Thanks to the inherent natures of chaotic sequences generated by chaotic systems, such as pseudo-randomness, strong sensitivity to initial conditions and control parameters, unpredictability, etc., chaos-based image encryption technology has a broad application prospect. In the last two decades, many chaotic image encryption algorithms had been presented and investigated extensively [2-7].

[a] Corresponding author: rsye@stu.edu.cn

Color image contains the red (R) , green (G), blue (B) color components, among which provides more abundant information. Many of existed color image encryption algorithms used the same method to encrypt R, G, B components, which means that the image is encrypted three times independently, ignoring the correlation between R, G, B components, and those components are easily attacked. In this paper, we present a novel self-adaptive color image encryption algorithm with a sort-based scrambling strategy for the 3D bit matrix and color components' diffusion in a cross way. The R, G, B color components of the plain-image with size of $H \times W$ and 256 grayscale levels are decomposed into 8-bit planes and one three-dimensional (3D) bit matrix with size $H \times W \times 24$ is yielded. One generalized Arnold map is used to generate pseudo-random sequences to scramble the resulted 3D bit matrix by sort-based approach. The scrambled 3D bit matrix is then rearranged to be one scrambled color image. Such a kind of operation changes the pixels' positions as well as pixels color components' intensity values. It reduces the correlation between R, G, B components and therefore improves the security and performance significantly. Another generalized Arnold map is applied to diffuse the resulted R, G, B components in a cross way to get more encryption effects. To achieve desirable key sensitivity and plaintext sensitivity, both the scrambling stage and the diffusion stage adopt self-adaptive strategy, where the key streams are all related to the content of the plain-image and therefore the encryption algorithm show strong robustness against known/chosen plaintext attacks. Some other performances are carried out, including key space, key sensitivity, histogram, correlation coefficients between adjacent pixels, information entropy and difference attack analysis. All the experimental results show that the proposed image encryption algorithm is highly secure and demonstrates excellent performance.

2 The Proposed image encryption algorithm

A color plain-image P can be expressed by a 3D matrix of size $H \times W \times 3$ meaning that the image is of height H and width W. We assume that the three base color components are denoted by 2D matrices R, G, B respectively. The three base color components R, G, B are all composed of 8 bit planes. We rearrange the color plain-image in bit planes mode to get one 3D bit-plane matrix *P3D* sized $H \times W \times 24$. One generalized Arnold map is appied to generate chaotic sequences to scramble *P3D* at bit-level and another generalized Arnold map is used to diffuse the resulted R, G, B components in a cross way to achieve more encryption effect. The complete proposed image encryption algorithm is composed of one round of 3D bit matrix permutation and one diffusion process of the R, G, B components. It is outlined as follows.

Step 1. Generation of pseudo-random sequences x, y for 3D bit matrix *P3D*'s permutation process. With cipher keys x_0, y_0, a, b, we iterate the generalized Arnold map (1) for N times and reject the transient points $\{(x_k, y_k): k=0, 1, \cdots, N-1\}$ to avoid the harmful effect. The values of (x_0, y_0) are reset to be (x_N, y_N) and the map (1) with new initial values (x_0, y_0) is applied to yield $\{(x_k, y_k): k = 1, \cdots, L+12\}$ where $L = \max\{H, W\}$. We note that N is set to be related to the content of plain-image to enhance the encryption algorithm's robustness against known plaintext and chosen plaintext attacks. N is calculated by mod(*sum1*, 100)+30 where *sum1* is the number of one in the 3D bit-plane matrix *P3D* and function mod(*e*, *f*) resturns the remainder of integer *e* divided by integer *f*.

$$\begin{pmatrix} x_{n+1} \\ y_{n+1} \end{pmatrix} = \begin{pmatrix} 1 & a \\ b & 1+ab \end{pmatrix} \begin{pmatrix} x_n \\ y_n \end{pmatrix} \bmod 1. \quad (1)$$

Step 2. Sort three sequences

$\{x_k, k = 1, \cdots, H\}$, $\{y_k, k = 1, \cdots, W\}$, $\{v_k, k = 1, \cdots, 24\} = \{x_{H+1}, \cdots, x_{H+12}, y_{W+1}, \cdots, y_{W+12}\}$

in ascendant order to get the new sequences $\{x_k^{'}, k=1,\cdots,H\}$, $\{y_k^{'}, k=1,\cdots,W\}$, $\{v_1^{'},\cdots,v_{24}^{'}\}$ and the position indices $\{t_k, k=1,\cdots,H\}$, $\{s_k, k=1,\cdots,W\}$, $\{u_k, k=1,\cdots,24\}$ such that $x_k^{'}=x_{t_k}$, $y_k^{'}=y_{s_k}$, $v_k^{'}=v_{u_k}$ respectively. We get three P-boxes T,S,U: $T=\{t_1,\cdots,t_H\}, S=\{s_1,\cdots,s_W\}, U=\{u_1,\cdots,u_{24}\}$.

Step 3. Permute the 3D bit-plane matrix *P3D* by P-boxes T,S,U respectively to get one new 3D bit matrix *P3D1*: $P3D1(i,j,k)=P3D(t_i,s_j,u_k), i=1,...,H; j=1,...,W, k=1,...,24$. The resulted 3D bit matrix *P3D1* is converted to be one color image *PI* with height H and width W such that each color component consisting of 256 grayscale levels. The corresponding color components for *PI* are still denoted by R,G,B.

Step 4. Generation of pseudo-random sequences w,z for the diffusion process. With cipher keys w_0, z_0, a_1, b_1, N_1, we iterate the generalized Arnold map (1) for N_1 times and reject the transient points $\{(w_k,z_k): k=0, 1,\cdots,N_1-1\}$ to avoid the harmful effect. The values of (w_0,z_0) are reset to be (w_{N_1},z_{N_1}) and the chaotic map (1) with new initial values (w_0,z_0) is applied to yield $\{(w_k,z_k): k=1,\cdots,HW\}$. The resulted $\{(w_k,z_k): k=1,\cdots,HW\}$ is used to generate the pseudo-random gray value sequences by

$$x(n)=\text{mod}(\text{floor}(x_n\times 10^{14}),256), y(n)=\text{mod}(\text{floor}(y_n\times 10^{14}),256), n=1,\cdots,HW,$$

where function floor(x) returns the largest integer less than or equal to x. The vectors $x(n), y(n), n=1,2,\cdots,HW$ are then converted into two 2D matrices X,Y with size $H\times W$.

Step 5. We Calculate the sum of all the pixels' gray values of R,G and determine the value of $k2,k3$ by

$$k2=\text{mod}(\sum_{i=1}^{H}\sum_{j=1}^{W}R(i,j),2),\ k3=\text{mod}(\sum_{i=1}^{H}\sum_{j=1}^{W}G(i,j),2).$$

Then we substitute the pixels values of G,B components by

$$G1=\begin{cases}\text{mod}(G+R+X,256),\text{if } k2=0,\\ \text{mod}(G+R+Y,256),\text{if } k2=1,\end{cases}\quad B1=\begin{cases}\text{mod}(B+G1+X,256),\text{if } k3=0,\\ \text{mod}(B+G1+Y,256),\text{if } k3=1.\end{cases}$$

The sum of all the pixels' gray values of $B1$ is then used to determine the value of $k4$ and change the values of R by

$$k4=\text{mod}(\sum_{i=1}^{H}\sum_{j=1}^{W}B1(i,j),2)\ ,\ R1=\begin{cases}\text{mod}(R+B1+X,256),\text{if } k4=0,\\ \text{mod}(R+B1+Y,256),\text{if } k4=1.\end{cases}$$

The resulted color cipher-image of plain-image Lena (Figure 1(a)) consists of the three base color components $R1,G1,B1$, as shown in Figure 1(b).

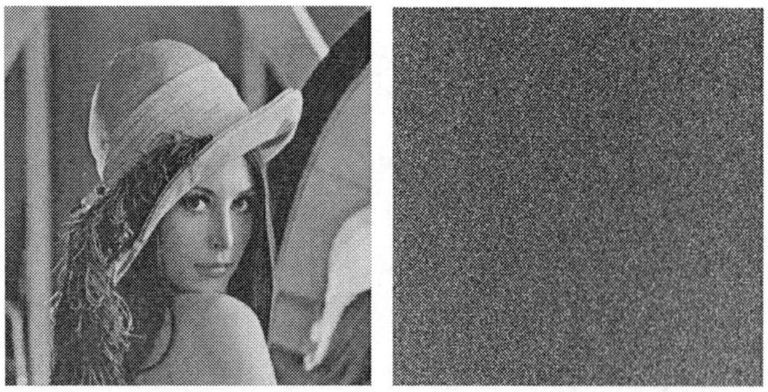

(a) (b)

 DOI: 10.1051/itmconf/20171106002

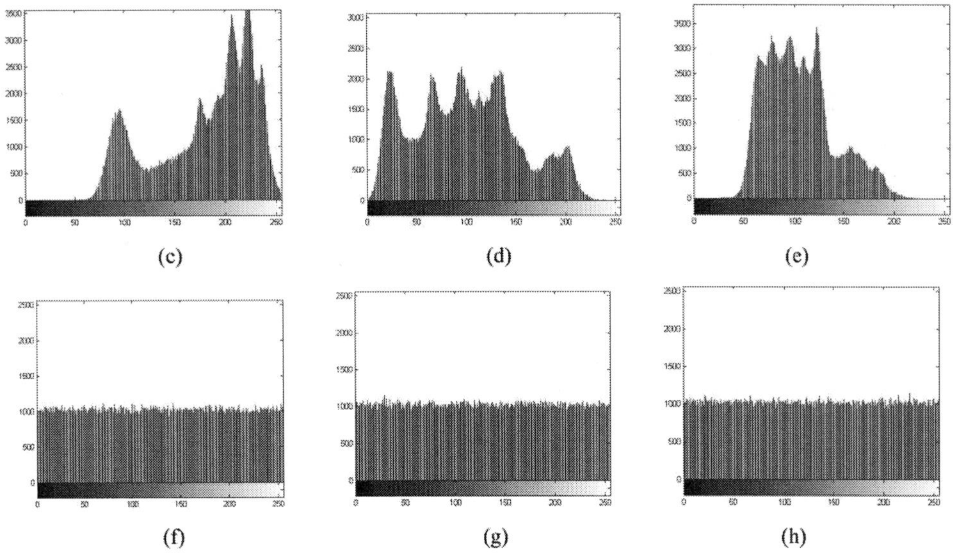

Figure 1. The encrypted results: (a) plain-image Lena; (b) cipher-image; (c)-(e) histograms for R, G, B components of Lena; (f)-(h) histograms for R, G, B components of cipher-image.

3 Performance analysis

An ideal cryptosystem requires high sensitivity to cipher keys, i.e., the cipher-text should have high correlation with cipher keys [1]. Furthermore, an ideal cryptosystem should have a large key space to make brute-force attack infeasible; it should also well resist various kinds of attacks like statistical attack, differential attack, etc. Some performance and security analysis will be carried out in this section, including the most important ones like key sensitivity, key space, statistical analysis (histogram analysis, information entropy analysis, correlation coefficients between adjacent pixels), and differential attack analysis. All the analysis shows that the proposed image encryption algorithm is secure enough thanks to its high sensitivity of the control parameters and initial conditions of the considered chaotic systems, large key space, and satisfactory self-adaptive approach.

3.1 Histogram analysis

Histogram analysis is applied to demonstrate the pixel distribution over the available intensity levels of an image. Regarding a 24-bit true color image, three histograms can be depicted for each 8-bit red, green and blue color components. We encrypt the color plain-image Lena one round with cipher keys $(x_0, y_0, a, b, w_0, z_0, a_1, b_1, N_1)$ to be (0.37, 0.59, 0.73, 0.81, 0.43, 0.59, 0.26, 0.41,100), and then plot the histograms of red, green, blue components of plain-image and cipher-image as shown in Figure 1(c)-(h). It follows from the histograms of the cipher-image that they are fairly uniform and significantly different from the corresponding histograms of the plain-image, and therefore the proposed image encryption algorithm is strongly robust against histogram analysis.

3.2 Correlation analysis between adjacent pixels

It is a common sense that each pixel is highly related to its adjacent pixels either at horizontal, vertical or diagonal direction for one nature image with definite visual content. An ideal cryptosystem should

 DOI: 10.1051/itmconf/20171106002

generate cipher-images with less correlation between adjacent pixels. We calculate the correlation coefficient of the whole pairs by

$$Cr = \frac{cov(x,y)}{\sqrt{D(x)}\sqrt{D(y)}},\quad cov(x,y) = \frac{1}{T}\sum_{i=1}^{T}(x_i - E(x))(y_i - E(y))\quad E(x) = \frac{1}{T}\sum_{i=1}^{T}x_i,\quad D(x) = \frac{1}{T}\sum_{i=1}^{T}(x_i - E(x))^2 \quad (2)$$

where x_i, y_i form the i-th pair of horizontally, vertically or diagonally adjacent pixels and $T = H\times(W-1), (H-1)\times W, (H-1)\times(W-1)$ for the three cases respectively. The correlation coefficients of horizontally, vertically, diagonally adjacent pixels for plain-image Lena and its cipher-image are given in Table 1. One can observe from Table 1 that the proposed image encryption algorithm significantly reduces the correlation between the adjacent pixels of the plain-image.

We also calculate the correlation coefficients between the red, green, blue components of the plain-image and the cipher-image. The numerical results are given in Table 2, Table3. We can see from Table 2 that the coefficients Crg, Crb, Cgb between the R, G, B components of the plain-image is close to 1, while those of the cipher-image is close to zero. The correlation coefficients between the red, green, blue components of the plain-image and cipher-image are all close to zero. All these results indicate that the proposed image encryption algorithm reduces the correlations of the three base color components significantly.

Table 1. Correlation coefficients between adjacent pixels of plain-image and cipher-image.

		Correlation between adjacent pixels		
		Red	Green	Blue
Horizontal	Plain-image	0.9753	0.9871	0.9634
	Cipher-image	-0.0020	-0.0022	0.0005
Vertical	Plain-image	0.9748	0.9872	0.9630
	Cipher-image	-0.0007	-0.0039	-0.0021
Diagonal	Plain-image	0.9532	0.9741	0.9334
	Cipher-image	-0.0002	-0.0011	-0.0001

Table 2. Correlation coefficients between the R, G, B components within the plain-image and cipher-image.

	Crg	Crb	Cgb
Plain-image	0.8856	0.6995	0.9191
Cipher-image	-0.0003	-0.0007	0.0005

Table 3. Correlation coefficients between the R, G, B components of plain-image and cipher-image.

		Plain-image		
		Red	Green	Blue
Cipher-image	Red	0.0016	0.0038	0.0039
	Green	-0.0007	-0.0010	-0.0004
	Blue	-0.0008	-0.0014	-0.0014

3.3 Information entropy analysis

Information entropy is an index to measure the randomness of information sequence [8]. It can be applied to measure the uniformity of image histogram as well. The entropy $H(m)$ of a message source m can be calculated by $H(m) = -\sum_{i=0}^{K-1} p(m_i)\log(p(m_i))$ (bits), where K is the total number of symbols m, $p(m_i)$ represents the probability of occurrence of symbol m_i and log denotes the base 2 logarithm so that the entropy is expressed in bits. Considering a random source with 256 outcomes, sharing equal probability, its entropy equals to 8. For a 24-bit color image, the information entropy for red, green, blue color components can be calculated respectively. We have calculated the information entropy for plain- image Lena and its cipher-image. The results are shown in Table 4. The values of information entropy for the cipher-image are very-very close to the expected value of truly random image, i.e., 8bits, implying that the proposed encryption algorithm is extremely robust against entropy attacks.

Table 4. Information entropy analysis.

	Red	Green	Blue
Plain-image	7.2634	7.5899	6.9854
Cipher-image	7.9994	7.9993	7.9993

3.4 Difference attack analysis

Differential cryptanalysis of a block cipher is the study of how differences in a plaintext can affect the resultant differences in the ciphertext with the same cipher key. It is usually done by implementing the chosen plaintext attack. Regarding image cryptosystems, attackers generally make a minor change (e.g., modify only one pixel) of the plain-image, and compare two cipher-images (obtained by applying the same cipher key on two plain-images having one pixel difference only) to find out some meaningful relationships between the plain-image and the cipher-image. If a meaningful relationship between plain-image and cipher-image can be found, it may further help the opponents to determine the cipher keys or equivalent key streams. If one slight change in the plain-image will cause significant, random and unpredictable changes in the cipher-image, then the encryption algorithm will resist differential attack efficiently.

Usually two most common measures NPCR (number of pixel change rate) and UACI (unified average changing intensity) are used to test the robustness of image cryptosystems against the differential cryptanalysis. If $C^{R/G/B}$ and $\bar{C}^{R/G/B}$ represent the R, G, B components for two cipher-images, then NPCR and UACI for each color component are calculated by

$$\text{NPCR}^{R/G/B} = \frac{\sum_{i=1}^{H}\sum_{j=1}^{W} D_{i,j}^{R/G/B}}{W \times H} \times 100\%, \quad D_{i,j}^{R/G/B} = \begin{cases} 1, \text{ if } C_{i,j}^{R/G/B} \neq \bar{C}_{i,j}^{R/G/B}, \\ 0, \text{ if } C_{i,j}^{R/G/B} = \bar{C}_{i,j}^{R/G/B}, \end{cases}$$

$$\text{UACI}^{R/G/B} = \frac{1}{W \times H}\sum_{i=1}^{H}\sum_{j=1}^{W}\frac{|C_{i,j}^{R/G/B} - \bar{C}_{i,j}^{R/G/B}|}{2^{L^{R/G/B}} - 1} \times 100\%.$$

We have performed the differential analysis by calculating NPCR and UACI on plain-image Lena. The analysis has been done by randomly choosing 10 pixels in plain-image, and changing one of the three color intensity values by one unit randomly at the selective pixel as well. The averages of 10 NPCR values and 10 UACI values thus obtained for all three color components are given in Table 5. It is clear that the NPCR and UACI values are very close to the expected values, thus the proposed image encryption technique shows good sensitivity to plaintext and hence invulnerable to differential attacks.

Table 5. Difference analysis of plain-image Lena.

Average NPCR (%)			Average UACI (%)		
Red	Green	Blue	Red	Green	Blue
99.5998	99.6110	99.6112	33.4212	33.4531	33.4738

3.5 Key sensitivity analysis

The key space of an encryption algorithm is composed of the total number of different cipher keys that can be used in the encryption procedure. The high sensitivity of the cipher-image to initial conditions and control parameters is inherent to any chaotic system. A good image encryption algorithm should contain sufficiently large key space. It should be sensitive to cipher keys as well, and thus can effectively prevent invaders decrypting original data even after they invest large amounts of time and resources. Strong key sensitivity is an essential feature of an effective cryptosystem. Key sensitivity of a cryptosystem can be observed and simulated from two aspects: (i) significantly different cipher-images should be generated even if keys with tiny difference are applied to encrypt the same plain-image; (ii) the cipher-image cannot be decrypted even if there is minor difference between encryption and decryption keys. We will use the following cipher keys to perform the simulations (one is master cipher key MKEY, the other keys are set by introducing a slight change to one of the parameters of master cipher key with all other parameters unchanged). Master cipher key is set to be $(x_0, y_0, a, b, w_0, z_0, a_1, b_1, N_1)$= (0.37, 0.59, 0.73, 0.81, 0.43, 0.59, 0.26, 0.41,100). Nine slightly different keys are

SKEY1 $(x_0 - 10^{-14}, y_0, a, b, w_0, z_0, a_1, b_1, N_1)$; SKEY2 $(x_0, y_0 - 10^{-14}, a, b, w_0, z_0, a_1, b_1, N_1)$;
SKEY3 $(x_0, y_0, a - 10^{-14}, b, w_0, z_0, a_1, b_1, N_1)$; SKEY4 $(x_0, y_0, a, b - 10^{-14}, w_0, z_0, a_1, b_1, N_1)$;
SKEY5 $(x_0, y_0, a, b, w_0 - 10^{-14}, z_0, a_1, b_1, N_2)$; SKEY6 $(x_0, y_0, a, b, w_0, z_0 - 10^{-14}, a_1, b_1, N_1)$;
SKEY7 $(x_0, y_0, a, b, w_0, z_0, a_1 - 10^{-14}, b_1, N_1)$; SKEY8 $(x_0, y_0, a, b, w_0, z_0, a_1, b_1 - 10^{-14}, N_1)$;
SKEY9 $(x_0, y_0, a, b, w_0, z_0, a_1, b_1, N_1 + 1)$.

(i) To estimate the key sensitivity for the first case, we encrypt plain-image Lena with MKEY and get the first cipher-image, then we encrypt Lena with SKEY1-SKEY9 and get nine cipher-images respectively. The correlation coefficients between the first cipher-image and the other nine cipher-images are calculated by Eq. (2). The experimental results are shown in Table 6. From the results, we can see that all the correlation coefficients are very small which indicate that even there is only slightly difference between the cipher keys, the cipher-images are greatly different. Hence the proposed encryption algorithm is extremely sensitive to the cipher keys.

(ii) Decryption using keys with minor difference is also performed in order to evaluate the key sensitivity of the second case. Firstly, we decrypt the cipher image using MKEY and we get the plain-image Lena. Secondly, nine decrypted images are produced as we decrypt the cipher-image using SKEY1-SKEY9 respectively. We have computed the correlation coefficients between Lena and nine decrypted images. The results are given in Table 7. It follows from Table 7 that there is even only a tiny difference between the decipher keys, the decrypted images have low correlation coefficients with the plain-image Lena. As for the second case, the proposed encryption algorithm also shows highly sensitivity to the cipher keys.

Since the permutation process is irrelevant to the diffusion process, the key space consists of the cipher keys in both the scrambling process and the diffusion process. We can conclude from the sensitivity analysis that the key space of the encryption algorithm is as large as $10^{14\times 8} \times 10^3 = 10^{75}$, if we set the seed N_1 to be one integer between 0 and 1000.

Conclusions

In this paper, we present a novel self-adaptive bit-level color image encryption algorithm using generalized Arnold maps. The 2D generalized Arnold maps are applied to generate chaotic sequences for both the sort-based scrambling stage and the color components' cross diffusion stage. The key streams are all related to the content of the plain-image and therefore the proposed image encryption algorithm show strong resistance against known-plaintext and chosen-plaintext attacks. All the experimental results show that the proposed image encryption algorithm is highly secure and demonstrates excellent performance.

Table 6. Key sensitivity analysis I.

	Correlation coefficients between the encrypted images obtained using MKEY and								
	SKEY1	SKEY2	SKEY3	SKEY4	SKEY5	SKEY6	SKEY7	SKEY8	SKEY9
Crr	0.0017	-0.0021	0.0007	0.0019	0.0004	0.0009	0.0009	-0.0015	0.0023
Crg	-0.0017	-0.0018	0.0033	-0.0003	0.0016	0.0021	0.0002	0.0010	-0.0001
Crb	-0.0017	0.0044	0.0008	0.0012	0.0031	-0.0011	-0.0012	0.0015	0.0014
Cgr	-0.0033	-0.0012	-0.0007	0.0012	0.0008	-0.0002	0.0015	-0.0039	0.0024
Cgg	-0.0002	-0.0013	0.0006	-0.0014	-0.0023	-0.0002	-0.0020	0.0032	-0.0024
Cgb	0.0017	0.0004	0.0003	0.0016	-0.0020	0.0016	0.0013	0.0009	-0.0004
Cbr	0.0005	-0.0041	0.0019	0.0016	0.0017	-0.0003	0.0003	-0.0026	0.0014
Cbg	-0.0001	-0.0010	-0.0012	0.0008	-0.0016	0.0012	0.0025	0.0016	0.0027
Cbb	-0.0022	0.0029	0.0001	0.0002	0.0013	0.0032	-0.0012	0.0001	0.0031

Table 7. Key sensitivity analysis II.

	Correlation coefficients between the decrypted images obtained using MKEY and								
	SKEY1	SKEY2	SKEY3	SKEY4	SKEY5	SKEY6	SKEY7	SKEY8	SKEY9
Crr	0.0031	-0.0065	0.0000	-0.0009	0.0009	-0.0028	0.0007	0.0010	-0.0003
Crg	0.0054	0.0001	-0.0020	0.0051	0.0001	0.0000	0.0016	0.0029	-0.0024
Crb	0.0039	0.0018	0.0090	-0.0068	0.0046	0.0038	-0.0001	-0.0037	0.0008
Cgr	0.0027	-0.0065	0.0005	-0.0015	0.0003	-0.0029	0.0001	0.0006	0.0004
Cgg	0.0062	0.0004	-0.0035	0.0052	0.0000	0.0002	0.0003	0.0022	-0.0021
Cgb	0.0051	0.0038	0.0073	-0.0040	0.0054	0.0036	0.0025	-0.0032	0.0008
Cbr	0.0000	-0.0037	-0.0021	-0.0031	-0.0001	-0.0027	-0.0003	0.0007	-0.0002
Cbg	0.0021	0.0009	-0.0014	0.0060	0.0002	0.0007	-0.0009	0.0011	-0.0018
Cbb	-0.0016	0.0032	0.0075	-0.0014	0.0049	0.0030	0.0041	-0.0017	0.0006

Acknowledgement

This research is partially supported by Entrepreneurship Training Program of Guangdong Colleges and partially by SRP of Science College of Shantou University.

References

1. D. R. Stinson, *Cryptography: Theory and Practice* (CRC Press, Boca Raton,1995)
2. J. Fridrich, Symmetric ciphers based on two-dimensional chaotic maps, Int. J Bifurcat. Chaos, **8**, 1259-1284 (1998)
3. R. Ye, A novel chaos-based image encryption scheme with an efficient permutation-diffusion mechanism, Opt. Commun., **284**, 5290-5298 (2011)
4. X. J. Tong, Design of an image encryption scheme based on a multiple chaotic map, Commun. Nonlinear Sci. Numer. Simulat., **18** , 1725-1733 (2013)
5. R. Ye, A novel image encryption scheme based on generalized multi-sawtooth maps, Fund. Inform., **133** , 87-104 (2014)
6. J. Chen, Z. Zhu, C. Fu, H. Yu, L. Zhang, An efficient image encryption scheme using gray code based permutation approach, Opt. Laser Eng., **67** , 191-204 (2015)
7. H. Liu, X. Wang, Color image encryption using spatial bit-level permutation and high-dimension chaotic system, Opt. Commun., **284**, 3895-3903(2011)
8. C. E. Shannon, Communication theory of secrecy system, Bell Syst. Tech. J, **28**, 656-715 (1949)

Performance Analysis of Multihop CC-HARQ over Lognormal Shadowed Nakagami-m Fading Channels

Jun-Mei HAN[a], Yong XI and Ji-Bo WEI

School of Electronic Science and Computer Engineering, National University of Defence Technology, Changsha, 410073 China

Abstract. The performance of truncated Chase Combining based Hybrid Automatic Repeat reQuest (CC-HARQ) in multihop relay network is analysed. Different from prior works, composite lognormal shadowed Nakagami fading channels are considered. By extending the Moment Generation Function (MGF) method to approximate the output signal-to-noise ratio to a lognormal random variable, the end-to-end outage probability is derived. The accuracy of the proposed approximating method is validated by simulations and the factors to affect such accuracy are thoroughly studied. The results have lots of potential usage in the analysis and design of practical networks such as power allocation, relay placement and optimization for energy efficiency etc.

1 Introduction

Hybrid Automatic Repeat reQuest (HARQ) protocols are widely employed to increase the reliability and efficiency of data transmission over wireless communication by combining forward error-correcting coding (FEC) with ARQ technique. Particularly, the Chase Combining based HARQ (CC-HARQ) scheme, in which the same packet is retransmitted in case of errors and combined with maximal-ratio combining (MRC), is widely used for the benefit of its simplicity and efficiency. HARQ schemes have been adopted in many wireless standards, such as High Speed Packet Access (HSPA), IEEE 802.15.4, IEEE 802.11 and Long Term Evolution (LTE). In addition, with the advent of its coverage extension and spatial diversity gain, multihop relay technique has gained considerable interest in the research community. Concepts such as smart home, smart grid and system control and automation have drawn considerable attention from researchers across the globle and it has been shown that multihop relay networks is one of the most promisising solutions for implementing such concepts [1].

Although various schemes have been proposed to analysis the performance of multihop networks or HARQ schemes, most of them considered only pure large-scale fading [1], [2] or small-scale fading [3]. No complete analysis of the performance for multihop networks adopting HARQ retransmission technique under composite shadowing-fading channels has been reported so far.

In this paper, a new approach of outage probability approximation is proposed for performance analysis of multihop CC-HARQ system under general channel conditions. We consider channel randomness from two channel fading components and the channel coefficient follows a composite

[a] Corresponding author: hjm.han@163.com

Nakagami- m /Lognormal distribution, where the small-scale fading from multipath propagation is modelled by a Nakagami- m Random Variable and large-scale fading from shadowing is approximated by a Lognormal random variable. Due to the complexity of Nakagami- m /Lognormal distribution and multihop CC-HARQ as well as the limit of maximum retransmission number, the analysis becomes very challenging.

In the following, first, the outage probability for single-hop CC-HARQ protocols is obtained by extending the Moment Generation Function (MGF) method to approximate the output signal-to-noise ratio (SNR) to a Lognormal random variable, whose cumulative distribution function (*cdf*) is obtained by numerically solving for its mean and standard deviation. Latter, the results are particularized for the multihop relay networks. The derived expressions are validated by Monte Carlo simulations. Due to the versatile and flexible features of Nakagami- m fading, it is worthy to note that the Nakagami- m /Lognormal channel has the advantage of including the Rayleigh-Lognormal and Rician-Lognormal channels as special cases.

2 CC-HARQ over Nakagami-m/Lognormal channels

We begin by extending the MGF-based approximating method to approximate the output SNR of Nakagmai- m /Lognormal fading with CC-HARQ, and the Gaussian-Hermite integral quadrature rule [4, *formula* (25.4.46)] is applied to approximately reduce the infinite nested integral to a finite number of weighted summations of Hermite polynomials. Then the tightness of the adopted approximation are studied and we examine performance scaling with respect to the SNR thresholds γ_{th} the Hermite polynomial order N_p and the maximum retransmission L.

We adopt truncated CC-type HARQ in the linear K -hop relay network with maximum retransmission number L over Nakagmai- m /Lognormal channels. The relay nodes purely help to forward the information bits from the transmitter to receiver, with half-duplex mode. We further assume that the L packets for the same hop suffer identically distributed and exponentially correlated Nakagami- m /Lognormal channels. The corresponding channel correlation matrix $\mathbf{R}$ is in a Hermitian Toeplitz structure, with the x -th column and y -th row element $\mathbf{R}_l(x,y)=\eta_l^{|x-y|}$, $\eta_l \in [0,1]$. For different hops $R_i \neq R_j$, the channel gains h_i and h_j are mutually independent and may assume different fading models. The instantaneous SNR of the k -th hop of l -th transmission is $\gamma_{k_l}=\left(P_{k_l}/N_0\right)\left|h_{k_l}\right|^2$, where N_0 is identical power of the additive Gassian white noises.

2.1 The Single hop outage probability

For the k-th hop, the output SNR in point-to-point transmission is the sum of L individual retransmission ($\gamma_k=\sum_{l=1}^{L}\gamma_{k_l}$). The desired outage probability, which is basically equal to the *cdf* of output SNR at a specific threshold γ_{th}, can be expressed as:

$$\begin{aligned} P_{out}(\gamma_{th}) &= \Pr\{\gamma_{MRC} \le \gamma_{th}\} \\ &= \Pr\left\{\sum_{l=1}^{L}\gamma_{k_l} \le \gamma_{th}\right\} = \Pr\{\gamma_k \le \gamma_{th}\}. \end{aligned} \tag{1}$$

DOI: 10.1051/itmconf/20171106003

The joint composite distribution of received SNR (γ_k) for all the L retransmission can be obtained by averaging the joint Nakagami-m distributed instantaneous SNR over the conditional density of the joint Lognormal distributed average SNR, whose *pdf* is given by :

$$p_{\gamma_k}(\gamma_k) = \int_0^\infty p_{\gamma_k|\bar{\gamma}_k}(\gamma_k \mid \bar{\gamma}_k) p_{\bar{\gamma}_k}(\bar{\gamma}_k) d\bar{\gamma}_k. \tag{2}$$

Note that (2) is composed of two components. The first component, i.e., the *pdf* of γ_k conditioned on the average SNR $\bar{\gamma}_k$, arises from multipath fading and is given by a Gamma distribution $f(\cdot)$ (Generally, $f(x;k,\phi)$ denotes the *pdf* of Gamma distribution with the shape parameter k and the scale parameter ϕ, given by: $f(x;k,\phi) = \frac{1}{\phi^k} \cdot \frac{x^{k-1}}{\Gamma(k)} \cdot \exp\left(-\frac{x}{\phi}\right)$, where $\Gamma(\cdot)$ is the Gamma function). Let m_k denote the fading severity measure. The first component can be written as:

$$p_{\gamma_k|\bar{\gamma}_k}(\gamma_k \mid \bar{\gamma}_k) = f\left(\gamma_k; \frac{m_k L^2}{u_k}, \frac{u_k \bar{\gamma}_k}{m_k L}\right), \tag{3}$$

with $u_k = L + \frac{2\eta_k}{1-\eta_k}\left(L \quad \frac{1-\eta_k^{\,L}}{1-\eta_k}\right)$. μ_k (dB) and σ_k (dB) are the mean and standard deviation of $10\log_{10}\bar{\gamma}_k$, respectively.

The second component of (3), $p_{\bar{\gamma}}(\bar{\gamma})$, is the joint *pdf* of average SNRs over all retransmission packets. The randomness of each average SNR is affected by the shadowing and is approximated by a Lognormal random variable:

$$p_{\bar{\gamma}_k}(\bar{\gamma}_k) = \frac{\lambda}{\sqrt{2\pi}\bar{\gamma}_k} \cdot \exp\left[-\frac{1}{2}(10\log_{10}\bar{\gamma}_k - \mu_k)^T (10\log_{10}\bar{\gamma}_k - \mu_k)\right] \tag{4}$$

where λ is the scaling constant ($\lambda = 10/\ln 10 = 4.3429$). By substituting ω_k for $(10\log_{10}\bar{\gamma}_k - \mu_k)/\sqrt{2}\,\sigma_k$, we obtain a simplified expression for the joint composite *pdf*,

$$p_{\gamma_k}(\gamma_k) = \frac{1}{(\sqrt{\pi})} \int_{-\infty}^{\infty} f\left(\gamma_k; \frac{m_k L^2}{u_k}, \frac{u_k \cdot g(\omega_k)}{m_k L}\right) e^{(-\omega^T \omega)} d\omega \tag{5}$$

Where $g(\omega_k) = 10^{0.1(\sqrt{2}\sigma_k \omega_k \mu_k)}$.

Due to the nested integral form, the closed-form m *pdf* expression for the composite Nakagami-m /Lognormal fading distributions is hard to get. However, it has been illustrated that the sum of composite Rayleigh-Lognormal fading random variables can be approximated by a Lognormal random variable by [5] and [6]. We extend those work to approximate the output SNR of Nakagami-

m /Lognormal fading with CC-HARQ to a new Lognormal random variable. Therefore, we can calculated the outage probability with only the means (μ_Γ) and standard derivation (σ_Γ) of the new Lognormal random variable, which reduced the computation complexity significantly. The *pdf* of the new random variable takes the form:

$$p_\Gamma(\gamma') = \frac{\lambda}{\sqrt{2\pi}\sigma_\Gamma\gamma'} \exp\left[-\frac{(10\log_{10}\gamma' - \mu_\Gamma)^2}{2\sigma_\Gamma^2}\right]. \quad (6)$$

We resort to an MGF-based approximating method to estimate the Lognormal characterized parameters μ_Γ and σ_Γ. Specifically, the corresponding parameters are estimated by matching respective MGFs at two different, real and positive value of s, namely, s_1 and s_2. This method consists of two independent equations as follows:

$$\Psi_\Gamma(s_k) = \Psi_{\gamma_{CC}}(s_k),\ k = 1,2. \quad (7)$$

The Gaussian-Hermite integral quadrature rule is applied to approximately reduce the infinite integral to a finite number of weighted summations of Hermite polynomials. Accordingly, μ_Γ and σ_Γ of the new Lognormal random variable Γ can be readily calculated. Through extensive derivations, the exact relationship between the original parameters and approximated one can be obtained as:

$$\begin{cases} \mu_{k'} = \mu_k + \lambda\left[\psi(m_k) - m_k\right] \\ \sigma_{k'} = \sqrt{\lambda^2\varsigma(2, m_k) + \sigma_k^2} \end{cases} \quad (8)$$

Where $\varsigma(2, m_k) = \sum_{i=0}^{\infty} \frac{1}{(m_k + i)^2}$ is the Reimann's Zeta function. $\psi(m_k) = -C + \sum_{i=1}^{m_k - 1} \frac{1}{i}$ is the Euler Psi function, C is the Euler's constant ($C \approx 0.5772$). The outage probability in (1) can be calculated by: $P_{out}(\gamma_{th}) \cong \int_0^{\gamma_{th}} p_\Gamma(\gamma')d\gamma'$.

2.2 The end-to-end outage probability

We now investigate the end-to-end outage probability of multihop relay networks which is given by:

$$\begin{aligned} P_{e2e} &= \Pr\left\{\min(\gamma_1, \gamma_2, \ldots, \gamma_K) \le \gamma_{th}\right\} \\ &= 1 - \prod_{k=1}^{K} \Pr\left\{\gamma_k > \gamma_{th}\right\} = 1 - \prod_{k=1}^{K} Q\left(\frac{(\log\gamma_k - \mu_\Gamma)}{\sigma_{\gamma_k}}\right) \end{aligned} \quad (9)$$

Where $Q(\cdot)$ is the Gassian Q-function (i.e., $Q(x)=\int_x^{\infty}\frac{1}{\sqrt{2\pi}}e^{-y^2/2}dy$). Roughly speaking, the desired outage probability at γ_{th} expressed in (9) is dependent on the retransmission number L, the number of hops M, the received SNR, and other location specific propagation characteristics of individual branches, e.g., severity measure of multipath fading m_l, local mean power μ_l' and standard deviation of shadowing σ_l'.

3 Analytical and simulation results

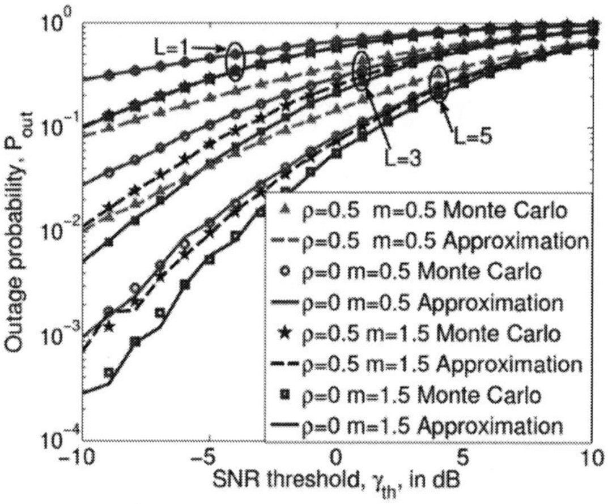

Figure 1. The Outage probability according to the SNR threshold.

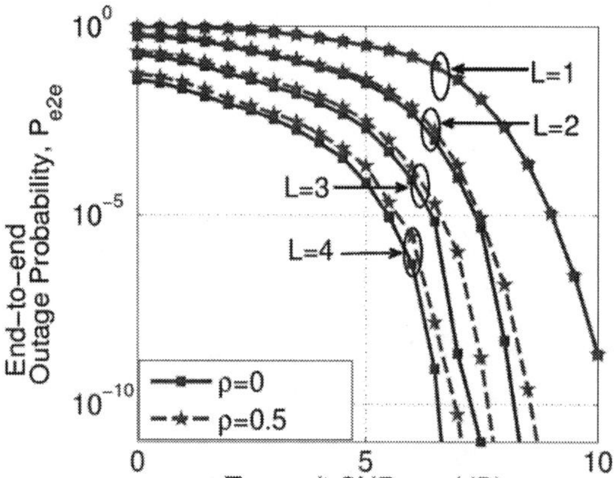

Figure 2. The end-to-end outage probability according to the transmit SNR for $M=3$.

In this section, the simulation and analytical results are presented. Fig.1 and Fig.2 show the outage probability performance. Fig.1 is the outage probability performance of exponential correlation model for single hop CC-HARQ at different SNR thresholds. The same mean path loss and standard deviation of shadowing are assumed to be μ = 0dB and σ_i = 6dB. Fig.2 is the end-to-end outage probabilities performance, and the results are generated by varying the transmit SNR while maintaining the ratio among individual hop noise power ration P_T / N_0 as $\gamma_1 : \gamma_2 : \gamma_3 = 1:2:3$. Three hop systems are considered with $\gamma_{th} = 5$ dB and severity measure of multipath fading factors for three hop are $m_1 = 0.5, m_2 = 2, m_3 = 1$. The Monte Carlo simulations with one million samples match with approximation method nicely, thereby validating the accuracy of the algorithm. The figures also display comparisons between two different levels of correlation (ρ = 0 or 0.5), as well as among different numbers of retransmission (L = 1,3,7).

As expected, increasing the correlation level ρ degrades the outage performance, while increasing the retransmission number L improves it. The efficient of correlation level ρ is more remarkable in the low γ_{th}. This is a consequence of the fact that the approximation underestimation is mainly affected by the fading effect on the composite showing-fading distribution and the showing effect is slighter. In particular, at the higher value of γ_{th}, the overall variability of composite showing-fading distribution is mainly cause by the Lognormal showing component, which is relate to transmit distance and is independent to other rounds. In addition, due to the multiplication between fading component and showing component, the disturbance effect of fading is much slighter at the lower value of transmit SNRs.

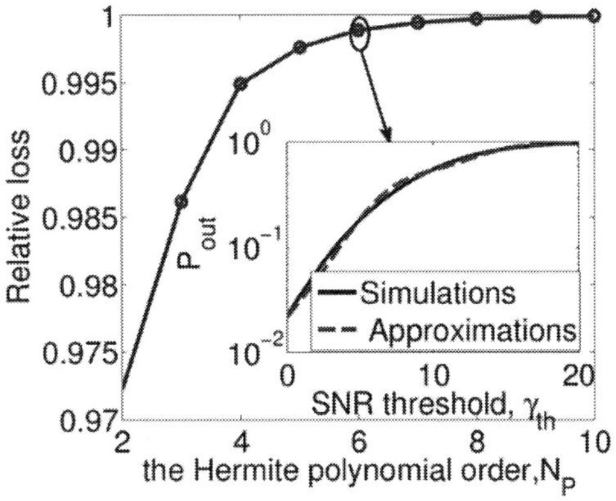

Figure 3. The relative loss of the proposed evaluation approaches under different N_P with $L = 4$.

The accuracy and efficiency of these approaches are dependent on the maximum retransmission number L and the Hermite polynomial order N_p. The corresponding parameters for Figure 3 and Figure 4 are as follows unless otherwise stated: $\mu = 0$ dB, $\sigma = 6$ dB, $\rho = 0.5$ and $m = 1.5$.

Figure.3 shows the relative loss for the proposed evaluation approaches N_p. Note that although the mismatch from the standard value will decrease when N_p increases, accurate results can be obtained even for small order of N_p. Additionally, increasing N_P will lengthen the runtime. As shown in the figures, $N_P = 6$ is the compromising values which guarantee both the accuracy and efficiency. It should be noted that $\mathbf{s}$ should be chosen appropriately to reduce the results mismatch. [5] provides guideline for $\mathbf{s}$ choosing according to the desired outage probability. In our scenarios, we find $(s_1, s_2) = (1, 0.1)$ provides a good fit as shown in the figures.

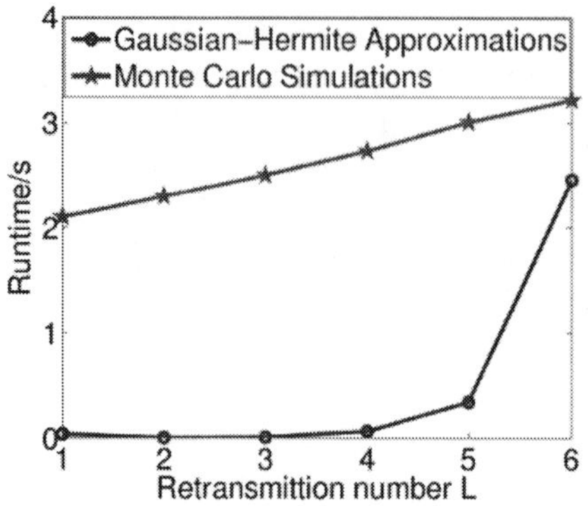

Figure 4. The runtime of the proposed evaluation approaches under different L levels with $N_P = 6$.

Figure.4 compares the runtime of the proposed evaluation approach with extensive Monte Carlo simulations for different L. The proposed approach is more efficient than the Monte Carlo simulations with one million samples. Note that the runtime is mainly affected by the complexity of the approach, the runtime of Gaussian-Hermite Quadrature is exponentially increases with the L. In fact, when L become larger ($L > 8$), the runtime becomes intolerable (more than 30 seconds). Fortunately, in most practical systems L is usually less than 8 due to the requirement of delay and efficiency.

Conclusion

This paper has presented a general numerical approach to evaluate the outage probability of multihop relay networks adopting CC-HARQ with L retransmissions under Lognormal shadowed Nakagami-m fading channels. An MGF-based method is proposed to approximate the output SNR by a new Lognormal random variable, whose characterized parameters are numerically solved. Based on the approximation, the outage probability can be calculated by the *cdf* of this approximating random variable at a specific threshold. This approximation is simple and is proved to be tight enough to address the outage probability. In addition, this evaluation approach is feasible to be used for the optimal design of system parameters, such as the optimal power and rate designs to achieve the maximum delay limited throughput.

References

1. Ankit.Dubey, Ranjan K.Mallik, Robert.Schober. :'Performance analysis of a multi-hop power line communication system over log-normal fading in presence of impulsive noise', *IET Commun.*, pp.1-9, **9**, 1 (2015).
2. Chinmoy. Kundu and Ranjan. Bose,: 'Joint optimal power allocation and relay location for decode-and-forward multi-hop relaying over log-normal channel', *IET Commun.*, pp.2197-2207, **9**, 18 (2015).
3. Peng.Wu and Nihar.Jindal.: 'Performance of Hybrid-ARQ in Block-fading Channels: A Fixed Outage Probability Analysis' *Wireless Commun. IEEE Trans on*, pp. 1129-1141, **58,** 4 (2010).
4. Milton Abramowitz and Irene A. Stegun: *'Handbook of mathematical functions with formulas, graphs, and mathematical tables',* (1964).
5. Mehta N B, Wu J, Molisch A F, et al.: ' Approximating a Sum of Random Variables with a Lognormal Anderson', *Wireless Commun. IEEE Trans on.*, pp. 2690-2699, **6** (2007).

6. Rui. Zhang and Jibo.Wei, etc: 'Outage Probability of MRC Diversity over Correlated Shadowed Fading Channels', *Lett. IEEE Wireless Commun.*, pp.516-519, **1**, 5 (2012).

Simulation of Logging-while-drilling Tool Response Using Integral Equation Fast Fourier Transform

Xiang-Yang SUN[1,a], Bao-Xin LI[1], Yong-Peng ZHAO[1]

[1]*High tech Zone(West), Chengdu, Sichuan, China Xi yuan Avenue, No. 2006, University of Electronic Science and Technology*

Abstract. We rely on the volume integral equation (VIE) method for the simulation of logging-while-drilling (LWG) tool response using the integral equation fast Fourier transform (IE-FFT) algorithm to accelerate the computation of the matrix-vector product in the iterative solver. Depending on the virtue of the Toeplitz structure of the interpolation of the Green's function on the uniform Cartesian grids, this method uses FFT to calculate the matrix-vector multiplication. At the same time, this method reduce the memory requirement and CPU time. In this paper, IE-FFT method is first used in the simulation of LWG. Numerical results are presented to demonstrate the accuracy and efficiency of this method. Compared with the Moment of Method (MOM) and other fast algorithms, IE-FFT have distinct advantages in the fact of memory requirement and CPU time. In addition, this paper study the truncation, mesh elements, the size of the interpolation grids of IE-FFT and dip formation, and give some conclusion with wide applicability.

1 Introduction

Logging-while-drilling tools [1-2] are based on the theory of waves and fields in inhomogenous media. In the field of petroleum well drilling and logging, electromagnetic wave resistivity sensors are frequently used to provide an indication of the electrical resistivity of rock formations surrounding an earth borehole. Such information regarding resistivity is useful in ascertaining the presence or absence of oil. A typical electromagnetic wave resistivity tool comprises a transmitter antenna and a pair of receiver antennas located at different distance from the transmitter antenna along the axis of the tool. The transmitter antenna is used to transmit electromagnetic waves. Due to waves received by two receiver antennas propagate through different distance, they are absorbed by the surrounding earth formation with different degree. So the voltages in the two receiver antennas have different phases and amplitudes. This is the reason that we use the phase different (PD) and amplitude ratio (AR) of voltages on the two receiver antennas to analyze the rock formation.

Simulation of LWD Tool response is of great importance for optimization and design the new tools, and interpretation the earth formation and son on. Numerical methods such as finite element method (FEM)[3-5]· finite difference time domain (FDTD), finite difference method (FDM) and moment of method (MOM) are flexible in dealing with 3-D formation. By contrast, the volume integral equation only require to divide the areas that are different with the background, so it has less

[a] Corresponding author: sunxiangyang@uestc.edu.cn

unknowns than FEM. One conventional method of solution for the volume integral equation is the method of moment (MOM). However, MOM methods are limited to relatively small problems because of their excessive CPU time and memory requirements. Therefore, Zhong Qing Zhang successfully proposed to improve the efficiency of induction logging problems with the CG-FFT method[6-10]. While CG-FFT require the uniform elements, it will create too many basis functions. Another method is MOM combine with multi-level adaptive cross approximation (MOM+MLACA)[11-14] used by the group of Zaiping Nie in UESTC, while MLACA is one method of pure mathematics. And the capacity to reduce computing time and memory is limited. In this paper, IE-FFT [15-16] is first used to solve the problem of the simulation of LWD tool response. IE-FFT method depends on the interpolation of the Green's function on the uniform Cartesian grids. And it takes advantages of the Fast Fourier Transform (FFT) to calculate the matrix-vector multiplication without needs to insure the uniform mesh elements. The superiority of IE-FFT is more attractively with the increase of the unknowns. This method is proved to be effective by contrast with the NMM, MOM, MOM+MLACA and MOM combine with multi-level adaptive cross approximation and singular value decomposition (MOM+MLACA+SVD). And it is clear that IE-FFT has significant advantages for reducing the memory requirement and CPU time.

2 The volume integral equation

In the model of the simulation of logging response, most of the area is homogeneous medium regarding as the background. The background is characterized by distribution of permittivity ε_b and conductivity δ_b, and the permeability is assumed constant $\mu_b = \mu_0$. While the inhomogenous formation are characterized by distribution of permittivity $\varepsilon(r)$ and conductivity $\delta(r)$, and the permeability is assumed constant $\mu_b = \mu_0$. Assumed that E^i is the excitation field, and the equivalent volume current is J_v in inhomogenous formation. The scattered field E_V^{sca} is the contribution of the volume current J_v, which can be calculated by

$$E_V^{sca}(r) = iwA_v(r) - \nabla\varphi_v(r) \tag{1}$$

where

$$A_v(r) = \frac{\mu_b}{4\pi}\int_v J_v(r)\frac{e^{ik_b|r-r'|}}{|r-r'|}dV' \tag{2}$$

$$\varphi_v(r) = \frac{1}{4\pi i\omega\varepsilon_b}\int_V \nabla\cdot J_V(r)\frac{e^{ik_b|r-r'|}}{|r-r'|}dV' \tag{3}$$

where ε_b' is the complex permittivity of background and k_b is the wave-number in the background medium given by

$$\varepsilon_b' = \varepsilon_b + i\delta_b / \omega \tag{4}$$

$$k_b = \omega\sqrt{\mu_b(\varepsilon_b + i\delta_b / \omega)} \tag{5}$$

In the volume region

$$D(\mathrm{r})/\varepsilon(r) = E_V^{sca}(r) + E^{inc}(r) \qquad r \in V \tag{6}$$

The unknown electric flux density can be expanded as

$$iwD(\mathrm{r}) = \sum_{n=1}^{Nv} f_n^v(r) \tag{7}$$

while

$$I_v(\mathrm{r}) = iw(k_b^2 / k^2(r) - 1)D(r) \quad \sum_{n=1}^{Nv} I_n^{Nv} \chi(r) f_n^v(r) \tag{8}$$

where χ is the contrast of the inhomogenous formation

$$\chi(r) = k_b^2 / k^2(r) - 1 \tag{9}$$

Substituting (7) (8) into (6) and using the GalerKin's technique yield a linear system with N unknowns

$$\sum_{n=1}^{Nv} I_n^V [f_n^V / iw\varepsilon f_m^V - iw(A_n^V f_m^V) + (\nabla \phi_n^V f_m^V)] = (E^i f_m^V) \quad \mathrm{m}=1,2......\mathrm{N}_V \tag{10}$$

Where

$$\begin{aligned} \phi_n^V(r) &= \frac{1}{4\pi i w \varepsilon_b} \int_{\Sigma T_n^{\pm}} \nabla \cdot \chi f_n^V \frac{e^{ik_b|r-r'|}}{|r-r'|} dr \\ &= \frac{1}{4\pi i w \varepsilon_b} \int_{\Sigma T_n^{\pm}} \chi \nabla \cdot f_n^V \frac{e^{ik_b|r-r'|}}{|r-r'|} dr - \frac{\chi_n^+ - \chi_n^-}{4\pi i w \varepsilon_b} \int_{a_n} \frac{e^{ik_b|r-r'|}}{|r-r'|} ds \end{aligned} \tag{11}$$

$$\nabla \phi_n^V f_m^V = \int_s \phi f_m^V(r) \cdot n dS - \int_v \phi \nabla \cdot f_m^V(r) dV$$

$$= \begin{cases} \int_V \phi \nabla \cdot f_m^V(r) dV & \mathrm{T}_n^{\pm} \in V \\ \int_S \phi dS - \int_V \phi \nabla \cdot f_m^V(r) dV & \mathrm{T}_n^{\pm} \in V \end{cases} \tag{12}$$

Let

$$Z_{1mn} = -iw(A_n^V f_m^V) + (\nabla \phi_n^V f_m^V) \tag{13}$$

3 IE-FFT method in the simulation of lwd tool response

The IE-FFT method is irregular mesh-based grid algorithm. The uniform grids are used for interpolating the Green's function. The action of Green's function on a vector can be computed efficiently using the FFT. For near interactions, correction of impedance is must, since the accuracy of the sampled representation is insufficient. The Green's function interpolated by Lagrangian polynomials can be approximated as

$$G(r,r') \cong \beta(r)\cdot G\cdot(\beta(r))^T \tag{14}$$

where

$$\beta(r) = \left[\beta_0^P(r)\ \ \beta_1^P(r)\ \dots\ \beta_{N_g-1}^P(r)\right]$$

$$= \begin{bmatrix} \beta_0^P(x)\beta_0^P(y)\beta_0^P(z) \\ \beta_1^P(x)\beta_1^P(y)\beta_1^P(z) \\ \\ \beta_{N_x-1}^P(x)\beta_{N_y-1}^P(y)\beta_{N_z-1}^P(z) \end{bmatrix} \tag{15}$$

$$G = \begin{bmatrix} G_{0,0} & G_{0,1} & \dots & G_{0,N_g-1} \\ G_{1,0} & G_{1,1} & \dots & G_{1,N_g-1} \\ \dots & \dots & \dots & \dots \\ G_{N_g-1,0} & G_{N_g-1,1} & \dots & G_{N_g-1,N_g-1} \end{bmatrix} \tag{16}$$

where N_x, N_y, N_z are the number of grid points in x, y and z coordinates. N_g is the total number of the grid points as N_g. Substituting (14) into (13)

$$Z_{mn} = -iw\mu_b \begin{Bmatrix} \Pi_3\cdot G\cdot(\Pi_1)^T - \frac{1}{k_b^2}\Pi_4\cdot G\cdot(\Pi_2)^T + \frac{1}{k_b^2}\Pi_4\cdot G\cdot(\Pi_5)^T \\ +\frac{1}{k_b^2}\Pi_6\cdot G\cdot(\Pi_2)^T - \frac{1}{k_b^2}\Pi_6\cdot G\cdot(\Pi_5)^T \end{Bmatrix} \tag{17}$$

where

$$\Pi_1 = \int_{V_n} \chi(r)\cdot f_n^V(r)\cdot\beta_l^p(r)dr$$

$$\Pi_2 = \int_{V_n} \chi(r)\nabla\cdot f_n^V(r)\cdot\beta_l^p(r)dr$$

$$\Pi_3 = \int_{V_n} f_n^V(r)\cdot\beta_l^p(r)dr$$

$$\Pi_4 = \int_{V_n} \nabla\cdot f_n^V(r)\cdot\beta_l^p(r)dr$$

$$\Pi_5 = (\chi_n^+ - \chi_n^-)\int_{V_n} f_n^V(r)\cdot\beta_l^p(r)dr$$

$$\Pi_3 = \int_{S_n} \beta_l^p(r)dr$$

When the near interactions are computed via the IE-FFT method, the results are highly erroneous. The correction value can be computed as the difference between the value directly computed by the MOM and the value computed via the IE-FFT algorithm

$$Z = Z_{MOM}^{near} - Z_{IE-FFT}^{near} + Z_{IE-FFT} = Z^{corr} + Z_{IE-FFT} \tag{18}$$

the matrix vector product can be compute via the FFT

$$\begin{aligned} V = \\ & Z^{corr} \cdot I - iw\mu_b(\Pi_3 \cdot IFFT\{FFT(G)\} \cdot FFT\left[(\Pi_1)^T \cdot I\right] - \frac{1}{k_b^2}\Pi_4 IFFT(FFT(G) \cdot \\ & FFT\left[(\Pi_2)^T \cdot I\right]) + \frac{1}{k_b^2}\Pi_4 IFFT(FFT(G) \cdot FFT\left[(\Pi_5)^T \cdot I\right]) + \frac{1}{k_b^2}\Pi_6 \cdot \\ & IFFT(FFT(G) \cdot FFT\left[(\Pi_2)^T \cdot I\right]) - \frac{1}{k_b^2}\Pi_6 IFFT(FFT(G) \cdot FFT\left[(\Pi_5)^T \cdot I\right])) \end{aligned} \tag{19}$$

4 Numerical results

eg1.The tolerance of 0.001 use GMRES iterations. The Green's function interpolate by the 2nd order Lagrangian polynomials. The size of interpolation grids is 0.1λ and the near gate for correction is $0.1\sqrt{2}\lambda$ (λ is the wavelength of the background medium). The inhomogenous formation has a thickness of 3m and the conductivity of 0.1S/m. The borehole has a 0.127m radius and filled with mud with conductivity of 3.0S/m. The mud conductivity is treated as background medium. The working frequency of the LWD tool is 500KHz. The two receiver antennas are located at 1.0m and 1.5m away from the transmitter antenna. The total unknowns is 47 854. The number of spatial samples are 41. The result is obtained on the computer with 3.3GHz, 8 core.

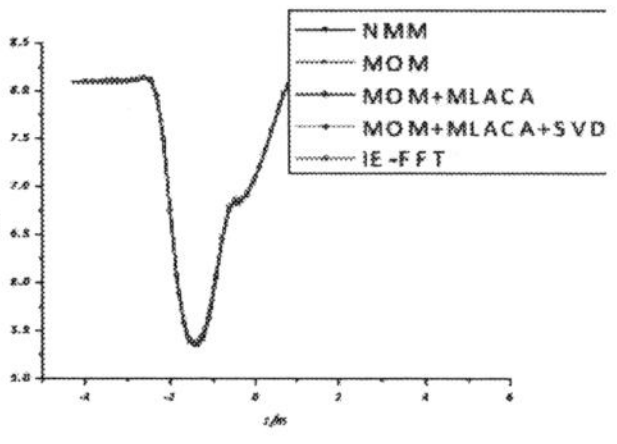

Figure 1 (a) Amplitude Ratio

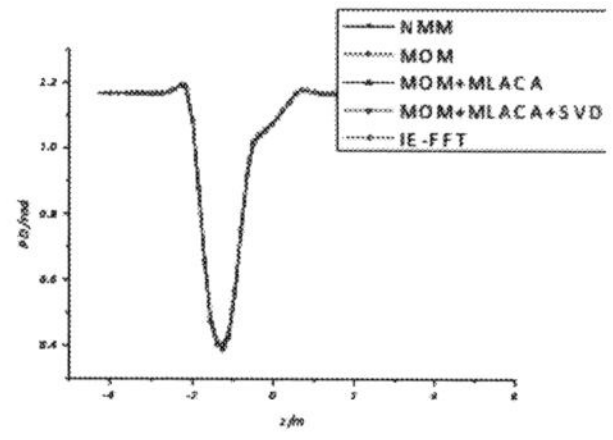

Figure 1 (b) Phase Difference

Table1 The contrast of the CPU time and memory requirement of MOM, MOM+MLACA

	Memory (G)	Time (S)
MOM	34	38 795
MOM+MLACA	9.3	994
MOM+MLACA+SVD	2.7	444
IE-FFT	2.6	274

eg2.The tolerance of 0.001 use GMRES iterations. The Green's function interpolate by the 2nd order Lagrangian polynomials. The size of interpolation grids is 0.1λ and the near gate for correction

DOI: 10.1051/itmconf/20171106004

is $0.1\sqrt{2}\lambda$ (λ is the wave length of the background medium). The inhomogenous formation has a thickness of 6m and the conductivity of 0.3S/m. The borehole has a 0.1m radius and filled with mud with conductivity of 8.0S/m. The mud conductivity is treated as background medium. The working frequency of the LWD tool is 450KHz. The two receiver antennas are located at 1.0m and 1.5m away from the transmitter antenna. The total unknowns is 414 926. The number of spatial samples are 41. The result is obtained on the computer with 2.27GHz, 16 core.

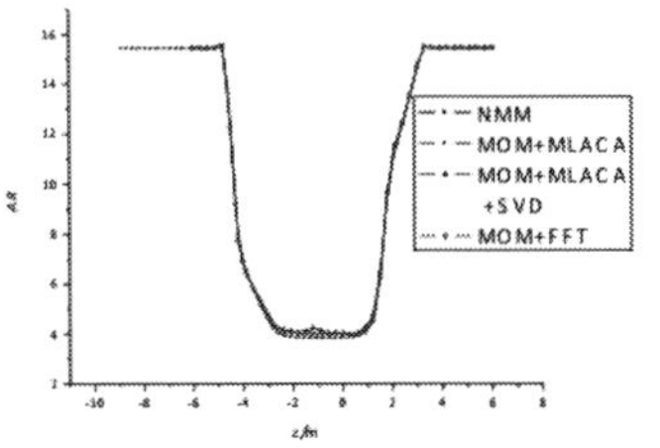

Figure 2 (a) Amplitude Ratio

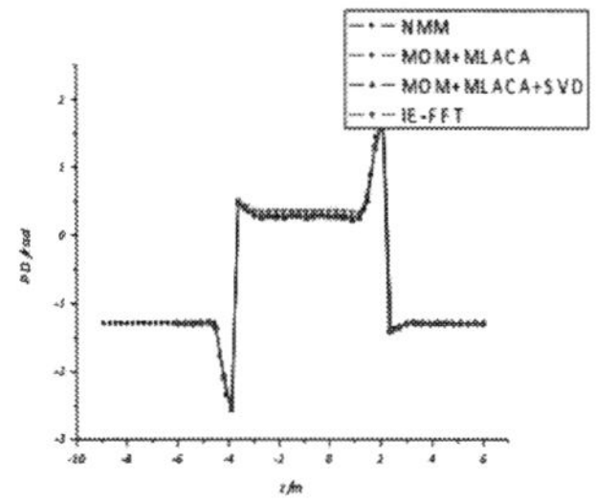

Figure 2 (b) Phase Difference

Table2 The contrast of the CPU time and memory requirement of MOM, MOM+MLACA , MOM+MLACA+SVD and IE-FFT in Fig2

	Memory (G)	Time (S)
MOM+MLACA	207	30945(8.6h)
MOM+MLACA+SVD	43	8476(2.4h)
IE-FFT	16	6781(1.9h)

The numerical results proved the effective of the simulation of LWD tool of response with IE-FFT. By contrast with the MOM, MOM+MLACA and MOM+MLACA+SVD, it clear that IE-FFT method has its own superiority in the fact of the memory requirement and CPU time. And the advantages will be more attractive with the increase of the unknowns.

Conclusion

The IE-FFT methods is irregular mesh-based grid algorithm. The IE-FFT methods is the interpolation of the Green's function on the uniform Cartesian tensor grids by Lagrangian polynomials. With the virtue of the Toeplitz structure of the Green's function, this method uses FFT to accelerate the matrix-vector product. The advantages of FFT are that it makes the computational complexity of $O(N^2)$ tend to $O(N\log N)$ and it makes the memory requirement of $O(N^2)$ tend to $O(N)$. So IE-FFT can heavily reduce the memory requirement and CPU time. Compared with MOM, MOM+MLACA and MOM+MLACA+SVD, it is proved that IE-FFT method has advantages in CPU time and memory requirement using solving the problem of logging. And compared with NMM, this method can use to solve the problem of 3-D.

References

1. H. G. Doll. Introduction to induction logging and application to logging of wells drilled with oil-based mud[J].Journal of Petroleum Technology, 1949, 1(6):148-162
2. Weng Cho Chew, Zaiping Nie, Qing-Huo Liu, Barbara Anderson. An efficient solution for the response of electrical well logging tool in a complex environment[J].IEEE Transaction on Geo-science and Remote Sensing, 1991, 29(2):309-313
3. B. Anderson, S. K. Chang. Synthetic induction logs by the finite element method[J].Log Anal., 1982, 23:17-29[J]. SPWLA 23rd Annual Logging Symposium, 1982, 23(1):17-29

4. S. K. Chang, B. Anderson. Simulation of induction logging by the finite element method[J].Geophysics, 1984, 49(11): 1943-1958
5. Sun Xiang-Yang, Nie Zai-Ping. 3-D Modeling of Electromagnetic Induction in Anisotropy Media Using Finite Element Method[J]. Antennas and Propagation Society International Symposium, 2008, AP-S 2008(1):1-4
6. Zhong Qing Zhang , Qing Huo Liu . The Hybrid Extended Born Approximation and CG-FFHT method for axisymmetric media[J].Antennas and Propagation Society International Symposium, 2001, 39(4): 710- 717
7. Qing Huo Liu ,Zhong Qing Zhang , Xue Min Xu . The Hybrid Extended Born Approximation and CG-FFHT method for electromagnetic induction problems[J].IEEE Transactions on Geo-science and Remote Sensing, 2001, 39(2):347-355
8. Zhong Qing Zhang, Qing Huo Liu. The Hybrid Extended Born Approximation and CG-FFHT method for axisymmetric media[J].IEEE Transactions on Geo-science and Remote Sensing, 2001, 39(4):710-717
9. Zhong Qing Zhang, Qing Huo Liu. Simulation of 3D EM fields by a weak-form biconjugate gradient FFT method [J].Antennas and Propagation Society International Symposium, 2001, 4(1):626-629
10. C.Garcia, Y. Alvarez. The adaptive cross approximation algorithm applied to a volumetric method-of-moments for electromagnetic analysis of inhomogeneous bodies[J].Antennas and Propagation Society International Symposium, 2010, 2010 IEEE(1):1-4
11. M.Astner, H. D. Bruns.Application of a hierarchical SVD-ACA compression technique to near-field calculation of monopole antennas[J].EMC International Symposium, 2007, EMC 2007(1):1-6
12. Kezhong Zhao, Marinos N. Vouvakis.The adaptive cross approximation algorithm for accelerated method of moments computations of EMC Problems[J].IEEE Trans.EMC, 2005, 47(4):763-773
13. Peng Li. Numerical simulation of response of electrical logging based on integral equation method[Master's thesis]. Chengdu: School of Electronic Engineering of University of Electronic Science and Technology of China, 2012
14. Seung Mo Seo, Jin-Fa Lee.A fast IE-FFT algorithm for solving PEC scattering problems[J].IEEE Transaction on Magnetic, 2008, 44(6):1398-1401
15. Nilufer A.Ozdemir,Jin-Fa LeeIE-FFT algorithm for a non-conformal volume integral equation for electromagnetic scattering from dielectric objects[J].IEEE Transaction on Magnetic, 2008, 44(6):1398-1401

Review on Development of Fault Diagnosis for Gyroscope

He SONG[1], Shao-Lin HU[1,2,a], and Ke-Yi ZHOU[1]

[1]*School of automation and Information Engineering, Xi'an University of Technology, 710048, Xi'an, China*
[2]*Foshan University, 528000, Foshan, China*

Abstract. Gyroscope is a core part of navigation system, whose working stability and reliability directly affects the navigation performance of navigation system. Therefore, in order to ensure the precision and reliability of navigation system, it is very important to develop the techniques of fault diagnosis for gyroscope. First, the development of gyroscope's history and the background and significance of fault diagnosis for gyroscope is introduced in this paper. Then, the influence factors of abnormal faults in the running of gyroscope are analyzed in this paper, and the faults are classified into different types according to the feature of faults for gyroscope. Second, there are some main algorithms of fault diagnosis for gyroscope, such as support vector machine, wavelet analysis and neural network etc. Finally, aiming at the development status of fault diagnosis for gyroscope, the current existing problems of fault diagnosis for gyroscope are summarized, and the future development and application of fault diagnosis for gyroscope are prospected.

1 Introduction

Gyroscope had already experienced four stages in the development of 100 years since it was first used in ship for orientation in 1910. The first stage was the development of the ball bearing gyroscope motor and gimbaled gyroscope, which used bearing or gimbals to support high-speed rotor rotating shaft steadily measure the angular position of the carrier, and were widely applied in the aviation gyroscope instrument and flight control system, but existing outer disturbing torque made its precision decreased. The second stage was the development of the liquid floated gyroscope and gas floated gyroscope in the late 1940s to the early 50s, which made the framework a thin wall airtight float, using liquid or gas support high-speed rotor to decrease the friction torque and improve accuracy, but it needed the high working accuracy and cost. The third stage was the development of the rotor gyroscope with dry power flexible support in the 1960s, using the flexible junction instead of gyroscope gimbals ring and precise shaft to drive high-speed rotor without floating fluid and temperature control system, getting widely application in the aircraft and tactical missile, but it could not bear a larger impaction and vibration because the thickness of flexible support was only zero a few millimeters. The fourth stage was the rapid development of static electricity, laser, optical fiber and vibration gyroscope[1], using electrostatic or optoelectronic technology to support high-speed rotor, which had been widely used in military and civil fields such as aerospace with high precision, small volume, impact resistance and strong practicability, and would become the research and development direction of gyroscope in the future.

[a] Corresponding Author: Hu Shaolin, hfkth@126.com

DOI: 10.1051/itmconf/20171107001

The inertia navigation system was a technology of autonomous navigation and developed in the middle of twentieth century, whose characteristics—full autonomy, all-weather, anti-disturbance, concealment and output a great number of real-time information—had not only led to provide the complete parameters(position, angular velocity and attitude angle) of navigation guidance and hence to widespread applied in the field of aerospace navigation, but had also selected as a standard and must to be installed navigation equipment. Especially, the increasing complex and intense relationship of national at present-day, the increasing dependence and requirement of inertia navigation technology changed more and more higher, and therefore it had become the key supporting technology in the competition of modern high-technology, and had the important significance to build the defense and security of national in strategic and practical.

As the core part of inertia navigation system, gyroscope can accurately determine the location of carriers and its reliability directly affects the navigation performance. According to the relevant statistics, approximately per sixty of fault is related to gyroscope in the inertia navigation system[2]. Therefore, it is great significance to ensure the safety and stability of carrier if the status of the performance of gyroscope had been judged in advance, and then timely accomplished fault diagnosis, prediction and remove for gyroscope.

2 Fault diagnosis for gyroscope

2.1 Classification of fault for gyroscope

The fault factors of gyroscope were divided into internal factors and external factors in the operational process. Internal factors mainly derived from the gyroscope itself, such as restriction of technological structure, the selection of component and the irrationality of circuit design. External factors is that the operating environment of gyroscope was relatively complex and poor, which made it easily suffer to the impaction of temperature, humidity, vibration and shock, electrical stress and other factors. For example, temperature factors can lead to gyroscope insulation aging, tensile strength aging, thermal decomposition and deformation failure. Humidity factor can cause gyroscope electrical short circuit, circuit board corrosion, surface damage and gyro motor stuck and other failures. Vibration and shock factors[3] can result in component fatigue fracture, poor contact and loose parts of the gyroscope. High-intensity and high-bandwidth radio interference can cause performance degradation and device failure and other failures.

Gyroscope will produce different patterns of abnormal failure due to the different fault inducing factors during operation. Based on the time length of failure, it may be classified into permanent failure with unrecovered, specifically as hardware damage or aging; irregular repeat intermittent failure resulting from poor contact between elements and bad environment; transient failure caused by surroundings change, such as exterior pressure change or electronic interference. Based on development degree of failure, it might be classified into unable to monitor and predict the mutability of fault in advance which could be easily checked and located, for example elements don't work suddenly; gradually failure (soft failure) varying by time and environment, such as the ones out of control leaded by decrease of accuracy and the degradation of performance.

Also, according to the common fault of gyroscope, many experts and scholars will be divided them into total failure, bias failure, drift failure and periodic disturbance failure[4], or according to the different characteristic of gyroscope output signal, the fault types can be considered as periodic failure, spike failure, pulse failure, offset failure and drift failure[5]. Despite the different types and classification of the fault for gyroscope, the occurrence of fault will lead to the reduction of accuracy and the performance degradation of gyroscope, and even affect its working safety and reliability. Therefore, it is important for ensuring the safe operation of gyroscope to investigate and seek an arithmetic which could timely, accurately and effectively deal with the detection, diagnosis and prediction of fault for gyroscope.

2.2 Fault diagnosis for gyroscope

At present, although the research of fault diagnosis for gyroscope had already made great progress, the key of the research is focused on the gradual fault diagnosis caused by gyroscope drift, and thus a number of different types of algorithms of fault diagnosis for gyroscope were proposed. If summarized in accordance with the structure of algorithms, it can be divided into the following categories:

2.2.1 Algorithms of fault diagnosis based on experience knowledge method for gyroscope

The algorithms of fault diagnosis based on experience knowledge method for gyroscope do not need to establish the mathematical model accurately, which can make full use of expert knowledge diagnose the fault of gyroscope by introducing the information of fault for gyroscope[6]. Currently used gyroscope monitoring methods are adequate for detecting failures that can happen in the short-term, to detect the performance degradation tendency of long-term fault, a fault detection model for gyroscope based on a fuzzy expert system solution is described and can improve the current operational processes of monitoring the gyroscope by detecting earlier on potential failures[7]; on the basis of the sequential adaptive learning algorithm, an improved evolving belief-rule-based learning algorithm based on the belief-incomplete criterion is proposed and used in the prediction of fault for gyroscope, and finally verify the validity of the algorithm and improve the precision of fault forecasting[8]; due to the existing method cannot evaluate the life of gyroscope quickly and exactly, a acceleration life evaluation method for gyroscope under temperature based on fault tree analysis is proposed and the steps of proposed method are simple and feasible[9]; in order to meet the reliability requirement of gyroscope, the problem of fault diagnosis need to be discussed and a expert system for gyroscope fault diagnosis based on Lab VIEW and Access is presented, which build the knowledge base and reasoning machine of expert system and write the corresponding software programme, the results show that the expert system can diagnose the location and reason of fault rapidly and accurately[10].

2.2.2 Algorithm of fault diagnosis based on support vector machines for gyroscope

Support vector machine(SVM)[11] is a new optimization algorithm which proposed by Vapnik and based on the principle of statistical learning theory and structural risk minimization, as the algorithm provided the solution of small sample, high dimension and nonlinear so that it is applied in fault diagnosis for gyroscope. A forgetting-factor least square SVM algorithm is given to build the forecasting model of drift-error-parameter of gyroscope based on the nonlinear measurement data, which used forgetting-factor to set different level of new-and-old sample and hence to avoid new information being covered by old information and enhance its self-adaptability and forecasting accuracy[12]; taking the time series of gyroscope's drift as study object, a prediction model based support vector regression is established and a pre-selecting algorithm based on the immune clustering in kernel function space is presented, and finally the method is rapid, high accuracy and practical[13], however, for improving the operational accuracy of gyroscope, the random drift error model based on wavelet analysis and least square SVM(LSSVM) is established to compensate the precision of nonlinear and weak-stability of gyroscope's random drift signal[14]; at the same time, in order to improve the learning performance and generalization ability of LSSVM, using CPSO algorithm to generate the initial chaotic particles and chaotic interrupt is added for the selection and optimization of the LSSVM, and then build the prediction model of gyroscope random drift and improve the precision of fault diagnosis[15]; for forecasting the tendency of gyroscope drift, a least square support vector regression model by introducing the wavelet kernel is presented and through genetic algorithm to optimize the model parameters, so its early forecasting ability of fault is improved and strengthened[16]; because of existing output error of gyroscope online, the online incremental LSSVM is utilized to build the dynamic model in order to obtain the real-time residual between real value and pre-estimating value, and then accomplish fast and accuracy online diagnosis[17]; to solve the classification accuracy reducing problem of SVM resulting from unbalanced samples and high noise of gyroscope output signals, an unbalanced FSVM fault diagnosis method of gyroscope based on DSP is presented, which can improve the diagnostic precision of fault samples and the disturbance of noise[18].

2.2.3 Algorithms of fault diagnosis based on wavelet analysis for gyroscope

The output signal of gyroscope is non-stationary, whose amplitude and frequency changed with the time. For these time varying signals, it is necessary to use the time-frequency analysis method which reflects its characteristics to analyze effectively and finds the fault signal. Wavelet transform can decompose the signal into multi-scale components, and selects the appropriate time domain sample step accordance with the different size of scale component to constantly focus on any small details of the processed signal[19]. For developing the model of gyroscope drift character, the multi-resolution theory of wavelet analysis is used to analyze and pretreated the signal of gyroscope drift and the result confirms its effectiveness[20]; aimed to the error fault of gyroscope drift, wavelet analysis is used to extract the error feature vector and then three-layers feedforward BP neural network is adapted to build fault model, finally fuzzy logic judgment makes diagnostic method more simple and quick[21]; Liu Luyuan extracted the tendency of the signal of gyroscope drift by the multi-resolution theory of wavelet analysis, and established the error model of gyroscope to improve the precision of model[22]; because gyroscope's drift output signal is weak and non-stationary random series, wavelet analysis is used to accomplish the hierarchical process of output data in frequency domain and use time series analysis method to build the model of gyroscope drift and finally improved the speed and precision of model[23]; according to the fault of gyroscope drift, a new prediction algorithm based on wavelet support vector machine is put forword for fault prediction and enhances the precision of fault forecasting while ensuring the safety of devices[24]; because of the mutation of the output signal of gyroscope, the signal is decomposed by three-layer wavelet package and extracts its feature to train RBF neural network, the result shows that the method can detect the fault accurately[25].

2.2.4 Algorithms of fault diagnosis based on neural network for gyroscope

Actually, the usage of neural network in fault diagnosis is achieve the classification of fault information without mathematical model, and adjusts the weight constantly while training to meet the requirement of precision in order to accomplish the nonlinear mapping between input and output and have the ability of self-organization and pattern recognition[26]. To solve the problem of gyroscope servo loop, the fault diagnosis using BP neural network and its software package had been simulated, the result is very satisfactory[27]; compared with BP algorithm, the LMBP algorithm which through optimizing standard BP algorithm with Levenberg-Marquardt(L-M) algorithm which had second-order convergence effects can improve the converges of neural network learning and the ability of fault prediction for gyroscope[28]; in order to accurately and reliably detect and predict the fault of gyroscope, a wavelet based on RBF neural network fault detect algorithm is proposed, which makes the output signal decomposed into eight nodes in different frequency bands and extracts feature, then to train RBF neural network and the result shows that it can accurately diagnose the type of fault and improve the precision of fault diagnosis[29]; for discerning in real time and predicting the tendency of gyroscope drift, wavelet extraction algorithm combined with neural network nonlinear prediction algorithm which can set up the fault prediction model, and hence to reduce the impaction of environment factors and improve the precision of fault prediction[30]; because the parameter of the performance of gyroscope had degradation, a new algorithm which uses the SOFM neural network to implement the feature information fusion for charactering its degradation and uses the HMM to transform the early weak fault signals into the easily observed information, thus predicts the faults of gyroscope and the results shows that the algorithm can easily and effectively extract the feature information on gyroscope's degradation[31]; according to the fault characteristics of gyroscope,

Hilbert-Huang Transform method is adapted to extract the feature of fault information and then uses fuzzy Kohonen neural network to build fault diagnosis model and finally improve the accuracy of fault diagnosis for gyroscope[32].

2.2.5 Other fusion algorithms of fault diagnosis for gyroscope

Of course, there are many other types of fusion algorithms of fault diagnosis for gyroscope. Aiming to the characteristics of gyroscope's fault, power spectra method is used to analyze the output signal eigenvalues whether fault occur or not, and then build the signal's AR model and power spectra chart so as to identify the classification of fault for gyroscope[33]; According to the tendency of gyroscope drift, a hybrid modeling method based on grey theory and stationary time series analysis is proposed and used in gyroscope drift forecasting, which has a higher forecasting precision[34]; Wang Jia has already use parameter identification method to complete performance analysis of gyroscope and the result shows that the method is very well[35]; in order to accomplish the problem of fault detection for gyroscope, an algorithm based on the sliding window least square method is designed and it can determine the fault type and fault time accurately[36]; to diagnose the fault for gyroscope when the redundancy of gyroscope cannot meet the requirement of odd-even equation, the nonlinear extended Kalman filter is adopted to estimate angular rate and can diagnose both abrupt and slow change fault of gyroscope[37].

Conclusions

In this paper, the mainstream algorithm of fault diagnosis for gyroscope is described in detail, but there are still many problems needed to be solved. First, fault diagnosis for gyroscope has a low degree of autonomy, and now most of algorithms of fault diagnosis still need researchers to identify in order to fail to achieve autonomous learning and diagnosis of fault completely. Secondly, the algorithm of fault diagnosis mainly researches the problem of single fault at present, if multiple faults occur, it is need to study how to classify and diagnose. Finally, in the big data environment, the investigation of fault diagnosis for gyroscope is just in the initial stage, and not makes great progress.

In recent years, the technology of machine learning and deep learning has developed quickly under the background of big data, which simulate the hierarchical structure of brain in order to obtain the multi-level characteristic expression from massive data, so as to improve the accuracy of classification and prediction. Therefore, the development of machine learning and deep learning will be the key technology in the research of fault diagnosis for gyroscope in the future.

Acknowledgement

This work is supported by National Natural Science Foundation of China under Grant 61473222 and Grant 91646108.

References

1. G.T. Liang, Aero. Miss. J., **(4)**, 38-40 (2006)
2. X. Z. Guo, *Theory of Gyroscope in Inertia Navigation System*, (1996)
3. Chen W, Xie Q, Luo Y. Com. Inf. Sci. (ICCIS) Int. Con. IEEE, 222-225 (2010)
4. Heredia G, Ollero A. IEEE Int. Con. Rob. Auto., **2**, 2229 (2005)
5. H.M. Qian, J.C. Ma, J. Elec. Meas. Ins., **21**, 538-541 (2007)
6. B. Yan, Q. Wei, Y. Li, Sci. Tec. Inf., **(31)**, 26-27 (2011)
7. A. Pereira, F. Moura-Pires, R.A. Ribeiro, ESM, 200-203 (2002)
8. X.S. Shi, C.H. Hu, Con. The. Appl., **12**, 1579-1586(2012)
9. L.X. Yu, L. Qin, J. Dete. & Con., **03**, 78-81 (2015)

10. X.D. Qin, Y.S. Li, Sci. & Tec. Vis., **21**, 110-111 (2016)
11. V. Vapnik, *The nature of statistical learning theory*, (Spr. Sci. & Bus. Med., 2013)
12. W. Zhang, C.H. Hu, J. Astr., **02**, 448-451 (2007)
13. Y.L. Cai, C.H. Hu, J. Chi. Ine. Tec., **05**, 593-597 (2007)
14. W.W. Qin, Z.Q. Zheng, J. Chi. Ine. Tec., **06**, 721-724+729 (2008)
15. Y.H. Gao, Y.B. Li, J. Sichuan Uni.(Eng. Sci. Edi.), **02**, 177-181 (2010)
16. Y.M. Cai, C.H. Hu. Sys. Eng. Elec., **30(1)**, 190-192 (2008)
17. Y. Shi, X.M. Li, Com. Meas. & Con., **21(1)**, 14-17+26 (2013)
18. Y. Li, Q.F. Luo, J. Shenyang Ligong Uni., **01**, 46-51 (2015)
19. S.R. Wang, H. Yang, J. Chi. Ine. Tec., **02**, 49-54 (1998)
20. L.N. Xu, Z.L. Deng, J. Chi. Ine. Tec., **01**, 50-53+62 (2003)
21. C.L. Fan, Z.H. Jin, J. Shanghai Jiaotong Uni., **01**,141-144 (2003)
22. L.Y. Liu, Y.Z. Chen, J. Chi. Ine. Tec., **01**, 62-66 (2004)
23. C. Li, J.H. Zhu, J. Pro. Roc. Miss. Gui., **SA**, 402-404 (2005)
24. W. Chen, C.H. Hu, Elec. Opt. & Con., **02**, 97-100 (2006)
25. L. Tong, W.M. Niu, Micro. Inf., **10**, 159-160+175 (2009)
26. H.M. Qian, W.S. Wang, Nav. Chi., **01**, 6-9 (2009)
27. J.T. Wu, H.K. Le, J. Chi. Ine. Tec., **01**, 38-40 (1999)
28. Y.J. Lv, C.H. Hu, Mech. Sci. Tec., **01**, 28-30 (2006)
29. L. Tong, W.M. Niu, Com. Meas. & Con., **11**, 2137-2139 (2009)
30. L. Yang, W. Zhao, Nav. Con., **09(2)**, 36-41 (2010)
31. Y.S. Shang, A.Q. Xu, Mech. Sci. Tec., **10**, 1711-1715+1720 (2012)
32. M.H. Wu, W.H. Li, Sci. Tec. Eng., **04**, 298-302 (2014)
33. J.N. Xu, Y.L. Gu, J. Naval Uni. Eng., **04**, 67-70+78 (2001)
34. Z.J. Zhou, C.H. Hu, Sys. Eng. Elec., **03**, 416-418 (2007)
35. J. Wang, X.F. Li, Appl. Res. Com., **03**, 817-819 (2013)
36. L. Yao, X.P. Han, J. Tele. Trac. Com., **01**, 19-23 (2013)
37. Y. Zhang, P.H. Wang, Aero. Shanghai, **03**, 22-25 (2005)

ITM Web of Conferences **11**, 07002 (2017) DOI: 10.1051/itmconf/20171107002
IST2017

Effect of Encoder Eccentricity on Rolling Speed Control and Elimination Method

Ren-Tao ZHAO[1,a], Xin-Long SHI[1] and Zi WANG[2]

[1]*School of electrical and control engineering, North China University of Technology, Beijing 100144, China*
[2]*State Grid Beijing Maintenance Company, Beijing 100054, China*

Abstract. Aiming to solve the problems of incremental photoelectric encoder eccentricity in the speed control system of rolling mill, this paper deduces the calculation model of actual speed, and gives a high precision approximation calculation method. Furthermore, the effectiveness and accuracy of the simplified model are verified by the simulation results. The online identification method of eccentricity and initial angle is also given in the paper. In addition, on the basis of continuous model, this article derives from the discrete model of traditional speed measurement scheme based on digital control system. This proposed algorithm has simplicity and excellent application value, and the effectiveness of the algorithm has been verified.

Introduction

Although the rapid development of the sensorless vector control system made a result that the application of speed feedback link in AC drive field is decreasing, roller speed regulation system which has wide-range and high-precision regulating speed still require to utilize incremental photoelectric encoder (referred to as optical encoder). Besides, DC speed regulating system still be widely used in speed closed loop system structure. According to the closed-loop control theory, the low frequency disturbance of feedback channel will have bad influence on the operation of the system, which may cause low-frequency oscillation of system. A simple eccentricity correction algorithm given in literature [1] can effectively overcome the low frequency disturbance caused by eccentricity of speed generator. But it is not suitable for digital system with incremental photoelectric encoder as speed feedback. Literature [2] uses SIMULINK to establish a simulation model of optical encoder, analyzes reasons about high-frequency noise of the velocity measurement of an encoder and their impact on system performance, and proposes a method to estimate the instantaneous speed of motor with speed observer. Although this method has a strong ability to suppress high-frequency noise, it still cannot eliminate the low-frequency signal generated by eccentricity. Literature [3] analyzes the expression forms of incremental optical encoder eccentricity, gives the realization method of eliminating eccentric effect by adding the diameter digital quantities. But the prerequisite of implementation of compensation is to add a set of photoelectric detection component in optical encoder. In order to eliminate the influence of eccentricity on velocity, we add two signals with 180 degrees phase difference in the external microprocessor together, which can play a very good

[a] Corresponding author: Ray_zhao@263.net

DOI: 10.1051/itmconf/20171107002

compensation effect.

Based on the derivation of the velocity eccentricity model, this article proposes a simple velocity correction algorithm which can obtain ideal effect speed compensation without special modification of optical encoder.

Establishment of eccentric model

As shown in Figure 1, assuming that the center position of the motor shaft is located at O, and the optical encoder center is at O', photoelectric detection device of optical encoder is installed in the horizontal axis direction, the margin of the grating disk in optical encoder and the horizontal axis intersect at P point. Postulating that OP is equal to ρ, and θ_0 is the angle between the photoelectric element that produces the Z pulse and the line OP, which will be a constant as soon as the optical encoder is installed [4, 5].

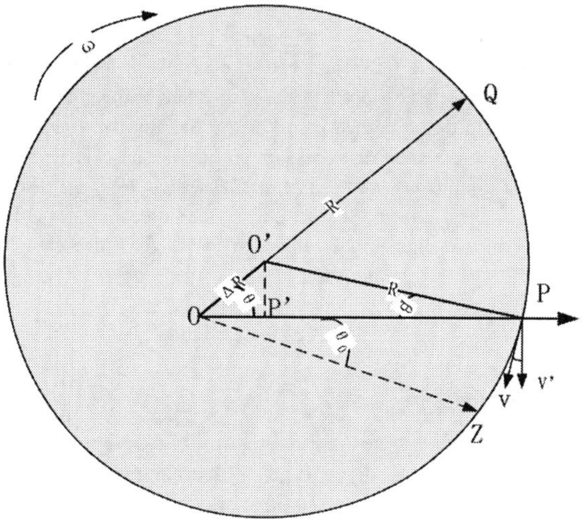

Figure 1. Diagram of eccentricity during the optical encoder installation process.

When the motor operates at angular speed ω, the center point O' of the optical encoder and the Q point on the edge of optical encoder rotate are around O point at the same angular speed [6, 7]. If the feature points' position on the optical encoder are shown in figure 1 at t time, the line OQ advances the horizontal axis by θ angle. According to the structure of the optical encoder, the frequency of pulse output from signal A or B is proportional to the line speed of P point (the tangential direction of eccentric circle) at any moment [8]. Accordingly, so long as the relation between OP and angle θ can be found out, it can be obtained that the relationship between optical encoder output frequency and angular velocity in the case of eccentric condition. The specific derivations will be given as follows.

This paper analyzes the situation that the optical encoder radius is 30mm, eccentric distance is 0.35mm. In order to derive mathematical model which is irrelevant to the radius of optical encoder, the radius R is normalized to 1.

According to the sine theorem, we can know that

$$\frac{R}{\sin\theta} = \frac{\Delta R}{\sin\beta}. \tag{1}$$

Another form is that

$$\sin\beta = \frac{\Delta R\cdot\sin\theta}{R}. \tag{2}$$

This formula can be further derived:

$$OP = OP' + P'P = \Delta R\cdot\cos\theta + R\cdot\cos\beta. \tag{3}$$

According to the formula (2), we can find out that

$$\cos\beta = R\sqrt{1-\left(\frac{\Delta R\cdot\sin\theta}{R}\right)^2} = \sqrt{R^2-\Delta R^2\sin^2\theta}. \tag{4}$$

Next, insert the equation (4) into equation (3), we can obtain equation (5) as follows after calculation.

$$OP = \Delta R\cdot\cos\theta + \sqrt{R^2-\Delta R^2\sin^2\theta} \tag{5}$$

Combined with figure 1, we can get an equation about the relation between optical encoder output frequency and angular velocity ω, as shown as formula (6).

$$f = K\cdot\frac{V'}{2\pi R} = K\cdot\frac{V\cdot\cos\beta}{2\pi R} = K\cdot\frac{OP\cdot\omega\cdot\cos\beta}{2\pi R}. \tag{6}$$

Among the formula (6), K is the number of pulses output from optical encoder for per revolution, namely the number of lines.

After that, insert the rotate speed formula $n = \frac{60f}{K}$ into the formula (6), we can obtain the relation between rotate speed n' and OP under the eccentric condition.

$$n' = K\cdot\frac{60\cdot OP\cdot\omega\cdot\cos\beta}{2\pi R\cdot K} = 9.55\frac{OP}{R}\cdot\omega\cdot\cos\beta. \tag{7}$$

And then, take equation (5) into equation (7), we can finally obtains the function relationship between the n' with the angle θ, as shown as equation (8).

$$n' = 9.55\frac{\left(\Delta R\cos\theta + \sqrt{R^2\,\Delta - R^2\sin^2\theta}\right)}{R}\cdot\omega\cdot\frac{\sqrt{R^2-\Delta R^2\sin^2\theta}}{R}. \tag{8}$$

Evidently, the equation (8) can be simplified as equation (9), when the optical encoder is installed without deviating from the center ($\Delta R = 0$).

$$n' = \frac{60}{2\pi}\cdot\omega = n. \tag{9}$$

In order to analyze the influence of eccentricity easily, we define the relative eccentricity as

$$e = \frac{\Delta R}{R}. \tag{10}$$

From Figure 2 we can see that the frequency fluctuation degree caused by optical encoder eccentricity is $0 \sim \pm\frac{\Delta R}{R} = \pm 10\%$, which means that the frequency fluctuation caused by eccentricity depends entirely on the relative eccentricity e.

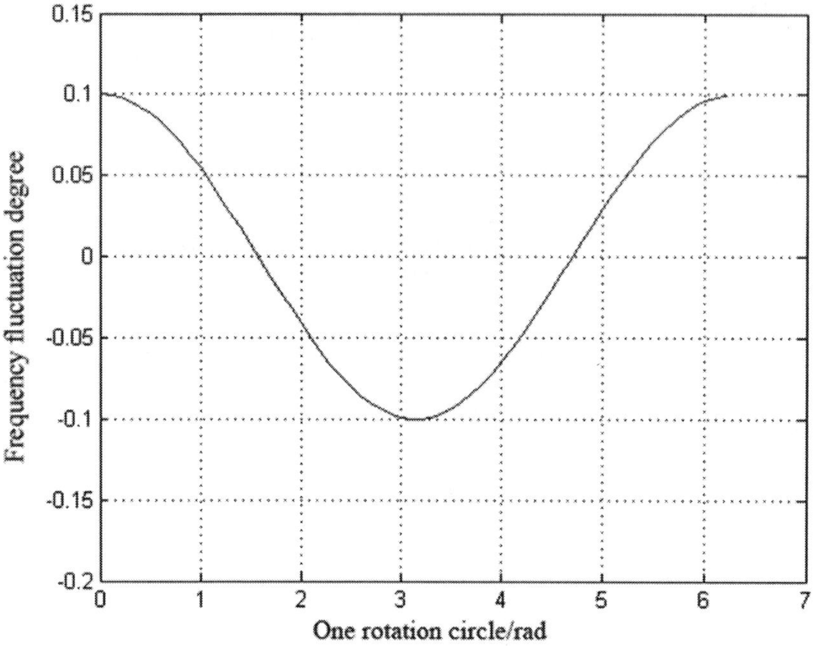

Figure 2. Normalized curve of optical encoder output frequency changing with angle θ for every rotation circle at constant speed (K=1024, ω=10.9, ΔR = 0.00035 meters, R=0.03 meters) .

Simplification of Eccentric Model

Aiming to apply the above model to the actual speed regulation system, the equation (8) should be simplified firstly to cut down the amount of computation, in order to facilitate real-time velocity correction to eliminate the effect caused by eccentricity [4].

Assuming relative eccentricity e is known, the relationship between the angle β and e can be calculated according to equation (2) and equation (10).

$$\sin\beta = e\cdot\sin\theta. \tag{11}$$

According to the Taylor series of $\sin\beta$ and $\cos\beta$, $\sin\beta$ can be approximately replaced by angle β when β is very small. Thus, the formula (2) can be adapted as

$$\beta \approx e\cdot\sin\theta. \tag{12}$$

$$\cos\beta = \sqrt{1-\sin^2\beta} \approx \sqrt{1-\beta^2} \approx 1-\frac{1}{2}\beta^2. \tag{13}$$

DOI: 10.1051/itmconf/20171107002

When the eccentricity reaches 0.125 %, it is less than 5 ppm that the error caused by approximate calculation with (13), which can be ignored. And put formula (10) and (11) into the formula (6), we can further get formula (14) by ignoring $\frac{1}{2}\beta^2$ and $\frac{1}{4}\beta^4$.

$$f \approx \frac{K}{2\pi}\cdot\left(e\cdot\cos\theta+1-\beta^2\right)\cdot\omega. \tag{14}$$

The formula (7) is predigested as

$$n \approx \frac{n'}{\left(e\cdot\cos\theta+1-e^2\cdot\sin^2\theta\right)}. \tag{15}$$

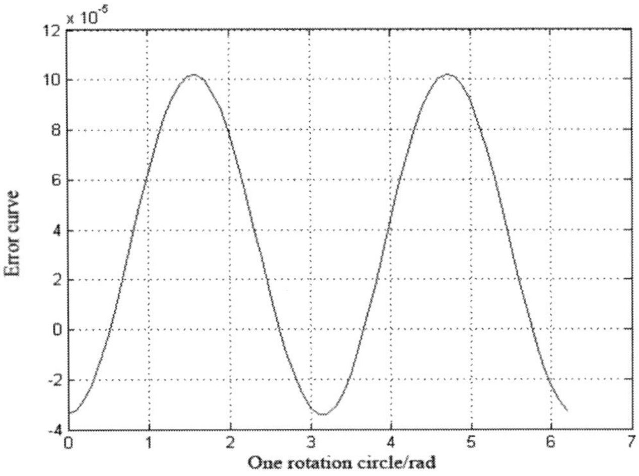

Figure 3. Error curve between the exact and approximate values of the rotate speed n' in a circle.

As can be seen from figure 3, the results of preliminary simplification are quite satisfactory. The maximum absolute error is less than $1.02*10^{-4}$ rpm, which is equivalent to the 0.001 ‰ of current speed 104 rpm (ω=10.9), completely meet the high-precision velocity measurement.

Further simplification of the formula (15) leads to the simplest model as follows:

$$n \approx \frac{n'}{\left(e\cdot\cos\theta+1-0.25\cdot e^2\right)}. \tag{16}$$

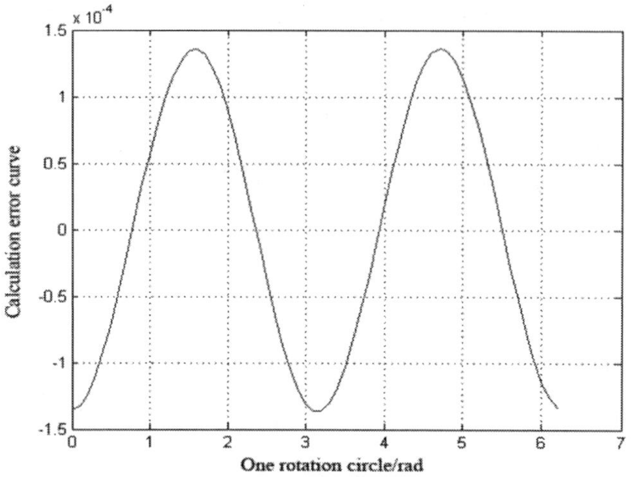

Figure 4. Calculation error curve of secondary simplification.

After observation of figure 4, we can find that the calculation error of the secondary simplified rotational speed model increases obviously. The maximum amplitude is close to $1.5*10^{-4}$ rpm, which is around 0.0014 ‰ of the current speed 104 rpm, and satisfy the requirements of higher precision velocity measurement.

Online identification method of eccentricity

Identification should be carried out in the case of no-load or constant load after the installation of optical encoder, for the purpose of ensuring the accuracy of identification.

(1) The output signal A of optical encoder should be connected to the pulse input port of the counter of microprocessor, and connects the signal Z to the input port of external interrupt.

(2) Motor operates at constant speed (n=100~500 rpm).

(3) Start online identification program.

a) When the microprocessor detects the Z pulse for the first time, it starts the counting and frequency catching process automatically, and stops this process automatically at the time of detecting Z pulse secondly. In the meantime, record the maximum cycle T_{max} (k_1) and minimum cycle T_{min} (k_2) of signal A and the corresponding counter values k_1 and k_2. According to figure 1, P and Q position coincide at k_2 moment, P is precisely on the OQ extension line at k_1 moment.

b) Calculate the highest frequency f_{max} and the lowest frequency f_{min} separately on the basis of T_{max} (k_1) and T_{min} (k_2).

$$f_{\max} = \frac{1}{T_{\min}}, \quad f_{\min} = \frac{1}{T_{\max}}. \tag{17}$$

c) Convert k_1 and k_2 into angle, as follows.

$$\theta_1 = \frac{2\pi \cdot k_1}{K}, \theta_2 = \frac{2\pi \cdot k_2}{K}. \tag{18}$$

d) Calculate initial angle θ_0 and relative eccentricity e.

$$\theta_0 = (\theta_2 + |\pi - \theta_1|)/2. \tag{19}$$

And e can be obtained through formula (15).

$$e = \left| \frac{f_{\max} / f_{\min} - 1}{\cos\theta_1 - \cos\theta_2 \cdot f_{\max} / f_{\min}} \right|. \tag{20}$$

Because the microprocessor chip is used in most of the speed regulating system [9], this paper needs to derive a recursive algorithm which can be directly applied to digital control system. The specific iterative algorithm is given as follows.

Assuming that the sampling period of velocity is fixed as T_s, the corresponding angular positions of the two adjacent sampling time are θ_k and θ_{k+1}. Accordingly, the results of the sampling can be expressed with the following integral expression:

$$n'' = \frac{1}{T_s}\int_{\theta_k}^{\theta_{k+1}} n' \cdot d\theta = \frac{n}{T_s}\int_{\theta_k}^{\theta_{k+1}} (e\ \cos\theta + 1 - \beta^2) \cdot d\theta. \tag{21}$$

Put formula (12) into the above formula, we can get that

$$n'' \approx \frac{n}{T_s}\int_{\theta_k}^{\theta_{k+1}} \left(e \cdot \cos\theta + 1 - e^2 \cdot \sin^2\theta\right) \cdot d\theta = n \cdot F(\theta). \tag{22}$$

In this formula, n is the result of speed calculation in the case of no eccentric, disturbance quantity is

$$F(\theta) = \frac{e}{T_s} \cdot (\sin\theta_{k+1} - \sin\theta_k) - \frac{e^2}{2T_s}(\theta_{k+1} - \theta_k) + \frac{e^2}{4T_s} \cdot (\sin 2\theta_{k+1} - \sin 2\theta_k). \tag{23}$$

Assuming that $M(k)$ is stand for the pulse count value at k moment and $M(k+1)$ is the pulse count value at $k+1$ moment in the digital control system. And both of them take K as modulus, which means that $0 < M(k) \le M(k+1) < K$. Then we can get equation (24) and equation (25). The actual rotational speed $n_0''(k)$ of any sampling period can be acquired by inserting equation (24) and (25) into formula (22).

$$\theta_k = 2\pi \frac{M(k)}{K}. \tag{24}$$

$$\theta_{k+1} = 2\pi \frac{M(k+1)}{K}. \tag{25}$$

$$n_0''(k) = \frac{n''(k)}{F(k)}. \tag{26}$$

The disturbance after discretization is

$$\begin{aligned} F(k) = {} & \frac{e}{T_s} \cdot \left(\sin\left(2\pi \frac{M(k+1)}{K}\right) - \sin\left(2\pi \frac{M(k)}{K}\right)\right) - \frac{\pi e^2}{T_s K}(M(k+1) - M(k)) \\ & + \frac{e^2}{4T_s} \cdot \left(\sin\left(4\pi \frac{M(k+1)}{K}\right) - \sin\left(4\pi \frac{M(k)}{K}\right)\right) \end{aligned}. \tag{27}$$

Because sine function can be cured to the proceeding space in advance, the perturbation $F(k)$ that seems cumbersome in the preceding paragraphs can be completely converted to simple algebraic

DOI: 10.1051/itmconf/20171107002

operations, which basically does not increase the computational burden to digital control systems.

Simulation and Verification

In the working process of rolling mill, low frequency disturbance of rotational speed caused by optical encoder eccentricity will have a great impact on product quality, such as steel plate creep deformation, uneven thickness. Meanwhile, the energy consumption of the rolling mill is increased obviously, and production decreased. Long time operation with fluctuation speed also shortens the life of the equipment seriously.

As we can see in Figure 5, the curves are the speed tendency of optical encoder (a) and output current (b), in the case of open-loop vector control system with 600 rpm rated speed and rotational speed is set to 17.35 % of rated speed. Obviously, the speed curve approximates to the sine curve and its fluctuation amplitude reaches to 4.8 rpm.

Figure 6 is a part of enlargement of figure 5, and it shows the speed curve of encoder output in one cycle. To eliminate eccentric disturbance, the iterative algorithm of the simplified model is embedded into the control system speed feedback channel. And the corrected encoder output is shown in figure 7. The corrected error is less than 0.5 rpm. Actual results prove that the elimination approach has a good correction effect, and can meet the general requirements of speed measurement.

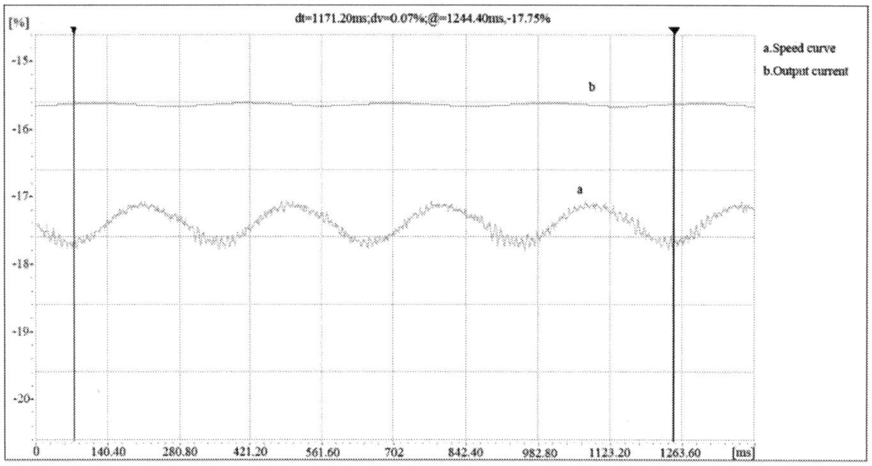

Figure 5. Curve diagram of the encoder speed and output current.

DOI: 10.1051/itmconf/20171107002

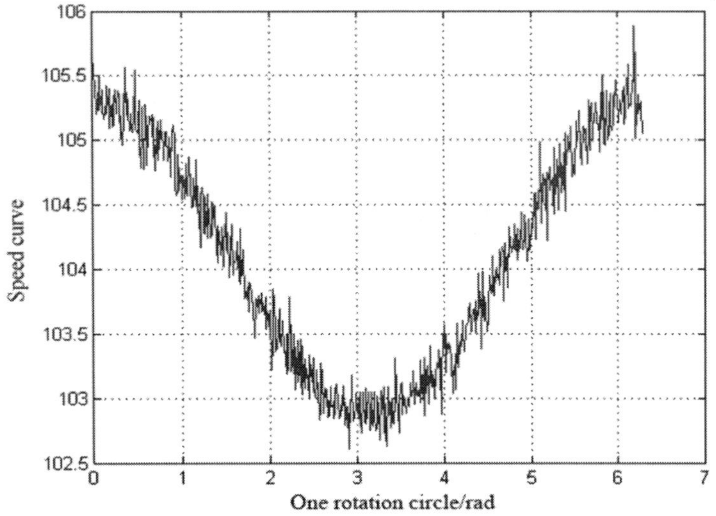

Figure 6. Curve of encoder speed.

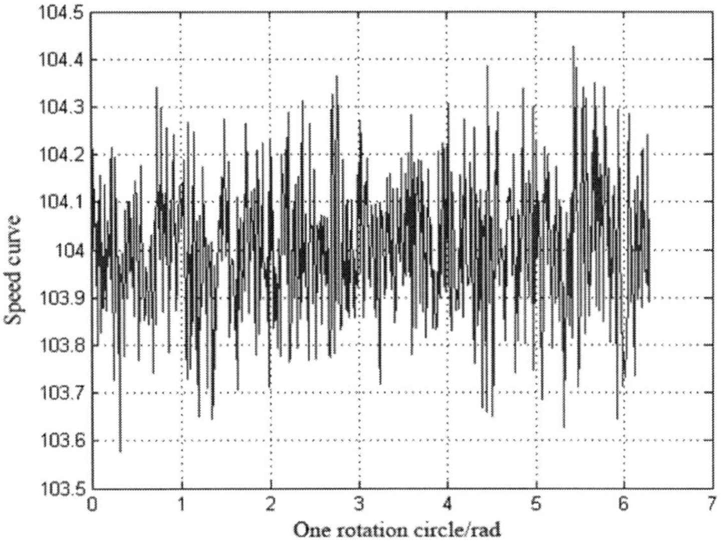

Figure 7. Curve of encoder speed output after eccentricity correction.

Conclusion

By mean of analyzing the eccentric mechanism, this paper establishes the simplified model that can effectively eliminate the low-frequency disturbance caused by the eccentricity in the speed feedback channel. Finally, a high accuracy recursive algorithm which can be applied to digital control system is presented, and it has a higher application value.

Acknowledgments

The authors wish to thank the financial support by the National Key R&D Projects of China (2016YFF0102407).

References

1. X. Tang, W. Chen. A simple method about eliminating eccentricity error. *Computation Technique*. **7**, 39-40(1996).
2. J. Tan, Y. Qin. Simulation Model of Optical Encoder and Estimation of Instantaneous Velocity for a Motor. *Electric Drive*. **2**, 41-43(2001).
3. Y. Fang. Studies on digital addition technology in incremental encoder. Master's Thesis Graduate University of Chinese Academy of Sciences.2005.
4. R. Zhao, Z. Zhang, J. Tie. Influence of Encoder Eccentricity on Speed Measurement and Elimination Approach. International Conference on Network Computing and Information Security. 63-66 (2011).
5. X. Ma, R. Zhao. High precision rotating speed measuring device. China. Utility Models. ZL200720141299.8. 2008-3-12.
6. Z. Cai, R. Zhao, F. Cheng. Research on Digital Estimation Method of Motor Speed and Rotor Position. *Electric Drive*. **37**(8), 12-14(2007).
7. Q. Yu, K. Liu, C. Wang, W. Yuan, W. Qian, C. Zhang. Choice of Optical-encoder and Measure of Speed and Rotor Place of Synchronous Motor. *Electric Drive*. **36**(4), 17-20(2006).
8. D. Mancini, M. Brescia, E. Cascone, F. Cortecchia, P. Schipani. Encoder system design: strategies for error compensation. *Proc. SPIE*. **3351**, 380-386(1998).
9. Y. Matsuzoe, N. Tsuji. Breadboard system and techniques to optimize the optical system of an encoder. *Optical Engineering*. **40**(2), 283-288(2001).

A GPU Heterogeneous Cluster Scheduling Model for Preventing Temperature Heat Island

Yun-Peng CAO[1,2,a] and Hai-Feng WANG[1,2]

[1]*School of Information Science and Engineering, Linyi University, Linyi Shandong, China 276005*
[2]*Institute of Linyi University of Shandong Provincial Key Laboratory of Network based Intelligent Computing, Linyi Shandong, China 276005*

Abstract. With the development of GPU general-purpose computing, GPU heterogeneous cluster has become a widely used parallel data processing solution in modern data center. Temperature management and controlling has become a new research hotspot in big data continuous computing. Temperature heat island in cluster has important influence on computing reliability and energy efficiency. In order to prevent the occurrence of GPU cluster temperature heat island, a big data task scheduling model for preventing temperature heat island was proposed. In this model, temperature, reliability and computing performance are taken into account to reduce node performance difference and improve throughput per unit time in cluster. Temperature heat islands caused by slow nodes are prevented by optimizing scheduling. The experimental results show that the proposed scheme can control node temperature and prevent the occurrence of temperature heat island under the premise of guaranteeing computing performance and reliability.

1 Introduction

After GPU (Graphic Processing Unit) was proposed by NVIDIA company and its birth, it has been developing rapidly beyond the speed of Moore's Law, its computing capability has been rising continuously. At SIGGRAPH conference in 2003, GPGPU(General-purpose computing on graphics processing units) was introduced. GPUs gradually shifted from dedicated parallel processors consisting of fixed functional units to architectures with primary general-purpose computing resources and secondary fixed functional units. GPU is composed of a large number of parallel processing units and memory control units, its processing power and memory bandwidth has obvious advantages compared with CPU. However, GPU cannot completely replace CPU, a lot of operating systems, softwares and codes cannot run on GPU. GPU general-purpose computing usually uses CPU/GPU heterogeneous mode, CPU executes complex logic and transactions and other tasks unsuitable for parallel processing, GPU implements compute-intensive large-scale data parallel computing tasks. With its high performance, low energy consumption and other advantages, CPU/GPU hybrid architecture has been widely used in graphics and image processing, video encoding and decoding, matrix computing and simulation, medical industry application, life science research, high-performance computing, signal processing, database and data mining and many other fields. With technology advances and breakthroughs, GPU is playing an important role currently in

[a] Corresponding author: lyucyp@163.com

large-scale parallel computing. With the rapid increase of problem scales of various application fields, single GPU's computing capability has become insufficient, so multi-GPU and GPU cluster general-purpose computing has become a new research hotspot. As an important approach of high-performance computing, GPU clusters have such advantages as low cost, high performance and low energy consumption for compute-intensive applications. In constructing GPU clusters, CPU and GPU cooperate with each other, participate in data processing, and form GPU heterogeneous cluster. GPU heterogeneous cluster can make full use of hardware resources, improve processing speed and throughput. It has become an important means of big data processing.

Processing big data, especially real-time big data stream needs cluster's continuous computing and processing, and it will inevitably require computer's high-load and continuous work, so the temperature of CPU, GPU and other components will continue to rise. On one hand, computing energy consumption increases, on the other hand, fans and air conditioners are needed for reducing temperature, thereby increasing cooling energy consumption. When temperature rises to a certain extent, the temperature of one or some nodes will be too high. The node with too high temperature is known as temperature heat island. The occurrence of temperature heat island will reduce computing reliability, ranging from result error to system's paralysis and halt. Once errors occur in computing results, recomputing is needed, resulting in time and resource waste, increasing processing costs. In this case, we must reasonably design cluster task scheduling scheme to minimize cluster overall run time, control temperature to appropriate range, prevent individual node from running so long that leading to over high temperature and forming temperature heat island, to ensure reliable computing results, reduce energy consumption as much as possible and achieve green computing.

This paper studied the task scheduling on GPU heterogeneous cluster, and proposed a task scheduling scheme of preventing temperature heat island. The scheme's main features and advantages are:

(1) strong robustness. The structure of GPU heterogeneous cluster is complex, each node's configuration is different, and the node is often changed and adjusted. This task scheduling scheme can sense and adapt to this complicated and changeable situation.

(2) high processing performance. A task is divided into some sub-tasks, and then they are scheduled to multiple nodes for parallel processing. The main problem is determining the mode of division and treatment. The concept of computing scale threshold and asymmetric partitioning method are proposed in order to adapt to the diversity and heterogeneity of node configuration, improve the parallelism and shorten the whole running time of cluster. This not only prevents temperature heat island from occurring because of individual node's overlong running time, but also improves processing performance.

2 Related researches

With the wide application of GPU heterogeneous cluster, its task scheduling, temperature and heat management and energy consumption optimization has become a research hotspot. Many scholars have put forward various scheduling schemes and methods to solve the problem of energy consumption and reliability. This has played a positive role in reducing cluster energy consumption and ensuring the reliability of computing results.

In [1] a dynamic task partition method was proposed. It divides parallel computing tasks according to execution speed to achieve best overall system performance. In [2] a multi-GPU self-adaptive load balancing method was proposed. GPU can self-adaptively select tasks to execute according to local free-busy state by establishing task queue model between CPU and GPU. In [3] a load balancing strategy that combines task partitioning and stealing was proposed. It takes into account task affinity and processor diversity to direct task scheduling between CPU and GPU. In [4] feedback controlling was combined with mixed integer programming, and the energy consumption controlling model of Web server cluster was constructed. In [5] model predictive controlling strategy was introduced from global perspective. The energy consumption state is changed by adjusting computing frequency and changing active stream multiprocessor. The feedback controlling and rolling optimization mechanism are used to predict future controlling to reduce redundant energy consumption. In [6] the energy loss at idle state is reduced by a specific node selection strategy. CPU resource utilization is improved by task type division, combination distribution and DVFS.

The above researches mainly focus on cluster task scheduling, changing CPU/GPU core voltage, frequency, hardware-based statistics, and so on to design cluster energy consumption model, study task scheduling algorithm and achieve energy-saving purpose, but do not consider temperature much. In GPU cluster computing, especially continuous computing, temperature has obvious relationship with energy consumption and reliability. When temperature is too high, energy consumption increases, reliability declines, and the probability of result error increases. Therefore, temperature should be controlled in a reasonable range to minimize energy consumption under the premise of ensuring reliability. The task scheduling scheme proposed in this paper distributes tasks reasonably among computing nodes to prevent the occurrence of temperature heat island and ensure the correctness of computing results.

3 Task scheduling model

In GPU heterogeneous cluster, CPU and GPU all participate in data processing. They are regarded as computing units uniformly when distributing tasks. The computers in cluster are classified as controlling nodes and computing nodes. The controlling node can be simultaneously used as a computing node. All tasks form a queue. Each task is decomposed into several sub-tasks to form sub-task queue. The controlling node runs the main scheduling process, Scheduler. Each computing node has a scheduling agent process, Agent. Scheduler and Agent cooperate to finish task scheduling. The architecture is shown in Figure 1.

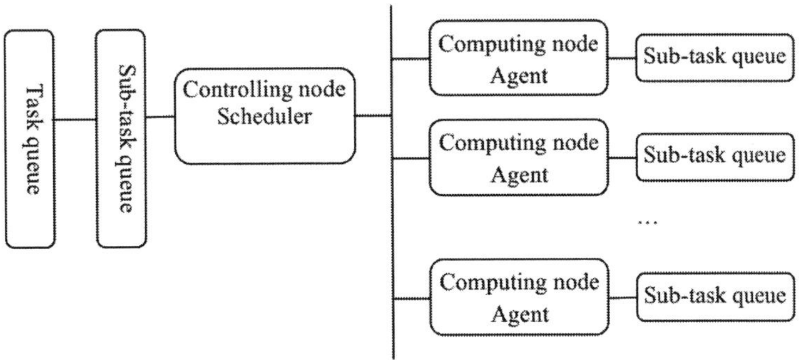

Figure 1. Task scheduling architecture

4 Task scheduling algorithm and strategy

Scheduler algorithm is as follows:

Algorithm 1 Controlling node Scheduler scheduling algorithm

1. Obtain a task from task queue
2. Obtain the hardware configuration and running status information of each computing node
3. Determine the number of computing nodes participating in parallel processing
4. Divide task into sub-task queue and assign sub-tasks to corresponding computing node
5. Wait for the results of each sub-task
6. Modify the status of corresponding sub-tasks and the associated tasks in queue.
7. Reschedule sub-tasks that timed out or requested to transfer, modify corresponding status
8. Go to 1

For each computing node, the sub-tasks that controlling node dispatches to it form a queue. The scheduling algorithm of Agent on computing node is as follows:

Algorithm 2 Computing node Agent scheduling algorithm
1. Obtain a sub-task from the sub-task queue of local node
2. Assign the sub-task to local node for processing
3. Wait for the result to be returned from local node
4. Report results to controlling node (completion, timeout, or requesting transfer)
5. Go to 1

4.1 Acquiring hardware configuration information

Scheduler first obtains the hardware configuration information of each node in cluster. The information can be manually created in advance and saved in file. When cluster is started, Scheduler loads cluster hardware configuration information file. It polls each computing node, Agent responds to the poll and reports hardware change information to Scheduler. Or, Agent reports hardware change information to Scheduler actively. Then Scheduler modifies cluster's hardware configuration information. In this way, controlling node can grasp the latest changes in cluster hardware configuration, avoiding unnecessary acquisition and reporting of hardware configuration information, thus adapting to actual hardware configuration changes and reducing network communication overhead.

4.2 Scheduling strategy

Computing scale is used to measure task size. Computing scale is the number of instructions to be executed or the amount of data to be processed to complete the task. A task contains parallelizable and non-parallelizable part. Suppose the computing scale of a task is T, $T=T_s+T_p$, T_s is the computing scale of non-parallelizable part, and T_p is the computing scale of parallelizable part. Let T_t be the critical value of the computing scale of parallelizable part, then task scheduling strategy is as follows:

(1) $0\le T_p<T_t$, the task does not have parallelizable part or has relatively smaller parallelizable part, it cannot or has no need to be divided into small sub-tasks, the computing unit with strongest computing capability is selected directly from idle computing units to process the task.

(2) $T_p\ge T_t$, the task has parallelizable part and it reaches a certain scale. The parallelizable part of task is divided into smaller sub-tasks, many computing units with strongest computing capability are selected from idle processing units to process them.

4.2.1 *Determining T_t and the number of computing units*

The processing capability is assumed to be C_s when task is processed separately by a single computing unit. Without loss of generality, assuming that when parallel processing, the number of computing units participating in processing is n, their processing capability is all C_p. In order to obtain better performance, then:

$$\frac{T_t}{C_s} \ge \frac{T_t}{nC_p} + Q \tag{1}$$

Where Q is the additional time overhead required for parallel processing, including parallel computing preparation, result merging, synchronization, network transmission, and so on. At the same time in order to ensure high processing efficiency, then:

$$\frac{T_t}{nC_p} \ge Q \tag{2}$$

Solving the inequality group consisting of above two inequalities will get:

$$T_t \geq \max\{nC_pQ, \frac{nC_pC_sQ}{nC_p - C_s}\} \quad (3)$$

The value of Q can be determined experimentally or by accumulating historical empirical data. C_p can be taken as the average of the current computing capability of all computing units, and C_s is the average of the current computing capability of all CPUs in cluster. Let $T_m = \max\{mC_pQ, \frac{mC_pC_sQ}{mC_p - C_s}\}$, $m=1,2,...,N_{idle}$, N_{idle} is the number of all idle computing units in current cluster. In order to increase the parallelization degree of task processing, change from N_{idle} in descending manner until the first number k which lets $T_p \geq T_k$ is found, then k is the number of units involved in parallel processing, the algorithm to determine it is as follows:

Algorithm 3 Determining the number of parallel processing units

1. get N_{idle}
2. $i \leftarrow N_{idle}$ $k \leftarrow 1$
3. if $i \leq 1$ goto 7
4. $T_i \leftarrow \max\{iC_pQ, \frac{iC_pC_sQ}{iC_p - C_s}\}$
5. if $T_p \geq T_i$ then $k \leftarrow i$ goto 7
6. $i \leftarrow i$-1 goto 3
7. end

If k<2 or qualified k value cannot be found, the task is handled by one CPU and not scheduled in parallel manner.

4.2.2 Partitioning parallel part

Assuming that the current computing capability of k computing units involved in parallel computing is $C_1, C_2, ..., C_k$, the scale of sub-tasks assigned to each processing unit is $T_1, T_2, ..., T_k$, then the time to complete the task is:

$$t = \max\{\frac{T_1}{C_1}, \frac{T_2}{C_2}, ..., \frac{T_k}{C_k}\} \quad (4)$$

Where $T_1+T_2+...+T_k=T_p$. It can be proven that when $T_i = \frac{C_iT_p}{C}$ $(i=1,2,...,k)$, t is minimum and $t = \frac{T_p}{C}$,where $C=C_1+C_2+...+C_k$. Therefore, the proportion of allocated task to total task scale being equal to the ratio of the current computing capability of the computing unit to the sum of the current computing capabilities of all computing units participating in parallel processing, can effectively reduce overall processing time, balance load, and avoid the case that some units are idle and some units run for long time and cause temperature heat islands to occur.

4.3 Estimating current computing capability

Current computing capability is related to its own hardware configuration and hardware's current state of utilization. For computing units with same configuration, the busier ones have stronger current computing capability than the idle ones. By referencing [7] and improving, the current computing capability is estimated. For any computing node N_i, consider its five hardware configuration parameters: CPU frequency $rate\_cpu_i$, memory size mem_i, cache size $cache_i$, GPU frequency $rate\_gpu_i$, GPU memory size mem_gpu_i and five state parameters: CPU utilization $utlz\_cpu_i$, memory

DOI: 10.1051/itmconf/20171107003

utilization $utlz\_mem_i$, cache utilization $utlz\_cache_i$, GPU utilization $utlz\_gpu_i$, GPU memory utilization $utlz\_gpumem_i$. The current computing capability of node N_i is:

$$C_i = k_1Q_1 + k_2Q_2 + k_3Q_3 + k_4Q_4 + k_5Q_5 \tag{5}$$

k_1, k_2, k_3, k_4 and k_5 represents the level proportion weight of influence on node current computing capability of CPU, memory, Cache, GPU and GPU memory respectively. Their sum is 1. Q_1-Q_5 respectively denotes CPU current capability, memory current capability, cache current capability, GPU current capability and GPU memory current capability after normalization of node N_i. Q_1 is calculated as:

$$Q_1 = \frac{rate\_cpu_i \times (1 - utlz\_cpu_i)}{(\sum_{j=1}^{N} rate\_cpu_j \times (1 - utlz\_cpu_j))} \tag{6}$$

The formulas for Q_2-Q_5 are similar. For a certain node, C_i, Q_1, Q_2, Q_3, Q_4 and Q_5 can be determined experimentally, and then the approximate value of k_1, k_2, k_3, k_4 and k_5 can be determined by regression method.

5 Experiment and analysis

The scheme proposed in this paper was verified experimentally. Two experiments were conducted on same cluster. The experiment program is: Some relative softwares (such as CPU-Z, HWMonitor, CoreTemp, etc.) were used to measure temperatures of CPU and GPU of each computing unit at different time during cluster's running, and the temperature curve of each computing unit was drawn according to them.

Seven computers were used to constitute GPU heterogeneous cluster. Five of them have the configuration: model is Lenovo Erazer X700, memory is 16G, CPU is Intel i7-3930k, GPU is NVIDIA GTX660i, operating system is Ubuntu12.04 LTS, cluster environment is hadoop2.2.0, Java version is JDK1.7. The other two have lower configuration: CPU is Intel Pentium (R) Dual-Core E5300 2.60GHz, memory is 4G, GPU is NVIDIA GeForce 9400GT, operating system is Windows 7 64-bit Ultimate. The experimental data is taxi GPS data and data generated continuously by loadrunner.

5.1 Conventional scheduling method

Firstly, conventional scheduling method was used. Only task balanced scheduling was considered, regardless of temperature changes. Every 1 minute temperature was sampled once. The result is shown in Figure 2, where C1, C2, ..., C7 is each computing node.

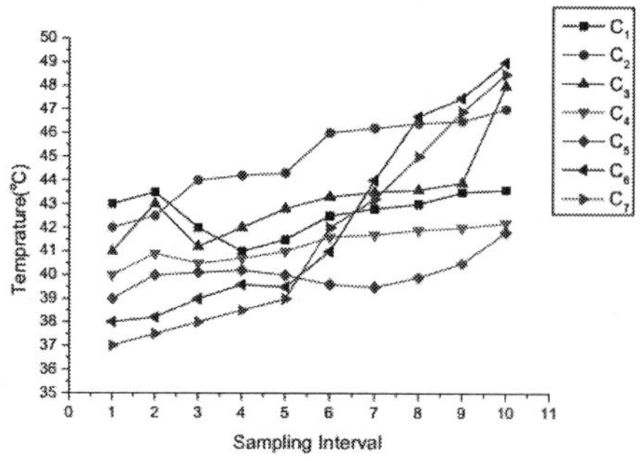

Figure 2. Temperature change in conventional scheduling method

The cluster processes taxi GPS data firstly. The data amount is larger, but because it is historical data, it does not take long time to process it. Temperature and power are measured with measuring instruments, temperatures of CPU, GPU and so on are monitored with softwares. It is found that the temperature and power of CPU and GPU are increasing during processing, but the task has been finished before temperature rises to the set threshold, and the problem of temperature heat island and reliability does not occur. Then simulation data that loadrunner software continues to generate is processed. At this time, CPU and GPU temperature continues to rise, energy consumption continues to increase. After a certain time, temperature exceeds the threshold and temperature heat island is formed, computing result error occurs. The difference between the lowest and highest temperatures of various computing nodes is about 12 °C.

5.2 Scheduling scheme proposed in this paper

In the second experiment, the same experimental environment and data were used, but the scheduling scheme preventing temperature heat island proposed in this paper was used. During processing task, temperature is collected. The result is shown in Figure 3.

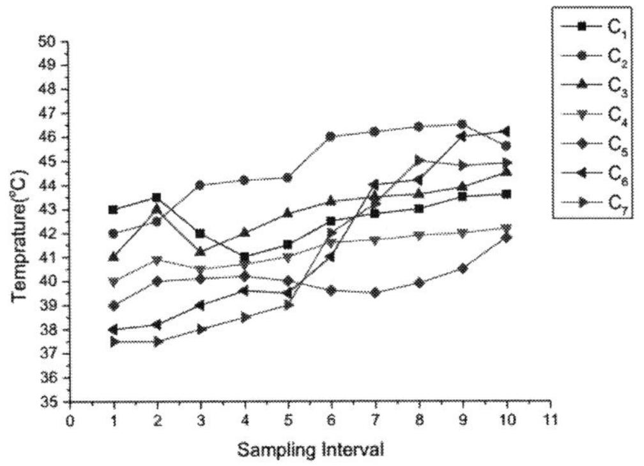

Figure 3. Temperature change in scheduling method preventing temperature heat island

The result of processing taxi GPS data is similar to the previous, but the result shows that the difference of temperature and energy consumption of each node tends to decrease. This shows that this scheme is more time-balanced in task scheduling to prevent temperature heat island from occurring and guarantee overall stability. Data streams generated continuously by program are processed by cluster. It was found that, although the temperature of CPU and GPU increased, the temperature and power did not increase continuously when temperature rised nearly to threshold value, and no temperature heat island and computing error occurred. When data supply amount was increased, the phenomenon that temperature and power increase did not occur. This shows that the scheduling scheme trys to balance running time, inhibit the increasing of temperature and energy consumption to prevent temperature heat island from occurring. The difference between the lowest and highest temperatures among various computing nodes is about 9 °C.

Analyzing above experimental results, it is shown that, if conventional method is adopted, the temperature of each computing node increases continuously with the processing of task, the temperature of some nodes exceeds threshold, and the temperature fluctuates greatly. However, when the scheduling method proposed in this paper is used, temperature is also rising, but because task division makes node running time be consistent as far as possible, the range of temperature fluctuation is small, the overall temperature change is relatively calm, thus it is avoided that the temperature heat island occurs.

Conclusion

The GPU heterogeneous cluster task scheduling scheme proposed in this paper avoids long running time of individual nodes as far as possible, prevents temperature heat island from occurring, guarantees computing reliability, controls energy consumption in a certain range, and also considers the constraints among temperature, reliability, performance and energy consumption, minimizes energy consumption or improves processing speed as far as possible under the premise of ensuring reliability. The main work of next step is to study how GPU heterogeneous cluster perceives and predicts cluster temperature and its variation, and apply it to cluster task scheduling.

Acknowledgments

This research project is supported by the joint special project of Shandong Provincial Natural Science Foundation (Project No.: ZR2015FL014) and the special project of Shandong Provincial Independent Innovation and Achievement Transformation (Project No.: 2014ZZCX02702).

References

1. C. Q. Yang, F. Wang, Y. F. Du, et al. *Adaptive optimization for petascale heterogeneous CPU/GPU computing. The 2010 IEEE Int'l Conf. on Cluster Computing*. (2010)
2. L. Chen, O. Villa, S. Krishnamoorthy, G. R. Gao. *Dynamic load balancing on single- and multi-GPU systems. The 2010 IEEE Int'l Symp. on Parallel & Distributed Processing (IPDPS)*. (2010)
3. E. Hermann, B. Raffin, F. Faure, T. Gautier, J. Allard. *Multi-GPU and multi-CPU parallelization for interactive physics simulations. The 16th Int'l Euro-Par Conf. on Parallel Processing: Part II (Euro-Par 2010)*. Berlin, Heidelberg: Springer-Verlag. (2010)
4. L. Bertini, C. B. Julius, D. Mosse. *Power optimization for dynamic configuration in heterogeneous web server clusters*. Journal of Systems and Software, **83**(4): 585-598. (2010)
5. H. F. Wang, Y. P. Cao. *GPU Power Consumption Optimization Control Model of GPU Clusters*. Acta Electronica Sinica, **43**(10): 1904-1910. (2015)
6. H. P. Huo, X. M. Hu, C. C. Sheng, B. F. Wu. *An energy efficient task scheduling scheme for node-layer heterogeneous GPU clusters*. Computer Applications and Software, **30**(3): 283-286. (2013)
7. H. Liu, J. G. Wang, Z. Z. Ge, et al. *Self-learning Load Balancing Scheduling Algorithm for GPU Heterogeneous Cluster*. Journal of Xi'an Shiyou University, **30**(3): 105-111. (2015)

ITM Web of Conferences **11**, 07004 (2017) DOI: 10.1051/itmconf/20171107004
IST2017

Theoretical and Numerical Study of Seismoelectric Logs for Logging While Drilling (LWD)

Xiang-Yang SUN [1,a], Yong-Peng ZHAO [2]

[1]*High tech Zone(West), Chengdu, Sichuan, China Xi yuan Avenue, No. 2006 , University of Electronic Science and technology*

Abstract. When the acoustic field propagates in the porous medium, the electromagnetic wave can be induced by the seismoelectric effects which can be used in the logging. This paper studies the seismoelectric wave field and deduces the formulations of the acoustic and electromagnetic field of the liquid in the well, and gives the acoustic and electromagnetic boundary conditions between the driller collar and the log liquid, when the driller collar is added. We also do the numerical simulation of the seismoelectric wave field excited by monopole source, study the velocity dispersion characteristics of the acoustic and electromagnetic field, and investigate the detective depth of the seismoelectric logs. Through the simulation we know the seismoelectric logs can avoid the interference of drill collar wave. This paper also provides theoretical guidance for the design of receiving antenna.

1 Introduction

With the development of the world economy, the shortage of oil and gas has become the main restricting factor of economic and social development[1].And the oil and gas are mainly stored in the porous media[2].So the application of seismoelectric effects in the exploration of oil and gas is very promising, especially in the search of "remaining oil"[3]. Seismoelectric effects refer to the excitation of electromagnetic wave excited by the seismic wave in the porous medium, It is a process of energy conversion between mechanical energy and electromagnetic energy in nature. Seismoelectric logs have better recognitive ability of oil and gas, and better detective ability than pure electric logging and seismic logging. Seismoelectric logs are also sensitive to the variation of formation parameters, so we can get more information.

A simplified method for Seismoelectric logs is proposed by Hu Hengshan and Liu Jiaqi, which ignores the influence of electromagnetic field and solve the acoustic field independently first, and then solve the electromagnetic field by using seismic and electric coupling relationship[4,5]. Guan Wei and Hu hengshan introduces the Maxwell equations with the percolation current as the current source, and uses the Hertz vector to represent the solutions[6]. Jin Zhiwen derived the expressions of the acoustic and the electromagnetic field in the porous medium excited by the multipole source[7].

Although there are a large number of theoretical researches about seismoelectric logs, but almost none considers the influence of drilling equipment such as the drill collar. Based on the above background, this paper studies the seismoelectric logs while drilling. And we give the analytical

[a] Corresponding author: sunxiangyang@uestc.edu.cn

solution of the seismoelectric field and study the propagating characteristics of the acoustic and the electromagnetic field. We also obtain the velocity dispersion characteristics of the seismoelectric field, and investigate the detective depth of the seismoelectric logs.

2 Formulation

2.1 Acoustic field

In the simulation, we use the LWD's model as shown in the Figure 1, with radial stratification, followed by mud liquid layer, drill tool layer, mud liquid layer in the borehole and porous medium.

When add the drill collar, there will be a cylindrical outward displacement potential function for the acoustic wave in the borehole. Excited by multipole source, the formal solution is

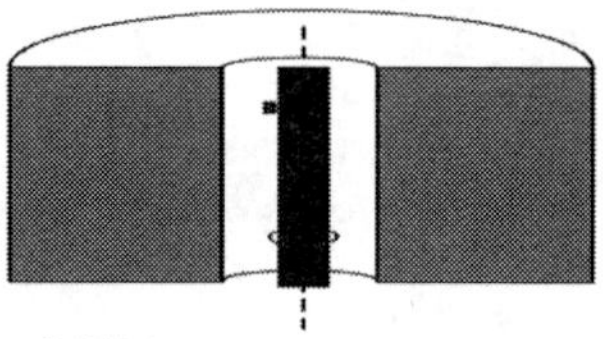

Figure1. model for logging while drilling(LWD)

$$\varphi(r,\theta,k,\omega)=\sum_{n=0}^{\infty}\varphi_n(r,\theta,k,\omega)=\sum_{n=0}^{\infty}\left[A_n^f I_n(\eta r)+B_n^f K_n(\eta r)\right]\cos n\theta \qquad (1)$$

k is the axial wavenumber, $\eta=\sqrt{l^2-(\omega/V)^2}$ is the radial imaginary wavenumber. The displacement and sound pressure can be calculated according to the relationship between the displacement (or the pressure)and the potential function in cylindrical coordinates in the flood.

$$u_r^o(r,\theta,k,\omega)=\sum_{n=0}^{\infty}\left\{A_n^o\left[\frac{n}{r}I_n(\eta r)+\eta I_{n+1}(\eta r)\right]+B_n^o\left[\frac{n}{r}K_n(\eta r)-\eta K_{n+1}(\eta r)\right]\right\}\cos n\theta \qquad (2)$$

$$P_f^o(r,\theta,k,\omega)=\sum_{n=0}^{\infty}\rho_f\omega^2\left[A_n^o I_n(\eta r)+B_n^o K_n(\eta r)\right]\cos n\theta \qquad (3)$$

With no source inside the drill collar cavity, there is only inward wave field.

(4)

$$u_r^i(r,\theta,k,\omega)=\sum_{n=0}^{\infty}A_n^i\left[\frac{n}{r}I_n(\eta r)+\eta I_{n+1}(\eta r)\right]\cos n\theta \qquad (4)$$

$$P_f^i(r,\theta,k,\omega)=\sum_{n=0}^{\infty}\rho_f\omega^2 A_n^i I_n(\eta r)\cos n\theta \qquad (5)$$

The wave equations for the displacement potential function of the acoustic field in the tool layer are: $\nabla^2\varphi+k_p^2\varphi=0$ $\quad\nabla^2\chi+k_{SH}^2\chi=0$ $\quad\nabla^2\Gamma+k_{SV}^2\Gamma=0$

Where $k_p^2=\omega^2/c_p^2, k_{SH}^2=k_{SV}^2=\omega^2/c_s^2, c_p=\sqrt{(\lambda+2\mu)/p}$, $c_s=\sqrt{\mu/p}$. and φ is the displacement potential function of the longitudinal wave in the tool layer, χ denotes the displacement potential function of the SH wave, Γ is the displacement potential function of the SV wave. The solutions of the three potential functions are:

$$\varphi(r,\theta,k,\omega)=\sum_{n=0}^{\infty}\varphi_n=\sum_{n=0}^{\infty}\left[A_nI_n(\eta_pr)+B_nK_n(\eta_pr)\right]\cos n\theta \tag{6}$$

$$\chi(r,\theta,k,\omega)=\sum_{n=0}^{\infty}\chi_n=\sum_{n=0}^{\infty}\left[C_nI_n(\eta_sr)+D_nK_n(\eta_sr)\right]\cos n\theta \tag{7}$$

$$\Gamma(r,\theta,k,\omega)=\sum_{n=0}^{\infty}\Gamma_n=\sum_{n=0}^{\infty}\left[E_nI_n(\eta_sr)+F_nK_n(\eta_sr)\right]\cos n\theta \tag{8}$$

We can obtain the displacement and stress of the acoustic field in the tool layer according to the relationship between the displacement and the potential function and the stress-strain's relationship in the elastic solid in the cylindrical coordinate[7].

In the porous medium, the displacement potential function of each body wave satisfies the following equations:

$$\nabla^2\varphi_l+k_p^2\varphi_l=0\,;\ \nabla^2\chi+k_{SH}^2\chi=0;\ \nabla^2\Gamma+k_{SV}^2\Gamma=0$$

Where φ_l is the displacement potential function of the longitudinal wave including fast longitudinal wave and slow longitudinal wave, χ denotes the displacement potential function of the SH wave, Γ is the displacement potential function of the SV wave [6].

2.2 Electromagnetic field

There is a certain proportional relationship between the solid displacement and the seepage displacement of each body wave in the porous medium.

$$w=\alpha_{pf}\nabla\phi_f+\alpha_{ps}\nabla\phi_s+\alpha_s\nabla\times(\chi\vec{z})+\alpha_s\nabla\times\nabla\times(\Gamma\vec{z}) \tag{9}$$

So the current flow can be calculated as

$$J_s=\nabla\psi_1+\nabla\psi_2+\nabla\times F_1+\nabla\times\nabla\times F_2 \tag{10}$$

According to the electromagnetic theory, when the excitation source is seepage current, we can get the equations of the Hertz vector as following:

$$(\nabla^2-\bar{\mu}\varepsilon\frac{\partial^2}{\partial t^2})\vec{\Pi}^m=-\vec{F_1}-\nabla\times\vec{F_2} \tag{11}$$

$$(\nabla^2-\bar{\mu}\varepsilon\frac{\partial^2}{\partial t^2})\vec{\Pi}^e=-\frac{\nabla\psi_1+\nabla\psi_2}{i\omega\bar{\varepsilon}} \tag{12}$$

When the source is individually $\nabla\psi_1,\nabla\psi_2,-\vec{F_1},-\nabla\times\vec{F_2}$, one obtains the particular solutions:

$$\vec{\Pi_1}^e=\frac{\nabla\psi_1}{i\omega\bar{\varepsilon}(k_{em}^2-k_{pf}^2)},\vec{\Pi_2}^e=\frac{\nabla\psi_2}{i\omega\bar{\varepsilon}(k_{em}^2-k_{ps}^2)},\vec{\Pi_3}^m=-\frac{\vec{F_1}}{k_{em}^2-k_{ps}^2},\vec{\Pi_4}^m=-\frac{\nabla\times\vec{F_2}}{k_{em}^2-k_{ps}^2}$$

Then get the solution of equations in the passive situation:

$$\vec{\Pi}_0^e = R_e \bullet A_e \bullet K_n(\eta_{em1} r) \quad \vec{\Pi}_0^m = R_e \bullet A_m \bullet K_n(\eta_{em1} r)$$

According to the Hertz vector above all, we can calculate the electromagnetic field in the porous formation .

$$\vec{E} = \vec{E}_1 + \vec{E}_2 + \vec{E}_3 + \vec{E}_4 + \vec{E}_0 \tag{13}$$

$$\vec{H} = \vec{H}_1 + \vec{H}_2 + \vec{H}_3 + \vec{H}_4 + \vec{H}_0 \tag{14}$$

There is electromagnetic field in the borehole which is not excited by the acoustic field but caused by the boundary conditions. The Hertz electric potential and Hertz magnetic potential in the borehole meet Helmholtz equation, respectively. When the drill collar added, there will be a cylindrical outward function for Hertz electric potential and Hertz magnetic potential in the borehole, individually:

$$\vec{\Pi}_0^e = R_e \bullet B_e \bullet I_n(\eta_{em1} r) + R_e \bullet C_e \bullet K_n(\eta_{em1} r) \quad \vec{\Pi}_0^m = R_e \bullet B_m \bullet I_n(\eta_{em1} r) + R_e \bullet C_m \bullet K_n(\eta_{em1} r)$$

Then we can obtain the electromagnetic field according to the relationship between the field and the Hertz potential.

2.3 Boundary condition

In the formal solutions of the acoustic and the electromagnetic field, there are unknown coefficients. These coefficients can be obtained by the boundary conditions of the acoustic and the electromagnetic field on the interface of different media.

The boundary conditions of acoustic field at the interface between drill collar and fluid inside or outside the drill collar satisfy:

Inner fluid

Continuity of normal stress : $u_r^i = u_r$

Continuity of normal stress : $-P_f^i = \tau_{rr}$

Continuity of tangential stress : $0 = \tau_{rz}$

Continuity of tangential stress : $0 = \tau_{r\theta}$

Outer fluid

Continuity of normal stress : $u_r^o + v_1^s = u_r$

Continuity of normal stress : $-(P_f^o + \sigma_1^s) = \tau_{rr}$

Continuity of tangential stress : $0 = \tau_{rz}$

Continuity of tangential stress : $0 = \tau_{r\theta}$

The boundary conditions of acoustic field at the interface between drill collar and fluid inside or outside the drill collar satisfy:

Continuity of fluid flow : $u_r^o + v_2^s = u_r^1 + w_r^1$

Continuity of Normal stress : $-(P_f^o + \sigma_2^s) = \tau_{rr}^1$

Continuity of Tangential stress : $0 = \tau_{rz}^1$

Continuity of Tangential stress : $0 = \tau_{r\theta}^1$

Continuity of fluid pressure : $P_f^o + \sigma_2^s = P^1$

i and o refer to the fluid medium inside and outside the drill collar, Respectively. 1 represent the porous medium. The matrix of acoustic boundary condition is

$$[m_{ij}]_{13\times13} \bullet \{a_j\}_{13\times1} = \{b_j\}_{13\times1} \tag{15}$$

Where a_j is the coefficient of the displacement potential function, b_j is the devotion of the source. The tangential components of electric field and magnetic field continue at the wall of the well, so we can obtain the equations:

$$E_{\theta A} = E_{\theta B}, \ E_{zA} = E_{zB}$$

The tangential components of electric field equal to 0 at the interface between the drill collar and the fluid outside the drill collar.

$$H_{\theta A} = H_{\theta B}, \ H_{zA} = H_{zB}$$

The matrix of boundary condition of electromagnetic field is

$$\left[m_{ij}\right]_{6\times6} \bullet \left\{a_j\right\}_{6\times1} = \left\{b_j\right\}_{6\times1} \quad (16)$$

Where a_j is the coefficient of Hertz vector potential. b_j is the the electromagnetic wave induced by the acoustic field in the porous medium.

2 Numerical simulation

The source is a monopole source with Richer wavelet as excitation function, and the center frequency is 7kHz, the receiving points are located at the wall of the well. The starting position is z=1.3713m, and the distance between each receiving point is 0.1524m, there are seven receiving points. The full waveform of the seismoelectric wave field is as Figure2.

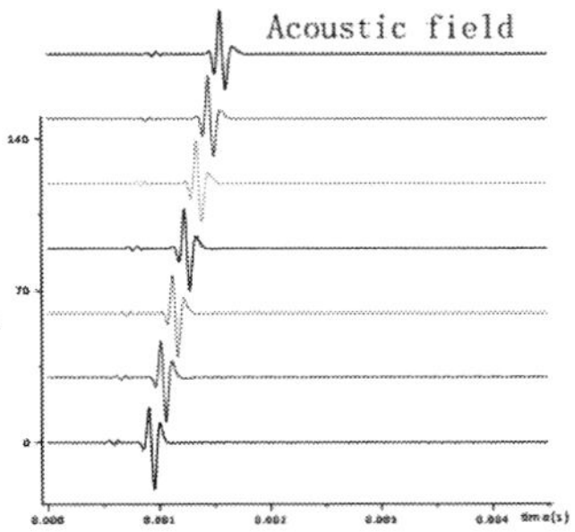

Figure 2a. Acoustic field

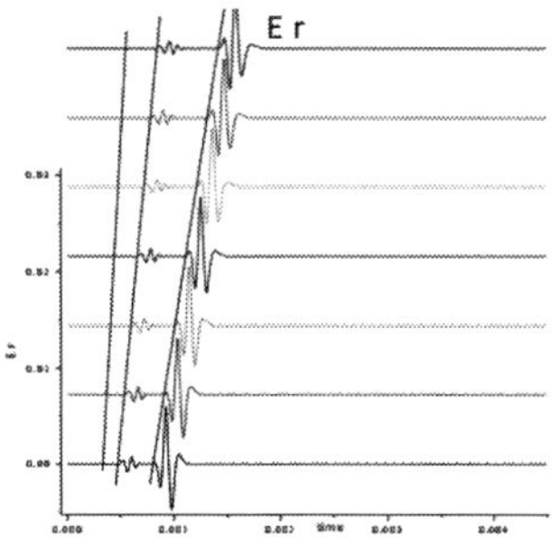

Figure 2b. Normal electric field

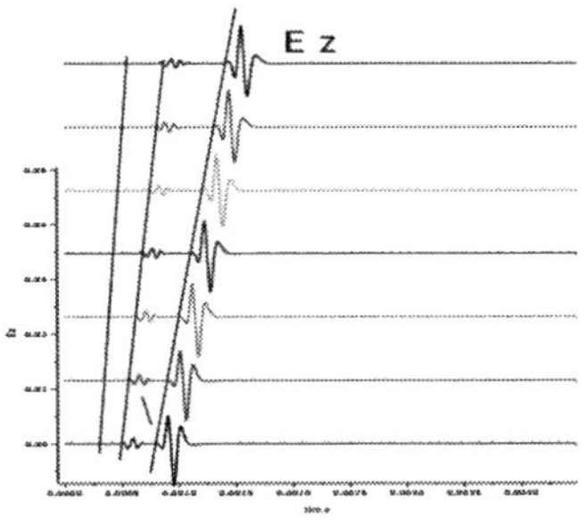

Figure 2c. Tangential electric field

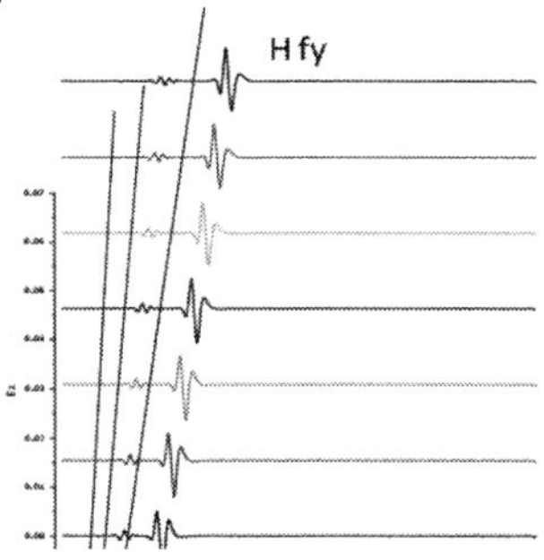

Figure 2d. Circumferential magnetic field

The three diagonal lines respectively go through the electromagnetic field coupled with fast longitudinal wave, transverse wave, Stoneley wave in Figure 2 b, c, d. Their slopes indicate the acoustic wave velocity. We can see form the figure that the coupled electromagnetic field can reflect

DOI: 10.1051/itmconf/20171107004

some properties of the acoustic field. The ratio of longitudinal wave and Stoneley wave or the ratio of shear wave and Stoneley wave of the acoustic field is less than that of the electromagnetic field.

We derive the velocity dispersion figures of the acoustic and the electromagnetic field by using multiple filter analysis method (MFT). We can see from Figure 3, when excited by monopole source, there is stronger drill collar interference for the acoustic field and less drill collar interference for the electromagnetic field.

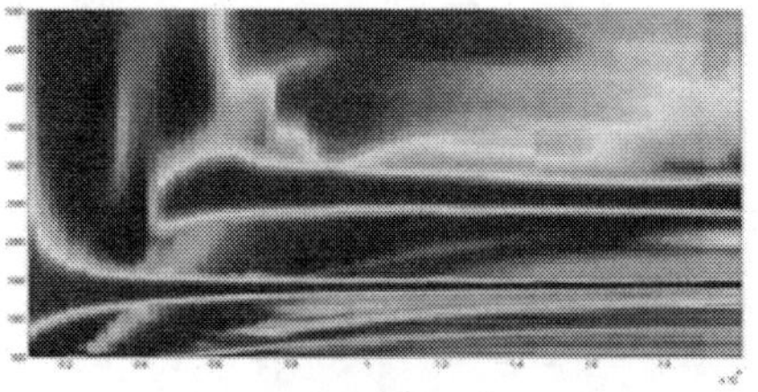

Figure 3a. Velocity dispersion of acoustic field

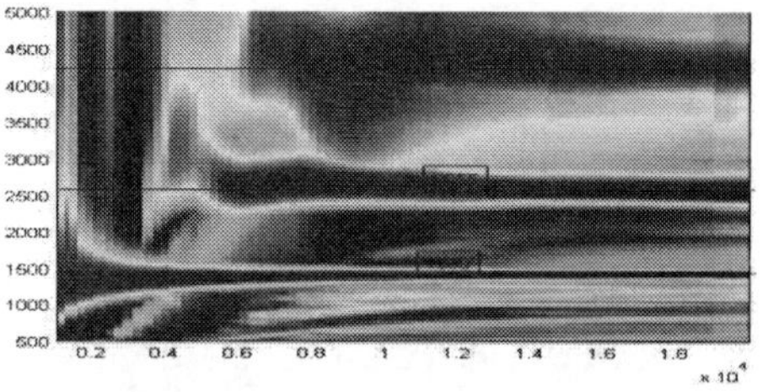

Figure 3b. Velocity dispersion of normal electric field

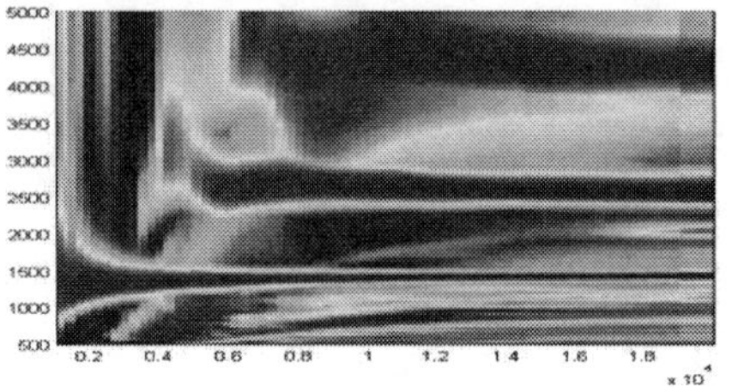

Figure 3c. Velocity dispersion of tangential electric field

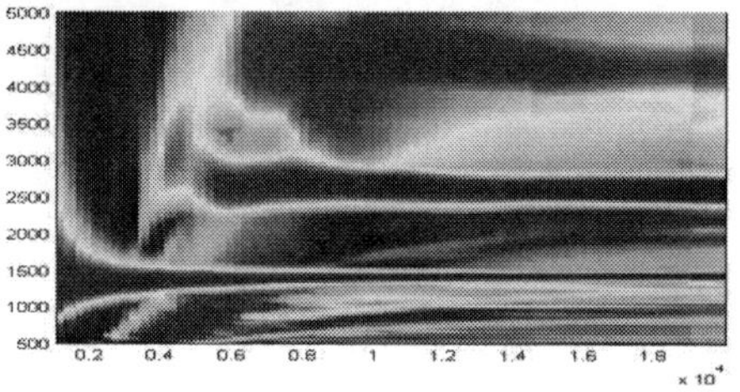

Figure 3d.Velocity dispersion of circumferential magnetic field

Figure 4a and Figure 4b respectively compare the acoustic field, electric field and magnetic field. The amplitude of the axial component of the electric field is about 3 orders of magnitude smaller than that of the acoustic field, while their phases are almost the same. The amplitude of the radial component of the electric field is almost

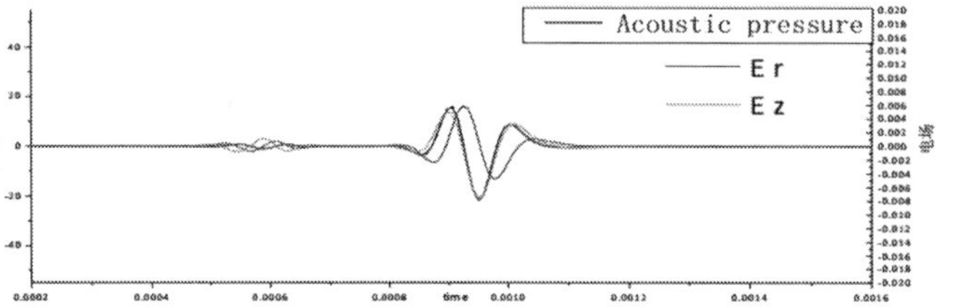

Figure4a. Contrast between electric field and sound field

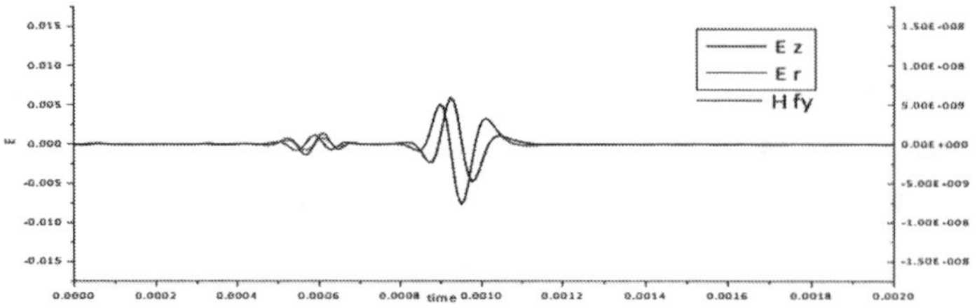

Figure 4b. Contrast between electric field and magnetic field

Now we study the detective depth of the seismoelectric logs. The model is shown in Figure 5a. The current signal excited by the acoustic signal is distributed in all regions of the porous medium, as shown in the red part of the Figure 5b. In order to investigate how far the electrical signals that can be received by the electric current, we assume the current signal is only distributed in a part of the formation, as shown in the red part of the Figure 5c. The thickness of the layer that does not excite the current is t. Investigate the change of the received signal, When t is changed.

Figure 6a investigates the change of the electric field the t value, and Figure 6b investigates the change of the amplitude of the electric field with t. As can be seen from the figure, the detective depth of seismoelectric logs is very shallow, there is one order of magnitude attenuation per 4cm, so the detective depth is about 2-3cm. At the same time, it is shown that the seismoelectric signal is mainly caused by the electric current of the electric double layer in the shallow stratum.

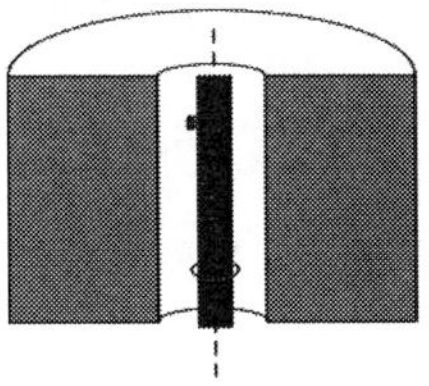

Figure 5a

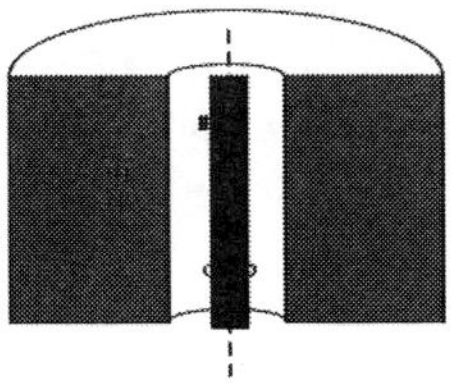

Figure 5b

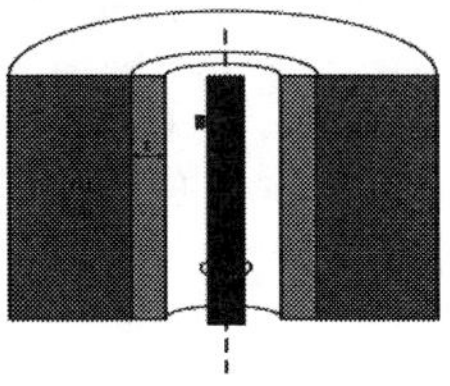

Figure 5c

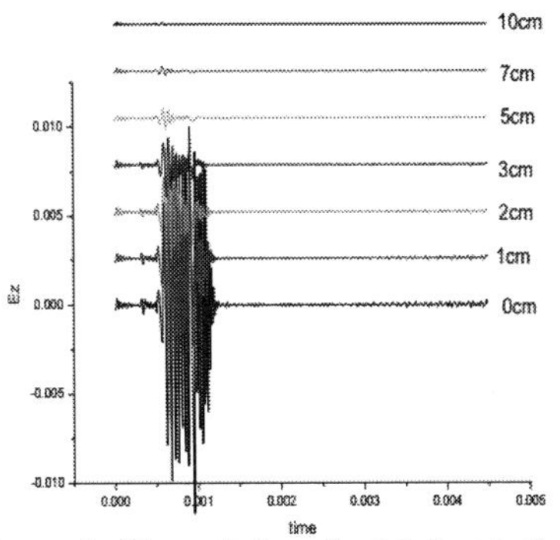

Figure 6a. The variation of axial electric field with t

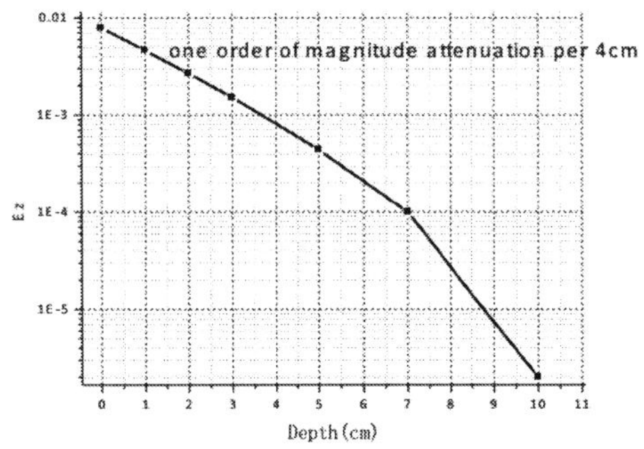

Figure 6b. The variation of axial electric field 's amplitude

Summary

Summarize the whole text, we can obtain the conclusions:

(1)Seismoelectric logs for LWD is feasible, the received signal can reflect acoustic wave velocity, which can be indirectly used in acoustic logging. It can be the response of P-wave, S-wave propagating along the formation and the Stoneley wave propagating along the borehole.

(2)Seismoelectric logs for LWD acoustic logging have certain advantages over acoustic logging: there is no collar wave interference for electromagnetic field when excited by monopole source.

(3)The simulation above, provides a reference for the design of the receiving antenna: There are 3 components in the electromagnetic field, namely, the axial electric field, the radial electric field and the circumferential magnetic field. We'd better receive the axial electric field.

(4)The receiving antenna can only receive the electric signal generated by the electric double layer of the shallow stratum, which is about 2~4cm.It is shown that the seismic signal is not generated by the interface between the wall and mud. At the same time, we can see that the electromagnetic field can reflect the characteristics of the acoustic field.

DOI: 10.1051/itmconf/20171107004

References

1. Guan Wei. Study on wave field simulation of coupling effect of elastic wave and electromagnetic field in porous media [D]. Journal of Harbin Institute of Technology, 2009
2. Liu Hong, Li Youming. Some views on the exploration of oil and gas water by using seismic effect [J]. petroleum geophysical exploration, 1994,02:94-101.
3. Zhang Yan. The refraction of plane wave on the interface between fluid and porous media under the effect of electric shock [D]. Jilin University, 2011
4. Hu Hengshan, Liu Jiaqi, Yan Yan, Yan. Comparative analysis of the wave equations of and Pride, [J].,, 2003,01:107-112.
5. Hu Hengshan, Liu Jiaqi, Wang, Wang, et al. Based on the simplified Pride theory to simulate the logging response of electro acoustic effect [J]. Journal of Geophysics, 2003,02:259-264.
6. Guan Wei, Hu Hengshan, Chu zhaotan. Hertz vector acoustic induced electromagnetic field representation and multipole acoustic logging simulation [J]. Journal of physics, 2006,01:267-274.
7. Cui Zhiwen. Theoretical and numerical study of acoustic model of porous media and multipole source acoustic logging and multipole logging while drilling. Doctoral dissertation of Jilin University. 2004:52-8

 DOI: 10.1051/itmconf/20171107005

Rule - based Fault Diagnosis Expert System for Wind Turbine

Xiao-Wen DENG[1], Qing-Shui GAO[1], Chu ZHANG[1], Di HU[2,a] and Tao YANG[2]

[1]*Electric Power Research Institute of Guangdong Power Grid Co., Ltd., Guangzhou 510600, China*
[2]*School of Energy and Power Engineering, Huazhong University of Science & Technology, Wuhan 430074, China*

Abstract. Under the trend of increasing installed capacity of wind power, the intelligent fault diagnosis of wind turbine is of great significance to the safe and efficient operation of wind farms. Based on the knowledge of fault diagnosis of wind turbines, this paper builds expert system diagnostic knowledge base by using confidence production rules and expert system self-learning method. In Visual Studio 2013 platform, C # language is selected and ADO.NET technology is used to access the database. Development of Fault Diagnosis Expert System for Wind Turbine. The purpose of this paper is to realize on-line diagnosis of wind turbine fault through human-computer interaction, and to improve the diagnostic capability of the system through the continuous improvement of the knowledge base.

1 Introduction

With more attention paid to the energy security, ecological environment, climate change and other issues, to accelerate the development of wind power has become the consensus of the international community to promote the transformation of energy development, to cope with global climate change and concerted action. According to statistics, by the end of 2015 the global wind power installed capacity of 432 million kilowatts, spread over the world in more than and 100 countries and regions [1]. Global wind power installed capacity continues to grow, fault diagnosis technology has gradually become a hot topic in the field of wind power.

For the working life of 20 years of the unit, the operation and maintenance costs generally account for the entire wind farm's total investment of 10% ~ 15%, while for the offshore wind farm, the overall ratio of up to 20% ~ 25% [2]. Statistics show that the determining time for the fault diagnosis takes up 70% to 90% of the total time, while the repair time takes up only about 10% to 30% [3]. Therefore, efficient and accurate fault diagnosis technology is an important way to ensure the economic and safe operation of wind turbine.

There are many fault diagnosis systems have been successfully applied in many kinds of technical processes to improve operation reliability and safety. Yang introduced a Web-oriented expert system for gear box in wind turbine using the fault tree model [4]. Yang developed an aviation fault diagnosis expert system, the reasoning machine based on the combination of fault tree and generalized regression neural network [5]. Yao presented an engine rotor fault diagnosis method based on random forests, that the failures be diagnosed timely and effectively to keep the engine in normal operation [6]. By using the fast diagnosis ability of expert system, the wind farm can greatly improve the efficiency of diagnosis.

[a] Corresponding author: 18140662310@163.com

This paper applies a rule based expert system [7] on wind turbine fault diagnosis, in order to make timely, accurate diagnosis for wind turbine and provide timely solutions. First, summarize the wind turbine fault symptoms and solutions, and the relationship between them is expressed in the form of rules. Then choose the C# language in the Visual Studio 2013 platform, use ADO.NET technology to access the database to establish the expert system. In this way, it can not only meet the requirements of rapid response to wind turbine fault diagnosis, but also prevent the emergence of human error, the valuable experience of experts can be retained to prevent lost, too.

Section 2 discusses the structure of the rule-based expert system, and the common faults of wind turbine and solutions. Section 3 discusses the rule-based wind turbine fault diagnosis expert system, mainly the establishment of the knowledge base and reasoning machine. Finally, Section 4 concludes.

2 The expert system based on production rules

Expert system is composed of man-machine interface (divided into user interface and development interface), knowledge acquisition module, knowledge base, reasoning machine, interpreter and comprehensive database. Experts or knowledge engineers in the development interface in the development of expert systems, increase, modify or delete faults, signs and rules, signs and rules stored in the diagnostic knowledge base, failure and other related information stored in the integrated database. The user in the user interface for rule-based diagnosis, the symptoms will be extracted into the rules of diagnostic module, the inference engine work to draw diagnostic conclusions, the interpreter of the system's reasoning conclusion to explain, feedback to the user. Rule based expert system schematic is shown in **Figure 1**.

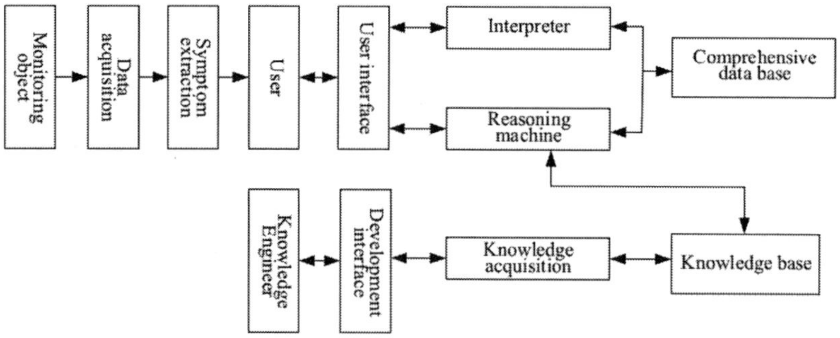

Figure 1. Rule based expert system schematic

The expert system based on production rules transforms the expert's diagnosis experience and knowledge into the production rule, and carries on the fault diagnosis through certain reasoning mechanism. It can clearly express the causality of the fault, and it is easy to add and modify [8]. Monsef H uses PROLOG to develop a rule-based fuzzy expert system for fault diagnosis of power system [9]. Soe S. M. M established a rule-based expert system for fault management of network devices [10]. Liu used depth-first search strategy as a control strategy, a rule-based fault diagnosis expert system is built, which solves the problem that some faults will be missed due to conflict in the reasoning process [11].

Production rules is composed of the first term If and the second term Then. The If is part of one or more conditions, conditions of each sub by logical connectives (and, or) composed of different combinations. The latter part of Then is one or more rear action should be taken or the conclusion, the premise condition is true conclusion. Rule reasoning is derived from If's preconditions Then the rear conclusion.

"If <Precondition true> then <Generate action> or <Draw a conclusion>"

The rule is the core of the expert system. The rule of good or bad determines the diagnosis effect of the expert system. It is necessary to improve the fault diagnosis and fault indication before

 DOI: 10.1051/itmconf/20171107005

establishing the diagnosis rule of the expert system. According to the fault history data of the wind turbine, the faults mainly focus on the key parts such as gear box, generator, low speed shaft, high speed shaft and blade. Now only list part of the common faults, fault phenomena and their causes of failure, as shown in **Table 1**.

Table 1. Part of the common fault in wind turbine

Fault	Fault phenomena	Causes of failure
High speed shaft unbalance	1. The spectrum of its 1X (X said multiplier) based 2. Radial runout 3. Amplitude increases with increasing speed 4. Axis orbit for a more round or oval	Rotor of the rotating machine due to the material density distribution, assembly factors, processing errors and movement of the erosion and deposition and other factors led to the center of mass and the rotation center there is a certain degree of eccentricity.
High speed axis misalignment	1. The spectrum is its 1X, 2X or higher harmonic 2. Axial vibration 3. The amplitude does not vary with the speed 4. Axis trajectory was banana-shaped or 8-shaped	Installation in the construction of the ultra-poor, the thermal expansion of housing, chassis deformation or displacement, high-speed shaft bending.
High speed shaft bending	1. The spectrum is its 1X, 2X or higher harmonic 2. When the rotor speed is fixed, the vibration amplitude is fixed	The bending of the shaft is permanent bending and temporary bending. The former is mainly caused by design and manufacturing defects, improper long-term parking methods, etc. The latter is mainly overloaded but can be recovered.
High speed shaft parts loosening	1. The spectrum is its 1X and harmonic 2. Vertical vibration greater 3. Vibration amplitude is not fixed	The fastener is not fastened, and the fastener is loose or the fastener is damaged under the vibration of the base.
High-speed shaft rubbing	1. Most of the spectrum is its 1X component, there are harmonics, sub synchronous and natural frequency components 2. Axis trajectory was banana-shaped or 8-shaped	The speed may be too fast or the internal temperature of the wind turbine may change abruptly or the distance between the rotating parts and the fixed parts may be too small or the part offsets may cause friction.
Blade fracture	1. The spectrum is $fz = ft \times Z$ ft-impeller frequency Z-Number of impeller blades	Long-term outdoor harsh environment of the work, the blade surface will be fouling or ice leaves, so that uneven stress due to the blade load fatigue crack, and ultimately fracture.

3 Realization of fault diagnosis expert system for wind turbine

Expert system development using C # has many advantages [12]. Therefore, the system is based on Visual Studio 2013 platform to select C# language for software development, using ADO.NET technology to access the database. In this section, the article will show how to use C # to represent the knowledge of fault diagnosis as a computer - recognizable form, to build the knowledge base of fault

DOI: 10.1051/itmconf/20171107005

diagnosis, and the forward reasoning method based on precise reasoning mechanism is adopted in the reasoning mechanism. Three important aspects of expert system: knowledge representation, knowledge acquisition, reasoning model. Finally, the article will show the man-machine interface.

3.1 Knowledge representation

In actual wind farms, the difference between different wind turbines increases the uncertainty relationship between fault symptoms and faults. In order to make the expert system have the ability to deal with these uncertainty information, and can make the corresponding judgment when the information is not very complete, the expert system in this system adopts the production rule based on the confidence degree, and uses the confidence degree to describe the degree of symptom determination.

A rule is a knowledge entity, itself has the function of advisory reasoning, which is implemented by the Query function of the rule class. A rule is a node in a chain of rules, and a chain of rules consists of a knowledge base.

Confidence-based production rule representation is as follows:

If *R1(W1, K1)* and *R2(W2, K1)* and...and *Rn(Wn, Kn)*

Then *T* With *(CF, K)*

Rl, R2... Rn represents the premise of a rule, also known as the failure symptom;

W1, W2..., Wn is the weight of each precondition of rules;

K1, K2... Kn is the threshold of confidence, prerequisite rules of each;

T is the rule conclusion; *CF* ($CF \in 0 \sim 1$) is the rules of the credibility of the conclusion

K ($K = 0 \sim 1$) is a rule established threshold, only when the true value is greater than or equal to *K* rules, this rule is activated.

For example, the design of a wind turbine generator shaft unbalance failure based on the confidence of the production rules, which are as follows:

If the spectrum (1X-based, spectrum into fir tree) Weight (0.4) Confidence threshold (0.8)

And phase (stable) weight (0.1) confidence threshold (0.8)

And Axis Trajectory (Oval) Weight (0.2) Confidence Threshold (0.8)

And rotation feature (forward movement) Weight (0.1) Confidence threshold (1)

And vibration direction (radial) weight (0.05) Confidence threshold (1)

And the critical vibration (the difference between horizontal and vertical direction is not significant) Weight (0.05) Confidence threshold (0.8)

And other (vibration varies with speed) Weight (0.1) Confidence threshold (1)

Then the rotor imbalance With ($CF = 0.98$, $K = 0.7$)

In the expert system based on the confidence production rule, we need to determine the confidence of the symptom in the fault diagnosis. If the symptom is deterministic, the user only needs to give an affirmative answer, which sets the confidence of the fault symptom to 1; in most cases, however, the symptom does not have an exact quantitative value, and the user can determine a confidence level based on what is observed.

3.2 Knowledge acquisition

The knowledge acquisition in this system is divided into two ways: one is manual input, the knowledge is input by the knowledge engineer in the development interface, and the other is the automatic learning of the machine, which can acquire the knowledge through the modification of the fault diagnosis process.

Two self-learning methods are designed in this system, which can self-study in the diagnosis process, improve the diagnosis rules and improve the correct rate of fault diagnosis, and finally achieve a better diagnostic effect on wind turbine fault diagnosis. The system self-learning process shown in **Figure 2**.

1. When the selected symptom matches a diagnostic rule successfully, it automatically increases the confidence level of the diagnostic rule. The new confidence level of the diagnostic rule is determined by the following equation (1), where k is a coefficient, and the smaller k, the faster the confidence increases. If the current trustworthiness of the rule is smaller, the more the rule credibility increases after the match is successful.

$$CF_{new} = CF + \frac{1-CF}{k} \tag{1}$$

2. When the selected symptom does not match the rule, the system will remind you whether to add a new diagnostic rule. If you choose to add a new rule, you need to select a fault as the diagnostic conclusion, and form a new rule together with the previously selected symptom to improve the expert system.

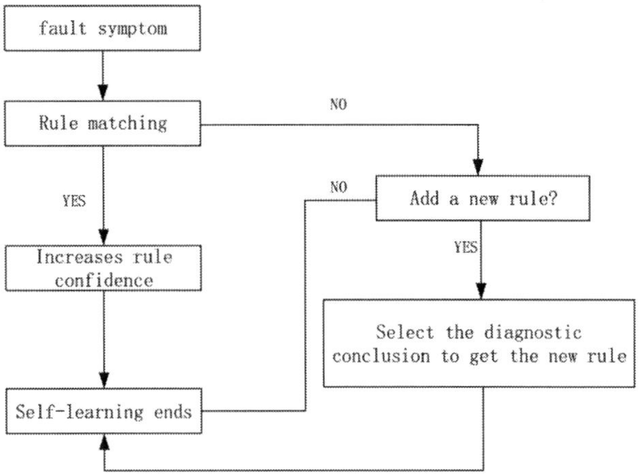

Figure 2. The system self-learning process

3.3 Rreasoning model

Expert system uses the reasoning model to solve the problem, so the reasoning model in the expert system is very important. The expert system in this system adopts forward reasoning. Fault diagnosis, through the parts monitoring parameters to determine its fault symptoms, fault diagnosis interface to select the appropriate symptoms, and then by the expert system to get the fault diagnosis results.
In this paper, the expert system's forward reasoning process is presented by the rule of "rotor unbalance", as shown in **Table 2**.
1. According to the symptom matching rule
Match the entered symptoms with all the rules one by one. If only one of these symptoms exists in a rule, the true value of the rule is calculated.
2. Calculate the true value of each symptom (rule sub condition)
When the confidence level of the symptom is greater than its confidence threshold in the rule, the true value is 1. When the confidence level is less than the confidence threshold, then the ratio of confidence level and confidence threshold is taken as the true value of the symptom. It is shown in **Table 2**.
3. Calculate the true value of the rule
The true value of the rule is determined by all the prerequisites in the rule. The calculation formula is as follows:

DOI: 10.1051/itmconf/20171107005

$$T = (\sum_{i=1}^{n} W_i \times T_i) * CF \tag{2}$$

The W_i is the weight of the corresponding prerequisites, T_i is the true value of this symptom, and CF is the credibility of the rule. In the above example, there are symptoms in the "rotor imbalance" this rule, then calculate the true value of this rule as follows:

$$\begin{aligned} T &= (0.4\times1 + 0.1\times1 + 0.2\times1 + 0.1\times1 + 0.05\times1 + 0.05\times1 + 0.1\times0.8) * 0.98 \\ &= 0.9604 \end{aligned} \tag{3}$$

4. Gives the fault diagnosis conclusion

It can be seen from the calculation that the true value 0.9604 of the "rotor unbalance" rule is greater than the activation threshold value 0.7, so this rule is activated. Therefore, the selected symptom matches the "rotor imbalance" rule, and the system extracts the fault name and fault explanation related to this rule according to the diagnosis result and outputs to the diagnosis interface.

Table 2. The process of forward reasoning

Rule "rotor imbalance"			Diagnosis		Result
Symptoms	Weight	Confidence threshold	Confidence level	True value	
spectrum (1X-based, spectrum into fir tree)	0.4	0.8	1.0	1.0	T > K Rule is activated
phase (stable)	0.1	0.8	1.0	1.0	
Axis Trajectory (Oval)	0.2	0.8	1.0	1.0	
rotation feature (forward movement)	0.1	1.0	1.0	1.0	
vibration direction (radial)	0.05	1.0	1.0	1.0	
the critical vibration (the difference between horizontal and vertical direction is not significant)	0.05	0.8	1.0	1.0	
other (vibration varies with speed)	0.1	1.0	0.8	0.8	
CF= 0.98 K=0.7			T=0.9604		

3.4 The man-machine interface

3.4.1 Login interface

The wind turbine fault diagnosis expert system can be accessed through the server. All operators enter the correct user name and password to enter the system's fault diagnosis interface, login interface shown in **Figure 3**.

DOI: 10.1051/itmconf/20171107005

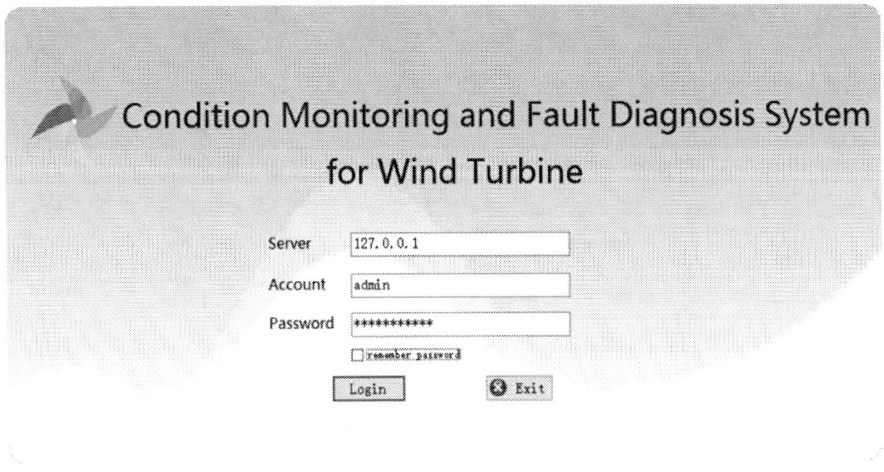

Figure 3. The Login interface

3.4.2 Fault diagnosis interface

After successfully logging into the system, click on the fault diagnosis button to enter the fault diagnosis module, fault diagnosis interface shown in **Figure 4**. Users can select the unit to be diagnosed, and then enter the fault symptom and the symptom of confidence, click the "Start Diagnosis" button, the system will automatically match the rules from the knowledge base to complete the fault diagnosis. In this interface, the system will automatically give the diagnosis of the credibility of the results and provide diagnostic details.

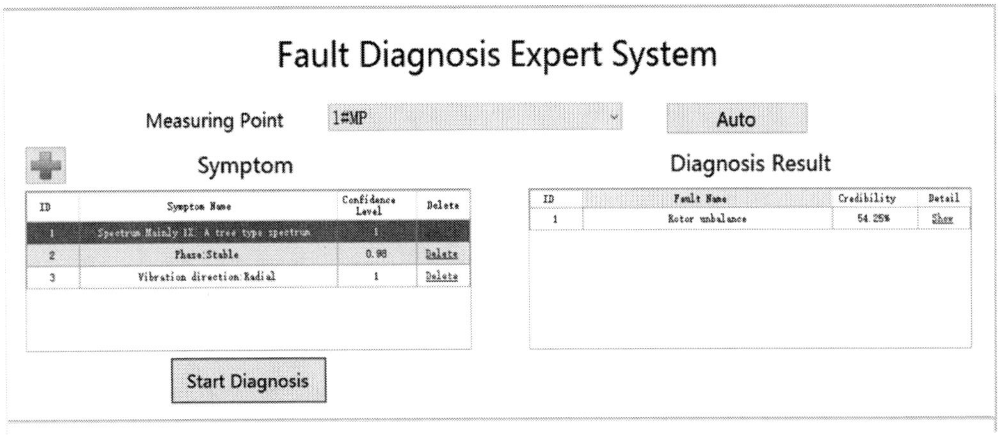

Figure 4. The Fault diagnosis interface

3.4.3 Rules management interface

Administrators can add, delete, and modify rules in the rule management interface. As shown in **Figure 5**, in this interface, the administrator can define the name of the rule, select the appropriate prerequisite, and set the diagnostic conclusion. In addition, the administrator can manually modify the priority of rule matching, the threshold of activation and the reliability of diagnostic results through historical diagnosis results, so as to improve the diagnostic knowledge base and improve the efficiency and accuracy of expert system diagnosis.

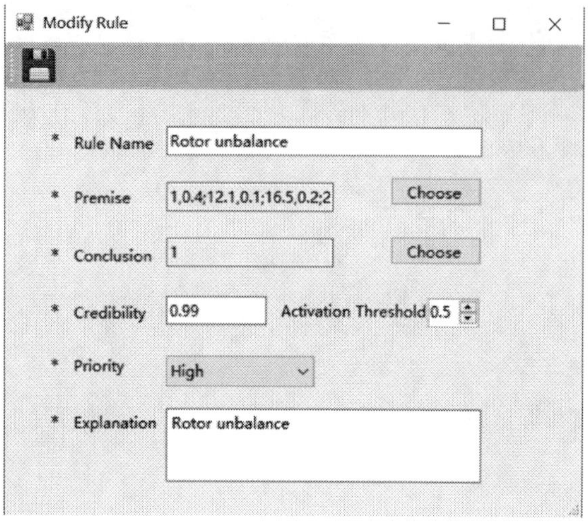

Figure 5. The Rules management interface

Conclusion

The development of computer science and artificial intelligence technology has greatly promoted the practical application of intelligent fault diagnosis technology. Based on the expert knowledge of wind turbine fault diagnosis, this paper designs a wind turbine fault diagnosis expert system based on production rules. In the process of establishing the knowledge base, a production rule based on confidence and an expert system self-learning method are designed, which can effectively increase the validity of the diagnosis result and expand the content of the knowledge base. In Visual Studio 2013 platform, we choose C # language, and use ADO.NET technology to access the database, and realize the development of wind turbine fault diagnosis expert system. The system, in combination with the fault signal detection and processing technology, can identify the state of the given environment and fault analysis, and provide recommendations to solve the problem. With the continuous accumulation of wind turbine operation data, the knowledge of the system diagnosis knowledge base is improved by strengthening the communication with field experts and improving the efficiency and accuracy of system fault diagnosis.

References

1. National Energy Administration. "Wind power development 13th Five-Year plan" [EB/OL]. http://www.nea.gov.cn/2016-11/29/c_135867633.htm, November 29, 2016
2. B Lu, Y Li, Z Yang. A review of recent advances in wind turbine condition monitoring and fault diagnosis[C]//Power Electronics and Machines in Wind Applications, 2009. PEMWA 2009. IEEE. IEEE, 2009, 1-7 (2009)
3. W Yi, F Xiaoyun. Electric locomotive fault diagnosis expert system based on fault tree. Electric Locomotives &Mass Transit Vehicles, **27**, 35-36 (2004)
4. Y Zhiling, W Bin, D Xinghui, L Hao. Expert system of fault diagnosis for gear box in wind turbine[J]. Systems Engineering Procedia, **4**,189-195(2012)

5. L Yang, J Wang, G Zhang, Z Ding. An expert system reasoning machine based on the combination of fault tree and generalized regression neural network[C]//Intelligent Control and Automation (WCICA), 2016 12th World Congress on.IEEE,1303-1306(2016)
6. Q Yao, J Wang, L Yang, S Haixia, Z Guigang. A fault diagnosis method of engine rotor based on Random Forests[C]//Prognostics and Health Management (ICPHM), 2016 IEEE International Conference on. IEEE,1-4(2016)
7. A Abraham. Rule-Based expert systems[J]. Handbook of measuring system design, (2005)
8. G Peixian, F Yongpeng. Research on the inherent defects of the integrated R & D system based on rule based expert system [J]. Computer Measurement and Control, **19(7)**,1711-1714(2011)
9. H Monsef, A M Ranjbar, S Jadid. Fuzzy rule-based expert system for power system fault diagnosis[J]. IEE Proceedings-Generation, Transmission and Distribution, **144(2)**,186-192(1997)
10. S M M Soe, M P P Zaw. Design and implementation of rule based expert system for fault management[J]. World Academy of Science, Engineering and Technology, **48**,34-39(2008)
11. L Jian, C Yichao, J Hong. Fault diagnosis method for general expert knowledge base based on rule [J]. computer and digital engineering, **38(6)**,72-76(2010)
12. L Jianhua. Design and Implementation of Expert System[J]. Information Technology, **30(4)**,150-152(2006)

ITM Web of Conferences **11**, 07006 (2017) DOI: 10.1051/itmconf/20171107006
IST2017

Channel Division Based Multiple Classifiers Fusion for Emotion Recognition Using EEG signals

Xian LI[1,2,a], Jian-Zhuo YAN[1,2] and Jian-Hui CHEN[1,2,3]

[1]*Faculty of Information Technology, Beijing University of Technology, Beijing 100124, China*
[2]*Beijing Advanced Innovation Center for Future Internet Technology, Beijing University of Technology, Beijing 100024, China*
[3]*International WIC Institute, Beijing University of Technology, Beijing 100024, China*

Abstract. With the rapid development of computer technology, pervasive computing and wearable devices, EEG-based emotion recognition has gradually attracted much attention in affecting computing (AC) domain. In this paper, we propose an approach of emotion recognition using EEG signals based on the weighted fusion of multiple base classifiers. These base classifiers based on SVM are constructed using a channel division mechanism according to the neuropsychological theory that different brain areas are differ in processing intensity of emotional information. The outputs of channel base classifiers are integrated by a weighted fusion strategy which is based on the confidence estimation on each emotional label by each base classifier. The evaluation on the DEAP dataset shows that our proposed multiple classifiers fusion method outperforms individual channel base classifiers and the feature fusion method for EEG-based emotion recognition.

1 Introduction

Human emotion which synthesizes the feelings, thoughts and behaviours, plays a critical role in our daily life[1]. With the rapid development of ubiquitous technology and computer technology, affective computing (AC) which is an interdiscipline related to cognitive science and artificial intelligence (AI) has gradually become a hot topic in the field of emotion research[2]. Emotion recognition as a key issue of AC has gained increasing attentions and applications such as brain-computer interface (BCI), psychology and clinical assistant diagnosis of mental disorders, etc. There are various physiological signals (e.g., ECG, skin conductance, respiration, etc.) used to perform emotion assessment, in which EEG-based emotion recognition is widely used because EEG signal from the central nervous system has real-time diversity, non-disguise and non-invasive.

Since EEG not only indicates emotional states, but also reflects other cognitive activity of the brain, recently researchers tried to find the correlation between the emotional changes and EEG signals. Some of these studies belonging to neuropsychology have focused on the question of asymmetrical activation of the cerebral hemisphere[3-4]. From these researches, a common conclusion that different brain areas are differ in the processing mode and intensity of emotional information can be obtained. In addition, more and more complex methods were proposed to improve the performance of EEG-based emotion recognition by presenting some novel feature extraction,

[a] Corresponding author: lixian1992@emails.bjut.edu.cn

DOI: 10.1051/itmconf/20171107006

feature selection and machine learning algorithms[5-10]. Most of these studies utilized a simple feature fusion strategy that is to combine extracted features and EEG channels to form a single feature vector as the input of classification model. However, EEG signals have low signal-to-noise ratio (SNR) and often mixed with much noise when collected. The more challenge problem is that, unlike image or speech signals, EEG signals are temporal asymmetry and nonstationary because the human brain can be seen as a complicated nonlinear dynamic system[11]. So these EEG-based emotion recognition methods using a simple feature integration or fusion are difficult to obtain stable recognition performance and even bring some negative effects. What's more, these methods cannot preserve the original domain information such as channels and frequency bands which are very important for understanding brain response.

Considering the problem mentioned above, this paper proposes an effective EEG-based emotion recognition approach with a novel decision fusion method based on multiple channels, namely multiple classifiers fusion (MCF). The rest of this paper is organized as follows. Section 2 briefly reviews the research background. Section 3 describes our approach in details. The detailed experimental settings, experimental results and analysis will be given in section 4. Finally, we give the remark and conclusion of this paper.

2 Emotion related EEG analysis and processing

2.1 Emotional models

An emotional state refers to a psychological and physiological state in which emotions and behaviours are interrelated and appraised within a context[12]. Many representations of emotional states, such as discrete scales[13] (e.g., anxiety, frustration, engagement and distress) and the arousal-valence space [14], have been used in emotion assessment studies. The bi-dimensionality theory of emotions proposes that nature of emotional experience, or at least its "affective core", is primarily determined by two main dimensions: arousal and valence. Arousal refers to the quantitative activation level ranging from calm to excited. Valence represents the quality of an emotion ranging from unpleasant to pleasant. Each discrete emotional state (e.g., happy, calm and sad) can be defined in the arousal-valence space as shown in Figure 1.

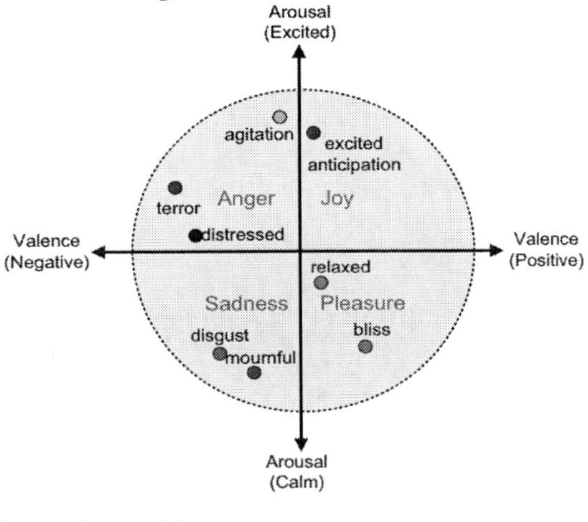

Figure 1. Two-dimension emotional model.

2.2 EEG acquisition and preprocessing

In this research, we used an open database for emotion analysis using physiological signals, DEAP, proposed by Koelstra et al.[15]. It is recorded over 32 participants aged between 19 and 37. Fifty percent of the participants are female and mean age is 26.9 years. EEG, peripheral physiological signals and facial videos are recorded while participants watched 40 excerpts of selected music videos. Participants performed self-assessment (SAM) ratings of their levels of arousal, valence, liking and dominance at the end of each video. These videos are gathered using a novel stimuli selection method from relatively large set of music video clips followed by subjective test, to select the most appropriate test material. EEG signals are recorded from 32 active electrodes with 512 Hz sampling frequency. Peripheral physiological signals are electromyograms (EMG), electrooculogram (EOG), blood volume pulse (BVP) using plethysmography, skin temperature, and galvanic skin response (GSR). The facial videos collected is available for 22 of the 32 participants. Figure 2 shows electrode placement for 32-channel EEG recording using the International 10-20 system.

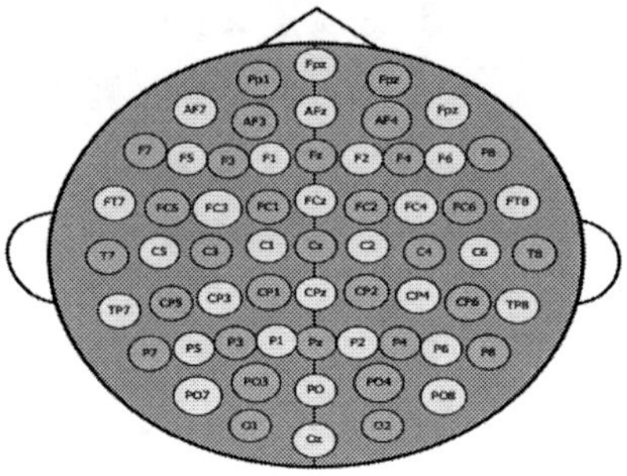

Figure 2. International 10-20 system for 32 electrodes (marked as gray circles).

The preprocessing operations of EEG signals include downsampled to128 Hz, bandpass filtered with cutoff frequency between 0.1 Hz and 45.0 Hz, EOG artifacts removal using blind source separation technique. All of the above preprocessing operations can be performed using EEGLAB toobox[16]. The artifact removal procedure was applied to all EEG epochs for every subject under different emotion conditions since it is hard for participants to keep eyes fixed during watching entire music videos. According to the response of the subjects, only the experiment epochs when the target emotions were elicited were chosen for further analysis. Hence, we extracted the EEG segments corresponding to the duration of each music video after performing the preprocessing. Each channel of the EEG data was divided into the same-length epochs without overlapping using time windows. Finally, all features discussed below were further computed on each epoch of the EEG data.

2.3 Feature generation

Suitable representation of EEG data makes informative patterns for a classifier to recognize emotion. The main task of feature extraction is to derive the salient features which can map the EEG data into consequent emotional states. Recently, a wide range of features which are relevant for emotion recognition from EEG signals have been proposed. Because feature extraction was not the research emphasis of this study, the typical features of three different groups, namely time-statistical domain, frequency domain and nonlinear dynamic domain, were extracted to more comprehensively and accurately represent the EEG patterns related to emotional states. The specific features of each domain extracted on EEG data are shown in Table 1. In this paper, the features of EEG signals are extracted on five frequency bands that are delta (0.1-4Hz), theta (4-8Hz), alpha (8-13Hz), beta (13-30Hz) and gamma (30-45) by Wavelet Transform. Then, each epoch from one channel was mapped to three groups of features on the above five frequency bands.

DOI: 10.1051/itmconf/20171107006

If all EEG features on 32 channels are analyzed in classification process, it will generate an enormous amount of computing cost, so the above typical feature values were computed merely on those channels related to emotion states. According to the analysis results in[7,15], 8 channels (namely, T7, CP5, P7, FC2, C4, T8, CP6, PO4) are selected to continue the following study.

Table 1. The extracted features from different domains.

Feature group	Feature name
Time-statistical domain	Skewness, Kurtosis, Peak-peak value, Hjorth parameters (activity, mobility, complexity), Hurst exponent, Mean value, Root mean square value, Root square amplitude value, Variance, Maximum value, Minimum value, Absolute mean value
Frequency domain	Power spectral density, Absolute power, Relative power, Band energy
Nonlinear dynamic domain	Renyi entropy, Approximate entropy, Shannon entropy, Sample entropy, Fuzzy entropy, Permutation entropy, Scale entropy, LZ complexity, Maximum lyapunov exponent, Correlation dimension.

3 Multiple classifiers fusion for EEG-based emotion recognition

3.1 Description of proposed method

As discussed before, many neurophysiological studies have proved that different brain regions have different intensity of processing emotion information. In addition, it was found that the performance of recognition changes with the varying channel positions in EEG-based emotion assessment researches. Traditional studies are to combine all the channels and features into one single feature vector using feature fusion method in order to represent the emotional patterns in EEG signals more adequately. However, it cannot improve the recognition performance stably because some bad-performed features bring negative influences. Furthermore, the simple feature concatenation always ignores the nature of emotion information processing in human brain and the non-linear structure of original EEG signals. To overcome these problems, this paper proposes an effective weighted fusion method of multiple classifiers constructed by channel division using Support Vector Machine (SVM). The framework of our proposed approach is shown in Figure 3.

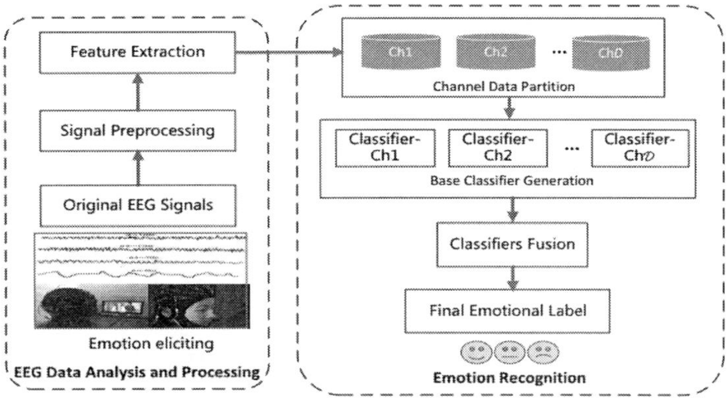

Figure 3. The framework of EEG-based emotion recognition approach using multiple classifiers fusion.

DOI: 10.1051/itmconf/20171107006

Firstly, D channel base classifiers based on SVM are constructed on the basis of D parts of channel training data, respectively. Secondly, the weight coefficients of each channel are learned based on the output of corresponding channel base classifier. Finally, a weighted fusion based multiple classifiers fusion model is constructed by integrating the outputs of D channel base classifiers with the weight coefficients to estimate the overall confidence of one sample belonging to each emotional class. Following the principle of minimum error, the class with the maximum confidence is outputted as the final emotion recognition result.

3.2 Base classifier-SVM

We used SVM to construct base classifiers on each channel sample data and evaluate the performance of our proposed approach on EEG-based emotion recognition. SVM is a supervised learning algorithm based on statistical learning theory [17]. The basic training principle of SVM is finding the optimal hyperplane where the expected classification error of test samples is minimized. It projects low dimension features into higher dimension using kernel functions $K(x,y)$ which can create nonlinear decision boundaries and solve the inseparable cases. Different kernels used in our work to find the best performance of SVM in EEG-based emotion recognition are defined as follows:

$$K(x,y)=\begin{cases} x^T\cdot y, & if\ kernel = linear\ kernel \\ (\gamma\cdot x^T\cdot y+coef)^d, & if\ kernel = polynomial\ kernel \\ \exp(-\gamma\cdot \|x-y\|^2), & if\ kernel = radial\ basis\ function \end{cases} \quad (1)$$

where $x,y\in R^n$, γ and $coef$ are the kernel parameters, d denotes the order of the polynomial kernel and T is the transpose operation. More information about SVM classifier can be found in[17].

SVM are known to have good generalization properties, to be insensitive to overtraining and to the curse-of-dimensionality. Finally, SVM has a few parameters (e.g., C, γ and d) that need to be defined. These advantages are gained at the expense of a low speed of execution. SVM can deal with over-fitting problem by having misclassified instances on training data. Due to these advantages, SVM is more appropriate for emotion recognition because physiology data is noisy[18].

3.3 Weighted fusion of multiple base classifiers

Multiple classifiers fusion (MCF), sometimes called decision fusion, is constructed by integrating the classification results of several base classifiers according to some combination strategies. In this paper, each channel is processed independently by the corresponding classifier and their outputs are integrated to generate the final result. It is different from the existing studies with feature fusion methods which are straight forward considering the synchronous characteristics of the involved features by concatenating the different features extracted from signals to form a composite feature vector. However, the brain activity is a complicate nonlinear dynamic system. Thus, the feature fusion sometimes brings negative impact. Especially, their outputs miss the non-linear structures in the signal during the dimension reduction. The MCF supports to model the asynchronous characteristics of channels flexibly. It has an important advantage over feature fusion is that since each of the channel data is processed and classified independently in MCF, it is relatively easy to employ an optimal weighting scheme to adjust the contribution of each channel to the final decision according to their reliability of the feature. In this study, EEG-based emotion recognition using MCF mainly include the following steps.

Step 1. Generating channel base classifiers.

We use the sample data of selected channels $\{\mathrm{Ch1},\mathrm{Ch2},\dots,\mathrm{Ch}D\}$ to build the base channel classifiers based on SVM algorithm: {C-AF3, C-FP1, C-P7, C-FC2, C-C4, C-T8, C-CP6, C-PO4}.

Step 2. Computing classification error rate.

The classification error rate of each base classifier on testing data set is calculated according to the following formula:

$$Error_t = \frac{Num(\sum_{k=1}^{N} F_t(X_k) \neq y_k)}{Num_{total}}, \quad t = 1,2, \dots, D \tag{2}$$

where $F_t(X_k)$ represents the predicted emotional label of testing sample X_k using the base classier built by the t-th channel training data and N is the number of testing samples. y_k is the true emotional label and the function $Num()$ is used to count the number of error-classification and total samples.

Step 3. Computing weight parameters.

We can get the weight of classification model of each channel by formula (3) which is computed as below:

$$\omega_t = \frac{1}{2} log\left(\frac{1-Error_t}{Error_t}\right), \quad t = 1,2, \dots, D. \tag{3}$$

Step 4. Computing output probability

For an input testing sample, the probability on each class is computed by the confidence estimation $conf_t$ on each emotional label :

$$P_{negative} = \sum_{t=1}^{D} \omega_t * conf_t^{negative} \tag{4}$$

$$P_{positive} = \sum_{t=1}^{D} \omega_t * conf_t^{positive} \tag{5}$$

Step 5. Obtaining the final results.

In the end, the emotional label with highest probability is the final decision output of this testing sample:

$$\text{Label} = \text{argmax}\{P_{negative}, P_{positive}\} \tag{6}$$

4 Experiment and results

4.1 Experimental settings

Our proposed MCF method for EEG-based emotion recognition on two emotional dimensions(arousal and valence) is evaluated on the DEAP dataset. In this study, the participants' ratings scales during the emotion elicitation experiment are used as the ground truth. According to the unnormalized SAM-ratings values on a scale of 1-9, the performance of the proposed method is investigated in a two-class problem about arousal and valence. For the binary classification, we transformed ratings for arousal, valence to two categories, namely positive and negative. On the 9-point ratings scales, the division threshold was simple placed in the middle.

In this study, each dataset about different classification task was first divided into training set and testing set according to the same way as existing already, and its evaluating results are expressed by classification accuracy. As described earlier, there have been a lot of researches that addressed the EEG-based emotion recognition problem recently. However, it is not easy to compare directly the accuracies with the results in the literature, since they are differ in experimental paradigms and conditions which include the kinds of stimuli, the types of emotions, the processing methods of EEG data, etc. Nevertheless, most of them reported that the support vector machine (SVM) showed the best performance compared with other classifiers in the EEG-based emotion recognition problems. In this paper, SVM integrated in the LibSVM library[19] is applied to construct channel base classifiers using 10-fold cross validation scheme for evaluating our proposed approach.

In order to find a better performance of SVM, the performances of three different kernel functions, namely linear, polynomial and radial basis function (RBF), were compared in our study. Furthermore, among the SVM-based approaches, C-SVC showed the best performances according to Horling's study[20]. Hence, we compared the results of the proposed method with those of C-SVC with three different kernel functions. The parameters of C-SVC were determined by 10-fold cross validation method. For all kernel functions, we estimated the classification accuracy using the same range of cost parameter $C: C \in \{2^{-4}, 2^{-3}, \dots, 2^{9}, 2^{10}\}$. The other parameter setting of different kernel is shown in the following table.

Table 2. Parameter setting for different kernel functions of C-SVC

Kernel function	Parameters setting
Radial basis function (RBF)	kernel parameter $\gamma: \gamma \in \{2^{-10}, 2^{-9}, \dots, 2^{3}, 2^{4}\}$
Polynomial	Degree parameter $d: d \in \{1,2, \dots, 14,15\}$
Linear	Cost parameter $C: C \in \{2^{-4}, 2^{-3}, \dots, 2^{9}, 2^{10}\}$

4.2 Experimental results and discussion

Table 3 shows the average arousal and valence classification accuracies using C-SVC with different kernel functions after testing the full parameter settings for each emotion classification model based on SVM algorithm. It can be observed that the average classification accuracy of SVM with RBF kernel function outperforms SVM with linear kernel and polynomial kernel for building any type of classifier on arousal and valence dimension. This definitely proves the robustness of the RBF SVM over the linear SVM and polynomial SVM, so the SVM with RBF kernel was chosen as the basic classifier in the remaining paper.

Table 3. Classification accuracies of C-SVC based classifiers with different kernels

Classifier	Arousal			Valence		
	RBF	Linear	Polynomial	RBF	Linear	Polynomial
C-AF3	**79.32**	78.04	78.43	**78.01**	77.21	77.85
C-FP1	**80.01**	78.25	79.17	**78.43**	76.37	78.22
C-P7	**73.48**	72.56	73.06	**72.17**	70.89	71.25
C-FC2	**78.21**	77.26	76.88	**76.33**	75.85	75.24
C-C4	**74.26**	73.67	73.80	**73.19**	72.81	72.65
C-T8	**74.85**	71.29	70.45	**72.79**	70.60	70.21
C-CP6	**75.32**	73.58	72.97	**74.31**	72.47	71.80
C-PO4	**66.54**	65.76	65.78	**64.79**	63.71	64.07
FF	**76.41**	75.19	73.69	**75.29**	74.37	72.78
MCF	**83.78**	80.46	79.33	**80.72**	79.25	78.17

In addition, it is found that the base classifiers C-AF3, C-FP1 and C-FC2, which are constructed by the sample data of AF3, FP1 and FC2 channel respectively, achieve relatively high accuracies compared with other channel base classifiers. The base classifier trained by FP1 sample data, namely C-FP1, has a highest average accuracy of 80.01% and 78.43% on arousal and valence respectively among all channel base classifiers. This results indicates that it is feasible to estimate emotion using single channel. Furthermore, it shows that accuracy in the frontal lobe seems higher than in other areas of scalp, which have reasonable interpretation in brain science that frontal lobe is associated with emotion, attention and motivation[21]. Locations of electrodes are dipcted in Figure 2.

A histogram is used to demonstrate the classification accuracies in order to compare our proposed MCF method with feature fusion (FF) method and other single channel base classifiers, as shown in Figure 4.

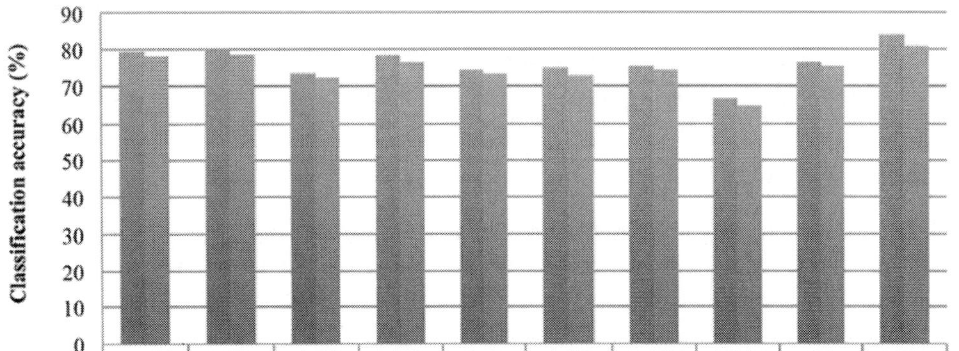

	C-AF3	C-FP1	C-P7	C-FC2	C-C4	C-T8	C-CP6	C-PO4	FF	MCF
Arousal	79.32	80.01	73.48	78.21	74.26	74.85	75.32	66.54	76.41	83.78
Valence	78.01	78.43	72.17	76.33	73.19	72.79	74.31	64.79	75.29	80.72

Figure 4. Classification accuracies of our proposed method and other classification models

From the Figure 4, it is observed that the feature fusion achieves the performances higher than the lowest performances but lower than the highest performance by base channel classifiers. In other words, the feature decision method can not improve the classification performance obviously. Our proposed MCF method achieved better performance than the best channel base classifier C-FP1 and feature fusion method. It achieves the 7.37% accuracy improvement on valence from feature fusion and 3.77% accuracy improvement from the highest base channel classifier C-FP1. As for the arousal classification accuracy, the MCF outperforms feature fusion for 5.43% and C-FP1 for 2.29%. These results show that our proposed MCF method based channel division is effective to improve the classification performance of EEG-based emotion recognition.

In order to evaluate the effect of different EEG frequency bands on emotion classification, we use the sample data on each frequency band to train and test emotion classification models. Figure 5 presents the classification accuracies of our method and feature fusion (FF) method across different frequency bands of EEG signal on arousal and valence emotional dimension.

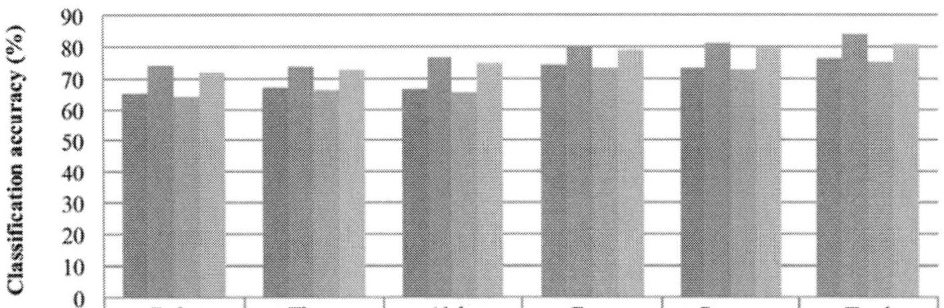

	Delta	Theta	Alpha	Beta	Gamma	Total
Arousal-FF	65.28	67.18	66.77	74.39	73.32	76.41
Arousal-MCF	74.22	73.7	76.59	79.66	80.91	83.78
Valence-FF	64.32	66.29	65.55	73.25	72.77	75.29
Valence-MCF	72.09	72.77	74.89	78.81	79.56	80.72

Figure 5. Classification accuracies of our method and feature decision method

We can find that the classification performances of feature fusion method and our proposed MCF method across all frequency bands is better than those based individual frequency bands under the

DOI: 10.1051/itmconf/20171107006

same conditions. In addition, it is found that the classification performance of beta and gamma bands is slightly better than those of delta, theta and alpha bands. This result shows that beta and gamma bands are the key bands in emotion recognition task. In other words, high frequency bands of EEG signals play a more important role in emotion activities than low frequency bands[22-23].

Conclusion

In this paper, we present an EEG-based emotion recognition approach by using multiple classifiers fusion (MCF) based on EEG channel division according to the neurophysiological theory that different brain areas have different processing intensity of emotion information. There are several important observations that can be drawn from our comparative experiments. Firstly, it can be observed that the classification performance of SVM with RBF kernel function outperforms SVM with linear kernel and polynomial kernel for building any type of classification model on arousal and valence emotional dimension. This definitely proves the robustness of the RBF SVM over the linear SVM and polynomial SVM for EEG-based emotion classification. Seconly, it is feasible to estimate emotion using single channel, especially those channels in the frontal lobe compared with other areas of scalp. Thirdly, gamma and beta frequency bands perform better than other frequency bands. It confirms that beta and gamma oscillation of brain activity are more related with emotional processing than other frequency oscillations. The last but the most important is that our proposed MCF method based on divisional channels outperforms all single channel base classifiers and the feature fusion method which combines all the channels and extracted features into one single feature vector. This indicates the effectiveness and reliability of multiple classifiers fusion in EEG-based emotion recognition.

References

1. Dalgleish T, Dunn B D, Mobbs D. Affective Neuroscience: Past, Present, and Future[J]. Emotion Review, 2009, **1**(4):355-368.
2. Healey J. Wearable and automotive systems for the recognition of affect from physiology[D]. Massachusetts: MIT, 2000.
3. Davidson R J. Anterior electrophysiological asymmetries, emotion, and depression: conceptual and methodological conundrums[J]. Psychophysiology, 1998, **35**(5):607-614.
4. Baumgartner T, Esslen M, Jäncke L. From emotion perception to emotion experience: Emotions evoked by pictures and classical music[J]. International Journal of Psychophysiology, 2006, **60**(1):34-43.
5. Gupta R, Laghari K U R, Falk T H. Relevance vector classifier decision fusion and EEG graph-theoretic features for automatic affective state characterization[J]. Neurocomputing, 2016, 174:875-884.
6. Jie X, Cao R, Li L. Emotion recognition based on the sample entropy of EEG[J]. Bio-medical materials and engineering, 2014, **24**(1):1185-1192.
7. Zheng W L, Lu B L. Investigating Critical Frequency Bands and Channels for EEG-Based Emotion Recognition with Deep Neural Networks[J]. IEEE Transactions on Autonomous Mental Development, 2015, 7(3):162-1175.
8. Duan R N, Zhu J Y, Lu B L. Differential entropy feature for EEG-based emotion classification[C]// *International IEEE/EMBS Conference on Neural Engineering*. IEEE, 2013:81-84.
9. Yoon H J, Chung S Y. EEG-based emotion estimation using Bayesian weighted-log-posterior function and perceptron convergence algorithm[J]. Computers in Biology & Medicine, 2013, **43**(12):2230-2237.
10. Sepideh H, Keivan M, Motie N A. The Emotion Recognition System Based on Autoregressive Model and Sequential Forward Feature Selection of Electroencephalogram Signals[J]. Journal of Medical Signals & Sensors, 2014, **4**(3):194-201.

DOI: 10.1051/itmconf/20171107006

11. Palus M. Nonlinearity in normal human EEG: cycles, temporal asymmetry, nonstationarity and randomness, not chaos[J]. Biological Cybernetics, 1996, **75**(5):389-396.
12. Salmeron J L. Fuzzy cognitive maps for artificial emotions forecasting[J]. Applied Soft Computing, 2012, **12**(12):3704-3710.
13. Lisa Feldman Barrett. Discrete Emotions or Dimensions? The Role of Valence Focus and Arousal Focus [J]. Cognition and Emotion, 1998, **12**(4):579-599.
14. Robinson M D. Measures of emotion: A review[J]. Cognition and Emotion, 2009, **23**(2):209-237.
15. Koelstra S, Muhl C, Soleymani M, et al. DEAP: A Database for Emotion Analysis Using Physiological Signals[J]. IEEE Transactions on Affective Computing, 2012, **3**(1):18-31.
16. Delorme A, Makeig S. EEGLAB: an open source toolbox for analysis of single-trial EEG dynamics including independent component analysis[J]. Journal of Neuroscience Methods, 2004, **134**(1):9-21.
17. Andrew A M. An Introduction to Support Vector Machines and Other Kernel-based Learning Methods [M]. *Printed in the United Kingdom at the University Press*, 2000.
18. Liu C, Rani P, Sarkar N. An empirical study of machine learning techniques for affect recognition in human-robot interaction[C]// *IEEE/RSJ International Conference on Intelligent Robots and Systems*. IEEE, 2005:2662-2667.
19. Chang C C, Lin C J. LIBSVM: A library for support vector machines[J]. ACM Transactions on Intelligent Systems & Technology, 2011, **2**(3):27.
20. Horlings R, Datcu D, Rothkrantz L J M. Emotion recognition using brain activity[C]// *International Conference on Computer Systems and Technologies and Workshop for Phd Students in Computing*. ACM, 2008:6.
21. Stuss D T. Functions of the frontal lobes: relation to executive functions[J]. Journal of the International Neuropsychological Society, 2011, **17**(5):759-765.
22. Klimesch W. EEG alpha and theta oscillations reflect cognitive and memory performance: A review and analysis[J]. Brain Research Reviews, 1999, **29**(2-3):169-195.
23. Oathes D J, Ray W J, Yamasaki A S, et al. Worry, Generalized Anxiety Disorder, and Emotion: Evidence from the EEG Gamma Band[J]. Biological Psychology, 2008, **79**(2):165-170.

ITM Web of Conferences **11**, 07007 (2017) DOI: 10.1051/itmconf/20171107007
IST2017

Modeling and Simulation of Linear Two - DOF Vehicle Handling Stability

Pei-Cheng SHI[a], Qi ZHAO and Shan-Shan PENG

Anhui Polytechnic University, Anhui Engineering Technology Research Center of Automotive New Technique, 241000 Wuhu, China

Abstract. Based on the theory of vehicle steering dynamics, a model of linear two-DOF vehicle handling stability was established in MATLAB / Simulink environment. Simulation analysis of state variable response such as vehicle yaw velocity and side slip angle was made under different vehicle speed conditions for step-input of front-wheel turning angle. The response curves of the state variables in the time domain are obtained under three vehicle speeds. The results show that the response curve of simulation is in good agreement with the actual situation, which not only verifies correctness of the established vehicle handling stability model, but also provides theoretical basis for subsequent design of handling stability control system.

1 Introduction

Vehicle handling stability is one of the important characteristics of vehicle, which directly affects driving convenience, vehicle dynamics and driver and passenger safety[1]. Vehicle handling stability includes two parts of controllabitity and stability. Controllabitity refers to the extent to which the vehicle is able to respond to driver's steering commands when the driver does not feel tired or nervous. Stability refers to the ability of the vehicle to maintain stable driving when encountering external disturbances (road disturbance or gust disturbance). The two are interrelated, affecting vehicle handling stability together. With the continuous improvement of vehicle speed, research on vehicle handling stability has attracted increasingly wider attention [2,3].

In the study of vehicle handling stability, yaw velocity and slip angle are generally considered as the optimal state variables to describe vehicle dynamics stability[4], which reflect vehicle stability from different sides. In this paper, a linear two-DOF vehicle handling stability model and analog simulation were established by MATLAB / Simulink. The vehicle yaw velocity and side slip angle changes were compared and analyzed under different vehicle speeds at front wheel turning angle step input. The results have certain engineering application value.

2 Vehicle handling stability modeling

In order to simulate the basic characteristics of vehicle handling stability, the vehicle model is reduced to an ideal linear two-DOF vehicle model. Two-DOF refers to two state variables: yaw velocity and

[a] Corresponding author: 18355311303@163.com

DOI: 10.1051/itmconf/20171107007

side slip angle. The model assumes that vehicle only makes plane movement parallel to the ground. That is, vehicle displacement along z-axis, pitch angle around the y-axis and roll angle around x-axis are zero. Also, the origin of the vehicle coordinate system coincides with center of mass of vehicle. The simplified vehicle model is shown in Figure. 1.

The modeling is also based on the assumption that the driving force is not large and effect of ground tangential force on laterodeviation characteristic is not taken into account, effect of the air resistance is not considered, and tire characteristic changes of the left and right wheel tires due to load variation and aligning torque of the wheel are ignored.

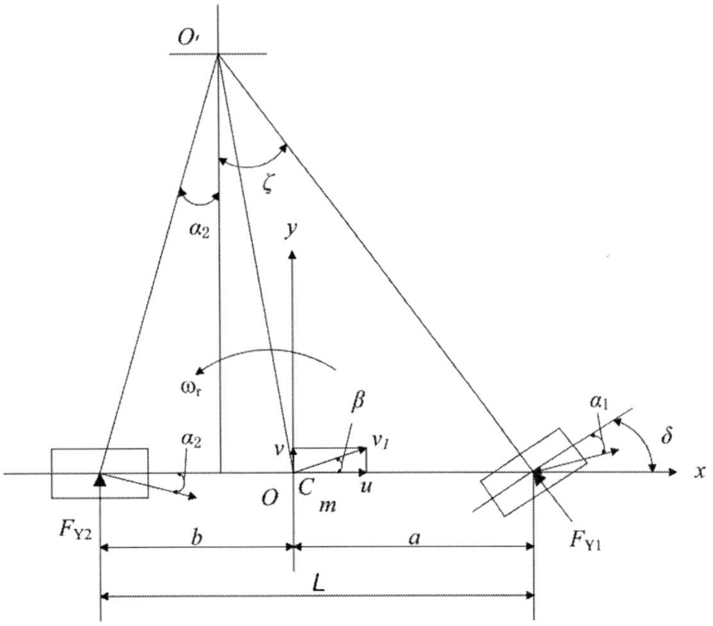

Figure 1. Two-DOF vehicle model.

In the Figure: a, b are respectively distance between the front and rear axles to the center of mass of the vehicle; L is vehicle wheelbase; ω_r is vehicle yaw velocity; δ is the front wheel angle; β is side slip angle; α_1 is the front wheel slip angle; α_2 is the rear wheel slip angle; m is the total weight; v_1 is velocity at center of mass; v is v_1 component at time t on oy axis; u is v_1 component at time t on ox axis; F_{y1}, F_{y2} are respectively cornering force of the ground on the front and rear wheel; ζ is the angle between the front wheel speed direction and the ox axis; O is the origin of the coordinate axis; C is the center of mass of vehicle; O' is the instantaneous steering center.

2.1 Establish differential equation of vehicle dynamics

According to the above-mentioned modeling analysis, the differential equation of vehicle motion at front wheel angle step input can be deduced as follows:

$$\begin{cases}(k_1+k_2)\beta+\dfrac{1}{u}(ak_1-bk_2)\omega_r-k_1\delta=m\left(\dot{v}+u\omega_r\right)\\(ak_1-bk_2)\beta+\dfrac{1}{u}\left(a^2k_1+b^2k_2\right)\omega_r-ak_1\delta=I_z\dot{\omega}_r\end{cases}\tag{1}$$

DOI: 10.1051/itmconf/20171107007

2.2 Two-DOF vehicle model Based on Simulink

According to formula (1), Two-DOF vehicle simulation model established in Matlab / Simulink software environment is shown in Figure.2. The assignment of each parameter is shown in Table 1.

Table 1. Two-DOF vehicle model simulation parameters

Model parameter	Value
Mass m(*Kg*)	1000
Rotational inertia Iz(Kgm^2)	2800
Distance from centroid to front axle a(*m*)	1.3
Distance from centroid to rear axle b(*m*)	1.2
Front wheel cornering stiffness k1(*N/rad*)	51000
Rear wheel cornering stiffness k2(*N/rad*)	45000

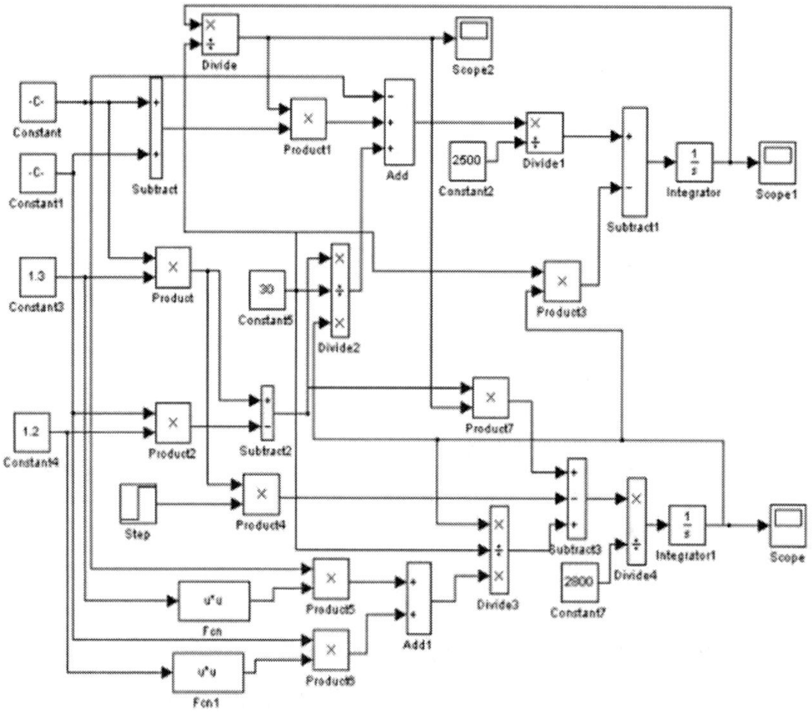

Figure 2. Simulation model of two-DOF vehicle.

3 Simulation analysis

According to the established simulation model, we set the front wheel turning angle input as the angular step signal, the amplitude is 0.4rad, and the simulation time is 5s. The response curve of the yaw velocity and side slip angle at three different vehicle speeds are obtained, as shown in Figure.3, 4.

 DOI: 10.1051/itmconf/20171107007

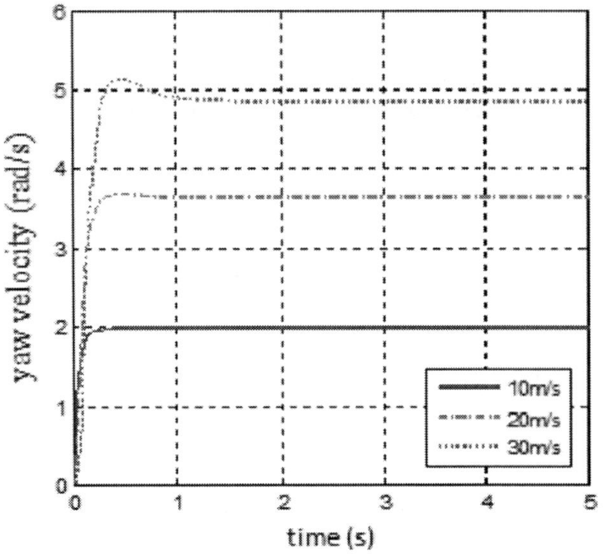

Figure 3. Yaw velocity curve.

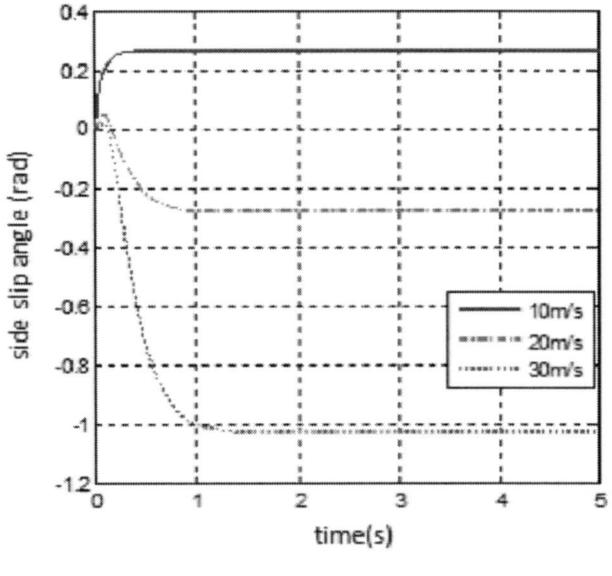

Figure 4. Curve of side slip angle.

It can be seen from Figure. 3 that, after a given angular step input, the vehicle yaw velocity response curve changes with the speed change. When the vehicle speed is 10m / s, the yaw rate reaches stable at about 0.3s after slight fluctuation and the steady state value is about 2rad / s, and the steady state response time is short. It can be seen from Figure.4 that when the vehicle speed is 10m / s, the vehicle side slip angle is stable at about 0.3s, and the steady state value is about 0.28rad. When the vehicle speed is 30m / s, the yaw rate reaches stable at about 1s, and the steady state value is about 4.8rad / s, the yaw velocity fluctuates more at high speed than low speed, and the steady-state response time becomes longer; The side slip angle is stable at 1.3s, and the steady state value is about -1.01rad, which is much higher than the value when the vehicle speed is 10m / s.

From the above analysis, we can see that when driving at a lower speed, vehicle enjoys better transient response characteristics. With the increase of vehicle speed, the response amplitude of yaw velocity and side slip angle becomes larger and the stabilization time becomes longer. This rule is in good agreement with the actual situation, which verifies correctness of the established model. Subsequently, the model can be used for vehicle handling stability control algorithm and experimental research.

Conclusion

Vehicle handling stability has a direct impact on steering characteristics, power output characteristics, driving safety, etc., so it is necessary to carry out further research on it. Based on the theory of vehicle handling stability, a simulation model of linear two-DOF vehicle handling stability is established. The model can be used to analyze the yaw velocity and side slip angle response at front wheel corner step input at any given vehicle speed. Through analysis of the simulation results, it can be seen that the response cure of vehicle yaw velocity and side slip angle in the time domain simulated by the model can more intuitively reflect change of vehicle handling stability, which has a certain reference value for the future experimental study.

Acknowledgement

The authors would like to thank Anhui province science and technology research key project (Grant No. 1604a0902158) and Anhui university scientific research platform innovation team building projects (2016-2018).

References

1. J. Liu. Dynamics Model and Simulation Analysis of Half-car Suspension Based on MATLAB/Simulink, J. Journal of Jiamusi University(Natural Science Edition), (06): 948-951. (2015)
2. J. Li, S.H. Yuan, D.M. Ju, R.Y. Li. Research on Test Methods for Special Vehicle Handling and Stability Based on Dynamics Simulation, J. Acta Armamentarii, (02): 262-267. (2014)
3. W. Huang, X.H. Wang, M. Zhang. Simulation on Handling Stability of Mult-iaxle Steering Vehicle, J. Tractor & Farm Transporter, (01): 70-73+81. (2011)
4. F.B. Bao. Analysis based on Vehicle Handling Stability, J. Western China Communications Science & Technology, (11):75-79. (2011)
5. Q.D. Wang, G.H. Zhang, W.W. Chen, H. Zhu. A Study of Vehicle Dynamics Stability Control Based on Variable Structure Control, J. China Mechanical Engineering, (05): 622-626. (2009)
6. H. Wang, L. Yang, S.H. He, C.W. Peng. Co-simulating the Vehicle Controlling Stability Based on ADAMS and MATLAB, J. Agricultural Equipment & Vehicle Engineering, (08): 38-41. (2012)
7. T.J. Chen, Y. Chen, F. Zhao, Q.L. Zhou. Control and Simulation Analysis of Handling and Stability of Electric Vehicle with All Motorized Wheels, J. Journal of System Simulation, (12): 3033-3038. (2013)
8. S. Chen, S. Meng, G. Li, Y.Y. Qin, X.Z. Qu. The Study on Co-Simulation Modeling of Automobile Ride and Handling, J. Agricultural Equipment & Vehicle Engineering, (04): 12-16. (2016)
9. X.W. Han, F. He, Y.D. Zhang, J.S. Chen. Roll Stability Analysis of Heavy Vehicles Based on Fuzzy Control, J. Coal Mine Machinery, (04): 7-9. (2016)
10. W.P. Li, S.J. Mo, J. Xiao, B.Z. Zhang. Control and Optimization of Vehicle Roll Stability with Considering of Ride Comfort, J. Computer Simulation, (08): 180-184. (2015)

11. S.B. Zhang, M. Li, Y.X. Liu. Simulation Analysis and Influencing Factor Study of Vehicle Handling Stability, J. Tractor & Farm Transporter, (02): 23-26+34. (2015)

The Design of Sobel Edge Extraction System on FPGA

Yu ZHENG[1,*]

[1]*School of software, Beijing University of technology, Beijing 100124, China;*

Abstract. Edge is a basic feature of an image, the purpose of edge detection is to reduce the amount of data in an image while preserving the shape information of objects .Field programmable gate arrays (FPGA) are best suited to implement image processing algorithms with the reason that it provides infinite reprogram ability and high parallelism.The aim of this paper is to design a real-time sobel extract system based on HLS method and the implement it on ZYNQ FPGA. The result shows the software processing time is almost 80 times than the hardware processing. The hardware acceleration has remarkable effect on sobel filtering.

1 Introduction

Edge is a basic feature of an image, the purpose of edge detection is to reduce the amount of data in an image while preserving the shape information of objects in an image. Edge detection is a preprocessing step for further image processing such as feature extraction and object segmentation. With the continuous research on edge detection algorithm, the noise immunity and quality of edge detection has been greatly improved, but the complexity of the algorithm is also greatly increased simultaneously. Furthermore, image processing systems are recognized as computational and data intensive systems. Such systems need high performance capabilities to meet the real time applications requirements. Those applications include real-time face/fingerprint recognition, video surveillance, military aerial systems. Designing special circuits for special applications is a thought of speeding up. Field programmable gate arrays (FPGA) are best suited to implement image processing algorithms with the reason that it provides infinite reprogram ability, high parallelism, and costs advantages when compared to ASIC with similar level of performance in most cases. Historically, the programming model of an FPGA was centered on register-transfer level descriptions and it is a great obstacle for software designers. High-Level Synthesis makes it possible that software engineer set up an SOC quickly when lacking of the knowledge of Hardware Description Language. The aim of this paper is to design and optimize a sobel filter system on Zynq based on HLS method.

2 The Sobel Edge Detection Algorithm

Sobel edge detection is a classical algorithm in the field of image and video processing for the extraction of object edges. Edge detection using sobel operators works on the premise of computing an estimate of the first derivative of an image to extract edge information. It takes advantage of the gradient

[a] Corresponding author: zhengyu@mails.bjut.edu.cn

differences of adjacent pixels between horizontal direction and vertical direction. And it judges whether the point is boundary point or not by comparing the gradient differences and the threshold.

Assuming that the function F(x,y) shows level of grey level of pixel in the original image, the function G(x,y) shows the grey level in the gradient image and θ is degree of elevation that shows the direction of the edge.The gradient can be expressed as :

$$G(x,y)=\frac{\partial F(x,y)}{\partial m}\cos\theta+\frac{\partial F(x,y)}{\partial n}\sin\theta \tag{1}$$

The magnitude form can be predefined as the sum of the magnitudes of vertical and horizontal gradient. In the partial derivatives of vertical and horizontal can be represented as Gx and Gy:

$$G(x,y)=G_x(x,y)\cos\theta+G_y(x,y)\sin\theta \tag{2}$$

The amplitude of gradient is:

$$G(x,y)=\sqrt{[G_x(x,y)]^2+[G_y(x,y)]^2} \tag{3}$$

Gx and Gy can be obtained by the convolution between regional template and image.

Figure.1 shows the 3*3 window of neighborhood of point(x,y), the horizontal gradient operator and vertical gradient operator.

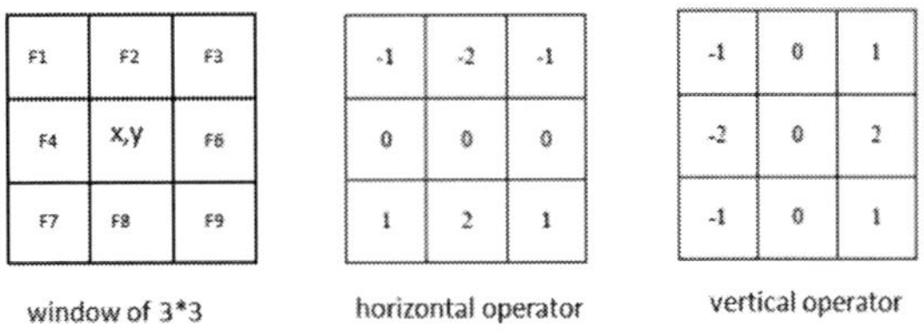

Figure 1. Sobel operator

The horizontal gradient and vertical gradient of F(x,y) is shown respectively:

$$G_x=(F_7+2F_8+F_9)-(F_1+2F_2+F_3) \tag{4}$$

$$G_y=(F_3+2F_6+F_9)-(F_1+2F_4+F_7) \tag{5}$$

After calculation of gradient for each pixel, threshold value t is selected. G(x,y) > t, is chosen to be the edge point.

3 The design of sobel IP core

The core of the system is sobel filtering, It's necessary to made sobel filtering IP core for the reason of reuse for other design and simplification hierarchical structure.

3.1 Memory architecture

When calculate the gradient of one pixel, the nine pixel points around it need to be accessible concurrently.

DOI: 10.1051/itmconf/20171108001

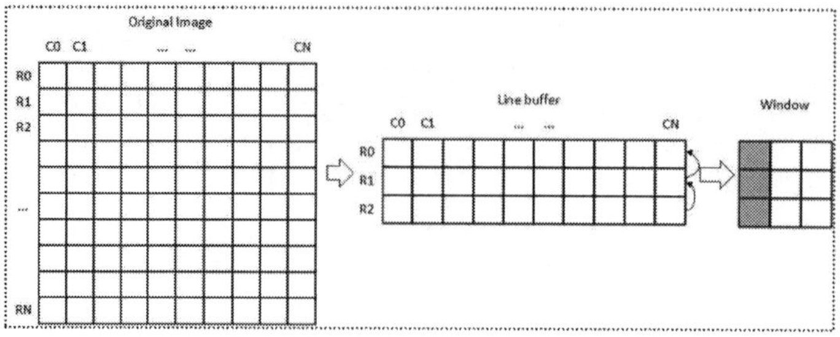

Figure 2. Original image pixels

As shown in Figure.2, when computing the output pixel of F, all the pixels around it need to be accessible.The line buffer is selected to meet concurrent multi-access requirement. To meet the 9-pixel-per-clock-cycle requirement, it is needed to add a memory window to the algorithm source code in addition to the line buffer. A memory window is a storage element implemented using the FF resources from the FPGA fabric. The purpose of this block is to store only the minimum number of pixels required for functional correctness and not to store the entire image. The overall data movement from input to computation through a tiered memory.The memory architecture is shown in Figure.3. At each clock cycle, the contents of the window shift left to make room for a new column from the line buffer. As Figure.4 shows the data reuse and distributed implementation of the window memory provides the nine memory operations required by the algorithm. No additional latency is introduced into the design by this memory. The window data movement operations occur concurrently with those of the line buffer. These memory structures can be implemented in C/C++ code as class window and class line buffer by using HLS library.

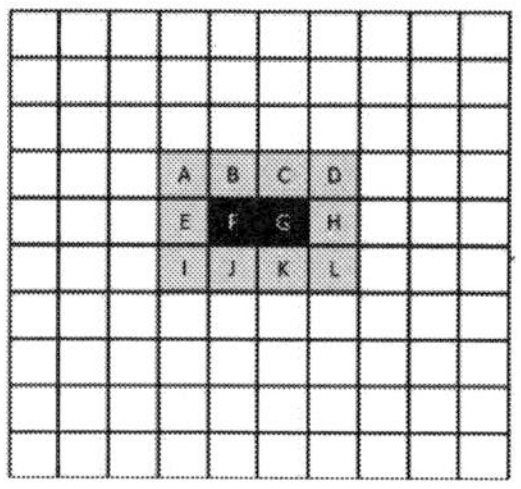

Figure 3. Memory architecture

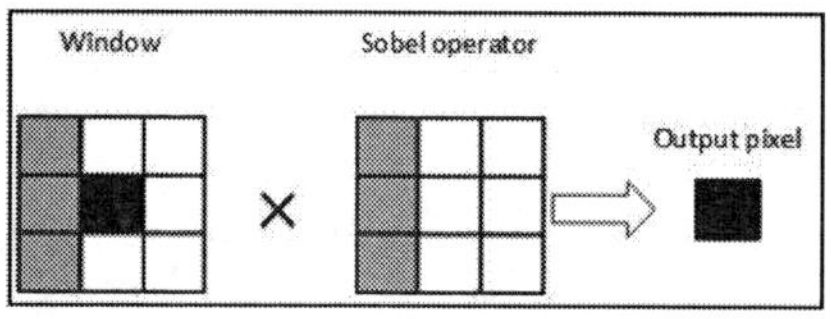

Figure.4. Calculation with sobel operator

3.2 Port-protocol

The design of the port protocol defines how the module starts and stops working and how to communicate with other modules. Xilinx provides the port protocol library and packed in ap_interfaces.h. This project uses ap_ctrl_hs block-level protocol and AXI4-Stream port-level protocol. The design is implemented in C/C++ and synthesized into RTL-level block in Vivado HLS. The IP core package diagram is shown in Figure.5

DOI: 10.1051/itmconf/20171108001

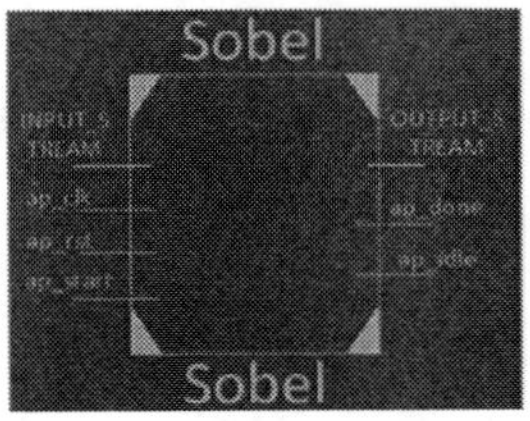

Figure 5. Sobel IP block

4 System design

4.1 Hardware system architecture

The processing result of sobel extraction is verified by a real-time video system. The original image is captured by the USB camera, after processing, the image is shown on the display device through the HDMI interface. The entire project is implemented on Zedboard, which is one of the Zynq family FPGA .It integrates a dual-core ARM Cortex based processing system (PS) and programmable logic (PL) in a single device. The hardware architecture is shown as Figure.6. An embedded linux runs on the PS and the camera acquisition control and memory data mapping control is responsible for the PS. PL is in charger of the implementation of sobel processing and control of display device. The block diagram in Figure.6 is implemented as IP core in the hardware design. Pixel date is first captured by a USB camera and is transmitted to from DDR to VDMA through memory map by AXI interconnect. Then the origin frame image is processed to extract the edge and the processed pixel date is stored in a VDMA again. A video display controller is then required to output the processed video. This project uses AXI4 Streaming protocol to communicate pixel data.

4.2 Software development

After finishing the hardware design, software can be developed based on it. The software design is divided into two main parts, embedded linux setup and the application software design.

In the context of a Zynq Soc runnning under Linux, applications based on Linux don't have access to the sobel IP in the FPGA logic. The kernel application program interfaces or system calls is used to make it possible to access to the hardware. These APIs or system calls interact with the Linux device driver to enable access to the hardware accelerator from the user application. Some files are needed to start an embedded linux on PS: u-boot.elf(Linux boot loader), bitstream (hardware configuration file), fsbl.elf (first stage boot loader), zImage(.linux kernal Image), devicetree. Dtb (device tree), embedded linux file systemAfter finishing the operating system transplantation, software of edge extraction can be developed based on the embedded linux. OpenCV library should be transplanted to control the USB camera. The flow chart of software is shown as Figure.7.

 DOI: 10.1051/itmconf/20171108001

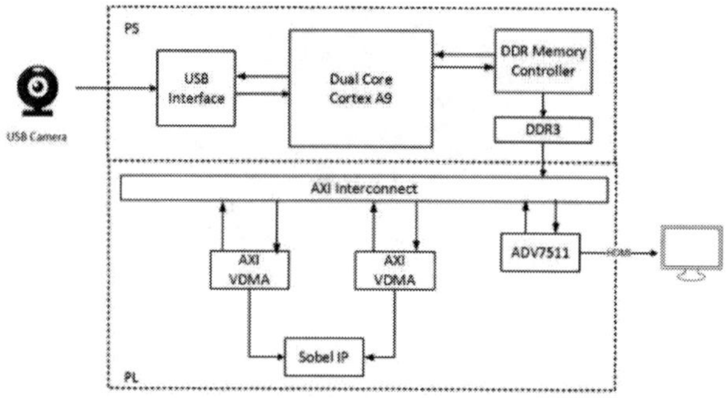

Figure 6. Hardware architecture

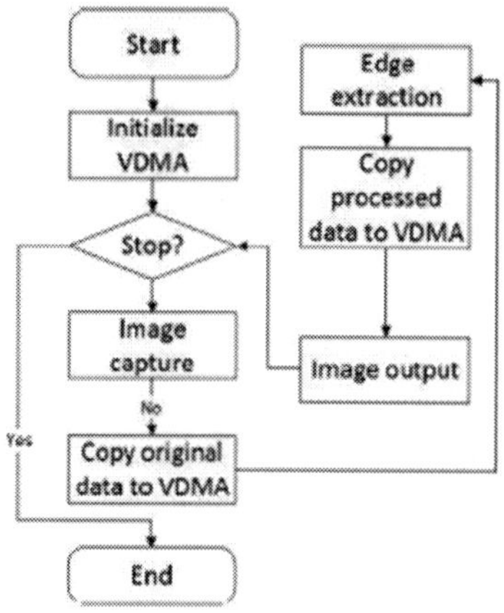

Figure 7. Software flow

5 Testing and results

A SD card with two partitions is needed to bring linux desktop. A FAT32 partition for Zynq Boot Images and an ext4 partition for root file system. Copy the generated Boot. Bin, zimage devicetree.dtb files to FAT32 partition and copy the file system files to ext4 partition. Start the linux and compile the software application and then test the system.

Different input images and their edge detected images are shown the Figure.8. The figures A, B are the input images and figures C,D are their edge detected results respectively.

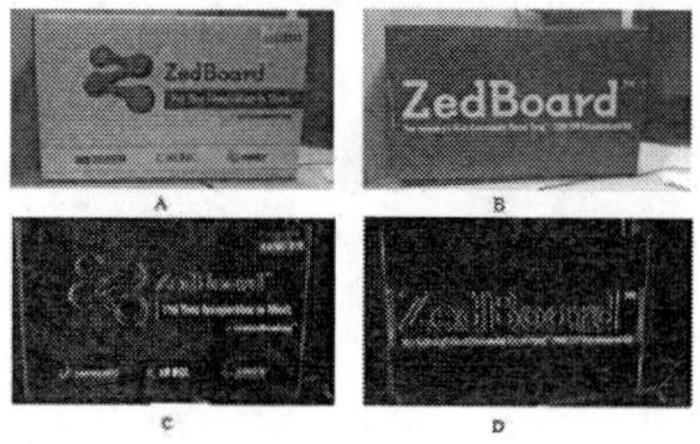

Figure 8. Sobel edge extraction results

 DOI: 10.1051/itmconf/20171108001

A comparative test is done to verify the hardware acceleration with software filtering on ARM. Two parameters are selected to measure the efficiency of the program. Latency represents the number of iterations of the image processing to one frame. Timing represents the processing time of one frame. The results are shown in Table 1.

Table 1 comparatinve test resulte

	Latency	Timing(s)
Software process	899	0.089134
Hardware process	129	0.001141

It's obvious that hardware process is more efficient than software process. Software processing time is almost 80 times than the hardware processing. The hardware acceleration has remarkable effect on sobel filtering. The reason of the reduction of latency is FPGA logic provides with parallel pipeline processing while CPU provides with serial processing.

Summary

The design of FPGA based sobel edge detection system is presented in this paper. High level synthesize method is used in the design of sobel IP core. The project is realized on ZYNQ FPGA kit. The original video is captured by a USB camera and processed video is shown on a HDMI display device. The FPGA supports high levels of parallel processing data flow structures that are important for efficient implementation of image processing algorithms. Through the software and hardware comparison test, it can be seen that the hardware processing time is reduced by nearly 80 times compared with the software, and it's necessary for a real-time system.

References

1. G. x. Yao, "Design of edge detection algorithm for image sobel based on FPGA," 2015 4th International Conference on Computer Science and Network Technology (ICCSNT), Harbin, 851-853.(2015)
2. J. Tian, J. Wu and G. Wang, "Realization of real-time sobel adaptive threshold edge detection system based on FPGA," Information and Automation, 2015 IEEE International Conference on, Lijiang, 2740-2743.(2015)
3. İ Koyuncu, Ö Çetin, F. Katırcıoğlu and M. Tuna, "Edge dedection application with FPGA based Sobel operator," 2015 23nd Signal Processing and Communications Applications Conference (SIU), Malatya, 1829-1832.(2015)
4. G. Chaple and R. D. Daruwala, "Design of Sobel operator based image edge detection algorithm on FPGA," Communications and Signal Processing (ICCSP), International Conference on, Melmaruvathur, 2014, 788-792 (2014)
5. Vanishree and K. V. Ramana Reddy, "Implementation of pipelined sobel edge detection algorithm on FPGA for High speed applications," Emerging Trends in Communication, Control, Signal Processing & Computing Applications (C2SPCA), 2013 International Conference on, Bangalore,1-5 (2013)

Fault Diagnosis of Planetary Gear Based on Fuzzy Entropy of CEEMDAN and MLP Neural Network by Using Vibration Signal

Xi-Hui CHEN, Gang CHENG[a], Chang LIU and Yong LI

School of Mechatronic Engineering, China University of Mining and Technology, Xuzhou, 221116, China

Abstract. A method of planetary gear fault diagnosis based on the fuzzy entropy of complete ensemble empirical mode decomposition with adaptive noise (CEEMDAN) and multi-layer perceptron (MLP) neural network is proposed. The vibration signal is decomposed into multiple intrinsic mode functions (IMFs) by CEEMDAN, and the fuzzy entropy that combines the fuzzy function and sample entropy is proposed and used to extract the feature information contained in each IMF. The fuzzy entropies of each IMF are defined as the input of the MLP neural network, and the planetary gear status can be recognized by the output. The experiments prove the proposed method is effective.

1 Introduction

Planetary gear often used in the key parts of the transmission system of large-scale complex equipment. However, it often suffered from the influences of heavy-duty and hostile environment, leading faults to occur [1]. Therefore, it is of great significance to study the fault diagnosis of planetary gears. Due to the influence of its complex structure, installation errors and operating environment, the vibration signal of planetary gear shows the characteristics with nonlinear and non-stationary [2]. Therefore, a fault feature extraction method that is suitable for processing the non-stationary vibration signal should be developed.

The time-frequency analysis method not only reflects the frequency characteristics of the signal but also shows the time-varying characteristics, making it is more suitable for the analysis of non-stationary vibration signals. Empirical mode decomposition (EMD) is a typical adaptive time-frequency analysis method, but it has a major drawback of modal aliasing [3]. With the development of research, ensemble empirical mode decomposition (EEMD) is proposed to solve the problem of modal aliasing. However, the reconstructed signal after EEMD contains more residual noise, and it is not a complete decomposition process. CEEMDAN is an improved EEMD algorithm, and the limited adaptive white noise is added at each decomposition stage. Each IMF is obtained by calculating the only remaining part, and the reconstruction error is almost zero. Therefore, CEEMDAN can overcome the modal aliasing phenomenon of EEMD, mitigating the incompleteness of EEMD, and a set of high quality and effective intrinsic mode function (IMF) can be obtained [4, 5].

Sample entropy is now applied in the fault feature quantification to reflect the complexity of the signal from the perspective of their similarity. However, in the calculation process of sample entropy,

[a] Corresponding author: chenxh@cumt.edu.cn

the similarity of the signal is reflected to a dichotomy, exhibiting both similarity and dissimilarity, it is inaccurate to describe the similarity. So the fuzzy entropy is proposed [6]. The fuzzy function is used to describe the signal similarity, and a more accurate calculation for the signal similarity is achieved. The complexity and stability of the signal are described more reasonably and effectively. The recognition of planetary gear status is important after extracting the feature information, and some intelligent classification technologies are widely used [7]. The MLP neural network has great practical value in pattern recognition in many fields, and it is composed of an input layer, an output layer and many hidden layers. MLP neural network is a type of belong to multi-layer feed-forward neural network, and it realizes the data transformation of input features by the transfer functions of the hidden layers. MLP neural network can be applied to recognize different planetary gear statuses, generating a structured network to achieve highly complex nonlinear mapping by data self-learning [8]. Therefore, in this paper, a fault diagnosis method of planetary gear based on fuzzy entropy of CEEMDAN and MLP neural network is established.

2. Model analysis

2.1 Complete ensemble empirical mode decomposition with adaptive noise

EMD is originally proposed by Huang [3], but it has the drawback of modal aliasing. EEMD is proposed to solve this problem, and the Gaussian white noise is added into the original signal to change the distribution of extreme points. However, the reconstructed signal of the decomposition result of EEMD still contains more residual noise, and EEMD is not a complete decomposition process. Therefore, CEEMDAN is proposed, and the limited adaptive white noise is added at each decomposition stage. Each IMF is obtained by calculating the only remaining part, and the reconstruction error is zero. Therefore, CEEMDAN not only can overcome the modal aliasing, but can also eliminate the incompleteness of EEMD. The reconstructed signal is identical to the original signal [9, 10]. The decomposition process of CEEMDAN can be described as follows:

Step1: Assume $E_j(\cdot)$ is defined as the first j IMF that is obtained by EMD [3], and $\omega_m(t)$ is the white noise with a zero mean unit variance. For the signal $x(t)+\varepsilon_0\omega_m(t)$, the first IMF that is expressed as IMF1(t) is obtained by EMD with M experiments, and it is expressed as follows:

$$\mathrm{IMF}_1(t)=\frac{1}{M}\sum_{m=1}^{M}E\{x(t)+\varepsilon_0\omega_m(t)\} \tag{1}$$

where ε_0 is the amplitude coefficient of the white noise.

Step2: The first remaining part can be described as follows:

$$r_1(t)=x(t)-\mathrm{IMF}_1(t) \tag{2}$$

Step3: The computation process of the second IMF of the original signal $x(t)$ by CEEMDAN is expressed as follows:

$$\mathrm{IMF}_2(t)=\frac{1}{M}\sum_{m=1}^{M}E_1\{r_1(t)+\varepsilon_1E_1(\omega_m(t))\} \tag{3}$$

Step4: For the other stages, namely, $k=2,3,...,K$, the calculation process of the first k remaining part is same as Step2 and Step3. The first k+1 IMF is as follows:

$$\begin{cases} r_k(t) = r_{k-1}(t) - \mathrm{IMF}_k(t) \\ \mathrm{IMF}_{k+1}(t) = \dfrac{1}{M}\sum_{m=1}^{M} E_1\{r_k(t) + \varepsilon_k E_k(\omega_m(t))\} \end{cases} \tag{4}$$

Step5: Step4 is continued until the remaining part of the signal can no longer be decomposed, and the criterion is that the number of extreme points is not more than two. The number of final IMFs is K, and the final remaining part is as follows:

$$R(t) = x(t) - \sum_{k=1}^{K} \mathrm{IMF}_k(t) \tag{5}$$

It can be seen from the realization process of CEEMDAN that the decomposition process is complete and can realize the reconstruction of the original signal. In each decomposition stage, the white noise can obtain an appropriate signal-to-noise ratio by adjusting the coefficient ε_k .

2.2 Fuzzy entropy

The calculation process of fuzzy entropy is as follows[11]:

Step1: Assuming $\mathrm{IMF}_k(t) = \{z(1), z(2), ..., z(n)\}$, a set of vectors that are used to calculate the fuzzy entropy is built, and they are expressed as follows:

$$A_i = \{z(i), z(i+1), ..., z(i+m-1)\} - u_0(i) \quad i = 1, 2, ..., n-m+1 \tag{6}$$

where m is the length of the vector. $u_0(i)$ is the mean of each vector.

Step2: The distances of each vector are calculated, and the distance between A_i and A_j can be defined as follows:

$$d_{ij}^m(A_i, A_j) = \max(|A_i(l) - A_j(l)|) \quad l = 1, 2, ..., n \tag{7}$$

Step3: The similarity between each set of vectors is described using a fuzzy function. An exponential function [12] is used, and it is defined as follows:

$$D_{ij}^m = \mathrm{e}^{-(d_{ij}^m / r)^n} \tag{8}$$

where n is the boundary gradient of the exponential function, and r is the similar tolerance.

Step4: The representation function B^m is defined as follows:

$$B^m = \frac{1}{n-m}\sum_{i=1}^{n-m}\left|\frac{1}{n-m-1}\sum_{j=1, j\neq i}^{n-m} D_{ij}^m\right| \tag{9}$$

Step5: Make m=m+1 and repeat Step1-Step4, B^{m+1} can be obtained, and the fuzzy entropy can be expressed as follows:

$$FuzzyEn = \ln^{(B^m / B^{m+1})} \tag{10}$$

2.3 Multi-Layer Perceptron Neural Network

The MLP neural network is composed of input layer, output layer and hidden layer, and the training process of the MLP neural network [13, 14] is expressed as follows:

Step1: The connection weights of the MLP neural network are initialized. The inputted features are sent to the hidden layer, and the calculation of each neuron of the hidden layer is expressed as follows:

$$s_h = f(\sum_j^J xi_j W_{jh} + \theta_h) \tag{11}$$

where xi_j is the *j*-th input feature, W_{jh} is the connection weight between input neuron *j* and hidden neuron *h*, θ_h is the bias of the *h*-th hidden neuron. *f*( ) is the activation function.

Step2: The calculation result of the hidden neuron is transmitted to the output layer, and the calculation of each neuron of the output layer is expressed as follows:

$$yo_k = g(\sum_h^H s_h W_{hk} + \eta_k) \tag{12}$$

where s_h is the output of the *h*-th hidden neuron, W_{hk} is the connection weight between hidden neuron *h* and output neuron *k*, η_k is the bias of the *k*-th output neuron.

Step3: Each output neuron has a target pattern corresponding to an input pattern t_k, and the error information of the output neuron is calculated as $\delta_k = t_k - yo_k$. The error information of the hidden layer is then calculated as:

$$\delta_h = (\sum_{k=1}^K \delta_k W_{hk}) s_h \tag{13}$$

Step4: The weight updating of the hidden neurons and the output neurons is expressed as follows:

$$\begin{aligned} W_{jh}(t+1) &= W_{jh}(t) + \alpha\delta_h xi_j + \mu[W_{jh}(t) - W_{jh}(t-1)] \\ W_{hk}(t+1) &= W_{hk}(t) + \alpha\delta_k s_h + \mu[W_{hk}(t) - W_{hk}(t-1)] \end{aligned} \tag{14}$$

where α is the learning rate, and μ is a momentum factor.

Step5: Determine whether the system meets the stop condition.

3 Test equipment and data acquisition

The fault simulation experiment of the planetary gear is carried out, and the basic layout of the experiment is shown in Figure 1. In the experiment, the motor speed is set to 40 Hz, and the load is set to 13.5 Nm. Five types of sun gears are simulated, and they are normal gear, broken gear, gear with one missing tooth, wear gear and gear with a tooth root crack. The sampling frequency is set to 12800 Hz, and the vibration signals of the five types of gears are collected.

DOI: 10.1051/itmconf/20171108002

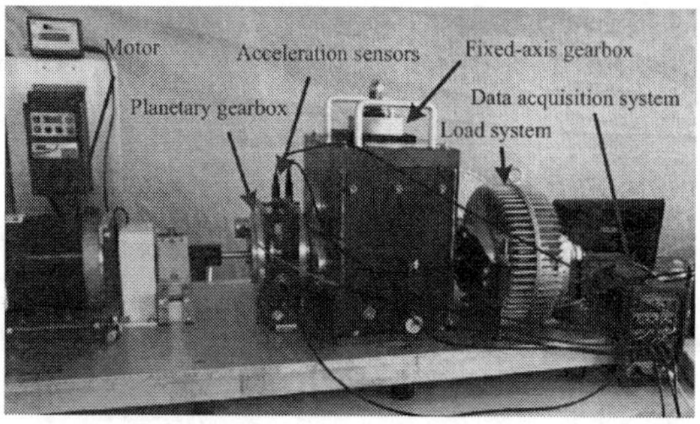

Figure 1. Fault experiment for the planetary gear

4 Experiment signal analysis

The five types of vibration signals for different gears are collected and shown in Figure 2.

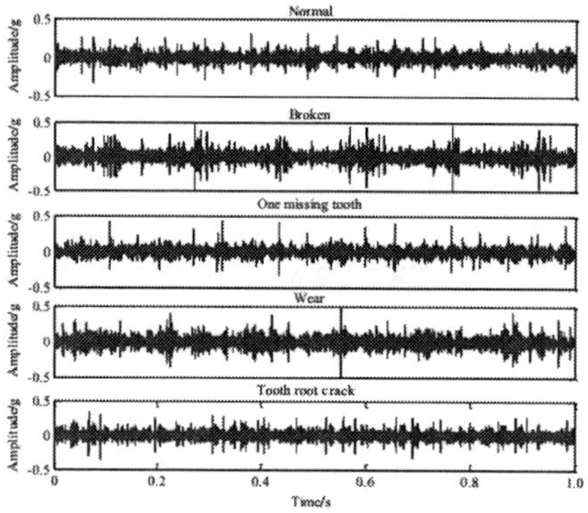

Figure 2. Five types of vibration signals for different gears

It can be seen from Figure 2 that five types of vibration signals for different gears have no obvious difference. It is not able to distinguish the gear status by comparing the time domain vibration signals, next, they are processed by the proposed method to verify the effectiveness of the method. The vibration signals are decomposed by CEEMDAN, and due to the limitation of space, the vibration signal of the broken gear is selected as an example to show the CEEMDAN process. To prove that the performance of CEEMDAN is superior to that of EEMD, the decomposition results using EEMD and CEEMDAN for broken gear are shown in Figure 3. It can be seen from Figure 3 that the vibration signal is decomposed into 12 IMFs and a residual signal, and for convenience of expression, the residual signal is called IMF13. IMF1-IMF13 are arranged from high frequency to low frequency. The decomposition result of EEMD still exhibits a serious modal aliasing phenomenon, as shown in IMF6, IMF7, IMF8 and IMF9. Meanwhile, some of them even are the illusive components, such as in IMF7 and IMF8. In the decomposition result using CEEMDAN, the quality of the obtained IMFs is greatly improved, and the modal aliasing phenomenon is further suppressed.

DOI: 10.1051/itmconf/20171108002

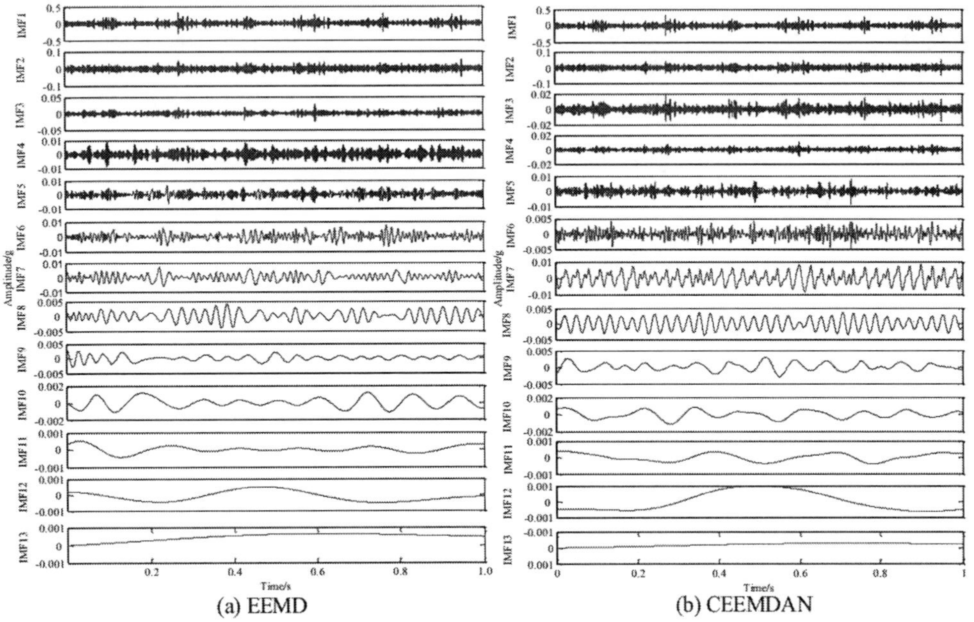

Figure 3. Decomposition result using EEMD and CEEMDAN for broken gear

Fuzzy entropy combining a fuzzy function and sample entropy is used to quantize the feature information contained in IMFs, and the fuzzy function is used to describe the similarity of each vector. The exponential function $D_{ij}^{m} = e^{-(d_{ij}^{m}/r)^{n}}$ is selected, in which there are some parameters that need to be determined: the similar tolerance r, boundary gradient n and length of the compared vectors m. r is usually set by the standard deviation of the signal, and in this paper, r=0.15sd. n is usually recommended to take a smaller integer value, so in this paper, n is set as 2. m is determined as 7000 after some experiments. To prove that fuzzy entropy has a better performance than sample entropy, the sample entropy and fuzzy entropy of each IMF are shown in Figure 4, respectively.

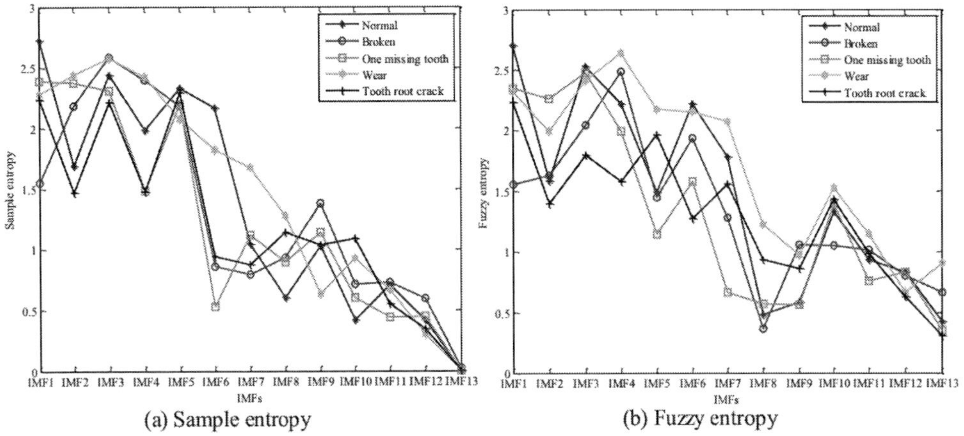

Figure 4. Sample entropy and fuzzy entropy of each IMF

It can be seen from Figure 4(a) that the complexity and stability of each IMF are described by the sample entropy. The sample entropies of the five types of gears are scattered in some IMFs, for example, IMF2 and IMF10, but in most of the IMFs, the sample entropies of some gears overlap together, for example, IMF3 and IMF4, etc. Especially in IMF5, the sample entropies of the five types of gears even coincide at a point, and those situations will interfere with the identification of five types of gears. In the calculation process of the sample entropy, the similarity description of the compared vectors is dichotomous, that causes the similarity of the compared vectors can not be described accurately, and the tiny differences among the signals can not be reflected effectively. The Fuzzy entropy is proposed, and the fuzzy function is used to calculate the similarity of the compared vectors in the calculation process. It can be seen from Figure 4(b) that the fuzzy entropies of the five types of gears are scattered in most of the IMFs. Only in IMF11 and IMF12, the overlap phenomenon is appear, but the overlap phenomenon is relatively minor. It can be found that the fuzzy entropy more easily distinguishes between the five types of gears, and it is thus superior to the sample entropy in the aspect of feature extraction.

Recognizing the planetary gear status is the most important step after extracting the feature information. Next, the fault diagnosis of the planetary gear is accurately achieved by applying a MLP neural network. The training sample set is prepared, and each planetary gear status has 30 samples, for a total of 150 samples. The fuzzy entropies of each IMF decomposed by CEEMDAN are defined as the input of MLP neural network, so that the input layer of MLP neural network has 13 input neurons. Because the training samples are divided into five types, so the output layer of MLP neural network has 5 output neurons. To train MLP neural network, different planetary gear statuses are denoted with different labels in the output layer: the normal gear is denoted as [1 0 0 0 0], the broken gear is denoted as [0 1 0 0 0], the gear with one missing tooth is denoted as [0 0 1 0 0], the wear gear is denoted as [0 0 0 1 0] and the gear with tooth root crack is denoted as [0 0 0 0 1]. The neuron number of the hidden layer is usually determined by trial-and-error. The learning rate of MLP neural network is set as 0.5, and the training step is set as 80. The mean squared error is used to evaluate the training performance of MLP neural network when the training process is completed. The changes in the mean squared error of the training process with different numbers of hidden neurons are shown in Figure 5(a). A testing sample set that includes different planetary gear status samples is prepared, and each planetary gear status has 40 samples, for a total of 200 samples. They are decomposed by CEEMDAN, and the fuzzy entropies of each IMF are inputted into the trained MLP neural network for use in verifying the recognition performance of the trained MLP neural network. The overall recognition rate for planetary gear with different numbers of hidden neurons is shown in Figure 5(b).

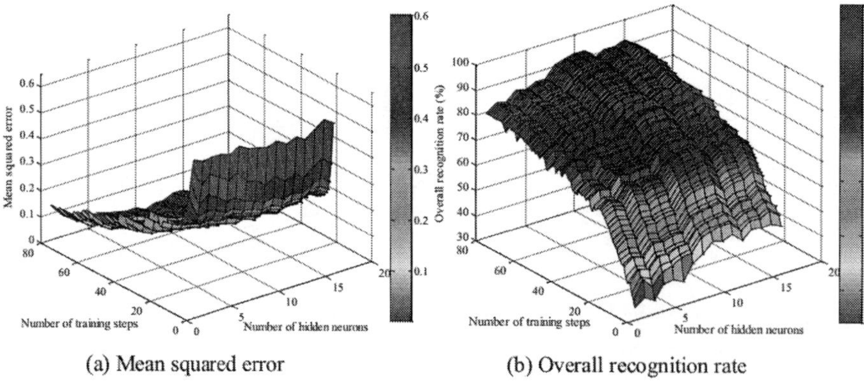

(a) Mean squared error

(b) Overall recognition rate

Figure 5. Mean squared error and overall recognition rate with different numbers of hidden neurons

It can be seen from Figure 5(a) that the mean squared error declines with the increase of the training steps, and it tends to stabilize when the training step is between 65 and 80, indicating that the training process of MLP neural network is completed. The final mean squared error has a minimum value when the MLP neural network has 11 hidden neurons, and it is 0.0035. It can be seen from Figure 5(b) that the overall recognition rate with different numbers of hidden neurons increases with the number of training steps, but the final overall recognition rate has a difference for different numbers of hidden neurons. The overall recognition rate for the planetary gear has a maximum value when the MLP neural network has 11 hidden neurons, and it reaches 91%. Hence, the MLP neural network with 11 hidden neurons has the best performance for the fault diagnosis of the planetary gear, and the detailed recognition rates of the MLP neural network with 11 hidden neurons for the different planetary gears are shown in Table 1.

Table 1. Detailed recognition rates of the MLP neural network with 11 hidden neurons

	Normal gear	Broken gear	Gear with one missing tooth	Wear gear	Gear with tooth root crack
Recognition rate	92.5%	95%	90%	87.5%	90%
Overall recognition rate			91%		

It can be seen from Table 1 that the overall recognition rate of the MLP neural network with 11 hidden neurons reaches 91%. Of different planetary gear statuses, the broken gear has the highest recognition rate, and it reaches 95%. While the wear gear has the lowest recognition rate, and it reaches 87.5%. The recognition rates of the normal gear, gear with one missing tooth and gear with tooth root crack are 92.5%, 90% and 90%, respectively. The experiments prove the planetary gear faults can be recognized by the proposed method based on the fuzzy entropy of CEEMDAN and MLP neural network, making it an effective fault diagnosis method for planetary gears.

Conclusions

A method of planetary gear fault diagnosis based on the fuzzy entropy of CEEMDAN and MLP neural network is proposed. CEEMDAN is used to decompose the vibration signal into multiple IMFs, the quality of the obtained IMFs and the completeness of the decomposition process are greatly improved. Fuzzy entropy combining a fuzzy function and sample entropy is used to quantize the feature information contained in the IMFs, and it can be found from data analysis that the fuzzy sample has a better performance than that of sample entropy, making it more suitable for extracting the feature information. The fuzzy entropies of each IMF are defined as the input of MLP neural network, and the mean squared error is selected as a criterion to train MLP neural network. The testing sample set is used to verify the recognition performance of the trained MLP neural network, and the overall recognition rate with different numbers of hidden neurons is calculated. The overall recognition rate for planetary gear has a maximum value when the MLP neural network has 11 hidden neurons, and it reaches 91%. The recognition rate of the broken gear reaches 95%, and followed by normal gear, gear with one missing tooth, gear with tooth root crack and wear gear. These results show that the proposed fault diagnosis method based on the fuzzy entropy of CEEMDAN and MLP neural network has a better recognition performance for planetary gear, making it an effective fault diagnosis method for planetary gears.

Acknowledgment

This work was supported by a Project Funded by the Priority Academic Program Development of Jiangsu Higher Education Institutions, the Natural Science Foundation of Jiangsu Province (grant number BK20141128) and Fundamental Research Funds for the Central Universities (grant number 2014ZDPY31); this support is gratefully acknowledged.

References

1. Y.G. Lei, D.T. Kong, J. Lin, M.J. Zuo, Fault detection of planetary gearboxes using new diagnostic parameters, Meas. Sci. Technol., **23** (2012) 055605-055615.
2. K.E. Ko, D.H. Lim, P.Y. Kim, J. Park, A study on the bending stress of the hollow sun gear in a planetary gear train, J. Mech. Sci. Technol., **24** (2010) 29-32.
3. N.E. Huang, Z. Shen, S.R. Long, The empirical mode decomposition and the Hilbert spectrum for nonlinear and non-stationary time series analysis, Proc. R. Soc. London., **454** (1998) 903-995.
4. X.M. Xue, J.Z. Zhou, Y.H. Xu, W.L. Zhu, C.S. Li, An adaptively fast ensemble empirical mode decomposition method and its applications to rolling element bearing fault diagnosis, Mech. Syst. Signal Proc., **62-63** (2015) 444-459.
5. J.R. Yeh, J.S. Shieh, N.E. Huang, Complementary ensemble empirical mode decomposition: a novel noise enhanced data analysis method, Adv. Adapt. Data Anal., **2(2)** (2010) 135-156.
6. L. Zhang, G. Xiong, H. Liu, Bearing fault diagnosis using multi-scale entropy and adaptive neuro-fuzzy inference, Expert Syst. Appl., **37** (2010) 6077-6085.
7. W. Guo, L.J. Huang, C. Chen, H.W. Zou, Z.W. Liu, Elimination of end effects in local mean decomposition using spectral coherence and applications for rotating machinery, Digit. Signal Prog., **55** (2016) 52-63.
8. M. Akhoondzadeh, A MLP neural network as an investigator of TEC time series to detect seismo-ionospheric anomalies, Adv. Space. Res., **51** (2013) 2048-2057.
9. X.H. Chen, G. Cheng, X.L. Shan, X. Hu, Q. Guo, H.G. Liu, Research of weak fault feature information extraction of planetary gear based on ensemble empirical mode decomposition and adaptive stochastic resonance, Measurement, **73** (2015) 55-67.
10. M.A. Colominasa, G. Schlotthauera, M.E. Torresa, Improved complete ensemble EMD: A suitable tool for biomedical signal processing. Biomed. Signal Process. Control, **14** (2014) 19-29.
11. D.R. Kong, H.B. Xie, Use of modified sample entropy measurement to classify ventricular tachycardia and fibrillation, Measurement, **44(4)** (2011) 653-662.
12. J.D. Zheng, J.S. Cheng, Y. Yang, S.R. Luo, A rolling bearing fault diagnosis method based on multi-scale fuzzy entropy and variable predictive model-based class discrimination, Mech. Mach. Theory, **78(16)** (2014) 187-200.
13. S. Souahlia, K. Bacha, A. Chaari, MLP neural network-based decision for power transformers fault diagnosis using an improved combination of rogers and doernenburg ratios DGA, Electr. Power Energy Syst., **43** (2012) 1346-1353.
14. V.N. Ghate, S.V. Dudul, Optimal MLP neural network classifier for fault detection of three phase induction motor, Expert Syst. Appl., **37** (2010) 3468-3481.

The Design and Simulation of High Impedance Surface in Airborne Telemetry Antenna

Yan-Lian ZHANG[1], Hai-Bo GONG[1,a] and Qian XU[1]

[1]Flight test establishment of China, Yanliang District, Xi'an, Shaanxi Province, China,

Abstract. Aiming to the problems that excessive reduction of airborne telemetry antenna's size will cause a sharp deterioration of the antenna's bandwidth and gain, this paper proposed that using a high-impedance surface in the airborne telemetry antenna. As the size and bandwidth of the high-impedance surface is far from being able to meet the application requirements, this paper designed a new high-impedance surface which can be applied to the telemetry transmitter antenna, and reduced the profile size of the telemetry antenna and increased the gain of the antenna at the same time. In addition, based on the equivalent circuit model, we have resolved the contradictory situation of small size and wide band gap in the high-impedance surface design. The results show that the low profile, high gain and wide bandwidth of the telemetry antenna can be achieved by using the new high-impedance surface. The antenna structure and design ideas presented in this paper can significantly improve the performance of airborne telemetry antenna.

1 Introduction

Real-time data processing and monitoring are often used in flight test. With the increasing number of high-risk item in flight test, real-time remote monitoring is becoming more and more important [1]. The telemetry transmit antenna used in the flight test is a microstrip antenna that adheres a thin metal conductor to a dielectric substrate. With the continuous improvement of aircraft performance requirements, airborne telemetry antenna in high-altitude and high-speed environment has a good aerodynamic shape and excellent performance has become a hot research area [2]. Conventional airborne telemetry antenna size will lead to over-reduction of other antenna performance of the rapid deterioration, in which the bandwidth and gain is particularly evident, so compromise between the various parameters and. Aiming at the problem, the parameters and performance of the telemetry antenna can not be taken into account, we have introduced the high resistance surface structure in the airborne telemetry antenna. The high impedance surface can exhibit high surface impedance in a certain frequency band, can cut off the surface wave propagation, at the same time for the incident plane electromagnetic wave has the same phase reflection characteristics, can replace the metal reflective surface as the antenna ground plate, thereby reducing the antenna profile [3].

The current low-impedance surface can be achieved, but the size and bandwidth is far from meeting the requirements of the application. This paper analyzes the miniaturization and wide bandgap design of the high resistance surface. The new high impedance surface structure can be

[a] Corresponding author: 13324521609@163.com

DOI: 10.1051/itmconf/20171108003

successfully applied to the aerial telemetry antenna, which can realize the low profile, high gain and wide frequency band design of the telemetry antenna. Simulation results using ANSOFT HFSS show that the new structure can make the telemetry antenna have a smaller profile size and better integration of antenna and fuselage without loss of bandwidth, and high antenna gain.

2 Airborne telemetry antenna and theoretical model of high resistance surface

In the airborne telemetry system, the telemetry transmitting antenna is a device for radiating electromagnetic wave. It is used to transmit the comprehensive information obtained from the airborne test to the remote telemetry receiving station, to realize the ground real-time data processing and real-time monitoring of the aircraft flight test result. The telemetry transmitting antenna used in aircraft flight test is microstrip antenna which sticks the thin metal conductor on the dielectric substrate. The microstrip patch antenna shown in Fig.1 is the most common aerial telemetry antenna, layer or multi-layer dielectric layer and covering the upper and lower sides of the radiation element and the metal grounding plate.

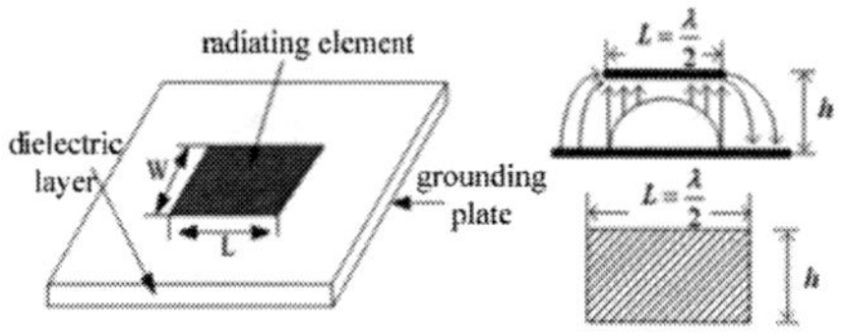

Figure 1. Airborne telemetry antenna and radiation field

A high-impedance electromagnetic surface is a electromagnetic band gap (EBG) structure consisting of a metal and a dielectric material. It is a resonant electromagnetic bandgap structure. The high-impedance electromagnetic surface is a textured surface consisting of a set of metal patches periodically arranged in a two-dimensional grid pattern on the dielectric substrate, and connected to the metal ground plane of the dielectric substrate through a vertical conductive via each metal patch [4]. It is not only the same as other types of electromagnetic bandgap structure with the role of suppression of surface waves, but also in a certain frequency range to achieve the same phase reflection, instead of metal reflective surface as the antenna ground plate, thereby reducing the antenna profile. Figure 2 is the surface structure of the most common high-resistance, square patch in the center with the ground through the hole, the square array arranged.

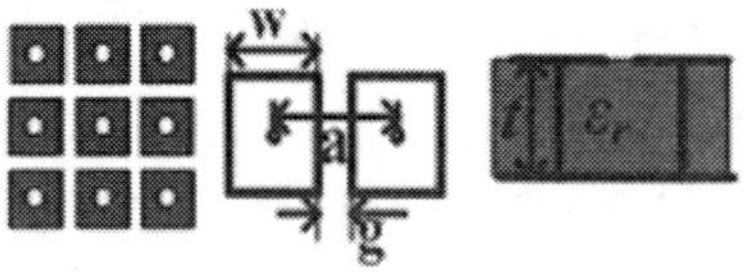

Figure 2. Top view, unit structure and side view

The cell size of the high resistance surface is much smaller than the operating wavelength, so its electromagnetic characteristics can be described by the lumped circuit components. Their characteristics are the same as the parallel LC resonant circuit, the capacitance between the adjacent metal units, the inductance of the conductive path. The equivalent circuit is shown in Figure

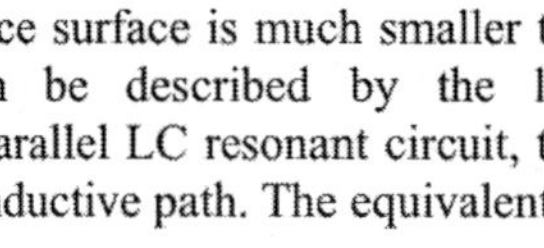

Figure 3. Equivalent circuit of High impedance surface

According to the equivalent surface impedance model, the resonant frequency of the high-resistance surface cell (the stopband center frequency of the high-resistance surface) and the bandwidth are:

$$\varpi_0 = 1/\sqrt{LC}, \Delta\varpi/\varpi_0 = \sqrt{L/C}/\sqrt{\mu_0/\varepsilon_0} \tag{1}$$

$$L = \mu_r \mu_0 t, \quad C = \frac{w(\varepsilon_0 + \varepsilon_1)}{\pi} \cosh^{-1}(\frac{a}{g}) \tag{2}$$

Where μ_0 is the permeability in vacuum, μ_r is the dielectric material relative permeability, t is the thickness of the dielectric substrate, ε_0 is the dielectric constant in vacuum, ε_1 is the substrate dielectric constant, w is the unit side length, a is the adjacent distance between the holes g is the gap width between the cells.

3 Compact design of high resistance surface

In order to improve the performance of the antenna and reduce the backward radiation, microstrip antenna generally placed under the antenna metal reflective surface. At this point, the metal reflective surface and the antenna need to maintain a quarter-wavelength height, profile size is relatively large. For the incident plane electromagnetic waves, high resistance surface in a certain frequency range has the same phase reflection characteristics, and no metal surface of the 180 ° phase difference, without a quarter-wavelength profile thickness, so the antenna and high resistance surface has great advantage and potential in realizing the low profile antenna with its great value of electromagnetic property, and it has a very high research value.

In practical application process, the high resistance surface structure must have sufficient number of units, or the electromagnetic properties are not obvious [5]. If the traditional electromagnetic surface structure shown in Fig 2 are used in the airborne telemetry antenna design, the size of 90mm ×75mm area, the number of units can accommodate no more than four, then the high-resistance surface of the electromagnetic properties simply can not be realized. Therefore, in order to integrate the high resistance surface structure into the design of airborne telemetry antenna, the high resistance surface needs to realize the miniaturization design.

By the high resistance surface equivalent circuit model, reducing the bandgap frequency can be realized by increasing the equivalent inductance L and capacitance C. The equivalent inductance is determined by the material of the high resistance surface, and the inductance is determined when the preparation material is determined. The factors that affect the capacitance are a lot, you can change the surface of the high-impedance surface of the structure of the cycle to change the amount of capacitance [6]. Thus we designed the L seam, F seam embedded structure, as shown in Figure 4 and Figure 5.

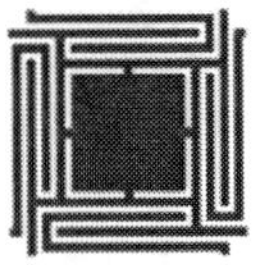

Figure 4. LSeam structure

Figure 5. F Seam structure

At present, the realization of compact high impedance surface design is mainly based on the equivalent capacitance to improve the structure to achieve, for example, three-tier structure, interactive embedding, three-tier structure of the implementation process is complex, technical requirements and costs are high, the practical application by restrictions. Compared with the traditional high-resistance surface structure shown in Figure 2, the inter-embedded structure can form a stronger coupling capacitor [7], reducing nearly 60% of the unit size. However, over a limited number of iterations, a limited patch area can not be fully utilized and the cell size can not be further reduced. It is found that the metal slit can make the path of the surface current flow longer and make the equivalent electric dimension of the patch larger, which can enhance the coupling capacitance between the cells. Therefore, the design of the slit structure and the embedded structure are the same, the combination of the two slotted embedded structure can be more effective use of patch area, thereby more effectively reduce the size of the unit. We designed the F-slot embedded structure which can reduce the cell size of more than 70%, to achieve high-resistance surface structure of the small size of the design effect is significant.

As shown in Figure. 6, the digital phase-change curve of the reflection phase corresponds to the L-shaped gap from the center of the patch to the close-to-close patch. The simulation of the slit-embedded structure shows that the width of the slit is constant. Slice edge of the process of change. Therefore, in order to effectively reduce the cell size, the L-shaped slot can be opened at the outermost side of the patch. F-type gap from the L-type gap and straight-line gap composition. To maintain the L-shaped gap in the outside of the patch, we adjust the F-shaped slot straight seam position, the reflection phase of the impact shown in Figure 7. The closer to the center of the patch, the greater the effect on the resonant frequency. F-type gap can adjust the edge of the patch and the inside surface current, to minimize the size of the unit. In addition to the location of the gap, the gap length of the resonant frequency of the greatest impact, the wider the gap, the longer the lower the resonant frequency.

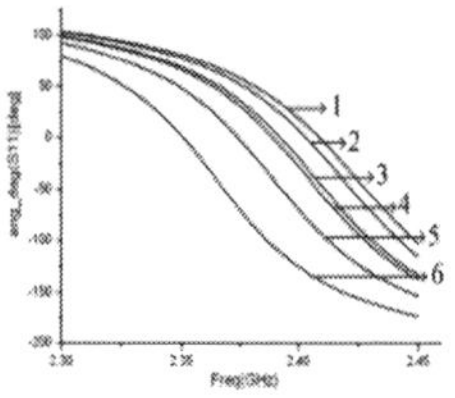

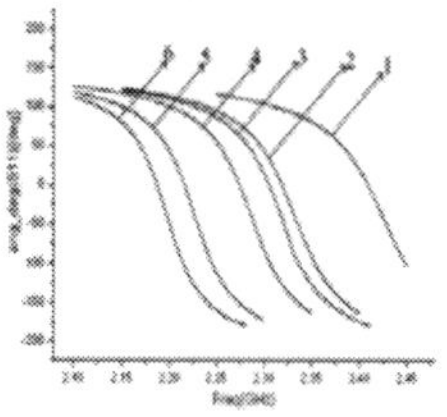

Figure 6. Change of L Slit phase Figure7 change of F Slit phase

F slit with embedded structure design, patch unit line width and pitch are 0.4mm, the unit side length of 13mm, 90mm * 75mm size of the area, the number of units can accommodate 42, the F-type crevice embedded structure of high impedance surface used in airborne telemetry antenna below the antenna simulation results shown in Figure 8, Figure 9:

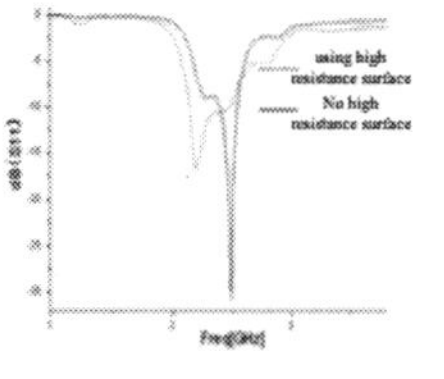

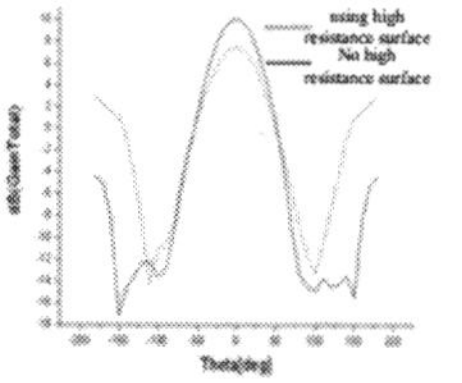

Figure 8. S11 curve **Figure 9.** Antenna gain

The experimental results show that the gain of the aerial telemetry antenna is increased by 2.5dBi and the posterior lobe of the antenna is reduced by 7.4dB after adding the high impedance surface of the F-type slot embedded structure. The high impedance surface is placed close to the antenna, The material is Rogers RO3210 (tm) with a thickness of 2 mm, so the thickness of the antenna profile is 2 mm and the profile size is rather small compared to the quarter-wavelength profile of the metal reflector. The experimental results show that the bandwidth of the telemetry antenna is reduced in the process of reducing the thickness of the profile, and increasing the gain of the telemetry antenna by adding a new type of high resistance surface structure. Because the high-resistance surface structure is a resonant electromagnetic band-gap structure, and the in-phase reflection band is narrow. In addition, the reduction of the cell size leads to a further reduction of the band gap of the high resistance surface, since the coupling capacitance is increased by the change of the cell shape to realize the small size

DOI: 10.1051/itmconf/20171108003

design but the inductance does not change. From the equation (1), as the coupling capacitance increases but the inductance does not change, the bandwidth of the high-resistance surface structure is reduced. Therefore, the size of the high-resistance surface structure is reduced and the bandwidth is also reduced during the miniaturization design.

4 Bandgap design of high resistance surface

In order to solve the problem of reducing the bandwidth while miniaturizing the design process by changing the shape of the cell, we first study the change of the reflected phase center frequency and the bandgap width from the different structural models of the high resistance surface. The mushroom-shaped patch structure, the butterfly-shaped patch-free structure, and the mushroom-shaped patch structure with short via were removed. We used different substrate materials to understand the change trend of the parameters of the high resistance surface, the purpose is to understand the relationship between the band gap width of the high resistance surface and the patch cycle.

As shown in Figure. 10, the horizontal axis represents the value of $a\varepsilon_r^{1/2}$, and the vertical axis represents the value of the bandgap width.

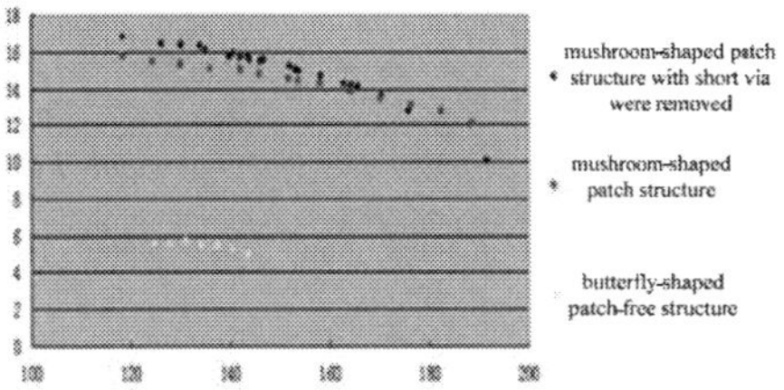

Figure 10. Bandwidth and patch cycle

It is found that the bandwidth of the same patch-like structure is the same curve with different substrate materials, but the patch shape of the butterfly shape is shorter than that of the mushroom-type structure, but the band width is smaller in the experiment, we found that the short-circuit via of the mushroom-type structure were removed, which still had the characteristic of high resistance surface structure, and the change of the center frequency and bandwidth of the reflection phase was not significant. The change of cell shape will not increase the band gap width.

The equivalent impedance and surface reflection coefficient of the high resistance surface structure are:

$$z = \frac{j\omega L}{1 - \omega^2 LC} = jX_0 \tag{3}$$

$$\Gamma = \frac{Z - \eta}{Z + \eta} = \exp(j\varphi_0) \tag{4}$$

from (3) and (4):

$$\frac{d\varphi_0}{d\omega} = \frac{-2\eta L\left(1 + \omega^2 LC\right)}{(\omega L)^2 + \eta^2\left(1 - \omega^2 LC\right)^2} \tag{5}$$

When $\omega = 1/\sqrt{LC}$, the surface impedance of the high resistance surface is infinite. When the resonant frequency is fixed, increasing the thickness will increases the value of L, which means decreasing C, which is beneficial to bandwidth broadening.

DOI: 10.1051/itmconf/20171108003

The bandwidth of the high resistance surface refers to the frequency range corresponding to the phase of $\varphi_0 = \pm 90^o$, so the formula (6) can be derived:

$$\Delta\omega = \frac{1}{\eta C} = \frac{\omega_0^2 L}{\eta} \tag{6}$$

From (1), (2), (3), we can get

$$\frac{BW}{f_0} = \frac{\Delta\omega}{\omega_0} = \frac{1}{2(\varepsilon_1 + \varepsilon_2)} \frac{\lambda_0}{w} \frac{1}{\operatorname{acosh}(a/g)} \tag{7}$$

$$\frac{BW}{f_0} = \frac{\Delta\omega}{\omega_0} = 2\pi\mu_r \frac{t}{\lambda_0} \tag{8}$$

In addition to the parameters of the chip structure, the dielectric constant of the substrate, the permeability of the substrate and the thickness of the substrate can be improved by using the substrate surface resistivity of the high resistance surface, from the formulas (7) and (8). Therefore, in order to improve the bandgap width, we can use a low dielectric constant substrate, high permeability substrate and to improve the substrate thickness to achieve. If the other parameters unchanged, the use of low dielectric constant substrate and improve the bandwidth at the same time, it will increase the resonant frequency of high resistance surface, which is not conducive to reducing cell size; high permeability substrate or substrate thickness can significantly increase the bandgap width, but also help to reduce the cell size. The high resistance surface structure of Figure. 2 is adopted to carry on the simulation, the simulation result is shown as in Figure.11, Figure.

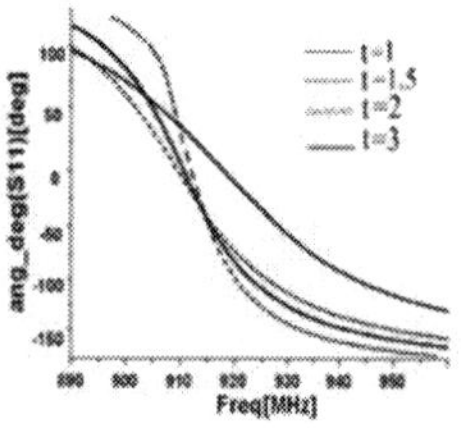

Figure 11. Thickness

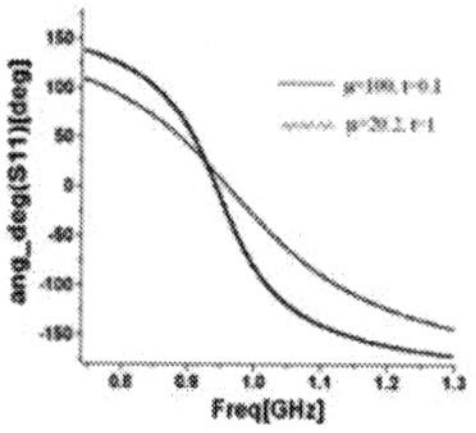

Figure 12. Magnetic

In order to observe the effect of increasing substrate thickness on improving the bandgap width, the patch period is kept constant and the inter-chip gap width is adjusted to maintain the resonant frequency. As shown in formula (7) and (8), the band gap width increases as the thickness of the substrate increases, and the increase is proportional to the result of Fig. Substrate thickness affects the magnitude of the equivalent inductance. As the thickness increases, the inductance increases and the resonant frequency decreases. It is feasible to increase the thickness of the substrate to increase the width of the bandgap compared with the height of the quarter-free-space wavelength of the metal reflector. It can be seen from Fig. 12 that the bandwidth of the substrate after using the high permeability material is obviously improved. Compared with the common substrate material of the same thickness, the band gap of the high permeability material substrate is remarkably improved, as shown in the formula (8) Large magnets and magnetic permeability is proportional to the size. Therefore, the permeability of the substrate increases, the substrate thickness can be very small, the patch size will be dramatically reduced, while also having a wide band gap width. Therefore, the use of high permeability material is to achieve high resistance to the surface structure of the ideal choice.

Conclusion

Based on the theoretical model of high resistance surface, a new type of slotted embedded structure is designed by analyzing the equivalent circuit model. Experimental results show that the new structure can greatly reduce the aerial telemetry antenna profile size while improving the antenna gain. In this paper, the equivalent circuit model of the high resistance surface structure is analyzed, and the parameters affecting the bandgap are pointed out. The method to increase the band gap is also found, and the contradiction between reducing the size and increasing the bandwidth is also solved. The structure and design ideas presented in this paper have practical significance for the design of modern airborne telemetry antenna.

References

1. P.F. Huo, H.H Li. *Telemetry transmission quality and adjustment of RF system*. measurement and control technology, 2008,27 (1): 4-6
2. Huang Wei, Xu Hengjie, Zhang Li. *Electromagnetic simulation analysis of airborne multi antenna system*. computer simulation, 2010,27 (5): 235-238
3. Yablonovitch E. *Inhibited spontaneous emission in solid-state physics and electronics*. Physical Review Letters. 1987, 58(20): 2059-2062
4. Wu Hao, Wang Lingmin, Tian L, et al. *Design of microstrip antenna based on high impedance surface microwave photonic crystal* . Journal of Jilin University (SCIENCE EDITION), 2014,52 (3): 583-586
5. Fu Yunqi, Yuan Naichang, Wen XISEN. *Microwave photonic crystal antenna technology*. Defense Industry Press.2006,24 (6)
6. M F Abedin, M Ali. *Effects of a smaller unit cell planar EBG structure on the mutual coupling of a printed dipole array* . IEEE Antennas and Wireless Propagation Let-ters, 2005, 4: 274-276.
7. Yan Dunbao. *Doctoral dissertation of artificial magnetic conductor structure and application of.* of national defense science and Technology University, 2006

Method for Estimating the Parameters of LFM Radar Signal

Chuan-Zhang TAN[1,a], Hong-Wei LI[1] and Chang-Zhou FAN[1]

[1]*School of Information and Navigation, Air Force Engineering University, Xi'an 710077, China.*

Abstract. In order to obtain reliable estimate of parameters, it is very important to protect the integrality of linear frequency modulation (LFM) signal. Therefore, in the practical LFM radar signal processing, the length of data frame is often greater than the pulse width (PW) of signal. In this condition, estimating the parameters by fractional Fourier transform (FrFT) will cause the signal to noise ratio (SNR) decrease. Aiming at this problem, we multiply the data frame by a Gaussian window to improve the SNR. Besides, for a further improvement of parameters estimation precision, a novel algorithm is derived via Lagrange interpolation polynomial, and we enhance the algorithm by a logarithmic transformation. Simulation results demonstrate that the derived algorithm significantly reduces the estimation errors of chirp-rate and initial frequency.

1 Introduction

As a non-stationary signal, LFM signal is widely applied to the fields of radar, sonar and communication. Scholars have done a lot of research on the parameters estimation of LFM signal. Among the numerous algorithms have presented, the FrFT is very suitable for LFM signal detection and parameters estimation because it can be interpreted as a decomposition of orthogonal LFM functions. FrFR was first proposed by Namias in 1980 [1]. It was not widely used until 1996 that Ozaktas presented the digital fractional Fourier transform (DFrFT) [2], which could be fast implemented by fast Fourier transform (FFT). However, the resolution of DFrFT is fixed, in order to solve this problem, a high resolution FrFT algorithm which named Zoom-FrFT and single point FrFT algorithm named SP-FrFT are proposed in [3], as an application, a new algorithm combing Zoom-FrFT with short-time Fourier transform (STFT) is presented to estimate the parameters of LFM signal [4]. Another method is using curve fitting over the spectral line via moving least square (MLS) [5], but it will produce an additional computation. The direct interpolation algorithm [6] can obtain high accuracy of parameters estimation while doesn't increase the computational complexity, and the iterative interpolation algorithm [7] further reduced the estimation error, but they are effective only to the no windowing signal. However, in fact, the windowed LFM signal also has to be considered [8, 9]. The Gaussian-weighted fractional Fourier transform (GFrFT) [10] is presented for the parameters estimation of low duty ratio signal, and it reduces estimation errors combining with fourth-order algorithm (F-GFrFT) [11], but the research found its performance can be further improved.

On the basis of analyzing the problem occurs in practical radar signal processing, a new method for estimating the parameters of LFM signal is proposed in this paper. Firstly, the basic principle of

[a] Corresponding author: kdytcz@163.com

parameters estimation based on FrFT is given. And then, aiming at the reality that the length of data frame is greater than the PW of signal, we establishe a new model for parameters estimation of low duty ratio signal, and windowed the data frame with a Gaussian window to improve the SNR. In order to realize the windowed LFM signal parameters estimation, a novel algorithm is derived from Lagrange interpolation polynomial, and its performance improved via logarithmic scale transform. We also compare the performance of the proposed algorithm with F-GFrFT and Cramer- Rao lower bound (CRLB) [12], simulation results demonstrate the validity and superiority of the proposed estimator.

2 Parameters estimation of LFM signal based on FrFT

Let $x(t)$ denote a continuous LFM signal, the pth-order fractional Fourier transform $X_\alpha(u)$ of $x(t)$ could be defined as

$$X_\alpha(u) = F^p[x(t)] = \int_{-\infty}^{\infty} x(t)K_\alpha(u,t)\,\mathrm{d}t \tag{1}$$

where $\alpha = p\pi/2$,p is an arbitrary real number, $F^p[\cdot]$ denotes the operator notation of FrFT. $K_\alpha(u,t)$ is the kernel function of FrFT, and its definition is given by

$$K_\alpha(u,t) = \begin{cases} A_\alpha \exp\{j\pi[\cot(u^2+t^2) - 2ut\csc\alpha]\}, & \alpha \neq K\pi \\ \delta(t-u), & \alpha = 2K\pi \\ \delta(t-u), & \alpha = (2K+1)\pi \end{cases} \tag{2}$$

where $A_\alpha = \sqrt{1 - j\cot\alpha}$, K is an integer.

It demands the implementation of discrete FrFT on a digital signal processor (DSP) in practical application, so we should get the digital computation of the FrFT. It is desirable that Ozaktas proposed a decomposition algorithm which is called DFrFT, it is widely used because of its low computation complexity. The model of a discrete LFM signal with an additive white Gaussian noise (with zero-mean and variance σ^2) is given by

$$x(n) = s(n) + w(n) = b\exp(j\theta + \frac{j2\pi fn}{f_s} + \frac{j\pi fn^2}{f_s^2}) + w(n), n\in[-\frac{N-1}{2}, \frac{N-1}{2}] \tag{3}$$

where N is the length of LFM signal, n is an integer, b is the amplitude, θ is the initial phase, f is the initial frequency, f_s is the sampling frequency and k denotes the chirp-rate. When the α rotates counterclockwise to the optimal order, the energy of LFM signal will be best gathered in the two-dimensional plane, and $|X_{\alpha_0}(u_0)|^2$ reaches its peak value at (α_0, u_0). Therefore, the chirp-rate and initial frequency can be estimated by

$$\begin{cases} \hat{k} = -\cot\alpha_0 \dfrac{f_s^2}{N} \\ \hat{f} = u_0 \csc\alpha_0 \dfrac{f_s}{N} \end{cases} \tag{4}$$

The estimation error comes from two aspects: (1) restriction of search step size in α domain, the estimation accuracy can be improved by reducing the size of search step while the computation cost is increased by series; (2) the fence effect caused by discretization in u domain. To improve the estimation accuracy and ensure the computation cost not significantly increased, the interpolation method is a splendid way.

3 Model for parameters estimation of low duty ratio signal

The chirp-rate and initial frequency of LFM signal are the most important measurements for radar signal sorting and identification. In practical signal processing, the length of data frame is much larger than the PW of LFM signal. We can get a coarse estimation of PW by envelope detection etc. to reduce the length of processing data, but it is still longer than the LFM signal. To avoid the SNR decrease by estimating the parameters directly, we can multiply the processing data with a Gaussian window function. Therefore, it becomes a problem of parameters estimation under low duty ratio. The diagram of processing model is as shown in Figure 1.

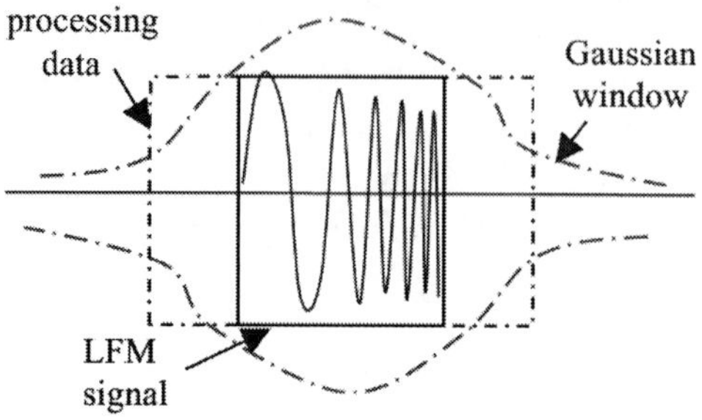

Figure 1. The diagram of signal processing model

According to Eq. (3), the expression of the signal processing model can be written as

$$x(n) = [s(n) + w(n)]g(n),\ n \in [-\frac{L-1}{2}, \frac{L-1}{2}] \tag{5}$$

where

$$\begin{cases} s(n) = b\exp(j\theta + \frac{j2\pi fn}{f_s} + \frac{j\pi kn^2}{f_s^2})\,\mathrm{rect}(\frac{n}{L}) \\ g(n) = \exp(-\frac{2c^2}{L^2}n) \end{cases} \tag{6}$$

where g(n) is a Gaussian function, c is an integer which takes control of the shape of the Gaussian window, L denotes the length of processing data. The $\mathrm{rect}(\frac{n}{L})$ is given by

$$\mathrm{rect}(\frac{n}{L}) = \begin{cases} 1, n \in [-\frac{N-1}{2}, \frac{N-1}{2}] \\ 0, n \in [-\frac{L-1}{2}, -\frac{N-1}{2}) \cup (\frac{N-1}{2}, \frac{L-1}{2}] \end{cases} \tag{7}$$

So the duty ratio is defined as

$$d = \frac{N}{L} \tag{8}$$

The output SNR of FrFT [13] is defined as

$$\mathrm{SNR}_{\mathrm{out}} = \frac{N^2\,\mathrm{SNR}_{\mathrm{in}}^2}{\frac{2N\,\mathrm{SNR}_{\mathrm{in}}}{d} + (\frac{1}{d})^2} \tag{9}$$

where $\mathrm{SNR}_{\mathrm{in}} = \frac{b^2}{\sigma^2}$, and the output SNR of the new signal processing model can be defined as [10]

$$\mathrm{GSNR}_{\mathrm{out}} = \frac{N^2\,\mathrm{SNR}_{\mathrm{in}}^2}{2N\,\mathrm{SNR}_{\mathrm{in}}(\frac{\eta_2 \rho d}{\eta_1^2}) + (\frac{\eta_2 \rho d}{\eta_1^2})^2} \tag{10}$$

where

$$\begin{cases} \eta_1 = \mathrm{erf}(\frac{c}{\sqrt{2}} d) \\ \eta_2 = \mathrm{erf}(c) \\ \rho = \frac{c}{\sqrt{\pi}} \end{cases} \tag{11}$$

$\mathrm{erf}(\cdot)$ is error function.

The same model is used in [10] and GFrFT algorithm is presented to estimate the parameters of LFM signal, but GFrFT only improves the SNR, although it improves the estimation accuracy combining with fourth-order algorithm, there still is a large gap compared with CRLB. In this context, we need to seek an algorithm with higher estimation accuracy.

4 Quadratic interpolation algorithm based on FrFT

The conventional interpolation algorithms are derived from properties of the rectangular window (no window), it is not suitable for the parameters estimation of windowed signal. The essence of the quadratic interpolation derived from Lagrange interpolation polynomial is parabolic fitting, so it can be applied to arbitrary windowed signal.

The Lagrange polynomial is given by

$$\begin{cases} \chi = l_{i-1}\chi_{i-1} + l_i\chi_i + l_{i+1}\chi_{i+1} \\ l_{i-1} = \frac{(\kappa-\kappa_i)(\kappa-\kappa_{i+1})}{(\kappa_{i-1}-\kappa_i)(\kappa_{i-1}-\kappa_{i+1})} \\ l_i = \frac{(\kappa-\kappa_{i-1})(\kappa-\kappa_{i+1})}{(\kappa_i-\kappa_{i-1})(\kappa_i-\kappa_{i+1})} \\ l_{i+1} = \frac{(\kappa-\kappa_{i-1})(\kappa-\kappa_i)}{(\kappa_{i+1}-\kappa_{i-1})(\kappa_{i+1}-\kappa_i)} \end{cases} \tag{12}$$

we can get a function via Eq. (12) and the graph of the function is a parabola, we can obtain the estimated value of the target parameter by calculating the vertex coordinates, the expression of the estimator is given by

$$\hat{\kappa} = \kappa_i + \frac{1}{2}\frac{\chi_{i-1} - \chi_{i+1}}{\chi_{i-1} - 2\chi_i + \chi_{i+1}} \tag{13}$$

DOI: 10.1051/itmconf/20171108004

By searching the spectrum peak in the two-dimensional plane, we can get the peak coordinates in α domain $(\kappa_{p_i},\chi_{p_i})$ and in u domain $(\kappa_{u_i},\chi_{u_i})$, and $\chi_{p_i}=\chi_{u_i}$. In α domain, the estimator can be obtained by substituting the coordinate of vertex and its adjacent points into the Eq. (13)

$$\hat{\kappa}_p=\kappa_{p_i}+\frac{1}{2}\frac{\chi_{p_{i-1}}-\chi_{p_{i+1}}}{\chi_{p_{i-1}}-2\chi_{p_i}+\chi_{p_{i+1}}} \tag{14}$$

But in u domain, the width of main lobe is less than three bins [14], we have to calculate the coordinates of other two adjacent points $(\kappa_{u_{i-0.5}},\chi_{u_{i-0.5}})$ and $(\kappa_{u_{i+0.5}},\chi_{u_{i+0.5}})$ to the vertex by SP-FrFT algorithm. The expression of estimator is given in three cases

Case1 $\chi_{u_{i-0.5}}<\chi_{u_i}<\chi_{u_{i+0.5}}$ or $\chi_{u_{i+0.5}}<\chi_{u_i}<\chi_{u_{i-0.5}}$

$$\hat{\kappa}_u=\kappa_{u_i}+\frac{1}{4}\frac{\chi_{u_{i-0.5}}-\chi_{u_{i+0.5}}}{\chi_{u_{i-0.5}}-2\chi_{u_i}+\chi_{u_{i+0.5}}} \tag{15}$$

Case 2 $\chi_{u_i}<\chi_{u_{i+0.5}}<\chi_{u_{i+1}}$

$$\hat{\kappa}_u=\kappa_{u_i}+\frac{1}{4}\frac{3\chi_{u_i}-4\chi_{u_{i+0.5}}+\chi_{u_{i+1}}}{\chi_{u_i}-2\chi_{u_{i+0.5}}+\chi_{u_{i+1}}} \tag{16}$$

Case 3 $\chi_{u_{i-1}}<\chi_{u_{i-0.5}}<\chi_{u_i}$

$$\hat{\kappa}_u=\kappa_{u_i}-\frac{1}{4}\frac{\chi_{u_{i-1}}-4\chi_{u_{i-0.5}}+3\chi_{u_i}}{\chi_{u_{i-1}}-2\chi_{u_{i-0.5}}+\chi_{u_i}} \tag{17}$$

Considering that the main lobe of Gaussian windowed signal is also Gaussian-shaped, we can use logarithmic scaling transform to the magnitude of the FrFT to improve the precision of parabola fitting. As an enhancement algorithm, its universal expression is the rewriting of Eq. (13)

$$\hat{\kappa}=\kappa_i+\frac{1}{2}\frac{f(\chi_{i-1})-f(\chi_{i+1})}{f(\chi_{i-1})-2f(\chi_i)+f(\chi_{i+1})} \tag{18}$$

where $f(\cdot)$ is the operator notation of natural logarithm, we can obtain the different expression form in u domain too, and the Eq. (18) is valid because $f(\cdot)$ is monotonic. Both the quadratic interpolation algorithm and its enhanced version are simulated.

5 Simulations and results analysis

5.1 The SNR gain with different *c*, *d* and SNR_{in}

In order to prove that the new signal processing model can improve the SNR, we defined R as

$$R=\frac{GSNR_{out}}{SNR_{out}} \tag{19}$$

DOI: 10.1051/itmconf/20171108004

Our destination is to get the optimal c with different values of d and $\mathrm{SNR_{in}}$, but R is a function of c, d and $\mathrm{SNR_{in}}$. Firstly, we can get the relationship between R and d, c while $\mathrm{SNR_{in}}$ is a constant (as shown in Figure 2), and then analysis the relationship between R and $\mathrm{SNR_{in}}$ while d and c are constants (as shown in Figure 3).

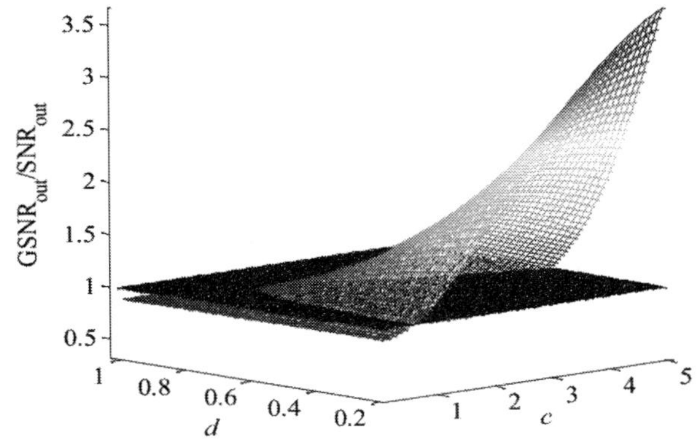

Figure 2. The relationship between R and d, c

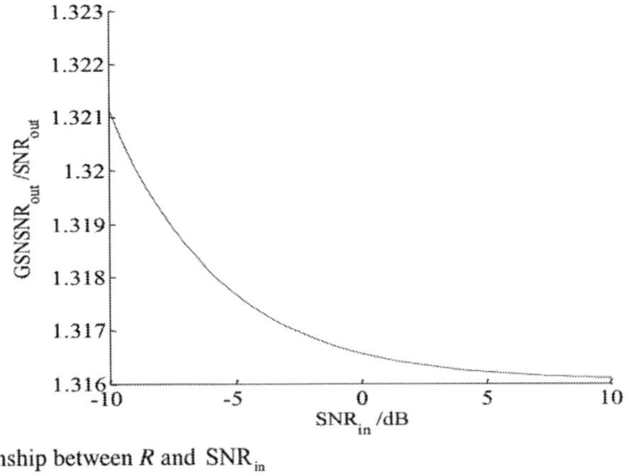

Figure 3. The relationship between R and $\mathrm{SNR_{in}}$

From the Figure 2 ($\mathrm{SNR_{in}} = 1$), we can see that the new signal processing model could improve the SNR under low duty ratio, and the lower the duty ratio is, the more the SNR improved. From the figure 3 (d=0.6, c=2.31), we can get that the lower the $\mathrm{SNR_{in}}$ is the more the SNR improved. In summary, the new signal model is especially suitable for the estimation of LFM signal under low duty ratio and low SNR environment. In order to obtain the optimal c for different d, we take $\mathrm{SNR_{in}} = 1$ as an example and get the following table

DOI: 10.1051/itmconf/20171108004

Table 1. Optimal c for different d ($SNR_{in} = 1$)

Duty ratio (d)	Optimal c	$GSNR_{out} / SNR_{out}$ (R)
0.2	5.00	3.6670
0.3	4.67	2.6321
0.4	3.50	1.9733
0.5	2.80	1.5783
0.6	2.31	1.3163
0.7	1.93	1.1331
0.8	1.56	1.0077
0.9	1.13	1.0044
1.0	0.01(0)	0.9203(1)

When the d=1, we can take c=0, and then the Gaussian window changes into a rectangular window.

5.2 The performance of estimator for different SNR_{in}

We take the latest algorithm F-GFrFT which combines the advantage of GFrFT and fourth-order algorithm as a contrast algorithm, and set N=513, L=1023, b=1, $\theta = \pi / 4$, f=24.3 MHz, f_s =100 MHz, k=4.76 MHz/us, c=2.8, and run 100 Monte Carlo simulations, and then calculate the normalized root mean square error (NRMSE) of chirp-rate and initial frequency. The CRLB is also simulated within the figure.

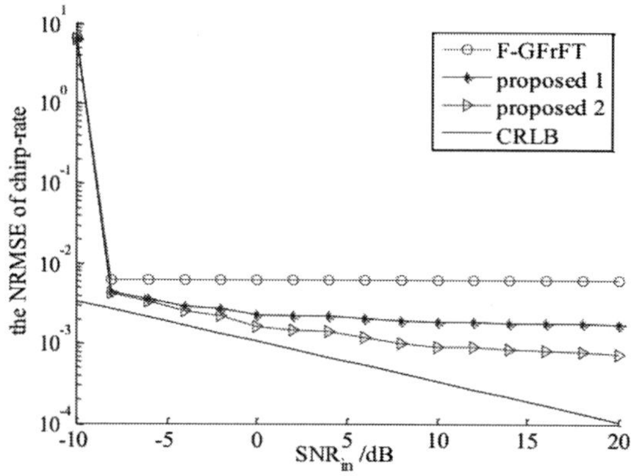

Figure 4. The NRMSE of chirp-rate as a function of SNR_{in}

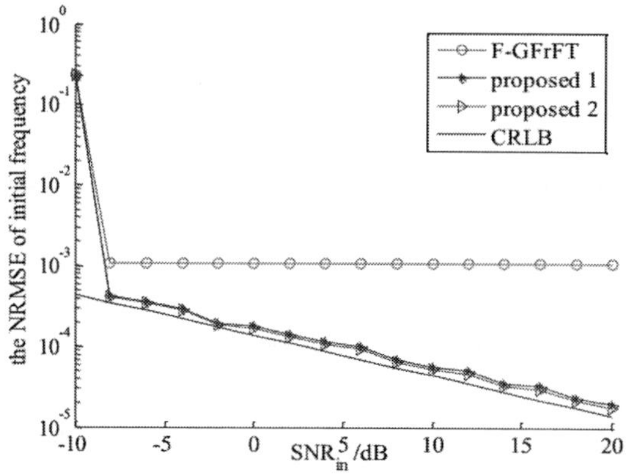

Figure 5. The NRMSE of initial frequency as a function of SNR_{in}

From Figure 4 and Figure 5 we can know that the proposed algorithms have a higher accuracy than the F-GFrFT algorithm both in estimating the chirp-rate and initial frequency, especially the in estimating the initial frequency. The enhancement algorithm has more advantages in the estimation of the chirp-rate while the initial frequency estimation performance is slightly better.

6 Conclusions and Future Work

According to the practical circumstances we have met in radar signal processing, a new model is established. Besides, the quadratic interpolation algorithm is proposed via Lagrange interpolation polynomial, and it can be applied to arbitrary windowed LFM signal. We demonstrated through simulations that the new signal processing model is very suitable for parameter estimation under low duty ratio and low SNR environment, and it can improve the SNR when the duty ratio is less than 0.9. And the quadratic interpolation algorithm we have proposed can effectively improve the accuracy of parameter estimation and outperforms the contrast algorithm in terms of NRMSE.

It should be pointed out that the new algorithm approaches the CRLB when estimating the initial frequency, but there still is an obvious gap between the CRLB when estimating the chirp-rate in high SNR. As the future work, we shall analyze the source of the error and further improve the accuracy of the algorithm.

References

1. V. Namias. The fractional order Fourier transform and its application to quantum mechanics. *IMA Journal of Applied Mathematics*. **25**.3 (1980) 241-265.
2. H.M. Ozaktas, O. Arikan, M.A. Kutay, et al. Digital computation of the fractional Fourier transform. *IEEE Transactions on signal processing*. **44**.9 (1996) 2141-2150.
3. X.H. Zhao, R. Tao, B. Deng, et al. New methods for fast computation of fractional Fourier transform. *Dianzi Xuebao(Acta Electronica Sinica)*. **35**.6 (2007) 1089-1093.
4. Y. Ding, L. Sun,H. Zhang, et al. A multi-component LFM signal parameters estimation method using STFT and Zoom-FRFT. *Communication Software and Networks (ICCSN), 2016 8th IEEE International Conference on. IEEE*. (2016) 112-117.
5. F. Zhang, L. Qi, E. Chen, et al. Parameter estimation of LFM signal in the fractional fourier domain via curve-fitting optimization technique. *Pervasive Computing Signal Processing and Applications (PCSPA), 2010 First International Conference on. IEEE*. (2010) 582-585
6. J. Song, Y. Liu, X. Zhu. Parameters estimation of LFM signals by interpolation based on FRFT. *Systems Engineering and Electronics*. **33**.10 (2011) 2188-2193.
7. J. Song, Y. Wang, Y. Liu. Iterative interpolation for parameter estimation of LFM signal based on fractional Fourier transform. *Circuits, Systems, and Signal Processing*. **32**.3 (2013) 1489-1499.
8. R. Chen, Y. Wang. Universal FRFT-based algorithm for parameter estimation of chirp signals. *Journal of Systems Engineering and Electronics*. **23**.4 (2012) 495-501.
9. L. J. Stanković, T. Alieva, M. J. Bastiaans. Time–frequency signal analysis based on the windowed fractional Fourier transform. *Signal Processing*. **83**.11 (2003): 2459-2468.
10. P. Wang, T. S. Qiu, et al. Parameters estimation of LFM signal based on Gaussian-weighted fractional Fourier transform. *Journal on Communications*. **37**.4 (2016) 107-115.
11. R. Chen, Y. Wang. Efficient detection of chirp signals based on the fourth-order origin moment of fractional spectrum. *Circuits, Systems, and Signal Processing*. **33**.5 (2014) 1585-1596.
12. B. Ristic, B. Boashash. Comments on" The Cramer-Rao lower bounds for signals with constant amplitude and polynomial phase. *IEEE Transactions on Signal Processing*. **46**.6 (1998) 1708-1709.
13. J. C. Liu, et al. SNR analysis of LFM signal with Gaussian white noise in fractional Fourier transform domain. *Journal of electronics & information technology*. **29**.10 (2007) 2337-2340.

DOI: 10.1051/itmconf/20171108004

14. X. W. Jin, M. F. Lu, Y. A. Xie, et al. Sampled signal analysis in the fractional Fourier transform domain. *URSI Asia-Pacific Radio Science Conference (URSI AP-RASC). IEEE.* (2016) 1489-1492.

A Micro-Doppler Modulation of Spin Projectile on CW Radar

Zhi-Xue LIU[a]

Baicheng Ordnance Test Center of China, Baicheng 137001, P. R. China

Abstract. To obtain the spin speed of projectile effectively, a micro-Doppler modulation model of rotating projectile measured by continuous-wave radar (CW radar) is introduced. High spin speed of projectile brings micro-Doppler modulation on echoes of CW radar, and there are many micro-Doppler modulation harmonic waves in the zero intermediate frequency (ZIF) echoes. The frequency interval of the adjacent harmonic waves is several times of rotational frequency, but the integral multiple is unknown. The simulation results prove correctness of the proposed mathematic model.

1 Introduction

The spin speed is a key test parameter of motive projectile and directly related to the design of various projectiles, guidance devices and fuses etc. The main methods to measure projectile spin speed in early stage, such as telemetry method and optical method, have some defects [1] . To the telemetry method, some sensors must be added in the projectile, so it will change the structure of projectile. The optical method could only measure a little part of the ballistic trajectory and it is affected greatly by the environment.

In fact, high speed spin of projectile bring modulation on echoes of CW radar, and there are many harmonic waves around Doppler signal, which called micro-Doppler effect [2]. In recent years, spin speed is measured by continuous wave Doppler radar, through grooving the bottom of the projectile, which can strengthen the micro-Doppler signal [3]. Compared with optical method, this method can measure the spin speed of projectile along with time, but it also changes the structure of projectile as the telemetry method. In order to measure spin speed with unbroken projectile, a method based on digital demodulation is proposed by extracting the micro-Doppler signal in the echo of CW radar, which is the first application of micro-Doppler technology on unbroken projectile [4]. But the mathematical model proposed by References 4 is incomplete. The method proposed in References 4 is incomplete, and the extracted spin speed is ambiguous. So, an emendatory micro-Doppler modulation of rotating projectile on CW radar echoes is proposed, which explains the reason of spin speed ambiguous.

2 Modulation of rotating projectile

The structure of uncontrolled projectile, such as cannonballs, rockets and etc, is symmetrical. Without loss of generality, it is supposed that there are N scattering pointers p_1, $\cdots$, p_i, $\cdots$, p_N, evenly

[a] Corresponding author: liuzx09@qq.com

 DOI: 10.1051/itmconf/20171108005

distributed on the bottom edge, which are l away from the center of the bottom shown as Figure 1. In the coordinate system of projectile axis, the coordinates of p_i is $X_i=(0, l\cdot\sin\theta_i, l\cdot\cos\theta_i)^T$, where $\theta_i=2\pi f_r t+2\pi i/N$, f_r is the spin frequency of projectile.

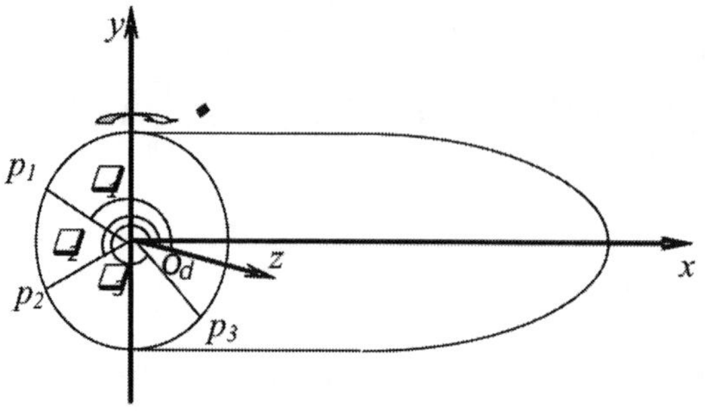

Figure 1. Rotation diagram of projectile

Radar measurement coordinate system O_rXYZ and reference coordinate system $O_dX_NY_NZ_N$ is established shown as Figure 2. The origin of radar measurement coordinate system is the radar, and the O_rX axis parallels the firing azimuth of the gun. The origin of reference coordinate is the center of the projectile bottom, and theO_dX_N axis parallels the direction of velocity. Reference coordinate system moves with the projectile. In the process of launching, the O_rX axis of radar measurement coordinate system almost parallels the direction of velocity. So the angular altitude β of velocity in Figure 2 is equal to the elevation E_l of radar in measurement coordinate system, and the azimuth ψ of velocity is equal to azimuth A_z of radar. Usually, radar is placed close to the firing azimuth of the gun, so the measuring azimuth A_z of radar is very small, and so it also can be considered A_z =0 here. After twice rotations, the coordinates of p_i in reference coordinate system can be transformed into the coordinates of p_i in the coordinate system of projectile axis. First, reference coordinate system rotates around the new Y axis with ψ, and then rotates around the Z axis with β. The β is elevation of the projectile axis and ψ is azimuth of the projectile axis. Therefore the coordinates of scattering pointer p_i in reference coordinates is shown as Eq. 1.

$$\begin{bmatrix} x_i \\ y_i \\ z_i \end{bmatrix} = \begin{bmatrix} \cos E_l & -\sin E_l & 0 \\ \sin E_l & \cos E_l & 0 \\ 0 & 0 & 1 \end{bmatrix} \cdot X_i \tag{1}$$

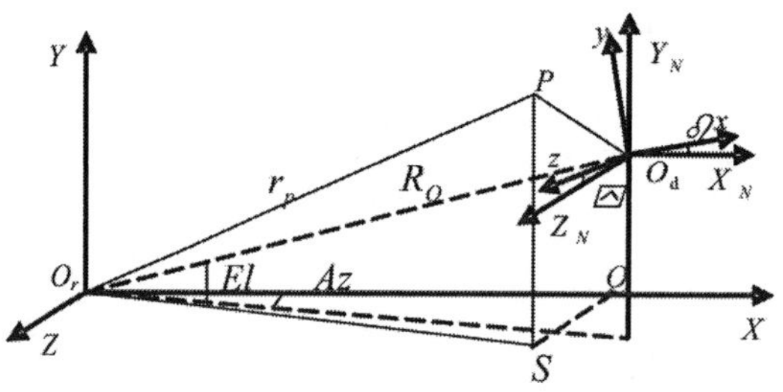

Figure 2. The relationship of coordinate systems

The slant range r_i between p_i and radar is shown as Eq. 2.

$$\begin{aligned} r_i &= [(R\cos E_l \cos A_z - l\cdot \sin E_l \cdot \sin\theta_i)^2 \\ &+(R\cos E_l \sin A_z + l\cdot\cos E_l\cdot \sin\theta_i)^2 \\ &+(R\sin E_l + l\cdot \cos\theta_i)^2]^{1/2} \\ &= [R^2 + 2R(a\cdot\cos\theta_i + b\cdot\sin\theta_i) + l^2]^{1/2} \end{aligned} \tag{2}$$

Where, $a = l\sin E_l; b = l\cos E_l \sin(A_z + E_l)$. Within a certain time, azimuth A_z, elevation E_l and β vary slowly compared with micro-motion, so they can be considered as constant. Because $R>>l$, r_i can be approximated as Eq. 3 based on Taylor expansion.

$$\begin{aligned} r_i &\approx R + (a\cdot \cos\theta_i + b\cdot\sin\theta_i)/2 \\ &= R + d\cos(\theta_i + \xi) \end{aligned} \tag{3}$$

Where, $d = (a^2 + b^2)^{1/2}/2; \xi = ctgE_l \cdot \sin(A_z + E_l)$.

The continuous wave radar transmits a single tone shown as Eq. 4.

$$s_T(t) = \cos(2\pi ft) \tag{4}$$

In Eq. 4, f is the frequency of single tone. While the single tone illuminates the rotating projectile, the echo from the scattering pointer p_i is shown as Eq. 5.

$$s_i(t) = m_{i0}\cdot\cos[2\pi f(t - 2r_i/c)] \tag{5}$$

In Eq. 5, m_{i0} is the amplitude of the echo from the scattering pointer p_i. Put Eq.3 into Eq.5, then

$$s_i(t) = m_{i0}\cdot\cos\{2\pi ft - 4\pi fR/c + \Delta\varphi_i\} \tag{6}$$

Where $2\pi ft$ is the phase varying with time of single tone, $4\pi ftR/c$ is the phase retardation caused by the range between the radar and the projectile, $\Delta\varphi_i$ is the phase shift caused by rotation of projectile and shown as Eq.7.

$$\begin{aligned} \Delta\varphi_i &= -4\pi fd\cos(\theta_i + \xi)/c \\ &= -4\pi fd\cos(2\pi f_r t + 2\pi i/N + \xi)/c \end{aligned} \tag{7}$$

In Eq. 7, the form of $\Delta\varphi_i$ is same with the phase of frequency modulation, which means that the phase shift is the frequency modulation [5]. According to the frequency modulation theory, while $|\Delta\varphi_i|>\pi/6$, the echo from the scattering pointer p_i can be expanded to a trigonometric series shown as Eq. 8, which coefficients are Bessel function.

$$\begin{aligned} s_i(t) = &\sum_{k=-\infty}^{+\infty} m_{i0} J_k(\beta_{FM})\cos(2\pi ft \\ &-4\pi fR/c + 2\pi kf_r t + 2\pi ik/N + k\xi) \end{aligned} \tag{8}$$

In Eq. 8, $J_k(\beta_{FM})$ is the kth Bessel function, $\beta_{FM}=4\pi fd/cf_r$ is the frequency modulation coefficient. The ZIF echoes are shown as Eq. 9.

$$x_i(t) = m_i \sum_{k=-\infty}^{+\infty} J_k(\beta_{FM}) \cdot \exp[j2\pi(f_d + kf_r)t + 2\pi ki / N] \quad (9)$$

In Eq. 9, m_i is the amplitude of the ZIF echoes from p_i, f_d the is the Doppler frequency. The ZIF echoes from all scattering pointers are shown as Eq. 10.

$$x(t) = \sum_{k=-\infty}^{\infty} M_k \exp[j2\pi(f_d + kf_r)t] \quad (10)$$

In Eq. 10, M_k is the amplitude of micro-Doppler modulation harmonic waves and shown in Eq. 10.

$$M_k = J_k(\beta_{FM}) \sum_{i=1}^{N} m_i \exp(j2\pi ki / N) \quad (11)$$

While the scattering are equal, the amplitude of echoes from different scattering points are equal, then $m_1 = m_2 = \cdots = m_N$. The amplitude of harmonic wave, which frequency is kf_r, is shown in Eq.11.

$$M_k = \begin{cases} NJ_k(\beta_{FM}) m_1 & k = NK \\ 0 & k \neq NK \end{cases} \quad (12)$$

In Eq.11, K is an integer, and the harmonic wave which frequency is not Nf_r disappeared.

The mathematic model in Eq. 10 shows that the ZIF echoes from the rotating projectile contain the micro-Doppler modulation harmonic wave. The frequency interval of the adjacent harmonic waves is the rotational frequency, and the frequency interval between the adjacent harmonic waves to the Doppler signal is also several times of the rotational frequency. In general, all harmonics should exist as the Eq. 11 shows, but in some case some harmonic are disappeared as the Eq. 12 shows. Compared Eq. 11 and Eq. 12, the frequency interval of the adjacent harmonic wave is indefinite in different conditions, and the spin frequency cannot be extracted directly from the frequency interval between the adjacent harmonic waves or the harmonic frequency.

3 Processing of micro-doppler signal

In the ZIF echoes from the rotating projectile, the micro-Doppler modulation harmonic wave is weaker than the Doppler signal, and the frequency interval between the harmonic waves and the Doppler signal is also very small, so the micro-Doppler modulation harmonic wave are submerged by noise in the power spectrum calculated by the Fourier transform. In the practical engineering, zoom-FFT is used for analyzing the spectrum of micro-Doppler modulation harmonic wave at high resolution .

After the Doppler frequency f_d is obtained, a local oscillator can be structured as Eq. 13.

$$s_1(t) = e^{-j2\pi f_d t} \quad (13)$$

Using $s_1(t)$, then the ZIF echoes $x(t)$ can be demodulated to a new signal shown in Eq. 14.

$$x_r(t) = x(t)s_1(t) = x(t)e^{-j2\pi f_d t} = \sum_{k=-\infty}^{\infty} M_k \exp[j2\pi(kf_r)t] \quad (14)$$

In the new signal $x_r(t)$, the Doppler signal is shifted to zero frequency, and the micro-Doppler modulation harmonic wave, which frequency is f_d+kf_r, are shifted to kf_r. Then the new signal $x_r(t)$ can be named as the micro-Doppler signal.

To improve the spectrum resolution and restrain the frequency aliasing, zoom-FFT adopts a low rate re-sampling and a low pass filter. Another Fourier transform can calculate the spectrum of $x_r(t)$, and the frequency peak in spectrum is the frequency of micro-Doppler modulation harmonic wave.

4 Experiments

In this section, the correctness of the proposed mathematic model is proved through two simulation experiment. The control parameters used in our simulation are summarized in Table 1.

Table 1. Parameters used in the simulation example.

Center frequency	10×10^{10} Hz
Sample interval	$20\mu s$
Radial velocity	$640-9.97t$ m/s
Spin speed	$100-1.2t+0.05*t^2$ Hz
Radial range	Eq. 2
Scattering point	2 or 4

In the first experiment, the amplitude of the echo from scattering pointer is a random number that obeys the (1, 0.5) normal distribution. The spectrogram and power spectral density are shown in Figure 3. In Figure 3 (a), the spectrogram of the micro-Doppler signal from the rotating projectile with 2 scatter is shown in Fig. 3 (a). Fig. 3 (b) shows the power spectrum curve at the first time point in Figure 3 (a). In Figure 3 (c), the spectrogram of the micro-Doppler signal from the rotating projectile with 4 scatter is shown. Figure 3 (d) shows the power spectrum curve at the first time point. It is shown from Figure 3 that, the frequency interval of the adjacent harmonic waves in the micro-Doppler signal from scatters with random scattering coefficient is the rotational frequency. The frequency interval of the adjacent harmonic waves is several times of the rotational frequency, but the integral multiple is unknown.

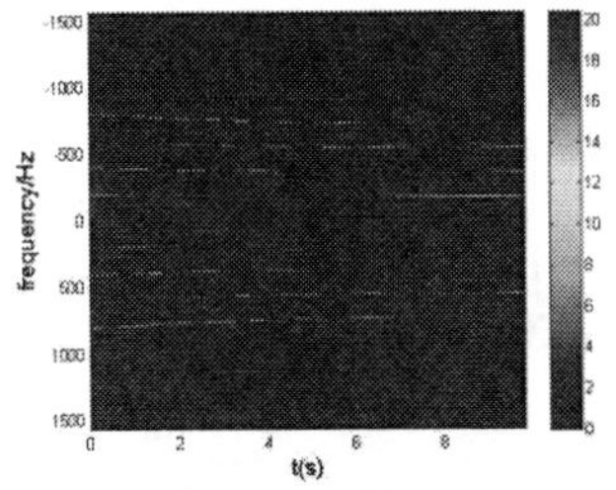

(a) spectrogram of 2 scatter

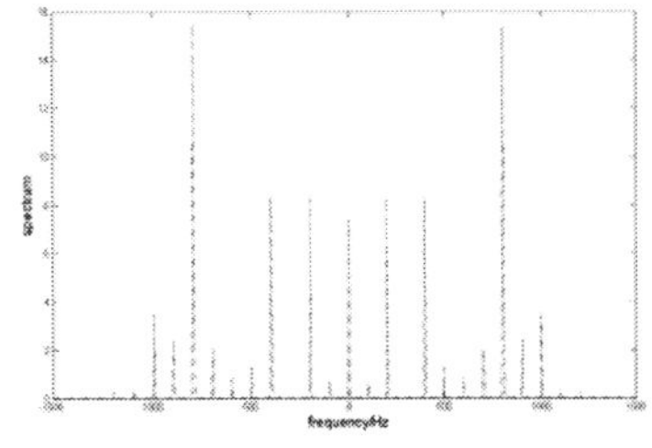

(b) spectrum on 1st point of 2 scatter

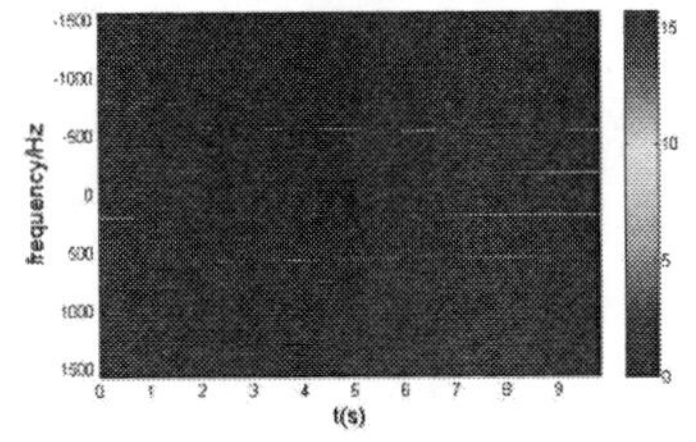

(c) spectrogram of 4 scatter

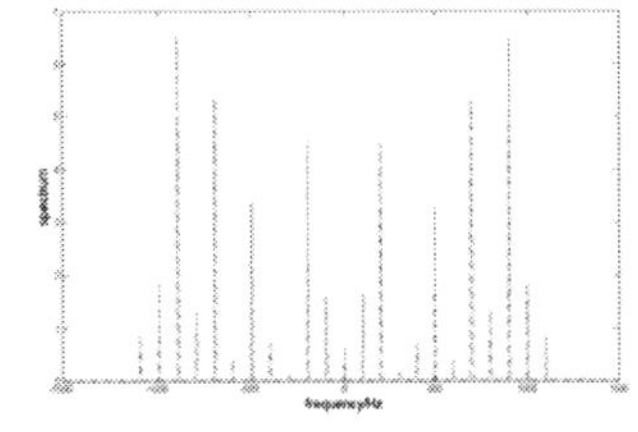

(d) spectrum on 1st point of 4 scatter

Figure 3. The Spectrogram and spectrum of random scattering

 DOI: 10.1051/itmconf/20171108005

In the second experiment, the amplitude of the echo from scattering pointer is equal instead of the random distribution. The results are shown in Figure 4.

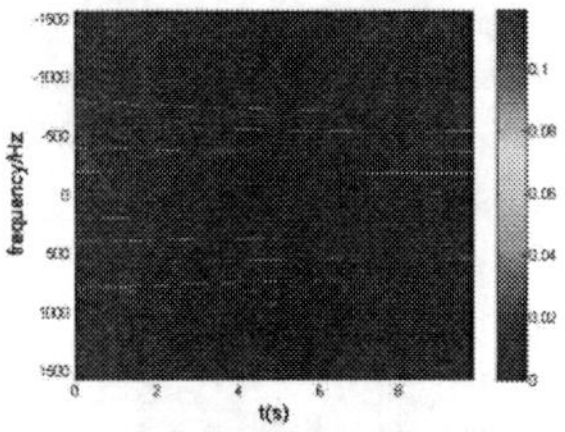

(a) spectrogram of 2 scatter

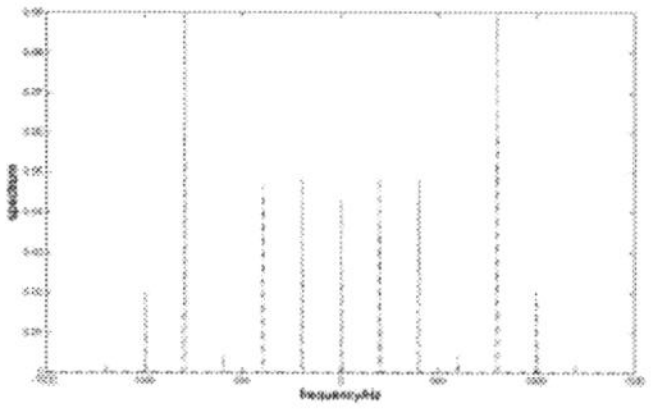
(b) spectrum on 1st point of 2 scatter

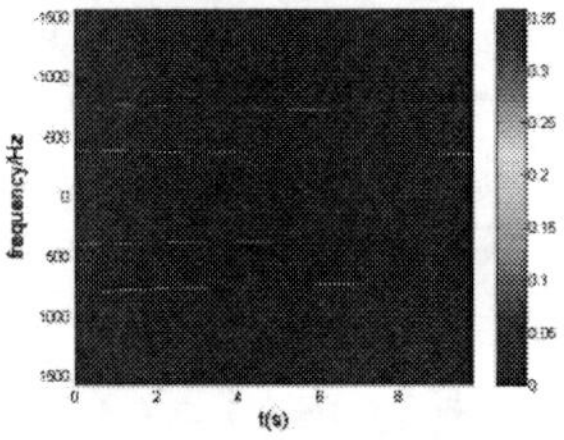

(c) spectrogram of 4 scatter

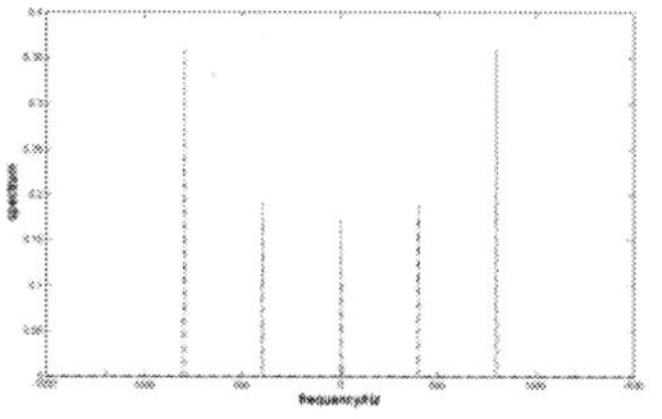
(d) spectrum on 1st point of 4 scatter

Figure 4. The spectrogram and spectrum of equal scattering

It is shown from Figure 4 that, the frequency interval of the adjacent harmonic waves in the micro-Doppler signal from scatters with identical scattering coefficient is several rotational frequencies. The frequency interval of the adjacent harmonic waves is the integer times of rotational frequency, and the integral multiple is the number of scatters.

Compare the result of Fig. 3 and Fig. 4, the frequency interval of the adjacent harmonic waves is indefinite in different conditions, it cannot be extracted directly from the radar echoes.

Conclusions

The micro-Doppler modulation model of the projectile rotation with multi-scatters is established based on the relationship between the ZIF echoes of projectile measured by CW radar and projectile rotation. It is deduced that the frequency interval of the adjacent harmonic waves in the micro-Doppler signal is several times of the spin speed of projectile, and the times of the frequency interval to spin speed cannot be processed directly from the micro-Doppler signal. In the practical, the multiple between the frequency interval and the spin speed can be calculated with the help of other equipment. From the results of simulation, it is concluded that the micro-Doppler modulation model proposed in the paper is correct.

References

1. Han Zipeng. Projectile *and Rocket Exterior Ballistics* [M]. Beijing: Beijing University of Aeronautics and Astronauts press, 2008, 153-162.
2. V C Chen, F Li,S Ho,et al. Micro-Doppler effect in radar-phenomenon, model and simulation study [J]. IEEE Transactions on Aerospace and Electronic Systems, 2006, 42(1):2-21.
3. Wang Yuan-qin et al. *A robust RCS periodicity estimation algorithm for ballistic target*[J]. Aerospace Electronic Warfare, 2008, 24(2): 5-8.
4. Zhang Wan-jun, Wu Xiao-ying, Leng Xue-bing, et al. Testing Method of Projectile Rotating Speed Based on Micro-Doppler Effect of CW Radars [J]. Journal of Academy of Armored Force Engineering. 2012, 26(5):47-50.
5. Proakis, J. G., Digital Communications, 3rd ed., New York, McGraw-Hill, 1995.

A Coarse-Fine Time-to-Digital Converter

Ya-Qian CHEN[1a], Li-Ya MENG and Xiao-Gang LIN

Key Laboratory of Optoelectronic Technology and System, Ministry of Education of the P. R. China, Chongqing 400044, P. R. China

Abstract. A design of time-to-digital converter (TDC) using a coarse-fine conversion scheme is presented. The coarse stage was accomplished by a delay line, and used a loop counter at the end of the delay line to achieve wide dynamic range. The fine stage utilized the dual DLL structure to achieve high precision. The proposed TDC can provide high resolution with less chip area. With an input reference clock of 125MHZ, the TDC achieves 8ps resolution, and the dynamic range achieves 1.5μs.

1 Introduction

Time to digital converter(TDC) is used to measure a short time interval, convert the time signal into a digital signal. With the rapid development of CMOS technology, time digitization had been widely used in physics, military and medicine science such as identify the particles by measuring their life time, in some high energy experiment, detect the distance between two target items by measuring the time interval between emission and reflection signals in laser range finder, rebuild the coordinate information of an annihilation event by measuring the particle's time of flight(TOF) in positron emission tomography(PET). Besides, TDC also plays an important role in logic analyzer, oscilloscope, etc[1].

There are two methods to design a TDC, analog approaches and digital approaches. Traditional analog approaches use time amplifier(TA)[2] or time to voltage converter(TVC) [3]to achieve high resolution, but these methods are area-consuming and with, higher cost, lower conversion rate and higher power supply comparing with digital approaches. As for digital TDC, high resolution is achieved by using the gate delay of the delay cell as TDC's quantization step. Several structures have been proposed before: The traditional structure is the single stage linear delay line, it can achieve wide range by sacrificing chip area. the Phase Locked Loop(PLL) and Delay Locked Loop(DLL) are also typically used, due to the difference of their configuration, DLL is preferred for its stability and fast locking time. Another structure named Vernier Delay Line(VDL), it provides excellent resolution but also suffer from large chip area if wide range is required.

Field-programmable gate array(FPGA) based TDC and application specific integrated circuit(ASIC) based TDC are the main technical ways to design a time to digital converter. Even the former take less time, it can hardly achieve high precision, while the ASIC based TDC has a better performance.

[a] Corresponding author: silhouette_c@foxmail.com

Resent years' research results are as follows: Richard C's team from the University of Florida proposed a novel Vernier ring TDC in 2010, this kind of TDC places the Vernier delay cells and arbiters in a ring format and reuses them for the measurement of the input time interval, finally it can achieve a large detectable range of 12 bits with a resolution of 8ps. In 2012, Professor Luca Vercesi's team from Italy improved Vernier TDC by using two dimensions Vernier line instead of the single dimension one, this new structure help Vernier TDC achieve wide range with on area sacrifice. It comes out with the resolution of 17.2ps and dynamic range of 160ns. After that, researchers form A&M university use the loop counter both in coarse quantization and fine quantization to get wide dynamic range, and the TDC realized with a time resolution of 8.12ps and wide dynamic range of 204.8ns.

Even though the researches above tried different structures to improve TDC's resolution, the cost of chip area and power supply are also very important, so how to optimize a TDC without the sacrifice of the factors above is still a research highlight. The TDC presented in this paper aims at achieving higher precision, wide range and small chip area. The paper is structured as follows: the principle of TDC is described in Section II. The architecture of the proposed TDC is presented in Section III. Section IV presented the circuit structure, the simulation and conclusions are drawn in Section V.

2 Principle of operation

Time to digital converters usually accept two asynchronous input signals: START and STOP, measure the time interval between these two signals can convert continuous time signal into discrete digital signal. A traditional method to measure the time interval is shown in Figure.1[4].

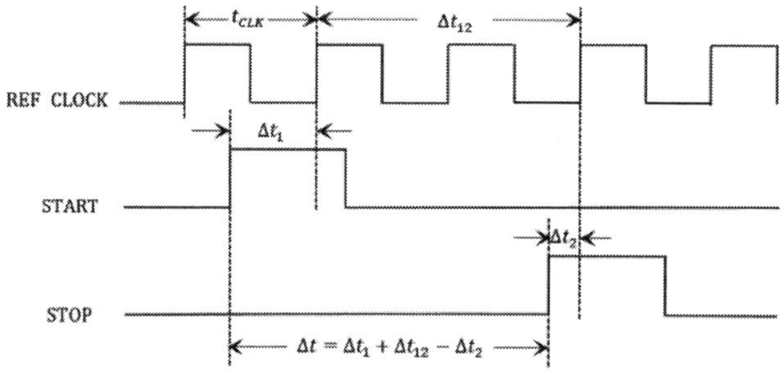

Figure 1. Timing diagram of conversion

The measured time interval consists of three parts: the time interval Δt_1 between START signal and the succeeding rising edge of the reference clock, the time interval Δt_2 between STOP signal and the succeeding rising edge of the reference clock, and the time interval Δt_{12} between the two rising edges mentioned above. Then, the time interval Δt between START and STOP can be determined as $\Delta t = \Delta t_1 + \Delta t_{12} - \Delta t_2$. In this architecture, TDC can get wide dynamic range but its resolution is limited by the frequency of the reference clock, so this kind of TDC usually used as the coarse measure stage.

Another typical architecture of TDC is based on delay line shown in Figure.2. The delay line consists of a set of tapped delay cells and D-flip/flops(DFF), and the delay time of every tapped delay cell is set to be τ, so that τ is the quantization step. When TDC works, the INPUT signal broadcast through the delay line, DFF start to sample the status of the delay line when STOP signal comes, the time interval can be calculated by counting the number of delay cell the START signal has passed. The sampling results of the DFFs are $P_0 \sim P_{n-1}$. Delay line can achieve gate resolution, but it may cost a lot of delay cells to match the wide range required. Besides, traditional delay line is suffered from error accumulation, with the addition of the delay cell, the delay time of delay cell becomes instable and the error will increase.

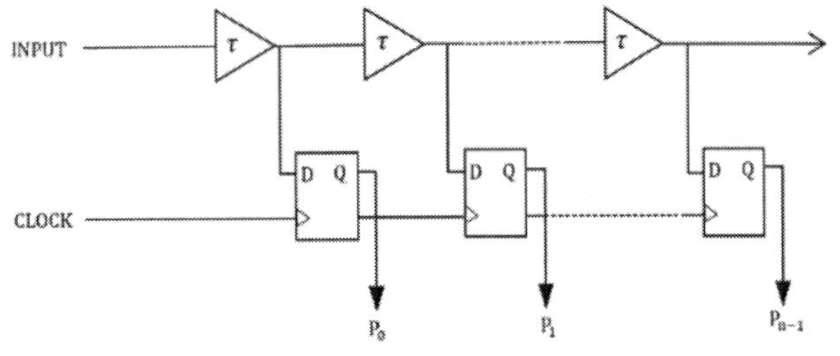

Figure 2. Architecture of tapped delay line

DLL is widely used in TDC in order to improve the precision. The block diagram of the conventional analog DLL is shown in Figure.3. DLL consists of four parts: a Phase Detector(PD) which sometimes be replaced by a Phase Frequency Detector(PFD), a Charge Pump(CP), a Loop Filter(LP) and the Voltage Control Delay Line(VCDL). In the DLL, the reference clock, CLK_IN, is propagated through the voltage control delay line. A PFD is used to compare CLK_IN with the output signal, CLK_OUT, at the end of the delay line. If PFD detect a phase difference between CLK_IN and CLK_OUT, the closed loop system will automatically correct it by changing the control voltage through the charge pump, which can finally change the delay time of the VCDL. However, if the initial delay time of the VCDL is shorter than $0.5T_{clk}$ or longer than $1.5T_{clk}$, the DLL may fail to lock or falsely lock to two or more periods. That means the DLL must lock the delay time to one clock cycle of the reference signal, the initial delay time of VCDL must between $0.5T_{clk}$ and $1.5T_{clk}$. DLL based TDC can achieve the resolution of CLK_IN/n, n is the number of delay cell in VCDL.

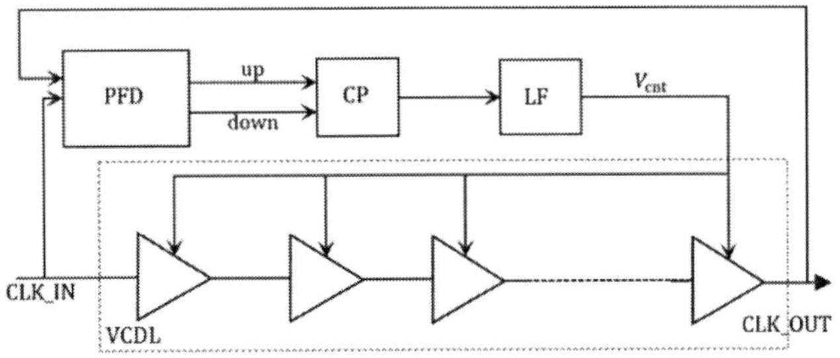

Figure 3. Block diagram of DLL

3 Architecture design

Considered both precision and dynamic range, the Coarse-Fine TDC we proposed in this paper including three stages as shown in Figure.4. At the first level, the time interval between the rising edge of the START and STOP signal is digitized by a looped delay line. The looped delay line comprises a set of delay cell and a digital 6 bits counter at the end of the delay line. The resolution of the first stage is set to be τ_{coarse}, which is the delay time of every delay cell in this stage. The looped architecture can effectively enhance the dynamic range of the whole TDC. Then the remained time interval which is shorter than τ_{coarse} are sent into the middle stage. In order to improve the convert efficiency and led to a small chip area, we add a middle stage with a resolution of τ_{middle}. The third stage use a dual-DLL based VDL to achieve high precision, two control voltage generated from dual-DLL controls fast delay line and slow delay line of VDL respectively, and the resolution is determined as T_{CLK}/n^2.

 DOI: 10.1051/itmconf/20171108006

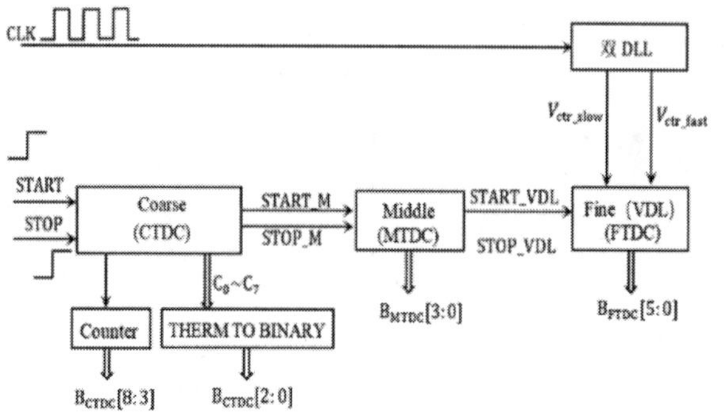

Figure 4. Proposed TDC architecture

3.1 A looped delay line

Conventionally, a delay line and a set of DFFs are needed in a phase sampler as Figure.2, a digital counter is added at the end of delay line to achieve wide range as shown in Figure.5[5]. When coarse quantization stage works, the rising edge of the START signal propagates through the delay line, the loop time of the START signal is stored in the counter. When the STOP signal comes, the propagate status are sampled to the DFFs and the digital counter stop to work. The time interval measured by the coarse stage can be determined as:

$$\mathrm{B} = B_{coarse} + n * B_{counter}$$

n is the number of delay cell, B_{coarse} is the sampling binary code while $B_{counter}$ is the binary code stored in the counter. We design the delay line with 8 delay cells and set every delay cell's delay time to be 4ns, the rising and failing edge of START signal propagate alternately through the delay line. The counter we used is 6 bits. The dynamic range of coarse stage can be infinite theoretically, in fact, the dynamic range is limited because of error accumulation and nonlinearity in the delay line. The proposed TDC in this paper can achieve the dynamic range of 1.5μs after simulation. Compared with the research results of recent years, 1.5μs is a very excellent dynamic range while most of them achieve a dynamic range of hundreds of nanoseconds.

The middle stage used a traditional delay line which consists of 16 delay cells with the resolution of 250ps and dynamic range of 4ns.

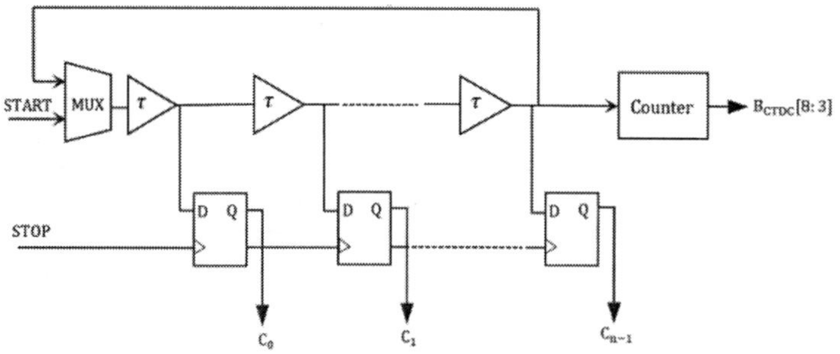

Figure 5. Coarse stage architecture

3.2 Dual-DLL

Traditional DLL has a single delay line, the precision is T_{CLK}/n, while T_{CLK} is the period of reference clock and n is the number of delay cells. In order to control the delay time of two delay lines of

VDL, a dual DLL structure is proposed as shown in Figure.6[6]. Dual DLL contains a fast DLL and a slow DLL, the fast DLL has shorter delay time while the slow one has longer. Each DLL consists of VCDL, PFD, CP and LP. When there is a phase difference between CLK_IN and CLK_OUT exist, the PFD generate UP or DOWN signal to control the charge pump, then the charge pump generates a control voltage to decrease or increase the delay time of the delay cell until the two signals are in phase.

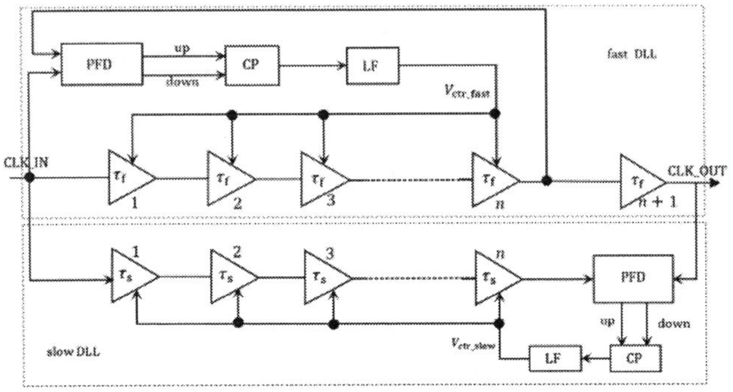

Figure 6. Dual DLL architecture

As shown in Figure.6, the fast DLL contains n delay cells, when CLK_IN and CLK_OUT are in phase, the delay time of every delay cell can be determined as $\tau_f = T_{CLK}/n$. We chose the (n+1)th output of the fast delay line to match the nth output of the slow delay line. It forces the delay time of slow DLL to be:

$$\mathrm{n} * \tau_s = (n+1)\tau_f \tag{1}$$

$$\tau_s = \left(\frac{T_{clk}}{n}\right) * \frac{n+1}{n} = T_{clk} * (n+1)/n^2 \tag{2}$$

This architecture has an important advantage that such a Dual-DLL needs only a single reference clock instead of two.

3.3 VDL architecture

The Dual-DLL we proposed before works for the fine quantization stage, VDL, shown as Figure.7. Obviously, the VDL architecture contains two tapped delay line with different delay time. Besides, the number of delay cells in VDL should be the same as in Dual-DLL. The resolution of the VDL architecture is determined as:

$\tau_{VDL} = \tau_s - \tau_f$, while $\tau_s > \tau_f$.

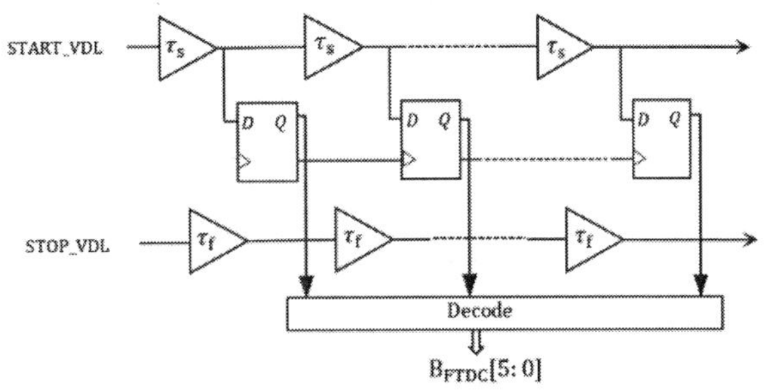

Figure 7. VDL architecture

DOI: 10.1051/itmconf/20171108006

The delay time of the two delay lines are controlled by the voltage provided by the Dual-DLL. According to the delay time determined above, fine quantization resolution is:

$$\tau_{fine} = \tau_s - \tau_f = T_{clk} * \frac{n+1}{n^2} - \frac{T_{CLK}}{n} = T_{CLK}/n^2 \quad (3)$$

In this paper, the reference clock is 125MHZ and n is 32, $\tau_{fine} = 7.8125ps$. The dynamic range of fine stage is $7.8125\text{ps} * 32 = 250\text{ps}$, which matches the resolution of middle stage.

4 Circuit description

This section describes the circuit scheme of some typical blocks.

4.1 Delay cell

We set the delay time of delay cell in coarse stage to be 4ns. The schematic of the delay cell with bias we chose is shown in Figure.8. It contains 3 nMOS and 3 pMOS, the voltage V1 and V2 is used to control the delay of rising edge and failing edge. The delay time can be set to be 4ns by changing the ratio of width and length of MOS.

The delay cell of the middle stage uses the same architecture above. Figure.9 shows the schematic of delay cell in fine stage[7]. The difference is that there is only one control voltage to control the delay of rising edge. Obviously, the control voltage here is generated from DLL we described before.

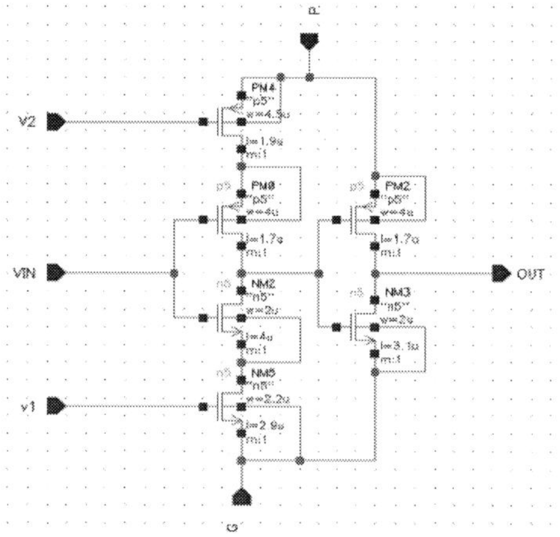

Figure 8. Schematic of the delay cell in coarse stage

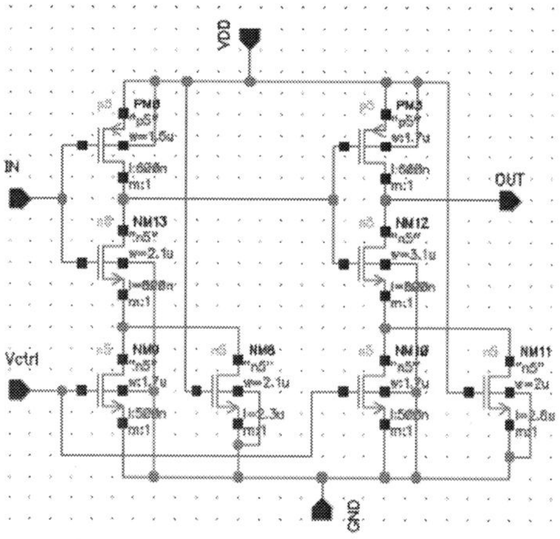

Figure 9. Schematic of the delay cell in fine stage

4.2 Symmetrical DFF

There is a set of DFFs match the delay cell in every quantization stage to sample the propagation state of target signal. The difficulty in designing the DFF lies in providing the same path for two signals propagate through DFF, so that the delay time of these two signals are the same, there is no extra error been brought in. That means we need a symmetrical DFF and its schematic shows as Fig.10.

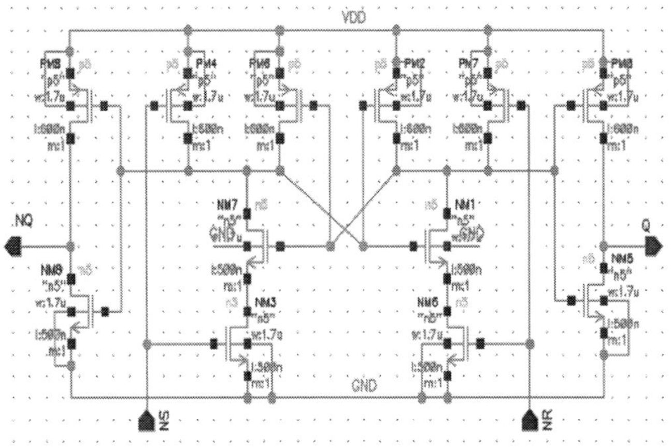

Figure 10. Symmetrical DFF

4.3 Control structure for DLL

The main problem of DLL is fail to lock or falsely lock to two or more periods. In order to make DLL lock correctly, we proposed a control structure for DLL shown as Fig.11 and Fig.12, and the former is for the fast DLL while the latter is for the slow DLL.

Take Fig.11 for example. A rising edge of SETUP signal generated when the first failing edge of REF_CLK comes, the first rising edge of REF_CLK is ignored so that the DFF won't fail to lock. The timing diagram is shown in Figure. 13.

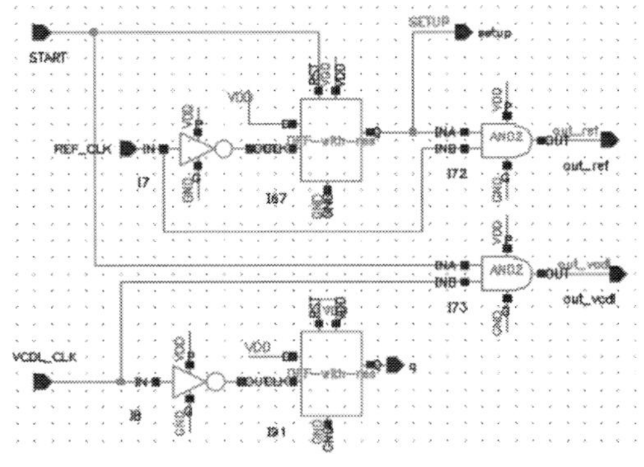

Figure 11. Control structure for the fast DLL

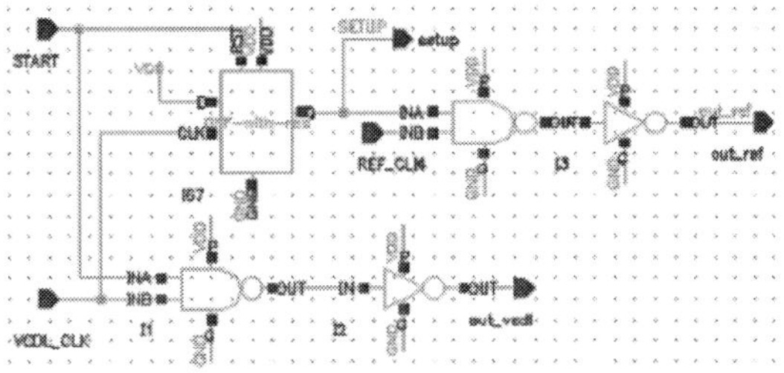

Figure 12. Control structure for the slow DLL

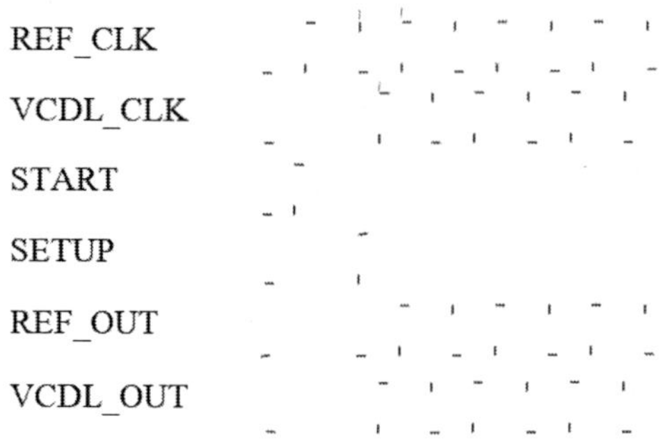

Figure 13. Timing diagram

5 Simulation and conclusions

The designed circuit is tested in Cadence Spectre software using SKYSILICON Co.Ltd CD035MVA 0.5μm CMOS process, and the simulation result of Dual-DLL is as Fig.14. The fast DLL costed 460.9ns to be stable while the slow DLL costed 582.6ns. The control voltage generated to control fast line and slow line of VDL are 1.798V and 1.59V.

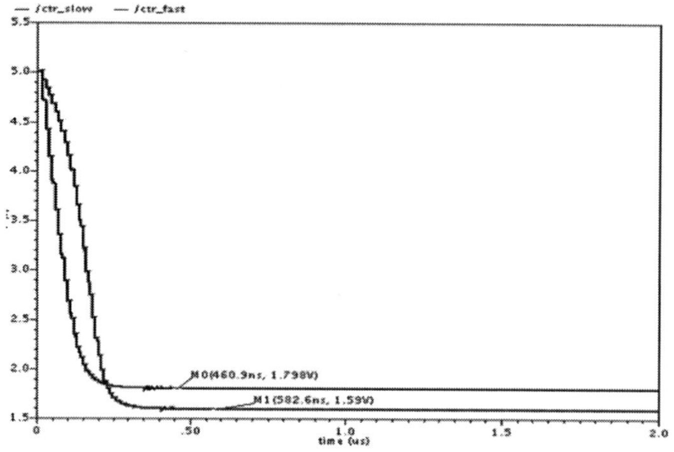

Figure 14. Simulation of Dual-DLL

We have proposed that the resolution of the fine stage is 7.8125ps, but the actual resolution from the simulation result shows 8ps~9ps, the error exist because the architecture of DLL will bring in some phase error, the propagation route of START and STOP signals in delay line can't be exactly the same, and even the DLL is locked, the jitter of control voltage still exists.

In this paper, a high-precision TDC using a three-level conversion scheme was proposed. With the development of integrated circuit technology, a TDC with both high resolution and wide dynamic range is need, only achieve one target is not enough. Compared with recent years' research results shown as Table.1, the TDC proposed in this paper performed well in the ratio of resolution and dynamic range.

Table.1 Recent years' research results

Year	Paper	Precision/Dynamic Range
2013	A 7 bit, 3.75 ps Resolution Two-Step Time-to-Digital Converter in 65 nm CMOS Using Pulse-Train Time Amplifier.	3.75ps/480ps
2013	A high-linearity, 17 ps precision time-to-digital converter based on a single-stage Vernier delay loop fine interpolation.	17.2ps/160ns
2014	A 15b, Sub-10ps resolution, low dead time, wide range two-stage TDC.	8.125ps/204.8ns
2017	This paper	8ps/1.5μs

References

1. M. Li, Y.H. Gong, M.Y. Yu, Microelectronics, **44**, 372(2004)
2. K. Kim, Y.H. Kim, W. Yu, S. Cho, Solid-State Circuits, **48**, 1009(2013)
3. P, Chen, C.C. Chen, Y.S. Shen. IEEE transaction on nuclear science, **53**, 2215(2006)
4. E.Raisanen-Ruosalainen, T.Rahkonen, J. Kostamovaara, MWSCAS, 197(1997)
5. N. Narku-Tetteh, A Titriku, S Palermo, MWSCAS, 13(2014)
6. C.S. Hwang, P. Chen, H.W. Tsao, IEEE Transactions on nuclear science, **51**, 1349(2004)
7. B Markovic, S Tisa, FA Villa, A Tosi, F Zappa, Circuits and Systems I Regular Papers IEEE Transactions on, **60**, 557(2013)

The Research on Full-speed Field Weakening Control Method of Electric Vehicle Interior Permanent Magnet Synchronous Motor

Run-Ze GAO[1,a], Li ZHAI[2] and Li-Wei SU[3]

[1]*From Research Institute of Highway Ministry of Transport (Beijing, 100088);*
[2]*From School of Mechanical Engineering, Beijing Institute of Technology (Beijing, 100081);*
[3]*From FAW-Volkswagen Automotive Co. Ltd. (Changchun, 130011)*

Abstract. The motor drive system represents a key technology for development of the electrical vehicles, and the permanent magnet synchronous motor becomes the mainstream of the new energy vehicle drive motor for the superior performances in power density, low-speed torque density, efficiency and reliability. The paper studies the field weakening control strategy for the interior permanent magnet synchronous motor (IPMSM) and provides a field weakening control strategy for the IPMSM at the full-speed range. By studying the mathematical IPMSM model and the methods of conventional vector control and analyzing the operating conditions of the IPMSM at the full-speed range, the paper divides the operating conditions into constant torque operation region I, constant torque operation region II, constant power field weakening operation region and high-speed field weakening operation region to confirm the control strategy algorithm in each region and the transition conditions between regions and provide the current control strategy that the d-axis current and q-axis current are confirmed by the reference torque and the feedback speed. Modeling of the field weakening control strategies in each region is made through the Matlab/Simulink, and simulation of the operating conditions with a steady-state load and a dynamic load is done to verify that the field weakening control strategy in each region is feasible. A co-simulation is made by combining the Matlab/Simulink-based control model, the RecurDyn-based virtual prototype and the RT-LAB to verify the feasible field weakening control strategy.

Introduction

The PMSM features a small size, the low inertia and the fast response to have the superior performances in power density, low-speed torque density, efficiency and reliability. The motor of the kind is very adaptive to the electric vehicle's drive system to become the mainstream motor for the new energy vehicles at moment. The PMSM is subject to the common strategies for variable voltage and frequency control, field-orientated control and direct torque control.

To ensure the fast, accurate and precise system, the vector control theory has been extensively applied in the PMSM control system design for years. As the PMSM has the permanent magnetic (p-m) rotor with the approximately constant flux, it is controlled by means of the rotor flux orientation

[a] Corresponding author: rz.gao@rioh.cn

DOI: 10.1051/itmconf/20171109001

in general. However, the field weakening expansion represents a key problem to hinder extensive application of the high-speed PMSM. For a decade, the domestic and foreign scholars have been attaching most importance to the problem and made great efforts to have a lot of study achievements. Unfortunately, these studies have the deficiencies in either the motor body or the control to combine speed, power and torque well. For this reason, the paper studies the field weakening strategy for the IPMSM to provide a field weakening strategy for the PMSM at the full-speed range.

1 Mathematical PMSM model

During analysis of the mathematical PMSM model, the following hypotheses are proposed to simplify the analysis process: The stator's armature winding generates a sine wave to induce the electromotive force and the rotor's permanent magnet also distributes the field of the sine wave form in the air-gap space; The eddy current and hysteresis losses are negligible for the core; The stator core has the negligible saturation with the constant inductance parameters and the magnetic circuit is considered linear; The damper winding is negligible for the rotor.

Based on the rotatory two-phase coordinates, the PM's fundamental wave exciter field axis is taken as the d axis and is rotated anticlockwise to surpass the d axis by 90° to take the electrical angle as the q axis. Both the d axis and the q axis are rotated at the rate of the electrical angle to determine the spatial coordinates with the electrical angle θr which is formed between the d axis and the reference axis A. The space sector of the PMSM in the coordinates is shown in Figure.1 below:

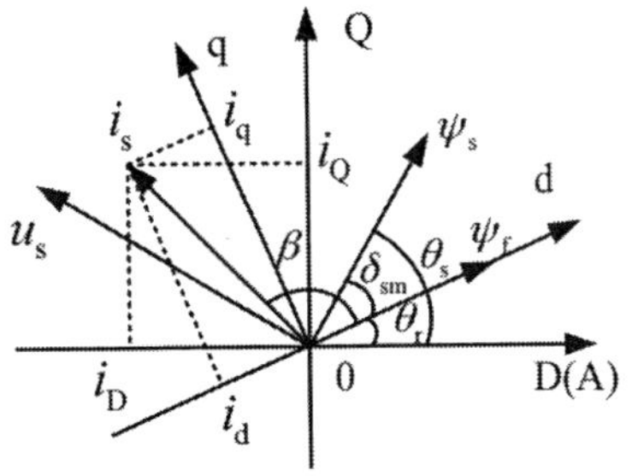

Figure. 1 PMSM Coordinate Sector Diagram

Where: The components of the d axis and the q axis may be obtained by shifting the three-phase stator winding in the coordinates (i.e. shift of the three-phase ABC coordinates to the rotatory dq coordinates).

$$\begin{cases} u_d = \dfrac{d\psi_d}{dt} - \omega_e \psi_q + R_s i_d \\ u_q = \dfrac{d\psi_q}{dt} + \omega_e \psi_d + R_s i_q \end{cases} \tag{1}$$

Where:
u_d and u_q—Stator Voltage Components at the d axis and the q axis (V);
ψ_d and ψ_q—Stator Flux-linkage Components at the d axis and the q axis (Wb);
i_d and i_q—Stator Current Components at the d axis and the q axis (A);
ω_e—Rotor's Electrical Angle (rad/s)
Flux-linkage Equation:

$$\begin{cases} \psi_d = L_d i_d + \psi_f \\ \psi_q = L_q i_q \end{cases} \tag{2}$$

$$\psi_s = \sqrt{\psi_d^2 + \psi_q^2} = \sqrt{(L_d i_d + \psi_f)^2 + (L_q i_q)^2} \tag{3}$$

Where:
ψ_s—Stator Flux-linkage (Wb);
L_d and L_q—Stator Winding Induction at the d axis and the q axis (H).
Back Electromotive Force Equation:

$$E_s = \omega_e \psi_s \tag{4}$$

Where:
E_s—Stator's Back Electromotive Force (V).
Torque Equation:

$$T_e = K p_n \psi_s \times i_s \tag{5}$$

Where:
T_e—Motor's Electromagnetic Torque (Nm);
K—Undetermined Coefficient;
i_s—Stator Current (A);
p_n—Pole Pairs of the Motor's Rotor.
In the paper, the torque is shown as follows:

$$\begin{aligned} T_e &= \frac{3}{2} p_n (\psi_s i_d - \psi_q i_d) \\ &= \frac{3}{2} p_n [\psi_f i_d + (L_d - L_q) i_d i_q) \end{aligned} \tag{6}$$

During the high-speed operation of the motor, the resistance's caused voltage loss is very little and negligible, so the equation (1) may be changed into:

$$\begin{cases} u_d = -\omega_e L_q i_q \\ u_q = \omega_e (L_d i_d + \psi_f) \end{cases} \tag{7}$$

For the IPMSM with the $L_d \neq L_q$, it is possible to control both the torque and the flux-linkage of the motor by controlling the quadrature-axis current and the direct-axis current respectively to improve the torque output capacity with the effective structural torque and change the flux-linkage for the field weakening control by controlling the direct-axis current.

2 Field weakening control algorithm

Restricted to the inverter output voltage and the motor current, the motor is limited to vary in current and terminal voltage in a specified scope and the stator current is limited by both the current limit circle and the voltage limit ellipse at the same time. i.e.:

$$\begin{cases} \sqrt{i_d^2 + i_q^2} = |i_s| \le |i_s|_{\max} \\ \sqrt{u_d^2 + u_q^2} = |u_s| \le |u_s|_{\max} \end{cases} \tag{8}$$

Where: i_s means the stator current sector and u_s means the stator voltage sector.

Combination of the equation (7) with the equation (8) may be simplified to obtain the current and voltage limit equations at the dq coordinates when the IPMSM is operating in a high-speed and stable state:

$$\begin{cases} \sqrt{i_d^2 + i_q^2} \le |i_s|_{\max} \\ (\psi_f + L_d i_d)^2 + (L_q i_q)^2 \le \left(\frac{|u_s|_{\max}}{\omega_e}\right)^2 \end{cases} \tag{9}$$

It is learned from the equation (9) that the current limit equation shows the circle (Dot: (0,0); Radius: $|i_s|_{\max}$) and the voltage limit equation shows the ellipse cluster whose center is located at the position of ($-\psi_f/L_d$, 0) and the lengths of the semimajor axis and the semiminor axis are inversely proportional to the rotor's angular speed ω_e. Both the current limit circle and the voltage limit ellipse cluster at the dq coordinates are shown in Figure.2. In the event of $-\psi_f/L_d<i_{smax}$, the center of the voltage limit ellipse cluster exists outside of the current limit circle (see Figure. 2(a)); In the event of $-\psi_f/L_d>i_{smax}$, the center of the voltage limit ellipse cluster exists in the current limit circle (see Figure. 2(c)); Therefore, any intersection exists in the areas represented by the current limit circle and the voltage limit ellipse at any rotary speed. But no point of intersection will exist in the areas represented by the current limit circle and the voltage limit ellipse at an excessive rotary speed. In this case, the rotary speed is deemed possibly maximum for the motor in theory.

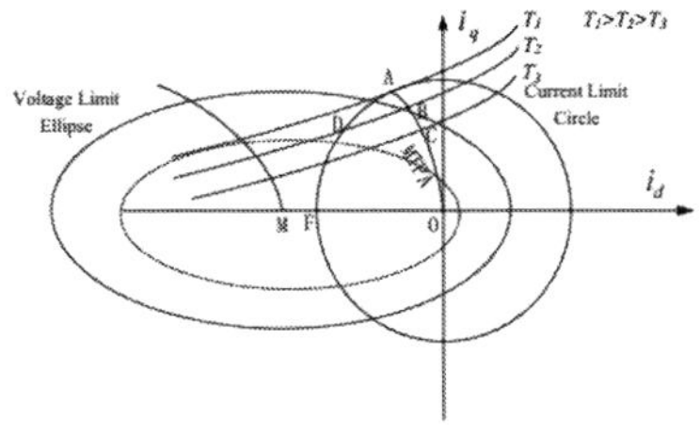

(a) $-\psi_f/L_d<i_{smax}$

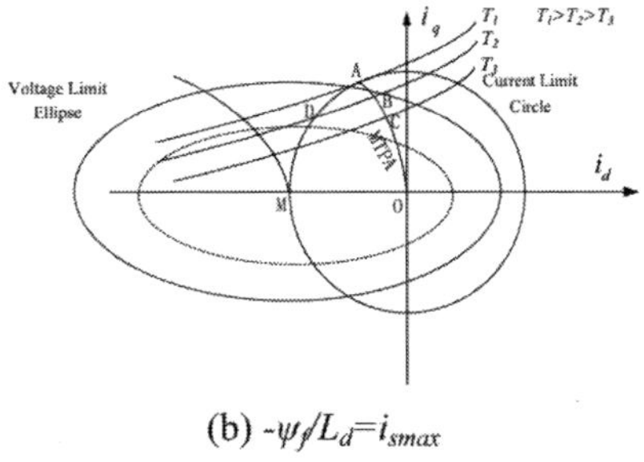

(b) $-\psi_f/L_d=i_{smax}$

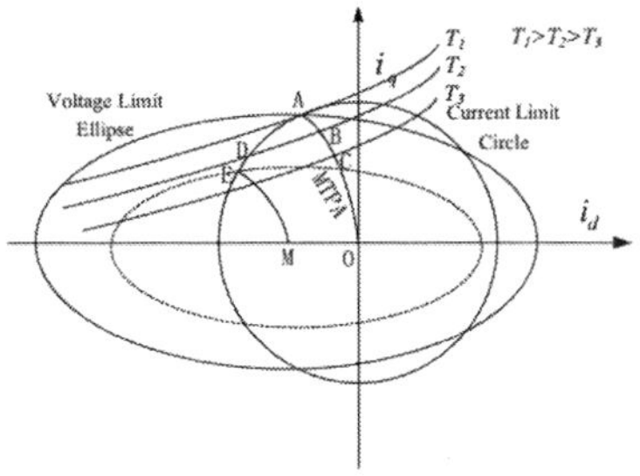

(c) $-\psi_f/L_d>i_{smax}$

Figure. 2 Diagram of current and voltage sector for the PMSM operating at the full-speed range

3 Full-speed and Field Weakening Control Strategy

The maximum torque/current ratio curve of the IPMSM is shown by OA in the Figure. 2. Just take for example the torque T2 as given in Figure. 2(c), in the event of a given expected torque T2, the stator current sector remains unchanged as OB and the voltage sector increases at a higher rotatory speed of the motor, but when the voltage sector reaches the inverter's maximum output voltage us max, it will fail to remain unchanged as OB and the motor will enter the constant torque region II. In this case, the appropriate rotatory speed of the motor may be defined as the turning speed from the constant torque region I to the constant torque region II to calculate A in the voltage limit ellipse equation (10). The Figure. 2 shows the greater the given expected torque, the lower the motor's turning speed from from the constant torque region I to the constant torque region II. The possible torque of the PMSM is indicated by the point A in the Figure. 2 to have the maximum stator current. Both the quadrature-axis current and the direct-axis current are shown in the equation (11) at the maximum torque.

$$\omega_A = \frac{u_{s\max}}{\sqrt{(L_d i_d + \psi_f)^2 + (L_q i_q)^2}} \tag{10}$$

$$\begin{cases} i_d = \dfrac{-\psi_f + \sqrt{\psi_f^2 + 8(L_d - L_q)^2 i_{s\max}^2}}{4(L_d - L_q)} \\ i_q = \sqrt{i_{s\max}^2 - i_d^2} \end{cases} \tag{11}$$

3.1 Gradient descent-based field weakening operation in the constant torque region II

When the motor operates in the constant torque region II, the voltage sector will continue the inverter's maximum output voltage and the stator current sector will increase at a higher rotary speed. According to the Figure. 2(c), the constant torque curve and the maximum input power curve have the point of intersection in or outside of the current limit circle, depending upon the variation in the given expected torque. When the constant torque curve and the maximum input power curve have the point of intersection in the current limit circle, the motor will transit directly from the constant torque region II to the maximum input power operation region bypassing the ordinary constant torque field weakening operation region at a higher rotatory speed. In this case, the turning speed ω_D may be determined through the voltage limit ellipse where the constant torque curve and the maximum input power curve have the point of intersection. When the constant torque curve and the maximum input power curve have the point of intersection outside of the current limit circle, the motor will transit to the ordinary constant torque field weakening operation region first at a higher rotatory speed. In this case, the turning speed ω_B may be determined through the voltage limit ellipse where the constant torque curve and the current limit circle have the point of intersection (see the equation (12)). In the event of the minimum rotary speed of entry into the maximum input power operation region, the motor will transit to the maximum input power operation region.

$$\begin{cases} i_d^2 + i_q^2 = i_{s\max}^2 \\ \omega_B = \dfrac{u_{s\max}}{\sqrt{(L_d i_d + \psi_f)^2 + (L_q i_q)^2}} \\ T_e = \dfrac{3}{2} \cdot p_n \cdot [\psi_f + (L_d - L_q) i_d] i_q \end{cases} \tag{12}$$

3.2 Ordinary constant torque field weakening operation

The stator current sector increases at a higher rotary speed of the motor. When the stator current sector reaches the maximum current $i_{s\max}$, the ultimate voltage ellipse and the constant torque curve will have the point of intersection outside of the current limit circle and the motor will fail to continue the constant torque output. Under this circumstance, to ensure continuous increase of the motor's rotary speed, it is possible to control the current sector changes along the point of intersection between the current limit circle and the voltage limit ellipse.

In the event of $i_d \geq -\psi_f/L_d$,

$$\begin{cases} i_d = \dfrac{-\psi_f L_d + \sqrt{\psi_f^2 L_d^2 - (L_d^2 - L_q^2)[\psi_f^2 - (u_{s\max}/\omega_e)^2 + L_q^2 i_{s\max}^2]}}{L_d^2 - L_q^2} \\ i_q = \sqrt{i_{s\max}^2 - i_d^2} \end{cases} \tag{13}$$

In the event of $i_d \geq -\psi_f/L_d$,

$$\begin{cases} i_d = -\dfrac{\psi_f L_d + \sqrt{\psi_f^2 L_d^2 - (L_d^2 - L_q^2)[\psi_f^2 - (u_{s\max}/\omega_e)^2 + L_q^2 i_{s\max}^2]}}{L_d^2 - L_q^2} \\ i_q = \sqrt{i_{s\max}^2 - i_d^2} \end{cases} \tag{14}$$

In the event of $\psi_f/L_d < i_{smax}$, the ordinary constant torque field weakening operation region is divided into $id \geq -\psi f/Ld$ and $i_d < -\psi_f/L_d$, depending upon the different functions for determination of the quadrature-axis current and the direct-axis current. During the transition from the $i_d \geq -\psi_f/L_d$ region to the $i_d < -\psi_f/L_d$ region, the turning speed ωE may be determined through the $i_d = -\psi_f/L_d$ and $i_q = \sqrt{i_{s\max}^2 - i_d^2}$ the voltage limit ellipse equation and its appropriate maximum torque T_{02} may be determined through the constant torque curve where the $i_d = -\psi_f/L_d$ curve and the current limit circle have the point of intersection. As shown in Figure. 3, the constant torque curve and the current limit circle have the point of intersection at the left or right side of the $i_d = -\psi_f/L_d$ curve for the different given expected torques. When the constant torque curve and the current limit circle have the point of intersection at the left side of the $i_d = -\psi_f/L_d$ curve, the equation (13) and the equation (14) may be applied simultaneously to solve the system of binary linear equations and obtain the stator current sector components at the quadrature axis and the direct axis respectively. When the constant torque curve and the current limit circle have the point of intersection at the right side of the $i_d = -\psi_f/L_d$ curve, the equation (13) and the torque equation (6) may be applied simultaneously to solve the system of binary linear equations and obtain the stator current sector components at the quadrature axis and the direct axis respectively. As mentioned above, when the motor operates in the ordinary constant torque field weakening region, the stator current sector will change along the current limit circle at a higher rotatory speed of the motor, and in the event of the minimum rotary speed of entry into the maximum input power operation region, the motor will transit from the ordinary constant torque field weakening operation region to the maximum input power region and the turning speed may be determined through the voltage limit ellipse where the current limit circle and the maximum input power curve have the point of intersection.

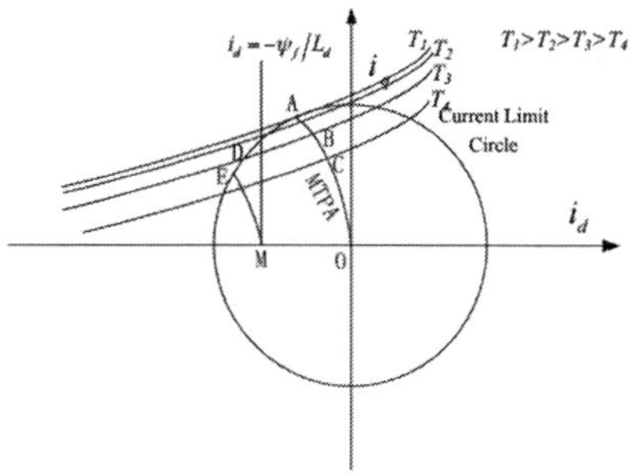

Figure. 3 Division of the ordinary constant torque field weakening region

3.3 High-speed and field weakening operation

The maximum input power control locus is shown in Figure. 2(c). The locus is intersected with the current limit circle at the point E which represents the minimum rotary speed C to provide the field weakening control at the maximum input power and may be determined through the voltage limit ellipse where the point E exists in the following equation (15). When the given expected torque is greater than the point A's appropriate maximum torque T01, the motor will bypass the constant torque field weakening region and enter the maximum input power operation region directly and the T_{01}may be determined through the constant torque curve where the point E exists in the equation (16). When the motor operates in the maximum input power region, the stator current sector will move along the maximum input power field weakening control locus toward the center point M of the voltage limit ellipse cluster. The point M has the coordinates of ($-\psi_f/L_d$, 0) to show the ultimate operation. That is, the demagnetizing field of the direct-axis current is equivalent to the exciter field of the permanent magnet at the point to make the motor speed infinitely great in theory. The motor speed will increase along the curve until balance of the electromagnetic torque and the load torque.

$$\omega_C=(\rho-1)\frac{\sqrt{2\rho+\left[3(\rho)^2-4\rho+1\right]\sqrt{4i_{s\max}^2\rho^2+4i_{s\max}^2+4\rho-3}+4i_{s\max}^2+5\rho^2-6\rho^3+2\rho^4+\rho^2-3}}{\rho\sqrt{2\left(4i_{s\max}^4-5i_{s\max}^2\rho^2+12i_{s\max}^2\rho-7i_{s\max}^2+\rho^4-6\rho^3+12\rho^2-10\rho+3\right)}} \tag{15}$$

$$\begin{cases} i_d=-\dfrac{\psi_f}{L_d}+\Delta i_d \\ i_q=-\dfrac{\sqrt{\left(u_{s\max}/\omega_C\right)^2-\left(L_d\Delta i_d\right)^2}}{L_q} \\ \Delta i_d=\left(\sqrt{L_q^2\psi_f^2+8\left(L_d-L_q\right)^2\left(\dfrac{u_{s\max}}{\omega_C}\right)^2}-L_q\psi_f\right)\Big/\left[4L_d\left(L_d-L_q\right)\right] \\ i_d^2+i_q^2=i_{s\max}^2 \\ T_{01}=\dfrac{3}{2}\cdot p_n\cdot\left(\psi_f+\left(L_d-L_q\right)i_d\right)i_q \end{cases} \tag{16}$$

DOI: 10.1051/itmconf/20171109001

$$\begin{cases} T_e = \frac{3}{2} \cdot p_n \cdot \left(\psi_f + \left(L_d - L_q\right) i_d\right) i_q \\ i_d = -\frac{\psi_f}{L_d} + \Delta i_d \\ i_q = -\frac{\sqrt{\left(u_{s\max} / \omega_D\right)^2 - \left(L_d \Delta i_d\right)^2}}{L_q} \\ \Delta i_d = \left(\sqrt{L_q^2 \psi_f^2 + 8\left(L_d - L_q\right)^2 \left(\frac{u_{s\max}}{\omega_D}\right)^2} - L_q \psi_f \right) \Big/ \left[4L_d\left(L_d - L_q\right)\right] \end{cases} \tag{17}$$

4 Simulation results

4.1 Simulation comparison between the MTPA control and the id=0 control

It is assumed that the expected torque is T_e=145Nm and the load torque T_L=50Nm, the waveform variation of the motor which is controlled through the MTPA and the id=0 is shown in Figure. 4~Figure. 9 in output torque, rotary speed, direct-axis current, stator current, stator voltage and flux-linkage.

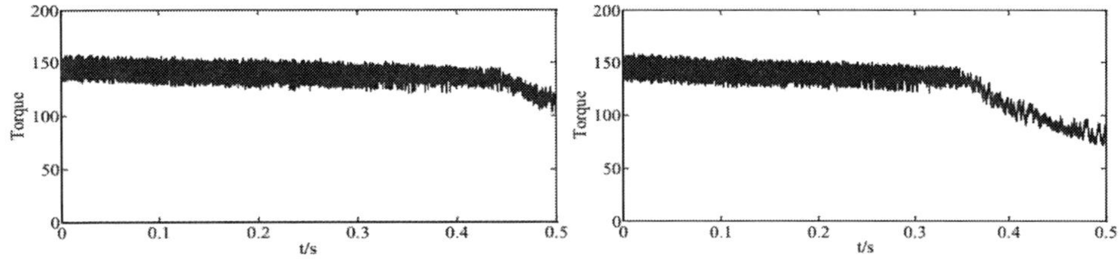

(a) MTPA Control (b) i_d=0 Control

Figure. 4 Torque change curve

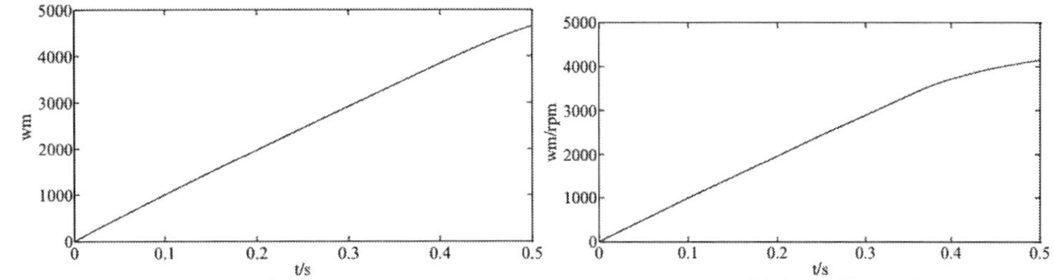

(a) MTPA Control (b) i_d=0 Control

Figure. 5 Rotary speed change curve

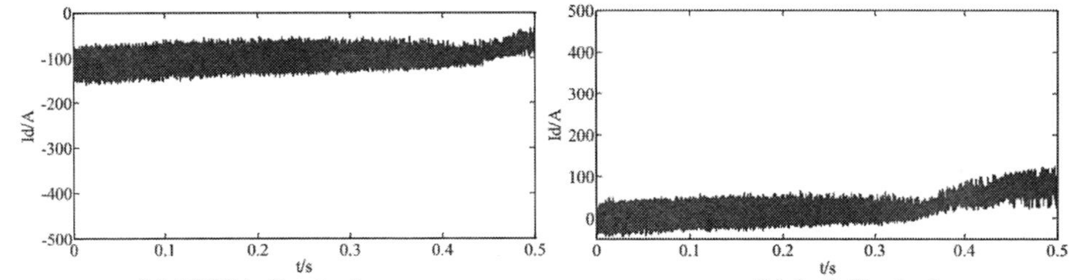

(a) MTPA Control (b) i_d=0 Control

Figure. 6 Direct-axis current change curve

 DOI: 10.1051/itmconf/20171109001

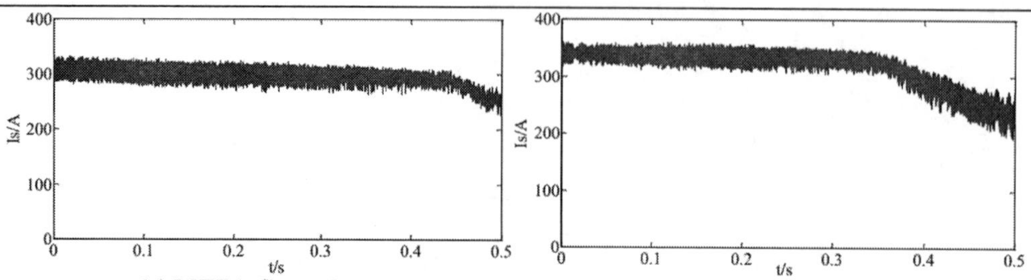

(a) MTPA Control **(b) i_d=0 Control**

Figure. 7 Stator current change curve

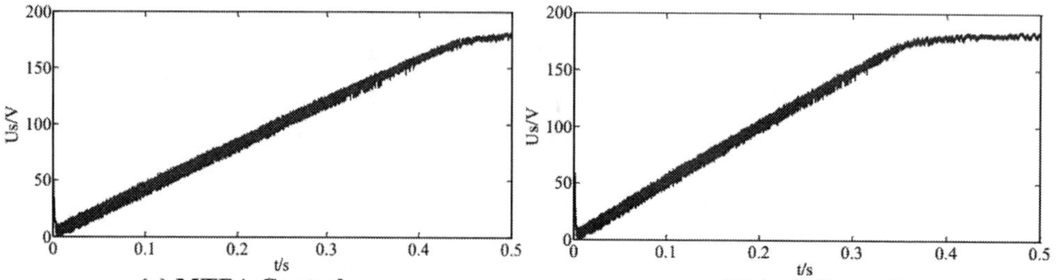

(a) MTPA Control **(b) i_d=0 Control**

Figure. 8 Stator voltage change curve

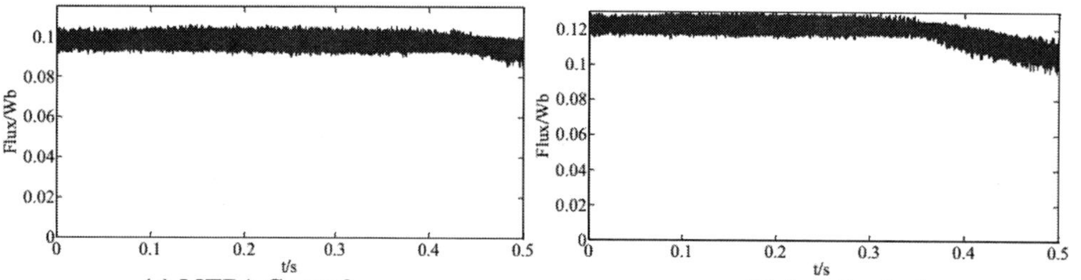

(a) MTPA Control **(b) i_d=0 Control**

Figure. 9 Flux-linkage change curve

According to the Figure. 4, in the event of the MTPA control, the motor maintains the output torque of 145Nm or so for about 0.45s before the automatic field weakening link; In the event of the id=0 control, the motor's output torque maintains for about 0.35s before the drop. Therefore, the MTPA may provide the expected output torque for a longer period of time when a similar torque is expected. According to the Figure. 5, in the event of the MTPA control, the motor will have the rotary speed of up to 4,500rpm at 0.45s, while in the event of the id=0 control, it will have the speed of no more than 3,500rpm at 0.35s. Therefore, the MTPA control may provide a higher turning speed when a similar torque is expected. According to the Figure. 6, in the event of the MTPA control, the direct-axis current Id will remain at the -100A or so with the existing reluctance torque. But in the event of the i_d=0 control, the direct-axis current I_d will be zero without the reluctance torque. According to the Figure. 7, in the event of the similar expected output torque T_e of 145Nm, the stator current of 300A is required for the MTPA control and the stator current of 350A for the $i_d=0$ control to show decrease of the current by 14.3%. Therefore, the MTPA control may improve the current utilization. The stator voltage change curve (see Figure. 8) indicates whether or not the stator has the maximum voltage to identify if the stator enters the field weakening control phase. According to the Figure. 9, the stator has the flux-linkages of 0.1Wb and 0.12Wb for the MTPA control and the id=0control respectively. Therefore, the MTPA is actually also the field weakening control, but the flux-linkage remains unchanged in the MTPA control phase (i.e. constant flux-linkage field weakening control).

4.2 Simulated field weakening control of the PMSM operating at the full-speed range

By applying the load force model in the field weakening control model for the PMSM, the expected torque of 100Nm is taken for the simulations as shown in Figure. 10~Figure. 15. Considering the selected expected torque of greater than TJ, the PMSM operates in one region after another (namely, the maximum torque/current ratio operation region, the constant torque region II, the ordinary constant power field weakening region and the maximum output power control region). The quadrature/direct-axis current, the stator current, the flux-linkage and the output torque remain unchanged in the constant value with the slow power increase at the beginning of the PMSM operation at the maximum torque/current ratio; At t=0.5s, the direct-axis current begins to increase inversely and the PMSM transits from the maximum torque/current ratio operation region to the constant torque region II where the output torque remains constant with the continuous reverse increase of the direct-axis current and the stator current begins to increase from the constant value for the maximum torque/current ratio operation region with the continuous power increase; At t=0.7s, the stator current becomes the highest; the PMSM transits from the constant torque region II to the ordinary constant torque field weakening region with the continued reverse increase of the direct-axis current; and the motor's output torque begins to drop with the absolute value of the direct-axis current remaining unchanged; At t=1s, the PMSM transits from the ordinary constant torque field weakening region to the maximum output power control region with decrease of the direct-axis current in the absolute value, drop of the stator current and power from the constant values and continuous reduction of the output torque until the PMSM tends to have the stable operation when the output torque is equivalent to the load torque at t=1.5s. According to the Figure. 12 and the Figure. 14, during the operation simulation, the motor has the continuous increase of the rotary speed to ensure the stability and balance, while the stator flux-linkage remains unchanged in the maximum torque/current ratio operation region and begins to decrease after entry into the constant torque region II until the motor has the stability and balance.

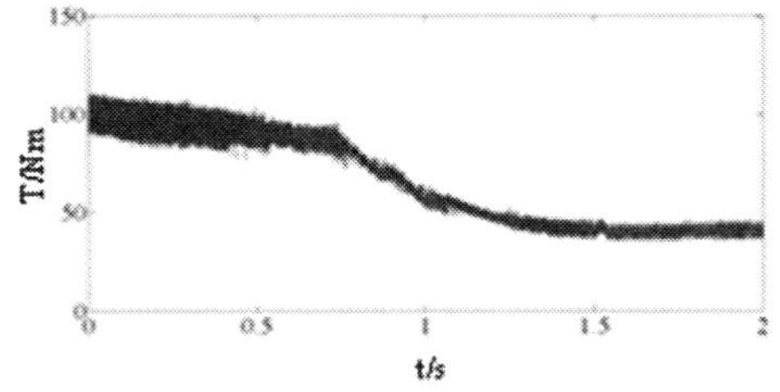

Figure. 10 Torque Change Curve

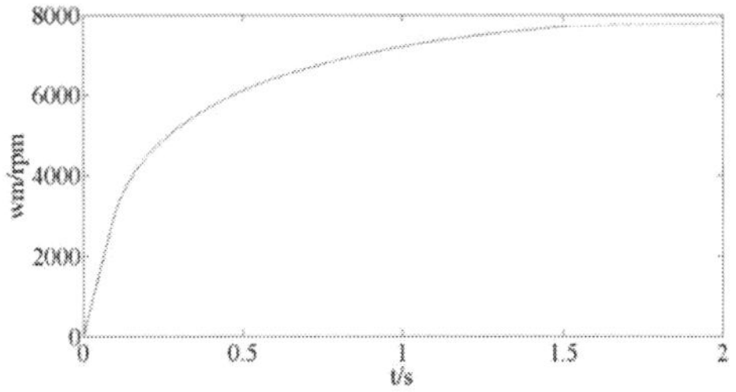

Figure. 11 Rotary Speed Change Curve

DOI: 10.1051/itmconf/20171109001

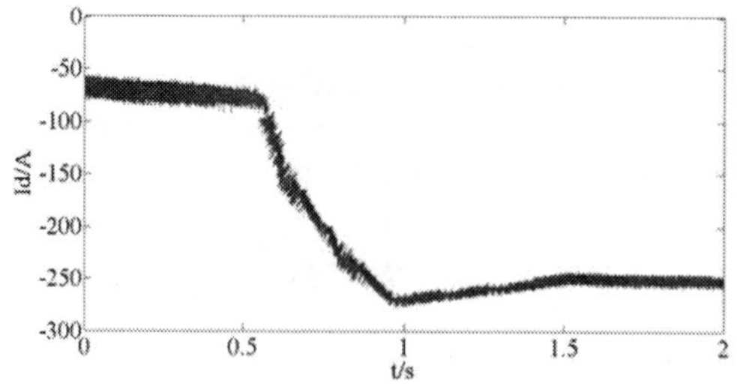

Figure. 12 Direct-axis Current Change Curve

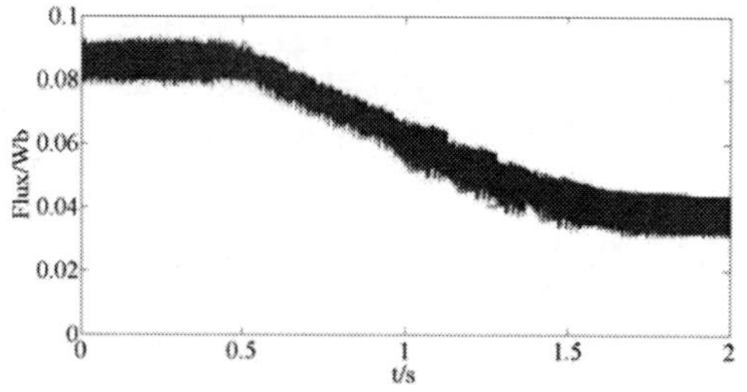

Figure. 13 Stator Flux-linkage Change Curve

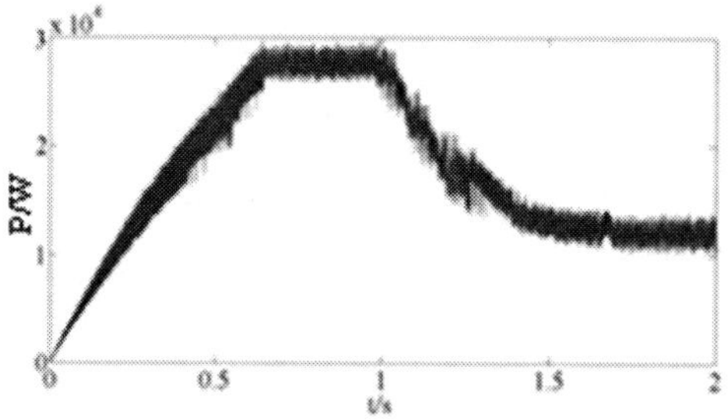

Figure. 14 Power Change Curve

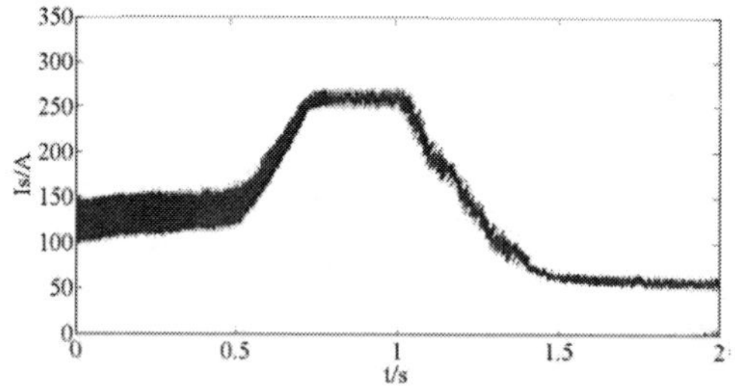

Figure. 15 Stator Current Change Curve

Conclusion

The paper studies the field weakening control strategy for the interior permanent magnet synchronous motor (IPMSM) and provides a field weakening control strategy for the IPMSM at the full-speed range. By studying the mathematical IPMSM model and the methods of conventional vector control and analyzing the operating conditions of the IPMSM at the full-speed range, the paper divides the operating conditions into constant torque operation region I, constant torque operation region II, constant power field weakening operation region and high-speed field weakening operation region to confirm the control strategy algorithm in each region and the transition conditions between regions and provide the current control strategy that the d-axis current and the q-axis current are confirmed by the reference torque and the feedback speed.

Acknowledgment

Funded by the National Natural Science Foundation of China (No.: 50975027).

References

1. Chen Qingquan, Sun Fengchun and Zhu Jiaguang, *Modern Electric Vehicle Technology* [M]. Beijing: Beijing Institute of Technology Press, 2002.
2. Sun Xudong and Wang Shanming, *Electromechanics*[M]. Beijing: Tsinghua University Press, 2006.
3. Dai Ying, Wang Lixin and Cui Shumei. *Review of the Permanent Magnet Synchronous Motor for Electrical Vehicles*[J], Micromotor, 2005, 38(3):84-86.
4. Wang Xiuhe, *Permanent Magnet Motor* [M]. Beijing: China Electric Power Press.
5. Guo Qingding, Sun Yibiao and Wang Limei, *Modem PMSM & AC-Servo System*[M]. Beijing: China Electric Power Press, 2006.
6. Wu Anshun, *The Newest Practice Speed Control System for AC Motor*[M]. Beijing: China Machine Press, 1998.
7. Zong Shiyong, *Hybrid Electric Vehicle Permanent magnet Synchronous Motor Vector Control*[D]. Hunan University: Control Science and Engineering, 2010.
8. Xu Yanliang, *Study of the PMSM for Electric Vehicles in Power Characteristics and Field Weakening Speed Expansion Capability* [J]. Transactions of China Electrotechnical Society, 2004, 6:58-62.
9. W. L. Soong, D. A. Staton, and T. J. E. Miller, Design of a new axiallylaminated interior permanent magnet motor [J]. IEEE Transactionson Industry Applications, vol. 31, pp. 358-367, 1995.
10. C. Deak, A. Binder, B. Funieru,.Extended field weakening and overloading of high-torque density permanent magnet motors[J],.in 2009 Energy Conversion Congress and Exposition, pp. 2347-2353, 2009.
11. S. Bolognani,S. Bolognani,L. Peretti.Combined speed and current model predictive control with inherent field-weakening features for PMSM drives[J].IEEE Electrotechnical conference, pp. 472-478, 2008.
12. Yasser Abdel-Rady Ibrahim Mohamed .Adaptive Self-Tuning MTPA Vector Controller for IPMSM Drive System[J] .IEEE TRANSACTIONS ON ENERGY CONVERSION, 2006,3:636-644.
13. ZHAI Li, DONG Shou-quan, SU Li-wei. Optimal DTC Strategy of PMSM in Electric Vehicle[C]. World Congress on Intelligent Control and Automation, 2012.7.6. to be pubulished.

ITM Web of Conferences **11**, 09002 (2017)
IST2017
DOI: 10.1051/itmconf/20171109002

Study on Automatic Solar Heat Insulated and Cooling Device of Car

Gui-Yue CHEN[1,a], Qi-Juan CHEN[2], Chang LIU[3] and Qi WANG[4]
[1,2,3,4]*School of Power and Mechanical Engineering, Wuhan University, Wuhan Hubei, China, 430072*

Abstract. In view of the common device for heat insulated and cooling of car, an improved new scheme which drove by solar energy is put forward. In this study, the transmission device are arranged inside the automobile, the thin-film solar is composited into the heat insulated and cooling material. Thus, the whole device can be driven by the energy from the photovoltaic conversion, which is clear and zero-pollution. The theoretical energy consumptions and preventable gas emissions are calculated to verify the environmental savings of the device. The results show that it has promising application prospect since it is not only environmentally friendly but also save and convenient as compared to the conventional device.

1 Introduction

In the case of serious shortage of parking spaces in China, the average annual growth rate of motor vehicles is still more than 15% [1-2].So that most of the private cars can often only be parked in the light of the sun. The test shows that temperature in car can be as high as 64.9□ after 15min at 32.5□ outdoor temperature.

Strong solar radiation will be harmful for the car's leather seats and dashboard as well as other facilities, produce formaldehyde, benzene and other harmful substances, accelerate the aging of components in the car, extremely easy to cause it to spontaneous combustion. There are great health and safety worries. In addition, with the increase of vehicle temperature and the time that the owner open the air conditioning to cooling before driving, the fuel consumption, carbon dioxide, PM2.5 and other harmful exhaust emissions has been increased. According to statistics, when the car is idling, the fuel consumption with the air conditioning opening is 15% higher than the normal. More than this, with the incomplete combustion of gasoline, the release of the CO, NO and other harmful gases reaches to 5 times as the normal state [3-4].Not only a waste of non-renewable energy, but also pollution of the atmospheric environment. Urban traffic pollution of China accounts for 70% to 90% of air pollution [5], and carbon dioxide emission ranks first in the world. Therefore, reducing carbon dioxide emission and gasoline consumption is a task which brooks no delay.

At present, the automotive insulated cooling devices on the market are mostly sucker sun block (plate), they have some disadvantages, such as manual arrangement, carrying inconvenient and not easy to fix. They do have some cooling effect, but it is poor, so that the frequency of use is not high. In addition, it is in 1978 that China used solar energy in the car for the first time, mainly about air conditioning and refrigeration technology [6-8].Thus, to provide simple and convenient vehicle

[a] Corresponding author: yue1020@whu.edu.cn

 DOI: 10.1051/itmconf/20171109002

insulation cooling device is in line with people's expectations and Chinese energy sustainable development goals.

On this basis, a new type of heat insulated and cooling device is presented in this paper. The transmissions and units are arranged in the vehicle body. After parking, the heat insulated device is automatically raised or lowered by the control circuit and the motor, and is fixed in the proper position. And the solar film and thermal insulation material are composited, to drive the entire device by the energy comes from photoelectric conversion. It can avoid the manual arrangement / removal of the sun shading device, which is convenient, and could achieve the energy saving and environmental protection.

2 Design

In order to reduce the occupancy of the interior space as much as possible, the device is arranged in the vehicle body of the front and rear window, to control its movements by the remote control. The control box is small, and placed on the instrument table. An intermediate sectional view of the mounting position of the integrated device is shown in Figure 1.

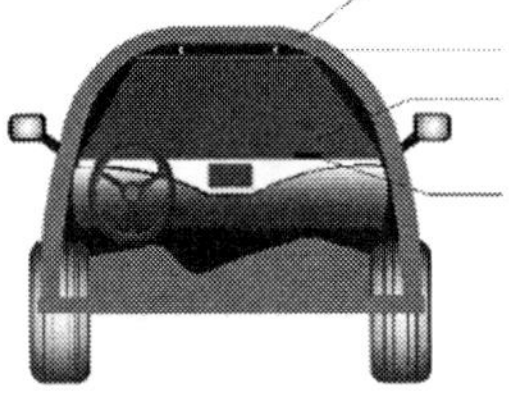

Figure 1. The intermediate sectional view of the mounting position of the device

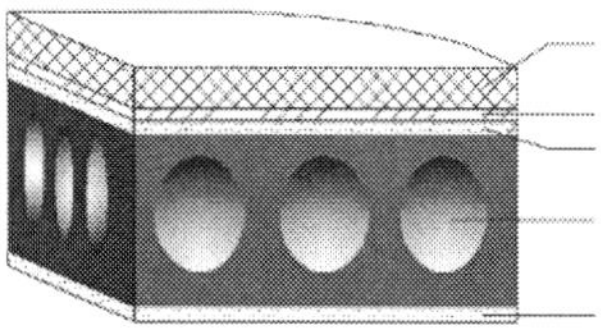

Figure 2. The schematic diagram of heat insulated and cooling and photoelectric conversion composite material

The material used in this project is composited by heat insulated and cooling material and photoelectric conversion material, the structure diagram shown in Figure 2.Dye-sensitized solar cell is used to achieve photoelectric conversion, which has the advantages of simple production process, stable performance, low cost and no pollution to the environment. Its development is very fast, researchers are constantly updating in materials, preparation techniques and basic research [9]. The current laboratory efficiency has exceeded 12%, and in standard light conditions, the highest photoelectric conversion rate can reach 11.18% [10-12].Insulation layer is a silver tape bubble diaphragm, in order to obtain a better heat insulation effect, the insulation layer adopts two layers of silver tape and the multiple bubbles separated form in the middle.

3 Theoretical calculation

3.1 Device selection

Taking into account the size of the space inside the vehicle and the energy consumption of the installation, the parameters of the motor and the battery are shown in Table 1.

Table 1. The parameters of the motor and the battery

Motor		Battery	
Type	DC	Voltage	12[*V*]
Rated power	120[*W*]	Model	6[*V*]4.5[*AH*]
Shaft diameter	8[*mm*]		
Outside diameter	9[*mm*]	Size	70×45×100[mm^3]
Axis length	30-50[*mm*]		
Voltage	DC 12[*V*]		
Rotating speed	12[*r/min*]	Net weight	0.65[*kg*]
Weight	460[*g*]		

3.2 Calculation of the energy consumption of the device and light time

Air quality can be derived from (1) type:

$$m=\frac{1}{cos(90-\theta)+0.50572(6.07995+\theta)^{-1.6364}} \tag{1}$$

Solar radiation flux is:

$$I_m=I_0y^m \tag{2}$$

In the formula, m is atmospheric quality; θ is the included angle between the incident light and the horizontal plane (θ=45°); I_0 is solar constant, and $I_0=1353W/m^2$; I_m is radiation flux of solar radiation through M atmospheric mass; y is atmospheric transparency. Under normal circumstances, the best sunny day desirable y=0.85, the good sunny day desirable y=0.80, the moderate sunny day desirable y=0.65, the poor sunny day desirable y=0.53 [13-15].This is calculated on a poor sunny day, take y=0.53. Substituting data can be obtained: m=1.4126, $I_m = 551.836\,W/m^2$.

The motor consumes energy is:

$$Q_1=2\times P_1\times t \tag{3}$$

The daily operating time of the motor is:

$$t=t_1\times N \tag{4}$$

The energy formula of dye-sensitized solar cell is:

$$Q_2=2\times\tau\times I_m\times\eta\times A\times t_2 \tag{5}$$

The energy formula of control box is:

$$Q_3=P_3\times t \tag{6}$$

By the law of conservation of energy we can see that the electricity energy of solar cells produced and consumed by the motor is equal, namely:

$$Q_1+Q_3=(1-\xi)Q_2 \tag{7}$$

In the formula, Q_1 is the energy consumed by the motor; Q_2 is the solar energy received by the dye-sensitized solar cell; t is the daily operating time of the motor; P_1 is the power of the motor; t_1 is the time of the motor lift and down once; Nis the number of movements within a day (take 4 times); A is the area of the dye-sensitized solar cells; η is the conversion efficiency of dye-sensitized solar cell, taking into account the conversion efficiency is difficult to achieve the highest in the practical application, here take 8%; τ is the automotive glass transmission rate; ξ is the loss of energy in the circuit (take ξ=0.2); Q_3 is the energy consumed by the control box; P_3 is the power of the control box (work for 30W, standby power is negligible); t_2 is the time of exposure of the dye-sensitized solar cell.

Taking t_1=20s, in accordance with the provisions of the State Ministry of Public Security traffic safety regulations, the transmittance of the front windshield must be greater than 70%. Therefore, taking τ=0.7 here. Dye-sensitized solar cell parameters: Radiation flux: $I_m = 551.836\,W/m^2$, Area: $A=100\times50=5000cm^2=0.5m^2$, it can be considered that the time of exposure of the dye-sensitized solar cell $t_2=777.842s\approx13min$.

From the above calculation can be seen, in the case of poor sunny days and moderate latitudes of 45°, it is need 13mins for sun exposure to meet the energy consumption of the device every day. If there is more sunny weather and lower latitudes, the time required will be less.

3.3 Device lift control

(1) The use of electronic controller to achieve the motor start and stop, forward and reverse

The circuit is controlled by the remote control device. When the controller emits a signal "L", the motor rotates forward and the heat insulated cooling device rises. After reaching the specified position, touching the limit switch SQ_1, cutting off the power supply, stopping the tubular motor, and limit the mechanical limit device on the tubular motor. On the contrary, when the controller emits a signal "down", the motor reverses and the heat insulated cooling device down. After reaching the specified position, touching the limit switch SQ_2, cutting off the power supply, stopping the tubular motor, and limit the mechanical limit device on the tubular motor. Control circuit ladder as shown in Figure 3.

(2) The use of remote control to achieve remote control

When touching the electric switch "on", at the same time trigger the electronic lock control circuit "open" and the electronic controller circuit "down", through the transmitter to send signals to achieve lock car at the same time the heat insulated cooling device automatically rising. Similarly, when touching the electric switch "lock", at the same time trigger the electronic lock control circuit "lock" and the electronic controller circuit "L", through the transmitter to send signals to achieve lock car while the heat insulated cooling device automatically rises. The schematic diagram shown in Figure 4.

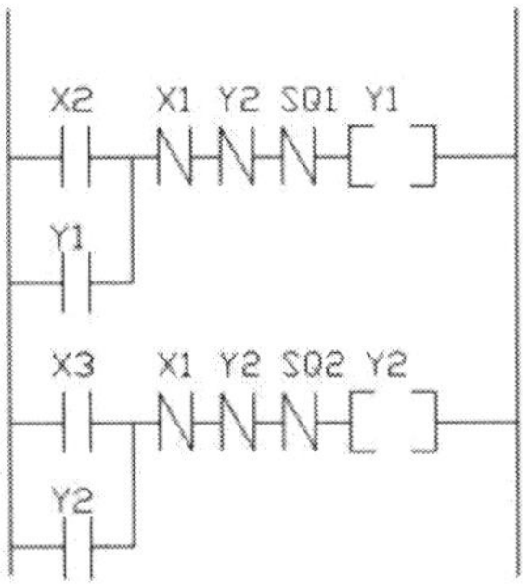

Fig. 3. Control circuit ladder

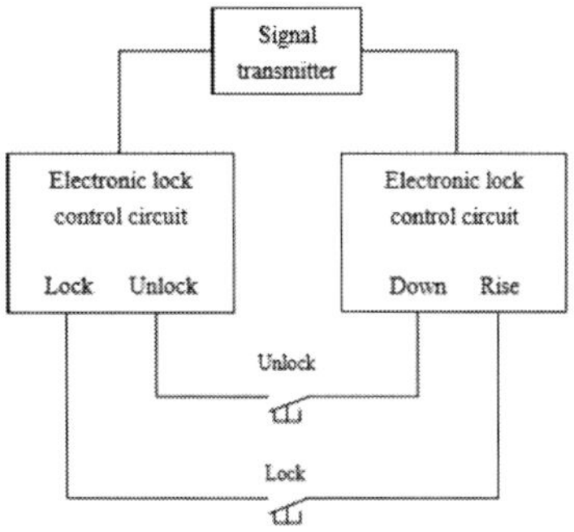

Fig. 4. The schematic diagram of remote control principle

 DOI: 10.1051/itmconf/20171109002

4 Test and analysis

4.1 Test program and effect

In order to estimate the time when the vehicle temperature dropped to 28°C in the absence of a sun shading device, the following tests were conducted in comparison with the case of a car with a shading device. Using two cars of the same color, displacement (both are 1.6L) and models as the object of this experiment. One installed the heat insulated and cooling device, and the other with a "naked sun". Before the test, the temperature inside the two cars was controlled at 28°C, and then exposed the two vehicles at the same time. The test of the warming-up phase began at 2 pm and ended at 3:15 pm, took place every 15 minutes to measure the outside air temperature and the inside air temperature. The measurement results are shown in Table 2.

Table 2. The change of the temperature inside the car

Time	outside air temperature[°C]	inside air temperature[°C]	
		With the device	Without the device
14:00	32.0	28.0	28.0
14:15	34.0	35.1	38.1
14:30	33.0	37.3	40.3
14:45	32.8	38.5	42.2
15:00	32.0	39.4	43.5
15:15	32.0	40.2	44.0

After rising the inside air temperature, cooling two cars immediately. According to the measurement, it required for 12 minutes and 03 seconds to cool the vehicle temperature down to the initial 28°Cof the car which was without the heat insulated cooling device by air conditioning, but it took only 7 minutes and 33 seconds for the car which was install the insulated cooling device. The use of insulated cooling device can reduce the air conditioning cooling time of 4 minutes and 30 seconds.

4.2 Vehicle Emissions Analysis

4.2.1 Automobile fuel consumption calculation

For the car with a displacement of 1.6L, idle fuel consumption when open air conditioning is 1.12L / h. Then the per minute fuel consumption of the parking idling state of the open air-conditioning is:

$$1.12L \div 60min \approx 0.0187\,L/min \tag{8}$$

Check the density of gasoline is 0.725kg/L. Then the consumption of gasoline quality of the car which is in the idle state of parking and taking more 4 minutes and 30 seconds to open the air conditioning is:

$$0.0187\,L/min \times 0.725\,kg/L \times 4.50min \approx 0.0610kg \tag{9}$$

4.2.2 Calculation of Carbon Emissions

The exhaust emissions of automobile engine cylinder accounted for about 65% of vehicle exhaust emissions [16]. According to the potential emission coefficient of CO_2 and the average low calorific value of fuel, the amount of CO_2 produced by fuel combustion can be calculated:

(1) The basic data

According to the data of the National Development and Reform Commission of the People's Republic of China Energy Information Dissemination Center released, the potential emission coefficient and the average low calorific value of CO_2 are shown in Table 3 [17].

Table 3. The potential emission coefficient and the average low calorific value of CO_2

Fuel type	the potential emission coefficient of $CO_2[kg/GJ]$	Energy name	the average low calorific value$[kJ/kg]$
gasoline	69.363	gasoline	43124
Diesel	74.024	Diesel	42705
natural gas	56.224	natural gas	35588

(2) The amount of CO_2 is calculated as follows:

$$m_{CO_2}=m_f Q_l k \tag{10}$$

In the formula, m_{CO_2} is the mass of CO_2 that produced by fuel combustion (kg); m_f is the quality of fuel consumption (kg); Q_l is the average low calorific value of fuel (kJ/kg); k is the potential emission coefficient of CO_2 (kg/GJ). After calculation, the quality of $CO_2(m_{CO_2})$ that produced by 1kg of gasoline combustion is 2.99kg. Then the mass of CO_2 that produces in the idle state of parking and taking more 4 minutes and 30 seconds to open the air conditioning is:

$$2.99\times 0.0610=0.1824(kg) \tag{11}$$

In the state of normal temperature and pressure, the density of CO_2 is 1.429g/L, then the volume of CO_2 that produces in the idle state of parking and taking more 4 minutes and 30 seconds to open the air conditioning is:

$$0.1824\times 10^3\div 1.429=127.642(L)\approx 0.128(m^3) \tag{12}$$

4.2.3 The amount of harmful gas produced by the automobile under different conditions

The amount of harmful gas produced by vehicles under different conditions is shown in Table 4.

Table 4. The amount of harmful gas produced by vehicles under different conditions

Vehicle type	Operating condition	Harmful gas emissions	
		$CO[\%]$	$HC[mg/L]$
Gasoline vehicles	Idle	4.0~10	300~2000
	Speedup 0~40$[km/h]$	0.7~5.0	300~600
	Uniform speed40$[km/h]$	0.5~4.0	200~400

For a car with the displacement of 1.6L (to four-cylinder machine, for example), taking the median CO emissions, a known: $\phi_{idle}=7\%$, $\phi_{speedup}=2.85\%$, $\phi_{uniform\ speed}=2.25\%$ (Since the proportion of HC is too small, it is ignored here). According to the calculation formula of CO emissions:

$$V_n=V\times f\times t\times\varphi_n \tag{13}$$

Then in the idle state, the engine speed of the car is about 600-1000 r/min, here take 800 r/min, the emission amount of CO is:

$$V_{idle}=1.6\times\frac{800}{60\times2}\times270\times7\%\approx0.202(m^3) \quad (14)$$

When speed of the car is up to 40 km/h, because of its engine speed rising, in order to make calculation convenient, here take the middle value of 1000 r / min, then the emission amount of CO in the accelerated state is:

$$V_{speedup}=1.6\times\frac{1000}{60\times2}\times270\times2.85\%\approx0.103(m^3) \quad (15)$$

When the car runs with a constant speed of 40km/h, the engine speed is about 1300r/min, the emission amount of CO is:

$$V_{uniform\ speed}=1.6\times\frac{1300}{60\times2}\times270\times2.25\%\approx0.105(m^3) \quad (16)$$

It can be seen that the emission of CO and HC is 1.96 times as fast as that of accelerating motion and 1.92 times of isokinetic velocity when the vehicle is running at idle. But in the crowded areas and traffic, exhaust emissions of pollutants accounted for about 40% of PM2.5. Moreover, in the idle state of operation, the resulting CO is 1.58 times of CO_2, indicating that in this state, the gasoline is not completely burned serious. The automobile exhaust is harmful to human health, it can cause eye irritation, tearing, headache, sore throat, cough, asthma, difficulty in breathing and other symptoms [18]. Therefore, it is particularly important to reduce vehicle exhaust emissions.

Conclusion

This study promotes a heat insulated and cooling device from install manually to lift and fall automatically with the open and close state of the car electric lock, which is more convenient and flexible. Meanwhile, the device use the environmental solar power as the energy source, which will not produce additional energy consumption. Theoretically, only 13 minutes of sunlight exposure can satisfy the energy requirement for a whole day. Thus, extra power from gas and vehicle exhaust emission can be both reduced, which confirms to the national energy conservation and emission reduction policy. Additionally, the device is set inside the automobile without obstructing the divers' sight, which is favor of diving safety. Based on the benefits listed above, this device is promising. In the future production process, the automobile makers can install these for cars before delivery to improve the performance and make them more impressive.

References

1. J. X. Wang. People's Public Transportation. **01**, 15-18 (2001).
2. F. C. Han, J. S. Wang. Journal of People's Public Security University of China (Science and Technology). **02**, 89-92 (2006).
3. Y. P. Wang, G. C. Jiao, B. C. Zou. Forest Engineering. **06**, 29-30 (1999).
4. Z. C. Xu. Anhui Agricultural Science Bulletin. **06**,100-101 (2008).
5. Q. Y. Yang, S. Y. Chen, Wang Zhengbin. Sichuan Environment. **01**, 84-87 (2004).
6. H. Meng, Y. J. Chen. Forum on Science and Technology in China. **05**, 96-101 (2009).
7. Z. Q. Yin, X. J. Meng. Acta Energiae Solaris Sinica. **05**, 575-588 (2003).
8. Y. F. Zhao, J. Wan, Z. P. Zhu, etc. Tractor & Farm Transporter. **05**, 16-19+24 (2011).
9. O' Regan Brian C, Grätzel Michael. Nature. **353(6346)**, 737-738 (1991).
10. A. Yella, H. W. Lee, Grätzel Michael, et al. Science. **344(6060)**, 629-633 (2011).
11. F. T. Kong, S. Y. Dai. Progress in Chemistry. **11**, 1409-1424 (2006).
12. X. Q. Fang, J. Zhang, Ding Yong, etc. Acta Energiae Solaris Sinica. **12**, 2222-2227 (2013).
13. B. Z. Wang, G. T. Pan. Acta Energiae Solaris Sinica. **01**, 13-22(1981).
14. X. J. Fang, Weng Duming. Acta Geographica Sinica. **01**, 52-59 (1988).

15. H. J. Li, C. Q. Zhu. Acta Energiae Solaris Sinica. **01**, 105-112(1983).
16. D. X. Shen, H. D. Chen, Q. Tian. Chinese Journal of Environmental Engineering. **06**, 24-34 (1997).
17. G. H. Wu. Theory Journal. **03**, 61-65 (2012).
18. Y. B. Cheng, Y. L. Jin, Y. C. Liu. Journal of Hygiene Research. **05**, 504-507 (2003).

Design of Logistics Route Planning for Printing Enterprises Based on Baidu Map

Zhong-Yue DA[1, a], Wen-Jie YANG[1],Pei-Pei RAN[1],Xing-Gen QIAN[1], Shuai SHAO[1], Shun PAN[1], Bing-Jie SHI[1],Yan LI[1],Rui-Li HE[1] and Yong-Hao XIAO[1]

[1]*School of printing and packaging engineering, Beijing Institute of Graphic Communication, Beijing, China*

Abstract. As traditional printing industry is facing fierce competition in the market and logistics becomes a new sources of growth, the traditional printing enterprises want to build and improve their logistics system. So in this paper, the author has designed the logistics planning system based on the Baidu map development kit. It has the function of route planning and location tracking. This system meet the printing enterprise logistics route planning and tracking demand.

1 Background

1.1 Industry background

The production of small and medium-sized printing enterprises is based on orders, so they are in a passive position in supply and demand [1]. Most enterprises are faced with high delivery requirements. Therefore, from the perspective of the enterprise logistics, it is the key of the survival and development of enterprises to realize the control of logistics cost and the more efficient management of logistics. Small and medium-sized printing enterprises need to use advanced management ideas and tools to help reduce costs, improve market response speed. In this paper, our aim is to design a route planning software for printing enterprise logistics.

1.2 Android platform background

Android occupies the largest mobile terminal operating system market. The open source and free features make it become the priority of the operating system for major mobile phone manufacturers [2]. Besides, it is easy for developers to operate and develop.

1.3 Baidu Map SDK

Baidu maps SDK is an application program interface. Developers can call the SDK interface, access to Baidu maps services and build a feature rich, interactive system [3]. The Baidu maps version we use in this paper is V4.0.0, which is based on Android.

[a] Corresponding author: dazhongyue@qq.com

2 System design

2.1 Technology platform

Owing to the advantages of Android, we choose Android as mobile terminal system. The tools that we need are Android studio and MyEclipse, first of which is a good use of Android development tools and last of which is a server development platform. Test environment is the Android device and Window system of the computer. The development tools are shown in Table 1.

Table 1. Development environment

Demand name	Platform and tools
Hardware platform	Android equipment + Computer
Development tool	MyEclipse + Android Studio
Development language	Java
Compile environment	Win7+JDK
Testing environment	Android
Database	MySQL
Software development kit	Baidu Map Android SDK

2.2 Requirement analysis

In order to find new revenue growth opportunities, the management of printing enterprises hope to improve profits through information management technology. However, their logistics is independent of the information management system. So printing enterprise manager want to have a logistics software which is able to compatible with the information management system. Specific requirements are as follows.

1. This software has route query based on mobile terminal.
2. Company management can know the location location at any time.
3. The path to the client should be recorded in the form of the start and end location.
4. The software should be extensible and compatible with other systems.

2.3 Design

2.3.1 Framework design

As Figure 1 shown, the whole system is composed of three parts, including Baidu Map Service Center, Mobile terminal and company server. The first part is provided by Baidu Maps API. In the following, we mainly discuss the latter two parts.

Baidu maps service provides route information. Mobile terminal is mainly composed of smart phones and mobile software. It provides man-machine interface and route planning function, while the server is mainly to complete the mobile location tracking and information recording function. Mobile terminal is the most important part of the whole system. So this paper focuses on the development of Android terminal.

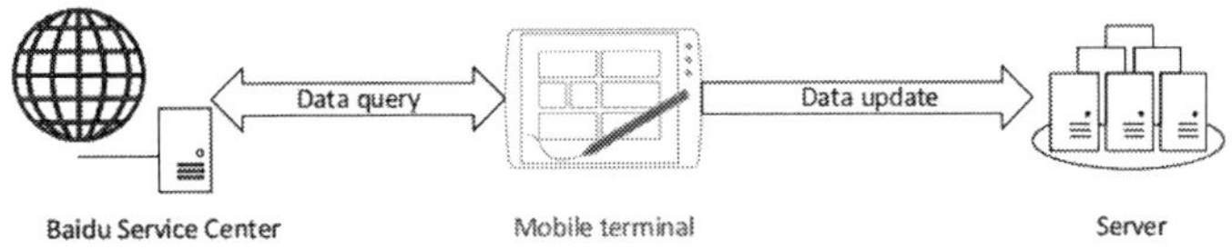

Figure. 1 System framework

2.3.2 Mobile terminal design

From the functional analysis, the client is divided into user login, route query, location coordinates query and upload the current information. The route query and coordinate location query are directly related to the efficiency of the client's distribution. So these functions are completed in the mobile terminal.

According to functional analysis, we divide the mobile terminal into three layers, which are business logic layer, presentation layer and data layer. We not only need to implement the interactive interface, but also to achieve business inquiries and monitoring.

The overall flow chart is shown in Figure two. After landing their account, the user can begin to search route and select the delivery route. In addition, according to needs, the user can choose the location model.

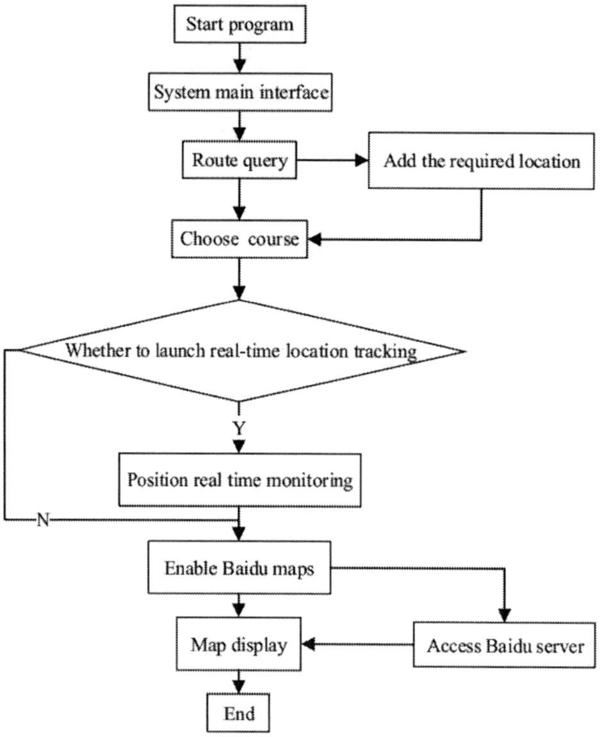

Figure. 2 Overall client flow chart

2.3.3 Server Design

Database is the most important part of server. Therefore design of database structure should be completed before server-side programming. The database is not only the support of the system, but also the support of management. The design of database model is the design server model.

According to the demand analysis, this paper designed user, route line two table. Table User is a table to record user information, including account number, password. Table route includes the starting location, the end location, and the distance of the route.

 DOI: 10.1051/itmconf/20171110001

Table 2. Table Route

Route properties	Data type	Meaning	Data sources
User	VARCHAR(128)	User name	User ID
Start	VARCHAR(128)	Starting position	Mobile terminal input
End	VARCHAR(128)	Destination	Mobile terminal input
Distance	INT(11)	Route length	Baidu map server
Flag	VARCHAR(128)	Logistics type	Mobile terminal
Datetime	DATATIME	Recording time	System

3 System implementation

3.1 Client implementation

The design of mobile terminal presentation layer is the interface design of software. The interface of the mobile terminal is mainly composed of the controls provided by Android and the map controls provided by Baidu Map SDK. We use dialog boxes and text boxes and other controls to ensure the simplification of the operation. Business logic layer is activity on Android platform. They implement logic operations and call Baidu maps API and data operation.

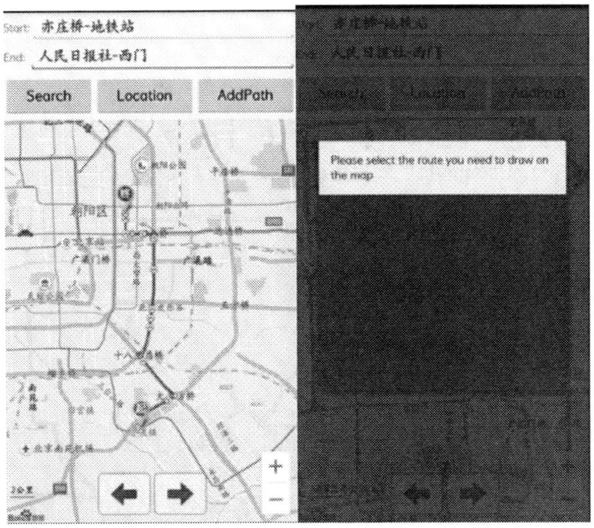

Figure 3. Route plan (left) and Results of the route (right)

The core meaning of the mobile terminal is to complete the route guidance. So we add the location function in the mobile terminal. As shown in Figure 3 and figure 4, the client can complete the basic route query, selection and navigation functions. On the route selection interface, it show the length of the route and the number of traffic lights. It help users choose a better route. In addition, we also add keyword recommendation function, which improve the accuracy of the input address.

Figure 4. Add locations (left) and results (right)

3.2 Server side implementation

The server is designed as two layers, which are business logic layer and data access layer. So, server is mainly data storage and data operation. When the mobile terminal is enabled, the server get the information of the mobile terminal in real time, including the location information and route selection information.

The administrator can understand the situation from the server in real time, and the design and implementation of the server can be merged into the information management system.

Conclusion

In this paper, we achieve the logistics planning and real-time location tracking by using the Baidu map SDK technology and the corresponding database technology. Mobile terminal map technology improves improve the timeliness and accuracy of logistics distribution. This design has certain significance for printing enterprises to excavate "the third profit source". However, the server administrator can not directly catch sight of the client position. Next, we will improve the server side and establish the relationship between logistics and inventory.

Acknowledgments

The study is supported by the 'Development and application of micron level vision quality detector (2013YQ140517)'.

References

1. ZH Tao, *The design and application of Logistics Oriented Management Information System for small and medium sized enterprises of printing*, University of Electronic Science and Technology (2008)
2. ZY Da, *Design of Query Software for Printing Enterprise Based On Android Platform* (2016)
3. ML Shi, *Based on Baidu maps Android application to build. Technology Research and Development*, 34-38 (2014)

4. SL Liu, *SZ printing company in the application of ERP demand analysis and process optimization*, Shandong University (2012)
5. Baidu maps SDK V 4.0.0[EB/OL]. http://lbsyun.baidu.com/index.php?title=androidsdk.
6. GG Sun, *Analysis and design of city logistics distribution system based on GIS*. North China Electric Power University (2013)
7. YP Chen, *Promotion of the Value Creating Capacity of Agricultural Products Logistics Industry from the Perspective of Resource Development.* Journal of Contemporary Finance and Economics, 99-112(2015)
8. Kenneth C. Laudon, Jane P. Laudon, *Management Information Systems* (13th Edition, 2016)
9. XY Shu, *Design of mobile web map service based on Android platform,* DMU (2009)
10. ZY Xia, *Logistics management of printing enterprises*, Print Today(2005: 65-66)

Efficient Data Integrity Verification Using CRC Based on HDFS in Cloud Storage

Yun-Hao XIA[1], Han-Shu HONG[1], Guo-Feng LIN[1] and Zhi-Xin SUN[1,a]

[1]*School of Internet of Things, Nanjing University of Posts and Telecommunications, Nanjing, China*

Abstract. Data integrity verification is becoming a major challenge in cloud storage which can't be ignored. This paper proposes an optimized variant of CRC (Checker Redundancy Cyclic) verification algorithm based on HDFS to improve the efficiency of data integrity verification in cloud storage through the research of CRC checksum algorithm and data integrity verification mechanism of HDFS. A new method is formulated to establish the deformational optimization and to accelerate the algorithm by researching characteristics of generating and checking the algorithm. Moreover, this method optimizes the code to improve the computational efficiency according to data integrity verification mechanism of HDFS. A data integrity verification system based on Hadoop is designed to verify proposed method. Experimental results demonstrate that proposed HDFS based CRC algorithm was able to improve the calculation efficiency and the utilization of system resource on the whole and outperformed well compared to existing models in terms of accuracy and time.

1 Introduction

With the rapid development of the big data era, data volumes are exploding grow, resulting in higher storage costs simultaneously with increasing the difficulty of data storage management. Cloud storage [1] serves as a kind of "infrastructure as a service" form of expression, which can provide a high performance. low cost. easy management and virtualization storage scheme. With the development of cloud storage technology [2] and the improvement of network bandwidth and reliability, more and more users can store data in the cloud server. However, the problem of data security [3] is still a major problem in cloud storage which can't be ignored. On the one hand, the security problem caused by data leakage; on the other, the data integrity problems caused by cloud service providers themselves. Data security can be guaranteed by the data encryption technology [4], and data integrity is verified by the verification algorithm [5].

Data integrity verification [6, 7] ensures that the acquired data is consistent with the previously saved data. It uses a specific algorithm to calculate the original data and gets a calibration value. At the same time the receiver uses the same algorithm to calculate once again. If the two check value is the same, the data is complete. Data integrity verification is generally used as the underlying, background or built-in module, and the most common three data integrity verification algorithms are CRC, MD5 and SHA-1.

[a] Corresponding author: sunzx@njupt.edu.cn

At present, many companies have launched cloud storage platform and cloud services, most famous the Hadoop [8], which was greatly welcomed by the industry. Pig, ZooKeeper, HBase, Hive and HDFS [9] are derived from Hadoop. The distributed file system HDFS has its unique value and advantage, and it is the basis of system development of Yahoo, IBM and Amazon and other Large Firm system. In the distributed file system HDFS, DataNode of the file system stores the metadata for CRC verification, and the whole process of data verification ensures the integrity and security of the data in the transmission process. However, it also brings about a series of problems, such as frequent switching of JVM, system load imbalance, non-ideal speed of read and write, degradation of the performance of IO, et al, bringing great burden to data processing system.

This paper does some research in data integrity verification mechanism of HDFS, and puts forward optimization of CRC verification algorithm and verification method to improve the performance of the system. This paper proposes an optimized variant of CRC verification algorithm based on HDFS, as the underlying, background or built-in module in the cloud storage system. It avoids the loss of data caused by the potential damage by outsourcing if the enterprise or individual stores its own data into the cloud storage space of a cloud service provider. The second section of this paper will introduce the CRC-n algorithm in detail, and seek to improve the method, and analyze the operating mechanism of the distributed file system HDFS guaranteeing data integrity. The third section of this paper will exhaustively describe the optimization method based on the second section. In fourth section, effectiveness of the proposed optimization method is verified by the experimental test data of the prototype system, and the contents of the paper are summarized in the end.

2 Related works

Currently, there are many algorithms for verifying data integrity [10-12] in the storage system. A class of methods based on the homomorphic techniques [13] which generate and store a check element for each data block to realize unlimited time verification. However, this kind of methods have a defect in the range of data coverage in the face of large data file verification, because the calculation is related with modular arithmetic in finite fields, and it need to consume a large amount of computing resources. The other is based on the hash algorithm to determine whether the data is complete, Using MD5 [14], SHA-1[15], CRC and other one-way hash function to generate hash value to verify the consistency of the two data objects. This kind of algorithm is characterized by small computational overhead, but it usually only supports once request for verification. HDFS of Hadoop has been involved in CRC32 and MD5.

CRC-n [16] (Checker Redundancy Cyclic) is one of the most common error check codes in the field of digital data communication, mainly using linear encoding theory. In data sending end, according to m bit binary code information sequence BCISm, produce n bit check code, that is, CRC code BCISn by a certain rule (verification algorithm rules). BCISn is attached to the information sequence BCISm, and finally send out a new (m+n) binary code information sequence BCISm+n. At data receiving end, according to the rules of the algorithm between the code BCISm and CRC code BCISn, verify the integrity of file to confirm if there is an error in the transmission process. Different constants correspond to different CRC algorithms, and when this constant is 32, that is the CRC32.

CRC-n generator polynomial is

$$(Mx^n + N) \bmod G = 0$$

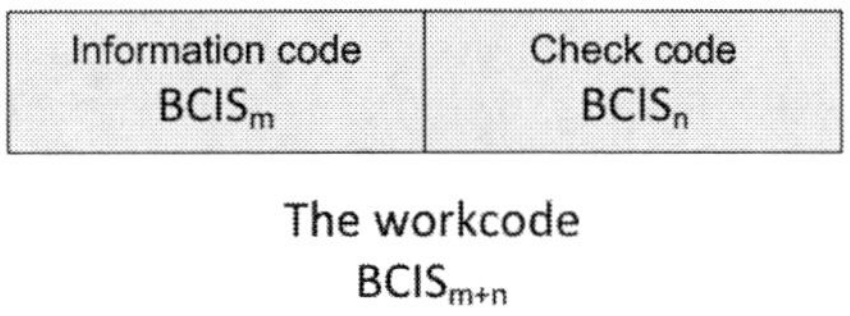

Figure 1. The binary code information sequence.

In the application of big data and high performance computing, the traditional CRC generation and inspection methods are faced with several problems. One problem is speed and another is data width. The size of the incoming bit stream in the execution process is different. An arbitrary number of invalid bits in the bit stream are required to be processed by the CRC calculation. The rate of CRC algorithm can be improved by hardware. However, due to the limited experimental conditions, coupled with the features that the low cost of cloud computing server to extend, we want to improve the verification efficiency by finding a variant of the CRC algorithm which seeks a suitable CRC-n algorithm and changes the number of bits checked and the size of the register during CRC calculation.

Kounavis and Berry [17] made some improvements in CRC algorithm of data integrity verification in cloud storage system. They improved CRC32 algorithm by seeking one single-bit table, and applied it in data processing platform Hadoop. The improvement was suitable for the data environment in that time and it has achieved some success. However, with the explosive growth of data and complex diversity of data types, the improvement that check 8 bits (a table) every time has been unable to meet the business needs of the current big data environment. In addition, HDFS need to switch JVM frequently in the data verification. Through the results of the experiments, the time of switching JVM accounted for 5/6 of the entire check time, bringing huge computational cost for data verification. Therefore, we need to further optimize the verification algorithm in facing with increasingly high performance computing applications demand.

Jing [18] presented a better optimization in the aspect of the method of seeking tables using CRC algorithm, and to a certain extent, it improved the efficiency of the algorithm. In this research, data integrity verification also optimized and improved CRC32 algorithm and used the method of seeking single-bit table, but the number of table increased, so that data integrity verification could verify more bits each time, hence improving the rate of data integrity verification. With the improvement of the hardware, memory expansion and the increase of bandwidth, at the same time CRC64 has a wider range of applications than CRC32 because the n of CRC-n is bigger, the algorithm is more reliable, there is room for further improvement of CRC-n data integrity verification.

Based on above-mentioned condition, this paper researches on data integrity verification technology in big data environment based on the open source cloud computing platform Hadoop, focusing on the problems existing in the optimization of the way to call checksum algorithm and the number of verified bits each time. This paper proposes a distributed file system verification model, optimizing verification algorithm and the way to call verification algorithm based on HDFS, in order to achieve the purpose of improving the system performance. This scheme not only ensures the high reliability of digital data in big data era, but also does not give the user and cloud server too heavy burden, while the process of verifying can protect privacy of user's data.

3 Improved CRC algorithm for data integrity verification

3.1 Problem description

Facing big data and high performance computing demand, there are a series of problems in data integrity verification in hadoop, such as frequent switching of JVM, system load imbalance, non-ideal speed of read and write, degradation of the performance of IO, et al,. For example, as shown in literature [13], nowadays in the HDFS, CRC32 verification algorithm was called by java.util.zip.CRC32 using Java Native Interface. Use the class java.util.zip to call the CRC32 function via the Java local interface (JNI). However, the efficiency of this method was low when it comes to calling the fine-grained file. If a file size is 100GB, the CRC32 value is only 800M, and does a CRC32 calculation each 512byte. During the process, it needs to switch the JVM frequently. The time of switching JVM will reach the entire verification time of 5/6. Thus, HDFS used the method of block storage strategy to improve the ability of system data backup and data fault tolerance, but also brought a huge computational cost.

3.2 Improved CRC algorithm

According to description in second section, this paper proposes a method of data integrity verification using CRC algorithm based on HDFS. In order to solve the problem of data integrity verification in current cloud storage, this paper researches system verification mechanism of hadoop, and makes efficiency optimization of the verification algorithm. Optimized method called CRC64_16_4 in the following paper can improve the verification efficiency of the distributed file system, raise system verification rate and ensure accuracy. The optimization in this paper is shown as follows: efficiency optimization variant of verification algorithm: choose more reliable CRC64 verification algorithm for reducing the impact of a collision and change the number of bits checked each time and the size of the register during CRC calculation; Optimize the code to solve a series of problems facing big data and high performance computing demand and improve the computational efficiency.

From the theoretical point of view, CRC could not complete reliably verify data integrity, because CRC polynomials are linear structures, and it is easy to reach CRC collisions by changing data. There is a more popular explanation, assuming a string with a CRC check code in the transmission, if a continuous error happens and when the number of error times reach a certain number, then almost certainly appear a collision(value is incorrect but the result of CRC is correct). However, with n of CRC-n increasing, the probability of collision will be significantly decreased. For example, CRC32 is more reliable than CRC16, and CRC64 is more reliable than CRC32.

Currently CRC32 verification algorithm used in Hadoop was calculated by checking tables. The number of tables was one and the method verified 8 bits each time by checking one table. However, this kind of method is not satisfied with computational requirements of big data nowadays. This paper will improve the verification efficiency by finding a variant of CRC algorithm which seeks a suitable CRC-n algorithm and changes the number of bits checked and the size of the register during CRC calculation. Put forward a new way to check tables: use CRC64 verification algorithm, check double-bite table, and provide four tables to check. Taking 16 as an incremental unit, 16 bit, 32 bit, 48 bit and 64 bit of verified data are calculated by XOR using CRC64 generating polynomial. Create (crc>>>16) ^T1, CRC (T4^T3^T2^T1). More bits of information field to be verified by checking fewer tables. The optimization accelerates the algorithm to guarantee and improve the verification rate. Considering the room which was used to store the tables, proposed method CRC64_16_4 would need more, but it has a very small impact on verification efficiency with storage devices nowadays, which could be seen in the following experiment. Calculation process of optimized variant of CRC-64 verification algorithm is shown in Figure 2.

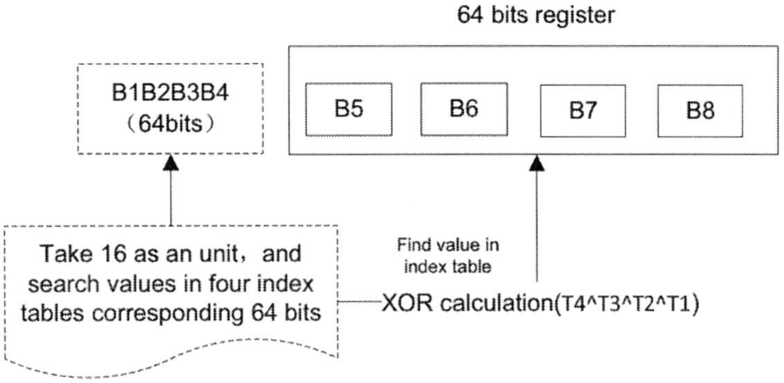

Figure 2. Calculation process of optimized CRC64.

In order to improve the work efficiency of verification, the quality of code must be improved combining with verification mechanism of HDFS. Therefore, quality of CRC64_16_4 code proposed in this paper was optimized to enhance the performance. Comparing with CRC algorithm called by

Sun Native and other optimized methods, proposed method used improved Java could enhance system efficiency.

4 System implementation and performance test

In our experiment, the data integrity verification system based on Hadoop was designed and realized. Hadoop version was 2.2.0, server configuration was apache-tomcat-7.0.42, operating system was CentOS-6.3-i386/Linux, Client was Chrome kernel browser, system architecture was B/S. The purpose of this system is to facilitate the user to manage cloud data and realize data integrity verification. The working process of system is shown in Figure 3.

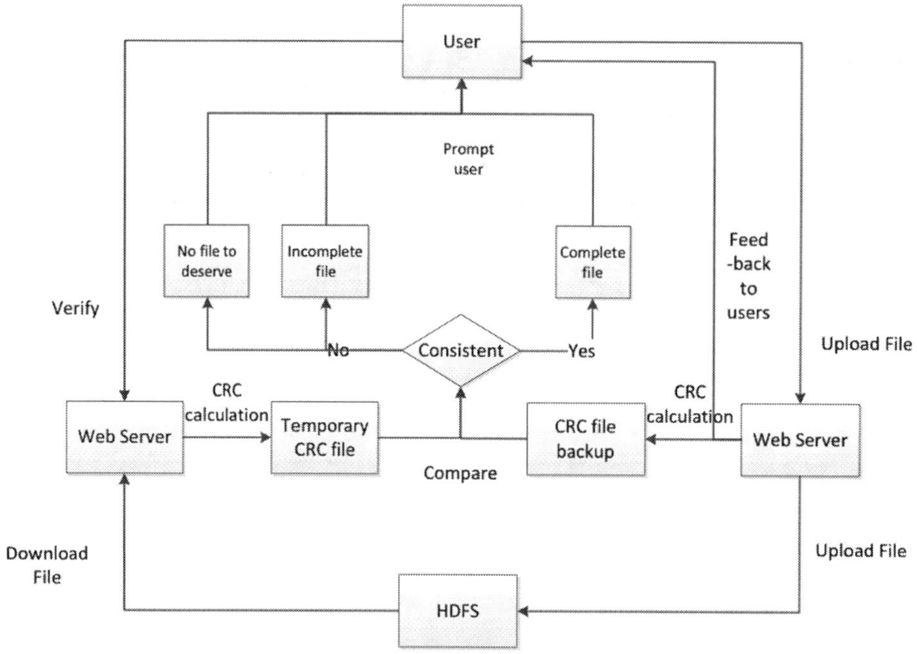

Figure 3. System architecture.

Possible outcomes of the system are as Table 1 shows.

Table 1. Possible outcomes of the system.

Results	Instructions	System states
Success	File is complete	Correct verification! Whether to download?
	File is incomplete	Verified file is incomplete! Please download carefully! Wrong location: the first 512 bytes
Failure	No CRC files to deserve	Could not find the corresponding CRC file on your server, and unable to identify the reliability of the file. If you upload this file, please download and verify it.

The objects of experiment were SunNative CRC32 of HDFS in the 2.2.0 version of hadoop, CRC32_8_8 checking eight single-byte tables and optimized CRC64_16_4 checking four double-byte tables. Experiments used JDK1.7, 64 bit, 3.10GHz machines for testing.

Verification process of the system is shown in Figure 4.

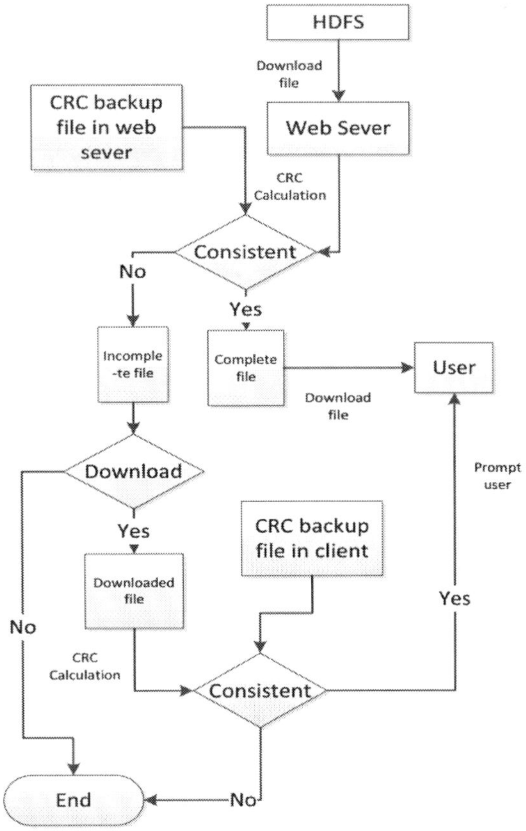

Figure 4. Verification process of the system.

In order to verify the correctness of the proposed method in this paper, choose a variety of different sizes of documents between 10M to 10G, and test them 2000 times in two cases that file error probability 1% and 0.5%. The results are shown in the following Table 2.

Table 2. Correctness of the proposed method.

Verification scheme	File error probability	Correct check probability	Success to report error	Error check probability	Fail to report error
Native CRC32	1%	99.9%	1998	0.1%	2
	0.5%	99.8%	1996	0.2%	4
CRC32_8_8	1%	99.95%	1999	0.05%	1
	0.5%	99.8%	1996	0.2%	4
CRC64_16_4	1%	100%	2000	0	0
	0.5%	99.95%	1999	0.05%	1

According to different chunk sizes in theory, CRC64_16_4 was faster than SunNative CRC32 and CRC32_8_8 vary between 1.2 and 8 times. But in practice, it will be affected by the network bandwidth or hardware. The performance of SunNative CRC32, CRC32_8_8 and CRC64_16_4 was compared. Experiments used JDK1.7, 64 bit, 3.10GHz machines for testing. The experimental results are shown in Figure 5.

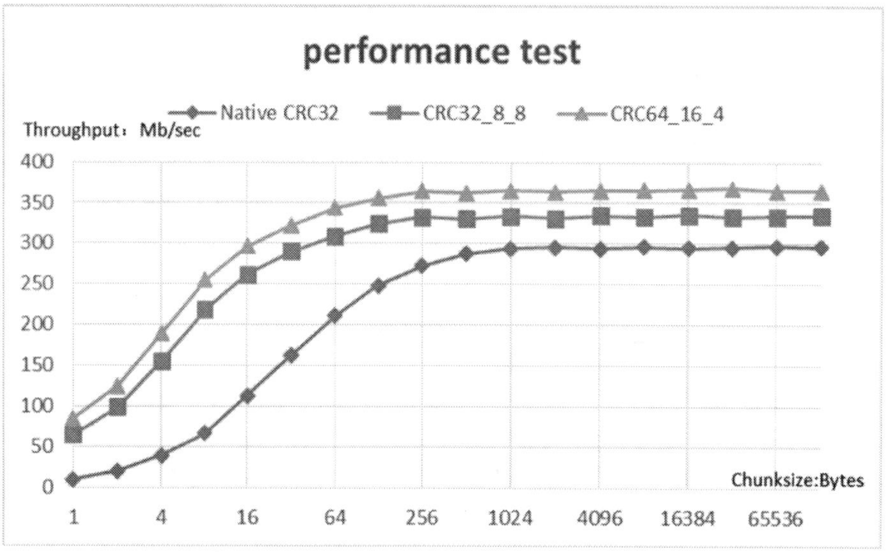

Figure 5. Comparison tests of three algorithms.

From the above, we can see that CRC64_16_4 has a significant effect on improving the throughput of the system. The difference between SunNative CRC32 and CRC64_16_4 was obvious, which means that SunNative wasted time in switching JVM and just verified 8 bits each time. The rate of CRC32_8_8 was limited because it verifies 64 bits each time but checking 8 tables, and there was room for improvement in the terms of the quality of code. CRC64_16_4 was optimized in two aspects, so that the experimental data show some advantages. But when chunksize reaches a certain number, the throughput will be affected by bandwidth, and it will not increase significantly.

The objects of our experiment were SunNative CRC32 of HDFS, CRC32_8_8 checking eight single-byte tables and optimized CRC64_16_4 checking four double-byte tables. Because the experimental data is greatly influenced by the hardware conditions, experimental data of proposed method fails to be compared directly with the experimental data in other literatures. But through the above experimental results, we can see the advantages of the proposed method in the theory and practical application.

Conclusion

This paper established CRC64 deformational optimization to improve verification reliability and provided a new method for checking table to accelerate the speed of the algorithm via researching characteristics of traditional algorithm CRC. At the same time this paper improves the quality of code by researching the defects of verification mechanism in hadoop and combining the features of CRC algorithm, in order to enhance verification efficiency. Those optimizations could guarantee and improve the verification rate on the whole, and thus could achieve the goal of improving system utilization.

In this paper, the verification mechanism of the distributed file system HDFS is optimized, and the efficiency of resource utilization is improved. But the system was still not perfect, and the network bandwidth has a certain impact on the data transmission. Nowadays along with the massive amounts of data and data types of diversification, computing requirements of big data become increasingly high. Higher requirements for data storage and data integrity verification are also presented. Based on this research direction, the author will continue to research and improve the data integrity verification technology, in order to achieve more efficient, more secure purposes.

Acknowledgement

This research is supported by the National Natural Science Foundation of China (NO.61373135, NO.61672299). The authors thank the sponsors for their support and the reviewers for helpful comments.

References

1. Dongju Yang, Chuan Ren. VCSS: An Integration Framework for Open Cloud Storage Services [J]. Services (SERVICES), 2014 IEEE World Congress on. June 27 2014-July 2 2014, Pages: 155-160
2. Machado G.S., Bocek T., Ammann M, Stiller B. A Cloud Storage overlay to aggregate heterogeneous Cloud services [J]. Local Computer Networks (LCN), 2013 IEEE 38th Conference on. 21-24 Oct 2013, Pages: 597-605
3. Pawar C.S., Patil P.R., Chaudhari S.V. Providing security and integrity for dta stored in cloud storage [J]. Information Communication and Embedded Systems (ICICES), 2014 International Conference on. 27-28 Feb 2014, Pages: 1-5
4. Arockiam L., Monikandan S. Efficient cloud storage confidentiality to ensure data security [J]. Computer Communication and Informatics (ICCCI), 2014 International Conference on. 3-5 Jan 2014, Pages: 1-5
5. Kavuri S.K.S.V.A., Kancherla G.R., Bobba B.R. Data authentication and integrity verification techniques for trustd/untrusted cloud servers [J]. Advanced in Computing Communications and Informatics (ICACCI), 2014 International Conference on. 24-27 Sept 2014, Pages: 2590-2596
6. Data verification_Baidu Encyclopedia [Z]. 2013
7. Chang Liu, Chi Yang, et al. External integrity verification for outsourced big data in cloud and IoT : A big picture [J], Future Generation Computer System, 2015, 49, Pages : 58-67.
8. White T. Hadoop: The definitive guide [M]. O, Reilly Media, 2012
9. Shvachko K, Kuang H, Radia S, et al. The hadoop distributed file system[C]. In: 2010. Pages: 1-10
10. Zhaoguang Peng, Yu Lu, Alice Miller, et al. Formal Specification and Quantitative Analysis of a Constellation of Navigation Satellites[J], Quality and Reliability Engineering International, 2016, 32(2), Pages : 345-361.
11. Yingjie Xia, Fubiao Xia, Xuejiao Liu, et al. An Improved Privacy Preserving Construction for Data Integrity Verification in Cloud Storage [J], KSII Transactions on Internet and Information Systems, 2014, 8(10), Pages : 3607-3623
12. Yu Lu, Zhaoguang Peng, Alice A. Miller, et al. How reliable is satellite navigation for aviation ?Checking availability properties with probabilistic verification [J]. Reliability Engineering & System Safety, 2015, 144, Pages : 95-116.
13. Khatri T.S., Jethava G.B. Improving dynamic data integrity verification in cloud computing [J]. Computing Communication and Networking Technologies (ICCCNT), 2013 Fourth International Conference on. 4-6 July 2013, Pages: 1-6
14. Danyang Cao, Bingru Yang. Design and implementation for MD5-based data integrity checking system [J]. Information Management and Engineering (ICIME), 2010 the 2nd IEEE International Conference on. 16-18 April 2010, Pages: 608-611
15. Matusiewicz K, Pieprzyk J. Finding good differential patterns for attacks on SHA-1[J]. Coding and Cryptography. 2006, Pages: 164-177
16. Peterson W.W., Brown D.T. Cyclic Codes for Error Detection [J]. Proceedings of the IRE. Jan 1961, Pages: 228-235
17. Kounavis M.E., Berry F.L. A systematic approach to building high performance software-based CRC generators[C]. In: 2005, Pages: 855-862
18. Rui Jing. Research and Improvement of Data Check Strategy in Distributed File System [D]. Jilin: Jilin University, 2013.

A Driving Violation Index Modelling Study at Intersections in Urban Precincts Using Big Data

Yan JIA[1,2,a], Da-lin QIAN[1] and Jin PU[2]

[1]*School of Traffic and Transportation, Beijing Jiaotong University, Beijing,100044, China*
[2]*Traffic Engineering and Technology Research Institute, Tianjin Public Security Traffic Management Bureau, Tianjin, 300040, China*

Abstract. Driving violations at intersections are profoundly prevalent in urban precinct in China. These violations, including failing to stop for a red traffic light or arrow, driving across single continuous dividing line, disobeying traffic lane markings, and illegal parking, have become a major issue not only impacting the overall safety of the cities, but also causing traffic delays and accidents. This article focuses on the behaviors of the driving violations at intersections, and investigates what the influencing factors and characteristics are. A model of Driving Violation Index (*DVI*) for these driving violations at intersections has been developed by utilizing the Big Data approach. Based on the actual traffic data from the intersections in the city of Tianjin, a relationship has been fitted and established between the driving violations and the influencing factors, and further yielded the model of calculating the related *DVI*. This research attempts to provide a mechanism to forecast the driving violations at intersections, and explore new strategies for managing the security and safety of the intersections.

1 Introduction

Road traffic crashes are a major public health concern particularly in developing countries. With the recent economic boom in China, vehicle volume and the number of traffic accident fatalities have become the highest in the world. Traffic accidents have become the leading cause of death in China. In 2015, more than 200,000 crashes resulting in damage or injury were reported in China. These crashes resulted in 67,759 deaths. Crashes at intersections account for about 30% of the total crashes in China [1]. Crashes often occur at intersections when drivers "scramble" to gain the right of way in violation of traffic regulations [2]. In the United States in 2011, more than 2.2 million police-reported motor vehicle crashes occurred at intersections or were intersection related.

In previous studies, it is well established that driving violation is one of the major risks threatening road safety in Western societies and in China [3, 4]. Violations among Western drivers mainly include drink-driving and speeding [5-7], and in addition to the violations mentioned above [8], there are distinctive violations in China, such as running the red light, driving across continuous dividing line, disobeying traffic lane markings, using a non-motor lane during traffic congestion, stopping on the road in prohibited areas. Despite most drivers believing red light running was problematic and

[a] Corresponding author: jiayan2010@sina.com

dangerous, approximately one in five respondents reported running one or more red lights when entering the last ten signalized intersections [9].

Depending on the environment and the personality of the driver, a particular situation may place the driver in an aggressive disposition. Studies, mainly conducted in the West, have identified some attitudinal and personality factors that are related to driving violations. Medina suggests that driver violation or error contributes to as much as 75% of all roadway crashes, which attempts to construct a generic taxonomy of driver errors and driver error causal factors, based on a synthesis of the available literature on human error and its causal factors [10]. Brosseau study the impact of waiting time and other factors on violations at signalized intersections [11]. Akaateba investigates the influence of three distinct variables: driver educational attainment, driving experience, and form of driver training on drivers' self-reported attitudes towards the frequency of commission of traffic safety violations [12].

In recent years, the comprehensive research on the influence factors of traffic safety is a lot, for example, Abdel-Aty developed a mathematical model that explains the relationship between the frequency of accidents and highway geometric and traffic characteristics, and they confirmed that shoulder and lane, widths, and sharp horizontal curve are found to affected the safety of a roadway, while AADT is significant factor [13]. Mehmood aimed to introduce the System Dynamics approach to simulate the driver behavior in relation of law enforcement, traffic monitoring, and education [14]. McCartt and Hu studied the effects of camera enforcement on red light violations, and got the result that red light violations at camera-enforced intersections declined significantly [15]. Al-Ataw assessed the characteristics of red light violations and analyzed the effect of intersection characteristics, such as geometric design, control system and location, on number of violations [16]. Yau study found that male drivers and young drivers are more likely to illegal driving [17].

2 Method

2.1 Big data sources

2.1.1 Traffic violations processing system

At present, more than 300 signal-controlled intersections in Tianjin have been installed video detection devices, which can get the data of drivers' traffic violations at area of the intersections and related data of traffic flow. The data of driving violation behaviors at intersections are obtained from the database of the Traffic Violations Processing System, maintained by the Tianjin Traffic Management Bureau. This database is used to process, store, and report information of traffic violations at intersections in Tianjin, China. The research violation data comes from the TVPS, which process the data covered all the signal-controlled intersections in Tianjin.

2.1.2 Traffic flow collection system

The data of traffic flow comes from the statistical database of Traffic Flow Collection System, which also maintained by the TTMB. Real-time traffic flow data are obtained through video analysis and geomagnetic detection. The traffic flow data in this study are collected by the hour.

2.1.3 Area coordinated system of signal control

The data of signal control is derived from the statistical data of Tianjin Area Coordinated System of Signal Control, and the system adopts the technology of Sydney Coordinated Adaptive Traffic System (SCATS). At present, Tianjin urban intersections are all using SCATS. This study collects the system control mode, the signal circle and the red light time data for analysis and research.

2.2 Measures

2.2.1 Design

The data obtained from the above systems show that the number of traffic violations and the objective conditions are related, because some of the intersection traffic violation data significantly more than others, while the number of violations will change over time and the occurrence of a certain pattern of changes. Therefore, this study aims to find the relationship between traffic violations and various external factors.

In the previous research, there are many methods of data source. Some scholars use the questionnaire [12,18-20], some are observational studies [21], and some use historical statistics [22].

Referring to the previous research methods, this study combines the quantitative data and qualitative data, including state data and dynamic data. Intersections were selected with characteristic differences all over the Tianjin city, in China. Tianjin, as one of China's four municipalities, is located in the south of Beijing. The city's population is more than 10 million, and the motor vehicles are more than 3 million. The traffic violations in Tianjin are prominent. According to the Tianjin Public Security Traffic Management Bureau statistics, in 2015 the Traffic Violations Processing System found and punished traffic violations in the intersections 1000 times. Among them, running a red light 200 times, driving across continuous dividing line 250 times, disobeying traffic lane markings 550 times.

2.2.2 Data processing

In consideration of detection errors of video detection devices, all the data used in this study has been dealt with through error analysis, data reduction and additional treatment of data incompleteness. Based on the statistical data of one intersection and one entrance lane of one day, this study selected the sample data of 300 days in 2015 in the selected 10 intersections in Tianjin, China.

In order to derive the Driving Violation Index (DVI), the general idea is to analysis of the relationship between traffic violations and the influence factors. This DVI is intended as a measure of the propensity for driving violation to be experienced at a signalized intersection. Hamdar got an aggressiveness propensity index for driving behavior at signalized intersections using the SEM method [23]. On the basis of previous studies, this study has established DVI at intersections through the analysis and the research of objective factors of urban intersections.

2.3. Analytical model

The Structural Equation Model (SEM) approach can handle a large number of endogenous and exogenous variables simultaneously, as well as latent variables specified as linear combinations of the observed variables. SEM is the combination of confirmatory factor model and causal model. The factor SEM includes is called measurement model, and its equation is called measurement equation which describes the relationship between latent variables and indicators. Besides, the causal model SEM contains is called latent variable model, also known as structural model, and its equation is called structural equation which describes the relationship among latent variables [24]. With the popularization of vehicles and the development of urban traffic, the influence factors and the complexity of traffic behaviors have increased significantly. Thus, SEM has been applied to traffic field by foreign scholars. Early in the 1980s, Golob applied SEM to the research of traffic demand model [25]. At the beginning of 20th century, foreign scholars were the first to apply SEM to the research of drivers' behavioral characteristics, and got a very good application. Golob using SEM to the study of travel behaviour, and de Abreu e Silva using structural equations modeling to unravel the influence of land use patterns on travel behavior of workers in Montreal [26-27]. Eboli explored land use and transport interaction through Structural Equation Modelling [28].

3. Results

3.1 Analysis of impact factor

Owning to the complexity of objective conditions of urban road intersections, the objective factors that influence driving behaviors are also a comprehensive and complex collection. Table 1-2 provides the factor variable classification, and also analyzes the impact factors through SPSS software. First, the data were tested through the test of KMO and Bartlett, and the KMO value is greater than 0.7, which illustrates that the data is suitable for factor analysis. Besides, the Sig value is less than 0.05, which shows the test is significant. Through the factor analysis of the data, this thesis got a coefficient matrix of factor scores.

Table 1. Observed exogenous variables' description in model

Variable	Abbreviation	Variable Description (Value Unit)
X_1	Legs	The number of entrances, e.g.: crossroad values four
X_2	Location	The location of intersections (Downtown area/non-central area/suburb, values 1/2/3)
X_3	Mlanes	The number of lanes of major road
X_4	Slanes	The number of lanes of minor road
X_5	Angle	The included angle of intersected roads (Degree)
X_6	Alanes	The number of accommodation lanes of all the entrances, and the accommodation lanes include left-lane and right-lane
X_7	Widthr	Width of main entrance road(m)
X_8	Widthl	Width of main entrance lane(m)
X_9	Divided	The number of parts road are divided
X_{10}	Dsd	Design speed of road (10 km/h)
X_{11}	Direct	One-way road values 1, and two-way road values 0
X_{12}	Control	Mode of control signal at intersection (Fixed period/induction/coordinated control value 1/2/3)
X_{13}	Mred	Average red time of main road (min)
X_{14}	Camara	The number of Video surveillance facilities at intersection
X_{15}	Vol	Daily traffic volume at intersection (thousand vehicles)
X_{16}	Hvol	Daily traffic volume of large scale vehicles at intersections (thousand vehicles)
X_{17}	Bvol	Daily traffic volume of non-motor vehicles at intersection (thousand vehicles)
X_{18}	Mque	Average queue length of main road (m)
X_{19}	Bsp	Is there a bus stop near the intersections? Yes values 1, and no values 0
X_{20}	Wea	Sunny/ Rainy/Snowy values 1/2/3
X_{21}	Time	Weekday/weekend/holiday (values 1/2/3)

Table 2. Observed endogenous variables' description

Variable	Abbreviation	Variable Description (Value Unit)
Y_1	RED	The number of running a red light
Y_2	LINE	The number of driving across continuous dividing line
Y_3	CROSS	The number of disobeying traffic lane markings
Y_4	PARK	The number of illegal parking

According to the analysis result, this thesis reduced the original five impact factors to four impact factors, excluding the environmental factor. Meanwhile, the factor scores of the angle of intersection, the width of lane, the design speed and the one-way road are all less than 0.1, so they are all excluded. Based on the actual experience, because the differences of lane width and design speed in this thesis are small, the two variables of lane width and design speed cannot be treated and analyzed as significant impact factors, which coincides with the analysis result of data software.

3.2 Selected model variables

According to the analysis result of impact factors, this thesis selected among the effective factors, and totally selected four exogenous variables and 1 endogenous variable as variables of structural equation model. The detailed descriptions of selected variables in the model are shown in Table 4.

Table 4. Selected model variables

	Factor	Variable	Abbreviation
Exogenous Variables	F_1	X_1	Legs
		X_2	Location
		X_3	Mlanes
	F_2	X_4	Slanes
		X_6	Alanes
		X_7	WidthR
	F_3	X_9	Divided
		X_{12}	Control
		X_{13}	Mred
		X_{14}	Camara
	F_4	X_{15}	Vol
		X_{16}	Hvol
		X_{17}	Bvol
Endogenous Variable	Index	Y_1	RED
		Y_2	LINE
		Y_3	CROSS
		Y_4	PARK

3.3 Model construction

This study uses the software of LISREL 8.8 to program and establish SEM. Applied the data samples of Tianjin intersections to model training, this thesis has obtained the measurement equation of exogenous latent variables and structural equation model. Establishing models and modifying them through software programming, this thesis has got a path diagram of the structural equation model to calculate driving violation index which includes factor loading and path coefficient, as shown in Figure 1.

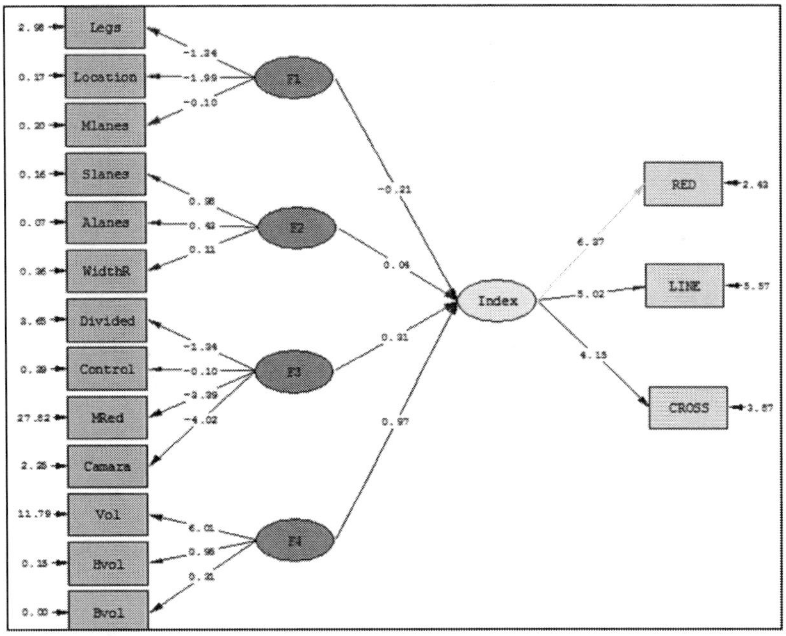

Figure.1 Final Driving violation index structural model by LISREL 8.8.

3.4 Calculation model of driving violation index

The results of calculation model can be acquired in accordance with SEM, among which *Err* is the error term. Models include the measurement model of endogenous variables, measurement model of exogenous variables and calculation model of violation propensity index. The result summarizing the model are presented in Table 5.

Table 5. Results of SEM

Exogenous measurement model		Endogenous measurement model	
1	X_1=-1.34*F_1 ; err=2.98	1	Y_1=6.37*DVI ; err=2.43
2	X_2=-1.99*F_1 ; err=0.17	2	Y_2=5.02*DVI ; err=5.57
3	X_3=-0.10*F_1 ; err=0.20	3	Y_2=4.15*DVI ; err=3.87
4	X_4=0.98*F_2 ; err=0.16		
5	X_6=0.43*F_2 ; err=0.07		
6	X_7=0.11*F_2 ; err=0.36		
7	X_9=-1.34*F_3 ; err=3.65		
8	X_{12}=-0.10*F_3 ; err=0.39		
9	X_{13}=-3.39*F_3 ; err=27.82		
10	X_{14}=-4.02*F_3 ; err=2.25		
11	X_{15}=-6.01*F_4 ; err=11.79		
12	X_{16}=-0.95*F_4 ; err=0.15		
13	X_{17}=-0.31*F_4 ; err=0.00		
	DVI=-0.21*F_1+0.04*F_2+0.31*F_3+0.97*F_4		

4 Discussion

4.1 Analysis of influencing factors

Through the model fitting of 300 data samples, this thesis uses structural equation model to obtain the calculation model of *DVI*. In the final fitting model, the Chi-Square value is 171.9, *RMSEA* value is 0.089, *GFI* value is 0.68 and *AGFI* value is 0.76. The fitting results are in an acceptable range when the sample size is much larger than observed variables. Because the model fitting is conducted with real data, it is inevitable that the data maybe uncertain and mutant. Therefore, it can be assumed that the result of model fitting is an ideal result.

The final structural equation model classifies the exogenous variables X_1 , X_2 and X_3 as impact factor F_1 which represents the characteristic index of intersections; classifies the exogenous variables X_4 , X_6 and X_7 as impact factor F_2 represents the characteristic index of entrance lanes at intersections; classifies the exogenous variables X_9, X_{12}, X_{13} and X_{14} as impact factor F_3 which represents the characteristic index of traffic control and traffic management; and classifies the exogenous variables X_{15} , X_{16} and X_{17} as impact factor F_4 which represents the characteristic index of traffic flow. The model fitting has excluded the exogenous X_{18} for its relevancy to the exogenous variable X_{15} is larger than 0.9. Through the comparison of path coefficient of impact factors, the sort of effects of impact factors on *DVI* is as follows: $F_4>F_3>F_1>F_2$. It shows that the traffic flow characteristic has the greatest influence on the traffic violation behaviors, and the impact factor of the entrance lane characteristics at intersections is the least.

Meanwhile, through the comparison of the path coefficients Y_1, Y_2 and Y_3, running the red light has the greatest influence on the *DVI* among traffic violation behaviours at intersections, followed by pressing the solid lines, and the third is driving not according to the guiding lanes. The illegal parking is eliminated by the model, which shows the low correlation between illegal parking at intersections and driving violation index.

4.2. Driving Violation Index Calculation

Making use of the model results obtained in this study, the *DVI* value of a certain intersection can be obtained. The violation propensity index of each intersection is related to traffic flow, traffic condition and other dynamic variables, so the average traffic data of intersections should be taken into account when calculating the violation propensity index of intersections. Meanwhile, the data of different entrance lanes should be averaged to calculate the result of *DVI*. According to the calculation model, the corresponding Fi value can be obtained by taking one factor in each factor, and then the Index value is calculated. At the same time, we can estimate the number of traffic violations according to the Index value. Research shows that with the increase of Index value, the tendency of traffic violations also increases. Table 6. presents the calculation results of the classical intersections in this study in Tianjin, China. Similarly, we can extend the results to other intersections or other Chinese cities, because of the similar characteristics of drivers and traffic. When the standard index is greater than 0.8, the intersection is considered to be more dangerous, it is recommended to take countermeasures, such as the number7, number 8 intersections in this study.

Table 6 *DVI* of the intersections in this study

Num	Intersection name	DVI Standard	Num	Intersection name	DVI Standard
1	Jiefang Road-Taian Street	0.76	3	Youyi Road-Shaoxing Street	0.65
2	Youyi Road-Waihuan Road	0.89	4	Waihuan Road-Xianfeng Road	0.98

Conclusions

In this paper, we have creatively proposed the concept of violation propensity index. Through collecting and organizing the data of illegal driving at intersections and other relevant data of road traffic, it established a SEM-based calculation model of violation propensity index. With the application of real data of Tianjin, it obtained the path coefficient and factor loading chart of SEM by programming with the software LISREL 8.8. Through analysing the impact factors of traffic violation behaviours at urban intersections in China, this thesis explored the relationship between traffic violation behaviours at intersections and intersection characteristics, road characteristics, traffic control characteristics and traffic flow characteristics. Besides, it also innovatively acquires the SEM-based calculation method of driving violation index at intersections through the combination of qualitative analysis and quantitative calculation, which provides new ideas and methods for safety evaluation of intersections. This study is not perfect, and further research in the following areas is suggested.

References

1. Pei, Y.-L., Ma, Y.-L. Journal of Harbin Institute of Technology **37**, 3 (2005)
2. Shi, Jing, et al. Accid Anal Prev **43**, 1540-1546 (2011)
3. Xie, Cheng-qiu, and Dianne Parker. Transport. Res. Part F **5**, 293-308 (2002)
4. Zhang, Guangnan, Kelvin K. W. Yau, and Guanghan Chen. Accid Anal Prev **59**, 18-25 (2013)
5. Bhalla, Kavi, et al. Injury 44, Supplement **4**, S49-S56 (2013).
6. Gheorghiu, Alexandra, Patricia Delhomme, and Marie Line Felonneau. Transport. Res. Part F **35**, 101-111 (2015)
7. MacLeod, Kara E., et al. Accid Anal Prev **81**, 134-142 (2015)
8. Zhang, Guangnan, Kelvin K. W. Yau, and Xiangpu Gong. Accid Anal Prev **64**, 30-40 (2014)
9. Porter, Bryan E., and Thomas D. Berry. Accid Anal Prev **33**, 735-741 (2001)
10. Medina, A.L., Lee, S.E., Wierwille, W.W., Hanowski, R.J. Proceedings of the Human Factors and Ergonomics Society 48th Annual Meeting, 2075–2080 (2004)
11. Brosseau, Marilyne, et al. Transport. Res. Part F **21**, 159-172 (2013)
12. Akaateba, Millicent Awialie, Richard Amoh-Gyimah, and Owusu Amponsah. Safety Science **75**, 156-162 (2015)
13. Abdel-Aty, Mohamed A., and A. Essam Radwan. Accid Anal Prev **32**, 633-642 (2000)
14. Mehmood, Arif. Accid Anal Prev **42**, 427-436 (2010)
15. McCartt, Anne T., and Wen Hu. Journal of Safety Research **48**, 57-62 (2014)
16. Al-Atawi, Attiyah M. IATSS Research **37**, 119-123 (2014)
17. Yau, Kelvin K. W. Accid Anal Prev **36**, 333-340 (2004)
18. Forward, Sonja E. Transport. Res. Part F **9**, 412-426 (2006)
19. Yagil, Dana. Transport. Res. Part F **1**, 123-135 (1998)
20. Yeh, Ming-Shan, et al. Transport. Res. Part F **32**, 35-45 (1998)
21. Yan, Fangfang, et al. Accid Anal Prev (2015).
22. Chen, Chen, and Yuanchang Xie. Accid Anal Prev **91**, 72-83 (2016)
23. Hamdar, Samer H., Hani S. Mahmassani, and Roger B. Chen. Accid Anal Prev **40**, 315-326 (2008)
24. Muthen, B. Psychometrika **49**, 115-132 (1984)
25. Golob, T.F., Meurs, T. Transport. Res. Part A **21**, 391-400 (1987)
26. Golob, Thomas F. Transport. Res. Part B **37**, 1-25 (2003)
27. de Abreu e Silva, João, Catherine Morency, and Konstadinos G. Goulias. Transport. Res. Part A **46**, 1252-1264 (2012)
28. Eboli, Laura, Carmen Forciniti, and Gabriella Mazzulla. Procedia Social and Behavioral Sciences **54**, 107-116 (2012)

Building Contour Extraction Based on LiDAR Point Cloud

Xu-Qing ZHANG[1], Heng WANG[1,a], Yong-Hua SHAN[1] and Liang LENG[2]

[1]*Jilin University, College of Geoexploration Science and Technology, China;*
[2]*Jilin University, College of Applied Technology, China;*

Abstract. This paper presents a new method for solving the problem of utilizing the LiDAR data to extract the building contour line. For detection of the edge points between the building test points by using the least squares fitting to get the edge line of buildings and give the weight determining of the building of edge line slope depend on the length of the edge line. And then get the weighted mean of the positive and negative slope of the building edge line. Based on the structure of the adjacent edge perpendicular hypothesis, regularization processing to extract the edge of the skeleton line perpendicular. The experiments show that the extracted building edges have the good accuracy and have the good applicability in complex urban areas.

1 Introduction

The application of airborne LiDAR point cloud for building edge extraction has been more extensive[1-8], Baltsavias, Zhang Zhiyou and Khoshelham etc. used aerial imagery and LiDAR data for building extraction comprehensively[9-11]. Due to the inherent error and resolution of the airborne LiDAR data, noise is often present in the edges of the building which can cause deformation of the edges of the building. It is mainly showed that the building of tiny twist, jagged or buildings connected to the two edge lines are not perpendicular to each other (as shown in Figure1). Zhang Yang-yang proposed a regularization method of building edge line based on minimal outsourcing rectangle[12]. You Hong-jian grouped the boundary points according to the change of the direction angle of edge points, and then the main direction of the building is calculated according to the boundary points of the groups, the outline of the outermost edge of the building is obtained finally[13]. Shen Wei proposed a method of "quadrangle method" for quadrilateral and a method of "categorical forcing orthogonal" for polygons (greater than four edges and even sides) to further regularize the edge lines[13].

[a] Corresponding author: hengwang15@mails.jlu.edu.cn

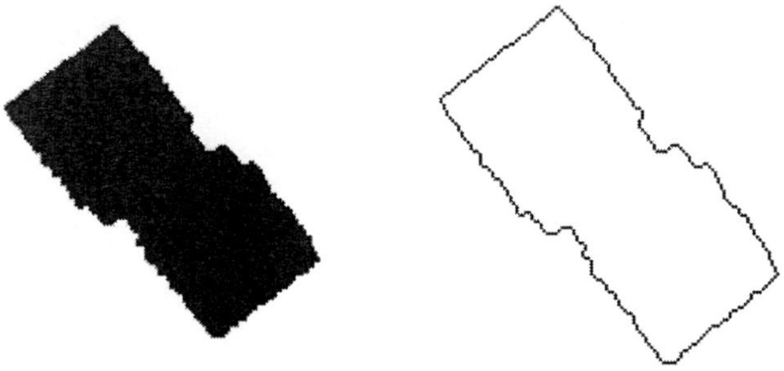

(a) (b)

Figure 1. the distorted and not vertical phenomenon of extracting the building outline by using LiDAR point cloud (a. Building point cloud; b. Extraction of buildings)

This paper based on the problem of deformation of the building using LiDAR point cloud extraction. The key points of the building are firstly detected on the basis of obtaining the building edge points, then the edge line of the building is extracted by using the least square method, and then the edge line of the building is regularized to lay the foundation for building the 3D model of the building later.

2 The building detection of key points

The key point of the building is the projection of the building to the corner or intersection of the planes. As shown in Figure-2, P_1.P_2.P_3.P_4 is the orderly building edge points. From point P_1, connect P_1 and P_2, the azimuth angle β_1 and the length l_1 of the straight line P_1-P_2 are calculated, P_2 for the straight line P_1-P_2 length d of the vertical line, from this we can calculate $\Delta\beta_1 = \tan^{-1}(\frac{d}{l_1})$, Connect P_1 and P_3, the azimuth angle β_2 and the length l_2 of the straight lines P1-P3 are calculated. Let $\beta = \beta_2$, $\beta_a = \beta_1 - \Delta\beta_1$, $\beta_b = \beta_1 + \Delta\beta_1$.

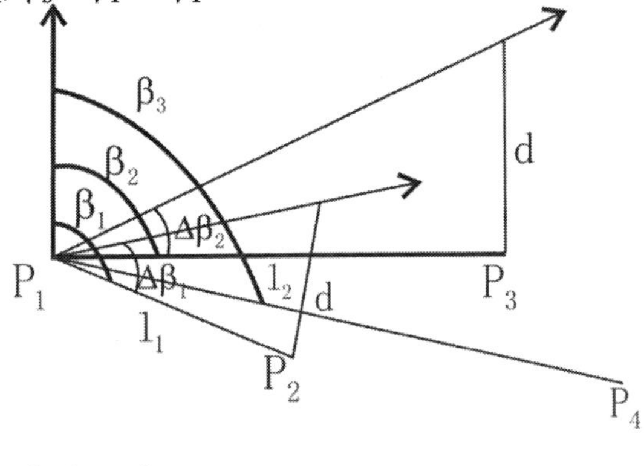

Figure2. the principle of testing key point

1) if $\beta \in (\beta a, \beta b)$, then P_2 is not a key point and remove it. P_3 for the straight line P_1-P_3 length d of the vertical line and calculate $\Delta\beta_2 = \tan^{-1}(\frac{d}{l_2})$. Connect P_1 and P_4 and calculate the azimuth angle β_3 of the straight line P_1-P_4. At this time, $\beta = \beta_3, \beta_a = \max\{\beta_1 - \Delta\beta_1, \beta_2 - \Delta\beta_2\}, \beta_b = \min\{\beta_1 + \Delta\beta_1, \beta_2 + \Delta\beta_2\}$, return to the first step.

2) if $\beta \notin (\beta_a, \beta_b)$, then P_2 is the key point and retain it. From P_2, connect the next point as the start judgment line, and repeat the above steps until the last point.

3) After all edge points are judged, the remaining points are the keys.

The key of this algorithm is to reasonably determine the value of d. Take the P_1, P_2, P_3 points in Figure-3 as an example, if the d is larger, $\Delta\beta_1$ is larger and the greater the range of change of β_2 for judging whether or not the point P_2 is a key point. Then the P_2 as a key point of the possibility of the smaller, the final effect is the detection of the key points less. In order to better extract the key points, not only to avoid changes in the direction of the edge of the smaller point as a key point, not the key points will be lost, d value of the selection should be based on the laser point cloud density and the actual building Complex situation specific to determine. As shown in Figure-3 is the key points (red dots) detected by the above algorithm.

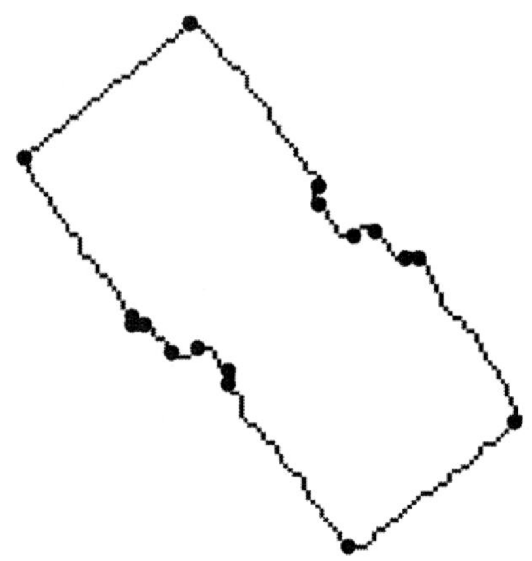

Figure 3. Using the above algorithm to detect key points (red point)

3 The generation of building edge skeleton line

After detection of the building key points was finished, the building edge skeleton lines were generated according to the detected key points. While when we detected the key points, many of the building edge points were considered non-critical points which may be filtered out. But these non-critical points still contain a large amount of useful information. Therefore, the generation of building edge skeleton line in this paper is not simply connecting the adjacent key points into line segments, but utilizing the adjacent two key points and all the building edge points located between these two key points to fit out a straight-line segment by least square method. And it is regarded as a building edge skeleton line in order to improve the generation accuracy of the building edge skeleton line. As shown in Figure-4, the skeleton line constructed by the least squares method is closer to the edge point of the building than the skeleton line constructed by the key point.

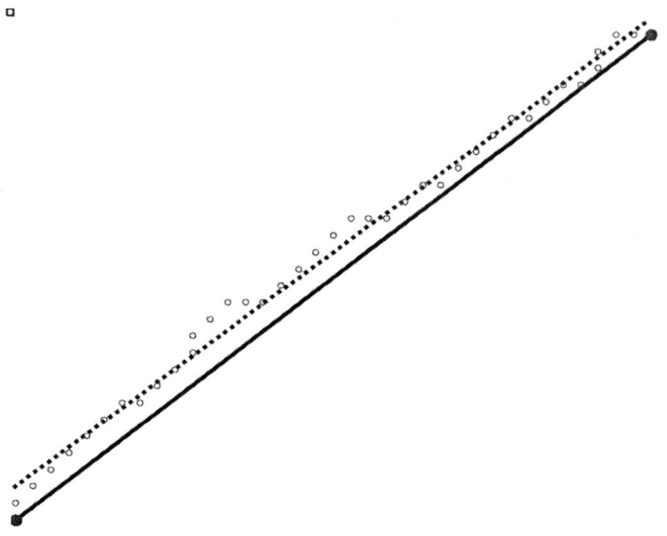

Figure 4. Key points of contour line compared with least-square fitting contour line

(The dotted line is obtained by least squares fitting, the solid line is the key point, the hollow point is the non-key point, the solid point is the key point)

After all the building edge skeleton lines are generated, theoretically speaking, the two slopes of the skeleton lines should be either equal in value (parallel) or the product of positive and negative is -1 (vertical). However, due to various factors (data accuracy, errors in building extraction, etc.) makes the actual situation which is not the case, there are often adjacent two skeleton line slope sign the same but not equal. This is because the detection of key points cannot really represent the key points of the building, therefore need to combine the two adjacent skeleton line segments.

An algorithm is required to merge the two skeleton lines. For example $L_1: y = a_1 * x + b_1$, $L_2: y = a_2 * x + b_2$ are the two connected straight segments. Their slopes are the same positive or the same negative and the length are the s1, s2 respectively. L_3 is the new straight merged line segment. How to determine the parameters (a3, b3) of line segment of L3? At this time, according to the length of the straight-line segment to weight, the weight of long line is large and using this method to calculate the parameters of L3.

The parameters of L3 is calculated as follows: $a_3 = a_1 * \frac{s_1}{(s_1+s_2)} + a_2 * \frac{s_2}{(s_1+s_2)}$, $b_3 = b_1 * \frac{s_1}{(s_1+s_2)} + b_2 * \frac{s_2}{(s_1+s_2)}$. After this treatment, the slope of any two adjacent skeleton lines are positive and negative on the contrary. As shown in Figure-5b, skeletal lines using least-squares fitting and merging are not vertical or parallel to each other, but the number of skeleton lines constructed using the key points is much smaller.

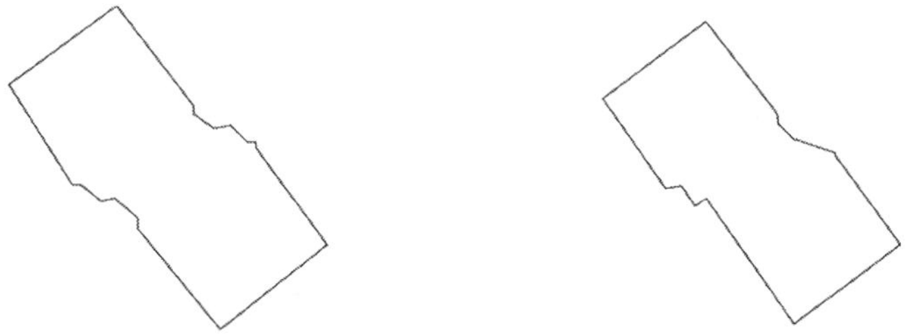

(a) (b)

Figure 5. The generated skeleton line (a.The skeleton line is constructed with key points; b. Least squares fitting and merging processing of skeleton lines)

4 Regularity of the edge of the building skeleton line

There are only two relations between the skeleton lines of buildings, that is, vertical or parallel, and the purpose of regularization is to adjust the skeleton lines of the two connected buildings so as to be perpendicular or parallel to each other.

After the completion of the building edge of the skeleton line generation, those trivial lines and redundant points is no longer exist, only leaving the edge of the building skeleton line. Regularization of the skeleton line of the building edge is carried out on the basis of the skeleton line, the regularization process is as follows:

1) All the skeleton lines are divided into two categories according to the positive and negative slope of the generated skeleton line, namely the positive slope of the skeleton line and the negative slope of the skeleton line.

2) After classification, calculate the weighted average slope of the positive and negative slant skeleton lines s_, s_ +. Such as for the positive slope of the skeleton line: $s_+ = \sum l_i * \frac{s_i}{l}, l = \sum l_i$, s_+ is the weighted average slope of positive slope skeleton line, s_i is the slope of the i-th skeleton line in the positive-slope skeleton line, l_i is the length of the i-th skeleton line in the positive slant skeleton line, l is the total length of the positive slope skeleton line. The weighted mean slope is calculated for the negative slope skeleton line in the same way. On account of the long skeleton lines have a higher accuracy of slope than the short skeleton lines, the weighted average slope of the skeleton line calculated in this way is more reasonable and more accurate.

3) Adjust the two weighted average slopes calculated in the previous step so that they are perpendicular to each other. As shown in Figure-6, OA is the direction of the positive slope of weighted averaged, OB is the weighted average of the direction of the negative slope of the weighted averaged, α is the angle between the OA direction and the X axis, β is the angle between the OB direction and the X axis, $\alpha = \tan^{-1} s_+$, $\beta = \tan^{-1}(-s_-)$, adjust the direction of the OA and OB direction to make $\alpha + \beta = 90$ ° Let the residual of angle is the c=α+β-90°, when c=0, OA⊥OB. In order to make c=0, the negative values of c are assigned to α and β in a certain way. Here α and β represent the total length of each line as the basis for distribution, the longer the length, the smaller the assigned value, $\alpha = \alpha - c * l_-/l$, $\beta = \beta - c * l_+/l$, l_+ is the total length of the positive slope skeleton line, l_- is the total length of the negative slope skeleton line, $l = l_+ + l_-$. After this treatment, OA will be strictly perpendicular to the OB, that means that the direction of positive and negative slopes is strictly vertical.

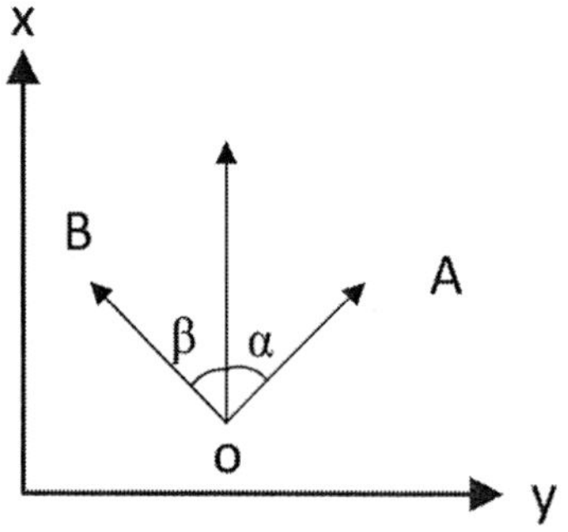

Figure 6. The weighted average slope vertical processing schematic drawing

1) Rotate each skeleton line around its center point to the direction of the weighted average slope of its category, after this step is completed, the adjacent skeleton lines will be strictly vertical.

2)If the length of the skeleton line is particularly small, the line may not be a real edge of the building, you need to remove it. After stripping, merge the two parallel skeleton lines on either side.

At this point, the building edge of the skeleton line of regular work completed, the effect is shown in Figure -7 below.

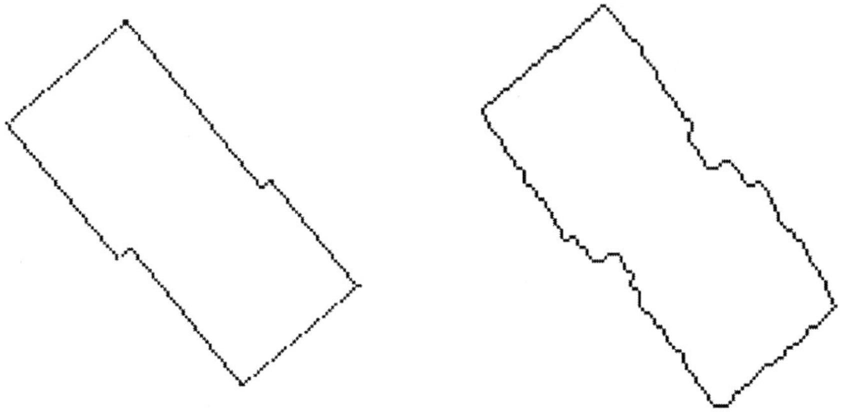

(a) (b)

Figure 7. The results of extracting building contour line (a. the edge skeleton line after regularization; b. the edge skeleton line before regularization)

5 Analysis and conclusions

The experimental results show that the edge extraction and regularization method used in this paper has a good effect, especially for buildings whose edges are at right angles.

The innovation of this paper: 1) According to the building key points to generate the building skeleton line is not simply connecting the key points of adjacent buildings, but to make the two building key points and all the building edge points between them are involved in the application of least squares to fit the skeleton line which will be closest to the original edge line of the building. 2) When the slope of the skeleton line is calculated, the length is weighted according to the length of the skeleton line, the length is proportional to the weight, and the slope is the slope of the weighted average.

References

1. Lai Xu-dong, Wan You-chuan. The study of the edge detection to the depth-image of light detection and ranging [J]. LASER&INFRARED. **6**,444-446. (2005).
2. Hu Y. Automated Extraction of Digital Terrain Models, Roads and Buildings Using Airborne Lidar Data [D]. University of Calgary, (2003).
3. Rottensteiner F. and Briese CH. A new method for building extraction urban areas from high-resolution LIDAR data[J]. IAPRS **,35-3A**,1682-1750,295,(2002).
4. Brunn A. and U.Weidner. Hierdner. Hierachical Bayesian nets for building extraction using dense digital surface models[J]. ISPRS Journal of Photogrammetry & Remote Sensing, **53**,296-307, (1998).
5. Alharthy A. and Bethel J. *Heuristic Filtering and 3D Feature Extraction from LIDAR Data [A].In: ISPRS Commission III, Symposium*,[C], Graz, Austria, September, **9-13**,(2002).
6. Liu Xiu-guo, Zhang Jing. Extract building quickly from Lidar point cloud data [J]. Earth Science-Journal of China University of Geosciences. **31**,5,615-618(2006).
7. Cheng Liang, Gong Jian-ya. Building boundary extraction using very high resolution images and Lidar [J]. ACTA GEODAETICA & CARTOGRAPHICA SNICA,**37**,3,391-393, (2008).

DOI: 10.1051/itmconf/20171110004

8. Elberink, S.O. and H.G. Maas. *The use of anisotropic height texture measurements for the segmentation of airborne laser scanner data* [C], IAPRS, **33,** (2000).
9. Baltsavias E. P. A comparison between photogrammetry and laser scanning[J]. ISPRS Journal of photogrammetry & Remote Sensing. **54**,2/3, (1999).
10. Zhang Z. Extraction and 3D Visualization of Buildings & Terrain Based on LIDAR Data and Aerial Image [D]. Beijing Jiaotong University, (2008).
11. Khoshelham, K. Building extraction from multiple data sources: a data fusion framework for reeconstruction of generic models [J]. IAPRS,**35**,B3,(2004).
12. ZHANG Yang-yang;MEN Lin-jie;LI Xiang-wei.Building regularization based on airborne LiDAR point clouds[J]. Engineering of Surveying and Mapping,**24**,10,59-61, (2015).
13. You H J, Li S K.Extracting Man-made Building from Sparse Laser Sample Point[J] .Journal of the Graduate school of the Chinese Academy of Science,**18**,2,154-158,(2001).
14. SHEN W, LI J, CHEN Y, DENG L, and PENG G. Algorithms Study of Building Boundary Extraction and Normalization Based on LIDAR Data[J]. Journal of Remote Sensing,**12,** 5, 692-698, (2008).

ITM Web of Conferences **11**, 10005 (2017) DOI: 10.1051/itmconf/20171110005
IST2017

LBS Mobile Learning System Based on Android Platform

Ya-Li ZHANG[a] and Xiao-Kan WANG

[1]*Henan Mechanical and Electrical Vocational College, Zhengzhou, 451191*

Abstract. In the era of mobile internet, PC-end internet services can no long satisfy people's demands, needs for App and services on mobile phones are more urgent than ever. With increasing social competition, the concept of lifelong learning becomes more and more popular and accepted, making full use of spare time to learn at any time and any place meets updating knowledge desires of modern people, Location Based System (LBS) mobile learning system based on Android platform was created under such background. In this Paper, characteristics of mobile location technology and intelligent terminal were introduced and analyzed, mobile learning system which will fulfill personalized needs of mobile learners was designed and developed on basis of location information, mobile learning can be greatly promoted and new research ideas can be expanded for mobile learning.

1. Introduction

With the constant development of mobile communication technology and the hardware support provided by smartphone for GPS, smartphone users' needs for location information are getting stronger every day, LBS is applied in various phones to increase rich experiences for user, the development and innovation of LBS are largely promoted, solid technical support is generated for LBS mobile learning based on Android platform. LBS usually consists of two parts: obtaining users' current location information through GPS positioning, base station positioning, WIFI positioning and etc.; provide related services to satisfy particular demands on basis of users' location information. The goal of mobile learning system is to build a circumstance in which learners can acquire knowledge at any time and any place, select proper learning contents according to their own needs and organize real-time communication with each other. There are connections and differences between mobile learning and online learning, the major difference is their applied technologies, mobile learning uses wireless communication technology which enables learners to learn without time and location constraints which online learners suffer, it is more flexible and freer. See Table 1 for comparison of characteristics of mobile learning and online learning.

[a] Corresponding author: zhang20021026@163.com

Table 1. Comparison of Characteristics of Mobile Learning and Online Learning

Characteristics	**Mobile Learning**	**Online Learning**
Learning Place	Any time and any place	Fixed Time and Place
Network Environment	Wireless Network/4G	Wired Network
Learning Mode	Online/Offline Learning	Online Learning
Learning Device	Smartphone, iPad and etc.	Computer
Communication	Any time and any place	Fixed Time and Place
Interaction Easiness	Relatively Limited People-device Interaction	Easy People-device Interaction

Combining characteristics of mobile learning, a mobile learning platform which changes with a learner's location was developed on basis of LBS, real-time location circumstance was obtained on Android platform of system client-end, real-time check-in, content push, help, sharing and other functions of mobile learning system were performed, Java programming technology was used, encapsulation and implementation of XML data document interface were realized in Eclipse environment, data were built and services were offered, and eventually, LBS mobile learning system based on Android platform was realized.

2. Selections on platform development

Compared with other systems, Android system has properties like open source, rich hardware equipment, no limitation and etc.; Android architecture is divided into four levels from top to bottom: Application Level, Application Framework Level, Support Base Level and Linux Kernel Level; Android application development mainly comprises four components: Activity, Service, Content Provider and Broadcast Receiver. Each component has its own purpose. Activity Component provides visible interaction interface for user and program; Service Component implements time-consuming operations on background of main thread; Content Provider Component provides a group of unified interfaces for storing and reading data to realize data sharing among different programs; Broadcast Receiver Component receives broadcast messages which meet certain conditions. Moreover, Android SDK also provides nice-looking basic map services. Developers can refer to specific API documentation and develop particular LBS applications which satisfy their own needs. Only by completing relative configurations and integrating SDK into own applications, developers can realize positioning function through LBS positioning interface provided by Android SDK. Therefore, application developments based on Android is the prior choices for realization of client-end of this system. See Figure 1 for positioning principle of Android SDK.

Figure 1. Positioning Principle of Android SDK

3. LBS mobile learning system based on android platform

3.1 Analysis of system mode

With the fast development of internet and information technology, organizing and obtaining modes of learning sources change continuously, mobile learning enters a new stage of circumstance perception from former single E-learning mode, exploring more on technology, resource, learning and

DOI: 10.1051/itmconf/20171110005

circumstance of internet era is beneficial for innovation of mobile learning mode. Mobile learning based on LBS is centered with real current location and circumstance information of learners, guided by actual learning activities of learners, real-time location and circumstance information are integrated, learning contents and information helps which satisfy information demands and circumstance interaction are provided for learners. See Figure 2 for information interaction model built based on location perception.

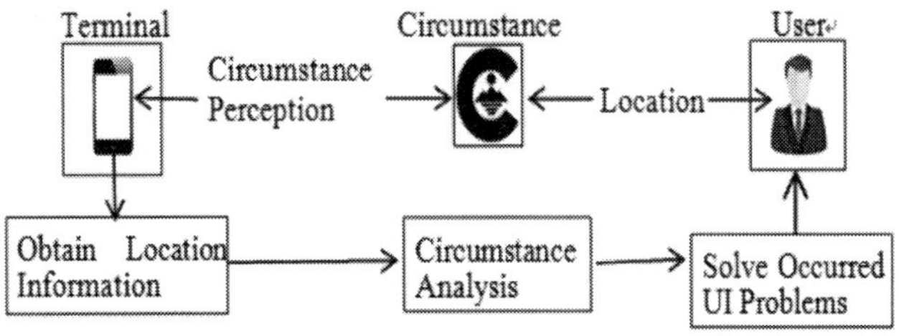

Figure 2. Circumstance Perception Mode Based on Location

3.2 System data push technology

Pushing data for learners is an important section in LBS mobile learning system based on Android platform. The push technologies commonly applied are: push based on association rules, push based on content, collaborative filtering push and etc., push based on content is used in the System. Items which users may perceive and push are presented by keywords, and weights of such keywords can be calculated with TF-IDF Method. Assume n-dimensional vector $\vec{d}_k = (W_{1k}, W_{2k}, \cdots, W_{ik}, \cdots, W_{nk})$ is item, $\vec{d}_l = (W_{1l}, W_{2l}, \cdots, W_{il}, \cdots, W_{nl})$ is tendency of User I, n is the number of keywords. According to TF-IDF Method, TF_{ij} value definition of keyword K_i in item set d_i is as shown in Formula (1):

$$TF_{ij} = \frac{f_{ij}}{\max_{zf_{zj}}} \tag{1}$$

IDF_i value definition of keyword K_i in item set d_i is as shown in Formula (2):

$$IDF_i = \log \frac{N}{n_i} \tag{2}$$

Final Weight Formula is obtained combining Formula (1) and (2), as shown in Formula (3):

$$W_{ij} = TF_{ij} \cdot IDF_i = \frac{f_{ij}}{\max_{zf_{zj}}} \cdot lob \frac{N}{n_i} \tag{3}$$

"N" refers total number of item sets, f_{ij} refers occurring times of keyword K_i in item set d_k, $\max_{zf_{zj}}$ refers the maximum occurring times of keyword K_z in all item sets, n_i refers number of items in keyword K_i.

 DOI: 10.1051/itmconf/20171110005

3.3 System design realization

3.3.1 Analysis of overall functional demands of the system

The System consists of two parts: resource supplying service end and resource user end. On resource supplying service end, corresponding support service platform was designed. Positioning accurately and obtaining terminal location circumstance and other function modules are required for client-end of the System, in order to assure successful learning, functions listed in Table 2 shall be available on client-end:

Table 2. Basic Functions on Client-end of LBS mobile learning system based on Android platform

Function Module	Function Realization
User Registration	Register basic information of users, follow and record their learning situations.
User Sign In	Users voluntarily report their location circumstances, the System automatically perceive users' location circumstances.
Circumstance Learning	Users use local resources to learn.
Learning Partner Sharing	Position users' locations, search for surrounding learning partners to share learning experiences, establish learning community.

3.3.2 System service architecture

The System applies a mixed system architecture of C/S and B/S, its service end is API resource support service platform based on LBS, its client-end consists of devices which can connect with network, including mobile device and PC. As shown in figure 3, learning resources, location, platform service and other function modules are integrated on service end (cloud end) through data interface (open API), resource services are provided for mobile devices, PC and other client-ends through internet.

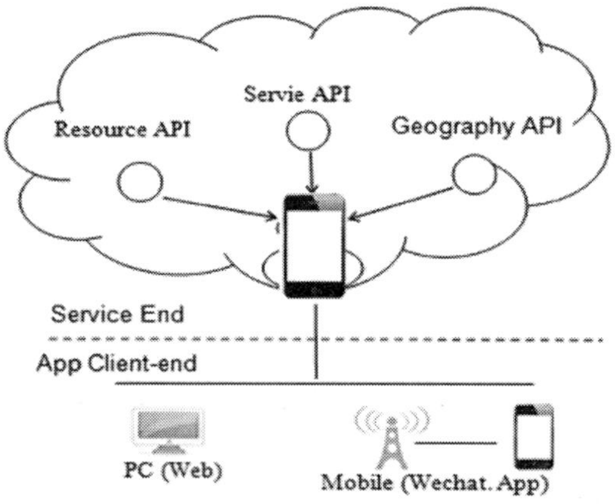

Figure 3. Architecture of Mobile Learning Service Based on Android Platform

3.3.3 Key technologies for realization of client-end functions of the system

There are two key technologies for realization of client-end functions of the System: The first is Android development technology; Android allows developers combine Internet data and local data, break distinctions between applications, third-party software can be conveniently called during client-end development process, assistant and support learning functions can be realized. Android provides application developers with a large number of local databases and utilities with which developers can establish their applications quickly. Android system is widely applied by mobile phone producers because of one of its characteristics -- open resource. The second is client-end network communication technology; there are mainly three communication modes between client-end and the server: HTTP, Socket and Web Service. In HTTP communication technology, client-end sends HTTP request to the server, the server receives the request from client-end, manages it and then responds client-end through HTTP; in Socket communication technology, external communication port is established inside application, while writing server-end and client-end codes, open the port and make communication protocol, verify safety and legality of data, after establishing connections, Socket directly realizes data communication without sending request to server-end; Web services are a kind of services based on XML and HTTPS technologies, they are deployed on Web server and managed by Web server. In order to offer satisfying user experiences, the most suitable communication mode will be selected according to demands of the System's transmitting data in realization of the System.

3.3.4 Function modules of client-end of the system

(1) User Registration Module

When learners start the application on mobile end, it will be checked if they ever registered or bind with basic information about their personal learning situations, if they never registered or bind, registration interface or binding interface will appear for them to fill in their basic learning situations. On one hand, bases can be provided to push personalized learning resources for learners; on the other hand, learning progresses of learners can be recorded continuously to provide bases for learning effects and evaluations.

(2) User Sign-in Module

User Sign-in Module is a process in which learners voluntarily report their location circumstances, acquire learning resources according to their location circumstances and learn online. In this module, it will be checked first if learners sign in as registered users, if not, it will jump to registration page. If users already registered and sign in successfully, mobile devices will automatically position locations of learners and report to the Platform, intelligent retrieval will be realized through perception reasoning, mobile client-end interface will be updated according to specific situations of mobile devices, knowledge will be presented in front of learners.

(3) Local Circumstance Resource Learning Module

One of the characteristics of Local Circumstance Resource Learning Module is downloading resources and storing them in local during idle hours of network. To-be-downloaded resources depend on pre-cached learning situations or pre-subscribed classified resources of learners. In environments with no or poor network, learners can retrieve resources fast for learning on client-end.

(4) Learning Partner Sharing Module

The client-end supports learning partner sharing function and learning community establishment. After obtaining and reporting current locations of learners, the information will be presented in form of POI data on real-time map, such POI information includes the problems which learners come across in learning, as well as their learning understandings and experiences, learner users within a certain range centered by learners will be searched, learning partnerships and community relationships can be established, real-time discuss and communication can be realized.

4. System test

On basis of System Design Realization Plan, in integrated development environment Eclipse, basic framework of service platform was realized through configuration files, basic functions were realized through writing organization codes, necessary function tests and application were conducted for prototype system. From aspect of operation and availability of the System, the Test was divided into two stages: the first stage is test of network resources and existing resources; the second stage is joint debugging of client-end and port. According to requirements of API closed design, ports are closed for resources which can be searched on platform, so that such resources can be called from client-end, resource sharing can be realized, resources can be retrieved by resource ID, resource open ports which are closed as SML data can be obtained through GET. "Key design codes of architecture ports which are closed as XML data" are as shown below.

```
public ComResource getResourceByIds(String resourceId)
{
    ComResource com = resDao.getResourceById(resourceId);
    if (com == null)
    {
        return null;
    }
    return com;
}
```

When users start client-end of mobile learning application based on LBS for the first time, current running environment of the Software will be checked, including network connection status, system positioning situation and whether it is the first time of using by users, initial data resources will be loaded.

Conclusion

In this Paper, LBS and currently popular mobile learning modes were combined, LBS mobile learning system based on Android platform was proposed. Mobile communication technology, LBS technology and mobile learning studies were analyzed, plan of mobile learning system based on LBS was established. It was suggested to apply LBS technology in mobile learning area and to integrate LBS and mobile learning. Application values of LBS in mobile learning were showed and improved, application of new technologies in education area was promoted to a certain extent.

Acknowledgment

This work was supported by the youth backbone teachers training program of Henan colleges and universities under Grant No. 2016ggjs-287, and the project of science and technology of Henan province under Grant No. 172102210124.

References

1. Yin Xixiang, Zhu Xianyuan, Chen Weiwei, "Design and Realization of Teaching Evaluation System Based on Android Platform" [J]. "Journal of Xinxiang University: Natural Science Edition", 2014, 31(2):31-34.
2. Qiu Bingfa," Research and Design of Mobile Learning System Based on LBS"[D].Chongqing Normal University ,2016.
3. Xiong Shuirou, "Design and Realization of Learning System Based on Android Platform" [D]. Beijing University of Posts and Telecommunications, 2012.
4. Yang Jia, "Location Based Service of Mobile Learning System Design"[J]."Chinese Educational Informational",2012,07:31-33
5. Kinshuk,Rory McGreal,Sun Hongtao,Shi Pengfeng,Compilation."Mobile Learning System Based on Position to Identify 5R Adaptive Framework"[J]."Modern Distance Education Research",2012,03:91-96

DOI: 10.1051/itmconf/20171110005

6. Zhang Gaoming,Ma Li,Zhao Jing."Campus LBS Application Research Based on Android Platform"[J]. "Journal of Xi 'an Liberal ArtsCollege: Natural Science Edition".2013,03

AUTHOR INDEX

AUTHOR INDEX